Papua New Guinea

Adrian Lipscomb
Rowan McKinnon
Jon Murray

Papua New Guinea

6th edition

Published by

Lonely Planet Publications

Head Office: PO Box 617, Hawthorn, Vic 3122, Australia
Branches: 155 Filbert St, Suite 251, Oakland, CA 94607, USA
10a Spring Place, London NW5 3BH, UK
71 bis rue du Cardinal Lemoine, 75005 Paris, France

Printed by

The Bookmaker Pty Ltd,
Printed in Hong Kong

Photographs by

Air Niugini	Ann Jelinek	Adrian Lipscomb	Yvon Perusse
Australian War Memorial	Holger Leue	Rowan McKinnon	Rainforest Habitat/Rocky Roe
Richard Everist	Mark Lightbody	Jon Murray	Liz Thompson

Front cover: Highlander wearing an *arse gras*, The Image Bank

First Published

April 1979

This Edition

February 1998

Although the authors and publisher have tried to make the information as accurate as possible, they accept no responsibility for any loss, injury or inconvenience sustained by any person using this book.

National Library of Australia Cataloguing in Publication Data

Lipscomb, Adrian.
Papua New Guinea.

6th ed.
Includes index.
ISBN 0 86442 402 7.

1. Papua New Guinea – Guidebooks. I. McKinnon, Rowan.
II. Murray, Jon. III. Title.

919.53045

Adrian Lipscomb

Adrian first visited Papua New Guinea in 1976, when he spent a few days of hard slog on the Kokoda Trail. This started a love affair with Melanesia and has resulted in frequent visits. Adrian combines travel writing with tourism industry consulting, and has a particular interest in Less Developed Countries. His academic background is in human geography, and he has travelled widely in Africa, the Middle East, Asia and the Pacific. His various careers have spanned international policy and intelligence with the Australian government, freelance journalism, small business operation, university lecturing and tourism planning. In 1994-95 he worked as a tourism adviser in the Solomon Islands. He is now based in Bellingen, Australia.

Rowan McKinnon

Born in country Victoria, Australia, Rowan spent some early years on Nauru, a tiny mid-Pacific island, and then grew up in outer bayside Melbourne. He worked as a kitchenhand, poster putter-upperer, taxi driver, packer, warehouse keeper, carpenter and rocket scientist, while studying philosophy at university and playing bass with a moderately successful arty band called Not Drowning Waving. After 10 years and too much poverty, he gave up the life of airports, tour buses, soundchecks, studios and rehearsal rooms to get a 'real job' with LP as an editor. Rowan first went to PNG in 1988 and has returned every couple of years since.

Jon Murray

Jon Murray spent time alternating between travelling and working with various publishing companies in Melbourne, Australia, before joining Lonely Planet as an editor. Resigning to go travelling again proved to be a great career move, as he was offered the job of updating Lonely Planet's guide to Bangladesh. Since then he has written, co-authored and updated LP guides to various destinations in Africa and the Pacific, including *South Africa, Lesotho & Swaziland* and *New South Wales*. Jon lives on some unruly bush acres near Melbourne.

From Adrian Lipscomb

Thanks to Air Niugini for its generous assistance and especially to John Siannos, in its Sydney office, and David Glover, in Port Moresby. Thanks also to Haus Poroman (whose staff put up with me during a particularly bad bout with influenza), Bird of Paradise Hotel, Gateway Hotel, Lae International Hotel, Smugglers' Inn, Ralf Stüttgen and the Angoram Hotel.

Many people assisted in providing information – or just pointed me in the right direction – so that a comprehensive and accurate revision could be made. I thank them all. They include:

Geoff Adlide (AusAID), Dominic Ashley (Tufi), Kiatit Batet (Madang), Steven Buku (Indabu), Colin Burdett (Port Moresby), Norman Carver (Goroka), Peter Clark (Lae), Fred Cook (Lae), Theresa Cullinan (Vanimo), Warren Daniels (Goroka), Steve Dawanincura (PNGTPA), John Fowke (Goroka), Peter Goleby (Tabubil), Phil Gregory (Tabubil), Bill Guile (Lae), Bryce Harding (Port Moresby), Dr Heino Hertel (Madang), John Hibberd (Popondetta), Yehiura Hriehwazi (Tabubil), Michael Hudson (Wau), Ray Japhse (Lae), Joe Kenni (Angoram), Vickson Kotaseao (Wau), Laurie Maher (AHC, Port Moresby), Glen McKenzie (Madang), Cosmas Makamet (Wau), Howard Mason (Tabubil), Alois Mateus (Ambunti), Maggie Mea (PNGTPA), Chris Mercer (Afore), Peter Mildner (Port Moresby), Wesbil Mukuwa (Tufi), Larry Orsak (Madang), John Morley Phillips (Kokoda and Gosford), Helen Pokapin (PNGTPA), Annie & Fritz Robinson (Afore), Rocky Roe (Port Moresby), Felix Rotsiyomana (Vanimo), Tim Rowland (Madang), Tony Salvadori (UPNG, Port Moresby), Erigere Singin (PNGTPA, Madang), Jacalea Swan (Mt Hagen), Malagui Tamilong (Madang), Pastor Nicky Tera (Wau), Francis Tike (Tabubil), Jane Urquhart (DFAT), Robyn Warkia (Lae), Keith & Maggie Wilson (Mt Hagen), Nane Winion (Lae), Jimmy Yarco (Tufi), Pindori Yorasa (Lae), Dr Don York (UPNG, Port Moresby).

Special thanks also to Barbera for her forbearance while I undertook the arduous task of writing.

From Rowan McKinnon

I would like to thank Maura Young and Jack Cashman at Air Niugini, Chris Abel, Wallace Andrew, Alison Chartres, Digby Holeong, Stephen Holliday, Shane Jenkinson, Demas Kavavu, Michael Lee, Noah Lurang, Glen Low, Gerry McGrade, Tabo Meli, Joe Moni, Peter Pilo, Bill Rochè, Greg Seeto and the Pacific Gold crew, George Telek, Jennifer Varssilly and John Wong. To Raymond Rangatin, I'm sorry I missed you. No thanks to the person who stole my shoes.

I would also like to thank Adrienne Costanzo at the Planet for having the faith; Deb, Lewis and Eadie; and Jane Hart.

This Book

Tony Wheeler researched and wrote the first two editions of *Papua New Guinea*. Mark Lightbody researched the 3rd edition, Richard Everist updated the 4th edition and Jon Murray updated the 5th edition.

For this edition, Adrian Lipscomb, the coordinating author, updated most of the mainland provinces, as well as Port Moresby. Rowan McKinnon updated the island provinces and the Milne Bay chapter. Both authors updated the introductory chapters and created the new glossary.

From the Publisher

This edition of *Papua New Guinea* was edited in Lonely Planet's Melbourne office by Rebecca Turner, with assistance from Adrienne Costanzo and Darren Elder. Janet Austin, Sue Harvey and Anne Mulvaney proofed the book, and Kerrie Williams and Rowan McKinnon helped to compile the index. Matt King and Helen Rowley produced the maps, with the help of Marcel Gaston and Lyndell Taylor. Helen handled the layout, with expert help from Marcel and others, while Matt and Mick Weldon created the illustrations. Thanks to Adam McCrow for the cover.

Many thanks to the travellers who used the last edition and wrote to us with helpful hints, useful advice and interesting anecdotes:

Serge Eric Abitol, Sue Alexander, Matt Andrews, Mike Bannock, Andrew Barber, GJ Bennett, Cameron Birch, B Bladon, Michael Bohm, Rob Campbell, Eduardo Castro, Dr Richard Chaikin, Barry Cheadle, Kelly Cunningham, John Duncan, Patti Eger, JulieAnn Ellis, Paul Falworth, Bob Findlay, Tad Glawthier, Shane Gleeson, William

Goldberg, Rogier Gruys, Tim Hilton, Stephen How Lum, Brent Howard, John Hunter, Alan Jacobs, Elizabeth Jansen, Dr M Juedes, Gary Kanaby, Chris Kauffman, Irma and Kai Keller, Marilyn Kelly, Don Kossuth, Axel Kummel, Sandy MacTaggart, Melvyn Maltz, Melanie-Jane Manley, Huw Mason, Charles McFadin, John Michalski, Mark Moller, Katrin Muller, Juliette Muscat, Iain Overton, Zane Perry, Mr and Mrs R Picton, Jess Ponting, Alisdair Putt, Lorraine Riddle, Nancy Roper, Martin Salmingkeit, Kim Shaddick, Rob Sherry, Barbara Slone, Dr Wolfgang Sterrer, Greg Stevenson, Ralf Stüttgen, Ludwig Stüttgen, Inbal Tubi, David Twine, Russ Ty, Andrew and Lisa Vallely, Dieter Van Camp, Peter Wagner, Douglas Whitman, Bruce Whittaker, Kilian Wolters, Don York.

Warning & Request

Things change – prices go up, schedules change, good places go bad and bad places go bankrupt – nothing stays the same. So, if you find things better or worse, recently opened or long since closed, please tell us and help make the next edition even more accurate and useful.

We value all of the feedback we receive from travellers. Julie Young coordinates a small team who read and acknowledge every letter, postcard and email, and ensure that every morsel of information finds its way to the appropriate authors, editors and publishers.

Everyone who writes to us will find their name in the next edition of the appropriate guide and will also receive a free subscription to our quarterly newsletter, *Planet Talk*. The very best contributions will be rewarded with a free Lonely Planet guide.

Excerpts from your correspondence may appear in new editions of this guide; in our newsletter, *Planet Talk*; or in updates on our Web site – so please let us know if you don't want your letter published or your name acknowledged.

Contents

Boxed Asides

Map Legend

BOUNDARIES

.... International Boundary
.... Provincial Boundary
.... Disputed Boundary

ROUTES

..... Freeway, with Route Number
.... Highway
.... Major Road
.... Minor Road
.... City Road
.... City Street
.... City Lane
.... Train Route, with Station
.... Metro Route, with Station
.... Cable Car or Chairlift
.... Ferry Route
.... Walking Track

AREA FEATURES

.... Building
.... Beach
.... Cemetery
.... Market
.... Park, Gardens
.... Pedestrian Mall
.... Reef
.... Urban Area

HYDROGRAPHIC FEATURES

.... Canal
.... Coastline
.... Creek, River
.... Lake, Intermittent Lake
.... Rapids, Waterfalls
.... Salt Lake
.... Swamp

SYMBOLS

✈	.... Airport		→	.... One Way Street			
⚱	.... Archaeological Site		℗	.... Parking			
🏖	.... Beach		)(	.... Pass			
⌂	.... Cave		⛽	.... Petrol Station			
⛪	.... Church		★	.... Police Station			
	.... Cliff or Escarpment		✉	.... Post Office			
◨	.... Dive Site		❖	.... Shopping Centre			
✪	.... Embassy		🏊	.... Swimming Pool			
✚	.... Hospital		☎	.... Telephone			
✳	.... Lookout		❶	.... Tourist Information			
▲	.... Mountain or Hill		⊝	.... Transport			
♆	.... National Park		🐘	.... Zoo			

■	.... Place to Stay	
⛺	.... Camping Ground	
⌂	.... Hut or Chalet	
▼	.... Place to Eat	
🍺	.... Pub or Bar	

✪	CAPITAL	.... National Capital
◉	CAPITAL	.... Provincial Capital
●	CITY	.... City
●	Town	.... Town
•	Village	.... Village

Note: not all symbols displayed above appear in this book

Papua New Guinea Map Index

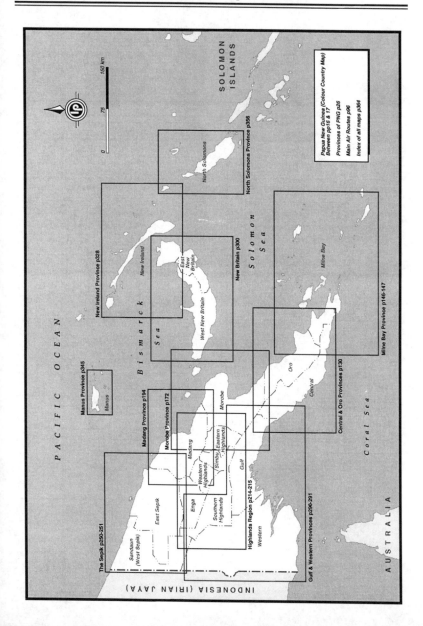

Introduction

Papua New Guinea is a last frontier for travellers. It can be a fascinating and rewarding experience and, in reality, PNG is not at all difficult to visit, although it takes a little ingenuity to avoid some of its steep prices. Travellers go to PNG for two main reasons – to experience the culture and explore the natural environment. Few places in the world can match its famed waterways, fascinating village culture, abundant wildlife, smoking volcanos, rainforest trekking and offshore diving experiences.

The diversity of PNG's attractions is overwhelming and, importantly, you can make your visit 'soft' or 'hard'. If you have enough money, you can get a taste of village life and culture and go bird-watching, butterfly-collecting or trekking, while staying in comfortable, tourist-oriented surroundings. If you are a budget traveller, once you get out of the cities, living is cheap and Papua New Guineans are the friendliest and most hospitable people you could meet, as long as you are willing to leave some of your cultural baggage at home. If you are invited by a villager to share their house, be prepared to open up to them, enjoy their hospitality and leave them with a heartfelt *'Mi laikim yu tru'* (I like you very much).

Images of 'primitive headhunters', everpresent and debilitating malaria and a country wracked by political and criminal violence abound in the western media. It is important to realise that such perceptions do not accurately reflect life in PNG and need not be the overwhelming deterrents they may seem.

No matter how you plan to travel, the important things to remember are: slow down, keep an open mind and enjoy what people are willing to share.

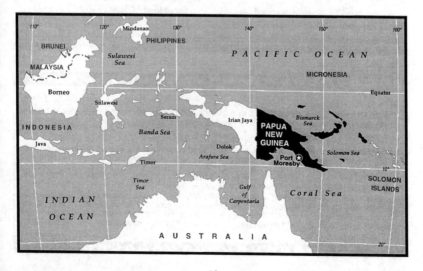

Facts about the Country

HISTORY

The First Arrivals

At no time was Papua New Guinea completely joined to South-East Asia, but it was joined to Australia by a land bridge which allowed migration further south. This bridge skirted a lake – possibly the largest ever known in Australia – which, with the rising sea-level about 6000 years ago, became the Gulf of Carpentaria. As a result, PNG shares many species of plants and animals (including marsupials) with Australia, but not with Indonesia.

It is believed that humans reached PNG and then Australia by island-hopping across the Indonesian archipelago from Asia at various stages, the first probably more than 50,000 years ago. This migration was made easier by a fall in the sea level caused by an ice age. Subsequent migrations account for the different language groups: Austronesian and non-Austronesian. The Austronesian languages are scattered along coastal areas of PNG and are also spoken elsewhere in the Pacific.

As the world's climate warmed, the sea level rose, isolating PNG and submerging the original coastal settlements. Parts of the Huon Peninsula have subsequently risen due to volcanic activity and eruptions continue in other areas to this day, the most recent of which is the 1994 Rabaul disaster.

While evidence of early coastal settlements has been uncovered, such as 40,000-year-old stone axes, it is believed that people reached the Highlands about 30,000 years ago and that most of the valleys were settled over the following 20,000 years. Evidence of human habitation going back 20,000 years has been found in the Kuk (or Kup) Swamp in the Wahgi Valley (Western Highlands Province) but, even more significantly, there is evidence of gardening beginning 9000 years ago. This makes Papua New Guineans among the first farmers in the world. The main food crops grown were sago, coconuts, breadfruit, local bananas and yams, sugar cane (which originated in PNG), nuts and edible leaves. Surprisingly, the South Papuan coast seems to have been mainly settled in the last 3000 years, although that's another figure which keeps receding with new finds. Trade between the Highlands and the north coast has been going on for at least 10,000 years.

The prehistory of the islands to the east has always been assumed to be shorter than that of the mainland, but new evidence shows

---

What's in a Name?

Few countries have a name with such a long and confusing history as Papua New Guinea. When the first Portuguese explorers came along, they named it Ilhas dos Papuas – Island of the Fuzzy-Hairs – from the Malay word *papuwah*. Later, Dutch explorers called it New Guinea because they were reminded of Guinea in Africa.

The German northern part of the island was assigned to Australia as a League of Nations Mandate after WWI and Australia had to run the two parts as separate colonies or, more correctly, a colony and a Mandated Trust Territory. After WWII, the two were combined and administered as the Territory of Papua & New Guinea, sometimes written as Papua-New Guinea or Papua/New Guinea. Finally, with independence, the country became simply Papua New Guinea.

In 1968 the *South Pacific Post* (now the *Post Courier*) held a contest for a more appropriate name. Suggestions included Genipapu, Pagini, Austrinesia, Bikpelaland, Blacksland and Pasifika, but a 10-year-old Port Moresby schoolgirl named Ade Asisa won the K50 first prize with Niugini, the Pidgin word for Papua New Guinea. The name has been retained by the national airline – Air Niugini. ■

that New Ireland and Buka (North Solomons) were inhabited around 30,000 years ago and Manus Island 10,000 years ago. People in New Britain have been trading with other islands for more than 10,000 years.

European Contact

The first European impact on PNG was indirect but important. The sweet potato was taken from South America to South-East Asia by the Portuguese and Spaniards in the 16th century and it is believed Malay traders then brought it to Irian Jaya, from where it was traded into the Highlands. Its high yield and tolerance for poor and cold soils led to its cultivation at higher and higher altitudes, and promoting greater population expansion, especially in the Highlands.

The next development preceding the permanent arrival of Europeans was the arrival of steel axes, which were also traded from the coast up into the Highlands.

D'Abreu, a Portuguese sailor, reached the island of Ceram in 1512 and was probably was the first European to sight the coast of New Guinea. The first known landing by Europeans was also Portuguese: Jorge de Meneses landed on the Vogelkop Peninsula, the 'dragon's head' at the north-west corner of the island in 1526. He got his name in the history books as the European discoverer of New Guinea.

In the following centuries, various Europeans sailed past the main island and its smaller associated islands, but the spreading tentacles of European colonialism had far richer prizes to grapple with. It was left pretty much alone.

Only the Dutch made any move to assert European authority over the island and that was mainly to keep other countries from getting a toehold on the eastern end of their fabulously profitable Dutch East Indies Empire (Indonesia today).

Indonesian and Malay traders had for some time carried on a limited trade with coastal tribes for valuable items like bird-of-paradise feathers. So the Dutch simply announced that they recognised the Sultan of Tidore's sovereignty over New Guinea. Since they, in turn, held power over the island of Tidore (a small island to the west of Irian Jaya), New Guinea was therefore indirectly theirs – without expending any personal effort. That neat little ploy, first put into action in 1660, was sufficient for over 100 years. During the 19th century, however, firmer action became necessary.

The British East India Company investigated parts of western New Guinea in 1793 and even made a tentative claim on the island but, in 1824, Britain and the Netherlands agreed that the latter's claim to the western half should stand. In 1828 the Dutch made an official statement of their sovereignty claim and backed it up by establishing a token settlement on the Vogelkop.

Nothing much happened for 50 or so years after that, although the coastline was gradually charted and the Australians, whose country was then evolving from a penal colony, started to make noises about those foreigners claiming bits of land which were rightfully theirs.

A series of British 'claims' followed; every time some British ship sailed by somebody would hop ashore, run the flag up the nearest tree and claim the whole place on behalf of Queen Victoria. The good Queen's government would then repudiate the claim and the next captain to sail by would go through the whole stunt again. In 1883 the Queensland premier sent the Thursday Island police magistrate up to lay yet another unsuccessful claim.

About this time, a third colonial power – Germany – was taking a definite interest in the north-east coast, so the British announced, in September 1884, that they intended to lay serious claim to a chunk of New Guinea. In response, the Germans quickly raised the flag on the north coast. A compromise was reached – a highly arbitrary line was drawn east-west in the 'uninhabited' highlands between German and British New Guinea. At that time no European had ventured far inland and it was nearly 50 years before it was discovered that the line went straight through the most densely populated part of the island.

New Guinea was now divided into three sections – a Dutch half protecting the eastern edge of the Dutch East Indies, a British quarter to keep the Germans (and everybody else) away from Australia and a German quarter because it looked like it could be a damned good investment.

The Germans were soon proved wrong: for the next 15 years the mosquitos were the only things to profit from the German New Guinea Company's presence on the north coast. They moved their administrative base from one centre to another until 1899, when they threw in the towel and shifted to the happier climes of the Bismarck Archipelago and quickly started to make those fat profits they'd wanted all along.

In 1888, Sir William MacGregor became the administrator of British New Guinea and set out to explore his possession, establishing a native police force to spread the benefits of British government. He instituted the policy of 'government by patrol' which continued right through the Australian period. In 1906 British New Guinea – the southern bit – became Papua and its administration was taken over by newly independent Australia.

WWI

In the early years of the 20th century, Britain was keen to devolve some of its imperial responsibilities to the 'dominions'. As a consequence of this policy, when the war with Germany broke out in 1914, the British government asked Australia to occupy German New Guinea. An Australian task force was despatched to New Britain in September 1914 and, after a few brief skirmishes, the Australian commander received the German surrender – although the German navy was still on the prowl elsewhere in the Pacific. The Australian military administration was slow to take control of the area and it was mid-1915 before all German posts were occupied. German planters, confident that the war in Europe would be won, had continued to develop their plantations between 1914 and 1919 and were amazed when their property was expropriated by the Australian authorities after the war, and sold for reparation. In 1920 the League of Nations officially handed PNG over to Australia as a mandated territory.

Between the Wars

Australia was quick to eradicate the German commercial and plantation presence from PNG, baulking only at the German missions. Beyond this, Australia enacted mercantilist legislation aimed at restricting the commercial exploitation of Eastern New Guinea to British nationals, and (more precisely) Australians. Sydney had become the de facto headquarters for all major commercial decisions concerning PNG, and the base of the head offices of the main plantation and trading companies: CSR (Colonial Sugar Refining Company), Burns Philp and WR Carpenter.

The main plantation commodities – copra, rubber, coffee and cocoa – experienced large price fluctuations in the 1920s and 30s, many of the smaller plantations falling under the direct management of their creditors, the trading companies. Needless to say, indigenous production was largely ignored by the colonial rulers but subsistence agriculture continued to provide for the needs of the majority of the population.

In 1929 the police and almost the whole local workforce in Rabaul, then capital of the mandated territory of New Guinea, went on strike for higher wages. It was short-lived and the leaders were rather savagely treated but it marked the first true Melanesian urban-based protest against the inequalities of the colonial system.

A significant improvement in the price of gold spurred further exploration for the commodity, and major finds were located at Edie Creek in 1926, followed by the discovery of large alluvial deposits in the Bulolo Valley. These finds reinvigorated the mining industry until war came along again. But the most significant consequence of gold exploration at this time was the discovery, by a small party of miners in 1930, of about a million people – almost a quarter of the total

Port Moresby Cultural Festival, National Capital District
Top Left: Duna traditional dress
Top Right: Daroa Komano traditional dress
Bottom: Inawi traditional dress

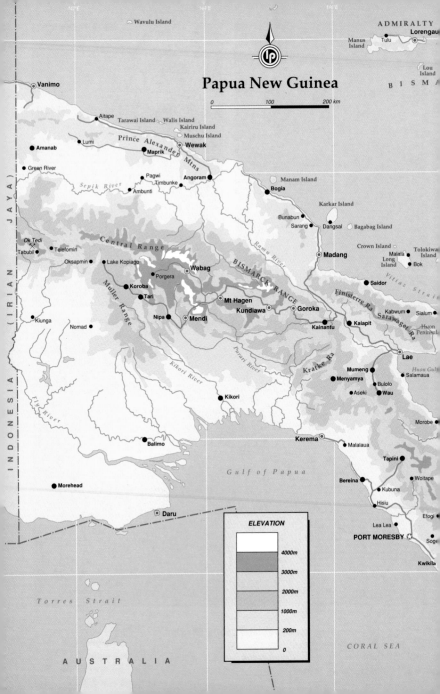

Left & Top Right: Mt Hagen Show, Western Highlands Province. The Highlands shows are a great opportunity to experience the region's artistic diversity. Highlanders wear their traditional dress and *bilas* (finery).
Bottom Right: *Doba* (traditional leaf money) from the Trobriand Islands

Melanesian population of PNG – in the secluded valleys of the central New Guinea Highlands. The Highlanders were physically separated, and culturally distinct, from the Lowlanders, who were already known to the Europeans but had long been trading in and social contact with each other. The fact that this discovery by Europeans happened so late in the colonial era is revealing of the enormous cultural gap between the colonists and colonised – and the blithe arrogance of the European *mastas*.

Under the Australian administration, government-by-patrol was the key to both exploration and control. Patrol officers, or *kiaps*, were not only usually the first Europeans to venture into previously 'uncontacted' areas but were also responsible for making the government's presence felt on a more or less regular basis. This situation persisted pretty well until independence.

WWII

By December 1941, when Japan bombed Pearl Harbour, Britain and her allies, including Australia, had been at war with Germany for over two years. With a population of just over 7.5 million, Australia had already devoted an inordinately large war effort to the European and North African campaigns. New Guinea was not a priority at this stage and consequently the expatriate population was very small.

In a well-orchestrated campaign, the Japanese simultaneously extended three prongs of their attack in the Asia-Pacific theatre: firstly, through Indochina to Malaya, Singapore, Sumatra and then Java; secondly, to the

AWM 026013

Papua, New Guinea, 1942. Diggers of B Company 55/53rd Battalion AIF have a smoke with a local family on their verandah, as they pass through a village during a patrol. Shown: Private L Scalon (1) and Staff Sergeant R Grey (2).

Philippines, Borneo and the Celebes; and thirdly, to New Guinea and the Solomon Islands, with a view to eventually occupying the north and east coasts of Australia.

The Japanese approached New Guinea boldly, rapidly leap-frogging along the north coast, occupying Rabaul in January 1942. They powered their way south along the rugged Kokoda Trail and came to within 50km of Port Moresby, the only remaining Australian stronghold on the island. In a flanking move, they also landed at Milne Bay but were repulsed after encountering heavy resistance from the Australians. Nevertheless, with an unsustainably extended supply line, they had run out of steam by September 1942 and with the Pacific War less than a year old, they started their long and bloody retreat back along the Kokoda Trail, harassed all the way by the Australians. In December, American and Australian forces captured Gona and Buna on the north coast in order to attack the enemy from the rear, but the Japanese tried to regroup near Lae to launch a counter-attack. The fighting around Salamaua and Lae proved to be some of the fiercest and most protracted of the war. Lae was eventually captured in September 1943.

It took until 1945 to regain all the mainland from the Japanese but the islands – New Ireland, New Britain, Bougainville – were not relieved until the final surrender.

Most Melanesians were militarily neutral in the conflict, although they were used extensively on both sides as labourers, guides, carriers and informers. But some were heavily involved, such as the Tolai of northern New Britain. It is estimated that the Tolai population was reduced by almost a third during these years.

Each year, 23 July is celebrated as Remembrance Day to honour Papua New Guineans killed during the war. It also marks the anniversary of the battle in 1942 between the Papuan Infantry Battalion soldiers and Japanese invaders. This took place near the Kumusi River in Oro Province.

Irian Jaya

The history of New Guinea island's other half, now known as Irian Jaya, has also been one of conflict and dispute. When WWII ended, Sukarno, leader of pre-war Indonesian resistance to Dutch rule, immediately declared Indonesia independent of the Netherlands and, for the next few years, the archipelago was racked by conflict. In 1949 the Republic of Indonesia was established, extending down the chain of islands presently comprising Indonesia but excluding Dutch New Guinea, which was retained by the Netherlands, and East Timor, retained by Portugal. But Indonesia argued that Dutch New Guinea was part of the former Dutch East Indies and should, therefore, be included in Indonesia.

A political union between the two halves of the island, the Territory of Papua & New Guinea and Dutch New Guinea, would have been logical. But Australia was not keen on the prospect of an independent PNG. Nor was it keen to inherit a Dutch colonial problem or antagonise its aggressively expansionary neighbour, Indonesia.

Indonesia was suffering at this time from significant unrest and its economy was in rapid decline. The government needed an external enemy to distract attention from the problems. The Netherlands proved an ideal target and the effort to 'regain' Dutch New Guinea became a national cause. The matter was brought to a head when Sukarno ordered amphibious landings and paratroop drops into Dutch New Guinea in 1961: the UN was stirred to act and prevailed upon Holland to turn the territory over to Indonesian administration.

Indonesia's economic collapse was rapidly accelerating by this time and the economy was in no shape to continue the massive investment projects the Dutch had initiated. By the time Sukarno lost power in 1965, Irian Barat (literally 'West Irian', as Dutch New Guinea was renamed) had suffered an asset-stripping operation with shiploads of Dutch equipment being exported and local businesses and plantations collapsing right and left. After Sukarno's overthrow, relations rapidly improved; the Indonesian half of the island was renamed Irian Jaya (literally 'Victorious Irian'), and Australia and Indonesia cooperated to accurately map the border area. ■

The End of Colonialism

The war left great destruction in its wake, but few villages were destroyed (except in New Britain and New Ireland). Everywhere roads, bridges, airstrips and equipment lay abandoned. Marston matting became the universal building material. Jeeps were salvaged and used for many years, with some Quonsett huts still in use today. But the main impact was social and political – the colonial rulers, who had been seen as the only possible form of government, were no longer beyond question.

The territory entered a new period of major economic development with a large influx of expatriates, mainly Australians. The expatriate population grew from about 6,000 to over 50,000, its peak, in 1971. Since then it has stabilised at around 24,000.

With many colonised countries seeking to end colonialism in the post-war years, Australia was soon pressured by world opinion to prepare Papua and New Guinea for independence. A visiting UN mission in 1962 stressed that if the people weren't pushing for independence, then it was Australia's responsibility to do the pushing. The pre-existing Australian policy of reinforcing literacy and education was supplemented by a concentrated effort to produce a small, educated elite to take over the reins of government.

Progress towards independence was fairly rapid through the 1960s. In 1964, a House of Assembly with 64 members was formed. Internal self-government came into effect in 1973, followed by full independence on 16 September 1975.

Post-Independence

A country rift by many mutually incomprehensible languages, where inter-tribal antipathy is common and where the educated elite accounts for a very small percentage of the population would hardly seem to provide a firm base for democracy. Yet somehow everything has held together and PNG has survived fairly well, especially by new-nation standards. Papua New Guineans have generally dealt with the problems of nationhood with a great deal of success, despite predictions of economic collapse. Dire predictions are still being made, particularly since the civil unrest surrounding the government's handling of the 1997 Sandline Affair (see The Sandline Affair aside).

The most significant issues to confront PNG in recent years have been:

- the Bougainville crisis (see the North Solomons Province chapter)
- border problems involving the OPM (*Organisasi Papua Merdeka*, or Free West Papua Movement; see the Gulf & Western Provinces chapter)
- major macroeconomic problems involving government overspending and requiring international debt rescheduling (see the Economy section)
- environmental concerns, particularly with respect to the overexploitation of forest resources (see the Ecology & Environment section)
- a crisis in health care, with malaria, tuberculosis, malnutrition and, most recently, HIV/AIDS cases reaching worrying proportions (see the Public Health aside in the Facts for the Visitor chapter)
- problems with law and order (see the Society & Conduct section in this chapter and the Personal Safety section in the Facts for the Visitor chapter)
- the volcanic destruction of Rabaul in 1994 (see the New Britain chapter).

GEOGRAPHY

The island of New Guinea is an effective transition zone, both geographically and culturally, between the Indonesian archipelago in the west and the PNG islands of New Britain, New Ireland and Bougainville, the Solomon Islands and other Pacific islands to the east.

A physical pattern in the mainland's geography is replicated on a smaller scale in the eastern islands: a mountainous central backbone descending sharply to coastal lowlands. On the mainland, this central range becomes wider, higher and more fragmented the closer it gets to the border with Irian Jaya. The larger of the Highlands valleys formed are up to 20km wide and have grass cover rather than the rainforest common at lower altitudes. The ranges here are very rugged with some valleys more than 1700m deep and slopes of 30° to 45°. The eroding power of two of PNG's major rivers, the Sepik and the Strickland, has combined with frequent earthquakes to create a massive gash in the grassland corridor of the mountain spine known as the Strickland Gorge. This is a rugged but awe-inspiring part of PNG, which offers some superb bushwalking for those who are fit enough.

Fringing the northern coastline are smaller mountain ranges, the Torricelli and Finisterre mountains, which contain the massive trough in which the Sepik and Ramu rivers flow. During floods, the Sepik's water spills over onto a flood plain up to 70km wide and covering an area of 7800 sq km. The Sepik basin was once an extensive inland sea up to 200m deep. To the south, the Fly River is almost as impressive and flows into the Gulf of Papua.

The lowland areas are notable for their large areas of swamp and grassland. In places, the central mountains descend right to the sea in a series of diminishing foothills, while in other regions broad expanses of mangrove swamps fringe the coast – gradually extending as more and more material is carried down to the coast by the muddy rivers.

The larger islands to the east have similar topography, although some east of New Ireland are the peaks of a submerged volcanic mountain chain, and the Trobriand and Muyua (Woodlark) islands are raised coral atolls; the highest point of the Trobriand Islands is only 60m above sea level.

PNG is endowed with striking coral reefs; there are reefs around much of the mainland coast and particularly among the islands of the Bismarck Sea and Milne Bay areas.

GEOLOGY

The landmass of PNG is marked by its rugged mountain spine of volcanic origins dating to 1.6 million to 1.9 million years ago.

There are, in fact, two distinct lines of volcanos in PNG – the first extending along the main spine of the mainland to West New Britain and the second following the line of the islands from Rabaul, south through Bougainville and into the Solomon Islands. The first line is relatively stable: there has been

no major volcanic activity on the mainland in recent history, apart from the unexpected and disastrous eruption of Mt Lamington in Oro Province in 1951.

The second line of volcanic activity is, however, much more potent and the eruptions of Tuvurvur and Vulcan in New Britain in 1994, which covered Rabaul's Simpson Harbour and Karavia Bay with metres of ash and rocks, are typical of the rapid devastation which can result. PNG's volcanos are of the explosive type and produce ash showers and lava flows which weather to fertile soils such as can be found on the Gazelle Peninsula of north-eastern New Britain.

Why is PNG so liable to volcanic devastation? It lies on the junction of two segments of the earth's surface – or tectonic plates. Volcanic and seismic activity is common in these areas.

Not all the landforms and rocks in PNG are of volcanic origin. Examples include the magnificent sheer limestone walls which can be seen stretching from Mount Mandala (in Irian Jaya) to the Strickland Gorge and beyond into the Western Highlands, and the spectacular steep-sided V-shaped valleys common in the Highlands.

PNG's geology has produced one of the country's main export income earners – mining. Vast commercial quantities of gold, copper and silver, as well as petroleum, have been found. See the Economy section.

CLIMATE

The climate is generally hot, humid and wet year round, but there are some exceptions. There are wet and dry seasons but in practice, in most places, the wet just means it is more likely to rain, the dry that it's less likely. The exception is Port Moresby, where the dry is definitely dry – the configuration of the mountains around the capital account for this two-season characteristic.

In most places, the wet season is roughly from December to March, the dry season from May to October. During the two transition months (April and November), the weather can't make up its mind which way to go and tends to be unpleasantly still and sticky.

Some places experience variations on this pattern, the most notable being Lae and Alotau, where May to October is the *wet* season. Some areas, such as Wewak and the Trobriand Islands, receive a fairly even spread of rain during the year and others, such as New Britain and New Ireland, have sharply differing rainfall patterns in different areas.

Rainfall is generally heavy but varies greatly. In dry, often dusty Port Moresby, the annual rainfall is about 1000mm (40 inches) and, like areas of northern Australia, the wet is short and sharp and then followed by long dry months. Elsewhere, rainfall can vary from a little over 2000mm (80 inches), in Rabaul or Goroka for example, to over 4500mm (175 inches) in Lae. In extreme rainfall areas, such as West New Britain Province or the northern areas of the Gulf and Western provinces, the annual rainfall can average more than 8m a year.

In mid-1997 El Niño, the climatic event which affects the south coast of PNG, produced unseasonably dry conditions in the Gulf region, choking the Fly River and limiting its use by the ships which come up the river to Kiunga to unload supplies and pick up ore concentrate. As a result, the Ok Tedi mine had to reduce output for some months.

Temperatures on the coast are reasonably stable year round – hovering around 25°C to 30°C, but the humidity and winds can vary widely. As you move inland and up, the temperatures drop fairly dramatically. In the Highlands, the daytime temperatures often climb to the high 20s but at night it can get quite cold. During the dry season, when there is little cloud cover to contain the heat, Highlands mornings can be very chilly. If you keep moving up into the mountains, you'll find it colder still. Although snow is rare, it can fall on the tops of the higher summits and ice will often form on cold nights.

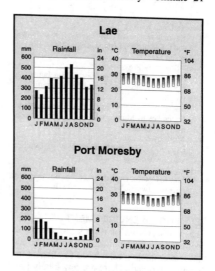

Gulf & Western Provinces
   The Gulf region is one of the wettest in the world with average annual rainfall of 8m, peaking between May and October. It is a little drier in

Western Province but heavy rain can occur between December and April.
Highlands
   In most of the Highlands, most rain falls between November and April. It is usually cooler and drier from May to October. In the southern Highlands, the wet lasts a bit longer at both ends and it is more likely to rain at any time of year. Cold nights and foggy mornings are common.
Madang Province
   Thunderstorms can occur from November to May. Drier months from July to September.
Manus Province
   Lorengau has drier months between September and December, but for most of the province there are no real seasons.
Milne Bay Province
   This maritime province has a wide variation in weather conditions. Alotau is wetter from April to October, with most rain in September. The Trobriand Islands have fairly even rainfall.
Morobe Province
   In Lae, it's hot and humid from November to February, wetter but slightly cooler from May to October; heaviest rainfall occurs between June and August. In Wau and Bulolo, it is the opposite and can get quite cool.
New Britain
   On the north side (including Rabaul and the Gazelle Peninsula), November to April is the wet season, while on the south side of the island, the wet season is from May to October with much heavier rainfall.

New Ireland Province
  Kavieng receives a fairly even spread of rainfall and the south of the island is wetter from November to May.
North Solomons Province
  It's the wet and cooler season from January to April; November and December are pretty hot.
Oro Province
  There is a poorly defined wet season from December to March, while it is drier between May and October.
Port Moresby & Central Province
  Dry, dusty and windy from May to October; wetter and cooler inland.
Sepik
  May to October is the drier season and the wettest time is between December and April.

ECOLOGY & ENVIRONMENT

The conservation of PNG's biodiversity is complicated by traditional land tenure and the government's reluctance to alienate the people involved. There are few totally protected areas. Prior to independence, only two national parks were established and only two have been since, but others have been proposed. A compromise concept is Benchmark Reserves which protect small parts of exploited areas.

The National Parks Board also recognises provincial parks and local parks, better known as Wildlife Management Areas. The latter are intended as multipurpose areas, especially for the management of specific types of wildlife used for food or other functions. They are popular in aiding local communities to prevent over-exploitation of wildlife, for example the eggs of scrub turkeys (megapode) and certain kinds of bird of paradise, and are the responsibility of the communities using the areas. An advantage of this arrangement is that, as with any plans for commercial exploitation of a particular area, the rights of the people living in the area are given priority. Guidelines are clearly established in local Land Use Management Plans.

Also important is the concept of Protected Species, in which all wildlife belongs to the traditional landowners but with the same restrictions as in Wildlife Management Areas. The list began in the 1920s to protect the bird of paradise and egret from extensive commercial exploitation of their valuable plumes. It later included most birdwing butterflies and long-nosed echnidas. Since independence, many more have been added as part of PNG's cooperation with international conservation objectives.

There seems to be a growing awareness of the necessity to conserve forests and wildlife. But traditional landowners are often torn between the rich rewards offered by foreign logging and mining companies and the destruction of their environment. Villager leaders also have limited experience from which to draw when making decisions regarding large-scale commercial logging. If, for example, you have never seen widespread clear-felling or experienced its long-term impact, but a bunch of white men or Malaysians tell you it will be all right, what should you believe? The problem is further exacerbated by the limited capacity of PNG authorities to police the activities of the logging companies which often overlog and operate outside the scope of their agreements. To cap all this, a growing population, which is still largely village-based and uses traditional slash-and-burn methods of agriculture, is rapidly reaching a size where traditional methods are unsustainable.

The growth of the mining industry is also causing some concerns at local village level. The demands and the accountability of large multinationals when dealing with villagers can sometimes leave much to be desired, for example the much-publicised Ok Tedi mine dispute a few years ago (see The Ok Tedi Mine & the Environment aside in the Gulf & Western Provinces chapter).

To PNG's credit, however, it was one of the first countries to introduce legislation against the movement of hazardous waste. Several years ago it rejected overtures from a US-based company wanting to dump radioactive waste in Oro Province.

FLORA & FAUNA

The Wallace Line, named after the 19th-century naturalist Alfred Wallace, marks a notable boundary – it lies in the deep water between Bali and Lombok, and Kalimantan and Sulawesi (in Indonesia), and separates markedly different flora and fauna. To the west of the Wallace Line can be found tropical vegetation, monkeys, elephants, Bengal tigers (very rarely now) and wild cattle, while to the east are more thorny arid plants, cockatoos, parrots, giant lizards and marsupials. The theory is that the more advanced placental animals which evolved in Asia stopped their advance at this deep-water boundary, allowing other species, such as marsupials and echidnas, to prosper because of the absence of carnivores.

Flora

About 9000 species of plants exist in PNG. More than 200 of these are tree-sized and found at lower altitudes. Pines and antarctic beech thrive around the 3500m mark and above this are predominantly sparse meadows and lichens. In the 1970s and 80s there were large afforestation projects in the Highlands – many of the stands of hoop and klinkii pine seen today date back to then. PNG has become known in recent times for its enormous variety of orchids – there are about 3000 kinds and the orchids come in all shapes and sizes, sometimes hardly recognisable as orchids. Probably the best places to see them are in Port Moresby's National Botanic Gardens or the Rainforest Habitat in Lae. PNG also has about 2000 different species of ferns and related plants.

Rainforest enthusiasts will find plenty to keep them occupied. Most of PNG is forested, with slash-and-burn cultivation widespread, even in steep areas. Commercial logging is generally localised, but expanding, often with clear-felling methods used. After extracting the commercial timber, the remainder is often burned to allow farming. In the south are extensive savannas similar to those of northern Australia.

Fauna

There are about 180 species of mammals in PNG categorised into eight families. These include bats and rats, about 60 marsupials (such as tree kangaroos and bandicoots), dolphins and whales. There are also two kinds of egg-laying echidnas (spiny anteaters).

But it is for its 700 or so bird species that PNG's wildlife is most renowned. A keen bird-watcher should try to include a visit to a swampy area like the Blackwater Lakes near the Sepik (for water birds), the Highlands (for birds of paradise) and the islands (for sea birds). PNG is home for 38 of the world's 43 spectacular species of bird of paradise, which have bizarre displays and mating rituals. Interestingly, it is the male bird of paradise which has the gaudy plumage (as it often is with human cultures in these regions). The closely related bower birds may lack the gaudiness, but more than make up for it in their skill in building not only bowers but elaborate maypoles and gardens, complete with a well-kept lawn and flower arrangements.

Among more familiar birds, PNG can boast more parrot, pigeon and kingfisher species than anywhere else in the world. All sizes and colours can be found, from the world's largest, such as the crowned pigeons, to the world's smallest, such as the pygmy parrots which scurry along small branches and feed on lichen.

Many other groups are represented and

PNG has more species of kingfisher than any other country

have a general similarity to Australian bird-life but are often more colourful. Perhaps the most notable are the giant cassowaries. Related to the Australian emu, they are stockier birds, adapted to forest areas and with a large, horny casque for crashing through undergrowth. Like the birds of paradise, cassowaries are of great ceremonial significance to many tribal groups.

Kokomos, or hornbills, are of impressive size and seem to be intelligent. Their flight is wonderful. If you're in the jungle and you hear what sounds like a small steam engine approaching, it's a kokomo skimming along like an elegant sculler. The big palm cocka-toos are also impressive: with their black feathers, sharply curved beak and spiky crest, they look like they belong in one of the Grimms' nastier fairytales.

Also represented in PNG are about 200 species of reptiles, including two crocodiles and 13 turtles, as well as about 100 snakes, which are much feared by the local people and often a cause for the repeated burning of some grassland areas, especially in the High-lands.

PNG is a paradise for insects and contains many thousands of species, notably a beau-tiful variety of birdwing butterflies, including the world's largest butterfly, the Queen Alexandra birdwing. Some insects, such as the brilliant green scarab beetles, are used as body ornaments although the most famous ornaments are, of course, bird of paradise plumes, seen at their best at the Highlands shows. They are very valuable not only for sing-sings, but also as bride prices, and are carefully stored for use over many years.

National Parks

For the latest information on national parks, write to the National Parks Service, PO Box 5749, Boroko. For information on Wildlife Management Areas contact the Wildlife Conservation Section, Department of Envi-ronment & Conservation, PO Box 6601, Boroko. No Wildlife Management Areas are listed here but there are now quite a few scattered through the country and it is best to

Stag beetles can be found in many of PNG's forest areas

find out the details for any particular prov-ince through the Wildlife Division. National parks include:

Varirata National Park This 1063 hectare park is 42km by road from Port Moresby and protects the western escarpment of the Sogeri Plateau, extending to the Astrolabe Mountains. There are upland rainforests and savanna areas here, with several walking trails. This is a good place for bird-watching. With an elevation of more than 600m, the cooler plateau is a popular escape from Port Moresby. A trip to the park can be combined with other activities, such as visiting the junction of the Kokoda Trail.

McAdam National Park This 2076 hectare park is between Wau and Bulolo, with one of its boundaries along the Bulolo River. The stream-dissected areas centred on the Bulolo River Gorge are found here. The park has lowland rainforest to about 1000m, then sub-montane oak-dominated forests to about 1800m and above this are beech-dominated forests with dense bamboo to about 2000m. The wildlife includes a large variety of mid-montane species. Echidnas, cuscuses (marsupials similar to large possums), casso-waries and birds of paradise are some of the highlights.

Lake Kutubu A national park has been declared in the Lake Kutubu area of South-ern Highlands Province.

GOVERNMENT & POLITICS
The Parliament
PNG is an independent parliamentary democracy within the British Commonwealth. It has a unicameral system of government based upon the Westminster model. The British monarch is head of state and appoints a governor general, on the recommendation of the PNG parliament, to represent the monarch. The PNG constitution provides for the parliament, judiciary and the public service. After each national election, parliamentarians elect a prime minister, who in turn appoints ministers from members of their party and/or coalition.

A provincial government system was introduced in 1976 when nineteen provinces and a separate national capital district were formed, each with a provincial assembly. Many of these were soon suspended for mismanagement or corruption, so, in 1995, as a result of the Constitutional Review Commission (the Micah Commission), the national parliament moved to radically modify the system. Now, provincial assemblies comprise national members from each province, including a governor. There are also over 150 local councils.

The Electoral System
The most important political forum is the national parliament and all citizens have voting rights in five-yearly elections. Voting is non-compulsory.

The national parliament is elected on a first-past-the-post system, where the candidate with the highest number of votes is successful and there is no limit to the possible number of candidates. In practice, this means that MPs are frequently elected with less than 10% of the total vote. This not only leads to widespread disenchantment at election time but also to corruption and tribalism. For instance, it is possible for a candidate to split the electorate's vote along tribal lines by encouraging representatives of each tribe in a constituency to stand. The candidate would then concentrate on ensuring the loyalty of their tribe and perhaps picking up a few votes here and there by spreading a little bit of 'financial goodwill'. The number of votes to win is consequently very small.

Such unstable arrangements also mean that very few MPs survive more than one electoral term, leaving the parliament short on experience and continuity. There has been considerable criticism of this situation but, as yet, no sitting parliament has had the political courage to challenge the status quo. In the 1997 election, over half the sitting members were not re-elected, including two former prime ministers and nine cabinet ministers. The majority of members of the new parliament are now Independents (including several women) – an understandable outcome, but one which may fuel further instability.

National Politics
National politics is a world of shifting alliances. No single party has ever governed in its own right – each successive government has been dependent on shaky, unreliable coalitions. Party discipline is also loose and party members are prone to act independently, changing allegiances overnight and voting as it suits them and, sometimes, their bank balances.

The political parties themselves are not distinguished so much by ideology as by the personality of their leaders and their regional bases. Generally, there appears to be a remarkable degree of consensus about the kind of society that should be created. All parties favour a mixed economy, with governments overseeing and, sometimes, operating alongside private enterprise; only the details and emphases differ.

The country's first prime minister, Sir Michael Somare (popularly known as 'the chief'), proved to be a remarkably astute politician with the ability to forge working compromises between diverse groups of people. In 1980, however, Somare's government fell to a no-confidence vote and Sir Julius Chan, an equally astute politician from New Ireland, became prime minister. With some manoeuverings which would have made Machiavelli proud, there was then a succession of prime ministers over the next

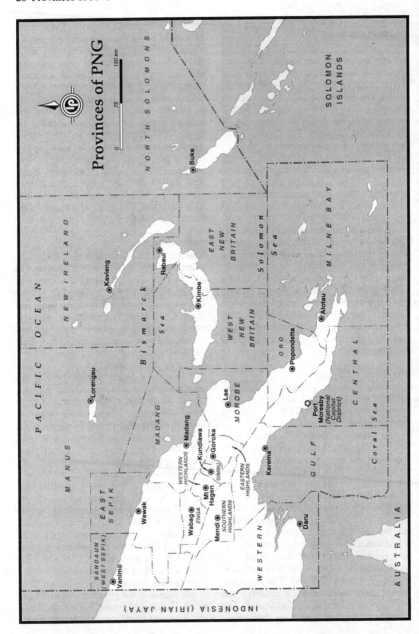

few years, culminating in the reinstallation of Chan as PM in 1994.

The Sandline Affair hit the headlines in early 1997 (see The Sandline Affair aside below) and Chan stepped aside briefly, only to reclaim the prime ministership two weeks before the June election. In a surprise outcome, probably reflecting the electorate's disenchantment with corrupt politics generally and the Sandline Affair specifically, Chan lost his seat and the prime ministership. The top job went to Bill Skate, a former

governor of the National Capital District, who allied himself with Chan's People's Progress Party.

ECONOMY

PNG has a population of approximately 4.2 million people, though only 225,000 (5.4%) are formally employed. Urban unemployment rates are particularly high. In 1995, PNG's gross domestic product (GDP) was US$4.8 billion, equating to a per-capita GDP of US$1228, which ranks it as a middle-

The Sandline Affair

The secessionist movement on Bougainville in the late 1980s and the closure of the Panguna mine dealt a seemingly insoluble blow to the PNG government (see the North Solomons Province chapter). The conflict became more and more entrenched as time went on to the point where, in late 1996, three members of the government – the then prime minister Sir Julius Chan, his deputy Chris Haiveta and the defence minister Mathias Ijape – decided to take pre-emptive action to resolve the matter using outside military force. This became known as the Sandline Affair and was to be a crucial factor in public perception of PNG's leaders in the lead-up to the June 1997 elections, described as the most important since independence.

With US$36 million (funded ostensibly by 'budget cuts'), Chan & Co employed a well-known mercenary company, Sandline International, which was tasked to provide men and equipment via an associated company, Executive Outcomes, to help train the PNG Defence Force in anti-guerilla tactics and to deploy in an attack on the secessionists. It was hoped that the result would be a speedy military victory on Bougainville, the kudos from which would sweep Chan's People's Progress Party back into power at the elections.

After learning of the plans in February 1997, Australia and a number of other regional governments urged Chan to negotiate with the secessionists rather than take military action. But the PNG leader was adamant and much of the money had already been spent on equipment and upfront payments; mercenary troops were, at that stage, stationed at Moem Barracks near Wewak and training was under way. The controversy became the subject of much public debate in PNG and, to complicate matters, the popular PNGDF Commander, Brigadier General Jerry Singirok, decided to do an 'about-face' and publicly condemn the government for undertaking such an affair. He was duly sacked, but the military stayed loyal, leading to rioting and looting in the streets of Port Moresby by his supporters. Widespread doubts that 'something was wrong' related to three issues: the source of the funding for the affair in this cash-strapped country, the way in which the money was spent and how the decision was made without wider consultation within parliament.

Bowing to pressure from both his parliamentary colleagues and the international community, Chan suspended the Sandline contract in March and announced a commission of enquiry into its circumstances. The mercenaries were sent home. As a result of further pressure, Chan announced, on 26 March, that he and his two associates would 'stand aside' pending the outcome of the enquiry. John Giheno was named acting prime minister in the interim.

The enquiry, conducted by Justice Warwick Andrews, cleared Chan of corruption. On hearing of this, in early June, Chan resumed his position as prime minister – until he lost his seat in the national elections two weeks later. However, the enquiry noted that it 'remains suspicious of Mr Haiveta's actions and motivations [concerning alleged insider trading associated with a trip he made to Hong Kong to meet Sandline executives], and, in parts, rejects his evidence as untruthful'.

With the alliance between new Prime Minister Skate and the People's Progress Party, it appears unlikely that the Sandline enquiry will be reopened (despite pre-election promises to that effect by Skate). That Haiveta is now foreign minister in the new government indicates the former regime is still very influential in the corridors of power. The affair's main legacy to PNG is a politicised and volatile defence force, with a strong antipathy to the police force and elements within government. ■

income country. But other social indicators such as income distribution, life expectancy, infant mortality and literacy rates are comparable with some of the poorest countries in the world.

PNG is the largest single recipient of Australian aid. Budget support and direct project aid between 1975 and 1995 totalled A$10 billion and is currently being provided at the rate of around A$300 million per annum. PNG's major revenue sources are gold, oil, copper, timber, coffee and palm oil.

One of the first things Sir Julius Chan did when he took over as prime minister from Sir Paius Wingti in 1993 was to devalue the kina by 12% to quash currency speculation and encourage export industries. This was followed, in October 1994, by the 'floating' of the kina, causing its value to fall dramatically almost immediately and then slowly decline further to the point where, in late 1996 (and for the first time since independence), the kina was worth less than the Australian dollar. It has been slowly declining ever since.

Most of PNG's economic activity is in the subsistence sector but this area is increasingly coming under threat for a variety of reasons. They include a greater access to western consumer goods, discontent – particularly among the youth – caused by increasing exposure to western media (many villages now have VCRs and radios) and greater access to PNG's larger cities and towns. Nevertheless, the subsistence village lifestyle does provides a 'safety net' for the wider population.

Most villagers undertake traditional economic activities such as slash-and-burn agriculture, fishing and pig-raising. But there is also a large number growing significant quantities of coffee, cocoa and copra (dried coconut kernel) for the international market. Growing vegetables in market gardens to sell in urban areas is also a growth industry, particularly in the Highlands.

There are persistent nutritional problems in some parts of the country (a shortage of protein is a long-standing difficulty), but virtually everybody is fed and clothed, even if they are unemployed in the cities. This is due in large part to the *wantok* system (see the Society & Conduct section), which continues to be a significant influence on the distribution of wealth, particularly where only one family member earns a wage – a single wage will often be distributed among dozens of people.

There is also an increasing gap between the expectations of those with an education and the number of available jobs and also between the growing need for cash and the few available opportunities to earn it. As yet, discontent has not manifested itself as a significant political force but it does show in urban shanty town crime and disputes over land-ownership in the Highlands.

There is virtually no manufacturing industry in PNG because of a shortage of skilled labour, high wages and the small size of the market. The country's imports include almost all manufactured goods and many basic foodstuffs, not a few of which could be produced locally (fish and rice in particular). Perhaps the most critical problem is that there is insufficient local capital to establish import replacement industries.

Until recently the formal economy was said to depend on copper, coffee, cocoa and copra. In recent years, however, this economic base has expanded to include and be dominated by a booming and increasingly diversified mineral sector and largely untapped forestry and fishing resources. Further reserves of gold, copper, silver, nickel, oil and gas are being frequently discovered.

Mining

Mining has taken over as the boom industry of PNG. In 1992, well over a billion dollars worth of gold, copper/gold concentrate and silver was exported from PNG mines. That was two-fifths of all exports. In the second half of that year, K300 million worth of oil was exported. In 1993, oil accounted for one-third of total exports and one-eighth of total government revenue. Although the government insists on partial equity in most mines, ownership and control rests overwhelmingly with overseas interests such as BHP, CRA, Rio Tinto Zinc, Placer, Renison and Kennecott.

Mining provides a significant proportion of government revenue – but it has been argued that large-scale, foreign-dominated, capital-intensive primary industries such as mining do not truly assist in the development process but help to promote inequalities and the development of a 'comprador' (middle man) class. No doubt the debate will continue and so will the mining.

Main mining developments in PNG are:

- Bougainville Copper Ltd (BCL) at Panguna on Bougainville Island, which produced mainly copper and a little silver and gold. It has closed temporarily because of the political situation.
- Ok Tedi, near Tabubil in Western Province, which produced mainly gold until the late 1980s and is now a major copper extractor
- Lihir, on Lihir Island in New Ireland Province, which produces large quantities of gold
- Misima Island in Milne Bay Province, which produces silver and a little gold
- Porgera in Enga Province, north of Mt Hagen, which produces gold and silver
- Kutubu in the Southern Highlands, which produces large quantities of oil and gas. There is talk of building a major pipeline from the Kutubu oilfields to take natural gas to north Queensland in Australia.

Agriculture

Coffee accounts for around 20% of total exports. Its significance is further heightened because it is one of the most important sources of cash income for the most populous area of the country – the Highlands; 70% of the total crop comes from small clan holdings.

Unfortunately, like most other crops, coffee is subject to major fluctuations in price. Coffee rust, a devastating fungal disease, is largely under control now.

After coffee, cocoa is the most important export crop. Tea has not been the great success once expected, although Highlands tea is quite pleasant. Rubber production has grown slowly but steadily.

Copra was the backbone of the economy for many years but has now slipped far behind coffee and cocoa. Production was something of a political football as the copra plantations were looked upon as a colonial relic which did not fit PNG's independent status, but the main problem was, and is, very low prices on the world commodity markets. Since independence, there has been a dramatic drop in output and a major fall in plantation employment – the work is simply too unrewarding.

Oil palms are partly responsible for the decline in the copra price as they are a considerably more efficient source of vegetable oils. There are now huge oil palm plantations in Oro, Milne Bay and West New Britain provinces.

The huge, sometimes barely accessible timber resources are being rapidly exploited, mostly by Malaysian companies, and the industry suffers from significant corruption and environmental abuse.

Fishing

The enormous potential of fishing around the coast is also now being exploited – the implementation of the 322km fishing zone has prompted Asian countries to involve themselves in fishing projects with PNG. Unfortunately, tinned fish remains a major import – even on islands surrounded by fish. There have been attempts at setting up canning plants in PNG, but the necessity for them to be at least partly foreign-owned has caused problems. At least one foreign company has taken advantage of the tax breaks offered, set up a trial plant, fished out the nearby sea, declared the trial a failure and gone home.

Tourism

Over 42,000 short term visitors came to PNG in 1995 – of these 49% were on business, 33% on holiday and 14% visiting friends and relatives. Australia (39%) remains the primary source, with the USA (11%), Japan (8%) and the UK (7%) contributing significantly.

Many people, both nationals and expats, are ambivalent about mass tourism. Some hotel managers say that a few more visitors would be welcome, but not too many. This cautious attitude might mean that PNG survives a push for tourism growth with its dignity and charm intact. Meanwhile, visitors are made welcome and treated as individuals rather than just another unit.

Village-based tourism is a relatively new phenomenon in PNG; it has great potential, but is unlikely to ever reach the stage where it attracts more than a trickle of tourists.

Foreign Aid
Development Aid Australia is the single largest donor of aid to PNG. It provided about two-thirds of all official development assistance over the last decade. Japan has recently emerged as a significant donor and, with Germany and NZ, provides the bulk of the rest of bilateral aid. The World Bank, the Asia Development Bank, the European Community and the United Nations Development Plan are the main multilateral and international agencies providing assistance to PNG.

In 1995, after an extended period of rapidly deteriorating economic conditions, the PNG government submitted to pressure from the International Monetary Fund (IMF) and the World Bank and agreed to undertake a financial stabilisation and economic recovery program: US$50 million was provided for the task. The recovery program is presently at some risk, however, and there are serious implications for the PNG economy should the loan be cancelled.

The recent Australian-sponsored *Simons Report* on Australia's overseas aid program recommended clearer objectives for the aid program and that Australian aid should no longer be 'muddied' with associated diplomatic and trade objectives; its objective should be 'poverty reduction through sustainable economic and social development'. The report noted the need for more efficient deployment of aid funds – and reinforced that aid should concentrate on basic education and health needs and the capabilities of PNG's government institutions to deliver the aid. Much of Australia's aid has, in the past, gone straight into PNG government coffers, leading to allegations of waste (nevertheless,

PNG officials have frequently complained about Australia's 'patronising' attitude, particularly in wanting tougher evaluation criteria for the programs it funds). It is likely, however, that over the next three years, all Australian aid for budget support will be replaced by direct program support, thus avoiding a corrupt and inefficient bureaucracy.

Military Aid PNG also receives significant military aid from Australia under what is, perhaps euphemistically, known as the Defence Co-operation Program (DCP). Estimated DCP expenditure in PNG in 1996-7 was almost A$12 million.

The programme comprises training and personnel assistance, as well as technical assistance and equipment grants. Among other things, Australian engineering units have been posted at various times to Vanimo and Mendi to assist in road construction, and financial help was given to refurbishing Lombrum patrol boat base wharf on Manus Island. Perhaps the most controversial aspect of the DCP was the donation of patrol boats and Iroquois helicopters to the PNGDF some years ago.

POPULATION & PEOPLE
More than a third of PNG's population of about 4.2 million live in the Highlands provinces. There are around 24,000 expatriates. Indigenous people are often referred to as nationals – never natives. But the term national is increasingly out of favour and many prefer to be described by their tribal or regional name or as Papua New Guineans. In more remote areas, you might find yourself referred to as *masta* or *missus* but most people, especially in the cities, now find this offensively colonial. The colonial era is still sometimes referred to as *taim bilong masta*.

Indigenous Peoples
The people of Papua New Guinea are related to people from other parts of the Pacific. They include the descendants of the Papuan people; Melanesians who are more closely related to the islanders of Fiji, Vanuatu and

New Caledonia; Polynesians related to New Zealand Maoris and Hawaiian islanders; and Micronesians related to the people of the Marshall, Kiribati and Nauru islands.

However, there's been much miscegenation and blurring of distinctions. One hundred years of plantation labouring has seen many people move from one part of the country to another and this too has changed the demographic. There are four regional groupings that reflect cultural and historical links: Papuans from the south, Highlanders, New Guineans from the north and Islanders.

There is a wide range of physical types – from the dark Buka people of the North Solomon islands, whose midnight black skins are said to be the darkest in the world, to the lighter, more Polynesian people of the south coast. After a spell in PNG, you'll soon learn to recognise the shorter, often bearded, Highlands men and many other distinct groups of people.

Grassroots is a slang term which has entered the language, and refers to, roughly, the village or peoples' level. A grassroots person lives in a village or town on a low income. Given the enormous diversity of cultures and a general clan-based parochialism the development of this unifying concept is a good thing for PNG. *Grassroots* was also a popular comic strip, now sadly defunct, but you can still see the amusing central character's image popping up in other media. Cut-out *Grassroots* cartoon strips are stuck to walls and fridges around the country.

Expatriates

There is still a large expatriate population, although it has fallen considerably from a 1971 peak of around 50,000 to a current figure closer to 24,000. You might be surprised to know that more than one-quarter are Irian Jayan refugees (around 7500) living in camps in Western Province. The next biggest expatriate group is Australians, who number around 6500, and there are small numbers of North Americans, New Zealanders and Filipinos. A large Chinese community has been in PNG for a long time and has intermixed much more than any other expatriate group.

More than half of the expatriates live in cities (mostly Port Moresby) and many of them are in the country on short-term, lucrative contracts with international companies. Often they lead lives that are divorced from reality, commuting between air-conditioned offices, company-provided houses (invariably surrounded by razor wire) and some sort of club. Many expats live in a strange 'other world' that coexists with the real local world but is removed from it. A culture of fear – a fear of ordinary people – breeds in these communities, fuelled by the media reports of violence that does occur in Port Moresby and elsewhere. But it is generally a misplaced anxiety and is unfortunate.

You'll also meet many long-term expats who defy the stereotype of the old colonial empire builder. That is an image that is breaking down these days. Some of the old characters that have been hanging around for most of their lives are often genuinely eccentric and fascinating to talk to. They say of the old days that you had to be a missionary, a mercenary or a misfit to come to PNG (the word mercenary has only recently taken on its broader meaning). Sometimes you feel like you're talking to all three at once.

The bible-thumpers in PNG seem to thump bibles harder than anywhere else and the church is a dominant factor in almost all ordinary lives. Mission workers have been in PNG for 100 years and their work has brought profound changes. Western religion has had a destructive impact on traditional culture and still expresses attitudes that are sometimes culturally inappropriate and difficult to reconcile with local traditions. The church has subjugated the Papua New Guinean people as much as any colonial power. But mission workers have done extremely valuable work setting up schools, farms, airports, hospitals and shipping companies and working among the hapless people lured by the 'big-city' aura of towns like Port Moresby. They continue to have a very strong influence on the country.

There's also a large and diverse volunteer

contingent, most working for low wages and as teachers, nurses, researchers or helpers with development projects.

When independence came in 1975, many Australian and Chinese residents were eligible for PNG citizenship, on the condition they renounced their original citizenship. Many did and some now hold positions of considerable political and economic importance. Ex-Australians regularly win seats in parliament.

EDUCATION

About 70% of children get some formal education, although this figure varies widely between provinces, and about 30% of those who make it through primary school go on to high school. Only about 1% of those who start school ultimately go on to a tertiary institution. The standard of education is generally very good and most villagers are articulate and highly literate. What is unfortunate is the lack of opportunities for them.

All kids must pay basic fees to attend school but, while fees are modest, most villagers are cash-poor and finding school fees can be difficult. The education system consists of government-run community (primary) schools which provide basic education and some government high schools (but so few that many pupils come from far away and have to board at the school). The churches run many primary and some secondary schools.

The government also runs the National High Schools, of which there are only six or seven throughout the country. They are matriculation senior high schools which prepare students for university, mostly attended by boarders.

Recent changes in curriculum have included teaching village schools (preparatory year, grades 1 and 2) in *tok ples* (local language). Education authorities found kids learnt the fundamentals of reading better in their own language.

Then there are private schools. The Internal Education Agency administers the International Schools which offer both primary and secondary education. There's quite a proliferation of international schools throughout PNG and they are attended mostly by the children of fee-paying expats. These schools often have foreign teachers and follow Australian syllabuses.

The country's tertiary colleges offer degrees in areas like teaching, forestry, agriculture and fishery, building trades and technical skills. The University of Technology at Lae offers science, engineering and accounting degrees, while the University of PNG in Port Moresby has arts, law, science and medicine streams.

SOCIETY & CONDUCT

The people of PNG belong to many different cultures. You'll find more information about arts and cultures in the various parts of this book, but understanding any one of the cultures is a lifetime's work, which explains the number of anthropologists in the country.

Nearly all Papua New Guineans are Melanesian and have some things in common. Even those who are not Melanesian share many of the following features.

Melanesian Society

PNG is changing fast, but the vast majority of people remain dependent on subsistence agriculture and live in small villages. Many aspects of life are still carried out traditionally; the social structure and an individual's responsibilities and privileges remain significantly unchanged.

In traditional PNG societies, despite sophisticated agriculture and, in some areas, extraordinary maritime skills, the main tools and artefacts were made of wood, bone, pottery or stone. There was no metal working, no domestic animal power and the wheel was unknown. Extensive trading networks existed and highly valued shells were used as currency. People traded widely and in some areas they were able to become specialised as gardeners, hunters and fishers, with trade items including pottery, stone tools, obsidian (dark, glassy volcanic rock), dyes, salt, sago and smoked fish.

The responsibility for the day-to-day work

of gardening and caring for animals lay with women, who were also responsible for the household. Men were concerned with the initial clearing of the bush, hunting, trade and warfare. Young men also worked for older men.

The social units were generally small, based on family, clan and tribe, with the most important obligations and responsibilities due to the extended family. Some observers have described these communities as democratic Edens, where ownership was communal and everyone's basic needs were met. But in reality, they were highly organised societies, often with hierarchical structures where power was vested in chiefs, village elders and *bigmen*. In some places, Bougainville and the Trobriand Islands for instance, clear-cut classes developed and a person's position in society was determined by birthright. In many island cultures, land and clan rights are inherited through a matrilineal system.

Individual ownership did not exist in the same way as in western societies. The accumulation of wealth and its grandiose display were often vital prerequisites for prestige and power. Ownership was a concept bound up with family and clan rights, controlled by a male elder. Within and between village households and beyond, there were complicated networks of obligation and privilege.

Fundamental to the society are notions of reciprocity (see The Wantok System aside) and family responsibility. Help, whether it be labour, land, food or pigs, is often given out of duty or in the expectation of some kind of return (perhaps loyalty in time of war or assistance in organising some future feast). Surplus wealth was not traditionally accumulated for its own sake but so it could be given away, creating prestige for the giver and placing obligations on the receiver.

In most cases, a bigman did not create a dynasty. Although a bigman's son had a head start in life, he still needed to demonstrate

The Wantok System

Common to many Melanesian societies and fundamental to every level of PNG culture is the idea of wantoks. In *tok pisin* (Pidgin) wantok simply means 'one talk' and your wantoks are those of your fellows who speak the same language – your kin and clanspeople. Every Papua New Guinean is born with a whole set of duties and obligations to their wantoks but they are also endowed with privileges that only wantoks receive. Reciprocity is the central idea of Melanesian generosity.

Within the clan and village, each person can reasonably expect to be housed, fed and to share in the community assets. And with any of the clanspeople, regardless of whether they are in Moresby or Madrid, all wantoks can expect to be accommodated and fed, until they can make more permanent arrangements.

The wantok system is both an organic safety net and social security system – and the plague of democratic politics. There's no level of PNG society that is not affected by the wantok system. If you tender out construction project and a wantok bids, then you will give the contract to the wantok. If your PMV driver is a wantok, you won't have to pay and if you have wantok in the judiciary, maybe you won't go to jail. Add the wantok factor to the highly-transient-population factor and the rapidly-developing-country factor and you begin to see how a simple village-community custom has come to be a truly dominating factor and there's really nothing anyone can do about it.

Some people say that the wantok system is simultaneously the best and worst thing about PNG and it's very true. For most of the country's people – rural villagers – it is an egalitarian way in which the community can share in its spoils. In a rapidly changing world the village and the clan can provide basic economic support as well as a strong sense of identity and belonging. PNG has no social security system and a very low rate of people in paid employment.

However, when these ideas are transposed to the political and public affairs arena, it simply becomes nepotism and, at worst, outright corruption. In the public service, the police, the army and especially in politics, this is a scourge. Candidates don't get to run without the generous support of their fellow wantok bigmen, who of course expect that when 'their' candidate is elected their generosity will be repaid in some form or another. Some local MPs get rural development grants worth almost a million kina and most of this money doesn't get spent on rural development. ■

qualities of his own: hard work, bravery, leadership, trading skill, magical knowledge. Different societies sought different characteristics in their leaders but economic ability was common to all. Wealth was necessary for a man to develop supporters.

The creation of wealth required hard work and, since women were largely responsible for agricultural production, it was essential for a man with any ambition to get married. It was the bigmen who monopolised the supply of female labour. They would sometimes help young men meet the bride price. Polygamy was often a feature of leadership.

In many areas, warfare and ritual cannibalism were commonplace and payback killings perpetuated an endless cycle of feuding. Each small group was virtually an independent nation – so any dealings with the next-door tribe were international relations. Although alliances were common, they tended to be shifting and expedient, rarely developing into large, long-term federations.

The world for most Papua New Guineans was determined by these factors and beyond their own clan, they were surrounded by hostile or suspicious neighbours who often spoke a completely different language. Although no quarter was ever given in war and women and children were not exempt from attack, fighting usually occurred in highly ritualised battles – and only after negotiations had failed. Bows and arrows and spears were the weaponry and generally, there were few casualties.

Traditional Wealth

Although the country has shifted to a cash economy to a great extent, traditional forms of wealth are still very important, particularly in the Highlands and on the Milne Bay islands. A wad of banknotes can never have the same impact as kina shells, cassowaries or pigs. A large sow might be worth around K600, but many people would rather have the pig. Another sign of wealth that is now displayed at ceremonial exchanges in the Highlands is a good stack of SP Lager.

Kina shells are large half-moons cut from the gold lip pearl shell and they are worn as personal embellishment, to show their wealth, particularly for ceremonial occasions in the Highlands. They were a traditional item of currency and, in other areas, other forms of shell money were equally important. The K1 coin (there's no note) has a large hole in the centre, perhaps with the idea that it too could be worn round the neck.

In the Highlands, another traditional display of wealth is the *aumak*, a chain of tiny bamboo rods worn around the neck. Each rod indicates that the wearer has lent out 10 or so kina shells. A long row of these little lengths of bamboo is an indication of great wealth.

In New Britain, shell money is still commonly used alongside the modern paper version, but only for small purchases – tiny shells strung along a piece of bamboo are worth about 10 toea a dozen. In Milne Bay *doba*, or leaf money, is made out of a bundle of etched and dried banana leaves worth K5 to K10. *Bagi*, the elaborate shell jewellery ritually traded around the Milne Bay Province islands, is the most important mark of prestige and wealth.

Law & Order

PNG is known world-wide as an 'unsafe' country, a reputation that is both overstated and simplistic. In reality, violence is a subtly different problem in PNG, and hence is more noticeable to western eyes. Violence plays a different role in PNG society – it occurs for different reasons, is handled in different ways and sometimes can have a cathartic effect on those involved. As you travel around the country and especially when you speak to white expats, it's hard to put these facts in perspective. Paranoia is contagious and crime is a favourite topic of conversation.

During the 1997 Sandline Affair, there was looting and rioting in the streets of Port Moresby. However, the violence was in no way aimed at foreigners and there was really very little danger to the average expat in the street. The object of the crowd's animosity

Pop Culture

There's a very strange mix of powerful influences on modern Papua New Guinean people. Almost everywhere, the history of European contact has meant domination by religious zealots and ruthless colonial empire builders. They inherited the legacies of WWII, and of slavery and exploitation.

Most people get to see TV regularly and there's a strong Chuck Norris movie culture that has developed – every second pet dog is called Rambo. However, perhaps because of the church's influence, overt sexuality is repressed and not shown on PNG TV, nor does it figure in toilet-wall graffiti. (Sexuality in many traditional cultures, such as the Trobriand Islands, is still liberally expressed.)

Almost all Papua New Guineans come from a village somewhere and their cultural traditions and beliefs remain a powerful influence throughout their lives. You'll meet university-educated and professional people who exhibit an amazing ability to straddle two worlds.

Perhaps the most confounding thing to outsiders is how Jesus fervour and traditional belief can sit side by side. Jesus is represented as a white European – in some remote areas, he will be the only white person some villagers have ever 'seen'! But Jesus is alive in the hearts of almost every person in the country – his image adorns T-shirts all over the country (with captions like 'life without Jesus is just HOPELESS!') and many people attend church weekly. But they also chew *buai* (betel nut) and believe in magic and between them they worship countless 'pagan symbols'. These traditional religious beliefs are strongly held and fiercely protected.

It's clear that the average Papua New Guinean is a very complex character. ∎

---

was its politicians; the street rallies and marches (traditional activities long associated with politics in PNG) loosened strong emotions in those involved, presenting them with enticing opportunities to acquire that VCR or ghetto blaster they had always wanted. So they broke into shops.

This sounds terrifying and dangerous to one unused to a culture which incorporates violence, or the threat of violence, to achieve many ends. It is in reality merely a way of life. During WWII, villagers near Wau watched the Australians and Japanese fight each other in much the same way that foreign researchers and voyeurs watch Highlands clans battle today. It was interesting and a little primitive.

But what appears to be uncontrolled anarchy is often nothing of the sort. For instance, tribal war is not necessarily regarded by the Highlanders as a breakdown of law and order but as the process by which law and order is re-established. A case that appears to be straightforward assault may well be a community-sanctioned punish-

ment. Looting a store may take the place of the traditional division of a bigman's estate.

The 'Rascal' Problem The term rascal has taken on a more serious meaning in PNG than the light-weight meaning it has most English-speaking countries. In short, a rascal is a thug, or a robber, especially one who belongs to a gang. Anyone who gets into gang mischief is a rascal and this can take the form of armed hold-ups (particularly on the Highlands Highway), house break-ins and even rape and murder.

Rascals are mostly disaffected (and often relocated) youths with few opportunities. There's no social security system in PNG and a very low rate of people in paid employment. Opportunities for most young people who aren't exceptionally gifted are very few and TV has brought its images of materialism and violence (see the Pop Culture aside).

These young, single men are drawn to the cities where they take advantage of wantoks who, traditionally, are responsible for feeding and housing them. Unfortunately there are just not enough jobs, so these bored young 'have-nots' wander the town, play cards and pool, drink beer and get into mischief. But the rascal problem is in no way race-related and relations between different races and nationalities are generally remarkably good.

A young, successful Computing Science student in Lae spoke to one author about his situation. He was brought up in a village near Popondetta and, after finishing his schooling, was confronted with the decision of what to do: 'whether to become a rascal in Moresby or to apply, with hundreds of other men, for a job with Steamships which might lead to a proper career'. An interesting choice and one which few young men in PNG would have the luxury of considering, let alone succeeding at. Fortunately he chose the latter and did succeed – but the alternative was a definite option.

Unfortunately, the rascal career path is one being chosen by far too many young men these days. The problem will not diminish over time – Port Moresby and Lae are likely to remain risky because of the continuing influx of unemployed young men. Mt Hagen has the same problem, made even more complex because it is the main centre of the volatile Highlands region (people go to town to settle paybacks, or compensation for a wrongdoing) and workers from the various mines spend their pay-cheques there. Most other Highlands towns are also edgy.

Clan loyalties also make police work extremely difficult. A village will not necessarily cooperate in the arrest of one of its members – if the rascal's actions have not affected the village negatively, they will often not be seen as wrong. To avoid police becoming involved in their own clan's disputes, they are often transferred to other areas where they have a better chance of being impartial. Police officers and their families are vulnerable to the threat of payback attacks – which, of course, are 'justified' if the police officer has arrested an 'innocent' relative.

One particularly worrying recent development is the escalation of robberies of banks and shops by gangs using high-powered automatic weapons, such as M16s and AK47s, which have been acquired either from the police or the military. The community response has been a massive, and often daunting, security presence outside shops and banks (every bank now has several guards with fierce dogs).

Solutions to such problems are never easy. On several occasions, the army has been called in, a state of emergency declared and strict controls placed on beer sales. The benefits of these crackdowns have been short-term at best. The rascals melt into the bush, or relocate to terrorise some other community, and are back as soon as the heat is off. The knee jerk response is 'more police and tougher sentencing' but this can never be a full answer – the problem would not have proved to be so intractable if it could. The private security industry is the fastest-growing in PNG.

'Dry' Towns, Gambling & Curfews Many attempts have been made to remedy the law and order situation. The Western Highlands, Simbu and Enga provinces have officially been declared 'dry' to reduce the impact of alcohol on crime. A boom-gate has been erected on the border between the Eastern Highlands and Simbu provinces to prevent the carrying of alcohol. (Alcohol is still available at tourist hotels, except in Enga Province where the ban is total.) It has helped a little to control the problem but it does not attack its root cause.

To make matters worse, poker machines are now common in PNG and gambling – with all its associated problems – is becoming endemic.

In November 1996, the government implemented a nation-wide curfew between 9 pm and 5 am in an effort to reduce the lawlessness. Anyone found outside during curfew hours was arrested, a somewhat draconian and unrealistic imposition in a country in which most of the population was isolated in rural villages. Effectively, a villager going night-fishing was in danger of being locked up and it was reported that

Domestic Violence

Domestic violence is said to affect about two-thirds of families in PNG. There are reports that up to 60% of PNG women have been victims of domestic violence – the second-highest rate in the world after Pakistan.

Cultural traditions in PNG have created an environment in which domestic violence can flourish. PNG is a patriarchal country and women are often totally dependent on their husbands. In most rural areas, the wife leaves her clan to join her husband's, leaving behind a well-entrenched support network; bride price is paid and the husband's relatives are usually loth to pay it back if the woman leaves her husband. The mere payment of bride price often leads to the belief that the husband has a right to beat his wife.

Domestic violence is not a phenomenon unique to PNG but the problem is exacerbated because there is no community welfare net for the women – they often feel alone and unable to cope, with no solution at hand. Following a recent report by the Law Reform Commission in Port Moresby, there has been much greater emphasis on this problem and attempts have been made to engender a wider awareness of women's rights. ■

people were being arrested by over-zealous police while going outside to relieve themselves in the bush. The cost of policing to the government has, however, been exorbitant and the benefits marginal. The curfew was lifted after the 1997 elections but could conceivably be reintroduced if the political situation hots up.

Dos and Don'ts

Travelling to PNG is like travelling almost anywhere else – you should respect that you're in someone else's home and that local people don't have the disposable income to go to your home. Be aware that people take their own ideas seriously and be prepared to show respect for local religious and customary practices but that doesn't mean you can't offer some spontaneous witticism or observation. Be interested in people and they will respond to you and forgive your every wrong move. Show that you are polite and respectful, but don't get hung up about it. Engage people rather than be aloof and you'll have no problems whatever your habits are at home.

RELIGION

PNG's constitution declares that it is a Christian country. The churches have played an important role in developing the country's health and education services but they are also responsible for the loss of traditional knowledge and cultural practices.

About 28% of people are Catholics, 23% Evangelical Lutheran, 13% belong to the United Church, and there are significant numbers of followers of the Evangelical Alliance, Seventh-Day Adventist, Pentecostal and Anglican churches.

Regardless of where PNG's people align their Christian beliefs, they all retain many of their beliefs in traditional religion and customary practices (see the Pop Culture aside).

Within traditional belief systems, people who live in danger of crocodile attacks are likely to give crocodiles an important place in their culture. The weather is important to farming communities and so they often celebrate fertility and harvest.

Most people, especially in the Highlands, traditionally lived in very small, independent communities, surrounded by communities which spoke different languages and could attack at any time. It isn't surprising that many traditional beliefs revolve around fear of the unknown and suspicion of difference. Placating the spirits of ancestors is a common theme in traditional beliefs, as is a fear of evil influences and of sorcery and witchcraft.

In most areas of PNG, traditional life continues but the various arms of the Christian church are extremely influential all over the country. The older churches seem to be able to cope with this dichotomy, concerning themselves with various education, health and development issues, but there are plenty of hell-fire fundamentalists, mainly Americans, up to who-knows-what in the remote areas.

LANGUAGE

More than 770 languages are spoken in PNG – about one-third of the world's indigenous languages. Linguists divide these languages into 14 major groups. Austronesian languages are spoken by a sixth of PNG's people and dominate in the islands and around the coast. Kuanua, the tok ples (literally 'talk of your place', or native tongue) of East New Britain's Tolai people, has the most speakers. Austronesian languages usually have a number system based on five.

Various dialects in the Highlands and Sepik regions are related and can be broadly understood across old clan boundaries. These are non-Austronesian languages and the Simbu Province dialect of Kuman has many speakers.

During the early days of British New Guinea and then Australian Papua, the local language of the Port Moresby coastal area, Motu, was modified to become Police Motu, and spread through Papua by the native constabulary. It is still widely spoken in the southern Papuan part of PNG and you can easily pick up a Motu phrasebook in Port Moresby.

Tok Pisin

Pidgin is a second language to most Papua New Guineans. It's a simple lingua franca that was developed in the early planters' days and is very easy to pick up. There's anxiety that Pidgin is corrupting proper clan languages and many young people are speaking Pidgin instead of their tok ples. It is sometimes known as Neo-Melanesian, but more frequently just as Papua New Guinea Pidgin. It resembles the Pidgin spoken in Vanuatu and the Solomons.

PNG Pidgin has taken words from many languages, including German, but is primarily derived from English. Since it first came into use around Rabaul during the German days, the Melanesian words used in Pidgin are mainly from the languages of East New Britain. There is, however, a number of words indicating other foreign influences. Milk, for example, is *susu* as in Indonesia, although in Pidgin susu can also mean breast.

Many educated people would often prefer to speak English to you, although they appreciate that you've tried to learn a few words of Pidgin. However, Pidgin is considered a crude and clumsy language by most educated people and it does have the old colonial ring to it.

You'll need to understand some basic Pidgin to get about the backblocks of PNG, even if it's only enough to glean what people are saying to you at a hundred miles an hour. Some people are shy about talking to an English-speaker (especially on the telephone) but even if you don't speak Pidgin well, they often relax if you throw a few Pidgin words into an otherwise English sentence.

Pidgin has at times been damned and condemned by everybody from the UN down. It's been called 'baby talk', 'broken English', 'demeaning' and much worse. There was a number of attempts to discourage its use but the language has proven to be vigorous and effective, supplanting Motu even in Port Moresby.

There are only about 1300 words in Pidgin and this frequently results in very roundabout and verbose descriptions. Despite this disadvantage, the language is easily learnt and often very evocative.

Learning Pidgin can be a lot of fun and long after you get home from PNG you'll hear yourself saying *'maski'* (don't bother) and *'tenkyu tru'* (thanks very much). Pidgin words and phrases generally make perfect sense if you just read them out slowly and thoughtfully, although if spoken rapidly they're not easy to follow. A sign outside a Madang cinema announced a film showing was a *piksa bilong bigpela man na meri tasol.* That is, it is a 'picture for big men and women only', in other words it was for adults only. And who was that uniformed Englishman at the independence day celebrations? None other than the *nambawan pikinini bilong Misis Kwin* – 'first-born child of the Queen' – Prince Charles! A public library? That's a *haus buk bilong ol man na meri.*

There are quite a few Pidgin words and phrases that have crept into everyday

English in PNG. You can always recognise somebody who has spent time in PNG by the way they say *tru* instead of 'really', 'that's right' or 'you don't say'.

No expat leaves PNG when their work is completed, they *go pinis*. It's never dinner time, always *kai* (food) time, which is followed not by dessert but by *switpela kai*. If something is unimportant or doesn't matter, then it's *samting nating* (ie something-nothing). And a private problem, your own affair, is *samting bilong yu*. The word *rausim* or *raus* harks back to the Germans (as does *haus* – house), and it loosely means to throw away or expel. If you say *'rausim'* to a person, it means 'get out of here'.

Conversely, modern English expressions, especially of Australian origin, are keeping Pidgin lively, such as *naiswan*, an expression of approval or congratulations – 'nice one'!

If your Pidgin is less than perfect, it is wise to append *yu save or nogat?* (literally 'you understand or not?') to just about any sentence. *Save* is pronounced by the Papua New Guineans as 'savvy'.

Note that *p* and *f* are pronounced (and often spelled) virtually interchangeably, as are *d* and *t*, and *j* and *z*; *qu* is spelled *kw*; *u* is pronounced like a short *oo*.

Avoiding Confusion

Be wary of words that may sound similar to English but have a different meaning in Pidgin. For instance, *kilim* just means to hit (but hard); to kill somebody (or something) you have to *kilim i dai*.

Bare Bones of Pidgin

Pidgin is simple and you'll find that having a basic grip of the language is useful in PNG. The following words and phrases provide the bare basics for communicating with locals in *tok pisin*. Remember that written Pidgin is very phonetic (as are the spellings of many people's names).

me	mi
me and my lot	mipela
you	yu
you and your lot	yupela
all of us	yumi
everybody	olgeta (note that *olgeta haus* means all of the houses)
he/she/it	em (note that *em* is followed by *i* as in *em i haus bilong yu i stap?* – where is your house?)
they	ol (note that *ol* indicates the plural as in *ol haus* – houses)
to think	tinktink
to forget	tinktink lusim
here	hia
there	hap (*long hap* is 'over there')
give	givim
receive, or to get	kisim
have	gat (*mi gat* ..., *yu gat* ...)
go	go
come	kam
shut, or fasten	fasim or pasim

Another very common and useful word is *long*, which means 'to' (as in '*mi go long haus*') or 'at' (as in '*long dispela haus* ...').

Probably the most confusing thing about Pidgin is tense. If you're talking about time in the past, you say *taim bipo* (time before), or *bipo long*. If you mean the very beginning of time, that's *pastaim*. To indicate that an event has happened the verb is appended with the word *pinis*, eg 'I have gone' is '*mi go pinis*'. If you're talking about the future that's *bihain* ('behind' as in the time *after* the current time). The word *pinis* can also be used to refer to a future event eg 'after he comes here' would be '*bihain em i-kam hia pinis*.

If you want to say 'I understand only a little Pidgin, but you will have to talk slowly', try '*Mi save liklik tok pisin tasol, yupela tok esi. Mi no ken save tok pisin sapos yupela tok kwiktaim*'. ■

Be careful of the sexual phrases – *pusim* means to copulate with, not to push. And while you can *ple tenis* (play tennis), *ple* is also a euphemism for intercourse. A man's trunk or suitcase may be a *bokis*, but a woman's *bokis* is her vagina. And a *blak bokis* is not a black suitcase but a flying fox or bat!

You'll love the standard reply to 'how far is it?' – *longwe liklik*. It doesn't actually mean a long way and not a long way – it translates more like 'not too near, not too far'.

Greetings & Civilities

Good morning.	*Moning.*
Good afternoon.	*Apinun.*
See you later.	*Lukim yu bihain.*
How are you?	*Yu stap gut?*
I'm fine.	*Mi stap gut.*

Questions & Phrases

May I take a photo?	*Inap my kisim poto?*
Show me.	*Soim me.*
Stop here!	*Stap!* [1]
Is it far?	*Em i longwe?*
near, close by	*klostu*
a very long way	*longwe tumas*
I would like to buy ...	*Mi laik baim ...*
Where is the ...?	*We stap wanpela ...?*
How much does that cost?	*Em i hamas?* [2]
I want something to eat.	*Mi laikim sampela kaikai.*
That is mine.	*Em bilong mi.*
Be careful!	*Lukautim gut!*
Go away!	*Yu go!* [3]
Don't touch/Put it down!	*Lusim!*

1   The word *stap* has many functions including to stay or to be present or to indicate the progressive form – *em i kaikai i stap* (he is eating).
2   Many townspeople add *kostim* (*Em i kostim hamas?*) but it is better Pidgin not to.
3   It is very impolite to say *raus*, it means 'leave (the house)' more than simply 'go away'.

Small Talk

What is your name?	*Wanem nem bilong yu?*
Where are you from?	*Ples bilong yu we?*
I don't understand.	*Mi no klia gut.*
I don't know.	*Mi no save.*
Speak slowly.	*Tok isi.*

Some Useful Words

Yes.	*Yes.*
No.	*Nogat.*
Please.	*Plis.*
Thankyou.	*Tenkyu.*
aircraft	*balus*
airport	*ples balus*
a little	*liklik*
bathroom	*rum waswas*
bedroom	*rum slip*
big	*bikpela*
brother	*brata*
child	*pikinini*
decorations/uniform	*bilas*
forbidden	*tambu*
hospital	*haus sick*
letter/book/ticket	*pas* [1]
luggage	*kago*
man/woman	*man/meri*
newspaper	*niuspepa*
photo	*poto*
plenty	*planti*
police station	*haus polis*
relative	*wantok*
sister	*susa*
toilet	*liklik haus*
towel	*taul* [2]

1   Anything with writing on it.
2   A towel used to be a *laplap bilong waswas* but that is now rather old-fashioned.

Food

food	*kaikai*
restaurant	*haus kaikai*
menu	*pas bilong kaikai*
tea	*ti*
coffee	*kopi*
eggs	*kiau*
sugar	*suga*
meat	*abus/mit*
unripe coconut	*kulau*
water	*wara*
drink	*dring*

breakfast	*kaikai bilong moning*
lunch	*kaikai bilong belo*
dinner	*kaikai bilong apinun*

Books

As with any language it takes a lot of study to understand Pidgin fully, but you can be communicating on at least a basic level with remarkable speed. Lonely Planet publishes the pocket-sized *Papua New Guinea phrasebook*, which includes grammatical notes, many useful phrases and a vocabulary.

There are a number of alternative phrasebooks and dictionaries that are easily available. The best places to look are the Christian bookshops in PNG; there is usually one in every town and they have all sorts of literature in Pidgin, including, needless to say, a Pidgin bible.

It's worthwhile buying the *Wantok* weekly newspaper, written entirely in Pidgin. As well as being a decent newspaper, reading it is a good way to learn the language. There are also comic strips, which are easy to follow even for beginners. EmTV broadcasts many programs in Pidgin, which will also help you pick it up.

Summer Institute of Linguistics (satellite ☎ 640 4400; PO Box 413, Ukarumpa) publishes a kit with two cassette tapes and a book. It is only available in PNG.

Papua New Guinean Arts

Papua New Guinea's arts are regarded as the most vital and varied in the Pacific. The lack of contact between different villages and groups of people has resulted in a rich and potent national heritage of indigenous art.

In traditional societies, dance, song, music, sculpture and body adornment were related to ceremonies. Art was either utilitarian (such as bowls or canoes) or religious. Since European contact, PNG's art has become objectified. There have always been master carvers and mask-makers but their role in traditional cultures was to enable the ceremonies and rituals to be performed correctly, and to serve the clan and chief. Art served the culture.

The production of artefacts is itself often ritualistic. On some of the islands secret men's societies build *dukduk* ritual costumes or carve *malangan* masks (totemic figures to honour the dead). Women are forbidden to look upon a dukduk or malangan until it is brought to life in a ceremony by a fierce anonymous character. But a dukduk is itself a spirit entity – art, religion and culture are European distinctions.

Traditional Arts

Traditional art and culture were bound together, with 'art' usually taking the form of carvings and artefacts used in ceremonies.

Highlanders are especially resplendent in their traditional garb and *bilas* (finery), and an afternoon at a local *sing-sing* (celebratory festival) or show will reveal just how artful and varied body decoration can be. Highlanders wear amazing headdresses of colourful bird feathers and *kina* shells, and paint their faces in fantastic designs (taking hours of preparation).

Artefacts

Pottery

The village of Aibom, near the Chambri Lakes, is virtually the only place on the Sepik to specialise in pottery. Aibom pots are noted for their relief faces which are coloured with lime; they are made by the coil method.

Other interesting pots can be found near Madang, in the Central Province, made by the Porebada people, and at Wanigela in Oro Province. The Amphlett Islanders in Milne Bay also make fine and fragile pottery. No pottery is glazed in PNG, and as it is often poorly fired, it can be extremely fragile.

Weapons

The Chambri Lakes carvers produce decorative spears which are remarkably similar to their masks. Shields are also popular artefacts – their spiritual role is just as important as their function of warrior protection. In the Highlands, the ceremonial Hagen axes are similarly half-tool, half-icon. There you will also see the lethal cassowary-claw tipped Huli picks, while in the Sepik region you will find the equally nasty bone daggers.

Spirit Boards, Story Boards & Cult Hooks

In Gulf Province, the shield-like hohao and gope boards are said to contain the spirits of powerful heroes or act as guardians of the village. Before hunting trips or war expeditions, the spirits in the boards were called upon to advise and support the warriors.

At Kambot on the Keram River, a tributary of the Sepik, story boards are a modern interpretation of the fragile bark carvings of the past. The boards illustrate, in raised relief, incidents of village life and are fantastic examples of PNG art.

Cult hooks – small ones are Yipwons, while larger ones are Kamanggabi – are carved as hunting charms and carried by their owners in a bag (the small ones, anyway) to ensure success on the hunt. Food hooks hang *bilums* of food from the roof to keep them away from rats, but they also have a spiritual significance.

Bowls

The Trobriand Islanders are prolific carvers of everything from stylised figures to decorated lime gourds and beautifully made bowls. The bowls are generally carved from dark wood and laboriously polished with a pig's tusk. The rims are patterned, often to represent a fish or turtle.

The Tami Islanders near Lae are renowned for their carved bowls. Further offshore the Siassi Islanders carve deep, elliptical bowls which are stained black and patterned with incised designs coloured with lime. In Milne Bay, the Muyua (Woodlark) Islanders carve bowls somewhat similar to those from the neighbouring Trobriand Islands.

Trobriands bowls are often created using fish motifs, and the rims are decorated with mother-of-pearl inlays.

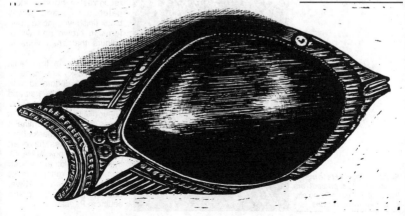

Malangan Carvings

In northern New Ireland, master carvers create malangan figures to fulfil their culture's mortuary rites. But malangan does not just refer to the carvings – it is a complex system of spiritual beliefs and rituals. There's a few regular master carvers on Tabar Island and Libba village near Konos; otherwise, the carvings are only created for village mortuary ceremonies (see the Malangan Death Rites aside in the New Ireland chapter).

Bilums

Bilums are colourful string bags which are made in many parts of PNG. They are enormously strong and expand to amazing sizes. Good bilums can be rather expensive, particularly in the towns. They are time-consuming to make since the entire length of string is fed through every loop. Bilums are now also made of synthetic cords which are sometimes ghastly and sometimes very striking and beautiful. There's a variety of styles – Highlanders make big 'woollen' ones made of cuscus fur.

Smaller bilums make handy daypacks and when you get home you'll never need a plastic supermarket bag again. The big bilums, worn with the strap around the forehead, can carry a staggering amount of stuff, but sometimes just a baby.

Simple, elongated face masks (often with lips pursed) are typical of the lower Ramu and lower Sepik river regions.

Masks

Masks in PNG are more often intended as decoration than as something to be worn. They are particularly found along the Sepik River but also in other parts of the country. The Chambri masks from the villages on the Chambri Lakes are the most modern of the Sepik masks – instantly recognisable by their elongated design and glossy black finish with incised patterns in brown and white, colours that are unique to Chambri.

At Korogo, in the Sepik region, masks are made of wood, then decorated with clay in which shells, hair and pigs' teeth are embedded. Other distinctive Sepik-mask styles are found at Kaminabit and Tambanum. Masks from the Murik Lakes have an almost African look. At Maprik the yam masks are woven from cane or rattan. Masks are also carved at Kiwai Island, near Daru on the southern Papuan coast.

Highland Hats

These hats are essential wear for Highlanders – you'll even see Highlanders wearing their colourful knitted hats down in hot Port Moresby.

Other Handcrafts

Buka baskets, from Bougainville Island in the North Solomons, are said to be the finest baskets in the Pacific and are very expensive. The style has been adopted elsewhere, but the Bougainvilleans still make the best. Similar, coarser baskets are found in the Southern Highlands. Figures of various types are carved on the baskets made around Murik Lakes, the Yuat River and the Trobriand Islands.

The Trobriand Islanders also carve very intricate walking sticks and some delightful little stools and tables. The walking sticks are often carved from ebony, which is now rare and found only on Muyua (Woodlark) Island.

Tapa cloth, made from tree bark, is beaten and decorated in the village of Yiaku in Oro Province and elsewhere. Shell jewellery can be found at many coastal towns, particularly at Madang and Rabaul.

Music

Indigenous Rhythms

In recent years there's been a strong revival of traditional PNG music, but the impact of missionary workers has meant many traditional musical forms have been lost.

The kundu drum is the most widely used traditional instrument, shaped like a tall and narrow egg-timer and covered with snake or lizard skin. Many cultures use garamuts, hollowed-out logs in any size from a pencil case up to a massive tree trunk. Garamut drummers play astonishing rhythms in hierarchical ensembles where the senior drummers play the trickiest patterns. The rhythms are specific to the region, but generally you can't tap your foot to them.

Shells and bamboo panpipes are blown, while rattles are made from gourds and bundled banana leaves. Highland flutes (simple throwaway bamboo tubes) are played in pairs and do an eerie call-and-response routine. Sepik flutes are highly decorated and hollowed from solid timber. They too are often played in pairs. Jew's-harps are also indigenous to PNG.

Sing-sings and provincial shows are good places to see many of the traditional instruments in use (see the Public Holidays & Special Events section in the Facts for the Visitor chapter).

Musical Instruments

Drums are available all over the country, with the large *garamut* drums and the smaller *kundu* drums the most common.

Other instruments include the sacred flutes always found in male-female pairs and generally reserved for initiation rites, the bull roarers which are spun round on a length of cord, the pottery whistles of the Highlands and the small jew's-harps which are also found in the Highlands.

Contemporary Arts

There are community-based drama groups as well as others associated with the universities and colleges. Theatre groups commonly work on local-legend themes and stories – some productions have brought to life old stories and traditional knowledge.

The Faculty of Creative Arts (also known as the National Art School) was established at the University of PNG in Port Moresby in 1972. With a strong emphasis on print-making and painting, some of its graduates have earned international reputations. Matthias Kuage, Jakuba, Cecil King, John Siune and Akis have works hung in overseas galleries; Kuage, in particular, is rapidly becoming famous (see the Matthias Kuage aside below).

Music

Western Influences

PNG has a thriving independent music scene and a prolific output from the two major recording studios, Pacific Gold Studios and CH Minh. Cassettes are cheap and sell well to a population that loves a good tune and a ghetto-blaster.

Missionaries brought hymns and songs and now there's a very strong gospel music tradition in PNG. This manifests in both a cappella groups and in a popular contemporary rock/soul sound.

However, it was the guitar that the people really took to – and the stringband was born. Stringband music is played by four or five guitarists and a ukulele player and based loosely around a 12-bar blues structure. The guitars are tuned in unorthodox ways (generally bright, 'majorish' tunings – EABEG#B is a standard Tolai tuning) and are often played with

---

Matthias Kuage

He sleeps through the morning on the concrete path outside the Port Moresby Travelodge, his head on his folded arms. His paintings are laid out near the door with a pebble on each corner, all very striking and filled with vivid images of helicopters and planes with huge faces in the windows. Kuage's people are generally villagers and the central theme of his work is the experiences of grassroots people thrust into the world of technology.

Kuage is in his 50s and comes from Simbu Province. His Highlands people have only had recent contact with the outside world. He can remember first seeing a helicopter first and, assuming it was a giant bird, trying to shoot at it with a bow and arrow.

In 1996, when Kuage was invited to exhibit his work at the Glasgow Museum of Modern Art and a London gallery, he was granted a short audience with Queen Elizabeth II, or *Misis Kwin*. He presented her with the portrait *Misis Kwin*, in which she was depicted with a tribal headdress and bone through her nose. Misis Kwin's graciousness and red outfit inspired Kuage to paint another series of portraits. Meeting the Queen was the best day of his life.

Kuage stirs and suddenly realises that someone is lingering over his paintings. He rouses and comes over to explain the pricing structure of his painted canvasses and paper. I vacillate endlessly and then buy two.

Rowan McKinnon

Telek

George Telek is PNG's most successful musician. A Tolai from near Kokopo, Telek says he chewed a magic *buai* (betel nut) when he was a boy which gave him his wonderful and unusual voice. Most of PNG's successful musical artists are graduates of universities and music courses, but Telek has a very grassroots background and little formal education.

Telek grew up near Rabaul when the PNG music industry was in its infancy. From the late 1970s he taught himself guitar while working in various rock and roll bands, and he kept his roots in stringband music by singing with the Moab Stringband and the Jolly Rogers Stringband.

Through the 1980s and early 1990s, Telek sold loads of cassettes as a solo artist and as a frontman for bands like Painim Wok (literally 'find work'), Kagan Devils and the wonderfully named Junior Unbelievers. He worked in Australia at world music festivals, touring and recording with the likes of Not Drowning Waving, Archie Roach and Kev Carmody.

'Eh, can you turn up the bass?'

In 1997 he released his first, self-titled album to an international market in Australia. *Telek* has some traditional material and some contemporary stuff, but most of it fits in between. To get a feel for his background (and for some fantastic Tolai stringband music), seek out the classic Moab Stringband cassette with the hammerhead shark on the cover (Pacific Gold label). ∎

an arpeggiated, hammer-on action. The stringband sound has a real swing to it in a lazy South Pacific kind of way, but it varies widely from the bright and happy Tolai (East New Britain Province) sound to the more dirge-like and sombre Manus stringband music. Virtually every PNG village has a stringband, whether for performances at festivals and sing-sings or just folks getting together to jam. Stringband music is a thriving musical form, and there are countless tapes from trade stores all over the country. Look out for cassettes of the now-defunct Moab Stringband which was fronted by George Telek (see the above Telek aside).

Most PNG rock musicians think stringband music is a bit unsophisticated and not too cool. They like good hard rock, maybe with a reggae feel. A strong musical culture, which nurtured the originally Rabaul-based recording studios, created a proliferation of bands and singers of all styles. Music shows on EmTV (the only PNG TV channel) play loads of local video clips. Both the original Pacific Gold and CH Minh studios are under Tuvurvur's ash in Rabaul and the companies now work out of Port Moresby.

There's no copyright law in PNG, which means that pirated cassettes of top-selling western artists sell for a mere K2.50 (the artist receives no royalty). Local music cassettes sell for around K7.

Buying Art & Artefacts

Like everything else in PNG, artefacts are expensive. The price mark-up on carvings can also be astonishing – some shop prices are many times the carver's sale price and there's another huge price jump if you buy PNG artefacts outside the country.

There are a couple of reasons for this (apart from plain profiteering). A dealer must gather stock and getting a broad collection together takes a long time – long buying trips, sometimes to remote places, are expensive. Transportation is a big problem because many PNG artefacts are large, unwieldy or terribly fragile.

The best advice to buyers is to buy one good piece you really like – it might even cost several hundred kina – rather than armfuls of small inferior carvings and artefacts. Bilums and Highlands hats are easy to get home in your luggage, but lugging more than one or two unwieldy artefacts around the country is going to be a hassle (one author left a carving bundled up in cardboard behind the Avis desk at Port Moresby's Jackson International Airport for three weeks – ask politely). Spears can be dismantled and are relatively easy to transport, as are Chambri masks, because they are solid without projecting teeth, horns or other features.

It's worthwhile to know what you're buying and it will help you select a good piece. The style of carving and artefacts varies so widely that general rules are hard to establish but look for the carver's deft touches and see how well the recesses are finished. Look at the details and feel the weight in the timber. Sometimes inferior timbers are rubbed down with shoe polish and passed off as high-quality ebony.

Don't haggle about the price – if you can't afford it buy something else. An artefact maker would feel insulted if you tried to bargain. There's sometimes room for negotiation, but bargaining is not a natural thing in Melanesian societies, and you're a rich tourist in their eyes. It is rare that a maker will over-inflate the price to allow room for it to be bargained down. There's perhaps more room for negotiation with the artefacts shops than with the makers themselves.

There are good shops in Port Moresby, Lae and a number of other towns – information on them is in the relevant regional chapters. In some places artefact sellers gather outside hotels.

You can buy one of the colourful Highlands hats in Port Moresby or at a Highlands market.

Aibom pots are very cheap on the Sepik, but rapidly become more expensive as you move further away from this region because, like other PNG pottery, they are very fragile.

Bows and arrows are available from a number of places, including the Highlands and Bougainville Island.

The Artefacts & Crafts of Papua New Guinea – a Guide for Buyers is a useful little booklet (see the Books section in the Facts for the Visitor chapter). If you want to get a preview of New Guinea art in Australia, visit New Guinea Primitive Arts, 6th floor, 428 George St, Sydney.

Facts for the Visitor

PLANNING

When to Go

The climate is the main consideration in deciding when to visit Papua New Guinea. You'll probably want to avoid rainy seasons (although a good tropical downpour is a sight to be seen) but they vary across the country. See the Climate section in the Facts about the Country chapter. Airlines run to capacity from before Christmas to early February (with a lull in January), ferrying people home on holidays and expats to and from Australia.

Maps

The National Mapping Bureau (NMB) in Waigani (☎ 327 6465; fax 327 6460; PO Box 5665, Boroko, NCD) has a wide selection of maps. The whole country is covered by topographic maps at 1:250,000 and 1:100,000 scale; topographic maps at 1:50,000 and 1:25,000 scale are available for selected areas; and 1:2,000 for principal town areas. The NMB also has cadastral maps, thematic maps, photo mosaic maps, complete coverage of PNG by aerial photography (dating back to the 1970s) and satellite imagery facilities. Some of the provincial Lands & Survey departments also sell these maps but the office in Port Moresby is more likely to have complete stocks.

Many of the topographic maps were produced by the Royal Australian Survey Corps in the 1970s and are a little out of date. It should be borne in mind when reading old maps that villages in PNG tend to move around over the years. A variety of reasons (including slash-and-burn agriculture, moving closer to newly made roads, or major deaths in the village) may cause some villages to move up to 20km from their original locations.

If you are planning to walk the Kokoda Trail, the NMB has produced a useful *Longitudinal Cross Section of the Kokoda Trail*, the latest version of which was printed in 1995.

Wirui Press (☎ 856 2479; PO Box 107, Wewak) has produced a handy and up-to-date map for those undertaking Sepik trips entitled *West and East Sepik Provinces*, which is available in Wewak from the publisher or either Ralf Stüttgen or Alois Mateus, both East Sepik guesthouse owners. Robert Brown & Associates (PO Box 1299, Coorparoo, Queensland 4151, Australia) has produced an easy-to-read political map of PNG showing provincial boundaries and main towns, and Hema Maps (PO Box 724, Springwood 4127, Queensland, Australia) has a good relief map.

What to Bring

The best advice, wherever you go, is to take too little rather than too much. Keep in mind that the domestic airlines have a baggage weight limit of 16kg, although as a tourist you can usually slip by if your bags weigh around 20kg. The generally warm climate makes things easy – even in the cool Highlands, a sweater is all you'll ever need for the evenings. Naturally, what you plan to do and how you plan to travel will shape what you need to take. For instance, the only time you'll need a coat is if you go mountain climbing: it snows on top of Mt Wilhelm.

Most of the time all you will require is lightweight clothing, T-shirts, sandals and swimming gear. Natural fibres, cotton in particular, will be most comfortable in the sticky, lowlands humidity – stay away from synthetics. Long-sleeved shirts are not necessary except on the most formal occasions, although they can be useful as sun and mosquito protection. Coats and ties are virtually never required. Men will find Australian-style 'dress' shorts can be worn for almost any occasion, but lightweight trousers are nice to have for restaurants and cool Highlands evenings. A hat, large enough to shade the back of your neck, and sunglasses will also be useful.

Unless you plan to spend all your time in

resorts, don't come laden with gaudy T-shirts, boardshorts and other 'beach culture' clothing. Other than the small rich elite, most people dress conservatively and many buy their clothes from secondhand stores. Flaunting your foreignness will make you stand out and could attract thieves.

Women must dress discreetly; the often scanty styles of traditional dress do not apply to foreigners and mission-influenced people can be very prudish. From a security point of view, it's not a good idea to call attention to yourself with revealing clothes. Shorts are not a good idea for women. A bikini is inappropriate at all but the most westernised and protected locations.

PNG is not a good place to buy clothes, unless you want to check out the ubiquitous secondhand shops. You can buy all the essentials in the main towns but they aren't cheap. On the other hand, the day-to-day western commodities that can be difficult to find in Asia (toothpaste, toilet paper, tampons etc) are easy to obtain. It is worth carrying a roll of toilet paper (handy if you're likely to be using bush toilets) and sunscreen and insect repellent are essential. A medical kit is also necessary – see the Health section.

The most flexible and useful items for carrying your baggage are travel backpacks. These are packs with internal frames and adjustable harnesses that can be zipped away into a compartment. You can use them as packs when you're bushwalking or looking for a hotel, and with the harness hidden you don't run into problems with straps snagging on airport conveyer belts or bus seats. A cheaper alternative is a sports bag with a shoulder strap. Unless you're on a tour or can afford taxis, you will have to do some walking, so make sure your baggage can be easily carried. Packing your things in separate plastic bags helps keep everything organised and dry.

A daypack is handy for carrying a camera and a water bottle (essential if you're walking or can't survive on Pepsi). If you don't need your daypack to be waterproof, buy a *bilum* (string bag) when you arrive. A money belt or pouch is essential. Because of the heat, a pouch or belt and its contents soon become sodden with sweat, so make sure paper items are sealed in plastic.

A mask and snorkel is worth having if you have space, as hire shops are few and far between, prices are high and virtually every beach is a snorkeller's delight. Consider taking some cutlery, a bowl, plate and mug so you can make your own breakfast or lunch. A Swiss Army knife with a can opener, bottle opener and scissors will be invaluable. A small torch (flashlight) is handy for late-night toilet expeditions (vital if you're in a village). Some light nylon cord, another all-purpose item, is useful for hanging mosquito nets, shoelaces, a washing line, tying parcels etc.

If you're not bushwalking, don't bother to bring a tent. If you anticipate spending much time in the Highlands, where the nights can get cold, it is worth considering a sleeping bag that is lightweight and compact. In other areas a sleeping sheet is just as useful and is lighter and smaller.

A mosquito net is essential if you're planning to stay in villages, but you can get these in Port Moresby or Wewak. See the Sepik chapter for details of items you will need on the river.

Poncho-style rain wear can fold out to be a ground sheet and is essential if you're travelling on dinghies between islands; it can cover your backpack, too.

HIGHLIGHTS

A cultural highlight of a PNG visit is attending one of the famed Highlands shows, with their spectacular dancing and colourful costumes – but you need to time your trip carefully to catch one. Otherwise, one of the more frequent *sing-sings* (celebratory festivals) will give you a sample of the colour and vibrancy of the culture.

If you're interested in the natural environment, cruising down the mighty Sepik River, and investigating village craftwork en route, or climbing Mt Wilhelm, the highest mountain in PNG, and taking in the panoramic views including the mainland's northern and southern coastlines are just two possibilities.

You can also dive or snorkel in the clean and clear waters around Madang, Tufi, Rabaul or Kavieng.

If you're keen on PNG's recent history, you could try trekking the historic Kokoda Trail, the scene of some of the heaviest fighting of WWII, or visiting volcano-ravaged Rabaul nestled on the beautiful New Britain coastline.

For those who want to rough it, PNG offers almost unlimited possibilities. You could spend months cruising the islands on small boats, or walking trails in remote areas. Just staying in a village for any length of time will be an introduction to a very different way of life.

TOURIST OFFICES

There are few outlets for general tourist information inside PNG. One of the best is Air Niugini. It plays a major role in promoting tourism and most offices are helpful and have some printed information.

There will be a tourist information office in the international arrivals hall at the new airport terminal in Port Moresby where you can get a visitors' guide and an annually updated accommodation directory.

A number of provincial governments have officials whose responsibilities include tourism; see the relevant sections in each regional chapter. But if you write to them, be prepared to receive no reply – ironically, public relations is almost invariably low on their agenda. Your best bet is to write to the Tourism Promotion Authority (PO Box 1291, Port Moresby), which approaches the task with some professionalism.

Overseas, Air Niugini offices are the best sources of information (see the Getting There & Away chapter). Embassies may help (see the Embassies section in this chapter), as can the tour operators.

VISAS & DOCUMENTS
Passport & Visas

The only essential document is your passport. It must have at least six months validity, even if you plan to visit PNG for only a few weeks.

The story on visas has made a number of abrupt about-faces over the years, so it is wise to check the regulations with a PNG consular office before you depart. In countries where there is no PNG consular office, apply to the nearest Australian office.

The latest change to the visa system has been the reinstatement of the one-month 'easy visa', granted to tourists on entry. You pay K13 and must have onward tickets. However, don't rely on this – it's better to get a visa before you leave home.

A standard tourist visa obtained outside PNG requires one photo, costs the equivalent of K13 and permits a stay of up to 60 days. Since they seem to give you what you ask for, ask for the maximum time rather than face the problem of extending. There are heavy penalties for overstaying your visa. The most lightly you're likely to get off is paying a K250 fee for 'late application for visa extension'. When applying for your visa, you may be asked to show your inward and outward ticketing, that you have sufficient funds and have made some sort of accommodation arrangements. Usually you will only have to show tickets.

To apply for a business visa, you'll have to provide letters of sponsorship from home and PNG, as well as details of your business. A multiple-entry visa allows up to 60 days stay each time and costs the equivalent of K250.

If you are seeking an employment visa, you must provide certain medical results, details for a police clearance, a copy of your employment contract and a letter from your country's department of labour and employment. A short-term visa will cost the equivalent of K333.

Church and aid volunteers can enter on a special K13 visa but the issuing authorities are required to wait for special immigration department approval. Researchers, film makers and journalists must submit their visa applications with a special application form from the National Research Institute (☎ 326 0300; fax 325 0531; PO Box 5854, Boroko). They cost K67 (journalists K133).

People coming in by yacht pay K100 for

a visa (which now must be obtained in advance) and possibly a K100 customs clearance fee when they leave.

In Australia, there is a PNG High Commission in Canberra, a consulate-general in Sydney and a consulate in Brisbane and Cairns. Allow at least a week for processing.

Jayapura in Irian Jaya is another exit point to PNG and there is a PNG consulate there. For more information, see the Indonesia subheading in this section and the Vanimo section in The Sepik chapter.

Visa Extensions Tourist visas can be extended for one month for a fee of K13. The immigration and citizenship office in the Central Government Offices in Waigani, Port Moresby, is (almost) the only place in the country where you can extend visas and the procedure is slow and frustrating – worth avoiding if you can. The immigration official in Mt Hagen is said to be helpful so, if you happen to be in the Highlands, try him first.

The immigration section (☎ 327 1026; fax 325 5206; PO Wards Strip, Waigani) of the Department of Foreign Affairs is on the ground floor of the Central Government Offices at Waigani. The office is open only from 8 am to noon and you'll have to battle hordes of agents who are on first-name terms with the staff. Extending a visa takes at least a week, officially, but one fortunate traveller reports managing it in a day.

Travellers who have tried extending their visas by mail from other parts of the country have generally found it impossible and have had to trek back to Port Moresby to retrieve their passports. If you do intend to do this, use a courier rather than mail. The address is: Immigration and Citizenship Division, Department of Foreign Affairs, PO Wards Strip, Waigani, NCD. If you have problems it might be a good idea to talk to an agent – see the Yellow Pages under Visa Services.

Indonesia The visa situation for people travelling to or from Indonesia is tricky. Regulations can change overnight and the left hand rarely knows what the right hand is doing. It pays to be flexible in your plans if you want to incorporate both Indonesia and PNG in your itinerary.

The main route is to Jayapura – the road from Vanimo to Jayapura should have been open by late 1997, Air Niugini has a regular flight to Jayapura every Sunday and there is a boat which does a quick trip from Vanimo to Jayapura weekly (see the Vanimo section in The Sepik chapter). If departing PNG from Vanimo by sea or air, you will be required to undergo PNG customs and immigration formalities in Vanimo. There will be a border post on the road to handle such formalities when it opens to traffic.

Although you can get a two-month tourist pass for Indonesia on arrival at certain international ports, if you have an onward ticket and your passport is valid for a minimum of six months, it's much better to get a visa before you arrive – the pass is actually distinct from a visa. Jayapura is *not* one of the ports where passes are issued, although there have been reports that some lucky EC (European Community) citizens have been given 14-day Indonesian transit passes on arrival in Jayapura from PNG and that these were converted to two-month tourist passes in Biak. Don't count on this.

You will need a Surat Keterangan Jalan (SKJ), or travel permit, if you want to leave Jayapura for other parts of West Irian – but this is easily obtained from the provincial police office in Jayapura for Rp 1500 (and two photos).

One-month visas to Indonesia are issued at the Indonesian Embassy in Port Moresby and the Indonesian Consulate in Vanimo (Sandaun Province). Apparently these can be extended in Indonesia. The visa usually takes between two and four days to be issued in Port Moresby, but only a day (or sometimes an hour) in Vanimo. You need an onward ticket from Jayapura, a couple of photos and K20. If you don't have the onward ticket (maybe you plan to leave by sea), try buying a return Vanimo-Jayapura ticket and cashing in the return half after you obtain a visa.

You do not need to present your application in person at the Port Moresby office, so you could use a courier (not the mail) to ferry your passport to and from wherever you happen to be. This system seems risky and with a consulate in Vanimo it should not be necessary, but it's used by many expats in PNG and there seem to be few problems, although sometimes phone calls are needed to hurry things along.

If you enter PNG from Indonesia and plan to exit through Indonesia, do not forget to get a new Indonesian visa in PNG – once you have left Indonesia, the original visa or pass is finished whether or not the time has expired. The easiest way is to pick up a new visa on *first* arrival in Vanimo as this will save time and trouble later.

For those travellers returning to PNG from Irian Jaya, visas are easily obtained at the PNG consulate in Jayapura. They take one day (but can do it within the hour if pressed!) and cost Rp 20,000.

Australia All nationalities (except New Zealanders) require a visa for Australia which is issued free at consulates and usually valid for six months. Extensions beyond the six-month period seem to be somewhat arbitrary – sometimes they will and sometimes they won't. Visitors aged between 18 and 26 from the UK, Ireland, Canada, the Netherlands and Japan can be eligible for a working holiday visa, and you should apply for this in your own country.

The Australian High Commission in Port Moresby seems to be pretty cooperative and very quick in issuing visas. Some travellers seem to use PNG as a convenient way of extending their stay in Australia without having to face the hassles of a straightforward extension. They travel around Australia for their initial six months, spend some time in PNG and come back to Australia for another six months.

Other Documents

You do not need an International Health Certificate in PNG, but you do for a number of Asian countries (Indonesia for one). A few two places to stay give discounts to members of the Hostelling International. A valid over-

seas licence is all you need to drive a car for up to three months from your arrival.

International Student Identity Cards are very useful, especially if you're under 26 years old. Air Niugini offers student discounts as do some of the smaller airlines. Airlines sometimes require an International Student Concession Form, which should be available from your institution or school.

EMBASSIES
PNG Embassies

PNG has diplomatic representation in a number of countries, including:

Australia
> High Commission, 39-41 Forster Crescent, Yarralumla; PO Box 572, Manuka, ACT 2603 (☎ (02) 6273 3322; fax (02) 6273 3732)
> Consulate-General, Somare Haus, 100 Clarence St; GPO Box 4201, Sydney 2001, NSW (☎ (02) 9299 5151; fax (02) 9290 3794)
> Consulate, Estates House, 99 Creek St; PO Box 220, Brisbane 4000, Queensland (☎ (07) 3221 7915; fax (07) 3229 6084)
> Consulate, level 15, National Mutual Tower, 15 Lake St; PO Box 8114, Cairns 4870, Queensland (☎ (07) 4052 1033; fax (07) 4052 1048)

Belgium
> Embassy, 17-19 Rue Montoyer, 1040 Brussels (☎ (02) 512 3126; fax (02) 512 8643)

Fiji
> Embassy, 6th floor, Ratu Sukuna House; PO Box 2447, Government Buildings, Suva (☎ 30 4244; fax 30 0178)

France
> Embassy, Apartment 272, Flatotel International Coenson, 14 Rue du Théâtre, 75015 Paris (☎ 01 45 75 62 20, ext 272; fax 01 40 58 12 22)

Germany
> Embassy, Gotenstrasse 163, 5300 Bonn 2 (☎ (0228) 37 6855/6; fax (0228) 37 5103)

Indonesia
> Embassy, 6th floor, Panin Bank Centre, Jalan Jendral Sudirman 1, Jakarta 10270 (☎ (021) 720 1012; fax (021) 73 4562)
> Consulate, Jalan Serui No 8; PO Box 854, Jayapura, Irian Jaya (☎ (967) 31250; fax (967) 31898)

Japan
> Embassy, Mita Kokusai Building, 3rd floor, 313, 4-28 Mita 1-Chome, Minato-Ku, Tokyo (☎ (03) 345 47801/4; fax (03) 345 47275)

Malaysia
> High Commission, 1 Lorong Ru Kedua, off Jalan Ru, Ampang, Kuala Lumpur (☎ (03) 457 4202/4; fax (03) 456 0998)

New Zealand
    High Commission, 11th floor, Princes Towers, 180 Molesworth St, Thorndon, Wellington (☎ (04) 473 1560; fax (04) 471 2942)
The Philippines
    Embassy, 2280 Magnolia St, Dasmarinas Village, Makati, Metro Manila (☎ (02) 810 8456/7; (02) fax 817 1080)
Solomon Islands
    High Commission, PO Box 1109, Honiara (☎ 20561; fax 20562)
UK
    High Commission, 14 Waterloo Place, London SW1R 4AR (☎ (0171) 930 0922/6; fax (0171) 930 0828)
USA
    Embassy, 3rd floor, 1615 New Hampshire Ave, NW, Washington DC 20009 (☎ (202) 659 0856; fax (202) 745 3679)
    Permanent Mission to the UN, Suite 322, 866 United Nations Plaza, New York 10017 (☎ (212) 832 0043; fax (212) 832 0918)

Foreign Embassies in PNG

All embassies are in Port Moresby. It's worth making a phone call if you plan to visit between noon and 2 pm (some, including the Indonesian Embassy, close for two hours).

Australia
    Independence Drive, Waigani; PO Box 9129, Hohola (☎ 325 9333; fax 427 1028)
France
    9th floor, Pacific View Building, 1/84 Pruth St, Korobosea; PO Box 1155, Port Moresby (☎ 325 3740; fax 325 0861)
Germany
    2nd floor, Pacific View Apartments, 1/84 Pruth St, Korobosea; PO Box 3631, Boroko (☎ 325 2988)
Indonesia
    Kiroki St, Waigani; PO Box 7165, Boroko (☎ 325 3544; fax 325 0535)
    Vanimo Consulate (Sanduan Province); PO Box 39, Vanimo (☎ 857 1371; fax 857 1373)
Italy
    Spring Garden Rd, Hohola; PO Box 6330, Boroko (☎ 325 3183)
Japan
    4th and 5th floors, ANG House, Cuthbertson St; PO Box 1040, Port Moresby (☎ 321 1800)
New Zealand
    Waigani Crescent, Waigani; PO Box 1051, Boroko (☎ 325 9444; fax 325 0565)
The Philippines
    Islander Village, Wards Rd, Hohola; PO Box 5916, Boroko (☎ 25 6414)

UK
    Kiroki St, Waigani; PO Box 4778, Boroko (☎ 325 1677; fax 325 3547)
USA
    Douglas St; PO Box 1492, Port Moresby (☎ 321 1455; fax 325 7026)

CUSTOMS

Visitors are allowed to import 200 cigarettes (or 50 cigars or 250g of tobacco), a litre of spirit and a small amount of perfume duty free. Personal effects that you have owned for a year (this might be difficult to judge!) are also duty free. You won't have any problem with your camera, film and personal stereo. There is sometimes quite a thorough check made of your gear at Jackson International Airport, Port Moresby. When arriving at Mt Hagen or some of the more unusual entry ports (like Tabubil), they also search your luggage for alcohol and weapons (both of which are forbidden imports in those areas).

There are also controls on what you can take out of the country – some items of cultural and historical significance are prohibited exports. This includes anything made before 1960, traditional stone tools, some shell valuables from Milne Bay and any item incorporating human remains or bird of paradise plumes. As a tourist, you are unlikely to be sold anything of this nature but if you are in doubt, you can get your artefacts and things checked at the National Museum & Art Gallery in Port Moresby. Stone tools and artefacts should definitely be checked because some can be incredibly old and may provide vital clues to PNG's past.

If you plan to buy artefacts, check your home country's import and quarantine regulations. If you are carrying the artefacts with you, you will also be subject to the regulations of countries you enter on your way home.

Once you clear customs, you have entered a country even if you are leaving again in a couple of days. The fact that you are an American tourist staying in Cairns for two days will not be an adequate defence against Australian regulations. Crocodile skin (it doesn't make any difference if it came from a farm), tortoise shell, some turtle shells and all birds of paradise (and their plumes) are prohibited imports to Australia because they are considered to be, or belong to, endangered species.

Australian quarantine regulations apply to all wooden articles (including all carvings), and all animal products (including bones and skins). If any of these things are judged to be quarantine risks you will have to pay to have them irradiated, a process that may take up to a week. This is a problem if you are catching a plane to the USA in two days or if you are clearing customs in Sydney and catching a connecting flight to Melbourne.

You can minimise the risk of this by checking potential purchases yourself. Bone will automatically be treated, signs of borer in wood will mean problems and hair or untanned skin will also require treatment. There are a number of ways around the problem if you simply must have that hairy mask with the boar's tusks. If you have a lot of artefacts, consider sending them all directly home. If you are a genuine transit passenger (that is, you will not clear Australian customs), Australian regulations will not apply to you. If you do clear customs you can have your goods kept in a quarantine bond store (controlled storage) for the duration of your stay, although this is not to be recommended for fragile or very expensive items. You can also, at considerable expense, have the artefacts shipped under quarantine bond to your port of departure (if you land in Cairns, say, and depart from Sydney).

MONEY

The unit of currency is the *kina* (pronounced 'keenah'), which is divided into 100 *toea* (pronounced 'toy-ah'). Both are the names of traditional shell money and this connection to traditional forms of wealth is emphasised on the notes too. The K20 note features an illustration of that most valuable of village animals, the pig. PNG has recently introduced plastic banknotes of a similar style to the new Australian banknotes.

Costs

PNG is an expensive place and you'll quickly realise how much a very ordinary room in a basic place to stay costs. It seems unreasonable. From a travellers' point of view, costs are pretty much at first-world levels and comforts are relatively few. How come? Overseas banking interests don't think that PNG is a very stable country and the trickle-down effect means that all financial loans to any PNG businesses or people must be repaid in five years. There are no 30-year mortgages in PNG, no long-term business loans, and the cost of doing anything is very high. There's no manufacturing base and high imports and no spirit of competition – domestic air legs are the same price with each carrier, goods in stores cost much the same. The Australian colonial administrators did nothing to encourage the development of industries that would compete with Australian producers and for many years regarded PNG as a captive export market.

There is no tradition of cheap hotels and restaurants (as in Asia) because when locals travel they stay with *wantoks* (relatives) or use their expense accounts and don't care how much they are charged. No real urban culture has developed (cities are a very new idea), so street life and nightlife are virtually nonexistent. Cheap, pleasant eating spots are extremely rare – there is no demand for them.

Once you get out of the towns, however, you can live for virtually nothing (there's virtually nothing to buy). The possibilities for budget travel are limitless and the rewards are terrific. You can walk through areas where roads don't exist, you can buy canoes and travel down rivers. All you have to do is get to the end of a secondary road and start walking or maybe jump in a coastal dinghy bound for wherever-they-said. There's always a place to stay – with a family or in village guesthouses, missions, schools or police stations – and your novelty value will assure you of hospitality.

You could virtually travel for weeks without spending much if you can survive for long periods on sago or sweet potato (breakfast, lunch and dinner) and enjoy walking and paddling. This kind of travel can be very demanding but there is no better way to see the country or meet the people. However, it is essential that you spend *some* money – paying your way is very important. Ten kina for a night's accommodation and some food is fair.

Melanesian hospitality is based on an exchange system with the aim of cultivating a long-term relationship. The tourist, passing through, has no role in this tradition of hospitality. When you do give or pay something in exchange for hospitality, traditional responsibilities are fulfilled, the village is supported and, hopefully, the next visitor is welcomed. There are villages in the Upper Sepik and elsewhere which have become pissed off with freeloading foreigners and are now wary of travellers. As one traveller put it, 'If you can afford to come here, you can afford to feed yourself and maybe someone else as well'.

Cash

In remote areas having enough small bills is important. People are cash poor and won't have change for K50. You'll need cash for small purchases and PMV (public motor vehicles) rides and it doesn't hurt to give a child a kina for showing you that WWII relic in the bushes.

Few wage-earners get paid in cash these days because of holdups. Banks have now instituted a cash card system for many employed people which can be used at banks and major supermarkets in the large towns. Consequently, most wages and salaries (in Port Moresby at any rate) get paid directly into bank accounts. This can mean *enormous* queues on pay Fridays.

You're not allowed to take out of the country more than K200 in notes and K5 in coins or more than K250 worth of foreign cash.

Travellers Cheques

You can change travellers cheques in every major town in PNG (including Buka), although the cashiers might only get to process a travellers cheque a few times a year

and might need to ring through for an exchange rate. Queues can be long at banks outside Port Moresby and nothing ever happens quickly in a PNG bank anyway.

Of the locally owned banks, PNGBC's K5 fee to change your travellers cheque into hard cash is much cheaper than the K12 fee of Bank South Pacific.

ATMs

ATMs and EFTPOS facilities are being installed in banks and supermarkets, respectively, particularly in Port Moresby – but there are separate groupings of banks, so you might have to line up at the right queue at the supermarket to use it.

There are also some ATMs popping up in Port Moresby. Unfortunately, they are not yet connected to the Cirrus network and are not much use to people who don't have a local bank account.

Credit Cards

Credit cards are not widely accepted but can be useful at hotels and restaurants, and if you get into a jam. Visa, MasterCard, American Express and Diners Club are accepted at various places around the country, but if you're planning on settling up your accommodation bill by credit card, check in advance that yours is accepted. There may also be a surcharge for using a credit card. Australia's Bankcard is not accepted in PNG.

Banks & International Transfers

PNGBC and Westpac branches are in most towns, and Bank of South Pacific (a member of the National Australia Group) and the Australia & New Zealand Banking Group (ANZ) also have branches across the country. Banking hours are from 9 am to 4.30 pm Monday to Thursday and from 9 am to 5 pm on Friday.

It's relatively simple and straightforward to have money transferred to a bank in PNG from overseas or you can open a passbook account when you arrive.

Currency Exchange

The kina has taken a bit of a tumble in recent

years and has fallen to just below the value of the Australian dollar. This is good for travellers whose trip was about 30% dearer a few years ago.

Australia	A$1	=	K1.04
Canada	C$1	=	K1.01
France	FF1	=	K0.24
Germany	DM1	=	K0.81
Indonesia	Rp 1000	=	K0.41
Japan	¥100	=	K1.18
New Zealand	NZ$1	=	K0.91
Singapore	S$1	=	K0.92
UK	UK£1	=	K2.29
USA	US$1	=	K1.41

Tipping & Bargaining

Tipping is not customary anywhere in PNG and the listed price of goods and services is what you'll be expected to pay. Importantly, there's no tradition of bargaining either and an artefact maker would consider it demeaning if a tourist was endlessly haggling over the price (see the special arts section).

Taxes

Provincial sales tax is set at between 2.5% and 7%. This is normally included in any prices quoted by hotels and restaurants – but not always. There was talk that a 10% value-added tax (VAT) would be introduced on all consumer items in 1998 to replace sales tax.

POST & COMMUNICATIONS
Postal Rates

The postal rates are: K0.25 for letters less than 50g within PNG; K0.50 for aerograms worldwide; K0.50, K0.65 and K1 for airmail letters less than 20g to Australia/New Zealand, Asia and Europe/North America, respectively.

Sending & Receiving Mail

Every post office now has its own postcode – there are only about 90 of them in PNG. They are included under destination headings in the regional chapters. When addressing mail you are meant to include the postcode 'to ensure prompt delivery'. But people rarely use postcodes and the mail gets delivered just the same. There is no letterbox mail delivery service, so if you're writing to people within PNG you must address your letters to post office boxes. Add the name of the relevant town and the province and, if you're keen, the postcode. For example:

Niugini Guest Haus
PO Box 108
Wewak 531
East Sepik Province

There's a poste restante service at most post offices. Underline the surname and print it clearly if you want the letter to arrive safely. Even then you have to cross your fingers.

The amount of time a letter takes to be delivered varies radically – it can take from three days to three weeks to travel between Australia and PNG. However, if you have a fixed address, mail usually seems to be quite reliable.

The overseas mail service from PNG is generally good. Wrap parcels carefully as surface mail can be very rough. Allow at least three months for parcel post from PNG to North America. If they're packed in cardboard cartons with paper packing, masks or other artefacts should get back OK.

Telephone

The international country code for PNG is 675.

The phone system in PNG, although limited to the main centres, is very good. You can direct dial between centres and there are no area codes to worry about, unless you're ringing a radio phone in which case you dial ☎ 019 for the operator. There's not too many international lines to PNG and bad weather can cause problems, so sometimes ringing home is difficult.

You can direct dial most of the world, even from payphones. However, in some areas, particularly parts of the Highlands (such as Kainantu and environs), the normal telephone network became so unreliable that it is no longer in operation and has been replaced by satellite phones, and these calls are expensive! Numbers for satellite telephones are not listed in the directory, so you must ring directory assistance.

Payphones charge K0.20 for local calls. For long-distance or international calls, feed in more money every time the red light shines. Unused coins are refunded. Payphones can be hard to find, particularly in Port Moresby where there are not enough phones to start with and some don't work. In Port Moresby, Lae, Mt Hagen and perhaps some other larger towns, you'll find payphones which take phonecards – post offices and a few shops sell the cards.

Some big hotels may allow you to use their phones by the front desk – this could be free (if they like you), but the cost could also be much higher than public phones (if they don't). Some hotels have fancy telephones in all the rooms but the phones are sometimes disconnected, so don't assume that a telephone in a hotel room means that you will be able to use it. If you need to make lots of telephone calls, a hotel room with a connected telephone can be a blessing.

Fax

Kwik piksa leta (fax) has taken off in a big way in PNG and many places have a fax machine. You can send faxes from post offices for a few kina and they can be a useful way of making accommodation bookings. Faxing might even save you money, as you can get through a lot of coins in a payphone when the clerk gives up on your Pidgin and goes off to look for an English-speaker. Fax numbers are listed in telephone directories.

BOOKS

There is a growing stock of books about PNG. The following is a small selection of the many that have been written.

General

For facts and figures, *A Fact Book on Modern Papua New Guinea* (2nd edition) by Jackson Rannells (Oxford University Press, 1995) is excellent. It's designed as a school reference but concisely covers most things you might want to know.

The volunteering experience is described by Inez Baranay in *Rascal Rain – A Year in PNG*. She worked as a volunteer in Enga Province and encountered more than her fair share of problems. It should be required reading for volunteers.

Yachties intending to visit should look for *Cruising Papua New Guinea* by Alan Lucas (Horwitz Grahame, Sydney, 1980).

If you are planning a trek on the Kokoda Trail, Clive Baker's *Do-it-Yourself Trekking – Kokoda Trail* (Australian Military History Publications, Loftus, Australia, 1994) is a necessity for your pack.

Lonely Planet's *Papua New Guinea phrasebook* is a good pocket-sized book with most of the basic words and phrases you are likely to need.

Anthropology

PNG has been a treasure house for anthropologists and from Malinowski to Margaret Mead, they've made their names here. They still come today.

Malinowski's three celebrated books, *Argonauts of the Western Pacific* (1922), *The Sexual Life of Savages in North-Western Melanesia* (1929) and *Coral Gardens and their Magic* (1935), were written about the Trobriand Islands. These writings brought anthropologists in droves.

Margaret Mead's *Growing Up in New Guinea* was first published in 1942, but is still available in a paperback Penguin. She conducted her studies on Manus Island and returned there after the war to investigate the dramatic impact of the wartime American base there. Her second Manus book was *New Lives for Old* (Morrow, New York, 1956). A good deal of controversy surrounds her observations but the books are well written and very readable.

The Crocodile, by Vincent Eri, was the first published novel by a Papuan (Jacaranda, Brisbane, 1970 – available in a Penguin paperback). It provides an interesting look at the contact between Europeans and locals from the side of the colonised rather than the coloniser.

Gardens of War – Life & Death in the New Guinea Stone Age by Robert Gardner and

Karl G Heider (Random House, New York, 1968, and also in a Penguin large format paperback) describes ritual warfare of New Guinea tribes, dramatically illustrated with many photographs. Fierce inter-village fighting was still common in the remote parts of Irian Jaya which the authors visited in the 1960s.

Cargo cults – a fascinating example of the collision between primitive beliefs and modern technology – have been much-studied. The classic book on these cults is *Road Belong Cargo* by Peter Lawrence (Melbourne University Press, 1964).

Gerry Schuurkamp's *The Min of the Papua New Guinea Star Mountains* (1995) is a big, well-illustrated book which gives some excellent insights into the Min people who live near the border with Irian Jaya. Its publication was sponsored by Ok Tedi Mining.

From Inside the Women's House by Alome Kyakas and Polly Wiessner (Robert Brown & Assoc, Queensland, 1992) gives some rare insights into Enga women's lives and traditions.

Culture & Arts

The magnificent two-volume hardcover *Art Oceanien*, by Anthony JP Meyer, has fine explanatory text in French, German and English. The artefacts are singly photographed with studio lighting and the two volumes have fascinating archival photos. In fact, it covers Micronesia, Polynesia and Melanesia, but its PNG material is very thorough and broadly representative. The publisher is Gründ and this book will cost about a week's wages.

Papua New Guinea (1981) by photo-essayist James Spiers is a large-format book with colour plates and good explanatory text.

The Artefacts & Crafts of Papua New Guinea – A Guide for Buyers is a very useful little booklet produced for the Handcraft Industry of PNG. It has over 250 pictures and short descriptions of a wide variety of PNG artefacts.

Contemporary Art in Papua New Guinea (1997), compiled by Susan Cochrane for Craftsman House, is a collection of paintings by such outstanding PNG artists as Taba Silau, Kaipel Ka'a and Martin Morububuna.

History & Exploration

It's difficult to find much information about the country before Europeans arrived. The simple truth is that not a great deal is known, although this glaring gap is now gradually being filled.

A Short History of Papua New Guinea by John Dademo Waiko (1993) is a good history of the country. Waiko was the first Papua New Guinean to get a PhD (Social Sciences at the Australian National University). He was professor of history at the University of PNG and a parliamentarian.

Papua New Guinea's Prehistory by Pamela Swadling (PNG National Museum & Art Gallery with Gordon & Gotch, Port Moresby, 1981) gives an excellent introduction to the early history of human settlement and the development of agriculture. It shows how painstaking archaeological research is beginning to piece together a picture of ancient PNG societies.

Sean Dorney, the Australian Broadcasting Corporation's long-time PNG correspondent, has written an interesting and informative book, *Papua New Guinea – People, Politics & History since 1975* (Random House, 1990), which makes sense of the country's recent history.

If you're interested in the OPM's (*Organisasi Papua Merdeka*, or Free West Papua Movement) struggle in Irian Jaya and the attitudes of the Indonesian and PNG governments, the best book to read is *Indonesia's Secret War – The Guerrilla Struggle in Irian Jaya* by Robin Osborne (Allen & Unwin, Sydney, 1985). It gives a fascinating and sometimes depressing insight into modern imperialism and politics.

For the full story of the Ok Tedi project and its environmental impact look for *Ok Tedi, Pot of Gold* by R Jackson (University of PNG), while Douglas Oliver's *Black Islanders – A Personal Perspective of Bougainville 1937-1991* sheds some light on the history of the island, leading to its present power struggle.

Voices from a Lost World, by Jan Roberts (1996), is subtitled 'Australian women and children in Papua New Guinea before the Japanese invasion'. The author's parents lived in Rabaul in the 1930s and this book began life as a PhD thesis in oral history. It's very readable and has some nice sepia photos from 1900 to 1940 from family albums.

If you visit Rabaul, you'll no doubt develop an interest in Queen Emma's highly colourful life which is described in *Queen Emma* by RW Robson (Pacific Publications, Sydney, revised 1979). A novel based around her life is *Queen Emma of the South Seas* by Geoffrey Dutton (Macmillan, Melbourne, 1976).

Pumice and Ash, by Sue Lauer, is a terrific book. It's an account of the 1994 Rabaul volcanic eruptions and includes fine photographs. Sue and her family lived in Rabaul (her husband was a vulcanologist). The book is self-published; see the Rabaul section in the New Britain chapter for information on how to get a copy.

WWII For a very readable account of the decisive fighting on the Kokoda Trail, culminating in the bitter struggle to recapture Buna and Gona from the Japanese, look for *Bloody Buna* by Lida Mayo. Originally published in New York by Doubleday in 1974, it is also available in cheap paperback.

The amazing courage of the coast watchers, who relayed information from behind Japanese lines, knowing that capture would mean a most unpleasant death, is also well documented. Look for Walter Lord's *Lonely Vigil – The Coastwatchers of the Solomons* (Viking Press, New York, 1978).

Some people find poking around the rotting relics from the war an interesting exercise – *Rust in Peace* by Bruce Adams (Antipodean Publishers, Sydney, 1975) tells you where to look, not only in PNG but also in other parts of the Pacific. *Battleground South Pacific*, with photos by Bruce Adams and text by Robert Howlett (Reeds, Sydney, 1970), also has much interesting material on

the war. *Pacific Aircraft Wrecks & Where to Find Them*, by Charles Darby (Kookaburra, Melbourne, 1979), is mainly devoted to WWII wrecks in PNG and has many fascinating photographs of these aircraft.

Wildlife

PNG's exotic and colourful bird-life has inspired many equally colourful books. For the amateur bird-watcher, the best field manual is *Birds of New Guinea* by Beehler, Pratt & Zimmerman (Princeton University Press, 1986).

A little more down-to-earth, in price at least, are two books you can find in Port Moresby. *Birds in Papua New Guinea* by Brian Coates (Robert Brown & Associates, Port Moresby, 1977) and *Wildlife in Papua New Guinea* by Eric Lindgrom (Robert Brown & Associates, Port Moresby, or Golden Press, Sydney, 1975) provide an interesting introduction with plenty of excellent photographs.

Travel Literature

Into the Crocodile Nest, by Benedict Allen (Paledin, 1989), is an account of travels and initiation ceremonies on the Sepik.

Islands in the Clouds, by Isabella Tree (Lonely Planet, 1996), is a contemporary account of the author's travels in the Highlands, and is one of the many titles in Journeys, Lonely Planet's new travel literature series. *In Papua New Guinea*, by Christina Dodwell (Oxford Illustrated Press, Yeovil, England, 1983), tells of an enterprising young Englishwoman's adventures through PNG on foot, by horse and during a four-month solo trip down the Sepik by dugout canoe. These books strongly reinforce the fact that England produces superbly eccentric travellers.

Bookshops

Port Moresby's bookshops have the best range of books, although Mt Hagen, Goroka, Madang and Lae also have shops with interesting selections. Probably the best bookshop in the country is Gordon & Gotch at Dogura Place, Six Mile, in Port Moresby.

The University Bookshop at the Waigani campus has recently changed hands after falling into decline. With any luck, its stock of books about PNG will be expanded as a consequence.

It is always worth checking out the shops attached to the major hotels as they often stock some of the books mentioned here – although their prices usually reflect the greater affluence of their clientele. The newsagent/bookshop at the new Jackson International Airport terminal may also have some stocks.

Every major town has at least one Christian bookshop and although books with angels and doves on the covers abound, they usually also have various Pidgin dictionaries and grammar guides and a range of books written in Pidgin, which are useful if you are making a serious attempt to learn the language.

ONLINE SERVICES

PNG is at the bottom end of the world of computer technology and the wired world hasn't really hit it. There are, however, some very good PNG websites. A couple of places in PNG now have Compuserve addresses but otherwise, 'online' means fishing in PNG.

Websites

There are in fact several good websites. Of course the place to start is the Lonely Planet website, where you'll find a country profile on PNG with some great photos (www.lonelyplanet.com/dest/aust/png.htm).

The *Post Courier* newspaper has a good site and publishes its stories daily (www.datec.com.au/postcourier/default.htm).

A site called Current News Reports has a strong slant on the Bougainville war issue, and publishes various writings (transcriptions of media reports etc) on the subject (www.magna.com.au/sashab/current.htm).

The *National* newspaper maintains another good website with weekly updates from its published stories (www.wr.com.au/national/home.html).

Wantok's Forum is a bulletin-board style website where interested people get to comment on all things Papua New Guinean and respond to other postings (www.niugini.com/wwwboard/wwwboard.html).

A site called Papua New Guinea is maintained and regularly updated by the Australian National University (coombs.anu.edu.au/SpecialProj/PNG/WWWVL-PNG.html).

FILMS

Kevin Costner never made it to PNG, but Errol Flynn did. Films about PNG are mostly made by outsiders and there's a fine tradition of documentary film making. Contact Ronin Films in Canberra, Australia (☎ (062) 248 0851), which can supply some of the following titles on all video formats.

Adventure in the Niugini Highlands is a documentary film shot on video by Albert Toro and Peter Dip. These two have made a few low-budget documentaries and this film deals with the history, geography and culture of the PNG Highlands. Toro and Dip also made a fine film called *Scattered in the Wind* which had UNICEF funding and deals with the impact of the Bougainville war on the women and children of the North Solomons Province.

Dennis O'Rourke's *The Shark Callers of Kontu* is justifiably famous and makes for compelling viewing. O'Rourke's film explores the ancient New Ireland art of shark-calling. He also looks at the bewildering dichotomies for Kontu villagers between their traditional ways and the impact of a rapidly arriving 20th century. Christianity, alcohol and breakfast cereal have all changed traditional ways of life.

Also set in a New Ireland village is Chris Owen's splendid documentary *Malangan Labadama*, which depicts the preparations, rituals and festivities surrounding the death of village *mi mi* (elder and chief) Buk Buk in the Mandak region of the island. It's really worth trying to see this film – it provides a wonderful insight into Malangan culture.

Islands of Fire and Magic is the story of sea-kayaker and adventurer Larry Gray and his team who make their way through the 'arc of fire' volcanic islands of PNG. Made by Gary Steer, the film visits various 'exotic' locations and has footage of Bainings fire dances.

Robin Anderson and Bob Connolly have made a series of excellent documentaries about PNG. *First Contact* is an extraordinary film, largely made from the film stock shot by the Leahy brothers when they went into the Highlands in 1933 in search of gold. Instead they found 100,000 people living in the Wahgi Valley who had no idea that the outside world existed. Try to see this film with its old scratchy black-and-white archival footage showing amazing scenes of Highlanders in traditional gear looking completely bewildered when the Leahy brothers land a plane, play music on a wind-up gramophone and when they see themselves in little mirrors. *Joe Leahy's Neighbours* shows a traditional society slowly coming to terms with the modern world. Joe is the son of Mick Leahy (to one of his Highlands concubines) and his profitable coffee plantation in the Highlands set him apart from the neighbouring Ganiga clanspeople whose subsistence lifestyles remain almost unchanged. *Black Harvest* completes the trilogy, showing Joe Leahy's coffee plantation expanding in partnership with the Ganiga clan. Just before the first harvest (after a five-year maturation), international coffee prices plummet and clan warfare breaks out.

NEWSPAPERS & MAGAZINES

One of the best ways to understand PNG is to read the papers. PNG has some good newspapers and enjoys a high level of media independence.

The *Post Courier* has the largest circulation selling more than 40,000 copies each day. It's quite a good newspaper and is principally owned by Rupert Murdoch's News Corp. The *National*, owned by a Malaysian company, began publishing each weekday in late 1993.

Wantok is a daily paper written entirely in Pidgin. About 14,000 copies are sold each week and its aim is to provide high-quality journalism to the people of PNG. It is produced by Word Publishing, a Christian organisation. If you doubt the vitality and utility of the Pidgin language, make sure you buy a copy – and reading the centre spread of comics is a good way to begin learning Pidgin.

Word Publishing also produces the weekly *Independent*. This is another good paper and offers analysis of political and economic affairs, both in PNG and abroad. The paper is rarely 'churchy' (except for the occasional editorial) and is well worth its K0.60 price. The *Eastern Star* is really a Milne Bay newspaper, but you can buy it all over the country. It, too, is very readable but confines itself more to local affairs.

RADIO & TV
Radio

The situation with regional radio has changed a lot recently. The federal government has handed funding back to the provinces, which are struggling to keep local radio stations alive. Some have gone under, some of them resurfacing, others not.

There are two national government-funded radio stations: Karai on the AM band and Kalang on the FM band. Both broadcast 24 hours. There's also two private commercial stations: NauFM ('now') broadcasts 24 hours in English and YumiFM ('you-me') has just started and broadcasts 24 hours in Pidgin. All of these stations have a pop-hits format and play a large amount of local music.

Short-wave Radio Australia (RA) broadcasts many news and current affairs programmes in PNG and is popular with nationals and expats alike. The Australian government has, unfortunately, recently decided to cut back on funding for this excellent service, so it is likely to diminish in quality over time. Nevertheless, in the short term, despite the cutbacks, the PNG RA service has actually managed to expand its broadcasts. You can catch it on 6080kHz or 7240kHz.

TV

There was a lot of anxiety about the introduction of TV in PNG – about whether the people really needed it and its effect on local cultures. The first domestic broadcasting began in 1987 by Niugini Television Network (NTN) and EmTV (Media Niugini) started about six months later; NTN quit broadcasting within 18 months.

Unfortunately, there's little local production and the bulk of EmTV's programmes comes from Australia's Nine Network, of which it is a subsidiary. EmTV produces its own news (Pidgin and English), music and religious shows, covers some local sporting events and produces many of its own advertisements.

Although EmTV is the only free-to-air broadcaster, most people can also pick up QTV, the north Queensland franchiser of the Nine Network. Subscribers have a choice of international broadcasters, including CNN and various others from America, Indonesia, the Philippines and Malaysia. They call it 'cable', but it's received on small domestic satellite dishes. The government regulations ban all forms of sexual content but allow an endless stream of mindless ultra-violent action movies to go to air.

But even channel surfing on PNG TV won't help you understand its role in PNG culture. You really have to go into a village (preferably in the early evening after dinner) to understand what it means. Most communities have a TV or two and most Papua New Guineans watch TV in highly animated groups of 20 or 30 or even more – true interactive TV. It's quite an experience.

Of course, the original anxieties about TV, trash culture and violence have all been well founded. There's a strong Rambo culture and a Sly Stallone T-shirt is a prized possession (even if it's faded, holey and limp), especially to the groups of generally disaffected (and often dislocated) urban youths who get into rascal mischief. More importantly, the commando action-man theme has truly scary manifestations in the Papua New Guinea Defence Force's (PNGDF) soldiers in Bougainville.

For the most part, however, you'll find TV in PNG quite entertaining and certainly enlivening. EmTV is a great way to catch on

to some simple Pidgin skills and the advertising is often as fun as any of the programmes.

VIDEO SYSTEMS

The standard PNG video system is VHS, the format for video hirers, and inexpensive VHS tapes are available at supermarkets and trade stores.

PHOTOGRAPHY & VIDEO

PNG is photogenic and you can easily run through a lot of film, particularly if you happen on an event like a big Highlands sing-sing. Bring more film than you'll need and then more again. Colour print film is readily available in the major towns but is fairly expensive; transparency film is available, but rarer. Fast film (eg ASA 400) is almost non-existent outside Port Moresby.

Protect your film and your camera from the dust, humidity and heat as much as you can. It's worth taking a small cleaning kit and spare batteries, as well as some silica gel sachets. Underwater cameras are particularly useful as they are sealed and waterproof. Olympus manufactures 'weatherproof' cameras which should handle the PNG humidity better.

Bear in mind that photography of dark-skinned people requires some different rules: a flash is almost an imperative, as otherwise the contrast with a light-coloured background can cause under-exposure.

While video cameras can give a fascinating record of your trip, they also make you stand out as a 'wealthy tourist' and are desirable items which can easily be snatched. They also help to create a barrier between you and the local people. Unless you plan to stick pretty close to large groups of tourists or the more upmarket tours, it is probably best to leave video cameras at home. If you *do* decide to take them, remember to follow the same rules regarding people's sensitivities as for still photography.

Photographing People

Never take a photograph in or of a *haus tambaran* (or any other spirit house) without asking permission. These are sacred places and you could quickly find yourself in trouble if you do not respect the wishes and feelings of your hosts. It's best to ask several of the male elders first, to make sure you do speak to someone who has the authority to grant your request. Even if you just glance through your viewfinder, people will assume that you have taken a photo, so be careful.

You'll find people are generally happy to be photographed, even going out of their way to pose for you, particularly at sing-sings. But do not assume that taking photographs is always OK – for instance, don't take a photo of someone washing in their bathroom, even if the bathroom is a jungle stream.

Some people, usually men dressed in traditional style, do request payment if they are photographed – a kina or two is average but it can be more. People are aware that western photographers can make money out of their exotic photos and see no reason why they shouldn't get some of the action. If you've gone ahead and taken a photo without getting permission and establishing a price, you may well find yourself facing an angry, heavily armed Highlander demanding K20 in payment. It would take some nerve to argue.

TIME

The time throughout PNG is 10 hours ahead of UTC (GMT). When it's noon in PNG it will be also noon in Sydney (except during the daylight saving months in NSW), 9 am in Jakarta, 2 am in London, 9 pm the previous day in New York and 6 pm the previous day in Los Angeles. There is no daylight saving (summer time) in PNG.

PNG is close to the equator, so day and night are almost equal in duration, and it gets dark quickly. The sun rises about 6 am and sets about 6 pm.

You will hear people refer to 'Melanesian time' – this refers to the habit throughout Melanesia (and indeed all of the South Pacific) of putting a low premium on punctuality. Do not expect people to be as obsessed with time as they are in the west.

Things will often be half an hour late – but they can also be half an hour early.

ELECTRICITY

The electric current on the national grid is 240V, AC 50Hz (the same as in Australia and New Zealand). While all the towns have electrical supplies most of PNG does not have power, other than that provided by the occasional privately owned generator. Blackouts frequently occur in all towns, even Port Moresby and Lae. These usually last for no more than half an hour, but sometimes can last for several hours. In some more remote areas, diesel generators operate for only a couple of hours in the morning and several hours at night – so don't expect that air-conditioner to keep you cool all day.

WEIGHTS & MEASURES

PNG uses the metric system. See the back pages of this book for conversion tables.

LAUNDRY

There are a few laundromats in Port Moresby, but they are almost nonexistent elsewhere. Often your place of stay will have a laundry service but it is generally outrageously expensive if all you're washing is a pair of shorts and a few limp T-shirts. Things aren't generally too formal in PNG, so you can afford to wear your tux a few days in a row.

HEALTH

Your health when travelling will depend on three factors: your predeparture preparations, your day-to-day health care while travelling and the way you handle any medical problems or emergencies that develop en route. While the list of potential dangers can seem quite frightening, some basic precautions should obviate anything more serious than an upset stomach. With the exception of malaria, there are no insurmountable health problems in PNG – for the visitor.

There are private doctors (but they are not cheap) in most main towns, and dentists in Port Moresby, Lae and Rabaul. And there are public hospitals in the provincial capitals –

but they are short of equipment and crowded, so if you do get seriously sick it is advisable to fly to Australia or home.

If you know you are going to be isolated for any length of time, it is advisable to take the necessary precautions – and do some research on how to treat yourself. In short, if you have access to a travellers' medical clinic, use it rather than a general practitioner, and buy a good book.

Travel Health Guides

If you are planning to be away or travelling in remote areas for a long period of time, you may like to consider taking a more detailed health guide.

Staying Healthy in Asia, Africa & Latin America by Dirk Schroeder (Moon Publications, 1994) is probably the best all-round guide to carry, as it's compact but detailed and well organised.

Travellers' Health by Dr Richard Dawood (Oxford University Press, 1995) is comprehensive, easy to read, authoritative and also highly recommended, although it's rather large to lug around.

Where There is No Doctor by David Werner (Macmillan, 1994) is a detailed guide intended for longer-term visitors to less developed countries, such as volunteer workers, rather than for the average traveller.

Travel with Children by Maureen Wheeler (Lonely Planet Publications, 1995) has basic advice on travel health for younger children.

There is also a number of excellent travel health sites on the Internet. From the Lonely Planet home page (www.lonelyplanet.com), there are links at www.lonelyplanet.com/weblinks/wlprep.htm to the World Health Organisation and Centers for Diseases Control & Prevention in Atlanta, Georgia.

Predeparture Planning

Health Preparations It may sound trite, but it does make sense to ensure that you are healthy before you start travelling, especially in the more remote areas – get a general medical checkup from your GP, make sure your teeth are OK and if you wear glasses, take a spare pair and your prescription.

Immunisations The further off the beaten track you go, the more necessary it is to take precautions. Be aware that there is often a greater risk of disease with children and in pregnancy.

Public Health

PNG is facing a health care crisis and the situation is worsening. The problem derives largely from limited finances, in combination with the difficulties of servicing a widely dispersed population living in rugged terrain. Medical services are vastly overstretched. In the more remote areas, there is a valiant (and technologically appropriate) 'barefoot doctor' system where basic health workers operate in the villages, but these workers are rarely highly trained, and facilities and drugs are often limited.

Infant mortality is also increasing, with one in three children underweight and one in 12 dying before their fifth birthday. PNG has one of the world's highest maternal mortality rates. There has been an alarming rise in the incidence of HIV infections and a growing death toll from tuberculosis, malaria and malnutrition.

One in 600 people has been infected with HIV, a ratio expected to double by the year 2000. To date, almost all have been heterosexual adults and nearly half of them women. And while 60% of reported cases have been from the Port Moresby area, the problem extends to people living in some very remote areas. Migration to the cities, high unemployment levels, changing social patterns, polygamy and promiscuity all help to exacerbate the problem. Public education on the subject is minimal and awareness programmes (especially necessary in the defence and police forces, at mining camps and among transport workers and young people) are practically nonexistent.

PNG has the highest incidence of tuberculosis in the Pacific, but it is unlikely to be a problem for the short-term visitor. Malaria accounts for nearly 10% of deaths in PNG, surpassed only by pneumonia and perinatal complications as the major cause of death. ■

Plan ahead to get your vaccinations: some of them require more than one injection, while some vaccinations should not be given together. It is recommended you seek medical advice at least six weeks before you set off on your travels. Record all vaccinations on an International Health Certificate, available from your doctor or government health department.

Discuss your requirements with your doctor, but vaccinations you should consider for this trip include:

Hepatitis A
The most common travel-acquired illness after diarrhoea which can put you out of action for weeks. Havrix 1440 is a vaccination which provides long-term immunity (possibly more than 10 years) after an initial injection and a booster at six to 12 months.

Gamma globulin is not a vaccination but is a ready-made antibody collected from blood donations. It should be given close to departure because, depending on the dose, it only protects for two to six months.

A combined hepatitis A and hepatitis B vaccination, Twinrix, is also available. This combined vaccination is recommended for people wanting protection against both types of viral hepatitis. Three injections over a six-month period are required.

Typhoid
This is an important vaccination to have where hygiene is a problem. Available either as an injection or oral capsules.

Diphtheria & Tetanus
Diphtheria can be a fatal throat infection and tetanus can be a fatal wound infection. Everyone should have these vaccinations. After an initial course of three injections, boosters are necessary every 10 years.

Hepatitis B
This disease is spread by blood or by sexual activity. Travellers who should consider a hepatitis B vaccination include those visiting countries where there are known to be many carriers, where blood transfusions may not be adequately screened or where sexual contact is a possibility. It involves three injections, the quickest course being over three weeks with a booster at 12 months.

Polio
Polio is a serious, easily transmitted disease, still prevalent in many developing countries. Everyone should keep up to date with this vaccination. A booster every 10 years maintains immunity.

Malaria Medication Antimalarial drugs do not prevent you from being infected but kill the malaria parasites during a stage in their development and significantly reduce the risk of becoming very ill or dying. Expert advice on medication should be sought, as there are many factors to consider including the area to be visited, the risk of exposure to malaria-carrying mosquitos, the side effects of medication, your medical history and whether you are a child or adult or pregnant. Travellers to isolated areas in high-risk countries may like to carry a treatment dose of medication for use if symptoms occur.

Medical Kit There are reasonably well stocked pharmacies in the main centres in PNG but it is a good idea to bring most of your medical needs with you and definitely a supply of any medication you take regularly. You will need to give careful thought to your medical kit if you plan to get off the beaten track. You should be in a position to treat malaria and dysentery, lacerations, sprains, insect and snake bites (some are highly venomous) and respiratory diseases (colds and even pneumonia are common in the Highlands). The kit should include:

- malarial prophylactics – such as chloroquine, mefloquine or doxycycline
- rehydration mixture – for treatment of severe diarrhoea or heat dehydration this is particularly important if travelling with children, but is recommended for everyone
- aspirin or paracetamol (acetaminophen in the USA) – for pain or fever
- antihistamine (such as Benadryl) – useful as a decongestant for colds and allergies, to ease the itch from insect bites or stings and to help prevent motion sickness; antihistamines may cause sedation and interact with alcohol, so care should be taken when using them
- antibiotics – useful if you're travelling well off the beaten track but they must be prescribed and you should carry the prescription with you
- loperamide (eg Imodium) or Lomotil for diarrhoea; prochlorperazine (eg Stemetil) or metaclopramide (eg Maxalon) for nausea and vomiting; antidiarrhoea medication should not be given to children under the age of 12
- antiseptic such as povidone-iodine (eg Betadine), which comes as a solution, ointment, powder and impregnated swabs – for cuts and grazes

- calamine lotion or Stingose spray – to ease irritation from bites or stings
- bandages and adhesive plasters – for minor injuries
- scissors, tweezers and a thermometer (note that mercury thermometers are prohibited by airlines)
- insect repellent, sunscreen, chap stick and water purification tablets
- a couple of syringes, in case you need injections; ask your doctor for a note explaining why they have been prescribed

Ideally, antibiotics should be administered only under medical supervision and should never be taken indiscriminately. Take only the recommended dose at the prescribed intervals and continue using the antibiotic for the prescribed period, even if the illness seems to be cured earlier. Antibiotics are quite specific to the infections they can treat. Stop immediately if there are any serious reactions and don't use the antibiotic at all if you are unsure that you have the correct one. Some individuals are allergic to commonly prescribed antibiotics such as penicillin or sulpha drugs. It is sensible to always carry this information when travelling.

Basic Rules

Care in what you eat and drink is the most important health rule; stomach upsets are the most likely travel health problem but the majority of these upsets will be relatively minor.

Water PNG is hot, at times very hot. You will sweat profusely and lose a lot of body fluid. Consequently it is very important to maintain a good intake of liquids. Don't rely on feeling thirsty to indicate when you should drink. Always carry a water bottle with you on long trips. Not needing to urinate or very dark yellow urine is a danger sign. Excessive sweating can lead to loss of salt and therefore muscle cramping.

The simplest way of purifying water is to boil it thoroughly. Simple filtering will not remove all dangerous organisms, so if you cannot boil water it should be treated chemically. Chlorine tablets (Puritabs, Steritabs or other brand names) will kill many pathogens, but not those pathogens causing giardia and amoebic cysts. Iodine is very effective in purifying water and is available in tablet form (such as Potable Aqua), but follow the directions carefully and remember that too much iodine can be harmful.

Food There is an old colonial adage which says: 'If you can cook it, boil it or peel it you can eat it – otherwise forget it'. Salads and fruit should be washed with purified water or peeled where possible. Thoroughly cooked food is safest but not if it has been left to cool or has been reheated. Of course, if you are staying with families in villages, this may be difficult. Hesitation to eat food offered because of doubts about hygiene may be interpreted negatively. In such circumstances the only advice is – use your discretion.

Medical Problems & Treatment

Self-diagnosis and treatment can be risky, so wherever possible seek qualified help. Although treatment dosages are given in this section, they are for emergency use only. Medical advice should be sought before administering any drugs. An embassy or consulate can usually recommend a good place to go for such advice. So can five-star hotels, although they often recommend doctors with five-star prices. (This is when that medical insurance really becomes useful.) In some places, standards of medical attention are so low that for some ailments the best advice is to catch a plane and get out. Provincial hospitals may, for example, provide adequate treatment for malaria (it is such a common malady), but anything more serious usually requires a trip to Port Moresby or Australia.

Environmental Hazards

Sunburn The sun can be a subtle and insidious enemy for those with white skins. You can get sunburnt surprisingly quickly in tropical areas like PNG, even through cloud, and it tends to sneak up on you when you are at altitudes (eg in the Highlands) where there is less atmospheric protection. Wear a hat that is broad enough to shade the back of your neck (especially if you're in a boat or a canoe), try to keep your skin covered and apply liberal quantities of an effective sunscreen. Take extra care to apply sunscreen to areas which don't normally see sun, such as your feet, and use zinc cream or some other barrier cream for your nose, lips and ears. Snorkelling can result in fiendish sunburn. Wear a T-shirt and use sunscreen; remember it does wash off, so reapply frequently. Calamine lotion is good for mild sunburn. Sunglasses are also a good idea, especially if you're on the water.

Prickly Heat Prickly heat is an itchy rash caused by excessive perspiration trapped under the skin. It usually strikes people who have just arrived in a hot climate and whose pores have not yet opened sufficiently to cope with greater sweating. Keep cool by bathing often, use a mild talcum powder, and take refuge in an air-conditioned room until you acclimatise.

Heat Exhaustion Dehydration or salt deficiency can cause heat exhaustion. Take time to acclimatise to high temperatures and make sure you drink sufficient liquids.

Salt deficiency is characterised by fatigue, lethargy, headaches, giddiness and muscle cramps and in this case salt tablets may help. Vomiting or diarrhoea can deplete your liquid and salt levels.

Heatstroke Long, continuous periods of exposure to high temperatures can leave you vulnerable to heatstroke. This serious, sometimes fatal, condition can occur if the body's heat-regulating mechanism breaks down and the body temperature rises to dangerous levels. You should avoid excessive alcohol or strenuous activity when you first arrive in a hot climate.

The symptoms are feeling unwell, not sweating very much or at all and a high body temperature (39°C to 41°C or 102°F to 106°F). Where sweating has ceased the skin becomes flushed and red. Severe, throbbing headaches and lack of coordination will also occur, and the sufferer may be confused or aggressive. Eventually the victim will become delirious or convulse. Hospitalisation is essential, but in the interim get victims out of the sun, remove their clothing, cover them with a wet sheet or towel and then fan continually.

Fungal Infections Fungal infections are frequently experienced by newcomers to PNG's heat and humidity. They are most likely to occur on the scalp, between the toes or fingers, in the groin and on the body (ringworm). You get ringworm (which is a fungal infection, not a worm) from infected animals or by walking on damp, infected areas, like shower floors.

To prevent fungal infections wear loose, comfortable clothes, avoid artificial fibres, wash frequently and dry carefully. If you do get an infection, wash the infected area daily with a disinfectant or medicated soap and water, and rinse and dry well. Apply an antifungal cream or powder like Tinaderm. Try to expose the infected area to air or sunlight as much as possible and wash all towels and underwear in hot water as well as changing them often.

Infectious Diseases

Diarrhoea Bali Belly, Montezuma's Curse or Delhi Belly – these are all forms of gastric disorder which are typically experienced by travellers as their bodies adapt to strange food and water. Although not nearly as severe in PNG as in some neighbouring Asian countries, it is likely you will get some kind of diarrhoea when you first arrive. But a mild bout of travellers' diarrhoea, involving a few rushed toilet trips with no other symptoms, is not indicative of a serious problem. A change of water, food or climate can all cause the runs; but diarrhoea caused by contaminated food or water is more serious.

Dehydration is the main danger with any diarrhoea, particularly for children who can dehydrate quite quickly. Fluid replacement is the main treatment. Weak black tea with a little sugar, soda water or soft drinks allowed to go flat and diluted 50% with water are all good. With severe diarrhoea, a rehydrating solution is necessary to replace minerals and salts. Commercially available oral rehydration salts (ORS) are very useful; add the contents of one sachet to a litre of boiled or bottled water. In an emergency you can make up a solution of eight teaspoons of sugar and half a teaspoon of salt to a litre of boiled water. Stick to a bland diet as you recover.

Lomotil or Imodium can be used to bring relief from the symptoms, although they do not actually cure the problem. Only use them if absolutely necessary.

Giardiasis The parasite causing this intestinal disorder is present in contaminated water. The symptoms are stomach cramps, nausea, a bloated stomach, watery, foul-smelling diarrhoea and frequent gas. Giardiasis (also known as giardia) can appear several weeks after you have been exposed to the parasite. The symptoms may disappear for a few days and then return; this can go on for several weeks. Tinidazole, known as Fasigyn, or metronidazole (Flagyl) are the recommended drugs for treatment. Treatment is a 2g dose of Fasigyn or 250mg of Flagyl three times daily for five days.

Dysentery This serious illness is caused by contaminated food or water and is characterised by severe diarrhoea, often with blood or mucous in the stool. There are two kinds of dysentery. Bacillary dysentery is characterised by a high fever and rapid onset; headache, vomiting and stomach pains are also symptoms. It generally does not last longer than a week, but it is highly contagious. Amoebic dysentery is often more gradual in the onset of symptoms, with cramping abdominal pain and vomiting less likely; fever may not be present. It is not a self-limiting disease: it will persist until treated and can recur and cause long-term health problems.

A stool test is necessary to diagnose which kind of dysentery you have, so you should seek medical help urgently. In case of an emergency the drugs norfloxacin or ciprofloxacin can be used as treatment for bacillary dysentery, and metronidazole (Flagyl) for amoebic dysentery. For bacillary dysentery, norfloxacin 400mg twice daily for three days or ciprofloxacin 500mg twice daily for seven days are the recommended dosages. In the case of children the drug co-trimoxazole is a reasonable first-line treatment.

For amoebic dysentery, the recommended adult dosage of metronidazole (Flagyl) is one 750mg to 800mg capsule three times daily for five days. Children aged between eight and 12 years should have half the adult dose; the dosage for younger children is one-third the adult dose.

Cholera Outbreaks of cholera are generally widely reported, so you can avoid such problem areas. The disease is characterised by a sudden onset of acute diarrhoea with 'rice water' stools, vomiting, muscular cramps and extreme weakness. You need medical help – but treat for dehydration, which can be extreme, and if there is an appreciable delay in getting to hospital then begin taking tetracycline. The adult dose is 250mg four times daily. It is not recommended for children aged eight years or under nor for pregnant women. Fluid replacement is by far the most important aspect of treatment.

Typhoid Typhoid fever is another gut infection that travels the faecal-oral route – ie contaminated water and food are responsible. Vaccination against typhoid is not totally effective and it is one of the most dangerous infections, so medical help must be sought. In its early stages, typhoid resembles many other illnesses: sufferers may feel like they have a bad cold or flu on the way, as early symptoms are a headache, a sore throat, and a fever which rises a little each day until it is around 40°C (104°F) or more. The victim's pulse is often slow relative to the degree of fever present and gets slower as the fever rises – unlike a normal fever where the pulse increases. There may also be vomiting, diarrhoea or constipation.

You must get medical help early because pneumonia or peritonitis are common complications, and because typhoid is very infectious. The fever should be treated by keeping the victim cool and dehydration should also be watched for.

Hepatitis A The symptoms are fever, chills, headache, fatigue, feelings of weakness and aches and pains, followed by loss of appetite, nausea, vomiting, abdominal pain, dark urine, light-coloured faeces, jaundiced skin and the whites of the eyes may turn yellow. In some cases you may feel unwell, tired, have no appetite, experience aches and pains and be jaundiced. You should seek medical advice, but in general there is not much you can do apart from resting, drinking lots of fluids, eating lightly and avoiding fatty foods. People who have had hepatitis must forego alcohol for six months after the illness, as hepatitis attacks the liver and it needs that amount of time to recover.

The routes of transmission are via contaminated water, shellfish contaminated by sewage or foodstuffs sold by food handlers with poor standards of hygiene. Taking care with what you eat and drink can go a long way towards preventing this disease.

Hepatitis B This is also a very common disease, with almost 300 million chronic carriers in the world. Hepatitis B is spread through contact with infected blood, blood products or bodily fluids, for example through sexual contact, unsterilised needles and blood transfusions or via small breaks in the skin. Other risk situations include having a shave or tattoo in a local shop or having your body pierced. The symptoms of type B are much the same as type A except that they are more severe and may lead to irreparable liver damage or even liver cancer.

Intestinal Worms These parasites are most common in rural areas and a stool test when you return home is not a bad idea. They can be present on unwashed vegetables or in undercooked meat and you can pick them up through your skin by walking in bare feet.

Tetanus This potentially fatal disease is found worldwide, occurring more commonly in undeveloped tropical areas. It is difficult to treat but is preventable with immunisation. Tetanus occurs when a wound becomes infected by a germ which lives in soil and in the faeces of horses and other animals, so clean all cuts, punctures or animal bites. Tetanus is also known as lockjaw and the first symptom may be discomfort in swallowing or a stiffening of the jaw and neck; this is followed by painful convulsions of the jaw and whole body.

Tuberculosis (TB) PNG has the highest incidence of TB in the Pacific. This is, however, unlikely to be a major problem for the short-term visitor. Typically many months of contact with an infected person are required before the disease is passed on.

It is a bacterial infection which is usually transmitted from person to person by coughing but may also be transmitted through consumption of unpasteurised milk. Milk that has been boiled is safe to drink and the souring of milk to make yoghurt or cheese also kills the bacilli.

Sexually Transmitted Diseases (STDs) PNG has very high rates of sexually transmitted diseases. Gonorrhoea, herpes and syphilis are among these diseases; symptoms include sores, blisters or rashes around the genitals and discharge or pain when urinating. In some STDs, such as wart virus or chlamydia, symptoms may be less marked or not observed at all in women. Syphilis symptoms eventually disappear completely but the disease continues and can cause severe problems in later years. Antibiotics are used to treat gonorrhoea and syphilis. There are numerous other sexually transmitted diseases, for most of which effective treatment is available, but there is no cure for herpes. While abstinence from sexual intercourse is the only sure preventative against STDs, condoms are potentially the next most effective method, but some health workers in PNG are reluctant to distribute them in the villages for fear of being seen as promoting promiscuity.

HIV/AIDS Any exposure to blood, blood products or bodily fluids may put you at risk of HIV infection. Apart from abstinence (highly recommended), the most effective preventative is to practise safe sex using condoms. HIV can also be spread through infected blood transfusions or by using dirty needles – if you do need an injection, ask to see the syringe unwrapped in front of you or, better still, take a needle and syringe pack with you. It is cheap insurance against infection with HIV. Vaccinations, acupuncture, tattooing and ear or nose piercing are similarly potentially dangerous if the equipment is not clean. So take care.

Insect-Borne Diseases
Malaria While discussing dosages for prevention of malaria with your doctor, it is often advisable to include the dosages required for treatment, especially if your trip is through a high-risk area that would isolate you from medical care.

Primary prevention must always be in the form of mosquito-avoidance measures. The *Anopheles* mosquitos are most numerous at dawn and at dusk, but are still active between those times. Travellers are advised to:

- Take malaria prophylactics regularly – while no antimalarial is 100% effective, taking the most appropriate drug significantly reduces the risk of contracting the disease
- Use mosquito repellents containing the compound DEET on exposed areas (overuse of DEET may be harmful, especially to children, but its use is considered preferable to being bitten by disease-transmitting mosquitos)
- Avoid highly scented perfumes or aftershave
- Use a mosquito net
- Wear light-coloured clothing
- Wear long pants and long sleeved shirts
- Longer-term residents should ensure their houses are screened

You will know if you catch malaria. But no one should ever die from it. Symptoms may include headaches, fever, chills and sweating (which may subside and recur), abdominal

The *Anopheles* mosquito can transmit malaria to humans.

pains and a feeling of ill-health. Without treatment, malaria can develop more serious, potentially fatal effects. But it can be diagnosed by a simple blood test, so seek examination immediately if you have any doubts.

Contrary to popular belief, once a traveller contracts malaria they do not have it for life. Two species of the parasite may lie dormant in the liver but they can also be eradicated using a specific medication. Most people who live in PNG for more than a few years come down with malaria, so getting the proper diagnosis and treatment (essential to avoid dangerous complications) is not difficult in towns but if you're planning to be out of touch for a while, you should talk to a doctor about diagnosing and treating yourself.

Adequate diagnosis and treatment could be a problem if you develop headaches and fever after you return home, where doctors rarely see malarial patients and are sometimes unfamiliar with the symptoms. You might be told to go away and take a couple of aspirin. If this happens, get a second opinion – fast!

Dengue Fever There is no prophylactic available for this mosquito-spread disease; the main preventative is to avoid mosquito bites. A sudden onset of fever, headaches and severe joint and muscle pains are the first signs before a rash starts on the trunk of the body and spreads to the limbs and face. After a further few days, the fever will subside and recovery will begin. Serious complications are not common but full recovery can take a month or more.

Cuts, Bites & Stings
Cuts & Scratches Skin punctures can easily become infected in hot climates and may be difficult to heal. Treat any cut with an antiseptic such as povidone-iodine. Where possible avoid bandages and adhesive plasters, which can keep wounds wet. Coral cuts are notoriously slow to heal and if they are not adequately cleaned small pieces of coral can become embedded in the wound. Simi-

larly, spines from sea-urchins can cause deep, painful and easily infected wounds. Any infection may result in tropical ulcers. These nasty, weeping sores are very difficult to get rid of once they take hold. You might need a course of penicillin.

Bites & Stings Insect stings are usually painful rather than dangerous. Calamine lotion or Stingose spray will give relief and ice packs will reduce the pain and swelling. Sandflies are tiny and you often don't know you've been bitten until the next day, when an itchiness unlike anything you've ever imagined descends on you. It can cause you a couple of sleepless nights. To make matters worse, sandfly bites often produce tiny sores and if you scratch off the minute scabs, they almost invariably become infected. Sandflies hang out on beaches, but not all beaches, so ask around.

Snakes Nearly a hundred different species of snakes are found in PNG but very few are dangerous, despite the general hysteria which greets the arrival of any snake in a village. PNG villagers tend to have an uncompromising and unreasonable fear of reptiles. Most snakes are not aggressive, however, and will quickly get out of your way before you are even aware of their presence. Nevertheless, there *are* some deaths each year from snakebite and, although unlikely, trekkers are at some small risk of being bitten.

There are very limited supplies of antivenins at hospitals in Port Moresby and (possibly) other major centres.

Jellyfish You should heed local advice about the presence of these sea creatures with their stinging tentacles. Dousing in vinegar will de-activate any stingers which have not 'fired'. Calamine lotion, antihistamines and analgesics may reduce the reaction and relieve the pain.

Leeches & Ticks Leeches are found in some areas; they attach themselves to your skin to suck your blood. Trekkers often get them on their legs or in their boots. Salt or a lighted cigarette end will make them fall off. Do not pull them off, as the bite is then more likely to become infected. An insect repellent may keep them away. You should always check your body if you have been walking through a tick-infested area, as ticks can spread typhus. A drop or two of kerosene or turpentine will loosen a tick's grip and it can then be carefully levered out of the skin, making sure that the mouth parts are also extracted.

Women's Health

Gynaecological Problems Poor diet, lowered resistance due to the use of antibiotics for stomach upsets and even contraceptive pills can lead to vaginal infections when travelling in hot climates. Maintaining good personal hygiene and wearing skirts or loose-fitting trousers and cotton underwear will help to prevent infections.

Yeast infections, characterised by a rash, itch and discharge, can be treated with a vinegar or lemon-juice douche or with yoghurt. Nystatin, miconazole or clotrimazole suppositories are the usual medical prescription. Trichomoniasis and gardnerella are more serious infections; symptoms are a smelly discharge and sometimes a burning sensation when urinating. Male sexual partners must also be treated and if a vinegar-water douche is not effective, medical attention should be sought. Metronidazole (Flagyl) is the prescribed drug.

Pregnancy Most miscarriages occur during the first three months of pregnancy, so this is the most risky time to travel as far as your own health is concerned. Miscarriage is not uncommon and can occasionally lead to severe bleeding. The last three months should also be spent within reasonable distance of good medical care. A baby born as early as 24 weeks stands a chance of survival, but only in a good modern hospital. Pregnant women should avoid all unnecessary medication but vaccinations and malarial prophylactics should still be taken where possible. Additional care should be taken to prevent illness and particular attention should be paid to diet and nutrition. Alcohol and nicotine, for example, should be avoided.

PERSONAL SAFETY

This section aims to help counter the bad press given to PNG, especially in Australia. It is true travellers are robbed, occasionally with violence, and there have been rapes, but the reality is that PNG is not the acutely dangerous place it is painted to be – as long as you are sensible.

Bear in mind that everything is saner and more relaxed in the villages. People quickly get to know you and you rapidly lose the anonymity that makes a stranger a target. The average person's natural friendliness and hospitality is not repressed as it is in an urban jungle. Which is not to say that you can throw caution to the wind when you leave urban boundaries – even in villages you need to use discretion and common sense. But in a village the villagers will take responsibility for you and that makes a world of difference.

Expats may tell you that PMVs are totally unsafe – but most resident expats have their own cars and have never caught one. PMVs are safe and, indeed, one big plus about PNG is that the usual Third-World nightmare of hurtling along in a totally unroadworthy bus with a maniac at the wheel doesn't apply. Most PMVs are in reasonable condition and most drivers are aware of the payback (compensation for a wrongdoing) problems they would have if they hit anything – even a chicken or a dog – or injured one of their passengers. You are most unlikely to have any trouble from other passengers on a PMV – they're more likely to share their food with you.

It is not worth considering walking the streets at night, especially if you are a woman. If you wouldn't walk around a tough neighbourhood in your own home town, then apply the same rule in PNG – and be particularly wary of drunks and young men in groups. Even in a crowd you are vulnerable – and there's very little night life to lure you anyway, even in Port Moresby. Make sure you find a good place to spend each night, and sleep securely. If you plan to go out to a restaurant or club, catch the last PMV there and get a lift or a taxi home (unless you are in places like Lae or Wewak where there are no taxis). It is worth being especially careful on the fortnightly Friday pay nights – things can get pretty wild.

In Port Moresby, try to avoid secluded urban areas, even in the daytime. Rascals are not strictly nocturnal. Walk up Paga Hill to look at the view by all means, but don't do it alone. Be careful walking past the shanty settlement on Three Mile Hill above Koki and behind Waigani around the golf club. And stay out of the shanty towns and Hanuabada unless you have a local guide.

Ask the locals about safe areas and activities as circumstances change from time to time. Sometimes roads or districts become prime areas for rascal activity – and then they quieten down again. Make an effort to communicate with everyone you meet – they can tell you a lot and you can make some good friends this way – and get to know the people who live in the area you are visiting. Not only will this add to your enjoyment, but also to your security – you will be identified as 'belonging' and have access to first-hand advice and information. There are few countries in the world where a smile and a greeting are so well received. Nevertheless, you cannot afford to be entirely naive about your popularity – you may well be regarded as a potential source of status, or even wealth. Use your common sense and be a little sceptical. Even if you do decide that someone is all right, don't put yourself in a vulnerable position.

If you are staying in villages, sleep with a family rather than in a village guesthouse or haus kiap (a house for kiaps, or patrol officers). It's safer and more fun. In most cases, you'll also be much better off with a guide who speaks the tok ples (local language). You won't be so likely to get lost, the guide can take care of the various permissions you will need (to camp, to cross someone's land etc) and you'll have automatic introductions to local people.

It's wise not to flaunt your wealth or possessions because people dressed expensively or as obvious tourists are potential targets for robbery. If you plan to frequent out-of-the-way places, wear a cheap watch, leave your expensive SLR camera at home, and keep just K25 or K30 in your wallet (to appease any would-be thief). Hide the rest in a money belt – or sew special hidden pockets in your clothing.

You should keep your possessions close to you and never leave anything unattended, even in the village haus of your 'best friend'. It isn't particularly common, but pickpockets and bag snatchers do exist in urban PNG, so be a little cautious in crowded places like PMVs, bus stops and markets. Take precautions such as concealing some emergency cash and making sure your travellers cheque numbers are written down somewhere safe. One traveller wrote that while his pack was stolen in a PMV hold-up, a dirty old bilum he had wasn't touched. You can insure your camera but not your precious exposed films, so think about mailing film home or to a secure address within PNG.

In short: be careful – but don't be paranoid.

WOMEN TRAVELLERS

Women should always dress conservatively, even when swimming. Outside the resorts, bikinis do not provide sufficient cover – a laplap (sarong) can come in handy as a wrap. Take your cue from the local women. Whether on a beach or in a city, lone women should restrict their movements to areas where there are other people around and never go off by themselves.

In many ways, Papua New Guinean women have a very hard time and this does affect the situation for visitors. Except in the cities, women are almost always subservient to men and physical abuse is common – the government feels it necessary to produce a brochure entitled 'Wife-beating is illegal'. In many parts of the country, a woman never initiates a conversation with a man and never talks to a male outside her family, never eats at the same table as men, and never even sleeps in the same house as any man, including her father or husband.

A lone, western female traveller has no local parallel and, to a certain extent, a special case will be made of her. Virtually throughout the country, however, it will be difficult for women to have a normal conversation with a man without being misinterpreted as a flirt. Similarly, but in reverse, a western man who attempts to initiate a conversation with a PNG woman can cause embarrassment and confusion.

Public displays of affection are almost unknown, and a western couple making physical contact in public – even holding hands – is regarded as an oddity and, especially in traditional rural societies, may be regarded with contempt. This can put the woman in danger.

It's recommended that women do not travel alone in PNG, especially if they haven't travelled in a highly sexist society before. But despite the obvious difficulties, we have received a number of letters from women who have clearly enjoyed travelling around by themselves. And throughout the country you'll find women working as administrators, entrepreneurs, pilots, teachers, nurses, missionaries and adventure travel tour guides, for example, so it definitely can be done.

Many towns have women's groups (which sometimes have guesthouses) and these are good places to find out about PNG women's lives and to see what is being done to help alleviate their problems.

GAY & LESBIAN TRAVELLERS

Homosexuality is illegal in PNG but the law has apparently never been enforced. Gays are sometimes made mild fun of, but there is no danger of physical violence. Indeed, homosexuality is far from a topical issue in Melanesian society. There are no gay organisations and the influence of the various churches tends to reinforce the view that homosexuality is morally reprehensible.

TRAVELLING WITH CHILDREN

If you are travelling with children, remember that they are likely to be harder hit than you by many diseases (especially dehydration caused by diarrhoea). Lonely Planet's *Travel with Children* gives some basic advice. Be warned that the local people will spoil your children shamelessly once they get to know you (which usually takes about 10 minutes).

USEFUL ORGANISATIONS
Volunteer Organisations

There are many hundreds of international volunteer workers in PNG, often located in remote areas. Their activities range from teaching and medical assistance to advisory roles with local area councils. Most are either associated with the churches or with international volunteer organisations which have field offices in major towns and cities. The exception is Australian Volunteers Abroad (AVA) which has between 20 and 30 volunteers in the country but no field office in PNG – it is administered directly from its Melbourne headquarters. The main organisations are:

Australian Volunteers Abroad (AVA)
    PO Box 350, Fitzroy, Victoria 3065, Australia
    (☎ (03) 9279 1788; fax (03) 9419 4280)
Canadian University Service Overseas (CUSO)
    PO Box 5726; 12 Mabata St, Gordons, PNG
    (☎ 325 4488)
German Development Service
    PO Box 1862, Boroko, PNG (☎ 325 5380; fax
    325 9377)
Japan International Co-operation Agency (JICA)
    PO Box 6639; Garden City, Boroko, PNG
    (☎ 325 1699)
Japan Overseas Co-operation Volunteers
    PO Box 6639; Gorogo St, Gordons, PNG
    (☎ 325 3949)
US Peace Corps
    PO Box 1790; 2nd floor, Garden City, Boroko,
    PNG (☎ 325 8355; fax 325 7026)
Voluntary Service Overseas (British VSO)
    PO Box 5685, Boroko; Tern St, Waigani
    (☎ 326 0026; fax 326 1010)
Volunteer Service Abroad (NZ VSA)
    PO Box 1501, Rabaul, PNG (☎ 982 7110)

Environmental & Development Organisations

There is a growing number of organisations concerned with environmental issues and community development. Some significant ones are:

Christensen Research Institute
> PO Box 305, Madang (☎ 852 3011;
> fax 852 3306; email cri@delphi.com)
> Situated next to the Jais Aben Resort near Madang, this organisation conducts scientific research and undertakes village-based development activities.

Foundation of the Peoples of the South Pacific, PNG (FSP/PNG)
> PO Box 1119, Boroko (☎ 325 8470;
> fax 325 2670; email fpsp@peg.apc.org)
> Funded by the World Wildlife Fund and US Aid, FSP is concerned primarily with integrating conservation and development activities at a village level, including ecotourism, ecoforestry, community awareness, literacy and work opportunities.

Oro Conservation Project
> PO Box 647, Popondetta (☎ 329 7556;
> fax 329 7558)
> Based in Popondetta and Afore, this organisation has Australian consultants advising on rural development and village ecology.

Research & Conservation Foundation of PNG
> PO Box 2750, Boroko (☎ 323 0699;
> fax 323 0397)
> RCF concentrates primarily on wildlife conservation and management, for example at the Crater Mountain Wildlife Management Area.

Village Development Trust (VDT)
> PO Box 2397, Lae (☎ 4721666; fax 472 4824;
> email vdt@global.net.pg)
> The VDT promotes self-reliance in village communities in ways that are environmentally, economically, and socially sustainable. It has been particularly involved in sustainable forestry and ecotourism.

Wau Ecology Institute (WEI)
> PO Box 120, Wau (☎ 474 6212)
> Funded by US and German aid, the WEI undertakes limited scientific research at a village level. It has an insect ranch (with some magnificent butterflies), a conference centre and zoo.

BUSINESS HOURS

Most offices are open from 8 am to 4 pm. Shops generally stay open later, especially on Friday nights and they're also open on Saturday mornings. Trade stores and snack bars usually have more liberal hours.

Post offices are open from 8 am to 5 pm weekdays. There's generally not much point in visiting government offices between 12.30 and 2 pm even though lunch officially starts at 1 pm and finishes at 1.30 pm.

PUBLIC HOLIDAYS & SPECIAL EVENTS

Each of the 19 provinces of PNG has its own provincial government day and these are usually a good opportunity to enjoy sing-sings. Generally, however, sing-sings are local affairs with no fixed yearly schedule, so you'll have to depend on word-of-mouth to find out about them.

Shows and festivals are held on weekends, so the dates change from year to year, usually only by a few days. Similarly, the public holiday associated with a provincial government day will usually be on a Friday or Monday.

January-May

New Year's Day (1 January)
Teptep Cultural Show, Madang (6-7 January)
New Ireland Provincial Government Celebrations & Kavieng Show (22 February)
Easter (March-April, variable date)
> traditional church services

Port Moresby Regional Cultural Festival
Oro Provincial Government Day (20 April)
Malalana Mini Cultural Show, Gulf Province (17-21 May)

June-August

Yam Harvest Festival in the Trobriand Islands (variable date)
Queen's Birthday (mid-June)
Port Moresby Show (mid-June)
> traditional and modern events

Central Provincial Government Day (mid-June)
Morobe Provincial Government Day (July)
Milne Bay Government Day (7 July)
Remembrance Day (23 July)
> mainly Port Moresby

Rabaul Frangipani Festival (16 July)
> commemorates the first flowers to blossom after the 1937 eruption of Matupit

Madang Provincial Government Day (early August)
Goroka Show (early August)
> this is *the* big Highlands sing-sing and well worth adjusting your travel plans around. A huge gathering of clans in traditional dress and *bilas* (finery).

Maborasa Festival in Madang (early August)
> includes dancing, choirs and bamboo bands

Manus Provincial Government Day (28 August)
Simbu Provincial Government Day (August)
George Brown Day (mid-August)
> celebrated in the New Britain and New Ireland provinces

Southern Highlands Provincial Government Day (August)

Mt Hagen Show (late August)
another major gathering of Highlands clans

September

Independence Day (16 September)
a great time to be in PNG, with many festivals and sing-sings all around the country

Hiri Moale, Port Moresby (16 September)
festival celebrating the Papuan trading canoes

Malangan Festival in New Ireland (16 September)
this two-week festival includes the famous tree-dancers

Tolai Warwagira in Rabaul (September)
a two-week festival of sing-sings and other events

Milne Bay Show (16 September)

October-November

Kundiawa Simbu Show (11-12 October)

Enga Provincial Government Day (October)

West New Britain Provincial Government Day (October)

East Sepik Provincial Government Celebrations (mid-October)

Oro Tapa Festival, Popondetta (mid-October)

Gulf Province annual celebrations (mid-October)

December

Gulf Provincial Government Day (1 December)

Western Provincial Government Day (6 December)

Christmas (25 December)

ACTIVITIES

Bushwalking

Considering the vast areas of rugged, mountainous terrain where the only way to get from village to village is to fly or walk, it is surprising that bushwalking in PNG has not caught on the same way trekking has in the Himalayas. For detailed information on walks and walking see the Lonely Planet book *Bushwalking in Papua New Guinea*.

Some of the walks are tough but, especially on the coast, it's possible to avoid the very steep ascents and descents characteristic of trails in PNG.

Once you're out in the bush, you'll find that your expenses plummet. Your major costs will be paying for guides, where they are necessary, or buying petrol for outboards on the river. Expect to pay a guide K15 to

K25 a day. You'll also have to provide or pay for their food and possibly some equipment.

A number of companies offer organised treks. They're not cheap but worth considering if you have limited time. It's hard to guarantee itineraries at the best of times in PNG but professional companies will probably have a better chance of sticking to them than you will. Some of them also go to places you would be hard pushed to reach yourself, even if you did find out they existed.

The Kokoda Trail is the best known walking track in PNG but there are literally hundreds of other lesser known but even more interesting walks. The whole country is criss-crossed with tracks, and in most parts of the country there is rarely more than a day's walk between villages. There really is no limit to the alternatives. Listed here are some of the more interesting walks; you'll find others covered in various places throughout this book.

Kokoda Trail (6-7 days) This is a difficult walk over the mountainous spine between the north and south coasts. The trail follows the route taken by the Japanese after they landed on the north coast. After almost reaching Port Moresby, they were driven back by Australian troops in some of the most bitter fighting of the war. There are relatively few villages and it isn't a particularly interesting walk from a cultural point of view, but the country is superb and getting from one end to another is a feat to be proud of.

The trail provides an important alternative to flying, as there are no roads between Port Moresby and the north coast or the Highlands. There are other possibilities, but this is the route most travellers use. See the Central & Oro Provinces chapter.

Lake Kopiago to Oksapmin (3-4 days) This is an extremely difficult but particularly interesting walk. Starting at the very end of the Highlands Highway, you cross the Strickland River's spectacular gorge. It is possible to continue on to Telefomin, which would take another six to eight days. From

Telefomin, you can catch planes to places in the Sepik Basin like April River. See The Highlands chapter.

Mt Wilhelm (3-4 days) Mt Wilhelm is the tallest mountain in PNG, and, at 4509m, it's a serious mountain by any standards. The climb is highly recommended – not only do you see traditional Simbu villages on your way to the mountain but the views from the top are spectacular. See The Highlands chapter.

Mt Wilhelm to Madang (3 days) A relatively easy way of getting between the Highlands and the north coast is to follow a 4WD track which takes off the main Mt Wilhelm Road just before Kegsugl and goes through Bundi and on to Brahman where, with a bit of luck, you'll find a PMV to Madang. See The Highlands chapter.

Wau to Salamaua (3 days) This is a very tough walk. You could fly from Port Moresby to Wau, spend some time around Wau, walk to Salamaua, relax there, then catch a boat to Lae. See the Morobe Province chapter.

Wedau to Alotau (3-4 days) This coastal walk is more a way to cut down on costs, do some swimming and snorkelling and experience village life than a tough slog through the jungle. You don't have to be particularly fit (there is a scramble over a mountain on the last day) and if you find that you're in no hurry to finish, you can extend the walk by another few days. See the Milne Bay Province chapter.

Woitape to Tapini (3 days) This is an interesting walk and there are airports at both places and a road to Fane, near Woitape. See the Central & Oro Provinces chapter.

River Journeys

PNG has some of the world's largest and most spectacular rivers. The Sepik is often compared to the Amazon and Congo rivers, while the Sepik Basin is an artistic and cultural treasure house.

There is a number of rivers that local people use as highways, including the Sepik and some of its tributaries (including the April, May and Keram), the Ramu, the Fly and many other rivers that flow into the Gulf of Papua. Local people can travel by river between the Irian Jayan border and, virtually, Madang, using the Sepik, Keram and Ramu. On these rivers there is often an assortment of craft, ranging from dugout canoes to tramp steamers.

If you do want to spend time on a river, there is a number of possibilities: you can buy your own canoe and paddle yourself; you can use PMV boats (unscheduled, intervillage, motorised, dugout canoes); you can charter a motorised canoe and guide/driver when you get to the river; you can go on tours of varying degrees of comfort; and you can sail in a cruise ship with all mod cons.

The larger tour companies also offer Sepik trips which vary considerably in the degree of comfort. Some are luxuriously based at the Karawari Lodge (eg Trans Niugini Tours), while others are based in the villages.

River Boats There are alternatives if you prefer to have something more substantial than a canoe beneath you. There are no longer regular passenger-carrying cargo boats on the Sepik, but you might get lucky.

Melanesian Tourist Services runs the *Melanesian Discoverer*, a luxurious cruise boat, from Madang to Green River, stopping off in the villages along the way, and Trans Niugini Tours has the smaller but also upmarket Sepik Spirit cruising the Sepik.

River Rafting Shooting down PNG's turbulent mountain rivers in inflatable dinghies is a sport still in its infancy, but one with tremendous potential. Not only is rafting great fun, you also get to see some spectacular country from an unusual perspective. There don't seem to be any regular trips operating from within PNG, but foreign adventure tour operators sometimes have them on their itineraries.

Sea Journeys

If you don't own a cruising yacht (and when you see PNG's islands and harbours you will wish you did), there are four alternatives left: use the regular coastal shipping, take a tour, charter a boat or crew a yacht. These options are covered in the Getting Around chapter. But with time, ingenuity and luck you can travel anywhere by boat. With a dense scattering of beautiful islands, PNG is a great place for sea kayaking.

Diving

Diving is one of the fastest growing attractions in PNG, with diving resorts opening all the time. PNG is said to be at least the equal of diving meccas like the Red Sea, the Caribbean and the Great Barrier Reef.

When you go to PNG, you *have* to look under the water – you'll see a world which is vivid and teeming with life. There's an amazing array of environments with reef and pelagic fish, dramatic drop-offs, shells and corals.

Those who like diving on wrecks will find the reefs are liberally dotted with sunken ships – either as a result of the reefs or WWII. The coast is surrounded by coral reefs, many easily accessible to snorkellers. There is, in general, excellent visibility and an abundance of fish.

PNG's best locations for divers are Alotau, Kavieng, Kimbe, Lae, Lorengau, Madang, Rabaul and Wuvulu Island.

Snorkelling is the cheapest and easiest way to have a look, but there are also a number of dive operators who offer courses, equipment and tours. Diving operators are found in all towns close to the good diving areas. See the regional chapters for details on locations and operators.

Overseas operators which book diving tours in PNG include:

Sea New Guinea
    100 Clarence St, Sydney 2000, Australia
    (☎ (02) 9267 5563; fax (02) 9267 6118)
Sea Safaris
    3770 Suite 102, Highland Ave, Manhattan Beach, CA 90266, USA (☎ 800-821 6670)

See & Sea Travel
    50 Francisco St, STU 205, San Francisco, CA 94133, USA (☎ (415) 434 3400; fax (415) 434 3409)
Tropical Adventures
    111 Second North, Seattle, WA 98109, USA (☎ 800-247 3483)

Surfing

Slowly surfers are making inroads to PNG and discovering the charms of staying in simple village accommodation and surfing breaks that have never been surfed before. Certainly there is surf in PNG, but there is no local surf culture and getting to know about reliable breaks is difficult. There's surf around Kavieng from November to April, and around Wewak from September to January and around Buka and Bougainville as well. The beaches west of Vanimo are sometimes good and Lido village even has a great surfers' guesthouse right on the beach. Plenty of other places have surf, but finding out about it isn't easy. It's best to avoid June, July and August when the prevailing winds are south-easterly.

The problem is that most accessible PNG beaches are in the lee of reefs or islands and don't open onto the ocean. If you have access to a boat and can get out to the reefs, there are plenty of waves, especially off the eastern coasts of New Ireland and Bougainville, and the unprotected East Sepik coast. This also means the surf breaks onto coral reefs, so these aren't for the inexperienced.

Kavieng is the most explored surfing location in PNG, with good breaks within a few minutes by dinghy or PMV from town. See the New Ireland chapter for information on surfing spots around Kavieng.

The Nusa Islands Retreat (☎ & fax 984 2247; PO Box 302), a new 'surfing resort' on Nusa Lik Island near Kavieng, can also arrange outer-island camping, sea kyaking, fishing and other activities. It recommends surfers bring a medium-length board.

The waves tend to be very fast-breaking over reefs but not often more than about 2m, so don't bother bringing a gun. You'll only need one good all-round board and a vest to protect you from the hot sun.

Diveco (☎ 325 25 4466; PO Box 1786) in Port Moresby offers surfing tours.

Windsurfing

The very characteristics which make surfing difficult in many areas make windsurfing viable: sheltered harbours, strong winds between June and August and, if you're interested, waves outside lagoons. Windsurfing is quite popular, particularly in Port Moresby and Madang. Although you won't always find it easy to get hold of a board, some top-end hotels on the coast have one or two for hire. The yacht clubs would also be good places to start your enquiries.

Fishing

Fishing in PNG has enormous potential. But unless they have permission from traditional owners, anglers can easily get themselves in trouble. You can't just walk up to a stream or the edge of the ocean and cast in a line – everything and every square inch of PNG is owned by someone, including streams and reefs. The fish are definitely there – including trout in the Highlands, reef and deep-sea fish offshore – and if you do get permission from the traditional owners, you should have some excellent fishing.

Several tours are offered by Sea New Guinea and, while it's possible to hire boats in several towns, most of the dive operators have boats that can be chartered (see the Diving section for addresses). Other fishing tour operators include:

Kavieng Hotel
  PO Box 4, Kavieng (☎ 984 2199; fax 984 2283)
New Britain Fishing Tours
  PO Box 1008, Kokopo (☎ 982 8370;
  fax 982 3043)
Reel Fish Charters
  PO Box 521, Madang (☎ 853 7496;
  fax 853 7468)
Trans Melanesian Marine
  PO Box 477, Port Moresby (☎ 321 2039;
  fax 321 1074)

Cycling

The lack of roads in PNG makes cycling impractical in most places. But New Ireland,

with good, almost traffic-free roads running along both coasts, is a paradise for cyclists. Rainbow Tours (☎ 984 2234) offers cycle tours of New Ireland and there are bikes for hire in Kavieng. Riding from Namatanai to Kavieng takes about four days, more if you take it easy.

The long Highlands Highway probably isn't very safe for cycling because of the risk of robbery (although cycling is so rare that your curiosity value might protect you), and some of the hills are damned steep! The excellent network of roads on the Gazelle Peninsula would be good (if often steep) cycling but finding a bike to ride is almost impossible.

Caving

Caves in the limestone regions of the Southern Highlands may well be the deepest in the world but to date they have been little explored. The Mamo Kananda in the Muller Range (near Lake Kopiago) is reputed to be one of the longest caves in the world at 54.8km and nearby Atea Kananda is the second longest in PNG at 34.5km. There are also caves around Bougainville (Benua Cave is thought to be the world's biggest cavern at 4.5 million cubic metres), Pomio (East New Britain Province) and Manus Province.

Bird & Butterfly-Watching

PNG is thick with bird-life and insects. See the Flora & Fauna section in the Facts about the Country chapter for details.

Visiting War Wreckages

At the end of WWII, the country was littered from end to end with the wreckage of Allied and Japanese aircraft, ships and army equipment. Most of it has been shipped out by bands of scrap dealers, but there is still much to be seen.

ACCOMMODATION

The one unfortunate generalisation that you can make about accommodation is that it is too expensive. Overall the quality is reasonable, although often not worth the price, and in most towns your options are limited.

ADRIAN LIPSCOMB

An American WWII fighter at the
Popondetta airstrip (Oro Province).

Booking ahead is a good idea, especially
for moderately priced hotels and guesthouses. Most are small and don't take many
people before they are full. Spend a few toea
to make a booking over the excellent phone
system and you could avoid arriving to find
that the one cheap place is full and the only
alternative is a luxury hotel room. Booking
ahead is especially important if there is a
festival. Transport between airports and
towns is sometimes difficult and often
expensive but most hosts will pick you up if
they know you're coming – another saving.
If you're booking by mail, remember there
is no postal delivery and you must write to a
post office box number. The fax machine has
become an important communication device
in PNG and it's the cheapest way of booking
your first night's stay from your home
country (request a confirmation fax).

Camping
Unless you're planning on doing some
serious trekking don't bother bringing a tent.
There's no organised camping facilities and
not really anywhere to pitch it (besides a
police station compound). All land has a
traditional owner somewhere and you need
to seek permission to camp. It may look like

empty bush but soon enough there'll be
people moving through on their way to and
from their gardens and workplaces. The land
owner may live just a few kilometres away
and by the time you've found them, you may
well be offered room in a hut anyway. And
then there's the problem with security –
you'd feel pretty vulnerable and over-
exposed out in the middle of the bush by
yourself in a jazzy high-tech tent.

Shelter is much easier to find than somewhere to pitch a tent. Unless you are going
to the Highlands, you'll find a sleeping bag
useless too – a sleeping sheet will be more
than enough. Cotton is cooler and cheaper
than silk (which may make you perspire
profusely) but is more bulky. Nights in the
Highlands can be cold and frosty (see the
What to Bring section).

If you are walking at low altitudes you are
most likely to be following a reasonably well
travelled route and come across either villages or bush shelters at regular intervals.
You will find local people enormously hospitable and you should make a modest
contribution to the local communities you
move through. If you are in a large group, a
tent is useful to take the pressure off limited
accommodation in villages.

A lightweight tent fly can help waterproof
a shelter and a well-ventilated tent inner can
prove handy as an all-in-one groundsheet,
mosquito net and changing room.

The space in your pack might be better
filled with a mosquito net, but even think
twice about taking that. In most places where
you'll need one, you'll find that if you
politely ask someone, a net can normally be
found. People do get malaria in PNG (locals
too) and if you're in the bush in the lowlands,
you have to be serious about avoiding mosquito bites (see the Health section).

Remember that the population density
drops and the weather becomes colder at
higher altitudes.

Inexpensive Accommodation
You can find somewhere inexpensive to stay
in most main towns. Inexpensive is a relative
term, though – the cheapest bed in Port

Moresby is K30 a night and elsewhere you'll sometimes pay a little less. There are some exceptions. In organised village guesthouses (bush huts) the rates are around K15, again with some exceptions.

Most of the cheaper places are mission-run guesthouses and hostels. Most exist for the benefit of visiting missionaries and church people. There are far fewer of these hostels than before and some no longer accommodate travellers. Lutheran hostels are reliably clean, comfortable and friendly. They usually offer generous servings of fairly plain food in their communal dining rooms, after a blessing. Despite this, hostels are good meeting places. The missionaries can also be helpful with local information and are often interesting people in their own right. Staying in one of the hostels will give you the opportunity to get a first-hand view of the church's role in PNG.

Around the country there are a growing number of provincial women's associations, some of which run hostels. Not only are the hostels inexpensive (usually), but they provide the opportunity to meet politically aware grassroots women. Men can sometimes stay in women's hostels. Although there are some YWCA hostels, most cater to permanent residents and are usually full. Still, women needing somewhere to stay could try them.

Some of the better hotels have cheaper rooms, costing not much more than at a mission guesthouse. Even if there is no cheap accommodation, it's sometimes possible to do deals at the more expensive hotels, especially if you arrive at the end of the day.

High schools are often quite isolated and all have boarding quarters, so you could get lucky and find a spare bed. It's likely you'll have to sing for your supper or at the very least do a lot of talking! The school headmaster is certain to be a good source of local information. Police stations around the country almost always allow you to camp on their grounds or use a spare room in their barracks, for no charge.

Some of the better-value options for budget travellers around the country are:

Haus Poroman Lodge near Mt Hagen, National Sports Institute in Goroka, the Wau Ecology Institute, the Oro Guesthouse in Popondetta, the CWA Guesthouse in Madang, the Kavieng Hotel, the Taklam Guesthouse in Kokopo and the Hamamas Hotel in Rabaul.

Staying in Villages If you're willing to rough it a bit and get well off the track, your accommodation costs will be much smaller. In most villages you'll find someone willing to take you in. You must pay your way and K15 is a fair amount to give to a family that has provided a roof and some *kai* (food).

In some villages you might find there's a haus kiap – a council house or some other structure where local people might think you will want to stay. Try to resist this, as not only is staying with a family in a traditional house more enjoyable than sleeping by yourself in a decaying colonial-era structure, it's *much* safer. As soon as you are involved with a community you become, to some extent, its responsibility.

There has been significant development of village guesthouses in recent years and they are particularly common around Madang, Tufi, on the Sepik and along the coast of New Ireland. Support them if you can – they help the tourist dollar filter down to the village level.

More Expensive Accommodation

Most of the top-end hotels are relatively recent constructions, often in a motel style with a few carvings tacked on. Prices range from a little to a lot higher than similar places in Australia. Singles range from about K80 to K180 and more. There's quite a wide variety of prices and you'd be wise to plan ahead carefully. The major centres all have at least one reasonably high-standard (or at least high-priced) place. Port Moresby has a Travelodge and several other five-star hotels but the prices are astronomically high.

Some Coral Sea group hotels have set stand-by rates on rooms still vacant at 5 pm and many hotels have weekend specials which can be good value. The Bird of Paradise Hotel in Goroka is perhaps the best upmarket hotel in the Highlands and Malolo Resort is best on the north coast.

There are two exceptional luxury resorts, whose nearest equivalents are the famous African safari lodges and which are worth the effort if you have the funds: the Karawari Lodge lies deep in the jungle on a tributary of the Sepik and, best of all, the Ambua Lodge perches at 2100m on a ridge in the Southern Highlands overlooking the extraordinary Tari Valley.

Another option combines the virtues of comfort and mobility: the *Melanesian Discoverer* is a well-appointed ship that cruises the Sepik and the north coast as far as the islands of Milne Bay, while Trans Niugini Tours' smaller *Sepik Spirit* also cruises the Sepik.

FOOD

While the food is generally uninspiring, you should manage to eat reasonably well, most of the time. Unless you get off the beaten track, however, you probably won't have much opportunity to try local food. To a western palate that is no great loss since the average diet is made up of bland, starchy foods with very little protein. Western-style food in PNG tends to be a little plain, although if you're prepared to pay top prices, the food in hotels and restaurants can be good. The big exception to this picture is the magnificent seafood, especially shellfish and crustaceans, available on the coast.

PNG's Asian community dines well at a proliferation of restaurants and often the Asian-style food is better than most of the food available.

Local Food

In much of the low-lying swamp country the staple food is *saksak* (sago) – a tasteless, starchy extract that is washed from the pith of the sago palm. In the Highlands the staple is the *kaukau* (sweet potato), a native of South America brought to Asia by the Spanish and Portuguese around the end of the 15th century. In taste, it is virtually indistinguishable from taro and yams, which, with bananas, form the starchy basis of subsistence communities' diets. The situation is

sometimes a little more inspiring along the coast because there is excellent seafood and the cooking makes heavier use of coconut and even, sometimes, spices like ginger.

Because of the country's limited animal life, protein deficiency has traditionally been a problem. In many regions, potential game (reptiles, birds, rodents and small marsupials) is scarce but hunting is still important. Small boys shooting at birds with slingshots aren't indulging in mindless destruction, they're trying to catch a meal.

Apart from fresh fish, only available on the coast and some of the rivers, pigs are the main source of meat protein, although they are not generally eaten on a day-to-day basis, but saved for feasts. Chicken is now quite popular. New varieties of vegetables are also being introduced and developed for local consumption and as cash crops, particularly in the fertile soil of the Highlands valleys.

The most famous local cooking style is the *mumu*, a traditional underground oven. A pit is dug, fire-heated stones are placed in the bottom, meat and vegetables are wrapped in herbs and leaves and placed on the stones. The pit is then sealed with more branches and leaves and the contents roast and steam. For feasts, the pits may be hundreds of metres long, and filled with hundreds of whole pigs.

The most recent staples to be added to the PNG diet are rice and tinned fish or bully beef – a legacy of WWII. Their importance is clear if you check a trade store's shelves: they stock rice, tinned mackerel, tobacco and salt. Many people who live in the cities, or who don't have access to a garden, have no other affordable choice. In some parts of the country tinned food helps to alleviate a natural protein shortage. It can be pretty awful, though. Sadly, the 777 brand (which had a cult status like Spear tobacco) is no longer on the shelves. Two-minute noodles are also becoming popular.

One modern addition to the PNG diet results from the 'dumping' of mutton flaps onto the market by NZ and Australian exporters. Mutton flaps are the belly portions of sheep and are 28% fat (compared to about 6% for lamb cuts). PNG is a ready market for these unwanted parts of carcass – they are cheap and have become extremely popular, mainly for stews with rice.

Restaurants

Many of the restaurants around the country are attached to the hotels and guesthouses, although there are a few restaurants in Port Moresby. Generally the prices are similar to Australia (K12 to K15 for a basic main course), but the cooking is not as interesting.

The cuts of red meat that come to PNG are the ones that don't get to go to Australian and NZ consumers and you might find them disappointing. Chicken, on the other hand, is local and the fish and seafood are splendid.

Some of the best food in PNG is prepared at the Loloata Island Resort in Central Province, Masurina Lodge in Milne Bay, Buka Luman Soho Lodge on Sohano Island, Bird of Paradise Hotel in Goroka and the Lae International Hotel.

Vegetarian Options

Proper vegetarian options in restaurants and hotels are few – vegetarianism is an odd idea to Papua New Guineans. If your 'vegetarianism' is broad enough to include fish and seafood you'll get through your time in PNG with no real grief, but you'll have some trouble if you are strictly herbivorous. Asian-style eating, where you can order vegetable dishes off the menu, is perhaps the way to go.

Fast Food

There are kai-bars everywhere. A kai-bar is often just a hole in the wall that serves food from a *bain-marie*. Perhaps the best thing about kai-bar food is that it is generally improving. The best way to tell which are better is to look for the busy ones.

Self-Catering

Those on a budget will want to cook for themselves as much as possible and many of the cheaper accommodation options provide access to well-equipped kitchens. PNG's markets have great fruit and vegetables, although what's available will depend on the

season, and the supermarkets have the familiar range of goods (and extra tinned fish).

Big, hard biscuits are popular and you should acquaint yourself with a packet of kundu crackers (once just a brand name and now a generic term). You can get them in beef and other flavours (you'll also see beef-flavoured Twisties!). They are inexpensive and it's worth stowing a few packets in your kit with a small jar of Vegemite or peanut butter or whatever your preference. A good kundu cracker is so tough you could stick a stamp on it and send it home as a postcard.

DRINKS
Nonalcoholic Drinks

It's a good idea to carry water because you loose a lot of fluid through sweating; you can get chilled water in kai-bars and supermarkets. The sugars (and caffeine) in some fizzy drinks might give you a lift when the midday heat is knocking you around.

Most of the coffee grown in PNG is arabica and the fresh coffee is excellent.

Alcoholic Drinks

South Pacific is now the only brewery in PNG and produces two beers. The everyday drink, which comes in a small bottle (known as a *stubby* to Australians), is known as an SP (or SP brownie). The more expensive and stronger export version comes in a colourful can. Wine and spirits are very costly, partly in an attempt to restrict their use.

DRUGS
Betel Nut

All through Asia people chew the nut of the areca palm known as betel nut or, in Pidgin, *buai*. Although it's a (relatively) mild narcotic and digestive stimulant and widely used in PNG, it's unlikely to attract too many western drug fans. It doesn't quite have the glamour factor required for trendy parties – the need to expel voluminous red spit is probably the reason why yuppies might prefer cocaine (and there's none of *that* in PNG). But it's really worth having a go, if only to break the ice with some locals (see the 'Do You Chew?' aside).

Marijuana

The Highlands, as well as other areas of PNG, are a source of potent marijuana and young traveller-types might be discreetly approached by somebody and asked whether they might like to buy some. There are, however, a few facts to know about the situation of marijuana in PNG.

Firstly, it is by law a controlled substance and there are stiff penalties for those charged as drug offenders. To carry any controlled substance across an international boundary is plain stupid and has legal implications way beyond simple possession.

Secondly, there is a lot of misinformation about who grows marijuana and why. Almost all of the marijuana grown in PNG is used by local people and grown as a simple

---

'Do You Chew?'

Virtually everybody in PNG (barring expats) either chews buai, used to chew buai or will some day chew buai. Ten years ago, betel nut was just being experimented with by most Highlanders, but nowadays it's part of their daily lives too. The expatriate community regards chewing buai as rather disgusting, mostly because chewers spit great streams of bright-red saliva – like an impressive spontaneous haemorrhage. It is, however, worth understanding buai culture and realising that most educated professional people (unless they are fervently Christian) will have a quiet chew too.

Betel nut takes up at least half of the selling space in every market in the country and people use it as a little pick-me-up during the day, a bit like a mid-morning cup of tea.

By the age of five, kids will be chewing buai with all the condiments and they start by gnawing on the husks of the nut that are discarded by others. Long-time chewers get badly stained teeth – first red and then black. The mild stimulant is brought about by the reaction of the nut, the mustard stick (*daka*) and the crushed-coral lime (*cumbung*) and it tastes awful! Nuts can vary in potency and a strong one might cause you to sweat and want to lie down for a few minutes. The lime used in the procedure is highly caustic and can cause ulcerated cheeks and mouth cancers.

ADRIAN LIPSCOMB

Preparing buai, near Tufi (Oro Province)

'Why Yes, Thank You!'

Take the husked nut between your back teeth and crack it near the stem end. Prise it open with your fingers, pluck out the kernel and chew it in the back of your mouth to one side. You'll suddenly be producing large amounts of colourless saliva and it's important not to swallow at any time (you can get a bit nauseated). So find somewhere where you can spit.

Once the nut is properly mashed (keep chewing!), take the daka between your fingers and lightly moisten an end with your mouth. Then dip the daka into the white powdery lime so that a few millimetres are 'frosted' with cumbung. Poke this into the back of your mouth, bite off the frosted part of the daka and chew and spit. Keep dipping your daka into the cumbung and keep biting it off (maybe three or four times), and chew and spit.

This is when your projectiles will turn a vivid red and (with luck) you'll feel the 'rush' come on; it can sometimes be just a little head-spin or it can be stronger. The effect will be largely determined by your chewing technique and you might be disappointed with the results of your first try. Watch how others do it.

Seeing a foreigner chewing a buai will bring broad smiles across the faces of local people and you'll immediately make friends. Be warned, however, that until you are practised you'll almost certainly ruin (or indelibly mark) the shirt you are wearing as the voluminous red spit escapes your mouth, runs down your chin and falls onto your favourite T-shirt. ■

cash crop in small gardens next to the taro and yams. There are stories about how it is cultivated in huge plots of land with sophisticated irrigation systems and traded to Australian black-marketeers for military hardware. This is simply not true (military hardware is much easier to get from your wantoks in the PNGDF). The government and media talk about gangs of rascals being whipped into violent frenzies by the effects of marijuana (ha!) and campaign vigorously about its evils.

Tobacco
Tobacco is an important cash crop and, as in many other developing countries, smoking is widespread and guilt-free. International brands are widely available. Locally made cigars are sold in many markets. They look crude but smell very tempting.

The grassroots' smoke was traditionally tobacco rolled in newspaper (the *Sydney Morning Herald* for preference) but are now tailor-made. They are called Mutrus and cost about K0.20 each. You puff one of these long cigarettes (the 'ettes' is redundant, they're like thin cigars) for a while, then put it behind your ear for later use. And they're not a bad wheezer, if you like that kind of thing.

When a company began tailor-making these long coarse-tobacco cigarettes, it was not allowed to use newspaper because of health regulations; instead, it made them with pristine rice paper. But there was market resistance to plain-paper smokes, so they had to print their paper to look like newspaper. Look closely at your aromatic Mutrus and notice that it is wrapped in paper inscribed with Latin!

ENTERTAINMENT
There's very little organised entertainment in PNG. Nightlife in the larger towns consists mostly of weekend discos at the upmarket hotels and there's likely to be a band playing somewhere (although this will probably be in a more low-brow venue). It's worth trying to break out of the expat and hotel-clientele circles and see how the real people let their hair down. Check the papers for entertainment listings.

SPECTATOR SPORT
The Papua New Guinean people love their sport, and ball games of all kinds fit simply into their communal outdoorsy culture. You'll see a raggedy volleyball net in many villages and kids playing cricket along a path; local teams play weekend sporting competitions in parks and fields everywhere.

Traditionally, rugby was the most popular game, but these days softball would be a genuine rival. Soccer is also played and you'll even occasionally see an Australian Rules football being kicked around.

Televised sport is important and everybody in the country aligns themselves fiercely (and arbitrarily) to the Blues or Maroons for the Australian Rugby League's state-of-origin match between Queensland and New South Wales. In Bougainville the sterns of boats bear two flags – one white, asserting neutrality in the fighting, and the other either blue or maroon. The fervour for this big event sees a rash of T-shirt sales and the hopes and dreams of half the country are dashed minutes after the game.

If you get to the Trobriand Islands, make sure you take in a game of Trobriands cricket (see the Local Customs aside in the Milne Bay Province chapter).

THINGS TO BUY
For information on buying PNG art, see the Papua New Guinean Arts section.

Getting There & Away

Although there are some wild and wonderful ways of getting to Papua New Guinea, almost everybody comes by air. And the vast majority of flights come to Port Moresby from Australia, although there are also direct connections with Singapore, Manila (the Philippines), Hong Kong, Honiara (Solomon Islands), Jayapura (Irian Jaya in Indonesia) and with Osaka (Japan). Otherwise, there are a few visiting yachts and the occasional cruise ship.

AIR
Airports & Airlines
Air Niugini, the national airline, operates in combination with a number of other airlines on the various routes. Australian connections are made with Qantas Airways. Solomon Airlines can take you to and from Honiara and some other Pacific islands. Singapore Airlines operates the Singapore route, Philippine Airlines has the Manila and Hong Kong routes and Japan Airlines flies to Osaka. Garuda Indonesia, Indonesia's national carrier, will get you as far as Jayapura in Irian Jaya (via Biak), from where you can fly to Vanimo in PNG with Air Niugini (Garuda Indonesia does not fly into PNG).

Milne Bay Air (or MBA, which was formerly devoted entirely to domestic routes) is now also flying Cairns-Alotau and Cairns-Port Moresby routes. Flight West Airlines, owned by Sir Dennis Buchanan, who previously owned Talair (a domestic airline in PNG which closed down a few years ago), is now operating four flights per week between Townsville and Port Moresby using Fokker F28s; these flights are timed to connect with Ansett Australia's Brisbane services and Flight West's other Australian services. Flight West (☎ (07) 725 3855; fax (07) 779 0007) can be contacted in Townsville at PO Box 7517, Garbutt 4814.

Port Moresby is by far the largest international gateway to PNG but there are now international flights to Alotau and Mt Hagen. MBA flies Daru-Cairns on Saturday and returns on Sunday; fares are K355 one way and K640 return. It also has return flights between Alotau and Cairns on Wednesday and Sunday for A$360 one way and A$650 return. From Vanimo, you can fly to and from Jayapura in Indonesia.

There is always talk of another international airport opening in PNG, with various local lobby groups arguing for Manus Island, Wewak, Madang, Vanimo and Lae to be chosen. No doubt it will happen someday, somewhere.

Air Niugini offices overseas include:

Australia
    Somare House, 100 Clarence St, Sydney 2000
    (☎ (02) 9290 1544; fax (02) 9290 2026)
    Level 6, 12 Creek St, Brisbane 4000
    (☎ (07) 3221 1544; fax (07) 3220 0040)
    Shop 2, Tropical Arcade, 4-6 Shields St, Cairns
    4870 (☎ (07) 4051 4950; fax (07) 4031 3402)
    Level 12, 520 Collins St, Melbourne 3000
    (☎ (03) 9614 0429; fax (03) 9621 1217)
Germany
    Waidmannstrasse 45, 60596 Frankfurt
    (☎ (069) 63 4095; fax (069) 63 1332)
Indonesia
    PT Ayuberga, Wisma Bumiputera, Jalan Jenderal, Sudiman Kva 75, Jakarta 13910
    (☎ (021) 578 0615; fax (021) 571 3013)
    PT Kuwera Jaya, JL A Yani No 39, Jayapura
    (☎ (967) 21427; fax (967) 32236)
Japan
    5th floor, Sunbridge, 2-2 Kanda Ogawamachi, Chiyoda-ku, Tokyo (☎ (03) 528 10444; fax (03) 528 10445)
Malaysia
    Pelancogan Abadi Sdn Bhd, 79 Jalan Bukit Bintang, 55100 Kuala Lumpur (☎ (03) 242 2311; fax (03) 241 2322)
New Zealand
    Walshes World (NZ) Ltd, 2nd floor, Dingwall Building, 87 Queen Street, Auckland
    (☎ (09) 379 3708; fax (09) 302 2420)
Philippines
    Fortune Office Bldg G/F, 160 Legaspi St, Legaspi Village, Makati, Metro Manila
    (☎ (02) 891 3339; fax (02) 891 3393)

Air Travel Glossary

Apex Apex, or 'advance purchase excursion' is a discounted ticket which must be paid for in advance. There are penalties if you wish to change it.

Baggage Allowance This will be written on your ticket: usually one 20kg item to go in the hold, plus one item of hand luggage.

Bucket Shop An unbonded travel agency specialising in discounted airline tickets.

Bumped Just because you have a confirmed seat doesn't mean you're going to get on the plane – see Overbooking.

Cancellation Penalties If you have to cancel or change an Apex ticket there are often heavy penalties involved; insurance can sometimes be taken out against these penalties. Some airlines impose penalties on regular tickets as well, particularly against 'no show' passengers.

Check-In Airlines ask you to check in a certain time ahead of the flight departure (usually 1½ hours on international flights). If you fail to check in on time and the flight is overbooked the airline can cancel your booking and give your seat to somebody else.

Confirmation Having a ticket written out with the flight and date you want doesn't mean you have a seat until the agent has checked with the airline that your status is 'OK' or confirmed. Meanwhile you could just be 'on request'.

Discounted Tickets There are two types of discounted fares – officially discounted (see Promotional Fares) and unofficially discounted. The lowest prices often impose drawbacks like flying with unpopular airlines, inconvenient schedules, or unpleasant routes and connections. A discounted ticket can save you other things than money – you may be able to pay Apex prices without the associated Apex advance booking and other requirements. Discounted tickets only exist where there is fierce competition.

Full Fares Airlines traditionally offer first class (coded F), business class (coded J) and economy class (coded Y) tickets. These days there are so many promotional and discounted fares available from the regular economy class that few passengers pay full economy fare.

Lost Tickets If you lose your airline ticket an airline will usually treat it like a travellers' cheque and, after inquiries, issue you with another one. Legally, however, an airline is entitled to treat it like cash and if you lose it then it's gone forever. Take good care of your tickets.

No-Shows No-shows are passengers who fail to show up for their flight, sometimes due to unexpected delays or disasters, sometimes due to simply forgetting, sometimes because they made more than one booking and didn't bother to cancel the one they didn't want. Full-fare passengers who fail to turn up are sometimes entitled to travel on a later flight. The rest of us are penalised (see Cancellation Penalties).

On Request An unconfirmed booking for a flight, see Confirmation.

Open Jaws A return ticket where you fly out to one place but return from another. If available this can save you backtracking to your arrival point.

Overbooking Airlines hate to fly empty seats and because every flight has some passengers who fail to show up (see No-Shows), airlines often book more passengers than they have seats. Usually

USA
Suite 3000 West Tower, 5000 Birch St, Newport Beach, Los Angeles, CA 92660 (☎ 714-752 5440; fax 714-476 3741)

Buying Tickets

The plane ticket will probably be the single most expensive item in your budget and there is likely to be a multitude of airlines and travel agents hoping to separate you from your money. It is always worth putting aside a few hours to research the state of the market.

The situation with PNG is particularly changeable, with new routes and small domestic airlines opening up and closing down and currency fluctuations causing fare changes. Nevertheless, it is wise to start early: talk to recent travellers – they may be able to stop you making some of the same old mistakes. Look at the ads in newspapers and magazines, consult reference books and watch for special offers.

Use the fares quoted in this book as a guide only. They are approximate and based on the general rates at the time of going to press. Quoting airfares does not necessarily constitute a recommendation for the carrier.

the excess passengers balance those who fail to show up but occasionally somebody gets bumped. If this happens guess who it is most likely to be? The passengers who check in late.

Promotional Fares Officially discounted fares like Apex fares which are available from travel agents or direct from the airline.

Reconfirmation At least 72 hours prior to departure time of an onward or return flight you must contact the airline and 'reconfirm' that you intend to be on the flight. If you don't do this the airline can delete your name from the passenger list and you could lose your seat. You don't have to reconfirm the first flight on your itinerary or if your stopover is less than 72 hours. It doesn't hurt to reconfirm more than once.

Restrictions Discounted tickets often have various restrictions on them – advance purchase is the most usual one (see Apex). Others are restrictions on the minimum and maximum period you must be away, such as a minimum of 14 days or a maximum of one year. See Cancellation Penalties.

Round-the-World Tickets The official airline Round-the-World (RTW) tickets are usually put together by a combination of two airlines and permit you to fly anywhere you want on their route system so long as you don't backtrack. There may be other restrictions. An alternative type of RTW ticket is one put together by a travel agent using a combination of discounted tickets.

Standy-By A discounted ticket where you only fly if there is a seat free at the last moment. Stand-by fares are usually only available on domestic routes.

Tickets Out An entry requirement for many countries is that you have an onward or return ticket, in other words, a ticket out of the country. If you're not sure what you intend to do next, the easiest solution is to buy the cheapest onward ticket to a neighbouring country or a ticket from a reliable airline which can later be refunded if you do not use it.

Transferred Tickets Airline tickets cannot be transferred from one person to another. Travellers sometimes try to sell the return half of their ticket, but officials can ask you to prove that you are the person named on the ticket. This is unlikely to happen on domestic flights, but on an international flight tickets may be compared with passports.

Travel Agencies Travel agencies vary widely and you should ensure you use one that suits your needs. Some simply handle tours while full-service agencies handle everything from tours and tickets to car rental and hotel bookings. A good one will do all these things and can save you a lot of money but if all you want is a ticket at the lowest possible price, then you really need an agency specialising in discounted tickets. A discounted ticket agency, however, may not be useful for other things, like hotel bookings.

Travel Periods Some officially discounted fares, Apex fares in particular, vary with the time of year. There is often a low (off-peak) season and a high (peak) season. Sometimes there's an intermediate or shoulder season as well. At peak times, when everyone wants to fly, not only will the officially discounted fares be higher but so will unofficially discounted fares or there may simply be no discounted tickets available. Usually the fare depends on your outward flight – if you depart in the high season and return in the low season, you pay the high-season fare. ■

Travellers with Special Needs

If you have special needs of any sort – you've broken a leg, you're vegetarian, travelling in a wheelchair, taking the baby, terrified of flying – you should let the airline know as soon as possible so that they can make arrangements accordingly. You should remind them when you reconfirm your booking (at least 72 hours before departure) and again when you check in at the airport. It may also be worth ringing round the airlines before you make your booking to find out how they can handle your particular needs.

Children Children under two travel for 10% of the standard fare (or free, on some airlines), as long as they don't occupy a seat. They don't get a baggage allowance either. 'Skycots' should be provided by the airline if requested in advance; they will take a child weighing up to about 10kg. Children between two and 12 can usually occupy a seat for half to two-thirds of the full fare and do get a baggage allowance. Push chairs can often be taken as hand luggage.

Australia

Air Niugini operates a combined service

International Fares

Air Niugini, in combination with Qantas Airways, Singapore Airlines, Philippine Airlines, Japan Airlines and Solomon Airlines, offers the following return fares to Port Moresby:

From	Frequency	Full Fare	Discount Fare	Details	
Cairns	Daily	A$780	A$504	APEX	– low season (there is also a $A399 Weekend Special)
Brisbane	3 per week	A$1306	A$820	APEX	– low season
Sydney	2 per week	A$1604	A$969	APEX	– low season (Qantas Airways also has 3 independent flights a week)
Singapore	2 per week	S$3894	S$1947	YEE45	– 7 to 45 days
Hong Kong	2 per week	HK$13,120	HK$9210	YEE45	– 7 to 45 days
Manila	2 per week	US$1702	US$860	YEE45	– 7 to 45 days
Honiara	2 per week	SI$2370	SI$1536	MEE30	– 5 to 30 days
Osaka	1 per week	¥305,800	¥126,000	GOKU	– 4 to 60 days

APEX, YEE45, MEE30 and GOKU are all excursion fares offered by Air Niugini/Qantas Airways, Singapore Airlines, Solomon Airlines and Japan Airlines. They must be paid for in advance and are valid for a maximum of 45 days in the case of APEX and YEE45 fares, 30 days in the case of MEE30, or 60 days with GOKU. Some minor details vary, but basically the high season is most of January, mid-April, mid-June to mid-July, mid-September to early October and most of December. YEE45 fares shown are applicable between March and December.

with Qantas Airways between Australia and PNG.

The flight time from Sydney is about three hours, plus an hour's wait in Brisbane. There are also daily flights from Cairns to Port Moresby (sometimes on the airbus and sometimes on F28s) and four from Cairns direct to Mt Hagen (returning via Port Moresby).

There isn't much discounting of tickets between Australia and PNG, but ask around and you might find something. Air Niugini's Weekend Special from Cairns to Port Moresby for A$399 is a good deal, but you must go on Friday and come back by Tuesday. Otherwise, it's worth contacting Air Niugini direct to see if there are any specials on offer.

STA and Flight Centres International are also major dealers in cheap airfares. The *Sydney Morning Herald* has a travel supplement every Saturday which is useful; also check the travel agents' ads in the Yellow Pages and ring around.

Niugini Tours (☎ (02) 9290 2055; GPO Box 7002, Sydney), Raging Thunder (☎ (07) 4031 1466; fax (07) 4051 4010; PO Box 1109, Cairns) and Terra Firma Associates (☎ & fax (07) 4055 0014; PO Box 357N, North Cairns) specialise in village-based tours and 'off-the-beaten-track' packages; they can organise Sepik or Kokoda Trail expeditions.

The Pacific

Air Niugini operates a combined service with Solomon Airlines to/from Honiara and Solomon Airlines sometimes offers an interesting circle fare between Brisbane, Honiara and Port Moresby, but it's fairly pricey unless the airline's offering special discounts at the time (which happens about once a year for a month). It also offers package deals to Fiji, Vanuatu and (of course) the Solomon Islands.

STA and Flight Centres International are popular travel agents in New Zealand, as they are in Australia.

Island-hopping all the way from the USA requires careful planning as some connections only operate once or twice a week. Options include Honolulu-Marshall Islands-Nauru-Honiara-Port Moresby; Honolulu-Guam-Nauru; Honolulu-Carolinas-Nauru; or Honolulu-Nandi (Fiji)-Honiara. The tiny island state of Nauru is the focal point for a lot of these routes and Air Nauru has an interesting network to its Pacific neighbours.

Airfares on these Pacific routes are a bit of a puzzle since Guam-Honolulu and other routes between the USA and Micronesia are treated like US domestic routes, with nice low fares.

Asia

Indonesia The short flight from Jayapura (K67) to Vanimo in PNG is currently the only air route between PNG and Indonesia. Garuda Indonesia does not even fly into PNG. Most other international flights out of Indonesia depart from Jakarta. There are daily flights from Jayapura to Jakarta for about US$529 (possibly cheaper if bought in Indonesia).

Once you're in Indonesia, you can take advantage of the country's excellent air-pass deals. There are also regular inter-island ferries. It might be possible to get a ticket written in Australia which will include stop-overs in Port Moresby and other PNG destinations, and Jayapura and other Indonesian destinations such as Bali.

The most important thing to remember on arriving in Jayapura is that you are no longer in PNG. Be on your guard and be prepared to be ripped off. Ask at the airport for the current official taxi fare into the town and don't be conned into 'chartering' the whole cab. If the driver won't be reasonable, and they usually get more reasonable the longer you wait, simply walk 300m straight down the road from the terminal to the main road where there is a taxi station at the junction, from where taxis depart regularly.

Elsewhere in Asia Air Niugini, in conjunction with Philippine Airlines, has twice-weekly Port Moresby-Hong Kong and Port Moresby-Singapore flights. The Hong Kong flight is usually expensive. A Singapore-Port Moresby low-season excursion return fare, valid for 45 days, costs around US$1380. From Manila to Port Moresby on Air Niugini, in conjunction with Philippine Airlines, a 45-day excursion return fare costs US$860. Both these fares would probably be cheaper if bought in Singapore or Manila.

Hong Kong is the discount plane ticket capital of the region, but its bucket shops are at least as unreliable as those of other cities. Ask the advice of other travellers before buying a ticket. STA, which is reliable, has branches in Hong Kong, Tokyo, Singapore, Bangkok and Kuala Lumpur.

The UK

Trailfinders in west London produces a lavishly illustrated brochure which includes airfare details. STA also has branches in the UK. Look in the listings magazine *Time Out* plus the Sunday papers and *Exchange & Mart* for ads. Also look out for the free magazines widely available in London – start by looking outside the main railway stations. The Globetrotters Club (BCM Roving, London WC1N 3XX) publishes a newsletter called *Globe* which covers obscure destinations and can help in finding travelling companions.

Most British travel agents are registered with ABTA (Association of British Travel Agents). If you have paid for your flight through an ABTA-registered agent which then goes out of business, ABTA will guarantee a refund or an alternative. Unregistered bucket shops are riskier but also sometimes cheaper.

Continental Europe

You can put together a ticket taking you from Europe to Hong Kong, Manila or Singapore and connecting with an Air Niugini flight to Port Moresby. A more complicated route would be to fly to Jakarta (Indonesia) and from there to Jayapura, from where it's a short hop to Vanimo in PNG.

A cheap ticket to Australia (possibly a Round-the-World ticket) plus an Apex return ticket between Cairns and Port Moresby might be the cheapest way to get to PNG from Europe.

There are a million and one deals on tickets from Europe to Australia and Asia, but check if there are any good deals on flights all the way to PNG. Singapore Airlines flies from Europe to Port Moresby and a low-season excursion fare from London, valid for a year and with a stopover in Singapore, might cost under £1500. Philippine Airlines (which flies from Manila to Port Moresby) doesn't seem to have particularly good deals on direct flights between Europe and Port Moresby, but it's worth checking out its specials between Europe and Australasia.

North America

There are three major alternatives from North America: fly to Australia, then on to Port Moresby; fly to Jakarta with Garuda Indonesia, then on to Jayapura and Vanimo in PNG; or fly to Manila or Singapore, then on to Port Moresby.

A return excursion fare from Los Angeles (LA) to Sydney costs around US$1090 return (with Qantas Airways). There is a lot of discounting on this route, so ask around.

You can fly with Garuda Indonesia from LA to Jakarta for about US$1300 return (some LA travel agents offer excellent deals), then to Jayapura from where the Vanimo Sunday flight costs about US$50. This is the easiest way into the Sepik region, but check connections carefully and remember that the international dateline will affect your calculations.

A return excursion fare (Apex – 30 days) on Philippine Airlines from LA to Manila costs US$1190 and the Manila-Port Moresby section is US$860.

The *New York Times*, *LA Times*, *Chicago Tribune* and *San Francisco Examiner* produce weekly travel sections in which you'll find any number of travel agents' ads. Council Travel and STA Travel have offices in major cities nationwide. The magazine *Travel Unlimited* (PO Box 1058, Allston, Mass 02134) publishes details of the cheapest airfares and courier pos-

sibilities for destinations all over the world from the USA.

Victoria Travel (☎ 805-962 0077; fax 805-966 1489; 11 West Victoria, Santa Barbara, CA 93101; email exotic@west.net) specialises in PNG travel – but mainly in the upmarket lodges and cruises. Mountain Travel – Sobek (☎ toll-free 1-800-227 2384, fax 510-525 7710; 6420 Fairmont Ave, El Cerrito, CA 94530-3606) offers Sepik and Trobriand Islands tours.

Travel CUTS has offices in all major Canadian cities. The *Toronto Globe & Mail* and *Vancouver Sun* carry travel agents' ads. The magazine *Great Expeditions* (PO Box 8000-411, Abbotsford, BC V2S 6H1) is useful.

SEA

Entering PNG by sea is now difficult or impossible unless you're on a yacht or a cruise ship. PNG is a popular stopping point for cruising yachties, either heading through Asia or the Pacific. If you ask around, it's often possible to get a berth on a yacht heading off somewhere interesting. Often yachties depend upon picking up crew to help them sail and to help cover some of the day-to-day costs. The best places to try are Port Moresby, Madang, Rabaul and around Milne Bay, although you can quite possibly find yachts visiting at almost any port around the country.

Australia

Unless you are a Torres Strait Islander, it is illegal to island-hop between Thursday Island (known as TI to locals) and PNG. You can exit Australia from TI but you must go directly to PNG, usually Daru. There are plenty of fishing boats doing the trip, but no regular direct flights. You are allowed to island-hop as far as Saibai Island, just off the PNG coast, but from there you cannot exit Australia and enter PNG – you must return to Australia. These rules were once much flouted but Australian patrols of the area have tightened up considerably and you're likely to be caught if you try to bend them.

Non-Australians entering Australia this way can be charged with illegal entry.

Solomon Islands

There was once a very interesting 'back-door' route into PNG from the Solomon Islands to Bougainville Island. This route is now used by the Bougainville Revolutionary Army to smuggle in supplies and by the PNG army on reprisal raids, so it's definitely out for the non-military traveller.

Indonesia

It is now possible to travel between Vanimo and Jayapura by land, sea or air; see the Sandaun Province section in The Sepik chapter. There are daily flights from Jayapura to Jakarta by Garuda Indonesia, Merpati or Sempati – and there are many international flights out of Indonesia through Denpasar (which is easier than travelling through Jakarta). There are also international flights from Ambon, Manado, Ujung Pandang and Kupang. The flight from Biak to the USA has been suspended, but there is talk of it being started up again. There are also plans for a Merauke to Darwin flight.

DEPARTURE TAXES

There's a departure tax of K15 no matter how you leave or where from. You have to buy a special stamp at a post office. If you've over-stayed your visa, expect to pay a very hefty fine before they let you on the plane. People on yachts might be hit for a K100 per person 'customs clearance fee', especially at Samarai Island in Milne Bay.

ORGANISED TOURS

The two main PNG-based inbound tour operators are Melanesian Tourist Services and Trans Niugini Tours, both of which have offices and agents worldwide. Air Niugini also has packages. There are many other tour operators, most of which can offer packages. See the Organised Tours section in the Getting Around chapter for names and addresses.

Melanesian Tourist Services also operates the luxury cruise boat *Melanesian Discoverer*, the Madang Resort Hotel and a couple of other upmarket lodges. For more information, contact its overseas offices listed below or any Air Niugini, Continental or Qantas Airways offices.

Germany
>   Alt-Schwanheim 50, 6000 Frankfurt am Main 71 (☎ (069) 35 6667; fax (069) 35 0080)

Italy
>   Via Teulie 8, 20136 Milan (☎ (02) 837 5892)

North America
>   Suite 10B, 302 West Grand Ave, El Segundo, CA 90245 (☎ (213) 785 0370; fax (213) 785 0314)

United Kingdom
>   32 Mossville Gardens, Morden, Surrey, SM44DG (☎ (0181) 540 3125; fax (0181) 540 5510)

Trans Niugini Tours is a large organisation similar to Melanesian Tourist Services, operating Sepik cruises (on the *Sepik Spirit*) and the award-winning Ambua and Karawari lodges and the Malolo Plantation Resort near Madang. Many tours are offered, including some for those on lower budgets. Its overseas offices are:

Australia
>   44B Aplin St, Cairns 4870 (☎ (07) 4051 0622; (07) 4052 1147)

France
>   21 Rue Valette, 75005 Paris (☎ 01 40 51 82 82; fax 01 43 29 68 05)

Germany
>   Blumenstrasse 26, 4000 Düsseldorf 1 (☎ (211) 80127; fax (211) 32 4989)

Italy
>   Via Ferdinando Galani 25/D, 00191 Rome (☎ (06) 329 3697; fax (06) 328 6261)

Japan
>   United Touring International, Koyata Building 3F, 2-5 Yotsuya 2-Chrome, Shinjuku-ku, Tokyo 160 (☎ (03) 335 52391; fax (03) 335 52438)

North America
>   Suite 105, 850 Colorado Blvd, Los Angeles, CA 90041, USA (☎ toll-free 1-800-621 1633 (CA), 1-800-521 7242 (USA & Canada); fax 213-256 0647)

United Kingdom
>   Suite 433, 52-54 High Holborn, London WC1V 6RB (☎ (0171) 242 3131; fax (0171) 242 2838)

WARNING

The information in this chapter is particularly vulnerable to change: prices for international travel are volatile, routes are introduced and cancelled, schedules change, special deals come and go, and rules and visa requirements are amended. Airlines and governments seem to take a perverse pleasure in making price structures and regulations as complicated as possible. You should check directly with the airline or a travel agent to make sure you understand how a fare (and ticket you may buy) works. In addition, the travel industry is highly competitive and there are many lurks and perks.

The upshot of this is that you should get opinions, quotes and advice from as many airlines and travel agents as possible before you part with your hard-earned cash. The details given in this chapter should be regarded as pointers and are not a substitute for your own careful, up-to-date research.

Getting Around

AIR

Civil aviation was crucially significant in the exploration and development of Papua New Guinea. The aeroplane has become almost symbolic of the way technology has intruded so successfully into what was, until relatively recently, a loose collection of hunter-gatherer societies. Geographic realities continue to rule: the population is scattered, often isolated in mountain valleys and on tiny islands, but even the most remote villages now have some familiarity with the ubiquitous *balus*, or aeroplane. A sketchy road network is beginning to creep across parts of the country but flying remains the predominant means of transport. Unfortunately, the geography and isolation also mean that flying is expensive and, if you are travelling with limited time, virtually unavoidable.

Many towns grew up around airstrips and there are still many important places where the arrival of a plane is the main entertainment for the day. People hang around airports the way they hang around railway stations in countries where trains still provide important transport links. How else are you to find out who is leaving town and who is arriving?

Domestic Air Services

There are two main carriers on domestic routes and numerous small operators, some only for charter but some running scheduled passenger routes. The main outfits are Air Niugini (the national carrier) and MBA (Milne Bay Air). Other regional airlines are MAF (Missionary Aviation Fellowship – known to some as the Missionaries' Air Force), Airlink, Islands Nationair, Northcoast Aviation and Island Airways. You may come across the distinction between first-level, second-level and third-level airlines for the first time when you visit PNG. First-level describes a carrier that operates internationally (Air Niugini and, to a lesser extent, MBA), second-level covers airlines that make the major domestic connections (mainly Air Niugini and MBA too) and third-level means an airline that operates between the tiny towns and villages (that is, all the others).

The airline industry in PNG is volatile and change is frequent – operators come and go, airstrips open and close, routes change and fares go up (but never down). The main second-level operator a few years ago was Talair, owned by Sir Dennis Buchanan, but it closed in frustration at political interference in the industry, leaving a gap which MBA was to fill. Other operators have also come and gone, bringing with them new routes and timetables. Wewak, Lae and Kainantu airstrips are built around disused airstrips which now form derelict centrepieces to those towns. A volcano buried Rabaul's old Rakunai airport in 1994 and the Kokopo-Rabaul area is now serviced by Tokua airport (although airline schedules still refer to this destination as Rabaul). Tokua can be closed if the wind blows the volcano's dust over the runway because it gets into the aircraft engines.

A problem unique to PNG is that most land is owned by customary title, often including the land associated with airstrips. Both Girua airport (POP) at Popondetta and Tadji airport (TAJ) at Aitape had their terminal buildings pulled down by irate locals when aviation authorities refused to pay rent. The Popondetta terminal has since been rebuilt, but at Tadji there is now just a clearing in the bush next to the windsock where trucks pull up to wait for flights. Porgera airport is often closed for the same reason.

Air Niugini operates half a dozen Fokker F28s (jets) and De Havilland Dash 7s (big turbo-props) on its domestic routes. MBA has grown in recent years from a third-level operator serving mainly the Milne Bay area to become second only to Air Niugini in its domestic coverage. It is rapidly expanding

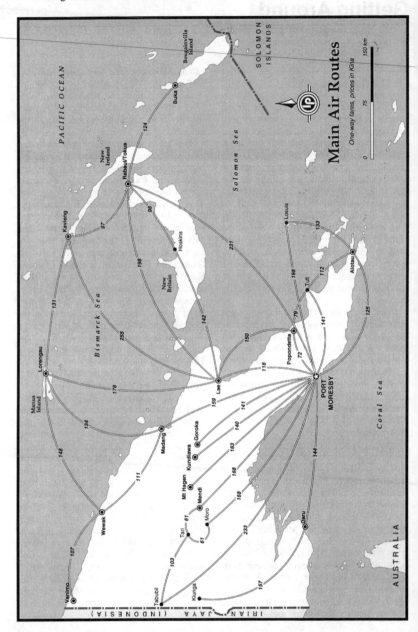

Main Air Routes

One-way fares, prices in Kina

internationally with flights from Alotau to Cairns and Townsville, as well as plans for routes into Irian Jaya, and flies mainly Twin Otters, Dorniers, Beechcraft and a larger Dash 8. The MAF fleet is dominated by small aircraft. MAF essentially supplies and transports missionaries rather than carrying passengers, so it has frequent and fairly regular flights, but you'll get a seat only if there is room for you. Many third-level operators fly charters rather than scheduled passenger routes; while you can often pay to go along on someone else's charter, this can take time (and beers) to arrange and isn't always possible. Most third-level operators are very approachable.

For the addresses of Air Niugini's overseas offices see the Getting There & Away chapter. Head-office addresses for domestic airlines are:

Airlink
    PO Box 1208, Madang (☎ 852 2933; fax 852 2725)
Air Niugini
    PO Box 7186, Boroko (☎ 327 3555; fax 327 3308)
Dovair
    PO Box 205, Vanimo (☎ 857 1056); flies mainly in the Sepik area
Island Airways
    PO Box 747, Madang (☎ 852 2601; fax 852 2353)
Islands Nationair
    PO Box 488, Boroko (☎ 323 3744; fax 325 5059)
MAF
    PO Box 273, Mt Hagen (☎ 545 1477; fax 545 1387)
MBA
    PO Box 170, Boroko (☎ 325 2011; fax 325 2219)
North Coast Aviation
    PO Box 350, Lae (☎ 472 1755; fax 472 0575)

MAF has bases (which operate fairly autonomously but not all have phones) in Anguganak, Goroka (☎ 732 1080), Mt Hagen (☎ 545 1317; head office, Kawito), Madang (☎ 852 2229), Mendi (☎ 549 1091), Nadzab (Lae; ☎ 472 3804), Tari (☎ 540 8014), Telefomin, Vanimo (☎ 857 1091), Wewak (☎ 856 2500) and Port Moresby (☎ 325 2668).

Air Niugini and MBA have computerised booking systems so bookings are usually quite efficient and can be made from anywhere in the world. This level of sophistication does not apply to every PNG airport – some terminals can be more accurately described as sheds.

Warning You have to check in on Air Niugini's domestic flights an hour before departure time. Take this seriously – half an hour before flight time, they may start giving seats to passengers on a waiting list.

As a general rule, it is also worth watching your luggage as it is processed through the check-in, loaded onto the trolleys and taken out to the aircraft. There have been instances, particularly when there is more than one aircraft on the tarmac, when luggage has been loaded onto the wrong plane.

The planes are small and fill quickly – many Air Niugini flights leave behind a long line of disappointed wait-listed passengers. Book ahead and always reconfirm. If you're told a flight is full, it's often worth trying again – they don't always seem to end up that way. Travel can be more difficult during the Australian school holidays. Many expats bring their children up from their boarding schools and flights are heavily booked around Christmas, early February, late June and late September.

Aircraft You may have to fly in light aircraft and carrying a 2m *garamut* drum under your arm might be difficult. Not only is your baggage weighed (16kg is the limit but 20kg is usually accepted) – so are you.

You should really try to make at least one flight in a small aircraft while you're in the country – preferably somewhere up in the mountains where flying can be a real experience. With over 450 licensed airfields there are plenty of opportunities – 18 could be described as second-level (large enough for F28s), while the rest are third-level (suitable for small aircraft only). A good way to experience this mountain-strip flying is to book a seat on MBA's 'milk run' out of Port Moresby. This only occurs on every second

Aviation History

After a hesitant beginning, it was the development of the Wau and Bulolo goldfields that really launched aviation in New Guinea. Cecil John Levien, one of the pioneers on these goldfields, soon realised that the goldfields would never be successfully exploited as long as getting men and supplies up from the coast involved a long, hard slog across difficult terrain populated by unfriendly tribes. After a number of unsuccessful attempts to interest Australian operators, Levien pushed through a proposal that his own Guinea Gold company should set up an air service, which they named Guinea Airways.

Their pilot, 'Pard' Mustar, had to do far more than just fly their first DH-37 biplane. First he arranged for an airstrip to be constructed at Lae (the local jail provided prisoners to build it), then walked from Salamaua to Wau to supervise the airstrip construction there. Next, he had to travel back to Rabaul where the DH-37 had arrived in pieces as sea cargo. Then he had to assemble it and fly to Lae – a 650km journey, much of it over sea or unexplored jungle, in a single-engine aircraft of dubious reliability.

In April 1927 Mustar took off on his first flight to Wau – and couldn't find it! He returned to Lae, took more directions and advice and tried again with an equal lack of success. Finally, on his third attempt, and with an experienced guide on board, he made the first of many 50-minute flights.

For the next couple of years, passengers and freight were shuttled back and forth. It cost £33 to fly to Wau, and only £10 to fly back, compared with K60 today.

Mustar quickly realised the need for more capacity and reliability and before the end of 1927, he went to Germany to buy a Junkers W-34 at the astronomical cost of £8000. It may have been expensive, but at the time it was the latest thing in cargo aircraft and could lift over a ton. A second W-34 soon followed, and with these aircraft Guinea Airways operated a service that proved the real possibilities of air transport just as convincingly as the much better publicised flights of Lindbergh or Kingsford-Smith. Wau became the busiest airfield in the world and more air freight was lifted annually in New Guinea than in the rest of the world put together!

Mustar left New Guinea but in 1929 was called back to attempt a scheme that, to many people at the time, must have seemed like something in the realms of science fiction. He had to find a way of flying gold dredges weighing 3000 tons onto the goldfields. Mustar's answer was to dismantle the dredges and buy another Junkers, the G-31, a three-engine, all-metal monster which cost £30,000 and could lift three tons. In the early 1930s, a fleet of these aircraft carried not just gold equipment but also workers and even the first horses ever to be transported by air.

Throughout the 1930s, more and more aircraft and operators came into New Guinea and the fierce competition dramatically forced down the air freight rates. In 1931, regular services started between the goldfields and Port Moresby on the south coast.

Holden's Air Transport Services developed but was later taken over by Guinea Airways. The air

Sunday, *if* the plane is reasonably full (ie five or six passengers). It takes a full day, lunch is provided, and the flight will take you on a circuit of some spectacular mountain strips in the Owen Stanley Range; the skill of the pilots in landing on these pocket handkerchiefs is quite amazing.

Unpredictable weather combined with mechanical problems and complex schedules can frequently lead to delays. If one plane is late at one airport, the whole schedule can be thrown out. Considering the terrain, the airstrips and the weather, reliability is fair and the safety record is very good. The pilots are extremely skilful – keep telling yourself this as you approach flat-topped ridges masquerading as airports. Many young pilots are intent on building up their

command experience so they can move on to a first-level airline, but others stay on because 'PNG has the best flying in the world'.

Discounts & Special Fares

Air Niugini offers special fares. These deals can and do change from time to time, so check before you leave home. They are reportedly limited to cash payment only – credit cards will not be accepted. The deals include:

Early Bird
These fares are available for the *first* flight of the day in each direction and apply to stays of between 10 and 21 days. Other conditions are similar to Weekend/Nambawan fares.
Hamamas Fares
These offer 30% off round-trip fares, maximum

service started by the island traders WR Carpenter & Co was longer lasting. In 1937, it absorbed Pacific Aerial Transport (originally formed by goldfields pioneer Ray Parer) and became Mandated Airlines Ltd (MAL).

In 1938, MAL started the first airmail service between PNG and Australia. Guinea Airways also expanded south into Australia, operating a successful service between Adelaide and Darwin via Alice Springs using the ultra-modern, twin-engine Lockheed Electra.

Also during the 1930s, pioneer missionaries proved that the aeroplane could be put to spiritual as well as secular use; possibly the first aerial mapping was conducted (in 1935); and aircraft supplied the prospectors and explorers who were opening up the final hidden parts of the country. One of the most spectacular forays was made by the wealthy American Richard Archbold, who used a Catalina amphibian and discovered the Grand Valley of the Baliem in Dutch New Guinea.

The arrival of the Japanese in 1942 abruptly ended civil aviation. Most PNG-based aircraft were caught on the ground by the first devastating raids on Lae, Salamaua and Bulolo. The aircraft that survived made a final desperate series of flights to evacuate civilians before the Japanese advanced.

When the war ended, aviation in PNG was a whole new story. In 1944, Qantas took over MAL's Australia-PNG connections and got its first toehold in the country. Guinea Airways was unable to obtain a licence to operate in PNG from the post-war Australian Labor government and Qantas became the dominant airline. Using DC3s and then DC4s, Qantas started regular passenger services between Australia and PNG and during the 1950s built up quite an incredible fleet of aircraft for internal use. Qantas operated everything from Beaver and Otter STOL aircraft, through DH-83 and DH-84 biplanes to Catalina, Short Solent and Sandringham flying boats. PNG was looked upon as a useful training ground for pilots who would later fly on Qantas' international network.

In 1960, the Australian government decided that Qantas should be a purely international airline and domestic services were handed over to Australia's domestic airlines, Ansett-ANA and Trans-Australia Airlines (TAA, which later became Australian Airlines), since PNG was considered part of Australia. MAL had been the main opposition to Qantas, swallowing smaller competitors such as Gibbes' Sepik Airways, but was in turn engulfed by Ansett. TAA and Ansett-MAL operated turbo-prop Lockheed Electras and, later, Boeing 727s between Australia and PNG. Internally, they supplemented their DC3 workhorses with Fokker F27 Friendships in 1967.

Air Niugini was formed on I November 1973, almost immediately after self-government, and took over Ansett's and TAA's PNG-based aircraft. In 1997 Air Niugini, formerly the state-owned flag carrier, was corporatised. It remains a substantial operator, with Airbus 310s on international routes and Fokker F28s and De Havilland Dash 7s on its domestic routes. ∎

30 days, minimum seven days. Other conditions are similar to Nambawan fares.

Student Discounts
Full-time students under 25 years of age get 25% off domestic fares (50% off if you're under 19). If you're making a booking outside PNG you need to have an International Student Concession Form, signed by your institution. You should also have one for booking flights within PNG.

Nambawan Fares
These are probably the most useful fares for travellers, as they offer round-trip tickets at a 45% discount. You have to stay a minimum of 10 days and there's a 21-day maximum, which allows plenty of time to explore your destination. You have to fly midweek. Like the weekend fares, these can be booked out, but it's less likely. You have to buy these tickets in PNG, from the town you'll fly from/to, in person. These fares might only apply at certain times of year.

See Niugini
These must be booked outside PNG, in conjunction with certain advance purchase tickets to/from PNG (including Apex fares). You get 20% off domestic flights and although you have to book flights while overseas, changes are permitted with certain conditions. Maximum stay is 45 days.

Visit PNG
You get four coupons for anywhere on the domestic network for US$299, plus additional flights for US$50. This could be a huge saving but tickets can only be bought from an overseas Air Niugini office and the holder must also have an international ticket.

Weekend Excursion Fares
These round-trip tickets cost only 60% of the standard fare. You have to fly out on Friday or Saturday and back on Sunday or Monday. Unfortunately, only a certain number of discount seats are allocated to any one flight and they're often

---

Call Signs

If you are planning a trip involving frequent travel to some small, out-of-the-way airstrips, you will need to come to grips with the fact that airstrip call signs often bear no resemblance to the names of the airstrips they represent. The major airports are reasonably easy to decipher: POM is Port Moresby, RAB is Rabaul, WWK is Wewak, MAG is Madang, HGU is Mt Hagen, and LAE is (can you guess?) Lae, although the Lae airport is actually called Nadzab and is 40km out of town.

But then things start to get a little less logical – TIZ is Tari, TBE is Timbunke, TBG is Tabubil and WUG is Wau. Alotau, which is becoming the second major international airport in PNG, has a call sign GUR because the airport is actually called Gurney. Wabag airport has closed for safety reasons, so if you fly to Wabag you land at Wapenamanda (WBM) which is an hour's drive away.

Equally confusing is Aitape. There are two airstrips at Aitape: Tadji (call sign TAJ) and Aitape (call sign ATP). Tadji airstrip is about 10km out of town and is where most flights land. It is a bumpy landing on often-overgrown grass but the strip is longer than the Aitape airstrip, which, although very close to the town centre, can only handle smaller aircraft.

Jayapura, the capital of the Indonesian province of Irian Jaya, has the call sign DJJ, which, although confusing, has a historical explanation – its old spelling was Djajapura. The Kundiawa call sign, CMU, also has a historical background – it probably stands for Chimbu (a former name of Simbu Province).

As for Wanigela (AGL), Moro (MXH), Namatanai (ATN), Porgera (RGE) and Nissan (IIS) – there's probably some logical reason for them, somewhere.

For the uninitiated, it is also worth having some understanding of the carrier abbreviations. Air Niugini flights all have the prefix PX, whether they are international or domestic. MBA flights begin with CG, Islands Nationair is CN, Airlink is ND and Northcoast Aviation is NCA. ∎

---

booked out long in advance. These fares might apply only at certain times of the year. There are also good-value weekend packages which include accommodation.

Only MBA and Air Niugini offer an across-the-board 20% discount on all advance purchases of domestic flight tickets to international travellers who can produce their international ticket. Air Niugini will automatically apply the discount to both its and MBA legs of your trip when the tickets are bought. If you are extending your journey by purchasing extra legs after you arrive in PNG, you must remember to produce your international ticket to get the discount (they will probably ask for it anyway).

MAF and some other third-level outfits offer student discounts, but they don't really get into fancy discount structures. They also offer discounts of 25% to overseas volunteers with identification. Islands Nationair has a special weekend fare – you can fly anywhere on its scheduled services for 40% off the normal adult airfare for most of the year. It also has special family fares and

Poroman (literally 'friend') packages which include accommodation.

ROADS

There is still a very limited network of roads around the country. The most important is the Highlands Highway, which is sealed from Lae to Mt Hagen, unsealed from Mt Hagen to Tari and becomes a 4WD track between Tari and Lake Kopiago, where it ends. Madang is also connected to the highway via the Ramu Highway at Watarais. A new road cuts across from Dumpu, joining the Highlands Highway at Henganofi, midway between Kainantu and Goroka.

Branching off the Highlands Highway are many secondary roads that go to numerous smaller places, such as Obura and Okapa in the Eastern Highlands; Chuave, Kegsugl, Kerowagi and Gumine in Simbu Province; Minj, Banz, Tabibuga and Baiyer River in the Western Highlands; Wabag, Porgera, Kompiam and Kandep in Enga Province; and Ialibu, Erave and Tambul in the Southern Highlands.

There are reasonable roads east and west along the coast from Port Moresby, along the north coast east and west of Madang and into the Sepik Basin from Wewak, while the Germans bequeathed excellent roads to New Britain and New Ireland. There is no road between Port Moresby and the Highlands or Port Moresby and the north coast.

PMVs (Public Motor Vehicles)

Wherever there are roads, there will be PMVs. PMVs are one of the secrets to cheap travel in PNG and a very successful example of local enterprise. Thirty years ago they didn't exist, now they are indispensable. Most PMVs are comfortable Japanese mini-buses but they can be trucks with wooden benches or even small, bare pick-up trucks.

Rural PMVs pick up and drop off people at any point along a pre-established route. You can more or less assume that anything with lots of people in it is a rural PMV, although officially they have a blue number plate beginning with P. In the urban areas there are established PMV stops (often indicated by a yellow pole or a crowd of waiting people). The destination will be indicated by a sign inside the windscreen or called out by the driver's assistant.

Stick your hand out and wave downwards and they will generally stop. PMVs have a crew of two: the driver, who usually maintains an aloof distance from the passengers; and the 'conductor', who takes fares and generally copes with the rabble. On most occasions, the conductor sits in the seat nearest the door, so when the PMV stops, he's the man to ask about the PMV's destination. If it's heading in the right direction and there's a centimetre or two of spare space, you're on.

If you're looking for long-distance PMVs, always start at the markets *early* in the morning. PMVs leave town when they're full, so if you're the first on board you can spend a very frustrating hour or two circling around looking for more passengers. Market days (usually Friday and Saturday) are the best days for finding a ride. On secondary roads, traffic can be thin, especially early in the week.

When travelling by PMV, it is wise to check the passengers ahead of you before you stick your head out of the window. Those streaks of *buai* (betel nut) spit along the sides of the vehicles are very nasty when met in the slipstream!

Costs Not only is PMV travel cheap, it's also one of the best ways to meet the locals.

There are standard fares for PMVs. Ask your fellow passengers if you want to be certain what they are. In the towns, you pay the conductor after you find yourself a seat. If you tell him where you want to go when you start, he'll let the driver know when to stop. If you make your mind up as you go, just yell 'stop driver!'.

In the country, they quite frequently collect the fare either midway through the journey or 15 minutes or so before your final destination. It seems too many passengers were escaping into the bush without paying. Because of fierce competition and general improvement in road standards, fares have only increased marginally over the last few years.

CAR

Any valid overseas licence is OK for the first three months you're in PNG. Cars drive on the left side of the road. The speed limit is 50 km/h in towns and 100 km/h in the country.

Bear in mind the tourist office's recommendations if you are involved in an accident: don't stop, keep driving and report the accident at the nearest police station. This applies regardless of who was at fault or how serious the accident is (whether you've run over a pig or hit a person).

Tribal concepts of payback apply to car accidents. You may have insurance and you may be willing to pay, but the local citizenry may well prefer to take more immediate and satisfying revenge. There have been a number of instances where drivers who have been involved in fatal accidents have been killed or injured by the accident victim's relatives. A serious accident can mean 'pack up and leave the country' for an expatriate.

Note that some towns such as Lae,

Wewak, Madang, Popondetta and Mt Hagen have no taxis.

Rental

It is possible to hire cars in most main centres, but because of the limited road network you usually won't be able to get far. The major car rental organisations are Avis, Budget, Hertz and Thrifty – their headquarters are listed in the Port Moresby chapter. Most have cars in the major towns, including on Manus, New Britain and New Ireland islands. Budget also operates from most of the Coral Sea hotels and offers special accommodation-car rental packages. There are a few smaller, local firms that are sometimes cheaper than these big rental companies; they are mentioned in the appropriate chapters.

Costs are high, partly because the cars have such a hard life and spend so much time on unsealed roads. All rental rates with the big operators are made up of a daily or weekly charge plus a certain charge per kilometre. A small economy car (like a Daewoo Cielo) costs K84 per day or K504 per week, plus K0.51 per kilometre. A 4WD wagon (like a Pajero) costs K165 per day or K990 per week, plus K0.86 per kilometre. Remote area surcharges of around K18 apply. The Highlands are regarded as remote.

HITCHING

It is possible to hitch-hike, although you'll often be expected to pay the equivalent of a PMV fare. In some places, any passing vehicle is likely to offer you a ride. That is, *if* there is a passing vehicle. You're wisest to wave them down, otherwise it's possible they'll think you're a mad tourist walking for the fun of it. If your bag is light, it's also sometimes possible to hitch-hike flights from small airports.

Hitching is never entirely safe in any country in the world and we don't recommend it. Travellers who decide to hitch should understand that they are taking a small but potentially serious risk. People who choose to hitch will be safer if they travel in pairs and let someone know where they are planning to go.

WALKING

The best and cheapest way to come to grips with PNG is to walk. See some of the walks suggested in the Activities section of the Facts for the Visitor chapter. With a judicious mix of walks, canoes, PMVs, coastal ships and third-level planes, PNG can change from a very expensive country to a reasonable one.

Accommodation and food is normally available in the villages – meaning floor space and sago or sweet potato, respectively – and once you're afloat or on foot, you will spend very little money.

BOAT

There is a wide variety of interesting sea transport, from ocean-going vessels to canoes. You can plan your trip around Lutheran Shipping's passenger boats or you can just wait under a palm tree and see what comes along.

The main ways of getting around by sea are: large boats, small boats, charters and yacht crewing.

Large Boats

Basically, there are boats taking passengers along the north coast between Oro Bay (near Popondetta) and Vanimo, as well as to the main islands off the north coast. There are no passenger vessels linking the north and south coasts or running along the south coast.

Most of the main cargo lines are very reluctant to take passengers on their freighters. However, if you make the right connections, usually via an expat in the shipping office (which are getting a little rare now) or directly with a crew member at the docks, you'll often manage to get a berth or deck space. The major companies list their schedules in the Shipping Notes section of the *Post Courier*, so you'll at least have an idea of when and where to look for a boat.

Conditions on many freighters can be grim. It is essential to take your own food and perhaps water. Your fare may include meals but these will amount to rice and tinned fish and may or may not be edible. If you're travelling deck class, a light sleeping bag or bed sheet, a mat and a tent fly (for shade and shelter) will be handy. Freighters often have schedules but they are very unreliable, due to delays in loading/unloading cargos. Also, many ships won't take passengers if they have dangerous cargo (including petrol). They often won't know what the cargo will be much in advance, so you can't rely on travelling on a particular voyage.

Fortunately, Lutheran Shipping runs a reliable, inexpensive and reasonably comfortable passenger-only service between Oro Bay and Wewak, with services out to New Britain.

Although there are a number of other smaller operations, some of the main shipping companies and their head offices are:

Coastal Shipping Company
    PO Box 423, Rabaul, East New Britain
    (☎ 982 2399; fax 982 8519)
Consort Express Lines
    PO Box 1690, Port Moresby (☎ 321 1288;
    fax 321 1279)
Lutheran Shipping
    PO Box 1459, Lae, Morobe Province
    (☎ 472 2066; fax 472 5806)
Pacific New Guinea Line
    PO Box 1764, Rabaul, East New Britain
    (☎ 982 1955)
PNG Shipping Corporation
    PO Box 634, Port Moresby (☎ 322 0420)

Lutheran Shipping has a virtual monopoly on passenger shipping along the north coast and services Oro Bay, Lae, Finschhafen, Madang, Wewak, Aitape, Vanimo and intermediate ports.

The two passenger-only boats, the *Mamose Express* and the *Rita*, have tourist class (air-conditioned seats and berths) and deck class (air-vented seats and berths). Some people say that the difference in quality between the two isn't enough to justify paying the higher fare, although deck class can get very crowded and you might miss out on a bunk. Both classes have video 'entertainment' and you might want to avoid bunks near the video. There is a snack bar which serves soft drinks, pies etc. You can get hot water to make tea or coffee, but you'll have to ask.

If you miss the boat, you'll get a 50% refund on your ticket up to 48 hours after sailing and nothing after that. Booking ahead might be necessary around Christmas.

Note that some boats go on to New Britain from Lae, so you might have to change if you're going further east or west along the coast. Students are entitled to discounts, although whether this is 50% or 25% differs between booking offices.

Lutheran Shipping's passenger-carrying freighters run at unpredictabe times between Oro Bay and Vanimo (and out to the islands), and at fares slightly lower than those on the passenger-only boats.

To/From the Islands Lutheran Shipping and Coastal Shipping have regular services from Lae to New Britain. Coastal Shipping also has frequent but unscheduled freighters sailing from Rabaul to Kavieng on New Ireland, sometimes continuing on to Lihir Island and the other island groups off New Ireland's east coast. Other freighters run to Nissan Island and on to Buka about weekly. Once a month or so, Coastal has a boat from Rabaul to Manus via Kavieng. A Lutheran Shipping freighter also plies the weekly route between Lae, Manus and Madang.

See the appropriate regional chapters for further details of these ships.

To/From the South Coast No freighters officially take passengers along the south coast. For unofficial berths try the shipping offices and docks in Port Moresby, where you'll also find small boats running to Gulf Province. You can village-hop east to Milne Bay, but it's probably best to start from Kupiano.

Small Boats
In addition to the freighters and passenger boats, local boats and canoes go literally everywhere. For these you have to be in the right place at the right time but, with patience, you could travel the whole coastline by village-hopping in small boats.

Work boats – small, wooden boats with thumping diesel engines – ply the coast, supplying trade stores and acting as ferries. They run irregularly but fairly frequently, and travelling on one will get you to some very off-the-track places. They aren't very comfortable and can be noisy and smelly, but for the adventurous there's no better way to travel. Once aboard, you are a captive client, so make sure the operator is trustworthy before you commit yourself to a day or two aboard.

If you're in a major centre, ask at the big stores, as they might have a fairly set schedule for delivering supplies to the area's trade stores. Take your own food and water on these boats.

Around New Britain and other places there are slightly more regular coastal services in small freighters, and in some places mission boats run set schedules and will take passengers.

For shorter distances, there are dinghies with outboard motors, often known as speedies or banana boats. These are usually long fibreglass boats which are surprisingly seaworthy despite their bronco-like mode of travel, leaping through the waves. The cost of running outboard motors makes them very expensive if you have to charter one, but there will often be a speedie acting as a ferry (taking people to church or market) and the fares are reasonable. There are still canoes with outboards around and you might even get to make a voyage in a sailing canoe on the south coast.

Boat Charter

Many dive operators charter their boats, some for extended cruises. A cheaper alternative, if you're not looking for comfort and the chance to dive, is to try to charter a work boat. Chartering is definitely possible in Milne Bay, Lae and probably elsewhere – for a group of five or six, it isn't ruinously expensive.

Yacht Crewing

There are thriving yacht clubs in Port Moresby, Lae, Madang, Wewak and Rabaul, and it is possible you might be able to find a berth, if you have some experience. Yachts often clear PNG customs at Samarai Island in Milne Bay.

ORGANISED TOURS

The two main inbound tour operators are Melanesian Tourist Services, based in Madang, and Trans Niugini Tours, based in Mt Hagen. Their PNG addresses and overseas contacts are listed in the Getting There & Away chapter. Listed below are some of the smaller inbound tour operators, ranging from 'grassroots' (which have much to recommend them) to some more upmarket operators.

Haus Poroman Lodge
    PO Box 1182, Mt Hagen (☎ 542 2722; fax 542 2207)
    Haus Poroman is one of the best places to stay in PNG and also offers Sepik canoe trips, treks of the Highlands and Mt Wilhelm, and other packages.
PNG Highland Tours & Treks
    PO Box 583, Goroka (☎ 732 1602; fax 732 3302)
    This small company is operated by the personable Norman Carver. It specialises in tours in and around Goroka and even as far away as Mt Wilhelm.
Sepik Adventure Tours
    PO Box 248, Wewak; PO Box 83, Ambunti (☎ 858 1291/856 2525)
    Operated by Alois Mateus, it is one of the few tour operations on the Sepik which is not owned by foreign interests. It is run in conjunction with Ambunti Lodge; staff can prearrange canoe tours.
Sepik Village Tours
    PO Box 35, Angoram (☎ & fax 858 3039)
    This, too, is a local organisation and is operated by Joe Kenni, who runs it in conjunction with the Angoram Hotel; Joe can organise canoe tours.
South Pacific Tours
    PO Box 195, Boroko (☎ 323 5245; fax 323 5246)
    This business offers general travel services including diving, adventure and trekking tours.
Tribal World
    PO Box 86, Mt Hagen (☎ 544 1555)
    Tribal World operates a chain of hotels and offers some tours, including canoeing, trekking and, sometimes, rafting.

Port Moresby

Land Area 240 sq km
Population 260,000
(National Capital District)

Port Moresby, the capital city of Papua New Guinea, is a large and sprawling metropolis noticeably lacking in character. It is located within the National Capital District (NCD), an administrative entity covering a geographic area which extends a little beyond the city boundaries.

As with many developing countries, there is a continuing urban migration of people from all over the country seeking opportunities in 'the big smoke'. People are attracted by Port Moresby's reputation for money, glamour and excitement. Nevertheless, most fail to find fame or even a job, and frustration mounts when 'excitement' is all around you but you have no money with which to participate. Consequently, a large number of disillusioned migrants end up living in squalid, unserviced squatter settlements and contribute to Port Moresby's high crime rate.

Port Moresby has the largest foreign contingent in the country (expats make up 7% of the population) and representatives of every cultural and/or tribal group in the country. About 17% of NCD residents were born in the Gulf region, 15% come from Central Province, 6% from Manus Province and 4% from the Oro and Eastern Highlands provinces. This mix is reflected in the city's housing – there are a small number of palatial residences dotting the hillsides, mainly occupied by wealthy expats, and ever-growing squatter settlements around the outskirts.

The NCD is situated in a rain shadow and is much drier than the rest of the country. The arid, brown, northern-Australian look of Port Moresby fades into the more prevalent lush green as you move away from the capital, both along the coast and inland to the rugged Owen Stanley Range. In the dry season, Port Moresby can suffer from extended droughts and there can be restrictions on water use.

HIGHLIGHTS

- Wandering through the manicured lawns and rainforest boardwalk of the National Botanic Gardens
- Checking out Parliament House in Waigani and, if your timing is right, catching a sitting of parliament
- Exploring the National Museum & Art Gallery
- Diving around the many islands, beaches and reefs near Port Moresby
- Taking a day trip by small plane to the picturesque and steep airstrips in the Owen Stanley Range
- Swimming in the cool waters of Crystal Rapids near Sogeri

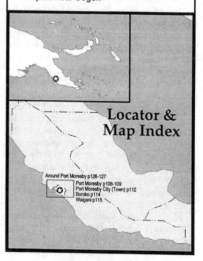

Locator & Map Index

Around Port Moresby p126-127
Port Moresby p108-109
Port Moresby City (Town) p112
Boroko p114
Waigani p115

Port Moresby's physical isolation is another major drawback. It is the only significant town in the southern half of the country and there are no road connections to any other important towns.

At present most visitors to the country are forced to go through Port Moresby, but this is slowly changing with the introduction of

105

international flights direct to Alotau, Mt Hagen and even Daru. Nevertheless, Port Moresby will remain an important city and it is well worth spending a couple of days here to look around.

History

There were two groups of people living in the Port Moresby area when the first Europeans arrived – the Motu and the Koitabu. The Motu were a seagoing people with an Austronesian language that has close links with other Melanesian and Polynesian languages. It seems probable that the Motuans were relatively late arrivals on the coast (possibly migrating from island Melanesia less than 2000 years ago) and lived in harmony with the Koitabu, who spoke an inland, non-Austronesian language.

The Motuan people were great sailors and their impressive boats, called *lakatois* and up to 15m long, were capable of carrying a large cargo and crew. They were rigged with one or two masts and strange crab claw-shaped sails.

The high point of the Motuan year was the annual *hiri* trading voyage – each Motuan village had a counterpart village in the Gulf region with which it traded clay pots for sago. The Motuans were not great farmers, perhaps because of the dry climate and limited agricultural potential of the Port Moresby area, as well as their seafaring heritage. So they were dependent on Gulf sago, which could be stored for long periods, for their survival.

Motu villages were built on stilts over Moresby Harbour. Hanuabada (the great village) was the largest of their communities and still exists today, although in a considerably changed form.

The first European to visit was Captain John Moresby in 1873, after whom the harbour was named. Moresby explored extensively along the south coast and spent several days trading with villagers at Hanuabada. He was impressed with the people and their lifestyles, posing the rhetorical question in his diary, 'What have these people to gain from civilisation?'

One year later, the London Missionary Society established its first outpost and the missionaries were soon followed by 'blackbirders' and traders, who recruited indentured labourers and were little better than slave-dealers.

The island's interior remained largely unexplored and 'unclaimed' by Europeans until 1888, as Britain already had sufficient colonial problems. Then, under pressure from colonists in Australia and with fears of the intentions of the Germans, who held the northern half of the island, the British formally claimed British New Guinea and Port Moresby became the capital. Under Sir William MacGregor's remarkable 10-year administration, the government in Port Moresby and a national police force were established. MacGregor also explored large tracts of the rugged island.

Between the wars PNG was administered in two parts: Papua, with Port Moresby as its capital, and Australian New Guinea (ex-German territory), with its capital at Rabaul in New Britain. Nevertheless, Papua was overshadowed by New Guinea, north of the central mountains, for much of the period between the two wars. The discovery of gold at Wau and Bulolo, plus the productive plantations on the offshore islands, made New Guinea much more important economically. WWII shifted the spotlight back to Port Moresby – the city became the staging post for the Allies fighting along the Kokoda Trail. Port Moresby remained in Australian hands throughout the war.

After the war, Papua and New Guinea were administered as one territory. Since the northern New Guinea towns were little more than rubble, Port Moresby retained its position as the country's administrative headquarters, a position it continues to hold despite occasional pressure to move it. Lae, with its central location and excellent communications to the important Highlands, is the usual suggestion.

Orientation

Getting your bearings in Port Moresby is no easy task because it spreads out around the coast and the inland hills. It takes a while to work out where things are. Luckily, PMVs run regular services between all areas of the city.

The centre of Port Moresby, if it can claim such a feature, is on a spit of land which ends in Paga Hill and is usually known as Town. Town has the majority of Port Moresby's few older buildings, the shipping docks and wharves, most of the major commercial office buildings, the conspicuous Port Moresby Travelodge and a large Steamships department store.

If you follow the coast round to the north from Town, past the docks, you'll be on the new dual-carriage highway which links up with Spring Gardens Rd and Geauto Drive en route to the airport. This part of the highway along the waterfront used to be known as Champion Parade but will report-edly be known as the Poreporena Highway. It runs between the Sir Hubert Murray Stadium (nowhere near the highway of the same name) and the new Royal Papua Yacht Club marina before veering inland to Gor-dons and the airport. If you turn left along the remains of Champion Parade, you will pass Hanuabada, the original Motuan stilt village built out over the water.

On the other, southern, side of Town, the main road runs alongside popular Ela Beach until you reach Koki, where there are shops, the Koki Markets and another, smaller stilt village. From Koki, the road divides into two one-way sections and climbs steeply up Two Mile Hill before dropping down to Boroko as the Sir Hubert Murray Highway.

Boroko (also known as Four Mile) has, in some areas, overtaken Town as the most important commercial and shopping centre. About 6km from town, it has numerous shops, restaurants, banks, airline agencies and a good post office.

If you continue along the Sir Hubert Murray Highway, you will link up with the new highway which leads to Jackson Inter-national Airport. A few kilometres past the airport the road divides, heading north to Brown River and east to the mountains, the Kokoda Trail and Sogeri.

The new highway, from Town through Hohola and Gordons to the airport, was due to be finished by the end of 1997 to coincide with the opening of the new airport terminal buildings. Whether these expensive projects are worth the prominence they have been given among PNG's competing develop-ment priorities is debatable. Nevertheless, the new highway will make a significant difference to the traffic flow in Port Moresby and help to speed the trip between the airport and Town. It will probably also mean that the PMV system will change dramatically – PMVs tend to create their own routes and stops over time. Sometimes these can change

---

! ! ! ! ! ! ! ! ! ! ! ! ! !

Warning
While Port Moresby has a deserved reputation for crime, visitors should not be deterred by overenthusiastic media reporting of the situa-tion. Rascals seem more concerned these days with robbing banks, holding up shops and breaking into houses than targeting travellers. You would be very unlucky to find yourself in trouble if you act carefully.

The golden rule is: don't walk the streets at night. Also, don't wander around the back-streets with a pack on your back or displaying valuables. Use the mini-bus airport services run by almost all the hotels and motels. PMVs are also a good way to travel, despite what resident expats may tell you. Remember that PMVs stop running when the sun goes down, so keep a few K10 and K5 bills handy for an after-dark taxi ride (taxi drivers will inevitably tell you they have no change).

It is wise to avoid secluded areas, particu-larly around the shanty settlements on the outskirts of the city, and if you see groups of young men loitering, head rapidly in the other direction. Be especially wary on Friday nights, as young men sometimes go on the prowl for beer money.

Residents take their security very seriously, as Port Moresby has a high incidence of break-ins, which have been known to occasionally involve rape. Hotels and motels employ armies of security guards and deploy kilometres of razor wire to ensure the safety of their guests. So you can feel pretty safe in your hotel room, but don't assume that pilfering is off the agenda and leave valuables lying around.

Also see the Personal Safety section in the Facts for the Visitor chapter. ■

! ! ! ! ! ! ! ! ! ! ! ! ! !

PORT MORESBY

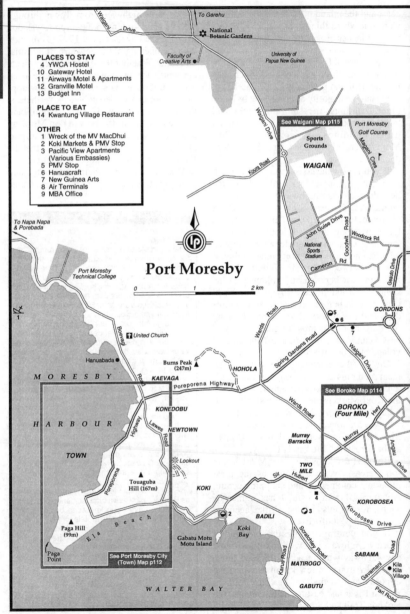

PLACES TO STAY
4 YWCA Hostel
10 Gateway Hotel
11 Airways Motel & Apartments
12 Granville Motel
13 Budget Inn

PLACE TO EAT
14 Kwantung Village Restaurant

OTHER
1 Wreck of the MV MacDhui
2 Koki Markets & PMV Stop
3 Pacific View Apartments
  (Various Embassies)
5 PMV Stop
6 Hanuacraft
7 New Guinea Arts
8 Air Terminals
9 MBA Office

To Garehu

National Botanic Gardens

Faculty of Creative Arts

University of Papua New Guinea

Waigani Drive

Koura Road

See Waigani Map p115

Sports Grounds

WAIGANI

Port Moresby Golf Course

Magani Cres

National Sports Stadium

John Guise Drive

Goodwit Road

Woodcock Rd

Cameron Rd

Gataba Drive

To Napa Napa & Porebada

Port Moresby Technical College

Port Moresby

0   1   2 km

United Church

Hanuabada

Boswigi Road

Burns Peak (247m)

HOHOLA

Wards Road

Spring Gardens Road

Waigani Drive

GORDONS

5
6
7

MORESBY

KAEVAGA

Poreporena Highway

KONEDOBU

HARBOUR

TOWN

Lawes Road

NEWTOWN

Lookout

Wards Road

See Boroko Map p114

BOROKO (Four Mile)

Murray Hwy

Angau Drive

Poreporena Highway

Touaguba Hill (167m)

KOKI

Murray Barracks

Sir Hubert

TWO MILE

4

KOROBOSEA

Paga Hill (99m)

Ela Beach

Paga Point

See Port Moresby City (Town) Map p112

2

Gabatu Motu Motu Island

Koki Bay

BADILI

3

Korobosea Drive

SABAMA

Scratchley Road

Kanu Road

Gavamani Road

Kila Kila Village

MATIROGO

GABUTU

Pari Road

WALTER BAY

unpredictably, particularly with a major traffic innovation like a new city highway. This book was updated some months before the highway was due for completion, so bear in mind that although its maps have incorporated the new information, PMV routes may change.

The new highway will create a major intersection with Waigani Drive which runs out to the north-west. Waigani Drive takes you (surprise, surprise) to Waigani, which is a sprawling development of office blocks, shops and hotels, including many government department offices, foreign embassies and high commissions. Also here are Parliament House, the National Museum & Art Gallery and the National Library. A little beyond Waigani you reach the University of Papua New Guinea (UPNG). After the campus, a branch road turns west back to the coast (joining the coast road 7km or 8km out from Hanuabada) and another continues to Gerehu, a fast-growing residential suburb.

The old air terminal was accessed via the Morea-Tobo Road in Six Mile (also known as Saraga). A number of accommodation places can be found on this route: the Gateway Hotel, Airways Motel & Apartments (overlooking the airport), the Granville Motel and Budget Inn. There is a good shopping centre at Dogura Place (where the Gordon & Gotch bookshop can be found) and a market nearby. With the new airport terminals and highway, which takes traffic to Town via a very different route, Six Mile may be in danger of becoming a bit of a backwater.

Information

Tourist Offices There will undoubtedly be a tourist information desk at the new airport terminal.

The PNG Tourism Promotion Authority (TPA) (☎ 320 0211; fax 320 0223; PO Box 1291, Port Moresby) is on the 2nd floor of NIC Haus in Town. It can provide some tourist and accommodation information but its primary mission is to promote and market PNG tourism.

The larger hotels can have excellent and

friendly staff at their reception areas, although staff can also be curt and surly. If you need information, go in and ask – the staff at the Gateway Hotel and the Port Moresby Travelodge were particularly helpful.

Don't be hesitant about asking the locals for advice – most of the time they'll be friendly and helpful, even in Port Moresby. Indeed, sometimes they can be too helpful and will insist on accompanying you wherever you want to go.

Foreign Embassies Most diplomatic representation is in Waigani. See the Facts for the Visitor chapter for addresses.

Money The head offices for PNGBC, Westpac, ANZ and the Bank of South Pacific are in Town not far from each other, with branches widely distributed around the city, including Boroko. Banks in most areas close at 4.30 pm Monday to Thursday and 5 pm Friday. Don't be deterred by the numerous security guards – but it is wise not to pat the dogs. There are always long queues in all banks – if you are cashing travellers cheques or dealing in international currency, go

---

Dealing with Bureaucrats

PNG is not unique in having unresponsive and sometimes inept bureaucrats – they can be found pretty well anywhere in the world. But dealing with the PNG variety requires a subtly different approach. You will come across all sorts of circumstances in PNG where petty bureaucrats have the power to make your life difficult – or easy.

If you are confronted by an unhelpful clerk at hotel reception who doesn't want to give you the discount to which you believe you are entitled, or an immigration clerk who demurs at your request for a visa extension, then it is best to remember that they are dealing with things which are more a part of your culture than theirs. The trappings of bureaucracy have been readily absorbed into PNG's administrative and commercial culture, but unfortunately competence and a wider perspective have not always accompanied them. Clerks may have been taught how to handle a credit card but may not understand the difference between American Express, Visa and Bankcard. Such bureaucrats really don't want to accept responsibility for a decision about something which is still a little strange to them. Their unfamiliarity leads to uncertainty, which leads to anxiety, which leads to obduracy and can (if you are not careful) lead to bravado ('Bugger this difficult person! Why should I help them?'). Frustration will consequently reign – correspondence may not be answered, urgent requests for information may be delayed and personal representations may be ignored.

Some PNG bureaucrats are wonderfully helpful and solicitous – but such people tend to be rare, and they rapidly rise through the ranks to positions where they no longer have to deal with the public. But others, probably the majority, are not very adroit. If you throw them a problem which is in any way out of the ordinary, their response will be to assume a sullen air and adopt one of these strategies:

- ignore you in the hope that you will go away, or take an inordinately long time to deal with your problem in the hope that you will give up in frustration and go away
- go in search of someone else who may know a bit more about it (and hope that in the meantime you will go away)
- tell you that it is not really their area of concern and that the person you should be dealing with is someone whose office is an hour away by PMV

How should you deal with this? Well, there may be no solution. You may just have to go away and come back another time when – with any luck – someone else will deal with you. But you can always try the following:

- always smile and be pleasant and do not get angry or aggressive. Keep the situation light and easy so that the person feels sympathy for you and actually wants to help you.
- make sure you know what outcome you want. If you can subtly suggest a solution to your own problem, the bureaucrat may jump at the opportunity to do just what you suggest.
- let your fingers do the walking. Don't do the rounds of offices all over Port Moresby – find a good telephone (sometimes a difficult task) and ring around to find out to whom you should speak. Then go and see them.
- learn to operate in 'Melanesian time' and have patience. ■

straight to the international desk, where the queues are always far shorter (the regular tellers will send you there eventually, anyway, if you get in the wrong queue).

There is a bank planned for the new airport terminal but arriving with some kina in your pocket isn't a bad idea.

Amex, Visa, Diners Club and MasterCard are accepted by top-end places and most airlines. Westpac in Town is the agent for American Express (☎ 322 0700; fax 321 3927; PO Box 706, Port Moresby). Bankcard is not accepted in PNG.

Post & Communications There is a poste restante desk at the main post office in Town, but for many travellers the post office at Boroko is much more convenient. At Boroko, go to the registered mail counter. Both post offices have philatelic counters. The hours are from 8.30 am to 4.30 pm Monday to Friday, and from 8.30 to 11.30 am Saturday.

Finding a serviceable telephone in a quiet area can be a problem in Port Moresby. There are phones outside the Boroko post office, some coin-operated and some card-operated. But they are located in the full morning sun and they can get quite hot. There are always long queues and broken telephones. There are one or two phones at the main post office in Town but there are also public phones inside the Steamships department store. The larger hotels always have public phones in their lobbies – or they will sometimes dial the number for you and let you use their phone.

You're less likely to have to queue at a card-phone and they are less often vandalised. Cards are available from post offices and some shops. Don't go overboard and buy the large denomination cards, as there aren't many places in PNG where you can use them (eg Lae has card-phones, but Wewak, Madang and Vanimo do not). A six-minute call to Australia will use up a K10 phone card.

Books & Maps There is a useful UBD street directory of PNG towns available at some newsagents. Maps are also available at the National Mapping Bureau in Waigani (☎ 327 6465; fax 327 6460; PO Box 5665, Boroko). It has a particularly useful two-part 1:10,000 street map of Port Moresby which is reasonably up-to-date (1990) but does not show the recently constructed Poreporena Highway.

There are several good places to buy books. Gordon & Gotch (☎ 325 4855) in Dogura Place at Six Mile probably has the best selection. The book section in the huge Town Steamships department store has a reasonable selection, including guidebooks and Pidgin dictionaries. City News in the Morgoru Motu building on the west side of Steamships is reasonably well stocked. The UPNG bookstore has a table devoted to publications about PNG and its stock should have picked up by now. It's also worth visiting the Institute of PNG Studies in Angau Drive, Boroko; it sells publications by local authors as well as films, videos and recordings of traditional culture and music.

Libraries There's a small Port Moresby public library in Town on Douglas St next to the Big Rooster. The big National Library (an independence gift from Australia) at the UPNG is excellent and houses a huge PNG collection. The National Archives, also at Waigani, houses an interesting collection, but you might wait for several hours before they can find what you are looking for. All of them are open to the public.

Emergency The Port Moresby phone number for emergencies (police, fire and ambulance) is ☎ 000, but this number doesn't apply elsewhere in the country. The Port Moresby General Hospital (☎ 324 8200) is on Taurama Rd, Korobosea, not far from Boroko.

Port Moresby City
• *postcode 121*
Port Moresby's CBD, commonly called Town, retains some sense of history, although there are few old buildings left and the number of high-rise office blocks is

PORT MORESBY

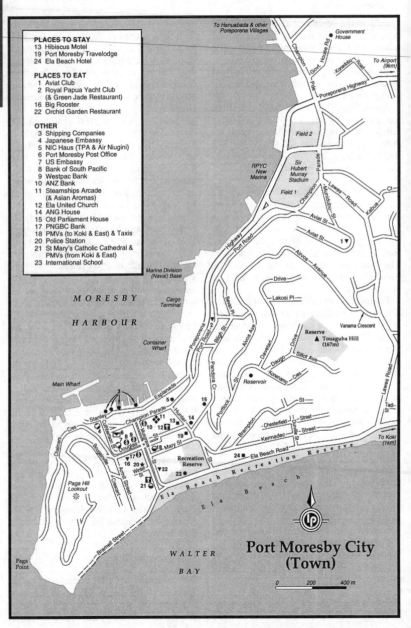

PLACES TO STAY
13 Hibiscus Motel
19 Port Moresby Travelodge
24 Ela Beach Hotel

PLACES TO EAT
1 Aviat Club
2 Royal Papua Yacht Club
  (& Green Jade Restaurant)
16 Big Rooster
22 Orchid Garden Restaurant

OTHER
3 Shipping Companies
4 Japanese Embassy
5 NIC Haus (TPA & Air Niugini)
6 Port Moresby Post Office
7 US Embassy
8 Bank of South Pacific
9 Westpac Bank
10 ANZ Bank
11 Steamships Arcade
   (& Asian Aromas)
12 Ela United Church
14 ANG House
15 Old Parliament House
17 PNGBC Bank
18 PMVs (to Koki & East) & Taxis
20 Police Station
21 St Mary's Catholic Cathedral &
   PMVs (from Koki & East)
23 International School

MORESBY

HARBOUR

Port Moresby City
(Town)

0   200   400 m

growing. Pacific Place (with a hemisphere on top), ANG House and the Port Moresby Travelodge dominate the skyline.

At the other end of Douglas St from the Travelodge is the PNGBC Bank, which has some interesting, traditional-style decorations on the facade. Also check out the gulf dugout canoe which hangs from the ceiling; at about 25m long, it's said to be one of the largest canoes ever made. An inscription describes its ceremonial use.

Paga Point is the harbour headland adjacent to Town. It's worth walking to the top of Paga Hill for the fine views over the town, the harbour and the encircling reefs. It's quite a popular spot at lunchtimes, but if you walk up you would be wise to go in a group – it can be a little too secluded to be safe.

St Mary's Catholic Cathedral is on Musgrave St, near Ela Beach; its frontage is in the style of a Sepik *haus tambaran* (spirit house).

The oldest building still standing in Port Moresby is the **Ela United Church** in Douglas St between Steamships and the ANZ building. It was opened by the London Missionary Society in 1890 and is one of the city's last links with the past.

Ela Beach Heading south down Musgrave St or Hunter St, you soon hit the long, sandy stretch of Ela Beach. It's a popular spot for lazing on the sand and there is a nice promenade along the beachfront for a kilometre or so, but it is not much good for swimming, particularly at low tide, because the water is very shallow and weedy. There are also many black sea urchins – be careful, as the spines can be very painful if you step on them. Windsurfing is popular.

Hanuabada

Past the docks to the north lies Hanuabada, the original Motuan village. Although it is still built out over the sea on stilts, the original wood and thatched houses were destroyed by fire during WWII. They were rebuilt in all-Australian building materials, corrugated iron and fibro-cement, and the surroundings are now littered with rubbish.

But it's still an interesting place and the people have retained many traditional Motuan customs.

It is not acceptable to wander around the villages if you are not a guest or don't have a local guide. In some senses, individual houses are more like single rooms in one great house, so if you wander around the walkways without knowing what you are doing and where you are going, you are certain to seriously offend people by invading their privacy.

The name Hanuabada is commonly used to describe six interlinked villages. In fact, Hanuabada correctly describes only one of the six villages that have grown together: collectively and officially they are known as the Poreporena villages.

Metoreai

The site of the first European settlement in Papua lies beyond Hanuabada on the ridge. The building there, which now belongs to the Ela United Church, was once the headquarters of the London Missionary Society and its first missionary, Reverend NG Lawes, who arrived here on 21 November 1874. There's a stone cairn and a plaque to mark the event and another monument commemorates the pastors from the South Sea islands.

Koki

Ela Beach runs up to the headland at Koki, where there is a cluster of shops and **Koki Market**. There's also a stilt village, smaller and more 'suburban' than Hanuabada, but still quite picturesque.

The Koki Market may not be the best market in the country but it is an interesting place. Saturday is the big market day although there's always plenty of activity – but watch out for pickpockets and thieves. Scores of people looked on with interest while several tourists were robbed at gunpoint recently among the crowded stalls. So take care here. The market is good for seafood; local anglers pull their boats up nearby. There are PMV stops on both sides of the road at the market.

Boroko
• postcode 111

Continuing up Three Mile Hill, past the YWCA, you come to Boroko (now less commonly known as Four Mile). It is becoming the most important business district, with its own post office, banks, airline agencies, a smallish market, several shopping plazas and a number of Chinese-owned general stores. But nothing matches the Steamships department store in Town.

There are also a number of restaurants and kai-bars and a few places to stay. There are even some civic touches, like a square, a pedestrian mall and a pedestrian overpass.

Boroko's success is due, in part, to its central position at the intersection of Waigani Drive and the Sir Hubert Murray Highway. Because of this, it also has the largest PMV station which is well worth avoiding at peak hours. PMVs leave from both sides of the Sir Hubert Murray Highway (linked by the overpass). With the comple-

tion of the new highway, however, things could change.

Gordons
Gordons is a couple of kilometres from Boroko. It is not a particularly attractive part of Port Moresby, unless you like breweries and factories, but it is the home for PNG arts and crafts.

There's also the bustling **Gordons Market**, one of the largest and busiest in the country. This market has an excellent selection of vegetables and fruit available. Open daily, it's a good place just to watch other people.

Gordons Market is the best place to catch PMVs for Bomana, Sogeri and nearby destinations. The market is just over 1km east of Waigani Drive, down Cameron Rd, or 1km north of the roundabout at the end of Spring Garden Rd (which now forms part of the city highway). PMVs, including No 4, run from Town to the market.

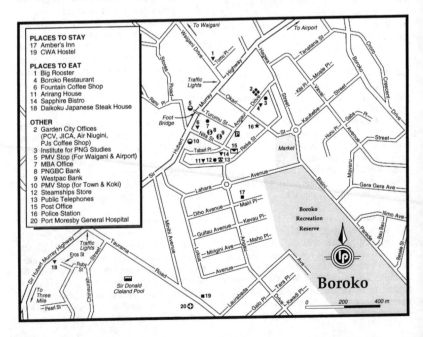

PLACES TO STAY
17 Amber's Inn
19 CWA Hostel

PLACES TO EAT
1 Big Rooster
4 Boroko Restaurant
6 Fountain Coffee Shop
11 Arirang House
14 Sapphire Bistro
18 Daikoku Japanese Steak House

OTHER
2 Garden City Offices
(PCV, JICA, Air Niugini,
PJs Coffee Shop)
3 Institute for PNG Studies
5 PMV Stop (For Waigani & Airport)
7 MBA Office
8 PNGBC Bank
9 Westpac Bank
10 PMV Stop (for Town & Koki)
12 Steamships Store
13 Public Telephones
15 Post Office
16 Police Station
20 Port Moresby General Hospital

Boroko

Waigani

• *postcode 131*

Waigani hosts most government offices. If you travel north along Waigani Drive past the Islander Travelodge on your left and then about half a kilometre to the right, you'll find the government centre housing many departments. Most PMVs let you get off on the main road before continuing towards Gerehu, although at peak hours there will be a PMV marked 'W'gani' or 'Office' that will travel direct to the Central Government Offices. No PMVs service the museum or the parliament.

On the corner of Waigani Drive and John Guise Drive is the Waigani Sports Complex, which was built for the 1991 South Pacific Games. It is a handy landmark if you've caught a PMV which doesn't run into Waigani proper and from here it's a 500m walk to the offices.

Waigani has been dubbed 'Canberra in the Tropics' and there's more than a little truth to that description. There's a handful of flashy, modern buildings with a lot of empty space between them and the only way you can get around is by car or on foot.

There are five main government buildings grouped together. The Haus Marea ('pineapple' building) is the distinctively ugly high-rise near the corner of John Guise Drive and Kumul Ave. On the opposite corner, the first building you come to, Haus Tomakala, is a more innocuous high-rise that has a Chinese restaurant out the front and a couple of snack bars inside.

The three-storey Central Government Offices, on the corner of Kumul Ave and Melanesian Way across from the Haus Marea, is home to the immigration section, a post office and an Air Niugini office. The National Mapping Bureau is behind the Central Government Office on Melanesian Way.

Parliament House The new parliament building was officially opened in 1984 with

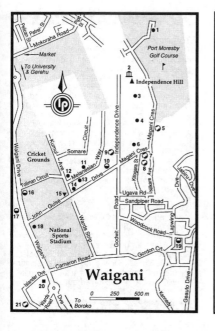

PLACE TO STAY
20   Islander Travelodge

PLACE TO EAT
15   Haus Tomakala & Golden Bowl Restaurant

OTHER
1   Port Moresby Golf Club House
2   National Museum & Art Gallery
3   Parliament House
4   Supreme Court
5   New Zealand High Commission
6   National Library & Archives
7   Indonesian Embassy
8   British High Commission
9   Australian High Commission
10   PMV Stop
11   National Mapping Bureau
12   Central Government Offices
13   Haus Morauta
14   Haus Marea ('Pineapple' Building)
16   PMV Stop
17   PMV Stop
18   Waigani Sports Complex
19   Gordons Market & Rural PMVs
21   Philipines Embassy

Prince Charles on hand. It's an impressive building, as it should be at a cost of K22 million. Built in the style of a Maprik haus tambaran, it sits on a hill fronted by fountains about 2km from the PMV stop on Waigani Drive. A taxi from Boroko costs between about K10 and K15.

The parliamentary proceedings inside are interesting as they require simultaneous translations into English, Pidgin and Motu, the three main languages of PNG. Even if parliament isn't sitting it's worth a look inside, although you can't take photos. There's a small shop with some interesting books, and some cases displaying PNG's amazing butterflies. It's usually open from 9 am to noon and from 1 to 3 pm. There's a cafeteria with standard kai-bar offerings under the front forecourt.

National Museum & Art Gallery The museum is not far from the parliament building. The displays justify the effort spent to reach it and, as a further reward, the building is air-conditioned. There's a shady courtyard area in front, with wooden tables and seats, which is serviced by a most uninspiring (and often closed) snack bar. If you have packed your lunch, this would be a pleasant place to eat it.

You'll need at least an hour to see the excellent displays covering the geography, fauna, culture, ethnography and history of PNG. There are superb examples of masks, shields and totems, a magnificent Milne Bay outrigger canoe decorated in cowry shells, as well as exhibits on local foods and shells. A small courtyard has some (usually live) birds, lizards and snakes.

The museum is open Monday to Friday from 8.30 am to 3.30 pm and Sunday from 1 to 5 pm. Admission is free, but you may be asked for a 'donation'. There is an interesting bookshop at the entrance. Although the selection of books is limited, there are publications about prehistory and culture that are hard to find anywhere else. The bookshop closes between 1 and 2 pm. There are plans to build a new constitutional park and heritage centre nearby, incorporating a modern

history museum, modern art gallery and national history museum.

University of Papua New Guinea
• *postcode 134*

After Waigani, you first come to the Administrative College, then to the attractive and spacious university. It's close to the main road and plenty of 'Gerehu' PMVs run by. There is a bookshop (to the right as you enter the main entrance) and a fairly comprehensive library in which visitors are free to browse. The bookshop has recently changed hands, after a period of decline, and is accumulating a worthwhile selection again.

To the right of the entrance is a long verandah with a well-executed mural extending the length of it, which is now battered and spattered with *buai*, or betel nut. At the end of the verandah is the students' dining room which serves pretty horrible food. Students may bring in guests for a fee of K2. There is also a coffee shop with decent, good-value

---

Tommaso Salvadori
Tommaso Salvadori was noted in the 19th century for the role he played as surgeon-general in Garibaldi's army during the Italian revolution. But his interests extended beyond medicine and into other sciences. He was particularly enthusiastic about ornithology and, in later years, was invited by the British Museum to assist in the classification of its bird collection. Here, in a long-forgotten trunk, he found a number of magnificent stuffed birds originating from an early expedition to New Guinea.

Perhaps overexcited by his discovery, he let his ego get the better of his professional ethics and named them all after himself. So we have – among other birds – Salvadori's teal, Salvadori's frogmouth, Salvadori's fig parrot, and Salvadori's bird of paradise (which now graces the PNG flag).

Strangely, Tommaso, who never set foot in New Guinea, had a PNG stamp issued in his honour in the 1970s. Moreover, in a curious twist of fate, his great-great-grandson, Antony Salvadori, also a keen amateur ornithologist, accepted a position in the mid-1990s as senior lecturer in Computing Studies at the University of PNG, where he recounted the above story with much relish. ■

meals. The uni is a good place to meet interesting people.

A little beyond the university entrance and on the opposite side of Waigani Drive, a road leads to the Faculty of Creative Arts (☎ 326 0390; PO Box 113, University). It's less than half a kilometre from the main road, an easy walking distance from the university.

National Botanic Gardens

Just north beyond the university on Waigani Drive is the National Botanic Gardens. After falling into decline for many years, they have now become one of the gems of Port Moresby. The gardens are an island of serenity and beauty in the midst of an otherwise lacklustre city. Don't miss them! They have more than 2km of boardwalk threading under and through the jungle canopy; manicured lawns and gardens displaying both PNG and exotic plant species; excellent wildlife displays including cuscuses, birds of paradise, plumed pigeons, cassowaries and various parrots; and an enormous shadehouse in the shape of a map of PNG exhibiting plants from the various regions. It also has what is probably the best collection

ADRIAN LIPSCOMB

The cassowary is Papua New Guinea's biggest bird.

of native and hybrid orchids in PNG. The entrance fee is K5 for visitors and K2 for locals (a very fair discrimination).

Islands, Beaches & Reefs

The wreck of the Burns Philp cargo ship MV *MacDhui* can be seen just breaking the surface in Moresby Harbour, off Hanuabada. It was sunk by Japanese aircraft in the early days of their WWII involvement. Its mast now stands in front of the Royal Papua Yacht Club; the Burns Philp offices in Town have the captain's report to the owners on how he came to lose the ship.

Many expats have boats and the yacht club is busy on weekends. If you play your charm cards right, you may get asked out for the day. **Manubada (Local) Island** is used for weekend beach trips but beware – there is no shade. The **Bootless Bay** area (south-east of Port Moresby) and the other islands around the harbour are also popular.

Idler's Bay, on the Napa Napa Peninsula just east of Port Moresby, is a popular beach. It's a pleasant drive out beyond here to **Lea Lea**, a large coastal village which you get to by crossing the creek on a dugout canoe 'ferry' service. **Napa Napa** was once a nautical training centre and is now a fisheries research station.

Close to Napa Napa is **Lolorua Island**, also known as Double Island because during WWII it was neatly chopped in two by a bomb. Nearby Gemo Island was established as a leper colony in 1937 but the colony was later moved to Laloki. **Tatana Island**, between Hanuabada and Napa Napa, is joined to the mainland by a causeway and has a village on the north-west side.

Basilisk Passage is the deep, narrow entrance to the harbour of Port Moresby and was named by Captain Moresby after his ship, HMS *Basilisk*. Next to it is **Nateara Reef** on which the ship SS *Pruth* was wrecked in 1924. An attempt to sink it during WWII broke its hull in two. **Sinasi Reef** is a very beautiful reef outside the passage and is joined to **Daugo Island**, also known as Fisherman's Island. It has very pleasant white-sand beaches and is a popular excursion from Port Moresby.

Activities

Clubs Expats come and go with some regularity in PNG, so the clubs in which they are involved tend also to have high membership turnovers. If you are looking for a specific type of club, there is always the Yellow Pages or you could rely on the expat 'grapevine'. The Australian High Commission sponsors regular meetings of Aussie Wantoks, a social club for Australian expats, which is useful for this sort of information-swapping.

The PNG Bushwalkers' Association has regular weekend walks, barbecues and picnics, which give you a chance to see the country in company. Contact Dr Don York at the UPNG (☎ 326 1020) or write to PO Box 1335, Boroko.

If bird-watching is your thing, then PNG has enormous possibilities. The PNG Bird Society conducts regular excursions. Contact Will Glynn (☎ 325 2862) or write to PO Box 1598, Boroko.

The Port Moresby Road Runners are popular in Port Moresby; venues are advertised in Friday's *Post Courier*.

It's reasonably easy to join boat crews if you hang around the Royal Papua Yacht Club. There are some serious yachties who have done very well in international bluewater races. Water-skiing, scuba diving and game fishing are other activities, that are organised from the yacht club. Hiri canoe races often take place along the coast.

Diving There are some good reefs and plenty of fish close to Port Moresby. Most diving is around the Tahira Marine Park at Horseshoe Reef. There are two small wrecks here, both scuttled in 1978; one is a 19.5m government trawler/patrol boat and the other a 12m work boat. Loloata Island Resort (☎ 325 8590) is also an excellent place to test the waters and Dick Knight is very knowledgeable.

The *Dive Centre* (☎ 320 1200; fax 320 1257) is based in Ela Beach Hotel and offers diving trips, courses (using the hotel swimming pool) and equipment hire.

Tropical Diving Services (☎ 321 1768, PO Box 1745, Port Moresby) is at the Tahira Boating Centre on Bootless Bay and runs regular dives.

Organised Tours

Aloha Tours (☎ & fax 325 9447) runs a number of day and weekend trips around Port Moresby. It offers half-day (K35) and full-day tours (from K40), including Parliament House, the National Museum, National Botanic Gardens, artefact shops and a drive out to Sogeri and Varirata National Park.

South Pacific Tours (☎ 321 3500; fax 321 3136) offers day tours to Varirata National Park, the Bomana War Cemetery and Owers' Corner, as well as organised Kokoda Trail treks.

MBA's small planes have 'milk run' circuits, including some picturesque and steep airstrips in the Owen Stanley Range. MBA calls it the Mountain Explorer Trip and it operates occasionally on Sundays if there are enough people interested. It takes in Ononge, Tapini (where the runway is quite hairraising), Woitape, and Fane. Lunch is provided and the whole experience is well worth it at around K120.

Special Events

In mid-June on the Queen's Birthday weekend there is a Port Moresby show with spectacular displays of traditional dancing.

The Hiri Moale, held around the Independence Day celebrations in mid-September, celebrates the giant Papuan trading canoes which once plied the coast. It sometimes seems to be more of an opportunity for Coke and Pepsi to battle it out than a cultural festival, but there are bound to be some events of interest.

Places to Stay

Places to stay are scattered around the suburbs and are generally pretty expensive. You'll find places near the airport, in Boroko, Waigani, Koki, Ela Beach and Town.

If you have a car, it doesn't matter where

you stay, but if you are dependent on PMVs, Boroko is the most convenient location.

Not much happens in Port Moresby on weekends, so it is worth considering a trip to Yule Island or the Hisiu Beach Resort, northwest of Port Moresby, or to Loloata Island, to the south-east, where there's a more expensive (but much more easily accessible) resort. See the Central & Oro Provinces chapter for details on these places. There are also a couple of places on the way to Sogeri which are popular weekend retreats. See the Around Port Moresby section.

Places to Stay – bottom end

Accommodation in PNG is notable for being unreasonably expensive. Port Moresby is no exception and some of the bottom-end options available a few years ago (such as the Salvation Army Hostel) no longer cater for travellers. So you are advised to make the best of what is available and book well in advance.

The CWA (Country Women's Association) has a hostel, *Jessie Wyatt House* (☎ 325 3646; mobile 693 1257; PO Box 1222, Boroko), on Taurama Rd across from the hospital. It's modern, clean and has a kitchen. Singles/doubles/triples cost K30/ 55/60 and there will be a key deposit. Each room has a fridge and there's free tea and coffee. There are only six rooms – five doubles and one triple – so it's advisable to book ahead.

It's some way from the Boroko shopping centre; it's easiest to get there by PMV. Most PMVs run to or from Town via Three Mile Hill and the Sir Hubert Murray Highway but some detour to the east through Badili, Kila Kila village and Korobosea (running past the hostel on Taurama Rd). Catch a PMV marked 'Kila Kila' and ask for the hospital. The closest PMV stop is near the hospital's Gate 4.

The *YWCA Hostel* (☎ 325 6522; PO Box 1883, Boroko) is at the top of Three Mile Hill between Koki and Boroko. PMVs run past regularly between Town and Boroko. There are only a few rooms for visitors (men are welcome which is not usually the case at YWCAs in PNG), otherwise it's all permanent residents. It costs K35 per person. During the week there's a 10.30 pm curfew (midnight at weekends) but Port Moresby's nightlife is unlikely to make this a problem.

Places to Stay – middle

Amber's Inn (☎ 325 5091/323 0624; fax 325 9565; PO Box 1139, Boroko) is probably the best value in town and is a very good mid-range hotel by PNG standards. There is a pleasant garden with a small swimming pool and *haus win* (gazebo-like structure).

It's on Mairi Place just around the corner from Angau Drive in Boroko. It offers a free airport pick-up (although it is not always reliable or punctual). Rooms with fans and clean shared bathrooms cost from K47/69 for singles/doubles and K89/109 for triples/quads. Rooms with TV, air-con and bathrooms cost K78/90 a single/double. All these prices include cooked breakfast. Dinners are available but are not great value at K15. There is a payphone next to reception which, frustratingly, is very temperamental, and there is an incomprehensible loudspeaker paging system which is meant to advise guests if there are incoming telephone calls.

The *Hibiscus Motel* (☎ 321 7983; fax 321 7396; PO Box 1319, Port Moresby) is in Town on the corner of Hunter and Douglas Sts, near the Travelodge. It is an old motel which has been refurbished and, after a period of vast overcharging, has settled down to a reasonable tariff – it is now quite good value. Singles/doubles/triples with shared bathroom and light breakfast cost K55/75/90. They have a special 'long stay' (monthly) rate of K40 per night. They also have a pick-up service from the airport but its reliability is doubtful.

The *Granville Motel* (☎ 325 7155; fax 325 7672; PO Box 1246, Boroko) is at Six Mile, only about a kilometre from the old airport terminal but it is not advisable to walk in this area, particularly at night. They can organise someone to pick you up; many PMVs run past its gate. It was built for Ok Tedi mine workers so the rooms are fairly spartan, but they're more than adequate and everything is clean. There's a pool, a tennis court, a haus win, and the meals are reasonable. Singles/doubles with shared bathroom cost K79/92 – pretty close to top-end prices – and there are also some self-contained units with weekly rates. They have hire cars available.

The *Budget Inn* (☎ 323 1611; fax 325 5991; PO Box 6361, Boroko) is at Six Mile, on the road to the old airport terminal. It is likely to be even less convenient with the opening of the new highway. It is reputed to be reasonably clean but not safe. People have complained of theft. It is also apparently noisy day and night, with drinking, prostitution and gambling. Rooms are from K35, but some are much more.

The *Lamana Motel* (☎ 323 2333; fax 323 2444; PO Box 495, Waigani) is reportedly worth trying. It is located in the centre of Waigani. Rooms are apparently nice and cost K80/90. They have a pick-up service from the airport and accept most credit cards.

Places to Stay – top end
The prices at this end of the market are simply outrageous, but it seems there are people who will pay them, especially those with expense accounts.

The *Ela Beach Hotel* (☎ 321 2100; fax 321 2434; PO Box 813, Port Moresby) is in a good location, looking out over the beach, a short stroll from the town centre. Despite being refurbished, it still feels a little like a high-security office block. There's a swimming pool and a popular bar and restaurant. Unfortunately, there is also a large area set aside for poker machines which has spoilt what limited atmosphere the place once had. Rooms cost from K120 (single or double) with K15 per extra person.

The *Gateway Motel* (☎ 325 3855; fax 325 4585; PO Box 1215, Boroko), part of the Coral Sea chain, is near the old air terminal. It has 95 rooms and 60 self-contained units with a swimming pool, gymnasium and squash courts. This is probably the most cost-effective of the top-enders. Rooms are very comfortable, clean and spacious, and the staff are friendly. There is a good restaurant, coffee shop and a couple of bars – one at poolside. Rooms are from K175.

The nearby *Airways Motel & Apartments* (☎ 324 5200; fax 325 0759; PO Box 1942, Boroko) overlooks the airport from Jacksons Parade and provides top-quality facilities. Rooms go for about K185, with special rates for apartments or weekly rental. There is an open-air bar overlooking the runways, a Greek restaurant, a sports club, a gym and a pool.

The *Islander Travelodge* (☎ 325 5955/ 325 3196; fax 325 0837; PO Box 1981, Boroko) is in Waigani between the Waigani central government complex and Boroko. It's part of the Travelodge chain and offers more space but less spectacular views than the Port Moresby Travelodge in Town. It has its own health club. Single/double rooms start at K200, but a 25% discount is available for company or corporate guests if they ask.

The *Port Moresby Travelodge* (☎ 321 2266/321 1987; fax 321 7534; PO Box 1661, Port Moresby) is the top-rated place to stay in Port Moresby. It's conspicuously located in Town on the corner of Douglas, Mary and Hunter Sts – right across from ANG House. Along with ANG House, it dominates the skyline. The rooms offer some stunning views over Port Moresby and the prices are similarly sky-high. Naturally the Travelodge offers all the features you'd expect – air-con throughout, restaurant, bars, souvenir shop, conference facilities, swimming pool and entertainment. Room prices start at K220, even with some form of corporate discount.

Places to Eat – budget
There are very few cheap, reasonably good quality places to fill the void between kai/ sandwich bars and expensive restaurants. If you are on a tight budget and can't stomach the thought of a staple diet of greasy fish and chicken, your best bet is to stay somewhere that has cooking facilities. Most of the kai-bars close fairly early, so by about 7 pm your options have shrunk to the hotels, clubs and restaurants.

The *Asian Aromas* coffee shop in the Steamships arcade is a good place for coffee and light meals. It has wonderful air-con to help escape the heat of the streets. A milkshake costs K3 and toasted sandwiches go for K5; they also have Chinese food. There is a cheap kai-bar upstairs in the same arcade.

Not far from Town, the *Royal Papua Yacht Club* sells snacks such as hamburgers and is a nice place for a beer. Theoretically you have to be signed in by a member.

In Boroko, the *Fountain Coffee Shop* on the first floor of Ori Lavi House (near the footbridge) is open for breakfast (K2.50 for eggs on toast) and lunch (K2.70 for toasted sandwiches or K5.50 for a mixed grill). On Tabari Place, the *Sapphire Bistro* is upstairs in the Hugo building, next to the post office. It's open daily from 8 am to 5 pm for breakfast and lunch. Breakfast is a little expensive, but toasted sandwiches are reasonable for K5, and staff still serve German specialities such as bockwurst, kassler and eisbein for lunch. *PJ's Coffee Shop* on the first floor of the Garden City Offices offers lunches of pork chops or pepper steak 'with garden vegies' for between K8 and K9. Obviously the nearby Peace Corps office has influenced this better-than-average nutritional offering.

American-style fast food has also arrived in Port Moresby in the guise of *Big Rooster*. There's one in Boroko on Waigani Drive, a short walk from Sir Hubert Murray Highway intersection, another in Koki on the main drag near the Salvation Army Hostel and another in Town on Douglas St. They're not cheap but they're open till 8 pm and offer standard variations on the chicken-in-a-box theme.

There are a few kai-bars around Waigani, but the best options are the snack bar under the forecourt of Parliament House and the two on the ground floor of Haus Tomakala, opposite the Haus Marea.

A good-value place for a sit-down meal is the *University Coffee Shop* and it's also a good place to meet people. If you enter via the main university entrance, it's to your left past the mural. It is hard to find, as there is no sign and if you walk too far you end up in the students' cafeteria where the food will probably turn you off whatever you intended

to eat in the coffee shop. Look for the poem on the wall and then an unmarked door on your right. It's open Monday to Friday from 9 am to 3.30 pm and you can get a hot meal for about K3.50, as well as sandwiches and coffee.

The nearby Gateway Motel has a *pizza bar* offering what are reputed to be the best pizzas in Port Moresby; a medium supreme costs K12. It has a daily takeaway service (6 to 10 pm). The Gateway's restaurant is also good value if you seek a little quality – a T-bone is K20 and lobster mornay is K25.

Don't forget the markets. Gordons is the best but Koki also has a good variety of fruit and especially seafood. There are a couple of smaller markets, including one at Boroko at the end of Okari St. Often the prices are clearly displayed, but even if they're not you're unlikely to be ripped off. Bargaining is out.

Places to Eat – mid-range & expensive

As well as the places listed here, it's worth checking out the various clubs, such as the *Port Moresby Golf Club* (☎ 325 5367) in Waigani, which often have relatively inexpensive meals, especially at lunch time. Most welcome visitors, although some have strict dress codes.

Town The *Green Jade* Chinese restaurant (☎ 321 4611) at the Royal Papua Yacht Club is open for lunch and dinner most days.

The Port Moresby Travelodge's *Mala Mala Coffee Shop*, more like a restaurant than a coffee shop, is open for lunch and dinner. The food is good and the prices are not too bad. A dinner buffet is served every night for K18.50 with different themes each night – Indian curry, Mexican, Asian, roasts, for example. Coffee and desserts are extra. The Travelodge's upmarket *Rapala Restaurant* has a good reputation and prices which reasonably reflect the good quality – entrees are from K12 and main courses from K24.

The *Orchid Garden Restaurant* (☎ 321 2765) is a popular Chinese place, opposite the Catholic church, and the *Aviat Club*

(☎ 321 4261), on Aviat St, is reputed to serve excellent food.

Boroko Check out the *Boroko Restaurant* (☎ 325 0338), at shops 5 and 6, Trophy Haus, Angau Drive, opposite the Garden City Offices. It has an extensive Asian menu with main courses between K12 and K20. It is open daily for lunch and dinner.

If you prefer Korean-style food, *Arirang House* (☎ 325 1395) on Reke St (a short walk from Amber's Inn) is open daily for dinner and for lunch from Monday to Friday.

The *Daikoku Japanese Steak House* (☎ 325 3857), above the Taurama supermarket between Boroko and Three Mile on the Sir Hubert Murray Highway, is a popular place.

The *Kwangtung Village* (☎ 325 8997) on Boio St, East Boroko, has good food – it's said to have the best Chinese food in Port Moresby. It is moderately expensive and if you drive to this place, it's not a bad idea to tip the guy outside to watch your car.

Elsewhere The Islander Travelodge in Waigani has a pricey *restaurant* and a more reasonable *coffee shop*.

The upmarket *Golden Bowl* (☎ 325 1656) is in front of Haus Tomakala and serves fairly pricey Chinese food daily except Saturday; the menu is large.

If you're not counting your kina too carefully and you've got an excuse for a special occasion (like a farewell dinner), try the Airways Motel & Apartments, which overlooks the airport and has an attractive open-air bar. Its *Bacchus Restaurant* is excellent, with a Greek-oriented menu. There's even a traditional wood-fired oven to make the pita bread. This is an ideal spot to sip a drink on a balmy tropical night or wait for a flight – there's a TV-link to the airport which displays flight information, but bear in mind that it will be a long hike to the new terminal buildings.

Entertainment

There has been little nightlife at all in Port Moresby over 1996 and 1997 because of the curfew which kept Moresbyites inside after 9 or 10 pm. Most socialising among expats inevitably takes place behind the doors of private homes or clubs – they can be an exclusive breed. Now that the curfew has been lifted, some life might be breathed back into Port Moresby's nights – but it is still not wise to wander the streets.

The Royal Papua Yacht Club holds a *disco* every Thursday night and the Islander Travelodge has *Party Night* every Friday, with happy hour drinks and a disco. It also has *Big Day Out* from 3 pm on Saturday, with live bands, and *Teen Zoo* on Sunday from 2 to 7 pm, with music, games and soft drinks specially for teenagers for K4.

You could also ask at the university to see if there's anything happening (check out the noticeboards at the Waigani campus).

Things to Buy

PNG Arts, a massive warehouse of artefacts from all over PNG, is on the new dual-carriage highway (formerly Spring Garden Rd) on the Gordons side of Waigani Drive. It can also be accessed from Goroa St and is open daily from 9 am (11 am on Sunday) to 4 pm. Its prices are quite reasonable, it accepts all major credit cards and travellers cheques and can organise freight and documentation on your behalf. A good booklet entitled *The Artefacts and Crafts of PNG* details the various regional styles of art and craft and is available for K7.

The other main artefact shop, Hanuacraft, apparently has a similar range. It is located near PNG Arts but in a back street on the other side of the highway. It too advertises that it is open seven days a week.

There is often a good display of artefacts and contemporary art on the footpath outside the Port Moresby Travelodge. It is worth stopping to have a look – these guys can be very good and are interesting to talk to.

You can buy *bilums* (string bags) and a few other types of artefacts at Gordons Market, although one traveller reports paying more here than at PNG Arts.

The Institute for PNG Studies at the northern end of Angau Drive in Boroka has some interesting tapes of traditional music for sale.

Getting There & Away

Port Moresby is the hub for domestic and international air travel, although international flights can now take you direct to Mt Hagen or Alotau. If you plan to spend most of your time in the Highlands, then it is probably better to fly direct to Mt Hagen (if you are coming from Australia); similarly, if you plan to see the eastern islands it is probably better to go direct to Alotau. There are more and more flights opening up on these routes, so you may be in the fortunate position of being able to miss Port Moresby entirely. The odds are, however, that at some stage you will have to visit here.

Some of the more remote places (eg Kundiawa) can only be accessed by air via Port Moresby – but there are other ways of getting around. You could, for example, walk the Kokoda Trail to Popondetta then fly to Lae (K150) or catch a boat to Lae with Lutheran Shipping (K23 deck class). Or you could get to Kerema by taking a PMV to Iokea, then a motor canoe to Malalaua (usually leaves Friday night and takes five hours), then catch a PMV to Kerema.

You might, if you're lucky, find a ship travelling from Port Moresby right around the eastern end of PNG to the north coast. There are no passenger ships or freighters officially carrying passengers, which isn't to say that ingenuity and persistence won't get you a berth. You could travel by PMV to Kupiano and from there hop by village boats around the coast to Alotau. The further east you go, the friendlier the people become.

Air The new international and domestic air terminals at Jackson International Airport were due to be opened in late 1997, so details of their layout and facilities will have to wait until the next edition. The international terminal will, however, have covered walkways extending right to the aircraft, so the traditional blast of hot air off the tarmac as you leave the plane will be a thing of the past. All the major domestic and international operators should have offices in the new buildings, so check there if you want to compare schedules and prices. There will be a new control tower too.

Air Niugini also has office in Boroko (Garden City Offices in Angau Drive) and Town (NIC Haus, opposite Steamships). For all reservations and reconfirmations phone ☎ 327 3555. Qantas' head office (☎ 321 1200) is behind ANG House in Town. British Airways (☎ 321 1211), Singapore Airlines (☎ 320 2222) and Solomons Airlines (☎ 325 5724) have representatives in Port Moresby.

Note that there is a K15 departure tax for all international flights.

The prices for flights to most centres from Port Moresby are given in their appropriate Getting There & Away sections. One-way fares from Port Moresby include:

Destination	Fare	Airline
Alotau	K125	Air Niugini/MBA
Daru	K144	Air Niugini/MBA
Kavieng	K288	Air Niugini
Lae	K118	Air Niugini/MBA
Lorengau	K254	Air Niugini
Madang	K159	Air Niugini
Mt Hagen	K163	Air Niugini/MBA
Popondetta	K72	Air Niugini/MBA
Rabaul	K231	Air Niugini
Wewak	K222	Air Niugini

Road

Rural PMVs run to a limited number of destinations from Port Moresby – there are a limited number of roads. Most leave from Gordons Market.

There are four car rental companies in Port Moresby. Undoubtedly they will all have offices at the new air terminal buildings. The Airways Motel & Apartments at the airport offers guests a discount on Thrifty cars. The Granville Motel offers slightly better rates than the major car rental companies. See the Getting Around chapter for rates.

Avis-Nationwide
    PO Box 1533, Port Moresby (☎ 325 8299;
    fax 325 3767)
Budget
    PO Box 1215, Boroko (☎ 325 4111;
    fax 325 7853)
Hertz
    PO Box 4126, Boroko (☎ 325 4999;
    fax 325 6985)

Thrifty
PO Box 1975, Boroko (☎ 323 2333;
fax 325 8293)

Boat There are no regular passenger boats sailing out of Port Moresby. Many of the large freighters do have passenger facilities, but none of the shipping companies officially allow passengers. Asking around at the wharves or meeting someone who works for a shipping company (most offices are near the wharves) might get you a berth. If you want to go to the gulf, ask around the smaller boats moored at the jetties north of the main wharf.

Heading east towards Milne Bay you might have better luck going to Kupiano and finding a small boat or canoe there. You're unlikely to find one running the whole distance, so allow plenty of time and be prepared to stay in villages.

Getting Around

The Airport Most places to stay will collect you from the airport if you ask when you make your booking. There will, no doubt, still be plenty of taxis hanging around outside the new terminal, except perhaps in the early morning. A taxi to Boroko will cost K10, to Koki K15 and to Town between K15 and K20.

PMV departures are frequent between 6.30 am and 6 pm, and a single journey anywhere in Port Moresby costs K0.50. PMVs will probably not be allowed near the terminal buildings (as was the case with the old terminal), but they should be a short walk away. See the following PMV section for some route numbers.

If you arrive after dark (that is, after about 6 pm), the only safe option for a newcomer is a taxi. It's much easier if you arrive in daylight, especially if you're a woman travelling solo.

Getting to the airport very early can be difficult, unless your accommodation can provide a bus. Consider staying nearby or book a taxi for the airport the night before. They usually show up, but often much later than you requested. They know the flight

schedules and will race you to the airport and arrive with a comfortable two minutes to spare!

PMV Port Moresby has an efficient PMV service, with frequent connections on all the routes between 6.30 am and 7 pm (or usually a bit later). The standard K0.50 for any trip in Port Moresby is great value. Pay the driver's assistant after you find a seat, but not with large bills. Yell 'stop, driver!' when you want to get off. In Town, established stops are indicated by yellow roadside poles.

Bear in mind that the PMV system might change with the opening of the new dual-carriage highway. At the moment, however, the main interchange point is in Boroko, a very busy place. Heading towards Town, PMVs stop near the dusty park; heading away from Town they stop near the pedestrian overpass. In Town, the main stops are towards the south end of Musgrave St.

The PMVs get very crowded at peak hours and especially on Friday evenings, when everyone is doing their weekend shopping, so it's worth avoiding them then if you can.

Most PMVs currently travel along the Sir Hubert Murray Highway between Boroko (Four Mile) and Town, but some head east through Kila Kila village (useful for the hospital and the CWA Hostel) and some head east through Hohola to Gordons or Gerehu, avoiding the traffic snarl around Boroko.

PMVs run set routes and have route numbers painted on the front. From the airport, No 5 runs down backroads to Boroko then down the Sir Hubert Murray Highway to Town, passing the YWCA Hostel and the Salvation Army Hostel in Koki. No 10 runs to Boroko, past the hospital and the CWA Hostel, down backroads to Koki and then into Town. No 15 runs to Boroko but not Koki. No 4 runs all the way from Hanuabada to Gordons Market. No 7 also runs to Gordons and past the turn-off to the Waigani government offices. No 11 runs from Boroko to Waigani.

As well as numbers, most PMVs also have destinations painted on the front. Outside peak hours, before 8 am and after 4 pm, few

PMVs run directly to the Waigani government offices; those that do are marked 'Office' or 'W'gani Office'. At other times look for the PMVs marked 'Gerehu' that run along Waigani Drive past the government offices and the university to the suburb of the same name. They'll drop you off on the main road, a short walk from the offices. If you're going to Town, look for PMVs going to 'Kone' (Konedobu, the old government centre between Town and Hanuabada) or 'H'bada' (Hanuabada). PMVs to the airport usually show a '7 Mile' sign.

Taxi Taxis are readily available at the airport, the big hotels and on the streets. While many have meters, most don't work. Agree on a price before you get in and be aware that there is some room for negotiation, but don't let it get acrimonious. It's considered a bit standoffish for men to sit in the back seat of a taxi. From Boroko it's between K10 and K15 to Waigani, Town or the airport.

Around Port Moresby

Port Moresby is the centre for a limited road network so there are a number of car or PMV trips you can make. There are also some interesting spots you can reach with short, relatively inexpensive flights.

If you continue out on the Sir Hubert Murray Highway, past the airport and turn right just before the Moitaka Showground & Speedway, a sealed road takes you along the Sogeri Gorge up to the cool Sogeri Plateau, the beautiful Rouna Falls, Varirata National Park and the beginning of the Kokoda Trail.

After the Moitaka Showgrounds, the road becomes the unsealed Hiritano Highway and turns north-west through Brown River, passing several attractive riverside picnic spots, continuing past the turn-off to Poukama (where there's a ferry to Yule Island) and on to Bereina and Iokea. To the south-east, the Magi Highway runs past Bootless Bay and the Loloata Island Resort and many fine beaches, continuing on to

Kupiano. See the Central & Oro Provinces chapter for details on wider travelling in Central Province.

SOGERI ROAD

The trip out to the Sogeri Plateau is one of the most popular weekend jaunts for Port Moresbyites. It's only 46km to Sogeri but there is quite enough to see and do to make it a full-day trip. You can get out there by PMV – some run regularly from Gordons Market and Boroko. The fare is K2. The road is surfaced to Sogeri and all the way down to the Varirata National Park.

Head out of Town on the Sir Hubert Murray Highway and turn right about 2km past the airport. There's a crocodile farm just before the turn-off and the Bomana War Cemetery is after the turn-off.

Moitaka Wildlife

Moitaka Wildlife is a few kilometres northeast of Port Moresby before the turn-off to Sogeri. Unless you make prior arrangements, it is only open to the public on Friday afternoon between 2 and 4 pm – feeding time for the crocodiles, who are hearty but infrequent eaters. The farm also has an enclosure of deer and some native animals and birds, including a raggiana bird of paradise which is quite an amazing show-off. Admission is K7.

Bomana War Cemetery

Not far past the turn-off to Sogeri is the large and carefully tended WWII cemetery where 4000 Australian and Papua New Guinean soldiers are buried. (The American soldiers who died in PNG were generally shipped home for burial.) It is a sobering experience to visit the graves of so many young men who died in a very bloody and horrific campaign.

Sogeri

A few kilometres past the cemetery, the road begins to wind up the Laloki River's gorge. Just past the turn-off to the Varirata National Park is a lookout point for the spectacular Rouna Falls ; before the hydroelectric power

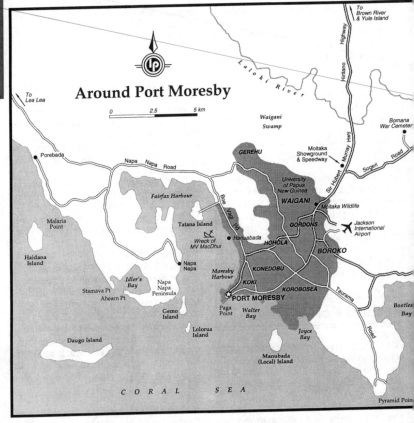

Around Port Moresby

plants were installed they were even more impressive. There are also good views back towards Port Moresby. You can have a look at the hydro plants and, just before reaching Sogeri, you pass the Kokoda Trail junction.

Apart from its cool climate (thanks to its 600m altitude), Sogeri has a pleasant Sunday market with a good selection of fresh vegetables. The road continues beyond Sogeri, via the popular swimming spot of Crystal Rapids to Musgrave River and the Sirinumu Dam. At Crystal Rapids they may charge a few kina to enter with a car. If you walk in (it's not far) it's less than a kina. The dam

controls the water flow to the Laloki River, which in turn supplies the Rouna hydroelectric station.

Places to Stay & Eat The *Bluff Inn Motel* (☎ 328 1223; PO Box 7347, Boroko) is on Sogeri Road at 17 Mile, by the river, and has rooms for around K100 per person, including all meals.

Also on Sogeri Road, the *Kokoda Trail Motel* (☎ 325 4403; fax 325 3322; PO Box 5014, Boroko) is about 40km from Port Moresby. It overlooks the river and has an open-air bar, a reasonable restaurant and a

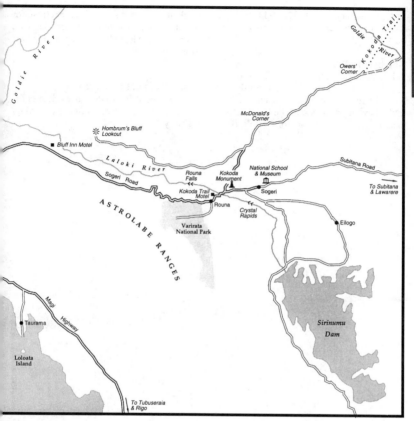

swimming pool. Because of the altitude the evenings are cool. Expats like this place as a weekend escape from the tensions of Port Moresby and there are often special rates – but even the regular rates are very reasonable. The staff can arrange transport, for a price.

Varirata National Park

The turn-off to the park, PNG's first national park, is right after the second hydro-station on the Sogeri Road. From this turn-off it's 8km to the park. There is a variety of interesting and clearly marked walking trails in the park and some excellent lookouts back to Port Moresby and the coast.

From June to November, in the early morning or evening, it is possible to see birds of paradise in a clearly signposted display tree above the circuit track.

Places to Stay It's possible to camp in the Varirata National Park but your belongings are not secure. Alternatively, there is the *Varirata National Park Lodge* where bedding and cooking facilities are provided, but you must bring your own food and utensils. For further information phone the ranger-in-charge on ☎ 325 9340 or the national parks service's assistant secretary on ☎ 325 4247.

Hombrum's Bluff

A little way down the Kokoda Trail road, a smaller road branches off back towards Port Moresby running parallel to Sogeri Road but high above it on the top of the Laloki River canyon wall. It leads to Hombrum's Bluff Lookout, which was used as a retreat for important military brass during the war. There are excellent views back towards Port Moresby.

East & West of Port Moresby

See the Central & Oro Provinces chapter for details on the unsealed Hiritano and Magi highways.

Central & Oro Provinces

Central Province

Land Area 29,940 sq km
Population 410,000
Capital Port Moresby

History
Evidence of human habitation around Kosipe up to 26,000 years ago has been found, but it is believed that coastal people arrived much more recently – within the last 2000 years. There were extensive trade networks along the coast using large two-masted *lakatois*, or sailing boats. The *hiri* trade, between Motuan villages and their respective counterparts in the Gulf region, revolved around sago and clay pots, although axes and shells were also common trade items.

The London Missionary Society established itself in Papua New Guinea in the 1870s and the Catholic Mission of the Sacred Heart made its headquarters on Yule Island in 1885. In 1908, the Seventh-Day Adventists started a mission near Sogeri.

In 1906 the colony was handed over to the newly independent Australia; in 1907, Sir Hubert Murray took over the administration of Papua, as it had been renamed, and ran it until he died in 1940, at the age of 78, while out 'on patrol' at Samarai in Milne Bay Province.

During WWII, the Kokoda Trail became a strategic route linking the north side of the island to the south and was the scene of fierce fighting between the Australians and Japanese.

Geography
Central Province consists of a narrow coastal strip, with a 500km coastline, rising rapidly to the Owen Stanley Range. Port Moresby, built around one of a number of natural harbours, is located in the centre of a large area of dry grasslands on this coastal strip; swamps and tidal flats can be found else-

HIGHLIGHTS
- Trekking on the Kokoda Trail
- Staying at one of the village guesthouses near Tufi and catching lobsters from outrigger canoes
- Tracking down the magnificent Queen Alexandra birdwing butterfly in its jungle habitat
- Seeing the sites of WWII battles at Buna and Gona
- Buying some of the Yiaku tapa cloth or Wanigela clay pots
- Diving and snorkelling at Loloata Island

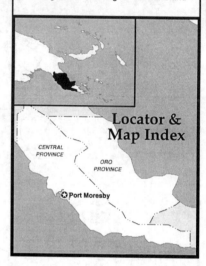

Locator & Map Index

CENTRAL PROVINCE

ORO PROVINCE

Port Moresby

where on the coast. The highest points are Mt Victoria (4035m) and Mt Albert Edward (3990m), both due north of Port Moresby in the Owen Stanley Range. Lake Sirinumu, near Sogeri, is one of Papua New Guinea's largest lakes.

People
Many of the coastal people of Central Province seem more closely related to the Polynesians of the Pacific Islands than to the

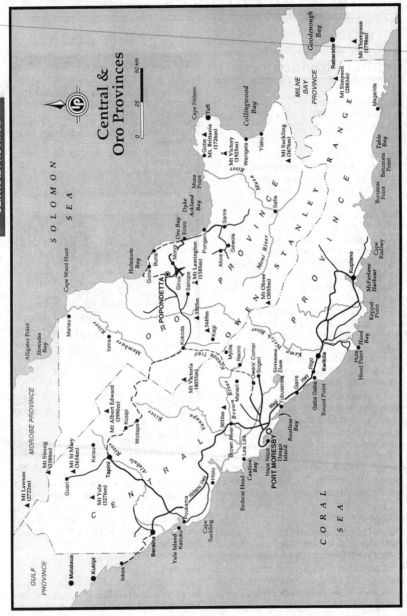

Central &
Oro Provinces

stockier inland people. The indigenous groups around Port Moresby were the Motu, a seagoing, trading people and the Koitabu, an inland people with hunting and gardening skills who coexisted with the Motu. Further into the mountains lived the warlike Koiari people and, to the north-west, the Mekeo.

During the early years of British and then Australian contact, the Motu language was adapted into a lingua franca called Police Motu. Its use as lingua franca has now been usurped by Pidgin, although many Papuans still speak Police Motu.

Getting There & Away

See the Getting There & Away section in the Port Moresby chapter for details on travelling to/from Central Province.

HIRITANO HIGHWAY

The coast west of Port Moresby, connected by road all the way to Bereina, is the home of the Mekeo people, who are noted for their colourful dancing costumes and face painting. On ceremonial occasions the men paint their faces in striking geometric designs.

You begin to escape the dry climate of Port Moresby by the time you get to Brown River, a popular picnic spot about 40km away, passing teak plantations on the way. You can get as far as Iokea in Gulf Province by PMV.

Brown River

Brown River is a pleasant spot for swimming and a good place for quiet rafting, either on inner tubes or a rubber dinghy. Take the road up the river – it turns off the Hiritano Highway about 1km before the bridge. It's best to have two cars: one to leave at the village by the turn-off and the other (preferably 4WD) to drive up the river to another village where you can leave the car right by the water. You then raft down to the bridge and drive back to get the other car.

The trip takes three to four pleasant hours. Don't be tempted to go downstream from the bridge – you can get tangled up in log jams and would, in any case, have trouble getting back to the bridge.

Yule Island

The missionaries who arrived at Yule Island in 1885 were some of the first European visitors to the Papuan coast of New Guinea. Later the island became a government headquarters, from which government and mission workers penetrated into the central mountains in some of the earliest exploration of the country. Today the district local government headquarters is on the mainland at Bereina, but there is still a large Catholic mission and Carmelite convent on Yule Island where you can stay.

One of France's top WWI air aces, M Bourgade, was an early mission worker and you can see his grave on Yule Island.

Place to Stay The *Carmelite Convent* (☎ 325 8023) is an operating convent but still welcomes visitors. You sleep in the original nuns' cells. You can cook your own food; fresh fish is available. It's a pretty place and worth the hassle of getting here.

Getting There & Away Turn off the Hiritano Highway about 38km past Agu Vari. From the turn-off, which is signposted, you travel another 20km to Poukama, where there is a car park and a canoe to take you to the island (K2 per person).

Poukama is about 160km (a three-hour drive) from Port Moresby. By PMV it's about 4½ hours and costs K9. A PMV leaves Gordons Market early but not every day.

There's an airstrip at Kairuku, the main village on the island, and it's possible to organise charters.

Hisiu

The *Hisiu Beach Resort* is a village-operated resort funded by the EU (European Union), although it bears no resemblance to the usual village guesthouses in PNG. It is very popular at weekends with expats from Port Moresby. There are six two-bedroom bungalows right on the beach and the area is excellent for fishing, surfing or swimming. Tennis and volleyball facilities are available. The bungalows are modern fibro and corrugated iron affairs with electricity, hot showers, toilets and fridges – so they can provide a degree of comfort unknown in most villages. But you must bring food, cooking utensils and linen. It is 100km north-west of Port Moresby or about 1½ hours along the Hiritano Highway. It costs K75 per night for a bungalow at weekends or K55 during the week. Book through Westpac Travel in Boroko (☎ 325 4500).

MAGI HIGHWAY

At Six Mile, instead of turning left to the airport, turn right onto Dogura Road. As you're leaving Port Moresby, the road passes through a shanty settlement. You have to slow down for speed humps in the settlement. The road circles round Bootless Bay to the small marina (Tahira Boating Centre) from which the ferry crosses to Loloata Island.

Loloata Island

Around 20km east of Port Moresby, Loloata Island in Bootless Bay is another popular weekend escape – midweek is even better. A day trip to the Loloata Island Resort (☎ 325 8590; fax 325 1369, PO Box 5290, Boroko) costs K30 or K15 for children. The resort has snorkelling, fishing, sailboarding and diving equipment for hire. A wrecked, but intact, WWII Boston Havoc bomber is on the reef near the resort. For the truly lazy there is a bar and a fine collection of old *New Yorker* magazines. There's a licensed restaurant and the dinners are excellent.

Loloata Island isn't a flashy place, but it's relaxed and a welcome escape from the tensions of Port Moresby.

To get there, drive out on the Rigo Road (which meets the airport road in Six Mile) to the Tahira Boating Centre on Bootless Bay. None of the PMVs runs all the way. The resort's ferry makes trips to the island at 8.30 am and 3.30 pm (5.15 pm on Friday).

The resort's comfortable accommodation costs K100 per person per day, with meals included.

Along the Coast

A little further on there is a turn-off to

Tubusereia, a big Motuan coastal village with houses built on stilts over the water. There are, unfortunately, few reminders of the attractive place it must have been. Corrugated iron, rusting car bodies and rubbish are the 20th-century additions.

The road continues past Gaire and Gaba Gaba, turns inland to Rigo and Kwikila, then back to the coast again at Hula on Hood Bay, another village close to the mouth of the Kemp Welch River. There are many fine beaches along this road.

TAPINI & WOITAPE

• *postcode 166*

If you want to look at the high country behind the coastal strip, experience one of the most heart-in-mouth airstrips in PNG or try a lesser known but interesting walk, then Tapini is a good place to visit. It is a pretty little station at a bit under 1000m altitude.

The airstrip is amazing. Carved into a hillside, it runs steeply uphill and ends in a sheer face so you can only come in one way. When you leave downhill, the strip drops off sheer at the end. You've got a choice of flying or falling.

Bushwalking

There are interesting walks around Tapini and most are not difficult. The Catholic fathers bequeathed the area an excellent network of well-graded tracks which closely follow the contours (that is, they're not steep, a rarity in PNG). The tracks are wide, well defined and, at one time, took mule-trains. Several missions in the area have accommodation.

Lonely Planet's *Bushwalking in Papua New Guinea* details a number of these walks; the Tapini Lodge and Owen Stanley Lodge in Woitape can give you information.

There is also a rough road from Tapini to Guari where the once-fearsome Kunimaipa people lived. In just 50km, the road climbs up to nearly 3000m and drops down to about 700m. Guari is just an airstrip with no real village but there are some nice walks in the valley below. You could do a circle trek out to the Kamali Mission.

June to October are the walking months; June to August are the best.

Places to Stay & Eat

Near Woitape, the *Fatima Mission* may still have accommodation, otherwise see if you can meet some local people and stay in a house. The two hotels in the area are very expensive.

The small *Tapini Lodge* (☎ 329 9237; PO Box 6972, Boroko) is near the airstrip and charges around K130 per person, including meals. The *Owen Stanley Lodge*, also known as Woitape Lodge (☎ 325 7999; PO Box 6036, Boroko), in Woitape, is a small place charging around K130 per person, including meals, snacks, guides for walks and fishing.

Getting There & Away

Woitape is connected to the coast by a spectacular road and there are PMVs to Port Moresby most days for about K12. It's a long trip.

MBA's Sunday milk-run of mountain airstrips includes Woitape. See the Organised Tours section in the Port Moresby chapter.

Kokoda Trail

Mention walking tracks in PNG and the famed Kokoda Trail is the one most likely to spring to mind. But while its historical connections make it a big attraction, there are better and more interesting walks.

Linking the north and south coasts, the trail was first used by miners struggling north to the Yodda Kokoda goldfields of the 1890s, but it was WWII that brought it to the attention of the world (see The Kokoda Trail aside).

WALKING THE KOKODA TRAIL

The Kokoda Trail is the most popular walking track in PNG. From a cultural point of view there are more interesting walks. But there are also good arguments in the trail's favour – it passes through spectacular country and is a practical link between the south and north coasts. And the trail's dramatic role in WWII provides an emotional appeal. Walking from one end to the other is a feat of which to be proud.

The straight-line distance between each end of the trail – Owers' Corner and Kokoda – is about 60km, but for the walker it is more than 90km. But this gives no impression of the actual difficulty; it's bloody hard work. The trail is a continual series of ups and downs – generally steep, exhausting ups and muddy, slippery downs. Over the whole trail you gain and lose 6000m (nearly 20,000ft) in altitude.

The walk can take as little as five (long) days but it could easily be spread over 10, if you throw in a few rest days. There are between 40 and 50 hours of walking involved, so most people average seven days.

Don't walk the trail during the wet season when the normally muddy trail is dangerously slippery and many rivers are high and hazardous to cross. The best months are usually August and September. Most people walk from south to north, but there's no reason not to do it the other way. It might even be easier, as walking from the south you encounter the hardest sections in the first few days.

As you may be starting to appreciate, the walk is no picnic, although anyone with reasonable fitness will be OK, as long as they stay within their limits (there are no prizes for speed) and have the right equipment. To get an idea of the fitness required, try walking up stairs carrying a 15kg pack. One tour operator recommends that you be able to do this for an hour before attempting the Kokoda.

Apparently the Kokoda National Park ranger will sell you a certificate for completing the trail.

Information & Maps

It is worth checking with the PNG Tourism Promotion Authority (TPA) in Port Moresby (☎ 320 0211) before undertaking the walk. Hideo Kameoka (a Japanese volunteer) and John Kambeoua work with the TPA and

The Kokoda Trail

Following the bombing of Pearl Harbour in December 1941, the Japanese made a rapid thrust down the Malayan archipelago and across to New Guinea. Their unsuccessful involvement in the Battle of the Coral Sea caused a brief pause in their advance and a reassessment of their strategy.

They decided to attack Port Moresby via a totally unexpected 'back-door' assault. The plan was to land on the north coast near Gona, travel south to Kokoda and then march up and over the central range to Sogeri and down to Port Moresby.

They made one serious miscalculation: the Kokoda Trail was not a rough track that could be upgraded for vehicles. It was a switchback footpath through some of the most rugged country in the world, endlessly rising and falling, infested with leeches, and hopelessly muddy during the wet season.

The Japanese landed on 21 July 1942 and stormed down the trail, battling an increasingly desperate Australian opposition. At that stage, with most of Australia's military effort concentrated in Europe, the only troops available to garrison Port Moresby were poorly trained and poorly equipped militia. It was not until they were reinforced by battle-hardened veterans of the Middle East conflict that the tide started to turn. The Japanese came to within 48km of Port Moresby before the Australians were able to reverse their advance and start the slow, bloody battle back up the Kokoda Trail. As the Japanese commander General Horii withdrew up the track, lines of defence were drawn first at Eora Creek, mid-way along the track, then at Oivi, on the road from Kokoda to Buna. Both were taken by the Australians after drawn-out and bloody fighting. Horii drowned while attempting to cross the Kumusi River. Finally, the campaign to dislodge the Japanese from Buna on the north coast resulted in the most bitter fighting of the Pacific theatre of the war, with disease and starvation taking as high a toll as actual combat.

Never again did the Allies meet the Japanese head-on during WWII. The policy for the rest of the war was to advance towards Tokyo, bypassing and isolating Japanese strongholds. Rabaul in New Britain, for instance, was sidestepped, while the front moved closer and closer to Japan.

The troops who fought here showed tremendous courage under horrendous conditions – it is no wonder the Kokoda Trail and the Buna and Gona campaigns retain such importance in the war histories of Japan, Australia and PNG. ■

monitor the state of the trail reasonably regularly.

Before you start out, contact the National Disaster, Surveillance & Emergency Service (☎ 327 6502/327 6666 for emergencies) to inform them of your party's plans and get up-to-date information on the trail. Don't forget to report in at the district office at Kokoda.

If you plan to walk the Kokoda Trail from the Kokoda end, talk to John Atkins at the Oro Guesthouse in Popondetta (Oro Province), as many trekkers stay there and pass on the latest information.

There are health centres (and radios) in Efogi No 1 and Kokoda, as well as at Sogeri.

Clive Baker's *Do-It-Yourself Trekking – Kokoda Trail* is a necessity, as is Lonely Planet's *Bushwalking in Papua New Guinea*, both of which have detailed descriptions of the walk. Up-to-date maps are available in Port Moresby from the National Mapping Bureau at Waigani. Do not leave without copies of the 1:100,000 topographic maps for Kokoda, Efogi and Port Moresby and the most recent *Longitudinal Section of the Kokoda Trail*, which has useful descriptive notes and detailed sections of tricky areas. In Australia, most of these maps are available from Mapworld at 371 Pitt St, Sydney (☎ 9261 3601).

Warning The biggest dangers are the usual ones of trekking in rugged, remote country. If you get lost you run the risk of exposure and the river crossings can be dangerous.

The main danger for lone trekkers is that they sometimes have difficulty finding the trail. Rascals are uncommon now but the possibility of a hold-up should not be ignored. As usual in PNG, the way to minimise risks is to talk to local people and become accepted by them. A guide will help and a guide from the local area is even better.

If walking from south to north, it's vital that you arrive at Owers' Corner early and walk a fair distance that day. Similarly, make a long day's walk all the way into Kokoda village rather than stopping for the night just short of the station.

Equipment

Local food can usually be bought in the villages but you should bring your own supplies. Small trade stores at Naoro, Manari, Efogi No 1, Kagi and Kokoda sell the usual tinned meat, tinned fish and rice, but they are very unreliable.

You'll need a comfortable pair of boots or a strong pair of running shoes. Grip is important. A tent, a fly or a large sheet of plastic is necessary to waterproof some of the shelters; you might get stuck on the trail overnight waiting for a river to subside. Also, the itinerary suggested here includes at least one night camping. A compass and a camping stove are also recommended. Bring a bottle as you'll need to carry water along certain sections of the trail. It can get quite chilly, so bring a sleeping bag; also bring some kind of wet-weather gear (even in the dry season). Make sure you take a comprehensive medical kit, and salt, matches or a cigarette lighter to detach leeches. The total weight of your pack should not exceed 15kg.

Guides & Porters

A guide might not be absolutely necessary, but you're strongly advised to take one, because of both the danger of getting lost and the slight danger of rascals (who seem to be thin on the ground these days). The best way would be to take different guides for different sections of the trail, so you always have someone with you who knows local people, but this might not be feasible. At least make sure that your guide comes from *somewhere* along the trail.

Having a porter might mean the difference between finishing the trail and giving up along the way. One porter between a few people might be a good compromise. Expect to pay a guide at least K20 a day (possibly more) and a porter about K10 a day. You have

to provide them with food and perhaps some equipment. Osborne Bugajiwai has been recommended as a good guide – he can be contacted through the TPA in Port Moresby (☎ 320 0211).

People do walk the trail alone but you're strongly advised not to, as sections are quite isolated. The safest number of people is three or more (too many might mean problems with accommodation), which allows one person to stay with an injured trekker and one to go for help. Ask around the hostels in Port Moresby to find out about other people planning to walk the trail.

Track Information

Information assumes a south-north trek. The following itinerary is suggested for those of below peak fitness (but who are still active and used to walking):

Owers' Corner to Va Ure Creek Campsite (10km, 6 hours)
  The campsite is about 1½ hours on from Imita Ridge.
Va Ure Creek Campsite to Naoro (17km, 10 hours)
  Naoro used to have a rest house but a traveller reports that the whole village has recently relocated to another site up the hill. But they may still be able to put you up. The track has been rerouted to follow the original wartime route and there are many interesting weapons pits, bunkers and relics to see.
Naoro to Efogi No 1 (19km, 7 hours)
  About halfway between these points there is a rest house in Manari village. There are two rest houses in Efogi No 1.
Efogi No 1 to Efogi Creek (12km, 7 hours)
  About 2½ hours past Efogi No 1 you pass through Kagi, where there's a good rest house. From Efogi Creek, you can walk to Myola in about two hours. A half-hour side-walk takes you to an intact wreck of a US Kittyhawk.
Efogi Creek to Alola (17km, 7 hours)
  There's a guesthouse in Alola.
Alola to Kokoda (19km, 7 hours)
  There is a new guesthouse at Kokoda attached to the hospital (see the following Kokoda Memorial Aid Posts aside).

Short-Cuts You could take a PMV from Port Moresby to the village of Madilogo. Doing this, you avoid the two hard days (possibly the hardest on the whole trail) it takes to walk from Owers' Corner to Naoro. It takes about two hours to reach the trail from Madilogo; from there it's 1½ hours to Naoro.

If you want a little taste of the trail without walking the whole distance, you can walk down to Goldie River from Owers' Corner in just an hour or so. If you have the energy, struggle up the Golden Staircase to Imita Ridge on the other side. Another option would be to fly in, walk a section and fly out. Flying to Kagi and walking to Manari (one day) or Naoro (two days) would be interesting. Myola also has an airstrip but it's only used by charter planes.

Organised Tours

Many companies offer organised Kokoda treks; while they aren't cheap, they do take care of the organisational hassles. Niugini Tours in Sydney has had some good reports. South Pacific Tours also conduct treks (see the Getting Around chapter for details).

Places to Stay & Eat

There are basic guesthouses in many villages and various shelters and campsites along the trail. Some of the guesthouses and shelters are small, so if you meet another party you might have to camp. Make sure you pay for village accommodation, even if you aren't asked. It's usually around K6 per person, with some of the better places charging more.

There's a good *guesthouse* at Myola, which is a bit off the main trail. It's recommended, although it costs around K30 for food and accommodation. The food is not too bad, there are (tepid) showers, the 'lakes' are interesting, and there are trout in nearby streams and some interesting war relics. You can fly in (charters only) and this would make a great weekend escape from Port Moresby. It is important to let the people know you're coming as Myola isn't really a village and there might not be anyone around or they may not be prepared for visitors.

Getting There & Away

When travelling from Port Moresby, the turn-off to the trail is just before Sogeri and

Kokoda Memorial Aid Posts

In 1994, in appreciation for the invaluable assistance given by villagers to Australian troops in WWII, Australian Rotary and the Returned & Services League (RSL) launched a joint Australia-wide appeal for funds to provide a much-needed health centre and several village aid posts in Oro Province.

An aid post at Waju village, 20km from Kokoda, was completed by a Rotary team in March 1994. A year later the Buna aid post and memorial cairn were completed, and on 16 September 1995 the Kokoda memorial hospital, the flagship of the project, was opened. More than 300 Rotary volunteers made the trip to PNG to assist in the project, as builders, carpenters and electricians.

Memorial aid posts have since been opened at Sairope, Kebara and Hanau villages. The Gona health centre has been extensively refurbished and upgraded. More projects are planned. The growing number of trekkers undertaking the Kokoda Trail will not only be closer to basic medical care, but will also be able to use a new guesthouse at the Kokoda Memorial Hospital. The hospital, guesthouse and museum built by Rotary were funded by the Australian government. ∎

there's a memorial stone at this junction. The road twists and turns and is rather bumpy, although quite OK for conventional vehicles (as long as it isn't raining). At McDonald's Corner there is a strange metal sculpture of a soldier; this is where the road once ended and the trail started, but the actual trail now starts further on at Owers' Corner (there's a sign – sometimes).

From Owers' Corner the trail is easy to follow and heads straight down towards the Goldie River. You can stroll down to the river if you just want an easy taste of what it's like. On the other side of the river, the endless 'golden staircase' crawls up to Imita Ridge, the turning point for the Japanese.

It's also possible to fly in to airstrips along the trail; several are near village guesthouses. PMVs run from Port Moresby to the start of the trail at Owers' Corner. They are infrequent and leave Gordons Market early in the morning. The 48km (two-hour) trip costs about K5. It might be worth taking a taxi to Gordons to ensure that you get there in time for the PMV.

If you miss the early PMV, you could take one running out the Sogeri Road and get off at the Owers' Corner turn-off. This means a long walk, although you could hitch. There's also an afternoon PMV to Owers' Corner, but if you take this one you'll have to stay overnight there.

There are airstrips at Naoro, Manari, Efogi No 1 and Kagi, as well as Bodinumu and Naduli, two villages near Kagi. From Kokoda, Air Niugini or MBA can fly you to Popondetta for K52 (if you are averse to travelling by PMV).

KOKODA
• *pop 600* • *postcode 244*

The Owen Stanley Range rises almost sheer behind the Oro Province village of Kokoda, where the northern end of the trail terminates. Grace Eroro (☎ 329 7446) is the postal agent in Kokoda and has been recommended as a very helpful person, whether you want PMV info, local guides or a telephone.

Places to Stay
The Kokoda Memorial Hospital has some new *hikers huts* set aside for trekkers for K25 per person. These are modern dormitories with proper toilets, showers, gas stoves and kitchen utensils. Money raised from the huts is used to buy much-needed medical supplies. Otherwise, accommodation may still be available at the Kokoda National Park headquarters for a few kina – see the ranger. Robberies are rare but some travellers have suggested staying in the police compound. Limited food is available from the trade stores.

Getting There & Away
The road between Kokoda and Popondetta is only a couple of hours drive (three by PMV). PMVs to Popondetta cost K7 and take nearly three hours, leaving at about 6 am. The Kumusi River is now crossed by a bridge near Wairopi (named after the 'wire rope' used to make the earlier footbridge). General Horii and hundreds of Japanese soldiers died near here while crossing the river during the retreat from Oivi Ridge. The road climbs steeply over the ridge and then drops into the Kokoda Valley, where the trail starts.

MBA flies Port Moresby to Kokoda and back every Wednesday and Saturday for K62 each way. A few years ago, some rascals came up with the innovative idea of welcoming the plane and then robbing its occupants – but all seems pretty quiet now. Northcoast Aviation may still have regular flights from Kokoda to Popondetta if you can't stomach the trip by PMV.

Oro Province

Land Area 22,800 sq km
Population 115,000
Capital Popondetta

Oro Province (often called Northern Province) is sandwiched between the Solomon Sea and the Owen Stanley Range. It is a little-visited region of the country but is physically beautiful, with a number of areas of interest.

Oro Province is the home of the world's largest butterfly, the Queen Alexandra birdwing, which is featured on the provincial flag. You might think that you've seen some big butterflies in PNG, but these are monsters, with wingspans of nearly 30cm. The first specimen collected by a European was brought down by a shotgun! That butterfly, a little damaged, is still in the British Museum. The Queen Alexandra Birdwing is now a threatened species, for the usual reason – it lives on the top layer of rainforests which are vanishing. It lays its eggs on a particular species of vine which is poisonous to most birds and animals; the butterfly is poisonous as well.

History
Early European contacts with the Orakaiva people, who live inland as far as Kokoda, were relatively peaceful, but when gold was

discovered at Yodda and Kokoda in 1895, violence soon followed. A government station was established after the first altercation between locals and miners. The situation did not greatly improve; the first government officer was killed shortly after he arrived. Eventually things quietened down and the mines, initially some of the richest in Papua, were worked out. Rubber plantations and other plantations superseded them.

WWII arrived in the Oro area unexpectedly and dramatically in 1942. The fighting on the Kokoda Trail was bitter, and the Japanese were slowly pushed to the northern strongholds at Buna and Gona. The Australian troops who had pursued the Japanese back up the track were strengthened by joint Australian-American detachments who came around the coast – but the Japanese held on suicidally. Although Kokoda was retaken at the beginning of November 1942, Gona and Buna did not fall until Christmas-New Year. It has been estimated that only about 700 of the 16,000-strong Japanese force survived this bloody campaign. The Australian-American forces then moved on Sanananda, where there was more heaving fighting, and then further westwards towards Lae and Wewak.

There are many war relics scattered around the area, most considerably covered with overgrowth. At Jiropa Plantation, on the Buna Road, a Japanese plaque commemorates the country's dead. Oro Bay, now the province's main port, was a major American base.

After the war, rebuilding the region proved difficult as the damage was especially severe. Strangled by their supply difficulties, the Japanese troops had scoured the country for food, even eating grass and bark off trees in an often-vain attempt to prevent starvation. The gardens and plantations were hardly back in shape after the war when Mt Lamington's 1951 eruption totally wiped out Higaturu, the district headquarters. The new headquarters town of Popondetta was established at a safer distance from the volcano.

Geography

The swamps and flatlands of the coast rise slowly inland towards the Owen Stanley Range, then with increasing steepness to the peaks, which stand at between 3500 and 4000m, despite being only 90 to 100km from the sea. The only roads of any length in the province run from the coast inland through Popondetta to Kokoda. The road between Popondetta and Oro Bay is sealed and in good condition, but as you head to Kokoda it becomes quite rough. South-east of the port at Oro Bay, a rough, unsealed road runs inland up some valleys to an inland plateau and the small administrative centre of Afore. Mt Lamington, near Popondetta, is a mildly active volcano that, in 1951, erupted with cataclysmic force and killed nearly 3000 people. In the east of the province there are more interesting volcanos near Tufi and there is a section of coast around Cape Nelson with unique tropical 'fjords', or *rias*; their origin is volcanic rather than glacial.

Arts

Tapa cloth, made by beating the bark of a paper mulberry tree until it is thin and flexible, is made at Yiaku. Natural dyes are used to make dramatic designs on the cloth. Tapa cloth is only worn by local people in the most remote parts of the province. Distinctive clay pots are fired at Wanigela in Collingwood Bay.

Getting There & Away

Oro Province is pivotal for budget travellers or anyone who wants to make the most of sea travel in PNG. Taking the short flight across the Owen Stanley Range to Kokoda (K62) and then PMVs to Popondetta (K7) and Oro Bay (K3) is a good way to see some interesting country, but is really little cheaper than flying direct from Port Moresby to Popondetta (K72). You could, of course, walk the Kokoda Trail if you are reasonably fit – but that option is considerably more expensive.

Oro Bay is the easternmost port serviced by Lutheran Shipping's passenger boats; from there you can head up the coast through

Lae and Madang to Wewak or Vanimo on a cargo boat. From Lae there are boats to New Britain, and from Madang you can catch one of the irregular freighters to Manus Island. From Lae and Madang there are road connections to the Highlands, and from Wewak you can access the Sepik River by road.

Heading in the other direction from Oro Bay, it's possible (but time-consuming) to take small boats along the coast to Collingwood Bay and perhaps from there to Milne Bay, from where boats run to the Trobriand Islands and the other island groups of Milne Bay Province.

POPONDETTA
• *pop 8000* • *postcode 241*
Popondetta, the provincial capital, is spread along the Oro Bay Highway a few kilometres from the old administrative capital of Higaturu, which has recently had a minor resurgence with the growth of the oil palm industry. Popondetta has all the basic facilities, including offices for Air Niugini and Northcoast Aviation (agents for MBA), banks, several shops, a baker and supermarkets. There is a war memorial with an interesting map of the battle sites and a memorial to the victims of the Mt Lamington eruption. Otherwise there is little of interest for the visitor. Oro Bay lies 43km to the north and Girua airport is 15km to the south on the main highway.

Popondetta is landlocked and inconveniently sited. Its name means 'place of the Popondo tree'. The provincial headquarters are located here only because the previous two sites were ill-fated: the one on the coast was invaded by the Japanese and destroyed, and the other – moved safely inland after the war – was destroyed by the eruption of Mt Lamington. The current site, a kunai grass plain, seems secure, but who knows?

Popondetta is currently experiencing a modest boom because of the huge Higaturu oil palm project. A British company, Higaturu Oil Palms, owns the factory which extracts the palm oil from the crop and also owns some of the oil palm estates around Popondetta (most are owned by villagers).

The network of good roads near here was made by the company for its trucks to collect the crop, those clumps of yellow-orange 'fruit' you might see lying by the roadside. The factory (which stinks) is a kilometre or so down a dirt road from the village of Doublecross, about 10km from Popondetta on the Kokoda Road. Doublecross is so named because there are two river crossings here, not because of the fickleness of the villagers.

A couple of kilometres past the factory is **Segeri**, Higaturu's company town. There's nothing much to see here but it's an utterly orderly place and surprisingly large. It has its own security force (with elaborate uniforms), school, hospital, sportsground, etc, and the houses come in different models depending on your position in the company. Electricity is generated by burning oil palm husks.

Out of town near the airport is a picnic spot and swimming hole in a river (dug by a WWII bomb). The local village may charge a kina or two to visit. To get there from Popondetta, turn right off the highway onto a dirt track by a store just before the entrance to the airport. Turn left onto a smaller track before the big, thatched Seventh-Day Adventist building and keep going. The total distance from the highway is about 1.5km.

Information
Basil Tindeba, from Buna, has been recommended as a guide around the WWII sites in the area, including the Kokoda Trail. Ask for him at the Oro Guesthouse or contact Kokoda Treks and Tours (☎ 329 7127; fax 329 7193; PO Box 2, Popondetta). John Gore, officer-in-charge of the Kokoda National Park office in Popondetta (☎ 329 7385; PO Box 285), is a useful source of information.

Mt Lamington
The 1585m peak of Mt Lamington (Sumburipa) is clearly visible from Popondetta (there's a good view on the road into town from the airport), but the original provincial headquarters were even closer – only

10km from the volcano. Like many other volcanos in PNG, Mt Lamington still shakes and puffs a little. Local residents paid no attention to a slight increase in activity in 1951 – then half of the mountain side suddenly blew out and a violent cloud of super-heated gases rushed down, incinerating all before it.

The European population of Higaturu and many Papua New Guineans died – around 3000 people. It was later estimated that the temperature stood at around 200°C for about a minute and a half and that the gas cloud rolled down at over 300km/h. Nearly 8000 people, or 10% of the province's population, were left homeless. It took a number of years for the region to recover.

Mt Lamington has been fairly calm since and keen bushwalkers can climb it today. You start from Sasenbata Mission, a little way off the Kokoda Road. Like most mountains the best time to reach the summit is in the early morning before the clouds roll in; there's a campsite on a ridge line. There's no crater but the views are excellent. Take water; there's none available near the top and it's thirsty work. Take care, too – it's still active. Some walkers have reported that there are two groups of landowners who own the mountain and may demand payment of K10 or so.

A guide from a nearby village (such as Duve) is almost essential to avoid hassles with local people.

Places to Stay & Eat

Oro Guesthouse (☎ 329 7127; fax 329 7246; PO Box 2) is reasonably good value, both for budget travellers and those with deeper pockets. It's comfortable and well designed. Good information about Oro Province and the Kokoda Trail is available; the manager, John Atkins, has travelled widely. John was temporarily back in Canada in 1997 and the place seemed to be getting quite rundown in his absence. Rooms and bathrooms were infrequently cleaned and there was a plague of biting midges. Things should improve with his return.

Many guests are government officials and you can have some interesting conversations. Meals are the same every night – simple but good, with a wide range of local vegetables.

There's quite a range of prices for rooms, although they are basically the same, with fan and shared bathrooms. Singles/doubles/triples cost K32/50/60 or K46/78/102 with breakfast and dinner. Add K4 for TV in your room and K3 per person to use the kitchen. There are cheaper beds if you're a student with ID, a volunteer, a YHA member or if you've walked the Kokoda Trail or (maybe) if you are just an impoverished backpacker – so ask.

To get there from the town centre, walk down the main street away from the direction of the airport and turn left at the hospital's 'in' sign. Go past the park and it's the fifth house on the left. Coming from the PMV stop at the market, head back to the main road, walk towards town and take the first right after the high school.

The *Lamington Lodge* (☎ 329 7222; fax 329 7065; PO Box 27) is noisy, frequented by drunks and has poker machines. It is part of the Coral Sea chain, but is probably the worst hotel in the chain. A standard room is vastly overpriced at K135, but there may be corporate or stand-by rates after 5 pm. Its restaurant is the only one in town, but the food is apparently not very good.

The country around Popondetta is very pretty, with stands of rainforest, kunai plains and huge tracts of oil palm. The dark aisles of oil palms are bathed in a deep green light and look as mysterious as the depths of Indian temples. The tidy villages are bright with flowers and most of the houses are of traditional design and materials.

The *Ondahari Village Guesthouse* is a small ecotourism lodge in a little hamlet in primary rainforest about 40 minutes north of Popondetta along a reasonable dirt road. You can go on forest walks or swim in the river – and there are four types of birdwing butterfly to be seen, including the Queen Alexandra, whose habitat is near the rainforest canopy. Bookings at the Ondahari Guesthouse can be made through the Oro Guesthouse or by writing to Russell or David Hauro, Ondahari Village, via Popondetta. It is a chance to support the income-earning efforts of rural people.

Another pleasant way to spend a day or two is travelling by canoe down the Embogo River, where you can experience river life in all its aspects. Stay at the *Embogo Women's Guesthouse* on the Oro Bay Highway – it is past the Embogo High School and just before the bridge by the aid post. PMVs from Popondetta cost about K3. You can book at the Oro Guesthouse or contact Humphrey Orere care of the Embogo Women's Council.

Things to Buy

You can sometimes buy tapa cloth from the vocational centre near the Oro Guesthouse; from the guesthouse, head down to the far end of the street and turn left. Enquire at the vocational centre canteen.

Getting There & Away

Air Girua airport is 15km from town and one of several wartime strips in the area. From the air, you'll notice that the area around the airstrip is scattered with horseshoe mounds – the remains of WWII emplacements. There is also a couple of well-preserved American WWII aircraft mounted at rather curious angles next to the air terminal.

The Air Niugini office (☎ 329 7022) in town opens at 8 am and the staff are competent and friendly. Air Niugini has daily flights from Port Moresby to Popondetta and back. The flight takes 40 minutes.

The Northcoast Aviation office (☎ 329 7219; fax 329 7209; PO Box 12) is three shops away from Air Niugini. Northcoast is also agent for MBA, which has return flights around the coast twice-weekly (Wednesday and Saturday), originating at Alotau and calling in at Wedau, Rabaraba, Cape Vogel, Wanigela, Tufi, Popondetta and Lae. It flies Popondetta-Tufi-Wanigela-Popondetta on Monday and Friday.

One-way fares from Popondetta are: Port Moresby K72, Lae K150, Tufi K79, Alotau K156.

PMV PMVs take about 20 minutes to get to the airport and about 40 minutes to get to Oro Bay. It's possible that when you want to leave for Oro Bay, all the PMVs in town will have already left to pick up passengers from the boat.

The Popondo area (around the Popondo Supermarket) is where most, but not all, PMVs depart from the town centre. For Kokoda (K7), they leave from under the tree at around noon; for Oro Bay (K3) and for the airport, the minibuses stop on the street between Popondo and the park – all marked Route No 1. Services are reasonably frequent (although less frequent on Sunday). On weekdays, the PMVs for Buna depart one street over in front of Price Rite Hardware, across from PNGBC.

Boat Niugini Agencies Pty Ltd in Popondetta (☎ 329 7061; fax 329 7467; PO Box 77) doesn't handle passenger business but may be able to tell you about sailing dates for freighters. Buy tickets on the wharf at Oro Bay.

Getting Around

The Airport No PMVs specifically service the Girua airport but you will get one on the nearby Oro Bay Highway heading either to Oro Bay or Popondetta. The fare from the airport to Popondetta is K1. There aren't very many PMVs and they are particularly sparse on Sunday. Otherwise, one of the locals will probably help with a lift. It is one of those small airports where there are always people about, so there are usually plenty of vehicles.

Getting to the airport is trickier, but Popondetta is a small town and if you ask around you'll probably hear of someone on the same flight who can give you a lift. The Oro Guesthouse charges K20 to deliver you to the airport.

Car Budget (☎ 329 7152; fax 329 7065) operates from the Lamington Hotel and has two cars available. Maoro Motors (☎ 329 7662) may have cheaper vehicles.

ORO PROVINCE

ORO BAY

This pretty bay has a new wharf complex, where the *Mamose Express* and the *Rita* dock. It's also where the palm oil is loaded for export. It has to be heated so that it's sufficiently liquid to flow into the tankers. Apart from that, there is not much to do or see. There are a couple of *villages* around the bay and you could probably arrange to stay in one if you're waiting for a boat. Otherwise try the *hospital*, across the bay from the wharf, or the *mission* at Emo.

Getting There & Away

Lutheran Shipping's *Mamose Express* or *Rita* leaves Oro Bay early Tuesday afternoon for the overnight trip to Lae (K23/35 for deck/cabin class) and continues as far as Wewak. There are also Lutheran Shipping freighters which take passengers on the trip, though less regularly and comfortably (K19/23 for deck/1st class). Check with Niugini Agencies in Popondetta.

If you're going further than Lae, insist on buying a through ticket, otherwise you might be sold a ticket to Lae and have to buy another there, which works out to be considerably more expensive.

If you're heading east you can find small dinghies at Oro Bay. Between K20 and K30 should get you to Tufi. Ask around the village nearest the wharf, but be careful not to pay until you are on board.

TUFI

• *pop 400* • *postcode 246*

Tufi is one of PNG's best kept secrets – a picturesque and peaceful spot. The people are very friendly and English is widely spoken. The climate is cooler than most other coastal areas and can provide welcome relief from the dust and heat of Port Moresby and Lae. There is also a palpable difference in the atmosphere – Tufi is remote and safe and the razor wire and armed guards of the larger towns are noticeably absent.

One of the great things about budget travelling in PNG is the opportunity to stay in villages and experience the culture and lifestyle up close and first-hand. This is where Tufi comes into its own. Not only are there a number of friendly villagers, with little traditional, bush-material guesthouses, who will welcome you warmly, but the yellow, sandy beaches and swaying palm trees will make it an idyllic experience. This form of tourism is not only cheaper and more culturally stimulating than hotels and resorts, but it benefits grassroots PNG because the money you pay stays in the village. Check out the village guesthouses wherever you can, but don't expect electricity or telephones; if you like your comforts, there is also a very pleasant dive resort in Tufi.

A suitably patriotic British sea captain named this scenic peninsula Cape Nelson after the legendary admiral and dubbed the three mountain peaks on the cape, Trafalgar (site of Nelson's naval victory over the French), Victory (his ship) and Britannia (she's the one who ruled the waves). He named the beautiful bay to the south Collingwood, after one of Nelson's captains. The cape was formed by ancient eruptions of its three volcanos and the lava which flowed down into the sea created the rias, for which it is now famous. The landscape is certainly reminiscent of both Scandinavia and fjordland in New Zealand, despite its very different geological origins. The water is always warm; beneath the calm surface of the sheltered bays there is beautiful coral waiting to be inspected.

Further south, on Collingwood Bay, is **Wanigela**, where there is also good snorkelling. Its market is supposed to be better than Tufi's and the village is known for its clay pots. You may be able to arrange canoe trips up the Murin River or over the coral reefs.

Yiaku village, south of Wanigela and quite close to the Milne Bay Province border, is the manufacturing centre for tapa cloth made by the Maisin people. Nearly all the tapa cloth you will have encountered will have been made in Yiaku, although other clans print their own designs on the cloth.

Things to See & Do

Diving Diving is one of Tufi's great attractions; there is consistent 30m-plus visibility.

Tony's Reef and Malua Reef offer excellent potential with deepwater drops – eels and hammerhead sharks are common. Nearby are some WWII ships easily accessible in shallow water. A couple of PT boats were reputedly sunk off the end of Tufi wharf, but, being timber, they have largely disintegrated. Apparently three torpedos and a machine gun can still be seen. The Tufi Dive Resort is well equipped to cater to your diving needs.

Fishing Local villages can provide outrigger canoes (the standard form of transport) if you want to go fishing or just want to potter around. The dive resort can organise fishing trips in its dive boat. Barracuda, Spanish mackerel, trevally and various sharks are common. It can get very windy between June and August.

Bushwalking There are many walking trails in the area, following the rias. Ask around and someone will probably insist on accompanying you. The villages and the resort can arrange boats to pick you up at various locations at the end of your walk.

Places to Stay & Eat

The *Tufi Dive Resort* (☎ & fax 61 1438; care of Tufi post office) is a middle-market resort offering bunk rooms, family rooms and duplex-style bungalows with clean bathrooms in the middle of each duplex. There is a bar, a good library and a video collection. It is a couple of hundred metres from the airstrip and has a great cliffside barbecue area with a spectacular view up the rias. Rates are K100 per person for bungalow accommodation – including three good meals (sometimes local lobster). It is primarily a dive resort but can also arrange fishing, windsurfing and bushwalking trips. There is a steep road going down the cliffside to the wharf below, where outriggers come and go from nearby villages, and where the resort moors its dive boat. Bookings can be made direct or as part of a package tour through MBA or most travel agents. Amex, Visa and MasterCard are accepted.

At Wanigela the *Anglican mission* may be able to offer accommodation. In Yiaku village see the mission or ask the local councillors.

The *village guesthouses* at Tufi have been operating for some years now and are run by local clans. The guesthouses are situated between the villages of Angorogo and Sai. Unfortunately they are not well supported by the Tourism Promotion Authority and their owners complain that tourist numbers have been declining in recent years, so please do your bit and support them. It may be worthwhile writing to the owners to let them know you are coming (write care of the Tufi post office), so they can prepare. They provide local food (the seafood is good), included in the daily rate of K30 to K35 per person. They can also arrange fishing and snorkelling trips – but bring your own gear.

All the guesthouses are near the sea, with pretty views. The *Kofure Guesthouse* (PO Box 6) is a short walk north of the airstrip and then a 10-minute trip by outrigger canoe. The *Konabu Guesthouse* (Hobson Fairi, PO Box 26) is on the point, a few minutes walk to the sea, while the *Tainabuna Guesthouse* is an hour by canoe from the airport and has been recommended. *Komoa Guesthouse* (Alphonces Kimai or MacKenzie Ruaba, PO Box 25) is a pretty spot, and *Jebo Guesthouse* in Sinofuka village (ask for Lancelot Gineri) also come highly recommended. Sinofuka literally means 'pig and dog' village!

Getting There & Away

See the Oro Bay section for information on boats to Tufi. The going rate seems to be between K20 and K30. A reader advises, however, to take care that the boat owner doesn't disappear once you have paid your money. The inlets between Oro Bay and Tufi have historically been the homes of pirates and, even in relatively recent times, coastal vessels have been boarded and cargoes stolen. The area seems pretty safe now.

To travel between Tufi and Wanigela you can hire a small boat, but the half-hour trip may cost about K30. If you wait patiently

ORO PROVINCE

and talk to people in Tufi, you will probably hear about a passenger boat for much less. It's a similar story with boats from Wanigela to Yiaku. You could perhaps continue eastwards by sea to Cape Vogel and Wedau in Milne Bay Province, but boats are not frequent and it's simpler to fly.

MBA makes three direct return flights from Port Moresby to Tufi on Tuesday, Friday and Saturday. These are mainly, but not only, associated with package diving tours at the Tufi Diving Resort. MBA also flies twice weekly around the coast from Alotau to Lae return, on Wednesday and Saturday, calling in at all the airstrips in between, including Tufi and Wanigela. Northcoast Aviation flies Popondetta-Tufi-Wanigela-Popondetta on Monday and Friday.

One-way fares are: Port Moresby-Tufi K141, Lae-Tufi K156, Popondetta-Tufi K79, Popondetta-Wanigela K79, Alotau-Tufi K112, Tufi-Wanigela K36 and Tufi-Cape Vogel K71.

AFORE

This tiny town is on a high plateau with sweeping views reminiscent of the African veld. There are good walks in the area, including one, close to Afore, to a reputedly bottomless volcanic vent. This deep, steep cave is full of bats and is considered to be a *tambu* (forbidden or sacred) site by the local villagers, so it is advisable to ask around for

a local guide and to offer a few kina for their trouble. It is too steep to explore without the help of ropes, but it is a good walk to the entrance, which in itself is quite spectacular.

In town, there's a school where you might be able to stay, and surrounding villages will probably accommodate you for a few kina. Sagarina Mission, most easily accessible on foot, is south of Afore and usually has accommodation.

Through one program run as part of the Oro Conservation Project in Afore, villagers are trying to create a sustainable industry selling butterflies to international collectors. The program teaches the villagers to promote the features of the environment conducive to the lifecycle of some of the spectacular butterflies found locally, particularly the Queen Alexandra birdwing.

Apparently MBA has flights (not strictly scheduled) from Port Moresby on Monday and Friday calling in at many small strips on demand, but only landing at Afore if someone is getting on or off. In the Dornier plane on this flight, every seat is a window seat.

Occasionally PMVs run from Popondetta to Pongani on the coast, but you might have more luck from Oro Bay. They aren't very frequent. From Pongani to Afore you might have to hitch, but the road is rough and vehicles are infrequent. In several places, the Australian army has built Bailey bridges to cross rivers and ravines.

Milne Bay Province

Land Area 14,000 sq km
Population 180,000
Capital Alotau

At the eastern end of mainland Papua New Guinea, the Owen Stanley Range plunges into the sea and a scatter of islands dots the ocean for hundreds of kilometres further out. This is the start of the Pacific proper – tiny atolls, coral reefs, volcanic islands, swaying palms and white beaches. Yet, this area has one big difference with the better-known areas of the Pacific – there are virtually no tourists. The Trobriand Islands are the only place in Milne Bay Province with any sort of a tourist reputation, but it would be a very busy week if they had 20 visitors!

More than 435 islands give the province 2120km of coastline, by far the most in the country, but poor transport infrastructure and limited arable land have hindered the region's development. Witchcraft is still widely respected and stories of its practice abound, but it's the *kula ring*, a ritual trading circle that encompasses the province's island groups, that is the most enduring cultural legacy of pre-European times.

Accommodation options are few and generally expensive, but this may soon change with direct flights from Cairns, Australia, to Alotau's Gurney airport. Many people in the region are excited by this link, as it's likely to increase tourism and give the local fishing industry much better access to the hungry markets of South-East Asia.

History

On many of the Trobriand Islands, there are remains of stone temples that bear resemblance to those of Polynesia and, despite centuries of miscegenation, the people have a distinctive Polynesian appearance. Trade between the islands had strong cultural and economic importance and the pre-European traders crossed vast distances of open sea in canoes, exchanging fish, vegetables, pigs,

HIGHLIGHTS

- Hanging around Alotau's colourful harbour area
- Catching a trade boat out to one of the many island groups
- Contemplating the former glory of tiny Samarai Island
- Visiting the Trobriand Islands during yam harvest

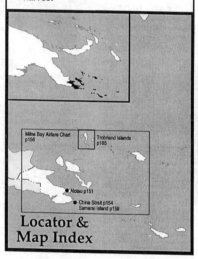

Milne Bay Airfare Chart p158
Trobriand Islands p165
Alotau p151
China Strait p154
Samarai Island p159

Locator & Map Index

MILNE BAY PROVINCE

stone axes, a rare jade-like stone from Muyua (Woodlark) Island and volcanic glass from Fergusson Island. The kula ring is the most famous of these trade routes and even today its rituals and customs are respected and honoured by people of the province.

The islands of Milne Bay Province were well known to other Pacific and Asian traders long before the first European contact in the 1600s.

In 1606, Spanish mariner Luis Vaez de Torres, after whom the Louisiades were named, abducted 14 children and took them to Manila in the Philippines to be baptised.

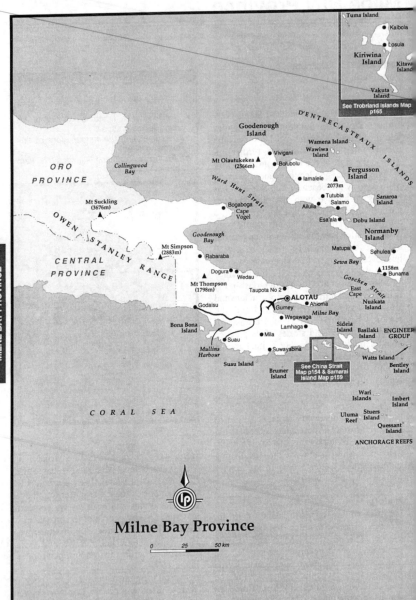

MILNE BAY PROVINCE

Tuma Island
Kaibola
Losuia
Kiriwina Island
Kitava Island
Vakuta Island
See Trobriand Islands Map p165

D'ENTRECASTEAUX ISLANDS

Goodenough Island
Vivigani
Mt Oiautukekea (2566m)
Bolubolu
Wamena Island
Wawiwa Island
Fergusson Island
Iamalele
2073m
Tutubia
Sanaroa Island
Ailulia
Salamo
Esa'ala
Dobu Island
Normanby Island
Matupa
Sehulea

ORO PROVINCE
Collingwood Bay
Ward Hunt Strait
Bogaboga
Cape Vogel
Mt Suckling (3676m)
OWEN STANLEY RANGE
Goodenough Bay
Mt Simpson (2883m)
Rabaraba
CENTRAL PROVINCE
Dogura
Wedau
Mt Thompson (1798m)
Taupota No 2
Godaisu
ALOTAU
Gumey
Ahioma
Milne Bay
East Cape
Nuakata Island
Sewa Bay
1158m
Bunama
Goschen Strait

Bona Bona Island
Wagawaga
Lamhaga
Suau
Mila
Sideia Island
Basilaki Island
ENGINEER GROUP
Mullins Harbour
Suwayabina
See China Strait Map p154 & Samarai Island Map p159
Watts Island
Bentley Island
Suau Island
Brumer Island

Wari Islands
Imbert Island
Uluma Reef
Stuers Island
Quessant Island

CORAL SEA

ANCHORAGE REEFS

Milne Bay Province

0   25   50 km

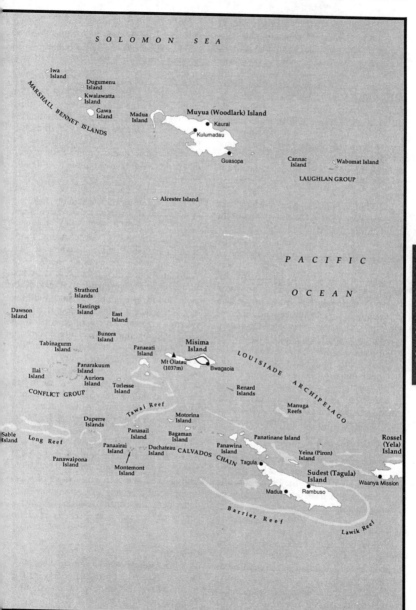

French explorer Bruny d'Entrecasteaux sailed through in 1793, depositing his cumbersome name on to the group that includes Fergusson, Normanby and Goodenough islands. However, it was not until 1847 that Europeans sought to settle the region; in that year, the first Marist missionaries arrived and established a mission on Muyua (Woodlark) Island that was to last a mere eight years – the locals, it seems, were unenthusiastic about Christianity. In the 1870s, the London Missionary Society (LMS) established missions on the south coast of the mainland and in 1891 the first Anglicans and Methodists arrived.

In 1873 Captain John Moresby happened upon the deep inlet at the eastern end of the mainland and named it Milne Bay after Alexander Milne, Lord of the Admiralty. He had already landed on Samarai Island and named it Dinner Island, after a meal he'd eaten there – he can't have been feeling too creative that day. Moresby claimed the area for Queen Victoria, running the Union Jack up a makeshift flagpole, but was subsequently slighted when the good queen repudiated the claim.

After Moresby's voyage, traders began arriving and soon there was a thriving trade in pearl shells and bêche-de-mer, a sea cucumber much prized as a Chinese delicacy. The region was also a source of labourers forcibly removed to work in northern Australian sugar plantations, a lothsome practice known as 'blackbirding'. Gold was discovered on Misima Island and later on Muyua (Woodlark) Island; while these finds eventually produced huge amounts of gold, the death toll of the miners who came in droves was enormous – they succumbed in huge numbers to disease, malnutrition and hostile locals.

Reverend Charles W Abel, a dissident member of the LMS, founded the Kwato Extension Association on Kwato Island, near Samarai, in 1891. This was the first church to provide skills training to the indigenous people of Milne Bay. The Kwato Church is alive and well today; many of its graduates and their children have been influential in the nation's development.

With so much trading and missionary activity in the region, tiny Samarai Island was established as its major port and capital, holding this position until after WWII.

The two major battles of Milne Bay are regarded as turning points of WWII in the Pacific. In the Battle of the Coral Sea (5-8 May 1942), the Japanese navy, rapidly moving south and intent on invading Port Moresby, was turned back by the Allies. It is regarded as a classic naval battle, but the warships did not come within 300km of each other; the fighting was confined to the air, with some of the heaviest dogfights above the Louisiades. There were heavy losses on both sides, but the Japanese navy, severely crippled, would cease to be a significant threat in the Pacific. And yet the Japanese resolve to capture PNG saw them land troops at Buna and Gona, in Oro Province, in July 1942 and move south along the Kokoda Trail. In August they attempted to invade Milne Bay, but poor intelligence resulted in their landing at Ahioma too far around the bay. They had to trudge through terrible swamps to meet the waiting Australian forces and attempt to take Gurney airstrip. The Australians had warning of this offensive and, after 12 days of heavy fighting in the Alotau area, they repelled the Japanese and secured the first Allied land victory in the Pacific. Afterwards, Milne Bay became a huge naval base for the Allies and the next few years saw hundreds of thousands of military personnel pass through. A few kilometres east of Alotau, near Ahioma, lies the rusted remains of a pontoon that the US forces used to load and unload their ships. During 1992, the 50th anniversary of these famous battles, many ex-servicemen from both sides of the conflict returned to remember and pay respects to their fallen comrades.

Geography

Mainland Milne Bay is extremely mountainous and most of its people live around the coast, where the mighty Owen Stanley Range tumbles into the sea. Coral limestone makes up the northern coast and the only large areas of flat land are the Gadaisu-Mullins Harbour area to the south-west of Alotau and at the eastern end of the 28km long bay itself. The south coast has many attractive bays, beaches and coral reefs; most of the province's islands are surrounded by coral reefs. The highest point of mainland Milne Bay is Mt Suckling at 3676m.

There are many islands in the province and they are enormously varied, from tiny dots that barely break the water surface to large mountainous islands like Fergusson, Normanby and Goodenough. Officially, there are 435 islands, but you can add to that countless little islets, atolls and reefs. Goodenough Island in the D'Entrecasteaux group is, for its size, one of the most mountainous places on the planet. While it's only 26km across, it soars to 2566m high at the summit of Mt Oiautukekea and is one of the most steeply sided islands in the world.

The islands are divided into six main groups: the Samarai group; D'Entrecasteaux group; the Trobriand Islands; Muyua (Woodlark) Island; the Conflict and Engineer groups; and the large 300km-long Louisiade Archipelago, which is made up of a number of smaller groups including the Calvados chain. Most of the islands in the Louisiades, Samarai and D'Entrecasteaux groups are extensions of the mainland and include several extinct volcanos.

Climate

Milne Bay Province can have unpredictable weather. Rainstorms can be sudden and heavy. There is considerable local variation in weather patterns within the province, although generally you can expect November to January to have the best and most consistent weather, and March to June to be the least windy period.

Fringing reefs protect the islands when the prevailing south-easterly winds blow, but from December to March, the cyclone season in northern Australia and the Coral Sea can cause high seas and big winds, although even then the weather is often even and pleasant.

Society & Conduct

There are 43 local languages in Milne Bay Province, 33 of them are Austronesian languages spoken by the coastal people and islanders. Eight distinct, but related, non-Austronesian languages are spoken by the mountain people of the Rabaraba region.

Although it's still regarded as something of a backwater, this eastern end of PNG has had contact with the outside world for a relatively long time and the impact of missionaries was felt here as early as anywhere in the country. Perhaps more than elsewhere in PNG, the church is central to the lives of Milne Bay people, although the confluence

The Kula Ring

Extending right around the islands of Milne Bay Province is an invisible circle, or kula ring, that binds the islands together in a system of ritual exchange. The ring encompasses the Trobriand, Muyua (Woodlark), Louisiade, Samarai and D'Entrecasteaux islands. It involved the trade of red shell necklaces, called *bagi* or *soulava*, in a clockwise direction and white shell armlets, *mwali*, in an anti-clockwise direction. Each trader had a kula partner on their nearest neighbouring island in each direction. Once a year, the trader and a delegation from his clan journeyed to the island of his kula partner to receive gifts in elaborate public ceremonies. Once a year, he would be visited by another kula partner who would receive gifts in similar ceremonies. Kula gifts were highly prized and were never displayed publicly or used for ornamentation.

Accompanying these ritual voyages (made on specific important dates) were other ceremonial objects and surplus fish and yams to be exchanged with neighbouring islands. Since the bagi and mwali rarely left the circle, this system ensured a distribution of wealth among the islanders, although it could take many years for the ceremonial items to return to their place of origin.

The exchange mostly involved trade between traditional families of high status and thus helped to reinforce clan-based hierarchies. The ceremonies associated with the kula trade were highly complex and even today some people are required to journey to the island home of a traditional kula partner bearing ritual gifts honouring the birthday or anniversary of a clan chief. ■

of traditional beliefs and contemporary church teachings can confound and confuse the outside observer.

Witchcraft is still widely respected and, especially on the islands, still practised. Contract killings can still be arranged with witch doctors, who sometimes employ the spiritual powers of cyanide from the old mining operations on Misima and Muyua (Woodlark) islands. A traditional landowner from the south coast had this to say:

I'm intrigued by witchcraft and sorcery – I can't believe in it, but it seems to work. I thought I'd test it, so I asked a sorcerer to teach me spirit-travelling. But his fee was too high. You have to kill a member of your family. Too expensive.

In most of the island societies, landownership and family rights are passed down in a matrilineal system. Clan leaders and paramount chiefs of these societies are still men, sometimes with many wives, and there's much pomp and ceremony associated with these titles, however, behind the scenes the women wield considerable power.

Woodcarving is important in the region and the carvers of the Trobriand Islands are justifiably famous. Their fine work, usually in high-quality ebony traded from Muyua (Woodlark) Island, is stunning and manifests mostly in bowls and walking sticks, often with inlays of pearl shell and decorated in fish, bird or shell motifs.

The people of the province have the second-longest life expectancy of any in PNG and the elderly folk are active and look pretty fit. The people also boast the highest literacy rate outside the National Capital District. English is spoken as the principal second language and if you hear *tok pisin* (Pidgin) spoken, it will indicate the speaker is from somewhere else in the country; labourers, especially Highlanders, have come to work on the copra and oil-palm plantations near Alotau, and there are many newcomers to the area. Making yourself understood in the Trobriand Islands used to be difficult, but these days the younger locals speak some form of broken English.

In many of the region's cultures, people were traditionally buried standing up, with their heads poking out of the ground and clay pots covering their heads. When the heads eventually separated from the bodies, the pots were removed and the skulls were placed in a skull cave. Skull caves are common in the area and clay pots are a traditional artefact of the region.

Mainland & China Strait

ALOTAU
• *pop 9000* • *postcode 211*

In 1968 the headquarters for the Milne Bay provincial government were transferred from Samarai Island to Alotau on the northern flank of Milne Bay. Access to Samarai Island was only possible by sea and the tiny island was already too overcrowded to handle any further expansion.

Alotau is a sleepy little town built on some steep, undulating hillsides on the edge of the bay. It has an attractive harbour and some magnificent views of the bay and the mountains to the south. It's a pleasant and friendly place, with a slow easy, pace. However, there's not really much to do here. You can walk around the harbour, go to the market, poke around the trade stores, climb up the hill to the commanding lookout near the hospital, read the inscription on the war memorial in the town centre and then try the whole lot in reverse. But if you want to get out to the Milne Bay islands, this is where to begin. There are banks in Alotau and supermarkets where you can stock up on food. On the islands beyond here there are no services and few phones, so if you've got business, do it in Alotau.

For many years, the national government has been talking about building a road link to Port Moresby, but it's not going to happen. The locals like their isolation, they're happy to pay high freight charges and most feel that a road would ruin their easy-going lifestyle and let all the riffraff in. And 10 minutes after your arrival, you'd have to concur: this is one of the most relaxed and stress-free towns in PNG.

Across Milne Bay from Alotau is Discovery Bay, where Moresby spent several days during his 1873 visit. The mysterious 'moonstones' in the hills behind this bay are, as yet, an unsolved archaeological riddle. There is very good fishing and excellent diving around Alotau.

Orientation

The commercial centre is laid out on a grid, with everything within a five-minute walk, basically around a single block. The Masurina Centre near the harbour is the closest thing to a shopping mall and houses most of the businesses that will be important to the traveller. The town's more affluent housing and the top place to stay are up a steep climb past the hospital behind the commercial centre. The busy harbour is a short walk to the east of town. Further around is the Masurina Trading wharf and then the international wharf, where big freighters dock.

Alotau's airport is Gurney, which is 15km from town and surrounded by a massive oil-palm development.

Information

The Milne Bay Tourist Bureau (☎ 641 1503; fax 641 0132; PO Box 119) is in the Masurina Centre, on the second floor at the very back. Jennifer Varssilli, its friendly and helpful tourism development officer, can arrange accommodation in the area, get you started on a trade-boat trip into the islands and is a great source of historical and cultural information about the province.

The major banks are represented and the shopping is adequate – you'll see the market on your right as you come in from the airport.

Harbour

The harbour is the most colourful part of town, with boats of all shapes and sizes from all over the province. You can entertain yourself for hours watching the comings and goings – the fishers in the bay and the brightly painted island boats loading and unloading, all against the backdrop of moun-

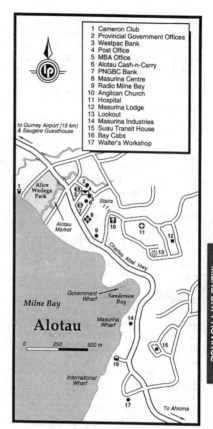

tains falling sheer into blue Milne Bay. Local kids spend hours goofing around at the end of the short government wharf, near where the trade boats tie up – they jump off into the water, climb up again, push someone else off and perform spectacular flips and dives, all the while squealing with laughter.

There are a few relics of the old government fleet rusting in the water. There used to be an excellent fleet of boats owned by the province but, with independence, their administration was taken over by the national government. The provincial government campaigned to have them returned, only to find that they couldn't afford their upkeep and subsequently sold them off. There is still local anger about this as people lament the loss of a once-great community asset. Maritime travel in the province is now largely confined to trade boats and dinghies. For a bird's-eye view of the harbour, walk up the steps in town to the hospital, take the right fork and keep going for a couple of hundred metres.

Activities

Swimming There isn't really a swimming beach in town. You could join the kids for a jump off the short pier, but the water in the harbour is a little sullied from all the boat traffic. There are several good black-sand swimming beaches to the east of town towards Ahioma, although they're not obvious from the road. PMVs run past and it's dead easy to hitch a ride along this stretch of road.

Diving There's great diving in and around Milne Bay and it's not just local dive-boat operators who visit the area. Rob Van de Loos runs Milne Bay Marine Charters (☎ & fax 641 1167, 641 1291; PO Box 270) and his boat *Cheetan* can sleep 12 passengers. The *Cheetan* has an extensive touring programme and favourite dive sites include Esa'ala, Nuakata, the Engineer group, East Cape, Cape Vogel and the Calvados chain. Rob's office is just past the high school; turn right off the airport road past the Mobil station.

Telita Cruises (☎ 641 1186; fax 641 1282; PO Box 303) operates the ten-berth *Telita*, which regularly plies through the waters of East Cape and the north coast, Normanby, Nuakata and the Engineers.

Niugini Diving (☎ 472 5692; fax 472 2455; PO Box 320, Lae) is managed by Rod Pearce out of Lae, but his six-berth boat *Barbarian* regularly comes to the waters of Milne Bay, particularly around the Cape Vogel area.

The 12-berth *Golden Dawn* is owned and operated by Craig Dewitt of Dolphin Enterprises (☎ 325 6500; fax 325 0302; PO Box 1335, Port Moresby) and frequents the waters of Milne Bay most of the year.

Organised Tours

The luxury *Melanesian Discoverer* runs tours between Madang and Alotau via the Trobriands. For details and schedule information contact Melanesian Tourist Services (☎ 852 2766; fax 852 3543; PO Box 707, Madang). The fortnightly *Eastern Star* newspaper, published in Alotau, sometimes advertises stand-by fares for the *Melanesian Discoverer*'s runs through the province, and while even these are expensive, the vessel certainly offers a high level of luxury and would be a nice way to see the region.

Special Events

The Alotau Provincial Show is held over three days in the second week in July.

Places to Stay

The cheapest place to stay in Alotau is the *Suau Transit House* (contact Jennifer Varssilli at the Milne Bay Tourist Bureau ☎ 641 1503), which is a little east of the commercial centre of Alotau in the hills behind the Masurina wharf. It's pretty basic with shared facilities and guest access to the kitchen. The plain rooms have no fan and single beds only, but the shared lounge area has a TV and an overhead fan. The nightly rates are K25 per person.

The KB Mission's *Saugere Guesthouse* (no phone; PO Box 32) is usually known as the KB guesthouse and is down by the bay just before town, off the road running in from the airport. It's about a 10-minute walk from town. This too is pretty basic and not especially cheap at K40/50 for a single/double.

Masurina Lodge (☎ 641 1212; fax 641 1406; PO Box 5) is the only other alternative in Alotau, and while it's a very comfortable and convenient place to stay, its tariffs are prohibitive. Masurina, with business interests including the lodge, shipping, fishing, constructions and finance, was established in the early 1970s by Chris Abel, grandson of the Reverend Charles W Abel who founded the Kwato Church. Rooms with overhead fan and shared facilities cost K112/153 per night single/double, and air-con rooms with private bathroom and phone cost K143/184. This rate includes all meals (and they're excellent), laundry and airport transfers. It's a friendly place, with a bar that's popular with expats and well-heeled locals, and has a small selection of artefacts and books for sale. The lodge also offers tours around the area. From the town's commercial centre, take the steps up the hill near the MBA office and Cash-n-Carry, which are a shortcut to the hospital, bear left at the first fork and keep climbing up past the hospital, and take the second road to the right. The lodge is about 200m down this street.

Places to Eat

Eating options are few in Alotau and your best bet for a hearty meal is the *Masurina Lodge*. Let them know you're coming and they'll provide breakfast at K8, lunch at K12 and dinner for K20 for non-guests. All meals are buffet style and they serve some of the better food in PNG. On Friday night they knock up a huge barbecue that is open to all comers for K10, which is good value.

The *Cafeteria* in the Masurina Centre is open during the day for lunch and snacks. It's a cut above the kai-bars in town and its atmosphere and air-con make it very pleasant, but don't expect anything too flash. Rice and stew, pies, fried rice, eggs and sandwiches are the fare available, all for about K3 or less. It also sells sliced fresh fruit, such as melon, pineapple and orange, and is clean and friendly.

Otherwise, you can get fresh fruit and vegetables at the market and there's several supermarkets and kai-bars in town. Several shops around town sell the good bread baked by the Alotau Bakery.

Entertainment

The bar at *Masurina Lodge* is the place to go for an evening drink, but if you want to see how the real people let their hair down, head down to the *Cameron Club*, which is on the waterfront past the market and the Alice Wedega Park. It's just behind the tennis courts and is a local workers' bar. Things can get a bit wild, especially on Friday nights (pay day), but if you're sensible and careful and make friends with a few locals, you'll have a fun time.

Things to Buy

There are couple of artefacts shops in the Masurina Centre. Reno Pty Ltd, on the ground floor in the arcade, sells a good range of regional artefacts, including carvings, baskets and bowls, but they are not cheap. Better value are the artefacts available from Barbara's Fashion Shop. Barbara sells some cheesy Milne Bay T-shirts and some other 'fashions', but her small range of artefacts is reasonably priced.

It's always worth having a close look in the trade stores for the weird and wonderful odds and sods that make their way to PNG from China and elsewhere – clothing, fuel lighters, Hawaiian-style painted ukuleles and loads of other kooky low-tech gadgets are available, but often you have to look hard to find the jewels in the junk heap.

Getting There & Away

Air Alotau's Gurney airport has recently been upgraded to handle the F-28s that MBA is flying from Cairns in Australia, alleviating the need to come through Port Moresby. There's a new terminal under construction, and customs and immigration agents meet international flights.

Gurney is 15km from town and was named after Bob Gurney, an Australian who began flying for Guinea Airways in 1929 and was killed in action with the RAAF in 1942.

Air Niugini and MBA have offices in town: Air Niugini (☎ 641 1100; fax 641 1636; PO Box 3) is in the Masurina Centre, and MBA (☎ 641 1591; fax 641 1559; PO Box 421) is near the big Cash-n-Carry building, next to the steps leading uphill to the hospital. Islands Nationair (☎ & fax 641 1273) has an agent at the rear of the Fifita Trading building in town.

Air Niugini flies daily direct between Port

Moresby and Gurney (K125); all its connections to Gurney are via Port Moresby.

MBA flies every day, except Sunday, between Port Moresby and Gurney, either direct or via Losuia in the Trobriand Islands (K125). MBA is the most useful carrier in the region, servicing remote airstrips in the province with its Dash-8 aircraft at least once a week. MBA flies between Gurney and Losuia on Monday and Wednesday (K133), connecting with flights to/from Port Moresby (K198 from Losuia). Islands Nationair flies to Losuia from Port Moresby

and Gurney on Tuesday, Thursday and Saturday.

The D'Entrecasteaux islands are serviced by MBA on Monday and Thursday. The fares from Gurney are: Esa'ala (Normanby Island) K61, Sehulaea (Normanby Island, Thursday only) K70, Salamo (Fergusson Island) K62 and Vivigani (Goodenough Island) K78. The route is slightly different on Monday and Thursday, and you can get from Esa'ala to Salamo (K34), but not from Salamo to Esa'ala.

To Misima Island, MBA flies from Port

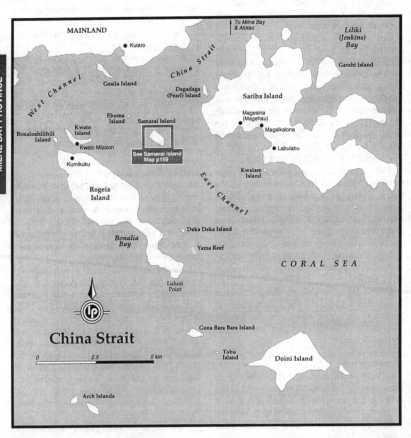

Moresby (K204) and Gurney (K113) on Monday, Tuesday, Thursday and Friday.

There's a flight from Gurney to Wedau (K37) and Rabaraba (K55) on Monday; to Rabaraba only on Tuesday; to Wedau and Rabaraba on Wednesday and flying on to Cape Vogel (K61); to Wedau and Rabaraba on Friday; and on Saturday to Wedau, Rabaraba and Cape Vogel.

All of MBA's inter-provincial connections to Gurney are via Port Moresby, except on Saturday flights to Popondetta (K156) and Lae (K203).

MBA manager, John Wild, lives on the China Strait Plantation, on the mainland near Samarai Island, which used to be a copra plantation. He is developing a tourist resort there soon. It's possible to stay there and easy to 'hitch' a lift on the daily flight from Gurney for K20. From China Strait, you can catch a dinghy to Samarai for K5.

Walking It's possible to walk to Alotau from Rabaraba or Wedau. See the North Coast section for details.

Boat There are no regular passenger ships to or from other provinces, although there are freighters from both Port Moresby and Lae. None officially take passengers, but you might get lucky. Most are Consort Line (☎ 641 1318 in Alotau) vessels.

Lutheran Shipping's north-coast run only operates as far east as Oro Bay, although by small boat you can get from Oro Bay right around the north coast to Cape Vogel and beyond. Moving in the other direction from Alotau, it would be possible to fly to Wedau (K37) on the north coast, or walk, and then catch dinghies up to Oro Bay and hook up with Lutheran Shipping's north-coast run. You can fly with MBA from Wedau to Wanigela (K88), but not in the other direction, and between Wanigela and Tufi (K36) in either direction.

To/from Port Moresby Travellers with time to spare could travel from Port Moresby to Alotau in local boats, sleeping in villages. You can travel by road from Port Moresby to Kupiano (where there's a guesthouse), by PMV from the Magi Highway turn-off, and from there to Domara by PMV. There's no formal accommodation east of here, but there is regular trade boat and dinghy traffic. In Domara there are work boats heading east, one or two most days travelling to Magarida, charging about K25 for the four-hour trip.

From Magarida you can catch a boat to the village of Suwayabina, where there's a health centre that runs a boat to Alotau once or twice a week. There are also other irregular boats.

Around Milne Bay Province There's much more sea than land in Milne Bay Province and, although there are regular flights to all of the island groups, the best way to see the region is by boat. Unfortunately, there are no regular passenger services. The old provincial government fleet has long been sold off, and so the dinghies and trade boats that service the trade stores on the islands are really the only option. These are primarily small work boats and catching a ride can involve lots of hanging around wharves, persistently asking about destinations and probably adding a few hours to the alleged times of departure. Unlike PMVs, boats aren't always a frequent and reliable way to get about, but once you're on the open water sitting atop a load of SP Lager, Kundu Crackers and margarine you'll begin to feel the real charm of the province.

In local parlance, a dinghy (banana boat or speedie) is an 18 to 23 foot open fibreglass boat with a 40-odd horsepower outboard engine. These are fast (depending on the load), safe and, at full throttle, an exhilarating way to get around. They can handle heavy seas much better than the average traveller, but with any undulations on the water's surface you are going to get wet – *very* wet – so do as the others do and keep your luggage off the boat's floor under the tarpaulin. Try to sit at the rear of the boat and hang on! The older-style heavy wooden work boats with a central diesel engine are known as 'putt-putts'; they're noisy and smelly, they roll a lot in the heavy seas and take about four times as long to get anywhere as the dinghies. They are best avoided unless there are no dinghies available. Remember that the boat operators are highly skilled mariners who for generations have plied these waters every day and value their own lives as much as you value yours. Remember also that what seems like a gentle breeze on terra firma can whip up high seas once you're beyond the point of turning back and can bring about the need for laundry by the time you get where you're going – the open sea can be very scary in a little fibreglass boat! Oh, and if you ask for a life jacket you'll just get blank looks.

Apart from hanging around the harbour (try the Masurina Trading wharf and the international wharf as well, and don't forget the small bay east of the market where dinghies often tie up) there are a few other strategies if you want to get around the islands.

The *Morning Star*, an ex-government boat now touring the province's missions, is one possibility, and the hospital in Alotau has a boat that it uses to call on the islands' medical clinics. The supermarkets will know about work boats carrying supplies; you can contact Bob Coleman (☎ 641 1246) at Alotau Enterprises in the big Cash-n-Carry building, or Fifita Trading (☎ 641 1373), which supplies many stores in the province. Radio Milne Bay gives shipping information at 7 am and 7 pm.

Osiri Trading (☎ 641 1088/642 1088) on Samarai runs a trade boat to and from the Masurina Trading wharf on Monday and Friday, and charges K20 for the trip. The tourist office will make a booking for you, or phone David Hall or Ian Poole at Osiri.

A number of work boats run to Esa'ala and Salamo in the D'Entrecasteaux islands for about K20.

The trade stores on Kiriwina in the Trobriands run boats to Alotau approximately weekly, and charge about K45 for the two-day trip. These boats pass by the D'Entrecasteaux islands and might be able to drop you off there.

There are a few charter options out of Alotau, but they're expensive unless you have a group – and not exactly cheap then. Both Telita Cruises and Milne Bay Marine Charters will charter their boats, although they are primarily dive outfits – see Diving in the Activities section earlier. The *Morning*

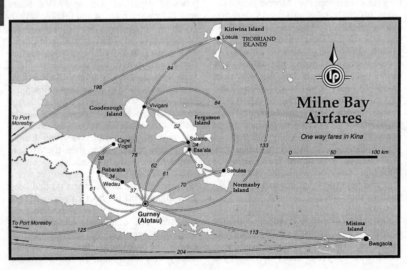

Milne Bay Airfares

One way fares in Kina

Star is also available for charter. Figure on about K450 per 24 hours.

Getting Around
The Airport Taxis meet most flights, but they charge K15 to get into town – a kina a kilometre. PMVs don't tend to come up to the terminal but run to town from the nearby main road (K2), a two-minute walk away. Allow yourself plenty of time if you're taking a PMV out to the airport. Masurina Lodge has free airport transfers for guests. However, the cheapest, best and probably most reliable way into town is simply asking someone for a lift.

PMV In town, PMVs heading for the airport can be found near the market and those going east stop near the PNGBC bank. The road continues east all the way to East Cape, the easternmost point on the PNG mainland. There are a couple PMVs a day that make it out that far, although the road fords several rivers and is bad after rains – it might sometimes be too much for the average minibus.

Car & Taxi Bay Cabs (☎ 641 1093) is the main taxi company and sometimes hires cars. It's located down near the BP fuel depot, near the international wharf. Walter's Workshop (☎ 641 1174) is also down near there and hires cars.

AROUND ALOTAU
East Cape
You can access East Cape from Alotau either overnight or as a day trip. You can get there by PMV for only K5, but they only run a couple of times a day and perhaps not at all, if the road's too wet. It's about two hours each way in a 4WD and the road fords several rivers and passes many pretty villages and black-sand beaches.

You could get there by dinghy from Alotau harbour if you were prepared to charter one for K20 or K30. Alternatively, you could organise a day trip with Masurina Lodge in Alotau complete with cut lunch for a hefty K150, perhaps worthwhile if you put a group together. There's terrific snorkelling and

diving, and a skull cave just a five-minute walk from the village.

Place to Stay There's the rustic *Oima Guesthouse* on the beach at Bilubilu village, only a few hundred metres from mainland PNG's easternmost tip. There's a radiophone at the nearby East Cape health centre on the VHF network where you could leave a booking, but you would have to be unlucky to find the place full. The guesthouse, a bush-materials hut right on the beach, is run by John Kailaga from the village. It's popular with yachties, who sometimes anchor just offshore, and charges K40 per night with kai-style meals included.

Wagawaga
This tiny settlement on the rugged and mountainous southern coast of Milne Bay has accommodation available. At the *Wagawaga Community Guesthouse* (☎ 641 1712; PO Box 94, Alotau), the cost is just K34 per person, including all meals. A dinghy from Alotau harbour would run you across the bay in about 30 minutes and only cost a few kina.

NORTH COAST
Wedau Area
There are good beaches and reefs around the small settlement of Wedau. Ethel Mercy Kaniniba runs the *Wedau Guesthouse* (no phone; PO Box 18 Dogura post office) and charges K35 per night. Nearby Dogura is worth a visit; there are views from the plateau and there's a fine church, but no accommodation. Gubanaona is a good place for swimming and snorkelling. Mt Pasipasi can be climbed in one long, hot day (take water) and there are good views from the top.

Cape Vogel
Towards Cape Vogel, there's the *Bogaboga Guesthouse* which you can contact on the radiophone VHF network – just ask the operator. Bevan Oscar Mogina is the person to talk to about the accommodation, which is just K15 a night. There are four rooms there. Bogaboga has a trade store but you would

want to bring some supplies. Local attractions include bush trails, waterfalls, good snorkelling (including gear for hire) and artefacts for sale. Contact the Milne Bay Tourist Bureau for more information.

Getting There & Away

MBA flies to Rabaraba, Wedau and Cape Vogel several days a week from Gurney. See the Alotau Getting There & Away section.

You can walk from Rabaraba or Wedau to Alotau, at least partly on a well-used path that runs along the coast. There are plenty of villages along the way, which means that you will have no trouble finding somewhere to sleep. Rabaraba to Wedau takes two days, and from Wedau to the tiny settlement of Taupota No 2 takes three easy days or two longer ones. From here, you can reach Alotau in a day by heading south across a low range, but you might want to take a guide for this section and there is a steep descent. Talk to Jennifer Varssilli at the Milne Bay Tourist Bureau about this walk; it's apparently not difficult. There's a couple of good routes across the range.

Alternatively, you can stay on the coast and walk from Taupota No 2 to East Cape, where there's the *Oima Guesthouse*, then around the cape and back towards Alotau where you'll meet a road on which PMVs run. This section takes three days. For full details and maps, see Lonely Planet's *Bushwalking in Papua New Guinea*.

SAMARAI ISLAND

• *postcode 215*

The tiny island of Samarai, just 24 hectares in area, is in China Strait (so named by Moresby because he thought it would be the most direct route from the east coast of Australia to China), some distance around the coast from Milne Bay. Like a verdant garden gone to seed, Samarai has seen better days: many of the old government buildings are derelict and worn, and the elements of nature have taken over. But it's still a pretty place in a very beautiful area. It has a faded-glory feel about it from the colonial days, when it was said to be one of the most beautiful

places in the Pacific. These days, some people and businesses rent the buildings from the provincial government but most are filled with squatters.

Samarai was long the provincial headquarters and the settlement predates Port Moresby. Before WWII it was the second-largest town in PNG, but during the war it was completely destroyed by the Australian administration, in anticipation of a Japanese invasion that never came.

Its post-war reincarnation was built in Australian country-town style, with lots of corrugated iron and cool verandahs along what passes for the main street. Well-mown grass grows on most of the narrow roads and sleeping dogs lie undisturbed in the middle of them. A path encircles the island; you can stroll around it in half an hour.

Samarai's decline began in 1968, when the provincial government headquarters moved to Alotau. When the international wharf closed in the 1970s, most businesses left. There are now only three or four expats on the island, from a peak of about 300. The old wharf, a big wooden structure, is now in terminal decay, but people fish from it and kids dive off it into the clear water.

David Hall and Ian Poole alternately run Osiri Trading, the only proper trade store left on the island. There are a couple of kiosk-size shops about but the Osiri trade boat supplies them anyway. There are almost no phones on the island, but Osiri Trading acts as a kind of information service for the island's population.

Information

Both David Hall and Ian Poole (☎ 641 1088, 642 1088) are interesting repositories of local cultural and historical information. If you arrive on their trade boat, they'll probably be waiting at the old wharf outside their store to meet the boat. Wallace Andrew, owner of the Kinanale Guesthouse, is also a good source of local information. He's a Kwato old boy, grandson of a cannibal, local entrepreneur and identity, and a fascinating character to talk to.

Things to See & Do

Well there really isn't much to see or do and certainly no organised entertainment. If you're there on a weekend you might be able to see some soccer or a cricket match on the sportsground. Other than that, you can walk around the island, climb the hill up to the old hospital, swim, watch other people swim, watch tropical fish swimming around the wharves and then walk around the island again.

In the middle of the town's main intersection, there is a monument to Christopher Robinson, the one-time administrator who committed suicide in June 1904. The inscription notes that he was an 'able governor, upright man and honest judge', 'his aim was to make New Guinea a good place for white men' and he 'was as well meaning as he was unfortunate and as kindly as he was courageous'.

Special Events

The Samarai Pearl Festival was a big hit when it happened once a few years ago. It attracted 9000 people to the tiny island and must have been standing room only, literally. There's strong local feeling that it should be held again on an annual basis, probably in November or December, and the provincial government is kicking in some financial support.

Places to Stay & Eat

The *Bwanasa Women's Association Guest-house* (contact Osiri Trading, ☎ 641 1088, 642 1088), commonly referred to as the Women's Guesthouse, is the only place to stay on Samarai and it's actually pretty nice. It's clean and plain, but nicely positioned halfway up the hill overlooking the wharves. Theresa and Genevieve look after the place and the rates are K40/25 per person with/without meals.

Wallace Andrew is the owner of *Kinanale Guesthouse* (contact Osiri Trading, ☎ 641 1088, 642 1088), which is not in operation due to financial problems and a certain point of principle: Sir Julius Chan's People's Progress Party held an all-in, eight-day, catered

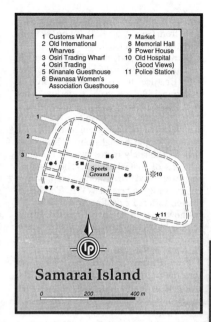

```
1 Customs Wharf          7 Market
2 Old International       8 Memorial Hall
  Wharves                9 Power House
3 Osiri Trading Wharf   10 Old Hospital
4 Osiri Trading             (Good Views)
5 Kinanale Guesthouse   11 Police Station
6 Bwanasa Women's
  Association Guesthouse
```

Samarai Island

0   200   400 m

conference there and then defaulted on payment. Wallace says this is the second time he's been burnt from hosting 'political conventions' and reckons he's owed a lot of money. He says he'll open again when he's been paid. The guesthouse is pleasant, with an airy beach-house feel about it, but wants a freshen-up anyway and is by no means luxurious. When it reopens, figure on about K65/45 per person with/without meals.

NEAR SAMARAI ISLAND

China Strait and the surrounding islands still have a reputation for witchcraft and, despite the strong influence of missionaries, superstitions linger. Strange lights, ghost ships and sirens (the singing kind) all crop up.

There are places to stay on islands around Samarai; *China Strait Plantation* (☎ 641 1019 or contact MBA in Alotau) plans to build a resort based around self-contained bungalows. There already are some facilities for guests and you can catch a dinghy from

Samarai for K5 or 'hitch' a lift on the daily flight from Gurney for K20. It's on the mainland near Samarai Island.

On **Kwato Island**, about 2 to 3km west of Samarai, the Reverend Charles Abel and his wife, Beatrice, founded a non-hierarchical church in 1891. Kwato Mission functioned as a successful educational and boat-building centre, although it wasn't until the 1930s that the last of the nearby cannibal tribes was 'saved'. People brought up on Kwato are disproportionately represented in the upper echelons of PNG business. The mission's boats were used to transport and supply Australian coastwatchers in WWII. The Kwato Church suffered a decline in the 1970s, but has now been officially recognised. It may be possible to stay here and a visit is worthwhile. Boats to Kwato are easy to catch from the wharf at Samarai.

Tiny **Ebuma Island**, just 1km off Samarai, has a house available for rent. This area gets so few visitors, however, that no-one is sure how much it costs. The house is a bit dilapidated and around K40 a night seems about right, but it's all pretty vague.

At neighbouring **Dioni Island**, a private island about 10km south-east of Samarai, there's accommodation available and a luxurious guesthouse in the making. The *Dioni Plantation Guesthouse* (☎ 641 1441; PO Box 46, Samarai) is managed by expat Tony Gallaway. The only people living here are a few workers on the coconut plantation. There are no villages. The island has walking tracks, plenty of reefs and sometimes surf at Clamp's Cove. The small white-sand beach near the manager's house is beautiful but plagued by sandflies.

Deka Deka, another tiny islet, is a popular beach and picnic spot, as is nearby **Logea Island**. The small cluster of the **Wari islands**, 45km from Samarai, is another boat-building centre and the people there are also fine potters.

It should be possible to stay in villages on many of the islands in the area for about K10. Island people come to Samarai to shop and sell produce at the market (busiest on Saturday morning but never very busy), so ask

around. A small sack of Trukai rice makes a good present for your hosts.

SOUTH COAST

The south coast of Milne Bay Province is the southernmost part of the PNG mainland and is beautiful, heavily forested country with very few services. The landowners of the Suau area plan to open a guesthouse on Delina Island and are negotiating with logging companies, which they hope will build roads into the area.

Island Groups

D'ENTRECASTEAUX ISLANDS

There are three large islands in the D'Entrecasteaux group that are separated from the north coast of the mainland only by a narrow strait. They are extremely mountainous – you pass directly over them when between Alotau and Kiriwina in the Trobriands. Whales, dolphins and dugongs move through the area.

Getting There & Away

MBA flies to Normanby, Fergusson and Goodenough from Gurney on Monday and Thursday. See the Alotau Getting There & Away section. A work boat from Alotau to Salamo on Fergusson or Esa'ala on Normanby costs about K20 and takes about 10 to 12 hours. Salamo probably sees the most traffic. From Salamo, a boat to the Trobriands costs about K20 and takes about 12 hours; to Muyua (Woodlark) a boat costs about K40 and takes two days.

Normanby Island

Esa'ala, the district headquarters, is at the entrance to the spectacular Dobu Passage. It's a tiny place, with a couple of stores, a market and electricity for a few hours each day. However, there are a few places to stay and a reef offering excellent snorkelling just offshore from the town. Trade boats from Alotau call at Esa'ala, but the airstrip is about an hour's drive away on a bad road.

Top: Stilt village near Koki, National Capital District
Middle: Beach scene at Kaibola, Trobriand Islands, Milne Bay Province
Bottom: Looking towards Cape Girumia, Wedau, Milne Bay Province

ROWAN MCKINNON

JON MURRAY

ROWAN MCKINNON

Top Left: Tidal flat mangrove on Loloata Island, National Capital District.
Top Right: Alotau harbour, Milne Bay Province
Bottom: Wharf, Samarai Island, Milne Bay Province

In the middle of the south-west coast is Sewa Bay, used by Allied warships during WWII and a port of call for small inter-island ships today. There are strange, unexplained rock carvings around the bay.

Places to Stay & Eat The *Esa'ala Guesthouse* is on the beach near the main wharf. Enquiries can be made through the Esa'ala post office on ☎ 641 1491, or the district office on ☎ 641 1217. It's friendly, the food is good and the K65 per person includes meals.

The *Inman's Weekend Retreat* (☎ 641 1209; PO Box 11, Esa'ala) is really just Tom and Val Inman's holiday house, but they open it up for guests at K30 per person. For K90, you can get six people into the three rooms, so if there's more than a couple of you, there's probably some room for negotiation on the room rate.

The *Kezzie Guesthouse*, at Dotaona village in the south of Normanby Island, is another accommodation option. The rates are K40 per person and breakfast costs K5 and dinner K10. Contact Ana-Latu Dickson at *Eastern Star* newspaper office in the Masurina Centre in Alotau (☎ 641 1141; fax 641 1370).

Dobu Island
In the passage is tiny, fertile Dobu Island, where the Methodists established their first mission in the area; the mountains rise sheer on both sides of the strait. This island has a reputation for sorcery, but it's also fervently Christian. Simple village accommodation is available in this beautiful place.

Fergusson Island
Fergusson is the central island in the group and the largest in size. Although mountainous, it pales in comparison with nearby Goodenough. The highest mountain here is only 2073m, with two other lower ranges from which the island's many rivers and streams flow. Fergusson's large population is mainly concentrated along the south coast. It is notable for its active thermal region – hot springs, bubbling mud pools, spouting geysers and extinct volcanos. Thermal springs can be found at Deidei and Iamalele on the west coast. There is a Methodist mission at Salamo on the south coast.

Salamo isn't a big place but it's the biggest town for some way, so there's a lot of boat and canoe traffic, especially for the Saturday market. It's not especially attractive, but is a good base for travel around the D'Entrecasteaux group and further afield.

Places to Stay & Eat Salamo has a couple of guesthouses. The *Salamo Women's Guesthouse* (☎ 641 1718; care of Salamo post office, Fergusson Island) and *Salamo Span* (☎ 641 1157; care of Salamo post office, Fergusson Island) both charge K20 a night, but you'll have to bring some supplies. In the mountains inland from Salamo is the *Sebutuia Mountain Lodge*, built and run by a local village. Accommodation costs around K30, including meals.

Nadi, about 45 minutes by boat from Salamo, is a pretty village with good beaches and a simple guesthouse. There are some strenuous but rewarding treks in the jungle, but apparently the spiders are 'as big as baseball mitts'.

Goodenough Island
The most north-westerly of the group, Goodenough is amazingly mountainous with a high central range that has two peaks topping 2400m and reaches 2566m at the summit of Mt Oiautukekea. It's only 26km across and one of the most steeply sided islands in the world. There are fertile coastal plains flanking the mountain range and a road runs around the north-east coast through Vivigani, site of the major airstrip in the group. There's only an open shelter here – 'one of the less exciting places to spend 12 hours waiting for a plane that didn't show up', reported one visitor.

Bolubolu is the island's main settlement, about 10km south of the airstrip at Vivigani. In the centre of the island there is a large stone, covered in mysterious black and white paintings, which is said to have power over the yam crops. The *Bolubolu Guesthouse*

MILNE BAY PR

(care of Bolubolu post office, Goodenough Island) charges K35 a night.

Amphlett Islands

The tiny Amphlett islands are scattered to the north of the main D'Entrecasteaux group. The people here are part of the kula ring trading cycle and make some extremely fine and very fragile pottery. By boat from Salamo, it's about two hours and costs around K10, or K40 if you charter.

TROBRIAND ISLANDS

The Trobriand Islands (locally referred to as the Trobes) lie to the north of the D'Entrecasteaux group and are the most famous islands in the province. They are also geographically very different from the rest of the province in that they are almost entirely flat.

Polish anthropologist Bronislaw Malinowski wrote a series of celebrated books – *Argonauts of the Western Pacific*, *Coral Gardens and their Magic* and *The Sexual Life of Savages in North-Western Melanesia* – after WWI. Since then, the islands have been the subject of much anthropological study. While the Trobriand Islanders are certainly an unusual lot, clinging to their traditions and fiercely resisting western culture, their 'exoticness' has been perpetuated as much by western anthropological fascination as their ability to keep their traditional society alive. These two things have fed each other. They do have some quirks – yam harvesting time is a colourful festival of clan prestige and free love, a strict hierarchical social system, enormous and highly decorated yam houses, and they are responsible for the most exquisite carvings. But in truth, had Malinowski been exiled to the Louisiades instead of the Trobriands, many of his observations would have been similar and no-one would ever have heard of the Trobriands. Many of the central elements of Trobriands culture are (were) common to many islands of the province.

However, the Trobriands are still a mecca for many travellers to PNG; they are accessible and a fascinating glimpse of a traditional culture that's not too corrupted by the 20th century.

The group takes its name from Denis de Trobriand, an officer on d'Entrecasteaux's expedition. The largest island in the group is Kiriwina, where the airstrip and district headquarters, Losuia, are situated.

The Trobriands are low-lying coral islands, in complete contrast to their southern neighbours, and lack the other islands' spectacular scenery. There are some very good beaches, it's possible to stay in villages and the fishing is apparently excellent.

There is almost no economic activity in the islands, apart from some bêche-de-mer harvesting and trochus shell collecting. Trochus shells are exported to Europe, where they are still used to make high-quality buttons. There's also some small-scale crocodile farming. Local lime, used with betel nut, is famed for its quality and traded around the province. Expats number only five or six and are either missionaries, lodge owners or working on the reafforestation programme. Be aware of the local sense of humour; practical jokes with the *dim dim* (foreigner) as the butt are greatly enjoyed. Communication can be a little difficult – Pidgin is not spoken, although the younger half of the locals speak at least some form of broken English, albeit shyly and hesitantly. English is taught at the 10 or so local primary schools; the one high school is on Kiriwina.

It's good manners to let the paramount chief know you have arrived and certainly if you are there as more than a mere tourist – to make any studies, shoot any film footage or the like – you should request an audience with him to explain why you've come. It's enough to ask almost anyone to pass on the message to the chief; it will reach him.

Society & Conduct

At the beginning of WWI, Malinowski was offered a choice of internment in Australia or banishment to the remote Trobriands. He sensibly chose the latter and his studies of the islanders, their intricate trading rituals, yam cults and sexual practices, led to his classic series of books.

Like other islanders of the region, Trobriand Islanders have strong Polynesian characteristics and a matrilineal society. The chief's sons belong to his wife's clan and he is succeeded by one of his oldest sister's sons. The society is strictly hierarchical, with distinctions between hereditary classes and demarcations in the kind of work each person can perform. The soil of the Trobriands is very fertile and great care is lavished on the gardens, particularly the yam gardens, which have great practical and cultural importance.

The villages are all laid out in a similar

Local Customs

Yams Yams are far more than a staple food in the Trobriands – they're also a ritual, a sign of prestige, an indicator of expertise and a tie between villages and clans. The quality and size of the yams you grow is a matter of considerable importance. Many hours can be spent on discussions of your ability as a yam cultivator, and to be known as a *tokwaibagula* (good gardener) is a mark of great ability and prestige.

The yam cult reaches its high point at the harvest time – usually June or July. The yams are first dug up in the gardens and before being transported back to the village they must be displayed, studied and admired in the gardens. At the appropriate time, the men carry the yams back to the village, with the women guarding the procession.

In the villages, the yams are again displayed, in circular piles, before the next stage takes place – the filling of the yam houses. Again, there are extended rituals to be observed. Each man has a yam house for each of his wives and it is his brother-in-law's responsibility (in other words, his wife's clan's obligation) to fill his yam house. The chief's yam house is always the first to be filled. Yams are not merely a food – they're also part of a complicated annual ritual and an important and ongoing connection between villages.

Sex Malinowski's tomes on the Trobriand Islanders' customs led to Kiriwina being given the misleading title of the 'Island of Love'. It is not surprising that such a label was applied by inhibited Europeans when they first met Trobriand women, with their free and easy manners, their good looks and short grass dresses, but it led to the inaccurate idea that the Trobriands were some sort of sexual paradise. The sexual customs are different to many other places, but are not without their own complicated social strictures.

From puberty onwards, teenagers are encouraged to have as many sexual partners as they choose until marriage, when they settle down with the partner who is chosen as suitable and compatible. Males leave home when they reach puberty and move into the village *bukumatula* (bachelor house). Here, they are free to bring their partners back at any time, although preference is usually given to places with a little more privacy. Even married couples, subject to mutual agreement, are allowed to have a fling or two when the celebrations for the yam harvest are in full swing.

It is said that despite all this activity few children are born to women without permanent partners. Perhaps there are herbal contraceptives, although there always seem to be plenty of kids in all the Trobriand villages. The people do not believe there is a connection between intercourse and pregnancy – a child's spirit, which floats through the air or on top of the sea, chooses to enter a woman, often through her head.

All this apparent freedom has absolutely no impact on visitors. Freedom of choice is the basis of Trobriand life, so why would any islander choose some ugly, pale dim dim who can't speak like a civilised human, doesn't understand the most basic laws and will probably be gone tomorrow?

Kula Ring Trobriands people sometimes block the ring to allow an accumulation of trade goods, then hold a big *uvulaku* (ring festival), which gives people an opportunity to display their wealth before trading it away again. Also see The Kula Ring aside earlier in this chapter.

Cricket A more modern custom is the unique sport known as 'Trobriands cricket'. Missionaries introduced cricket as a way of taking the Trobriand Islanders' minds off less healthy activities and it's since developed its own style, which is quite unlike anything the MCC ever had in mind. The fact that the Trobriands cricket rule book contains no mention of how many players make up a team goes some way to explaining how it works. If there's a game scheduled while you're on the island, don't miss it! There's only a couple of villages inland that take it seriously and the dancing that accompanies the game can be provocative. ■

pattern – which you can see most clearly from the air as you fly in or out of Kiriwina. The village yam houses form an inner ring, surrounded by sleeping houses, and the whole lot is encircled by a ring of trees and vegetation.

The islanders are wonderful carvers and examples of their fine work will be keenly pressed upon you as soon as you step off the plane at Losuia by the people milling around (the cash economy is very small and your tourist kina are keenly sought). Bowls, sticks and stools are the most common carvings, with forms and styles specific to a village or clan. A master carver is a position of high prestige in the Trobriands and is a role bestowed upon people at birth. This is also true of dancers, singers and most other roles in the society. A carver cannot fell his own timber, as this is another role given to others in the hierarchy, and must purchase it from the landowner where it is grown. The two kinds of ebony grown on the islands are now rare, and another finer timber gets traded from Muyua (Woodlark) Island. Ebony is an extremely hard and brittle timber, and difficult to work.

Highly decorated yam houses are a feature of the Trobriands; the tall structures seem like skyscrapers against the flat land. The building of a yam house is the exclusive privilege of a clan leader or big man, but there's been some trouble in recent years with Trobriand Islanders returning home after being educated, working and amassing some money in the cities. Some of these people have erected their own yam houses, acting above their station and undermining traditional hierarchy. Clan warfare is still practised and ensuing deaths and paybacks are not uncommon.

Staying in Villages

The people are proud and fairly aloof and certainly know the value of a kina. They are adept at separating you from your money, so make sure you establish the price of *every-thing* in advance with the village chief. Nothing is free.

This attitude might be partly explained by the islanders' expertise as traders (see The Kula Ring aside) and traditional notions of reciprocity, but also by the fact that herds of naive and nosy anthropologists keep turning up. Remember too that there's almost no cash economy and your hard cash buys goods from stores.

You need to be fairly hardy to cope with the rigours of village life because, although it may look like paradise, it is in reality pretty tough. There is a fair degree of overcrowding, the hygiene levels leave something to be desired and the food is uninspiring. You should take in your own water.

Most people who come want to stay at least one night in a village and for most of those it is a fantastic experience. Certainly you must be prepared to pay for what you use (hardly a shocking concept for good capitalist tourists), but you are also likely to meet friendly, interesting people and gain an insight (however limited) into an extraordinary culture.

Orientation

By far the largest island is **Kiriwina** and the airstrip is here. Most of Kiriwina is flat, although there is a rim of low hills (uplifted coral reefs) that runs down the eastern side. The central plain is intensely cultivated, to the extent that there are no decent trees left, and hot and flat. The airport is here and south of it on the coast is the main town, **Losuia**, a 15-minute drive away. North of the airport is Kaibola. The bay on the western side of the island is a huge expanse of very shallow water – so shallow that the canoes are punted along with poles. Towards the southern end of the island, the eastern beaches are backed by beautiful rainforest, and although they all have reefs they look out onto the open sea.

Information

Losuia, the only real town and generally known as 'the station', has a wharf, a couple of schools and churches, a police station, health centre, a couple of government offices, a few small trade stores and that's about it. It's more like a sprawling village than a town. Its postcode is 221.

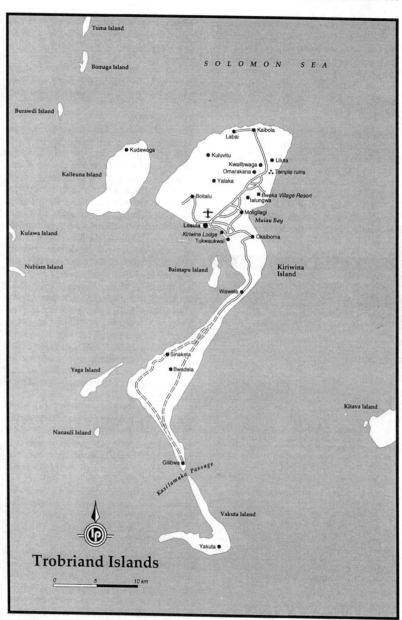

The Trobriands have only recently been connected to the telephone network and the lines still go down fairly often. There is no bank, so you must bring all the cash you will need with you. If you plan to stay in the villages, make sure you bring small denominations. Kiriwina Lodge might change travellers cheques for guests.

Special Events

The Trobriand Islands Yam Festival is an annual event, usually held in June. This is the most colourful time to come, as there's much ritual associated with the yam harvest. The spirit of free love is at its most heightened at this time, when the women take as many lovers as possible into the bushes for a bit of wanton lustful activity. However, visitors

Naughty Words

Malinowski, in his studies, made a detailed foray into the Trobriands language, which has a wide variety of sexual terminology including different ways of referring to male and female genitals, depending on whether they're yours, your partner's or somebody else's. Just so you have your sexual terminology lined up before you get there, remember that it is:

Female	Male
my wiga	my kwiga
your wim	your kwim
her wila	his kwila

Since *wila* is pronounced 'Wheeler', my surname has an unfortunate translation. Once they had got over the sheer amazement that anybody could be so dumb as to call himself Wheeler (or *wila*), the girls at the Kiriwina Lodge took great pleasure in calling me wila as frequently as possible.

There's plenty of other fun to be had with the local language. If male readers would like something nice to whisper in their girlfriend's ear, try '*yoku tage kuwoli nunum, kwunpisiga*' or when things get a bit heavier, try '*wim, kasesam!*' For female readers, say '*kaykukupi kwim*' if you want to belittle your male friend. You can further enhance your stock of questionable Trobriands phrases at celebrations during the yam harvesting season.

Tony Wheeler

with boiling loins might have to make their own entertainment because, while yams are considered objects of great beauty, dim dims are not.

This is also the time when the Trobriands get most visitors, including more documentary makers than you can poke a camera at.

Places to Stay

Formal Lodgings The *Village Birth Attendant Centre* (call the district office on ☎ 641 1502), near the health centre in Losuia, was established by a PhD student, Joseph Anang from Ghana, as a centre for training village midwives. It's now run by Sue, who replaced Joseph after nearly a decade of service to the Kiriwina community. There are five huts, each sleeping two people, and you can stay here for K20 a night. Bedding and mosquito nets are provided and conditions are very clean but basic – if you don't like this, you won't cope at all in a village.

The *Bweka Village Resort* (☎ 640 4500; PO Box 75, Losuia), also known as the Workers' Lodge, is a new place run by John Kasaipwalova and his Malaysian wife, Mary. John was once a student radical and has published some books of poetry. The lodge is near the beach on the eastern edge of Kiriwina Island and charges K50/80 for a single/double including some meals. Mary is a terrific cook.

The *Kiriwina Lodge* (☎ 641 1326; PO Box 1, Losuia) is the top place to stay, but it's expensive and badly positioned. Single/double rooms with attached bathroom cost K103/133 for a single/double room with fan, and K115/145 in an air-con room. These rates include all meals, which feature a lot of seafood and are quite reasonable. The lodge has undergone some recent renovations but even those don't justify the expensive room rates. It's now managed by a former speaker of parliament, Dennis Young.

The lodge is on the coast, several kilometres east of Losuia. It is on the lagoon side of the island and a small section of garden runs down to the water, which is, unfortunately, shallow, swampy and no good for swimming. A few small crocs are fattened up for slaughter in a pond. Sitting on the balcony, drink in hand, watching the outrigger canoes being poled across the bay and chatting to local people and expats as they come and go is pleasant enough, up to a point. If you want to do any snorkelling or see anything, however, you'll have to organise transport. See the Getting Around section.

Villages Kiriwina Lodge arranges village stays for about K10 a night, including basic food, and will transport you (for a fee) to and from the village, but to take advantage of this you have to stay a night or two at the lodge. Doing it this way might cost considerably more than arranging everything yourself but at least you won't be ripped off by the village and you will be guaranteed of transport back to Losuia in time to catch your flight, an important consideration on an island with little public transport and infrequent flights.

The villagers are well aware of what the Kiriwina Lodge charges for accommodation and feel cheated if you pay too much less than you would there. North of Losuia it is possible to stay in some villages from about K10 a night. You must make the arrangements with the village chief. Make sure you know exactly what you're paying for, or you'll have endless small additions made to the bill. Two villages not far from the airport that have been suggested are Ialungwa and Omarakana . Kapwapu , with a chief called Tobuguota, is apparently a 15-minute walk from Kaibola Beach. This village charges a very negotiable K20 a night including meals. It's also possible to stay in villages south of Losuia.

Things to Buy

By far the best known artefacts in the province are the Trobriands carvings. Certain villages specialise in certain styles and types of carvings. Trobriand Islanders are astute businesspeople, so you should avoid rushing into any purchases. The prices will have some room for negotiation, but you'll be much more pleased with yourself with one fine object than a few inferior ones. Look closely at the carvings and expect to pay for what you get – a master carver's work will be immaculately finished in all the recesses and details, with pearl-shell inlays, and a good stick might cost K80 to K100 or more. You'll also be offered some objects knocked up for tourists, sometimes blackened by shoe polish to make them look as if they've been made with high-grade ebony.

Kiriwina Lodge has a good collection of carvings and other artefacts, and most are for sale. Check this out before you visit the villages so you have some idea of the quality and price to aim for. You might end up buying from there anyway, as the prices aren't unreasonable.

There's a variety of artefacts, ranging from bowls and stools to walking sticks. The bowls, popular for use as salad or fruit bowls, often have decorative rims or flat surrounds carved like fish or turtles, with shells for eyes. But, again, there's good ones and dodgy ones, so be discerning. These goods are available in Alotau and elsewhere, but prices rise the further you are from the Trobriands. The best carvings are made from ebony.

Stools are also made and a tiny one costs about K30, but the big stools cost about K800 – plus the excess baggage charges to get these monsters off the island. Three-legged tables are also popular. Lime containers made from decorated gourds, and chains carved from a single piece of wood are other items you may see.

Other than carvings, you can get shells and bagi, although the latter is likely to be very expensive. The shell money is made on Rossel Island – it's meticulously ground shell discs with a diameter of about 5mm strung like a necklace. If it's genuine, it will cost about K1 a centimetre – beware of plastic imitations. *Doba* (leaf money) is also still used as negotiable currency; it's a bundle of banana leaves with each leaf incised with patterns.

Getting There & Away

MBA flies between Gurney (Alotau) and Losuia on Monday and Wednesday (K133), connecting with flights to/from Port Moresby (K198 from Losuia). Islands Nationair flies to Losuia from Port Moresby and Gurney on Tuesday, Thursday and Saturday.

The two main trade stores in Losuia run work boats to Alotau approximately weekly. One of the stores is owned by the Kiriwina Lodge people, so you could ask there. They charge K45 for the trip, which takes two days (stopping at an island for the night) and passes by the D'Entrecasteaux group. You can probably arrange to be dropped at the island of your choice, but take your own food and water.

Getting Around

Most of Kiriwina's main roads are in fairly good condition and this is yet another place in PNG where cycling would be a joy if there was a bicycle to ride. You could perhaps hire one from a local – there are certainly bicycles about – but negotiations are likely to be protracted, involving the rider's cousin or brother whose next-door neighbour's uncle actually owns the bicycle and he might be fishing that day.

The island's six PMVs run infrequently but are cheap – K0.60 should get you from Losuia to the north coast. Almost all private vehicles (there aren't many) operate as de facto PMVs. Otherwise, you'll have to walk, and this can get very hot.

You can organise tours and transportation using the Kiriwina Lodge's 15-seater bus. This costs from K1.20 per kilometre and can get expensive unless you can share costs. From Kiriwina to Wawela is around 20km, to Kaibola is around 30km and a day trip to either, with lunch, is K40, although there might be a discount for solo travellers.

AROUND KIRIWINA ISLAND

Going north from Losuia is 'inland' to the locals. This area has most of the island's roads and villages. **Omarakana**, about halfway between Losuia and Kaibola, is where the island's paramount chief resides. You'll know you're there by the large, intricate, painted yam house not far from the road. The paramount chief presides over the island's oral traditions and magic and strictly maintains his political and economic power. He oversees the important yam festival and kula rituals.

Caves used for swimming and fresh water are found at Tumwalau, Kalopa, Lupwaneta, Neguya, Bobu, Sikau, Kaulausi and Bwaga. Large coral megaliths still exist and, together with designs on some ancient pottery, have linked the Trobriands to possible early Polynesian migrations.

At **Kaibola** village there's a school and excellent swimming and snorkelling at its picture-postcard beach. In the village, you can see traditional boats, fishing gear and other items. Ask one of the kids to take you to nearby Luebila village, past the neat gardens of yams, taro, bananas and tapioca.

About 90 minutes' walk from Kaibola is Kalopa Cave, near Matawa village. There are several deep limestone caves housing burial antiquities and skeletal remains. Stories are told of Dokanikani, a giant whose bones are said to be buried with those of his victims in one of the caves. Also along the beach at Kaibola look for the little glow worms at night, clinging to the rocks along the shore.

The trip to Kaibola from Losuia takes about 30 minutes and covers nearly 30km along the narrow, coral road. Bring snorkel,

---

Trobes Tok Ples

Here are some useful words in Trobriands *tok ples* (local language):

good morning	*bwena kau kwau*
good afternoon	*bwena la lai*
good night	*bwena bogie*
very good	*sena bwena*
very bad	*sena gaga*
yes/no	*eh/gala*
you/me	*yokwa/yegu*
What does that cost?	*Aveka besa?*
food	*kaula*
What is your name?	*Yokwa amiyagam?*
go away	*kula*
I am going to sleep	*Ye bala masisi* ■

mask and fins to explore the underwater caves at Moligilagi, near the east coast.

South of Losuia, the road is even less frequently used and the population is smaller. **Wawela** village is on an excellent, curving sand beach edging a cool, deep, protected lagoon. On a falling tide, beware of the channel out to sea from the bay: the current can be very strong.

Further south, the road squeezes through thick jungle. At **Sinaketa** there are a couple of traditional kula canoes on the beach.

There are several islands off Kiriwina that would be great to visit, but getting to them is expensive. The fuel accounts for much of the cost and there isn't anything you can do about that except find a canoe. Kiriwina Lodge, as usual, is the most reliable place to find a boat. The cheapest return trip costs about K80. Negotiating hard, you might get a local boat for K55. Of course, if you find a boatload of people who are already going somewhere, you might be able to go along for a lot less. **Labi Island** is one of the nicest and is good for swimming. **Kitava**, a larger island east of Kiriwina, is also pretty. There's a good beach on the island about 1km off the main wharf in Losuia.

MUYUA ISLAND

Muyua (Woodlark) Island is east of the Trobriands and north of the Louisiade Archipelago. It takes its European name from the Sydney-based ship *Woodlark*, which passed by in 1836.

The island is a continuous series of hills and valleys and is highly populated. It was the site of the biggest gold rush in the country until the later discovery of gold at Edie Creek near Wau. A form of 'greenstone', similar although inferior to the greenstone or jade of New Zealand, was also found here and made into axes and ceremonial stones.

Today the people are renowned for their beautiful ebony carvings. Kulumadau is the main centre, although there is now an airstrip at Guasopa.

The Laughlan group is a handful of tiny islands and islets 64km east of Muyua.

LOUISIADE ARCHIPELAGO

The Louisiade Archipelago received its name after Louis Vaez de Torre's 1606 visit, but was probably known to Chinese and Malay sailors much earlier. The name was originally applied to the whole string of islands, including that now known as the D'Entrecasteaux group.

The largest island in the archipelago, **Sudest (Tagula)** had a small gold rush at about the same time as Muyua Island. It consists of a similar series of valleys and hills, the highest of which is Mt Rattlesnake at 915m.

Rossel (Yela) Island is the most westerly of the islands, if you discount the uninhabited Pocklington Reef. Rossel's rugged coastline ends at Rossel Spit, which has had more than its fair share of shipwrecks. An airstrip was built here in 1980.

The **Calvados chain** and **Conflict group** are a long chain of islets and reefs between Sudest and the mainland and make navigation through the province an exacting and often dangerous operation. None of the islands is of any great size. To the west, they terminate with the three islands of the Engineer group.

Misima Island
• *postcode 222*

Mountainous Misima Island is the most important in the group, with the district headquarters at Bwagaoia. Mt Oiatau at 1037m is the highest peak on the island. Misima too had a goldrush, although this took place between the wars, much later than on the other islands of Milne Bay Province.

A major gold and silver mine is now in operation, and estimations on the size of the deposit just keep getting bigger. There's a lot of people travelling to and from the island, although these numbers will drop off once it's fully operational. There's been gold mining on Misima off and on since the late 1800s.

During the brief span when PNG was a British colony rather than an Australian one, the people of Misima were thought of as the most dangerous and difficult in the country. Today, Misima has about half of the total population of the archipelago.

The *Misima Guesthouse* (☎ 643 7001; PO Box 24, Bwagaoia, Misima) in Bwagaoia is expensive at K85 with meals and often booked out by mine workers.

MBA flies to Misima from Port Moresby (K204) and Gurney (K113) on Monday, Tuesday, Thursday and Friday.

Morobe Province

Land Area 34,500 sq km
Population 430,000
Capital Lae

The province of Morobe curves around Huon Gulf and includes the rugged Huon Peninsula. The provincial headquarters, Lae, is Papua New Guinea's second-largest city. The province's main river, the Markham, bisects the mountains with a broad, open flood plain. Morobe has the best road connections in the country. From Lae, you can drive west to the Highlands along the Markham Valley, north-west to Madang, or south to the highland areas around Wau and Bulolo, the centre of the 1920s goldrush.

History

Some of the earliest remains of human civilisation in PNG have been found in this province; axe heads discovered at Bobongora by students of the University of PNG have been dated at 40,000 years old. It is believed the earliest settlements were in coastal areas. These were subsequently flooded by rising sea levels (after the Ice age), so most of PNG's prehistory has been lost under the sea. But in some regions, like parts of the Huon Peninsula, these coastal areas have subsequently risen and exposed the remains of these early settlements.

The first contact the coastal people had with Europeans came when the German New Guinea Company made an unsuccessful attempt to colonise the mainland.

In 1885 the Germans established their first settlement at Finschhafen; it soon started to disintegrate due to the effects of malaria and various other tropical ills, boredom and alcohol. These problems followed them along the northern coast and were only left behind (at least partially) when they transferred to the island of New Britain. The Lutheran Mission arrived during this time, but remained after the company moved on. Finschhafen is still a major Lutheran base.

HIGHLIGHTS

- Visiting local villages like Busama, where you can go fishing, bushwalking and swimming
- Watching leatherback turtles come ashore to lay their eggs on the beaches around Maus Buang and Labu Tali
- Exploring the Rainforest Habitat in Lae
- Spending some contemplative moments at the Lae War Cemetery
- Walking in the cool mountain forests around Wau
- Inspecting the butterfly and insect collections at the Butterfly Ranch in Wau or the Insect Farming & Trading Agency in Bulolo

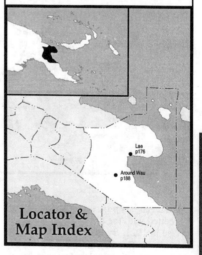

Lae
p176

Around Wau
p188

Locator &
Map Index

MOROBE PROVINCE

After the Australian takeover Morobe became a fairly quiet place. Until the discovery of gold, no-one cared to disturb the region's ferocious warriors. At Ho'mki ('outcrop of rocks'), by the Butibum River, large boulders mark the site of the last raid on Lae by hostile tribes from up the valley. This final clash, in 1907, killed 67 people.

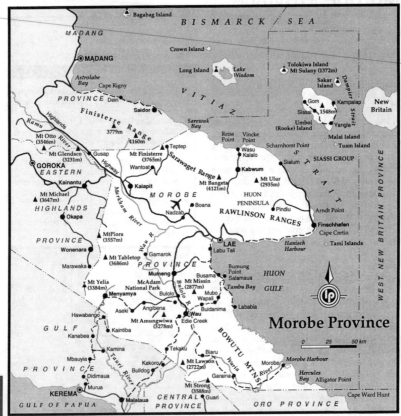

Morobe Province

The legendary prospector 'Sharkeye' Park is credited with the discovery of gold close to Wau in 1921. By the mid-1920s the gold hunters were flooding in, arriving at the port of Salamaua and struggling for eight days up the steep and slippery Black Cat Track to Wau, a mere 50km away. As if the conditions of the track, the wet and often cold climate and the tropical diseases were not enough, the miners also had to contend with hostile tribes. Frequent reprisal raids by angry miners hardly helped matters.

In 1926 a richer field was discovered at Edie Creek, high in the hills above Wau.

Although miners made quick fortunes here and at the earlier Koranga Creek Strike, it soon became evident to the more far-sighted prospectors that to really squeeze the most out of these gold-rich streams, large investments and heavy equipment would be needed.

The rough trail from the port of Salamaua up to Wau, Bulolo and Edie Creek was totally unsuitable for transporting heavy equipment, so the New Guinea Gold Company took the brave step of flying in the equipment. An airstrip was prepared in Lae and a shuttle service began. At one time, more air freight was lifted in PNG than in the rest of the world put together.

The goldfields continued to be productive until after WWII, when the recovery rate started to drop, gold was pegged at an artificially low price (US$35 an ounce) and the costs of production increased. One by one, the eight huge dredges were closed down – the last one in 1965. Although many people still work the fields, it is now a small-scale cottage industry. You can see many small prospectors on the Bulolo River as you drive up the road to Wau.

Lae, or Lehe as it was originally spelt, was a tiny mission station before the goldrush. It soon became a thriving community clustered, in true PNG fashion, around its central airstrip. The town and aviation remained closely linked. In July 1937 the pioneer aviator Amelia Earhart took off from Lae on one of the final legs of a round-the-world flight and disappeared over the Pacific without trace.

The volcanic eruptions at Rabaul in 1937 prompted a decision to move the capital of New Guinea to Lae, but WWII intervened before the transfer was really under way. Lae, Salamaua and Rabaul became the major Japanese bases in New Guinea.

In early 1943, the Japanese, reeling from defeats at Milne Bay and the Kokoda Trail, and their naval power devastated by the Battle of the Coral Sea, decided to make one more attempt to take Port Moresby. This time they attacked towards Wau, marching up over the mountains from Salamaua in late January 1943. Australian troops in Wau were quickly reinforced by air from Port Moresby and the Japanese advance was repelled.

The Battle of Wau was fought hand-to-hand after the ammunition ran out. Villagers watched the battle in much the same way that foreign researchers and voyeurs watch Highlands battles today.

A grim campaign to clear the Japanese from Morobe followed. It took six months to struggle through the mud and jungle to the outskirts of Salamaua. Australian troops landed on beaches 25km east of Lae on 4 September, and the next day a huge Allied force parachuted onto Nadzab airstrip, up the Markham Valley from Lae. Transport aircraft then flew vast numbers of men and huge amounts of materials in for the advance on Lae.

Salamaua was captured on 11 September, and once Lae was surrounded it was easily taken on 16 September. Many Japanese escaped into the mountain wilderness of the Huon Peninsula and started on the incredible retreat that was eventually to come to an end at Wewak.

Lae, Wau, Bulolo and Salamaua were badly damaged during the fighting and Salamaua was never rebuilt. Today it is just a tiny and very pretty village.

Post-war, things looked a little bleak for Lae – the gold was petering out in the mountains and Port Moresby was chosen as the capital of the new united Territory of Papua & New Guinea. But Lae soon had a new reason for existence: it was to become a major transport hub for goods shipped to and from the Highlands. The road between Wau

LBJ & The War

During WWII, former US president Lyndon Baines Johnson, then a Texan congressman and member of the US Naval Reserve, was sent by congress on a fact-finding mission to the south and south-west Pacific, becoming the first congressman to see active duty.

On 9 June 1942 he joined the crew of a B26 Marauder as an observer on a bombing run to Japanese-held Lae. This was a one-time-only assignment and he was initially assigned to one aircraft in the formation but switched to another shortly before take-off. The formation was attacked by Japanese Zeros over the Huon Gulf and while Johnson's aircraft survived intact, the one to which he was initially assigned was shot down with all hands.

General Douglas MacArthur awarded him the Silver Star for Gallantry – America's third-highest decoration – for spending 13 minutes under enemy fire.

LBJ's accidental involvement with PNG continued – unbeknown to him – with another series of events on Lavongai (New Hanover) Island in the 1960s (see The Johnson Cult aside in the New Ireland chapter). ■

MOROBE PROVINCE

and Lae had been built during the war and work on a road along the Markham Valley from Lae into the Highlands had started. It was clear that the economic development of the Highlands also meant development for Lae, if the highway could be finished. Two of the major export industries – coffee and tea – were prospering in the Highlands, but access to a port was needed. So completion of the highway was given priority. The mineral boom of the 1980s and 90s in the Highlands, with its need for massive heavy cargo shipments, resulted in Lae becoming the major port and industrial centre of PNG. It still has the most important road links to the interior.

Geography

The Huon Peninsula is the hump in the New Guinea 'dragon's back', an area of steep ranges leading down to northern coastal grasslands and coastal swamps to the south, between Lae and Finschhafen.

The Finisterre, Sarawaget and Rawlinson ranges form a rib along the Huon Peninsula, which is detached from the mainland's spine. They are raised mountains of coral limestone that march right down to the sea and pop up again as the backbone of the mountainous island of New Britain (an unusual skeletal structure). The lower slopes of the ranges are blanketed in one of the most tangled and impenetrable rainforests in PNG.

The mountains in the south-west are equally inhospitable. Central in the province is the Markham River, which rises both in the Finisterre Ranges and the foothills of the central spine and travels for 190km before venting into the gulf near Lae. The wide and fertile Markham Valley has become a major cattle-grazing area. The valleys in the south of the province, near Wau and Bulolo, were once densely forested now but many trees have been cut down now for timber and in the search for gold. Reafforestation is, unfortunately, no longer a priority.

Morobe also has a number of volcanic islands between the Huon Peninsula and New Britain.

Climate

The climate varies throughout the province. The Lae-Finschhafen area's rainy period is from May to October and it has only a slight seasonal variation in temperature. Wau and Bulolo receive between 1500 and 2000mm, mainly between November and April, and have a daily temperature range of 18°C to 29°C. Wau is a welcome relief from the heat and dust of Lae.

Annual rainfall figures for the main centres are: Lae 4617mm, Finschhafen 4417mm, Wau 1843mm, and Menyamya 1769mm.

Society & Conduct

Many parts of Morobe were virtually uninhabited when Europeans first arrived, including the fertile Wau and Bulolo valleys. The Leiwomba people, however, were long established in the Lae area and the Anga people lived in the central mountains in the Menyama district.

Frequently incorrectly and offensively referred to as the Kukukuku, the Anga averaged less than 1.5m (five feet) in height and were renowned fighters. They lived a nomadic existence interspersed with violent raids on more peaceful villages at lower altitudes – or upon each other. Despite the bitter climate in their high mountain homeland, they wore only a tiny grass skirt, like a Scotsman's sporran, and cloaks made of beaten bark, known as *mals*.

JK McCarthy, who between the two world wars made some of the first contact with these people, describes them vividly in his book *Patrol Into Yesterday*. His contact even extended to receiving an arrow in the stomach; the warriors are excellent bowmen who make up for their imperfect aim with an incredibly rapid delivery.

McCarthy also recounts their first sight of an aircraft: men took turns at crawling underneath it to inspect its genitals, unsure whether the bird was male or female. Their first reaction to McCarthy was less confident. When the first white man arrived in an Anga village, many of these otherwise fearless people fainted.

Lae

• *pop 90,000* • *postcode 411*

Lae is a place of contrasts. It is a city adjacent to a fine harbour and scenic coastal views but is inward-looking (in every sense of the phrase) and turns its back on the sea. Looming mountains, rather than the blue waters of the Huon Gulf, pull the eye. Here can be found fumy streets, the clamour of traffic, the bustle of shoppers and laid-back, idle watchers. And yet here too are manicured lawns at the University of Technology (Unitech), the shady greenness of the Rainforest Habitat and the melancholy peace of the war cemetery. Lae has one of the best airports in PNG. And here can be found the most potholed and roughest urban roads in PNG leading to some of the finest, and underutilised, sporting facilities available – all left over from the 1991 South Pacific Games. And in Lae, you can discover some of the nicest, and most expensive, accommodation options in the country, as well as some of the cheapest (but definitely not the worst).

The city is laid out around the Botanical Gardens in much the same way that New York is laid out around Central Park. And, like Central Park, you should approach a stroll in the gardens with a degree of caution – rascals have been known to frequent them. The gardens are now fenced in with an effective (and aesthetically pleasing) fence to improve security.

Tourism is a growing industry here, particularly in activities associated with the blue waters of the Huon Gulf. The recently established Rainforest Habitat is a jewel in the city's crown. But Lae is also a leader in commerce and manufacturing, with the Ramu hydroelectric scheme giving plenty of scope for industrial expansion (but blackouts are common). Current industries include cement, poultry, soap, paint, chemical products, metal products, soft drinks and printing.

As in all parts of PNG, Christianity is widely adhered to. The German influence has persisted in few aspects of life in these north-coast former German settlements, but religion is one that remains dominant. Lutherans make up 78% of the population, with the remainder being mainly Catholic and Seventh-Day Adventist.

Orientation

Lae is built on a flat-topped headland, which ironically gets almost no benefit of a view over the beautiful Huon Gulf. Before the war, the city was better oriented. The old airstrip, where the airlines have their offices, lies at the foot of the steep hill to the west of the town centre and runs up beside the Botanical Gardens. It was, for many years, Lae's main airport – centrally located and convenient. But with the expansion and upgrading of Nadzab airport (which also dates to the war) the old airstrip fell into disrepair, and it is now overgrown and deserted. The only wheels rolling along the tarmac these days belong to cars taking short-cuts from the town to the market.

Voco Point is south-east of the airport and

! ! ! ! ! ! ! ! ! ! ! ! ! ! !

Warning

In past years Lae has had a bad reputation for crime. Things have definitely improved, but visitors should still take care: the volatility of life in PNG could swing the pendulum rapidly back to 'dangerous'.

It pays to stay off the streets at night, especially as Lae has no taxis. PMVs are a great way to get around during the day, but they stop running after dark. You will need to organise your return transport carefully if going out at night, but the lack of nightlife in Lae may limit your desire to stray too far anyway. If possible, eat your evening meals at the place where you are staying. If you plan to visit friends, ask them in advance if they will escort you home at the end of the evening.

It's not wise to wander through secluded parts of the botanical gardens or around Mt Lunaman unless you're in a large group. The Lae War Cemetery is relatively safe because there are usually security guards (with enormous dogs) stationed there.

Also see the Personal Safety section in the Facts for the Visitor chapter. ■

! ! ! ! ! ! ! ! ! ! ! ! ! ! !

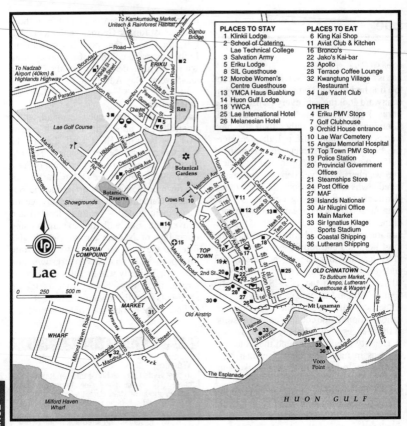

PLACES TO STAY
1 Klinkii Lodge
2 School of Catering, Lae Technical College
3 Salvation Army
5 Eriku Lodge
8 SIL Guesthouse
12 Morobe Women's Centre Guesthouse
13 YMCA Haus Buablung
14 Huon Gulf Lodge
18 YWCA
25 Lae International Hotel
26 Melanesian Hotel

PLACES TO EAT
6 King Kai Shop
11 Aviat Club & Kitchen
16 Bronco's
22 Jako's Kai-bar
23 Apollo
28 Terrace Coffee Lounge
32 Kwangtung Village Restaurant
34 Lae Yacht Club

OTHER
4 Eriku PMV Stops
7 Golf Clubhouse
9 Orchid House entrance
10 Lae War Cemetery
15 Angau Memorial Hospital
17 Top Town PMV Stop
19 Police Station
20 Provincial Government Offices
21 Steamships Store
24 Post Office
27 MAF
29 Islands Nationair
30 Air Niugini Office
31 Main Market
33 Sir Ignatius Kilage Sports Stadium
35 Coastal Shipping
36 Lutheran Shipping

MOROBE PROVINCE

where the shipping companies have their offices. There's also a wharf at the end of Milford Haven Rd. Down here on the seaside flatlands are also several sporting venues, built for the 1991 South Pacific Games.

Huon Rd is the main through street, running in from the Highlands Highway, past the Eriku PMV stops and the main rural PMV stop, through the city centre (still sometimes known as Top Town) and connecting with Markham Rd, another major thoroughfare which leads down past the airport and Voco Point, then runs out to Ampo and beyond.

Nadzab airport is 40km west of town, just off the Highlands Highway.

Maps For maps, see the Department of Surveying & Land Studies at Unitech (☎ 473 4951) or the Department of Lands in the provincial government buildings in town.

Information

There is an active Lae Tourist Association; the current contact is Bill Guile at the Lae International Hotel (☎ 472 2000). Fred Cook of Morobe Tours (☎ 472 3647) is also a mine of information and has been involved in tourism around Lae for a long time.

For information, try contacting the province tourism officer, Joe Kewere (☎ 473 1688; fax 472 4745; PO Box 294) or cultural officer Nane Winion (☎ 473 1758), both of whom are based in the provincial government centre in the middle of town.

Lae is well supplied with all the major banks and shops, including sports stores (for snorkelling gear) and bookshops. There's a good public library in town.

The post office is efficient, opens at 8 am and sells phonecards. There are public telephones nearby, most of which work but all take only phonecards (one of the rare places outside of Port Moresby where phonecards are accepted). There's a useful noticeboard outside the post office and another one at the Bali news agency on Coronation Drive that advertises dances, club meetings, lost dogs, prams for sale and other useful things. Andersons supermarket in Eriku also has a noticeboard.

There are several dentists in Lae (dentists are rare outside of Port Moresby, Rabaul and Lae).

Botanical Gardens

These gardens are being revitalised. There are huge trees virtually smothered in vines and creepers, brightly coloured birds that call out raucously and electric-green lizards that scuttle through the undergrowth. The gardens also boast an exotic orchid collection.

Within the garden boundaries is the **Lae War Cemetery**, with the graves of thousands of Allied servicemen, mainly Australian and Indian, who died during the last war. There are 2808 graves here – 2363 of which are Australian. If the war seems rather distant and unreal, pay a visit and read some of the headstones – this is a peaceful and well-maintained place, just a short walk from the screeching traffic of downtown Lae. The names are frighteningly ordinary, and many of their owners were extremely young. There are security guards with dogs patrolling here these days, so it is quite safe to visit, even on your own.

Mt Lunaman

The hill in the centre of town – Mt Lunaman or, more correctly, Lo' Wamung (First Hill) – was used by the Germans and the Japanese as a lookout point. The Germans named it Burgberg (Fortress Hill); the Japanese riddled it with caves and tunnels. Ask around whether it's still safe to visit, but bus tours do come here.

Unitech

Unitech, about 8km out of town, is located in some nice landscaped parks and gardens. It actually feels like a university and you can even stay here (see the Places to Stay section). Its Matheson Library is the largest library of technology in the South Pacific and Duncanson Hall has 36 Sepik-style carved pillars, while the coffee house is built like a traditional haus tambaran (spirit house). Unitech also has the only public collection of artefacts, including many rare pieces, in the province. From the city centre, take PMV No 11A or 11B.

Rainforest Habitat

Next to the university is the Rainforest Habitat, a big new attraction in Lae and well worth visiting. It comprises about 3000 sq m of reconstructed rainforest inside a covered shadehouse – similar to the shadehouse in Port Moresby's National Botanic Gardens. It incorporates a lake, raised walkways and an abundance of plants and birds. Many of the birds are tame and will land on your shoulder, and the native flowers are superb. Outside is a mini-zoo with cuscuses, echidnas and tree wallabies. If you want to come to grips with the variety of flora and fauna in PNG, this is a microcosm of it and a great place to start. There's a breeding program, which has had some notable successes. If you ask, you can get an informative guided tour.

It is open every day from 10 am to 4 pm and lunch is available on weekends. It also conducts educational workshops and has

MOROBE PROVINCE

accommodation facilities in a nearby guest-house (see the Places to Stay section).

Markets

Lae has three markets. The main market on the west side of the airstrip is quite interesting and has food and a few local curios. The Butibum market is a smaller, village market out of town on the Butibum Road. The third market is the Kamkumsung market, just past the Bumbu Bridge on the way out to the Unitech. It serves the Kamkumsung suburb and surrounding villages.

Activities

The Lae Explorers Club mainly consists of expats who are interested in outdoor activities; it welcomes visitors who want to take part in bushwalking, boating or rafting on *gumis* (rubber tyre rafts). The current contact is Ed McArdle (☎ 472 1044; fax 472 2748).

If you are interested in watersports, ask someone at the yacht club (☎ 472 4091) or Rod Pearce from Niugini Diving (☎ 472 5692; PO Box 320), who can help with diving information. He operates the *Barbarian*, a well-equipped dive boat.

Mainland Holdings has a large crocodile farm, run in conjunction with a chicken farm, a few kilometres out of town on the Nadzab Road. It is a commercial, not a tourist, operation, so guided tours aren't offered – but it's open every Monday afternoon if you want to wander out and have a look.

If golf is your game, the Lae Golf Course is one of the best in PNG and has a fine clubhouse.

Morobe Tours (☎ 472 3647; fax 472 5788; PO Box 245) operates air-con bus trips in and around the town. Assuming you have at least four people on the bus, a half-day city tour will cost K35 and a full-day tour of city and environs K48. It also hires cars, and has a fully air-con 35ft luxury cruiser which you can charter for day trips or game fishing.

Places to Stay – bottom end

The *Salvation Army* (☎ 472 2487; PO box

PNG has two types of echidna – the short-beaked echidna (pictured above) and its long-beaked relative, known as the giant spiny anteater.

259) is on the corner of Bumbu and Huon Rds near the Eriku PMV stop, a couple of kilometres from the centre of town. The staff will still let you sleep on the floor of the recreation hall for K2, but you might have to share with other people. See the Places to Stay – middle section for details on its units.

The YMCA's big *Haus Buablung* (☎ 472 4412; fax 472 2654; PO Box 1055) on Cassowary Rd is a multi-storey concrete block building which clearly has potential but is becoming a little dilapidated. Verandah railings, showers and basins need major repair and the whole place needs a good scrub down. Nevertheless, for its price, it is a good place to stay – it's secure, cheap and near the city centre. It's also a good place to meet local people, as most of the 96 rooms are taken by long-term residents, mainly young working people. They have a TV room and satellite dish, so you can catch up on Australian or CNN news. The rooms are small (all are singles) and they can get hot as there are no fans, but the staff may take pity on a poor traveller and install one in your room for you – they are very obliging people. The price has not changed for about five years; K12 gets you a room, breakfast and dinner. Despite its limitations, this must still be one of the best-value accommodation houses in PNG. The food, however, is not inspiring.

To get there from the town centre, walk east on 7th St from Huon Rd and when 7th St turns right (you're now on Hawk St), turn left at the bottom into Cassowary Rd. It is a little way along on your left; there's no sign.

The *Lutheran Guesthouse* (☎ 472 2556; PO Box 80) is at Ampo on Busu Rd, opposite the Balob Teachers' College. Ampo (pronounced 'Umpo') is the main administration centre for the Lutheran Church and the colonial-style guesthouse buildings are about 200m on the right from the main road, set in green, attractive grounds. The shared rooms (two to five beds) are very clean, as are the bathrooms, and there are lounge rooms with coffee-making facilities. Bed and breakfast costs K35; with three good meals it's K40.

The guesthouse's priority is to look after people who are associated with the church;

although they welcome travellers, you may be unlucky and find it full, so phone first. As in other Lutheran guesthouses in PNG there are rules, but if you don't mind making a few concessions you'll meet some very friendly, interesting people in a calm, relaxing environment. The gates are closed between 10 pm and 6 am.

It's too far out of town to walk to the guesthouse, but PMVs are frequent. Catch one from the Top Town PMV stop on 7th St near Huon Rd. You want a Butibum PMV (No 13A), but check with the driver's assistant that it goes to Ampo.

The *Morobe Women's Centre* (☎ 472 5881; PO Box 1468) guesthouse is not great value as far as accommodation goes, but is a good place to meet people. It's on Huon Rd near 10th St and both men and women can stay; floorspace costs K2, and dorm beds are K13. There are cooking facilities. The guesthouse was founded by and for grassroots mothers and runs programs to improve subsistence agriculture. Most of the association's members are rural women who stay at the guesthouse when they come to Lae.

The *YWCA hostel* on 7th St between Huon Rd and Cassowary Rd is close to town. It's almost always full of permanent residents and doesn't take men. A shared room costs K5 per night and is called a transit room (which is a little more private) costs K25 per night. If there's no-one there when you call in, try the YWCA centre (☎ 472 1691) on Huon Rd near the corner of Cassowary Rd.

There might be accommodation available in the *Unitech student hostel* during vacations. Check with the director of student services (☎ 473 4377). There's also a very good guesthouse (see the Places to Stay – middle section).

The *Rainforest Habitat* (☎ & fax 475 7839) can also offer accommodation at a middle-to-budget price in a comfortable guesthouse near Unitech, provided a workshop is not running at the time. Ring first to enquire.

Places to Stay – middle

There is a guesthouse out at *Unitech* which

MOROBE PROVINCE

is excellent value. It's a pleasant house rather than a hostel and there are only a few rooms (two singles, two twins and one double) which cost K40 each, whether there are one or two people in them. Breakfast costs K5 and a good dinner is K12. Benedicte is the name of the current manager.

People staying at the guesthouse can use the university's staff club, which has cheap meals. To book, phone the vice chancellor's secretary (☎ 473 4201). See the Unitech section for details on how to get there.

The Summer Institute of Linguistics (SIL) missionary group runs a *guesthouse* (☎ 472 3214; fax 472 5516; PO Box 342) on Poinciana Rd, off Kwila Rd, which runs into Milford Haven Rd opposite the Botanical Gardens. It's an easy walk from the Eriku PMV stops. It is clean and quiet; smoking and drinking are banned. There are six rooms with shared bathrooms at K52/65 for a single/double; six units which share a bathroom are K58/70. There are cooking facilities and a small above-ground swimming pool.

The *School of Catering* (☎ 472 6805), at Lae Technical College (not Unitech) on Milford Haven Rd, has four motel units. They look as though they were designed by a committee in the early 1960s and are becoming shabby but are reasonable value at K55/65 for a single/double. They have air-con (the building gets very hot), fridges, toasters and electric kettles, but no cooking facilities.

Meals are available during the week; on weekends you can eat in the student mess by prior arrangement. There's a small shop on campus. If you plan to arrive after hours or on a weekend, make sure you have the name of the person who is supposed to give you the key. If they aren't around, ask to see someone in housekeeping.

The *Salvation Army* (☎ 472 2487, PO Box 259), on the corner of Bumbu and Huon Rds near the PMV stop, has four self-contained motel-style units with kitchenettes. They are quite comfortable and centrally located. If you play golf, you can walk out the back onto the golf course – quite a pretty area. It cost K65 for one or two people and then K10 for additional people. The current contact is Captain Arivusu Moha.

Close by, on Klinkii St, which runs off Huon Rd, is *Klinkii Lodge* (☎ 472 6040, PO Box 192). The rooms are basic but clean enough. With shared bathroom they cost K67; two rooms with attached bathroom and air-con are K88. Meals are available and staff will take you out to the airport for K30.

The newest place in Lae is *Eriku Lodge* (☎ 472 2612; fax 472 2116; PO Box 1391) on the corner of Gurney and Chayter Sts, a short walk from the Eriku shops. It is a well-maintained but spartan place and reasonably clean; it charges K65 for one or two people or K87 for three. The rooms can get pretty hot, but all have air-con and (here's the catch) they charge an extra K20 per day to turn it on. There is a dining room where breakfast costs K4 and dinner K20. Staff will also rent you a car for K95 per day (plus K0.69 a kilometre) or they have special rates for room-plus-car.

Places to Stay – top end

The *Huon Gulf Lodge* (☎ 472 4844; fax 472 5023; PO Box 612) is one of the Coral Sea chain – but is not one of its best. It is on Markham Rd, in what must once have been a prime location, nestled into a corner of the Botanical Gardens and close to the now-defunct airport. It looks a little forlorn now, and while it's the cheapest of Lae's top-end places, K135 for a room is exorbitant. What's more, it now has a casino with poker machines, so don't expect a pleasant clientele. If you arrive after 5 pm (and if you haven't already booked) it may have stand-by rates.

The *Melanesian Hotel* (☎ 472 3744; fax 42 3706; PO Box 756), on 2nd St, is also in the Coral Sea chain but is a little more pleasant. It has a choice of bars and restaurants, and a pleasant swimming pool. There are 68 rooms costing K170 each; meals are good but not cheap.

The top hotel in Lae is the *Lae International Hotel* (☎ 472 2000; fax 472 2534; PO Box 2774). It is a few blocks from the town centre at the end of 4th St. It was, until a few years ago, a gracious old colonial lodge but has now been converted to a modern and luxurious hotel with spacious and secluded grounds and tropical gardens; it has retained its grace and style. There's an excellent 25m pool, a *haus win* (gazebo-like structure) and a small zoo. Rooms cost from K185, but they may give corporate discounts – if you want to be pampered, it may be worth it.

Places to Eat

As with most PNG cities, there is a range of eating places to suit your budget and taste. There is, however, not much entertainment available apart from eating out and this is limited at night because getting around is so difficult. There are no taxis, it is unsafe to walk anywhere after dark and you are restricted to eating at your lodgings if you don't have your own transport. There are some good places for lunch or breakfast.

The *Terrace Coffee Lounge* on 2nd St is good and Paul Menzel, the German expat who runs the place, is an interesting guy to talk to. What's more, it has air-con. Omelettes are about K6 and good coffee is K2. It's open from 9 am to 4.30 pm on weekdays and on Saturday morning.

The *King Kai Shop* in Eriku looks more like a western fast-food chain shop, but with better food and greater variety. It is a good place to sit down and relax; it is clean, has air-con and serves both European and Chinese food as well as takeaway. Hamburgers are K3.50, milkshakes K2.30, and proper scooped ice cream is K2 per cone. It even has healthy salads. It's recommended.

Jako's Kai Bar on 4th St is Indian-run and has some curries and sambals on the menu for about K3.50. *Lae Fish Supply* has more choices than the average kai-bar and is clean and cheap. A spring roll or a piece of fish costs K1 and a good serving of chow mein K2. *Bronco's*, on Coronation Drive between 7th and 8th Sts, is a kai-bar with tables.

The most pleasant spot for a meal is the *Lae Yacht Club* (☎ 472 4091). At the time of writing it was located amid the shipping offices overlooking the water at Voco Point, but it is due to relocate to a nearby spot with an even better view of the harbour. Meals here are bistro-style and good, and the beer is cold. Roast beef is K8.50 or a T-bone is K10 for lunch. There are also cheaper snacks. This is a good place to link up with ocean-going yachts or to find out what's going on in the local nautical scene.

The *Aviat Club* on Huon Road near the courthouse is open from 11am and has a bistro serving lunches and dinners six days a week for between K3 and K5, including nice roasts. The *Aviat Club Kitchen*, next door, serves Chinese food with main courses between K10 and K20. The *Kwangtung Village Restaurant* is run by the same people as the Aviat Kitchen and has a similar price range. It's rather inconveniently located on Mangola St, out beyond the market on the other side of the old airstrip. The *Apollo*, in town on 2nd St, is open for lunch and dinner on weekdays.

The *Huon Gulf Lodge* and *Melanesian Hotel* have restaurants, with main courses from about K16. The *Lae International Hotel* has a popular poolside lunchtime barbecue on Sunday. Its *Vanda Restaurant* is first class but pricey, but there is also *Luluai's Italian Restaurant* (how's that for multiculturalism) and the *Kokomo Coffee Shop* where you can get more reasonably priced meals in very pleasant surroundings. Both the Melanesian and the International also sell pizzas – reports indicate that the International's are better.

Things to Buy

The Melanesian Arts Centre (☎ 472 2659) has a good collection of artefacts including many pieces from the Trobriand Islands and the Sepik region. Owned by Robyn Leahy, daughter-in-law of Highlands explorer Mick Leahy, it's open Monday to Friday from 9 am to 4.30 pm and from 9.30 am to 11.30 pm Saturday. It has moved around a bit over the last few years and plans were for it to operate from the Melanesian Hotel foyer, where you will probably be able to find it. Prices for artefacts are similar to, maybe a little cheaper than, those in Port Moresby. The centre will ship your purchases home for you; its staff are friendly, helpful and knowledgeable.

Small, inexpensive crafts are also available from street sellers who spread their wares on the pavement around the city-centre stores, particularly the Steamships store. Good *bilums* (string bags) are quite cheap here.

Getting There & Away

There's a wide choice of transport into and out of Lae; it's the major centre on the north coast, the major north-coast port, an important airport and the coastal access point for the Highlands Highway.

There are frequent air connections to all main centres, including the islands; regular shipping services along the coast and to New Britain; and numerous PMVs running between the Highlands and Madang.

Air Lae's airport is at Nadzab, 40km from town. It was an important airstrip during the war and it is much bigger and better than the derelict airstrip in town. But in a planning decision which owed more to military logic than civic responsibility, it was situated out of town, about a 45-minute drive away. The old airport has now closed permanently.

If you're heading for Madang, you should seriously consider taking a PMV, which will cost a great deal less than a plane (about K20, which could be a lot less than just getting to Nadzab) and take not much more time, once you add up the time taken to get to Nadzab, the check-in time and the flight time.

The main airline offices are a remnant of older times – they are located beside the old, disused airstrip a short walk from the centre of town. Air Niugini (☎ 472 3111) has frequent flights to all major centres. MAF (☎ 472 1555) also flies from Lae into the province and up to the Highlands. The MAF office is in town on 2nd St, next to the Terrace Coffee Lounge. Islands Nationair (☎ 472 5277; fax 472 3072) also services Lae and has an office on the other side of the Terrace Coffee Lounge, also on 2nd St.

PMV PMVs to Wau, Goroka and Madang

leave Lae between 8 and 9 am every day; there are fewer on weekends. The main long-distance PMV stop is in Eriku on Bumbu Rd. But some also leave from the Main Market on the west side of the old airstrip.

Car Avis (☎ 472 4929; 472 4644), Budget (☎ 472 4889, 472 2069), Hertz (☎ 472 5982) and Thrifty (☎ 472 7977) are all represented in Lae. Both Avis and Budget have offices at Nadzab airport and in the town. Hertz's office is on 9th St. Avis' city office is at the Lae International Hotel and Budget is at the Melanesian Hotel. Some smaller motels (like the Eriku Lodge) also have accommodation-car packages (see the Places to Stay section).

Boat There are frequent connections west along the coast as far as Vanimo and east as far as Oro Bay (Popondetta) and regular connections with New Britain and Manus Island. Usually they give a couple of weeks notice, but not necessarily. If any passenger-carrying freighters load (or expect to load en route) dangerous cargo such as petrol, they will not accept passengers.

Lutheran Shipping (☎ 472 2066, 472 2823; fax 472 5806; PO Box 1459) and Coastal Shipping Services (☎ 472 3180; fax 472 1686; PO Box 1721) both have their offices and wharves at Voco Point. The Lutheran ticket office is open five days a week, but is closed for an hour (or perhaps two) from 1 pm for lunch; it is also open Saturday morning. Get there early as there are queues. Tickets are sold up to a week in advance of sailing.

Other freight lines run to Lae but don't officially take passengers. You might have more success getting on a freighter by talking directly to the ship's captain rather than the office people.

To/From Port Moresby Flights from Port Moresby climb up and over the central mountain range. In the old days you flew through, rather than over, the mountains. These days you whistle over the top in 45 minutes, but in an Air Niugini F28 you are

MOROBE PROVINCE

still not too high to appreciate the dramatic geography.

Both Air Niugini and MBA have frequent direct flights to/from Port Moresby costing K118. Islands Nationair has both direct flights and flights routing through Kerema.

To/From Wau & Bulolo Islands Nationair flies from Lae to Bulolo for K56. The PMV fare from Lae to Bulolo is K6; to Wau it's K8. The road is sealed and quite good as far as Mumeng (K4), then it is unsealed and gets quite rough. Most PMVs running this route are trucks with wooden benches for seats; try to sit near the front, and definitely not over the rear axle. It takes about 3½ hours to Bulolo and an extra 45 minutes to Wau. The road follows the Bulolo River for part of the way and the scenery is spectacular.

To/From the Highlands MBA flies to Goroka (K77) and Mt Hagen (K107) every day except Sunday. Air Niugini has direct flights to Mt Hagen on Thursday and Sunday, but no direct flights from Lae to Goroka.

See The Highlands chapter for details on PMVs and the Highlands Highway. The PMV fare to Goroka is K12 and the distance is about 330km. The view from the Kassam Pass looking back up the Markham Valley is spectacular.

To/From Madang Air Niugini has daily flights to/from Madang. The fare is K84.

The road is OK and is sealed as far as Ramu, although potholes are frequent. All up, it's about 360km. When it's open, it can be covered by virtually any vehicle, but when it's closed (which now happens less frequently), even a 4WD won't get through. The problem is, as usual, the river crossings.

PMVs leave from the long-distance Eriku PMV stop around 8 am, cost K20 and take about six hours. After turning off the Highlands Highway, the road runs through a flat valley cultivated with the cane fields of the Ramu Sugar Refinery before climbing over the hills on the approach to Madang.

The boat trip is much more enjoyable.

Lutheran Shipping's passenger-only *Mamose Express* and *Rita* service all the main north-coast ports. Fares to Madang are K31/48 in deck/cabin class. The through fare to Wewak is K36/53. Lutheran Shipping also operates less regular, slower and much less comfortable passenger-carrying freighters on the route. By comparison with the passenger boats, they're not a bargain but the trip is still enjoyable.

To/From New Britain Both Air Niugini and Islands Nationair have daily flights to Rabaul/Tokua via Hoskins, costing K198 (but Islands Nationair doesn't fly on Sunday).

Lutheran Shipping has a weekly passenger boat (the *Maneba*) sailing to Rabaul from Lae on Monday afternoon, arriving on Tuesday. To Rabaul, deck class costs K46 and cabin class K54.

Coastal Shipping has the *Kimbe Express*, a mixed passenger/cargo boat with deck-class accommodation only; it runs once a week between Lae and Rabaul via Kimbe. To Kimbe it's K38 and Rabaul K46. The *Astro I* departs for Rabaul on Wednesday, running via the south coast of New Britain and stopping at Kandrian, among other places. This is not a passenger boat but there may occasionally be cabins available for around K100.

To/From Oro Bay The *Mamose Express* or the *Rita* sails from Lae for Oro Bay on Monday evening, taking about 18 hours. Deck/cabin class fares are K23/35. There are also freighters.

To/From Other Destinations Northcoast Airlines flies between Lae and Finschhafen on Monday, Wednesday and Friday for K85. Virtually all the Madang-bound boats call at Finschhafen. Speedboats can also be chartered for the trip, although they can be somewhat costly. Lutheran Shipping has a number of ships doing the Finschhafen run; the fare is around K15. The most recent addition to their fleet is the 'luxury' passenger catamaran, the *Gejamsao*; it is fully

MOROBE PROVINCE

air-conditioned and has seating for 170, plus 12 in VIP class. Sealand Pacific also runs the *Sea Lark* and the *Avonmore*.

The *Lalada* is a boat owned by Busama village that takes supplies to Salamaua and places in-between. The journey from Voco Point takes between one to 1½ hours to Busama and costs about K3.50, or 2½ hours to Salamaua and costs K5.

The Lutheran Shipping freighter *Maneba* plies the weekly route between Lae, Manus and Madang; the fare to Manus is K42/49 deck/cabin class (students half-price).

Getting Around

The Airport Travelling the 40km between Lae and Nadzab airport is probably the most difficult part of any visit to Lae. There is the Nadzab bus, a common garden-variety PMV, which (reportedly) meets every flight and charges K2 for the trip to Lae. To get out to the airport, you can pick it up at the main market by the old airstrip. There is also the occasional passing PMV which comes into the terminal area, or you could walk the few hundred metres or so out of the airport to the Highlands Highway and flag down a PMV there, but there are few after about 4 pm.

Morobe Tours (☎ 472 3647) has a luxury air-con minibus which will pick up and drop off at Nadzab for K40/60/70 for one, two or three people – or half that price if you happen to be staying at the Lae International or the Melanesian hotels.

Otherwise, you can always cadge a ride with a local.

PMV PMVs around Lae cost K0.40. The local PMV stop in Eriku is on Huon Rd. The other local PMV stop (also known as the Top Town PMV stop) is on 7th St. There are route numbers painted on urban PMVs but these are fairly vague.

Listen to the driver's assistant, who leans out the window and calls the destination and the names of stops in a semi-automatic, rapid-fire incantation. Even if you don't understand a word, people will point you in the right direction. You can't go too far in the wrong direction because the urban PMVs all have circular routes; sooner or later you'll end up back where you started.

SOUTH OF LAE

The Labu Lakes, right across the Markham River from Lae, were used to hide ships during the war, but the maze of waterways and swamps are now only home to crocodiles. The beaches on the ocean side are beautiful and are an important breeding site for leatherback turtles, incredible reptiles that can live to a great age, weigh up to 500kg and measure up to 2m in length.

Maus Buang & Labu Tali

From the end of November until early February, leatherback turtles come ashore along the beaches around Maus Buang and Labu Tali villages and dig deep nests where they lay up to 100 eggs, which hatch about two months later. It is one of the most extraordinary sights and this is one of the few places where it can be witnessed.

Traditionally the eggs are gathered by people from the villages, but over the years the demand for the eggs has increased to the point where the turtles are in danger of dying out. To save the turtle and improve the villagers' very basic living standards, researchers from Lae Unitech have convinced the people to set aside the 3km beach between the two villages for conservation.

If you are fortunate enough to see the turtles, please make an effort not to disturb them; some human-being-type animals apparently have an overwhelming urge to torture them by shining torches in their eyes, riding them up the beach, poking them with sticks etc.

Busama (also known as Busamang) is a pretty village halfway between Lae and Salamaua. Apparently the village is immaculate and villagers have organised themselves well to tackle tourism. They can take you fishing, bushwalking or swimming.

Places to Stay There are now village guesthouses at Maus Buang and Busama. Contact Joe Kevere or Fred Cook for more information; see the Lae Information section to find out how. Fred has a special relationship with Busama – he was naturalised there a few years ago.

Getting There & Away Boats leave frequently from Voco Point in Lae – just go down to the point, ask around and wait. The *Lalada* takes supplies to Salamaua, stopping along the way. The journey takes one to 1½ hours to Busama and costs about K3.50; to Salamaua it takes 2½ hours and costs K5.

Salamaua

There is little to suggest that the picturesque peninsula of Salamaua that we see today played such a significant part in the development of Wau and Bulolo in the goldrush days or a pivotal role in the course of the Pacific theatre of war during 1942 and 1943.

Two small villages now occupy the site: **Kela** and **Lagui**. Close by, there's excellent diving, good walks and a few interesting war relics. It's becoming a popular place for people to escape the dust, heat and urban strife of Lae.

The original town cemetery is disappearing under the bush but can still be reached by following a rough path that begins in the north-west corner of the school oval. This path also leads past a small reef which is good for snorkelling. Near the start of the path is the entrance to a Japanese tunnel. A steep path leads up the hill to four Japanese gun emplacements and there's a great view.

You can also visit Coastwatchers Ridge where Australians were stationed to report on Japanese shipping and troop movements. If you want a full day's walk, Mt Tambu has spectacular views and a huge battlefield where the Australians met the Japanese as they advanced towards Wau. Local guides are available.

Place to Stay The *Salamaua Guesthouse* is still standing but is not in a fit state to take guests. Many expats holiday in Salamaua and some are trying to restore the guesthouse after years of neglect under provincial government management. Ask Joe Kevere or

Fred Cook about it; see the Information section for their contact details.

Getting There & Away As with Busama, look around at Voco Point in Lae for PMV boats going to Salamaua. The *Lalada* makes the trip to Salamaua most days; it takes 2½ hours and costs K5.

Alternatively, you could disembark at Busama and walk along the beach to Salamaua in about five hours. If you are adventurous, you could walk along the beach all the way from Lae to Salamaua in about two days. Two major rivers must be crossed: the Markham and the Buang. You can wade across the second but you must definitely get a boat across the first.

From Salamaua you could head south to Lababia.

Lababia

An area of 69,000 hectares near the village of Lababia (population approximately 500), about 30km south of Salamaua on the coast, has been declared a Wildlife Management Area. It comprises forests, mangroves, sandy beaches, coral reefs, waterfalls, rivers and lakes. Here you can see gigantic leatherback turtles laying their eggs at night (between November and February). The village will rent canoes for paddling the rivers or coast, there are some good snorkelling sites (bring your own gear) and walking tracks crisscross the area.

Places to Stay Lababia villagers, with the help of the Village Development Trust (VDT), have built an ecotourism training centre and tourist lodges. Three small bunkhouses and a dormitory are available; there are showers, toilets, solar and generator power, and dining facilities. The place is new, and is operated primarily as a training/conference centre, but visitors are welcome as long as you don't arrive unannounced. They charge about K25 per night, with food extra. Book through the VDT (☎ 472 1666; fax 472 4824: PO Box 2397, Lae).

Getting There & Away The village is buying

a small passenger boat to transport visitors to the site. PMV boats make the two-hour trip from Voco Point in Lae, stopping en route at Salamaua. Another alternative is to walk the Black Cat Track from Wau to Salamaua and catch a boat from there. There is no airstrip at Lababia.

Around Morobe Province

FINSCHHAFEN AREA
• postcode 435

The town of Finschhafen was the German New Guinea Company's first, unsuccessful, attempt at colonising New Guinea. Between 1885, when they arrived here, and 1892, when they moved west to Stephansort, the Germans had a miserable time and many died from malaria and assorted tropical ills.

They did not do much better at Stephansort and soon moved to Madang and then to Rabaul, where they finally found relief from the mosquitos. Today Finschhafen is an idyllic coastal town. The modern town of Finschhafen was moved from its original site after WWII. Little remains of the original town apart from one old Lutheran building, which is now used by holidaying missionaries. Its tower was once used as a lookout.

Towards the end of WWII the town was used as a staging post for US troops and vast numbers of GIs passed through. The war's abrupt end left them with millions of dollars worth of redundant aircraft and equipment, so the whole lot was bulldozed into a huge hole. There are a number of well-preserved sunken ships and aircraft offshore.

Nearby **Malasiga** village was settled by Tami Islanders and here it is possible to buy the famous Tami Island bowls. A reader suggests visiting the Ngasegalatu Church, which has some amazing carvings by David Anams, on the way to Malasiga. The beautiful **Tami Islands**, south of Finschhafen, are only 12km from the coast. The islanders are

renowned for their beautifully carved wooden bowls. Malasiga is a good place to look for transport to get out to the islands.

A two-hour drive north of Finschhafen is **Sialum**. It was a major holiday resort for the expat community during colonial times, but has, in recent decades, fallen from favour. Locals are trying to resurrect their tourism industry, and the town is well worth a visit. Nearby, natural terracing forms an interesting feature. There are good bushwalks here, fishing is excellent and the Paradise Spring River waters are crystal clear for swimming. The **Butaweng Waterfalls** are also worth a visit.

Places to Stay
The *Fisika Guesthouse* (☎ 474 7073; fax 474 7093; PO Box 177) is a modern three bedroom house with a kitchen for guest use and a haus win in the backyard. Rooms each have two beds and cost K30/40 a single/double. A produce market is only 100m from the house, and there are two stores within 1km, as well as a kai-bar, bank and post office. The airport is 2km away. Some Peace Corps volunteers have helped to establish it as a guesthouse; they welcome visitors.

Dreger Lodge (☎ 474 7050; PO Box 126) was built and run by Dregerhafen Provincial High School, 3km from Finschhafen. It has five rooms, each with two or three beds, and costs K35 for one or two people or K55 for three. It has communal cooking facilities – no food is provided. There is good snorkelling nearby.

In Sialum, the *Paradise Inn* has seven simple and comfortable rooms available. It is prettily situated by the seaside, near the Paradise Spring River. Ask for Mana Gasawe. Bookings can be made through the Fisika Development Authority (☎ 474 7073) in Finschhafen.

There is talk of a major hotel development to be built at Finschhafen in the next few years. Hopefully this will not spoil the peace and quiet and the beauty of the area.

Getting There & Away
Virtually all Madang-bound boats call at

Finschhafen. Lutheran Shipping has a number of boats, the most recent of which is the *Gejamsao*, a fully air-conditioned passenger catamaran which has seating for 170 plebeians plus 12 in VIP class. If you are willing to pay through the nose, you can rent a speedboat between Lae and Finschhafen.

Northcoast Airlines flies between Lae and Finschhafen on Tuesday, Thursday and Saturday for K85; MBA flies direct from Port Moresby to Finschhafen on Friday and Sunday for K154.

There's a road from Finschhafen to Sialum and a rough road further still to Wasu (where there is a village guesthouse).

It's possible to walk between Finschhafen and Lae; students from Dregerhafen Provincial High School regularly do this walk. See the school principal for advice. The walk along the coast, sometimes on the beach, takes three days.

WAU & BULOLO
Wau • pop 5000 • postcode 422
Bulolo • pop 8000 • postcode 423

The nicest thing about Wau (pronounced 'wow') and Bulolo is the weather. The coolness is a welcome change from the stifling heat and humidity of coastal towns like Lae. The abundant pines give a refreshing new slant on equatorial vegetation. Nights can get chilly at this altitude of about 1300m.

Wau and Bulolo were the sites of New Guinea's goldrush in the 1920s and 30s, but the gold began to peter out by the start of WWII and the mines never got back into full swing afterwards. The construction of a road down to Lae during the war has encouraged the development of timber and agricultural industries. If you're interested in the history of gold mining, the mountains and their people, bird-watching or butterfly-collecting, Wau and Bulolo are well worth a visit.

Many people still work small claims in the area and fossickers turn up the occasional nugget. Gold traders indicate their business with signs placed outside their houses in Wau and Bulolo: *'Salim Gol Long Hia'* (gold sold here).

A couple of the pre-war dredges, weighing

2500 tons, which were flown in by the old Junkers tri-motors from Lae, could be seen for many years by the river, but the Japanese bought them and cut them up for scrap. Between Bulolo and Wau, the road winds through the deep Wau Gorge, crossing first Edie Creek and then Little Wau Creek – the two creeks which formed the basis of the goldrush activities.

After the goldrush, the hoop and klinkii pine forests were decimated by a logging company formed by the gold dredgers. Many of the bare hillsides riddled with erosion are the result of this.

McAdam National Park
This 20-sq-km park was established in 1962 to preserve the last virgin stands of hoop and klinkii pine and over 200 species of birds that have been recorded in the area. The bird-life includes cassowaries, eagles and 10 species of bird of paradise. There are also orchids, ferns, butterflies and tree kangaroos. Note that this is not the McAdam Memorial Park, south-east of Wau.

Unfortunately, there are no tourist facilities yet, but you can view the park from the road adjacent to the boundary. There's also a walking track into the park which leaves the Wau-Bulolo Road just as you enter Bulolo Gorge.

Wau Ecology Institute
The Wau Ecology Institute (WEI) has seen better days, but is still an excellent place to stay (see the Places to Stay section). Its aim is to research grassroots ecology and save PNG's rapidly disappearing rainforests and biodiversity. Unfortunately it is now a little rundown and needs a massive injection of funds to maintain its existing programs. Its small zoo is becoming overgrown; when visited by one author, a dead snake was lying in its cage and a lone crocodile looked stunned and totally bored, far from its natural coastal habitat.

The institute also has a small museum and conference centre, the Somare Environmental Centre, which seemed to be maintained, although underutilised. The museum has an

MOROBE PROVINCE

interesting collection of photos of Wau in its heyday in the 1930s. The hostel run by the institute is large and comfortable, but even it was showing subtle signs of decay.

Perhaps the most viable of the WEI's activities is its Butterfly Ranch (☎ & fax 474 6212). It supplies collectors around the world with examples of PNG's astounding variety of insects. The philosophy is that villagers earn money by collecting and selling butterflies, beetles and other insects which have usually already laid their eggs, thereby ensuring the procreation of their species. While earning an income, villagers also interact more closely with their environment (and become less tempted to cut down trees for a fast buck). The ranch can show you some amazingly well-camouflaged stick insects, enormous creepy spiders, and a wonderful array of large and multi-coloured butterflies.

Insect Farming & Trading Agency

Another place that operates in similar fashion to the Butterfly Ranch is the Insect Farming & Trading Agency (☎ 474 5285; fax 474 5454; PO Box 129, Bulolo) in Bulolo on Godwin St, uphill and to the left

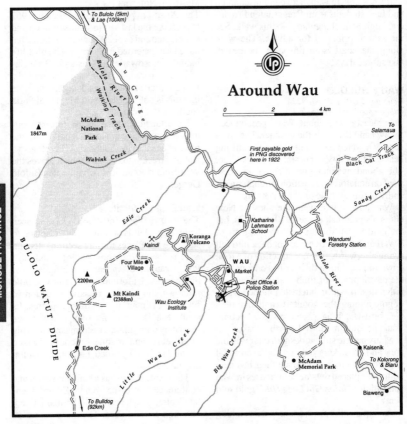

Around Wau

from the post office. Well worth a visit, it is run in conjunction with Lae's Rainforest Habitat and Unitech.

Rafting the Watut River
PNG has countless rivers ideally suited for whitewater rafting; the Watut is one of the best. Unfortunately it has had a reputation as a dangerous place because of rascals but it is possible to raft all the way from Bulolo down to the Markham River. You might check with Ed McArdle at the Lae Explorers Club (☎ 472 1044; fax 472 2748) to see if there's any recent information.

Walking in the Wau Area
There are many interesting walks on local footpaths and roads around the WEI. An hour will get you to Four Mile village, which has some spectacular views of the Wau Valley. It is a hard walk beyond there to the Edie Creek area. Allow at least four hours to get there and three to return. Those planning longer treks in the area should talk to the people at the WEI as they may be able to help find reliable guides and can often drive you to the trailhead.

There is a WEI field station at **Kolorong**, about an hour's drive south-east of Wau on the Biaru Road. It was established by the WEI as a base from which to conduct research, particularly bird-watching, but there are interesting walks here too (see Places to Stay).

If you are going deep into the bush, prepare properly. These walks are adventures, not merely treks. Guides are highly recommended; expect a hard slog and be properly equipped. For more information on the Black Cat Track and other trails in this area, see Lonely Planet's *Bushwalking in Papua New Guinea*.

Black Cat Track The Black Cat Track, which begins 14km from the WEI near Wandumi Forest Station, is the old gold-miners' route between Wau and Salamaua. Some Australian soldiers described the Black Cat as the hardest walk they'd ever done, mainly because the trail heads straight

for its objective rather than following the less difficult ridges – a common problem with PNG trails. One local expat described it as 'suitable only for masochists and Israeli paratroopers'.

The track reaches the lowlands by way of the Francisco River. The track between Buidanima and Wapali is hard. The remainder of the trail is generally easy to walk but there are numerous potentially dangerous crossings of the Bitoi River between Wapali and Mubo. Water is plentiful throughout the walk but there are no stores along the trail.

June, July and August are the best months, although May and September can also be quite nice.

Bulldog Track The old WWII Bulldog Track, intended to link Wau with the south coast, runs on from Edie Creek. The track never actually got to the coast – from Bulldog you had to travel by river. Since the war, the track has deteriorated and been cut by landslides and slips in many places. Fit walkers, preferably with a guide, can walk to Bulldog in about three days; from there they may be able to get a boat down river to the south coast. Serious planning is required and this walk should definitely not be undertaken lightly.

Tekaku & Kakoro The Foundation of the Peoples of the South Pacific (FSP/PNG) (☎ 325 8470) is establishing an ecotourism walk on part of the Bulldog Track involving the two villages Tekaku and Kakoro, both of which are near the Morobe-Gulf border. A scientific research centre will be established at Tekaku, to look at flora, fauna and ecological issues, and there is already a tourist guesthouse at Kakoro. It offers packages ranging up to eight days with charter flights in and out to Tekaku. If you want to see grassroots PNG, this area is highly recommended.

Places to Stay & Eat
Remember that in Wau you're up at an altitude of about 1300m, so come prepared for chilly nights.

The *Wau Ecology Institute* (WEI) (☎ 474 6218; fax 474 6381; PO Box 77) is clean and comfortable. Twin rooms with clean shared bathrooms cost K30 per night, and you have access to a well-equipped kitchen with tea and coffee-making facilities. At most times you will get a room to yourself, but if there is a research conference under way (you would have to be unlucky) you may have to share or sleep elsewhere – but they will put you up somewhere. There may be cheaper beds available in a duplex bunkhouse. Food is only provided if there is a conference, so stock up in the shops in Wau before heading for the WEI. It's a couple of kilometres out of Wau on a hillside above the town and the walk can get a little arduous, particularly if you do it several times in the same day.

You can stay at the *Kolorong Guesthouse* for a few kina. It is an hour's drive from Wau, and is a particularly good bird-watching area. It has three double bunk beds in three rooms, plus a classroom. Ask at the WEI about getting there and back and give plenty of warning that you are coming. It is a long way and uphill most of the way.

About 2km before Wau on the road from Bulolo, the *Katharine Lehmann School* (☎ 474 6232; PO Box 81, Wau) has two and three-bedroom houses which they let as holiday homes for around K30 a night. You can do your own cooking or you can eat with the students during term. They may still have a car which you can rent for just a few toea per kilometre. The PMV from Lae goes right past it, so ask the driver to let you off.

The *Wau Hotel* (☎ 474 6391) is centrally located in Wau. If you want to experience a wild west-type saloon, then this will suit you. The rooms are apparently not too bad – but the pokies, bars, brawls and loud music may turn you off.

The *Pine Lodge Resort* (☎ 474 5220; fax 474 5284; PO Box 90) in Bulolo is owned by Melanesian Tourist Services, so the hotel is suitably luxurious and expensive. There are 14 comfortable, furnished bungalows, each with a private balcony overlooking the Bulolo Valley. The resort has a swimming pool and aviaries in landscaped gardens. The

staff can also organise tours to the surrounding areas.

Also in Bulolo, there's very basic and cheap accommodation at the *PNG Forestry College*. To get there, head towards Wau on the main road and turn right at the market and keep going until you come to the plymill, where you turn right.

Getting There & Away
Air Wau airstrip has nothing to remind you of its former level of activity. It's one of the steepest airstrips in PNG, falling 91m in its 1000m length (definitely one-way!).

Islands Nationair flies from Port Moresby to Bulolo for K128 and from Lae to Bulolo for K56. North Coast Aviation also services Wau.

PMV Coming from Lae, several PMVs (trucks) leave from the Eriku long-distance PMV stop on Bumbu Rd fairly early in the morning, say before 9 am. In Wau, PMVs stop near the market and most going to Lae leave early.

Walking Another way to get to Lae, particularly for travellers seeking a challenge, is to walk to Salamaua (three days) and from there catch a boat to Lae (around K6).

MENYAMYA & ASEKI
• *postcode 427*
Menyamya is in the heart of the old Anga country and is now a coffee-growing centre; it's not particularly interesting in itself. Some people still wear traditional dress and the area has been recommended for walks.

The Anga used to smoke their dead and leave the mummified bodies in burial caves. They now practise Christian burials. It is possible to see some of these mummified bodies at Aseki, but the most accessible place to see them is at **Angibena**, a 2½ hour drive from Wau on the Aseki road. There will be a charge of between K5 and K10. Ask around near here, and a guide will turn up to show you three bodies in a cave close to the road, one holding a baby. But *please* show respect – these are the ancestors of your guides. A group of European tourists recently made fun of the genitalia on one of the bodies and as they left the site they narrowly avoided an avalanche, convincing the local guide that his ancestors were unhappy with the group's behaviour.

The market days in Aseki are Tuesday, Thursday and Saturday and in Menyamya, Monday, Thursday and Saturday. You can see people in traditional dress, but ask permission before taking photos; they will probably charge you.

If you have a less-than-enthusiastic welcome around here, it might be because some visitors show disrespect or haggle bitterly over prices for photos or accommodation. Use your common sense, otherwise it makes life difficult for later visitors.

Walking in the Menyamya & Aseki Areas

For full information on the trails mentioned here see Lonely Planet's *Bushwalking in Papua New Guinea*. Guides and thorough planning are essential on these walks, as the country is remote and the inter-clan squabbles can cause problems.

Menyamya to Kerema This beautiful walk passes through the rugged heart of Anga country. June, July and August are the best months to walk although May and September can also be OK. The suggested itinerary takes eight days but you could shorten it to six by flying out of Kamina rather than walking all the way to the Kerema.

A guide is not necessary between Menyamya and Mbauyia, and between Didimaua and Murua. But one is essential from Mbauyia to Didimaua. In Menyamya, the district office or the Anga Development Authority can probably help you find someone reliable.

Food can usually be bought in villages along the trail and there are basic trade stores in Menyamya, Hawabango, Kanabea, Kamina and Kerema. There are unreliable trade stores in Murua and along the road between Meware and Wemauwa.

The first section, Menyamya to Mbauyia, basically follows a track on which patrol

officers in the 1970s rode motorcycles. A road, used rarely, links Kaintiba, Kanabea and Paina, a small village half a day's walk south of Kanabea. The rest of the track is narrower but easy to follow.

Between Mbauyia and Didimaua, the trail follows a difficult path through tough terrain where it's very hot and humid. It's the most difficult section of the walk and requires a fair degree of fitness. But it's possible to bypass it by flying out from Kamina, half a day's walk due east of Ivandu.

From Didimaua another rough road is followed down to Murua Station. From here Kerema can be reached by either road or motorised canoe down the Murua River.

Menyamya to Marawaka Expect five or six days of walking on this route. It takes you through the villages of Yagwoingwe, Yakana, Andakombe, Gwalyu, Yamuru and Wauko.

Places to Stay

If you want to stay up in the Menyamya district, contact the Anga Development Authority (☎ 474 0211; PO Box 61), which has a *guesthouse*. Meals may be available, but it is advisable to come well-stocked. Otherwise, ask at the Menyamya Police Station where to stay. As in most parts of PNG, if you get to know the people, you can usually find someone to spend the night with – and it is far safer to sleep with a family in a village than on your own.

The Lutheran missionaries may still operate a very basic *guesthouse* in Aseki.

Getting There & Away

Air North Coast Aviation should have regular flights to both Menyamya and Aseki. You may also be able to charter with MAF.

PMV A road runs from Bulolo up to Aseki then on to Menyamya through some extremely rough and absolutely spectacular country. There are PMVs on the route, although they may not run every day; Bulolo to Menyamya costs about K10; from Wau it's about K12 but you'll usually have to change

MOROBE PROVINCE

at Bulolo. In Bulolo, PMVs usually leave from the Wabu Trade Store. The road actually bypasses Aseki, so if you're going there make sure the driver knows so he can take you into the village.

SIASSI GROUP

The Siassi Group is between the mainland and New Britain. **Umboi (Rooke) Island** is the largest, with a total area of 777 sq km and a number of settlements. Siassi is the main village; there are two good boat anchorages at Marien Harbour and Luther. On the southeast side of Umboi is Lablab mission where there's a guesthouse.

Slightly north of Umboi is the sometimes violently volcanic **Sakar Island**, only 34 sq km in area. **Tolokiwa Island**, a little to the west, is wooded and inhabited, but it too has a conical volcano, 1377m high. All these islands are in the volcanic belt which extends through New Britain and down to the north coast of New Guinea.

Getting There & Away

North Coast Aviation services Lablab (K112) and Siassi (K112) on Umboi from Lae and Finschhafen on Tuesday, Thursday and Saturday. Lutheran Shipping's passenger vessels sail to Lablab from Lae; its passenger-carrying freighters sail to Siassi. The fare on a local boat from Finschhafen to Siassi is about K5.

ANN JELINEK

JON MURRAY

RAINFOREST HABITAT/ROCKY ROE

Top Left: Called a *kokomo* by locals, Blythe's Hornbill is a lowland rainforest bird.
Top Right: Goodfellow's Tree Kangaroo
Bottom: Butterflies at the Insect Farming & Trading Agency, Bulolo, Morobe Province

Madang Province
Top: Kranket Island's lagoon, a snorkeller's paradise
Middle: Guesthouse built in traditional style on Siar Island
Bottom: A Japanese WWII bomber near Amron

Madang Province

Land Area 28,000 sq km
Population 290,000
Capital Madang

Madang Province is a fertile coastal strip backed by some of the most rugged mountains in Papua New Guinea – the Adelbert and Schrader ranges to the north and the Finisterre Ranges to the south. A string of interesting, and still active, volcanic islands is offshore. More or less in the middle of the coastal stretch stands Madang – quite possibly the most beautiful town in the whole country, even, some claim, in the Pacific.

History

Settlements dating back 15,000 years have been found near Simbai in the Schrader Ranges. The Bilbil and Yabob people traded pots from Karkar Island with what is now western Morobe Province. This network extended to the Highlands and involved such items as shells, salt and clay pots.

The Russian biologist Nicolai Miklouho-Maclay was probably the first European to spend any length of time on the PNG mainland. He arrived at Astrolabe Bay, south of the present site of Madang, in 1871 and settled in for a 15-month stay before leaving to regain his health, which was badly affected by malaria. His interest in New Guinea led to two further, equally lonely visits.

Unlike many explorers who followed him, his relations with the local tribes were remarkably good and his studies still make fascinating reading. He was suitably amazed by the large, two-masted sailing canoes of the Madang people and named the islands in Madang Harbour the 'Archipelago of Contented Men'.

The German New Guinea Company turned up 13 years later but its stay, although longer, was rather less successful. As Maclay had found, to his cost, the northern New Guinea coast was unhealthy and rife with

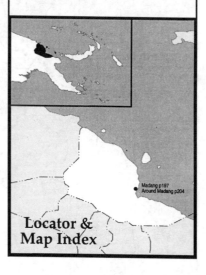

Madang p197
Around Madang p204

Locator & Map Index

malaria; the disease followed the Germans as they moved first from Finschhafen to Bogadjim on Astrolabe Bay and then on to Madang. If malaria didn't get them, then blackwater fever usually did.

From 1884 to 1899, 224 officials worked for the company, of whom 41 died and 133 either resigned or were dismissed. On the point of failure, the German government

MADANG PROVINCE

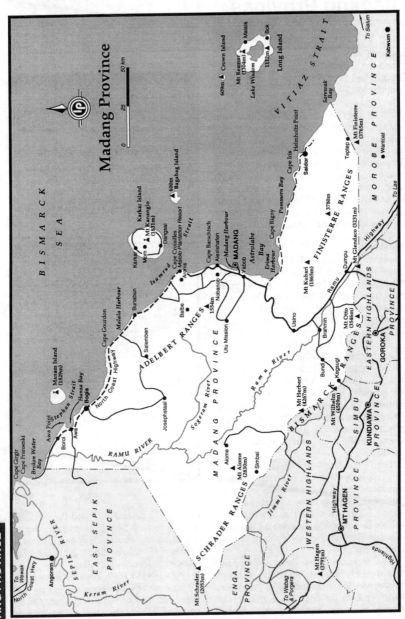

took over and moved the settlement to the healthier climate of Kokopo, near Rabaul, on New Britain Island. The coast still has many German names and mission stations, although gravestones are almost the only reminders of the old company.

In WWII, the Japanese soon took Madang, but after the recapture of Lae, Australian troops slowly and painfully pushed the Japanese along the coast to their final defeat at Wewak. The bitter fighting for control of Shaggy Ridge and the route over the Finisterre Ranges to Madang started in late 1943; it took a month to push the Japanese down to the coast and on towards Wewak.

Madang was virtually demolished during the war and had to be totally rebuilt. Even the old German cemetery bears scars from the vicious fighting. Madang's importance as a major north-coast port, from where freight was flown to the Highlands, changed drastically when the Highlands Highway shifted business to Lae. Now that a new road has shortened the distance between Madang and the Highlands, things might pick up again. Madang Province has 1762km of road but only some 100km of it is sealed – between Madang town and Malolo, and inland along the Ramu Highway.

Logging has since brought money into the town – a woodchip conveyor belt and a smoking pulp mill disfigure the harbour – but clear-felling is destroying the inland jungles and threatening the province's bird and animal life.

Geography

Madang Province comprises strips of lowland and mountain. Coconuts and cocoa have been grown along the fertile coast since the German days. Inland, mountain ranges rise parallel to the coast then slope down to the Ramu River valley, which also parallels the coast. This is productive cattle country and home to the Ramu Sugar Refinery, which meets almost all of PNG's sugar requirements. Only a low divide separates the Upper Ramu from the Markham Valley, in which the Highlands Highway runs to Lae.

Inland from the Ramu, the Bismarck and Schrader ranges rise to the highest peaks in the country, including Mt Wilhelm which stands on the border with Simbu Province.

There are 45 islands off the coast of Madang Province – three of these are still active volcanos: Manam, Karkar and Long islands. Lake Wisdom is a crater lake in the middle of Long Island; it is 180m above sea level and PNG's largest lake in terms of volume.

Society & Conduct

The diverse geographic nature of this province is reflected in the make-up of its people. They can, by virtue of their lifestyle, be broken into four distinct groups: islanders, coastal people, river people and mountain people. These groups are alike in physical appearance, apart from the small-statured Simbai tribes which inhabit the Highlands foothills.

Traditional dress is rarely worn, but the majority of people still live in villages at a subsistence level. The coconut is used extensively, except in the mountains. Islanders depend on seafood; the coastal people grow a variety of different root crops, bananas and tropical fruits; the river people's staple is sago; and the mountain people base their diet on the sweet potato, although it is now supplemented by many western vegetables.

The Manam Islanders live around the base of a volcano and their society is dominated by a hereditary chief, known as the *kukurai*. Although there are different language groups, the Manam clans are related to the people who live along the lower sections of the Ramu River, the north coast of the province and the lower Sepik. The artefacts produced on Manam Island are not unlike those produced on the Sepik.

There are even closer artistic links between the Ramu and the Sepik people. The mighty Ramu is almost linked to the Keram River, and thence to the Sepik, so probably there was extensive trade and cultural interchange for thousands of years. Their way of life is similar and the Ramu people are also great wood carvers, like the Sepik people.

The nearby coastal villagers of Yabob and

A mask from the Astrolabe Bay area.

Bilbil are famous for their earthenware pots and, like the Motuans of the Port Moresby area, they once traded these items far up and down the coast in large *lalaoika* (trading vessels). Their attractive houses are made from sago and toddy palms, usually without nails. The walls and fold-out windows are made from sago palm leaf stems tied into frames and panels with the leaves, either intertwined or sewn into long shingles. On Karkar Island, and in the lower Ramu district, some traditional houses have two storeys.

MADANG
• *pop 29,000* • *postcode 511*

The title of 'prettiest town in the Pacific' may not be an official one but it has often been applied to Madang. The town is perched on a peninsula jutting out into the sea and is liberally sprinkled with parks, ponds and waterways – frequently decked in water lilies.

The warm, wet climate and fertile soil has created luxuriant growth; many of the huge trees, particularly casuarinas, survived WWII and still tower over Madang's gently curving roads (and house huge colonies of flying foxes). A scattering of picturesque islands around the town's deep-water harbour completes the picture. Unfortunately, as in so many other towns in PNG, the beautiful rain trees are being severely lopped or cut down – they have a nasty habit of dropping their huge branches on people and property.

Madang is the most tourist-oriented city in PNG and this, fortunately, translates into a wide range of facilities but falls a long way short of being plastic. It is not, however, the place to come to if you want to see untouched local cultures. By far the greatest attraction is what lies beneath the surface of the sea. There are some excellent places to stay beside the sea, in all price brackets.

Orientation

Madang is built on a peninsula. Coronation Drive, on the south-eastern side, faces across Astrolabe Bay to the beautiful Finisterre Ranges. On the north-western side, the town looks out across the still waters of Binnen and Madang harbours to the airport and the palm-lined coast. The tip of the peninsula, on the north-western side, faces the entrance to the harbours and Dallman Passage, which separates the peninsula from Kranket Island. The main shopping and business area is here, at the end of the main road (Modilon Rd) running the full length of the peninsula.

The airport, about 7km from the main area of town (you have to cross the Wagol River and skirt Binnen Harbour), is not within walking distance. See the Getting Around section.

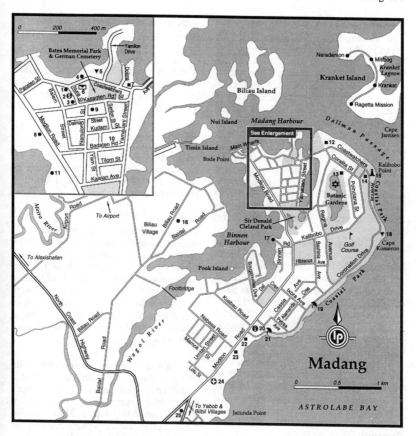

PLACES TO STAY
7   CWA Guesthouse
12 Madang Resort
    Hotel
13 Lutheran
    Guesthouse
14 Coastwatcher's
    Motel
22 Smugglers'
    Inn
23 Madang
    Lodge

PLACES TO EAT
5   Madang Club
18 Golf Club

OTHER
1   Air Niugini
2   Westpac Bank
3   Island Airways
4   Yacht Club
6   Post Office
8   Rab-Trad
    (Rabaul Trading)
9   Steamships
    Store
10 Market
11 Lutheran Shipping
15 Coastwatchers'
    Memorial
16 Pulp Mill
17 Coastal Shipping
19 RSL Park Beach
20 Madang Visitors &
    Cultural Bureau
21 Lion's Reserve
    Beach
24 Hospital
25 Provincial
    Government Offices

Information

The Madang Visitors & Cultural Bureau (☎ 852 3302; fax 852 3540; PO Box 1071), in Haus Tumbuna on Modilon Rd near the intersection with Coronation Drive, should be your first stop for information. It combines a small but interesting museum with a tourist information office and is well stocked with brochures and literature on things to do around the area (a rarity in PNG). The museum has displays of local artefacts such as weapons, jewellery and musical instruments, as well as many photographs from the German occupation period. There are also models of traditional local boats. The bureau is run by the provincial government, with the Tourism Promotion Authority also represented.

The shopping in Madang is not as extensive as in Lae but you'll have no problems with essentials. It is a more pleasant place to just wander around. There's a post office and banks, and Air Niugini and Lutheran Shipping have offices here. The third-level airline Island Airways (☎ 852 2601; fax 852 2244; PO Box 747), not to be confused with Islands Nationair, is based in Madang.

Melanesian Tourist Services (☎ 852 2766; fax 852 3543; PO Box 707), which runs the *Melanesian Discoverer* and a number of tours and places to stay in PNG, is based at the Madang Resort Hotel, where there's also a travel agency.

Cemetery

In the centre of town, near the market, is the old German cemetery. Madang was the German New Guinea Company's last attempt at a foothold on the mainland before they packed it in and moved to New Britain. This rather bleak little cemetery attests to the malaria that was, and still is, extremely virulent.

Coastwatchers' Memorial

This 30m-high beacon is visible 25km out to sea, a reminder of those men who stayed behind the lines during WWII to report on Japanese troop and ship movements. It is a somewhat stark concrete memorial but provides some nice shady corners for idlers wanting to sleep away the sultry daytime hours.

The 3km coast road south of the memorial is one of the most pleasant in Madang, fringed by palm trees and poincianas and backed by the golf course with fine views across Astrolabe Bay.

Market

The colourful and popular market is at its busiest best on Saturday. Apart from the vegetables and fruit, there is a section for handcrafts and artefacts. The local shell jewellery can be a bargain.

Activities

Kranket and Siar islands are commonly visited and easily accessible for day trips. See the Around Madang section; it's possible to stay cheaply on both these islands. Wherever you stay, take advantage of the harbour and the superb underwater scenery, whether through glass-viewing boxes, snorkelling or skin diving. You can get out on the exceptionally beautiful harbour by yourself using local boats, or with a cruise.

Snorkelling & Diving The snorkelling and diving in Madang are excellent and the area is justifiably world famous. There is excellent visibility, superb coral and, if you're diving, many WWII wrecks. There is a wide range of dive locations within 15 minutes of town and many more up the coast.

There are three dive shops in Madang:

Madang Aquaventures
    PO Box 166 (☎ 852 2023)
    Based at Smugglers' Inn
Niugini Diving Adventures
    PO Box 707 (☎ 852 2766)
    Based at the Madang Resort Hotel
Jais Aben Resort
    PO Box 105, Madang (☎ 852 3311;
    fax 852 3560)
    Based 20km north of Madang and specialises in diving

You can hire gear from all three places and all have packages including accommodation and dives. If you are just snorkelling, have a word to the dive shops about locations but you could try Lion's Reserve Beach, Siar Island, the reef in the beautiful Kranket Lagoon, Pig Island and around Sinaub Island. Dugout canoes are available at Siar or Kranket to use as dive platforms. Make sure you take someone with you: there are very strong currents in some places and the boat could easily drift away, leaving you stranded.

You can hire snorkelling gear on Siar and Kranket for a few kina but it might not be good quality. It is best to rent in town.

Golf The golf course in Madang is attractive and well maintained. It follows the coast road on the east side of the peninsula and you can enjoy views of the sea and islands as you play a round or two. The clubhouse is a good place for a cold beer or snack afterwards. Check out the thousands of flying foxes in the casuarina trees lining the road skirting the golf course.

Swimming The small Lion's Reserve Beach, just north of the Smugglers' Inn, has excellent coral and tropical fish just a few strokes from the shore. It's not so good at low tide, however, when sea urchins and sharp coral wait for the unwary foot. Not far away, there are two or three tiny bays with minuscule beaches along Coronation Drive near the end of Ixora Ave. You can also swim in the inlet by the CWA Guesthouse.

Other favourite – and much better – spots are Siar Island, Kranket Lagoon, Pig Island (an exceptionally beautiful little island, despite the name) and Wongat Island. Be careful of jellyfish and their stingers – it is worth taking a small bottle of vinegar for first-aid.

Do-it-Yourself Harbour Cruises If you want to organise your own voyage around the harbour, you can do it easily and cheaply. Wander down behind the Lutheran Shipping office or just behind the Madang Club and you'll find a ferry service that shuttles across to Kranket Island for just K0.40. It's irregular, but usually fairly frequent, and you could hardly do it cheaper. Sundays are quiet and the boat makes fewer trips.

Another method is to take a PMV to Siar village for K0.50 (you might be dropped off on the highway and have to walk a few kilometres to the village), then negotiate a ride across to Siar Island. Although it's only a short distance, you can expect to pay at least K2. You can also find canoes for longer cruises.

Shark-Cleaning at Barracuda Point

A Madang diver, Tim Rowland, has reported an unusual phenomenon he has observed only five times in 15 years of diving around the area.

At the Barracuda Point dive site, he has noticed that grey reef sharks sometimes hover expectantly over a particular ledge and then flip up to stand on their tails, balancing against the current. The shark snaps open its jaws with an audible click, at which point a blue-and-white wrasse, which has been hovering nearby, enters its mouth and proceeds to clean around its teeth and gills.

With the wrasse in its mouth, the shark swims off to do a circuit of the area for a few minutes before returning to its original position, flipping up on its tail again, opening its mouth and releasing the 'cleaner fish'. If the job is not complete, the wrasse stays put and the shark does another circuit until the wrasse is finished.

As this apparently only happens at Barracuda Point, it seems the wrasse there have a nice little cleaning business. ■

The Madang area is good for bird-watching – you might see a sulphur-crested cockatoo.

A third alternative is to rent your own transport. Smith Keenan and Saimon Tewa on Siar Island hire canoes for a few kina, and canoes are also available at Jais Aben Resort. Afternoons tend to get windy, stirring up waves and making it hard to paddle, but this is a great way to get around. Definitely take a T-shirt and suntan lotion: you can really fry out there.

Organised Tours

All the resorts and hotels in Madang can organise harbour cruises.

The Madang Resort's cruise departs every day at 9 am and costs K35 for a half-day and K60 for a full day, with a minimum of two people. You will be picked up from your hotel and taken to see the rusting wreckage of Japanese landing craft; Kranket Island, where you can view the fish and coral formations through glass-bottomed viewing boxes; and Siar Island, where you get a chance to wander around or snorkel for an hour or so.

Several places, including the Madang Resort Hotel and the Malolo Plantation Resort on the north coast, offer tours of villages. These tours could be interesting if you haven't yet managed to see a *sing-sing* (celebratory festival) and don't plan on visiting areas of PNG where traditional culture remains strong, but don't expect spontaneity.

There is plenty of bird-life in the area (although the heavy-handed logging of the inland rainforest is threatening it) and Malolo Plantation Resort can take you to some good bird-watching places.

Places to Stay – bottom end

Madang has a permanent holiday feel and has a better range of accommodation options than most other large towns.

One of the best is the *CWA Guesthouse* (☎ 852 2216; PO Box 154), which raises money for worthwhile women's causes. Its location on the waterfront near the town centre is excellent. It is an agreeable spot, well operated and clean. The five bedrooms inside the main cottage are let on a shared basis. A bed costs K25 per night and if you are a single traveller you may be lucky and have a room to yourself, otherwise you will have to share. There is also a self-contained family unit which sleeps four (two adults and two children) for K70 per night. No meals are served but there are good kitchen facilities and a pleasant barbecue overlooking the water.

The *Lutheran Guesthouse* (☎ 852 2589; 852 2895 (AH); PO Box 211) on Coralita St, about midway between the Madang Resort Hotel and the Coastwatcher's Motel, is friendly and clean and the rooms have fans and attached bathrooms. It can get busy on weekends so it's worth booking ahead; as with the CWA Guesthouse, solo travellers may be asked to share a room. The manager isn't always there but the caretaker lives in, so you can arrive at any time. Accommodation is K40 per person (including breakfast and dinner) or K35 (for bed and breakfast only). There's a well-equipped kitchen. Bear in mind that this is a church guesthouse, despite Madang's resort-town atmosphere.

Ask here about the cheaper *Lutheran Hostel*, although it's usually full of permanent residents and is pretty grubby.

There is also an *SIL Guesthouse* (☎ 852 3254; PO Box 675), with self-contained flats for K45/65 a single/double. It is located near the provincial government offices, 1km or so from the town centre.

There are other bottom-end alternatives in and around town. One writer advises that the fire station will take in guests as long as they are presentable and contribute to the communal *buai* (betel nut) fund. There are also some locally owned bush-material places with loads of character on some of the islands in the harbour. Siar Island has two competing village guesthouses and Kranket has a good hostel as well as more expensive accommodation. They're definitely worth considering if you're planning to be in the area for more than a day or two. See the Around Madang section.

Places to Stay – middle & top end

From the street, the *Madang Lodge* (☎ 852 3395; fax 852 3292; PO Box 59) looks uninspiring and a little daunting, but once inside it is a pleasant and well-maintained place with gardens and water views. At the budget end, you can have a small motel-style room with shared bathroom for K45/55. Middle of the range rooms have en-suite bathroom and air-con for K65/75, and garden terrace rooms are K95/110. Monthly rates are also available. There is a dining room and bar, but no swimming pool.

The *Coastwatcher's Motel* (☎ 852 2684; fax 852 2716; PO Box 324) is on Coastwatcher's Ave, behind the Coastwatchers' Memorial. Although a little characterless – it is a typical motel – it is newer than the two other top-enders. All rooms have air-con, a fridge, TV and telephone. It also has a restaurant and a swimming pool; the bar is a friendly spot for a cold beer and can get quite lively in the evenings. The motel is part of the Coral Sea chain.

Smugglers' Inn (☎ 852 2744; fax 852 2267; PO Box 303) is one of Madang's better and more established resorts. It is built on the waterfront on Modilon Rd and has a superb open-air restaurant with louvred windows leading to a wide terrace and superb coastal views. The food is good – see the Places to Eat section. There's a swimming pool or you can snorkel at the Lion's Reserve Beach only 50m away. Madang Aquaventures have a shop in the grounds.

Prices at Smugglers' are the same as for Coastwatcher's (they're part of the same chain) – between K100 and K125 per room for one or two people (excluding breakfast). If this is your price range and you want something new and modern, choose Coastwatcher's, but if you want a little charm and great water views choose Smugglers'. Both Smugglers' and Coastwatcher's are clean and comfortable (they even share a minibus).

The *Madang Resort Hotel* (☎ 852 2655; fax 852 3325; PO Box 111) is the top of the range hotel in Madang. It has a superb setting, looking over the harbour and across to Kranket Island. The hotel has a swimming pool and restaurant. Rates range from K65/75 in the garden wing to K160/170 for apartment suites and K250/260 for top-of-the-range bungalows. What you get is what you pay for: the top end is luxury and self-contained waterfront bungalows, while the bottom end (which is not too bad at all) is a motel-type room with a TV and coffee-making facilities. The grounds are superb and include the Elizabeth Sowerby Orchid Collection and cages with cuscuses, hornbills, cockatoos and other wildlife. Niugini Diving Adventures has its shop by the water and there's a jetty for the *Melanesian Discoverer* which journeys to the Sepik and around Milne Bay. It costs K45 for one dive, plus K20 gear hire, or K180 for a four-dive package.

Places to Eat

Steamships has the usual lunchtime sandwiches and fried food; across the road is the market where you can buy fresh produce, and there's also several kai-bars.

The *Little Dumpling* (☎ 852 1020) at the Madang Club offers medium-priced Chinese dishes or western snacks like hamburgers, sandwiches and mixed grills. It's a relaxed, friendly place and open daily from 11 am to 1.30 pm and 6 to 10 pm. Foreign volunteers working in the area often eat here. The club is meant to be for members only, but overseas visitors should have no problems gaining access. It offers transport to and from the club for diners and is pretty low-key, with snooker, darts and raffles the main entertainment. There's a good view of the harbour from the bar. The dress regulations ban singlets but that's about all (and doesn't seem to deter members from wearing them). You can still see some old German steps near the club.

The *golf club* on Coastwatcher's Avenue is pleasantly situated between the golf course and the sea. Cheap meals and snacks are available but you may have to be signed in. There is also a bar, of course.

All the middle and top-end accommodation places have restaurants with prices reflecting their niche in the market. All have both ambience and good food. The restaurant at *Smugglers' Inn* would make a perfect setting for a remake of *Casablanca*; the food is excellent, with main courses costing around K20. The restaurant at *Madang Lodge* is a little cheaper and has nice water views; they have Lobster Hawaiian for K19.

The restaurant at the *Madang Resort Hotel* is in a *haus win* (gazebo-like structure) overlooking the sea and has a barbecue lunch every Sunday for K15. The resort also has a coffee shop open for breakfast and lunch. A hamburger here will cost you K9 and fish and chips K12. Pizzas are also available.

Things to Buy

The clay pots from Bilbil village are the most interesting traditional local items. If you buy them, make sure they are very carefully packed as, like most PNG pottery, they are extremely fragile.

There are thriving artefacts workshops and marketplaces at Smugglers' Inn (where you can see carvers in action) and the Madang Resort Hotel, dominated by women from the Sepik and the Ramu areas. There

are excellent selections of *bilums* (string bags), shell jewellery and carvings. Don't rush into your purchases, and remember there is often a 'second price'.

Getting There & Away

Air The airport is about 7km from town, which is too far to walk unless you are very keen – see the Getting Around section for local transport details.

Both Air Niugini (☎ 852 2255) and Island Airways (☎ 852 2601) have offices at the airport. MAF (☎ 852 2229) has a few flights in the province.

Air Niugini has flights from Port Moresby (K159), Lae (K84), Mt Hagen (K83), Goroka (K66) and Wewak (K111), as well as weekend packages offering fares from Port Moresby and accommodation in Madang.

The flight from Goroka is brief and quite interesting as you climb up and over the southern fringe of the Highlands, then over the Ramu Valley and drop down to the coast. Flying to/from Wewak, you can see the mouths of the Ramu and Sepik rivers as they meander and loop to the coast, joined by many tributaries.

Island Airways flies to Bundi (on the way to Mt Wilhelm; K62), Saidor (east along the coast; K63), Karkar Island (K50) and many other small strips.

There are daily 40-minute flights with Air Niugini to Wewak for K111.

Road There are coastal roads to the north and south of Madang. The North Coast Highway is sealed as far as Malolo but continues as far as Bogia and Boroi. The road to the south is unsealed and less interesting. Madang is linked to both the Highlands and Lae by the Ramu Highway, which goes inland from Madang to the Ramu Valley, where it turns south-east for 90km and then splits – one road going to the Highlands and one continuing into the Markham Valley to Lae. There is a new, shorter route which has recently been constructed between Dumpu and Henganofi.

PMVs for the north coast leave from near the big *pikus* (fig) tree on Bates Oval, behind the post office. All other PMVs leave from the market area, a block away. You might have to walk around for a while to find the right place to wait as they are not concentrated in one area.

Heading north, the PMV fare to (or near) Siar village is K0.50, Riwo/Jais Aben is K0.50, Alexishafen is K1, Malolo is K3 and to Bogia, near the end of the North Coast Highway, it's K6. Heading south, the PMV fare to Yabob and Bilbil villages is K0.60, Usino is about K7 and Ramu Sugar is K10.

The PMV fare from Madang to Lae is K20.

Avis (☎ 852 2804) has a desk at the airport and at the Madang Resort Hotel; Budget (☎ 852 3044) operates from Smugglers' Inn; Thrifty (☎ 852 2655) also has cars available; and the Lutheran Guesthouse (☎ 852 2589) may give you a cheap deal on its car.

There are no taxis in Madang.

The Highlands The Ramu Highway joins the Highlands Highway at Watarais and while it is quite OK, it can still be closed by floods. The new road cuts across from Dumpu, joining the Highlands Highway at Heganofi, between Kainantu and Goroka, but PMVs still prefer the older, better-known route. PMVs leave from the Madang market. Bus fare to Goroka is K20 but reportedly a discounted fare of K15 is offered to students.

It's an interesting drive along the Ramu Highway, through many isolated villages, past beautiful mountain and jungle scenery. There are still some unbridged rivers to be forded.

It is possible to walk along a very rough road from Brahmin Mission via Bundi to Kegsugl, at the foot of Mt Wilhelm, from where you can catch a PMV to Kundiawa in Simbu Province. This would probably take a minimum of four or five hot, hard days; it is much easier to walk in the opposite direction. The Catholic Mission Guesthouse in Bundi is highly recommended at K15 for a bed, three good meals and a hot shower. See the Walking to Madang information in the Simbu Province section in The Highlands chapter.

Boat Madang is on the main north coast shipping route, well serviced by Lutheran Shipping (☎ 852 2577; fax 852 2180; PO Box 789) on Modilon Rd.

Once again, the most important options are Lutheran Shipping's *Mamose Express* and *Rita*. Eastbound boats depart for Lae at 9 am on Sunday morning. Westbound, you arrive in Madang on Thursday morning and leave at 5 pm on Friday, so you get nearly two days in Madang, which is enough time to have a good look around. Tourist/deck class fares from Madang to either Lae or Wewak are K31/48; Madang-Oro Bay through fares are K36/53.

Lutheran Shipping has several considerably less comfortable freighters that also call in to Madang on their way west to Wewak and Vanimo or east to Lae then Oro Bay or West New Britain. It occasionally has freighters running to Lorengau on Manus Island for K21/26.

The MV *Thompson*, owned by the Wuvulu-Aua community, does a trading circuit between Madang and Wuvulu, Aua, Manus and Wewak, but there is really no fixed schedule. The *Tawi*, operated by the Manus provincial government, was under repair at the time of research, but it normally plies between Madang and Lorengau, the outer islands of Manus and Wuvulu, as well as Wewak.

A boat runs to Karkar Island daily from the Rab-Trad (Rabaul Trading) wharf, near Lutheran Shipping, stopping at Biabi (K7) and Kulili (K8).

Getting Around
The Airport The middle and top-end places in Madang (and the Jais Aben Resort a little north) offer free airport transfers. You can also take a PMV into town from the small Rotary Park across the road from the terminal, but only during the day. Most of the people in the park will be waiting for a PMV, so ask around.

PMV There are frequent PMVs around Madang with a standard K0.30 fare in town. There are also plenty going further out – see

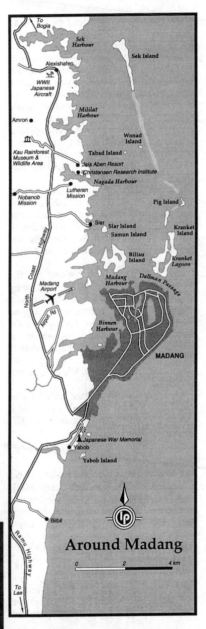

Around Madang

0   2   4 km

the Getting There & Away section. The market is the PMV hub.

AROUND MADANG
Kranket Island

Kranket Island, just across the Dallman Passage from Madang town, is a large island with several villages and an absolutely beautiful lagoon. Once you're on Kranket Island, you can wander around, swim, snorkel or find somebody to take you further out on an outrigger canoe.

At the other end of the island, on the eastern side of the lagoon, there's a picnic area; it can get a bit busy at weekends. In the days immediately following WWII, this was a rest area for wounded Australian soldiers.

Places to Stay The Dum clan (pronounced 'doum') operates the lodges and hostel adjoining the picnic area. The cheaper option is the *hostel*, a large, clean house with four or five bedrooms, a pleasant lounge and a kitchen with a gas stove and refrigerator. It's much better than the average village guesthouse and a steal at K15 per person in shared rooms. Bring your own food. Their betterclass accommodation, *Kranket Island Lodge* (PO Box 800, Madang), has two well-built bungalows, both with private bathrooms, kitchens and hot and cold water. Each has a dining room, a bedroom with four or five beds, plus a large, furnished lounge room overlooking the water. The all up cost is around K70 per night – and you really get all the comforts of home. You can book the lodge (but not the hostel) through the Madang Resort Hotel (☎ 852 2655) which will organise transfers.

Getting There & Away Small boats run to Kranket from near Madang's Town Clinic, on an inlet behind the CWA Guesthouse, for K0.40 for the 10-minute ride. There are boats hourly or so from 7 am to about 5.30 pm. They take you to the end closest to Madang; the accommodation is up the other end – about a 45-minute walk. You might be able to persuade the driver to drop you at the hostel for another K1 or so.

Biliau Island

There are three wrecked Japanese freighters and a small landing barge on Biliau Island, the large island right in the middle of Madang Harbour. More Japanese barges can be seen further to the right. You can reach the island by canoe while staying at Siar village. Most harbour cruises also call in.

Siar Island

Siar is a small island and a popular spot for picnics, barbecues and snorkelling. Just a short boat ride from town, Siar has a beach with large chunks of WWII aircraft wreckage. There are reefs on both sides of the island.

The best thing about Siar is its cheap accommodation, which allows you to make the most of the beach and reefs and learn something about village life. Two locals have set up simple, basic accommodation for budget travellers. The conditions are not luxurious (there's no electricity on the island, for example) but are adequate – even families stay. For some people, this is a highlight of their PNG trip. The houses are built in traditional style with sago walls and roofs and you are, effectively, living on the edge of a village with pigs and chickens and all. It is very pretty and the beaches are superb. Meals are included in the tariff, including local fresh food such as fish, *kaukau* (sweet potato), greens and coconut.

The families running these two places are serious rivals in the competition to attract budget travellers and have become quite well known. The competition has kept prices very low and it's possible you could bargain if things are quiet. In a way, it's a pity that prices have stayed so low – another kina or two on the price of a bed and the standards might be higher. Travellers have complained that the 'deep drop' toilets were full to overflowing and consequently unusable. There have also been complaints of pilfering from the guesthouses, so take care not to leave anything unattended.

Saimon Tewa (PO Box 887, Madang), one of the guesthouse operators, can be contacted through the Madang Club (PO Box 2). He is an amiable guy who takes particular delight in showing a framed letter thanking him for helping with a 1970s visit from the Duke of Edinburgh. He is building a more substantial stilt house by the beach. *Smith Keenan* (PO Box 792, Madang) lives nearby and has a guesthouse close to the beach, just like Saimon's. You can book through the CWA Guesthouse (☎ 852 2216) in Madang. The tariff for both places is K15 per night (including meals). The food is adequate, but it's worth bringing some extra provisions for lunch or to supplement what can be a limited menu (rice and tinned fish).

You can usually rent a mask and snorkel although you're taking a chance on quality and availability – renting in Madang is a safer bet. Canoes can also usually be rented.

Saimon drops in at the Madang Club occasionally to see if anyone wants to go to Siar Island – you might also check at the Madang Visitors & Cultural Bureau. Smith does the same, but at the CWA and Lutheran guesthouses. Both charge K2 for the boat trip and it's a nice ride. Alternatively you can take a PMV to (or near) Siar village for K0.50 and catch a boat for the short ride from there. If you ask Smith or Saimon for an airport transfer they can drop you off on the beach by the airstrip, from where you can follow a path to the terminal building.

Samun Island

Not far away from Siar Island is smaller Samun Island, a similarly picturesque spot. Moses Kalup (☎ 852 3362 or care of PO Box 1241, Madang) and his family have a village guesthouse here. Their prices are similar to those at the Siar guesthouses.

Yabob

If you take Modilon Rd south out of town, shortly before the right turn to the airport and North Coast Highway, a road branches off left to Yabob village. You pass a lookout point and a Japanese war memorial on the way to this pretty little village. There's an island nearby, which you can easily arrange to visit by canoe.

Long before Europeans arrived in the area,

MADANG PROVINCE

Yabob was known for its fine clay pots which were traded far up and down the coast, but unfortunately the villagers have recently stopped making them.

Bilbil

This is another attractive village and pottery is still produced here. Take the first road on the left after the Gum River, off the Ramu Highway; this loops back to the highway. A PMV from Madang market costs K0.60.

Around Madang Province

NORTH COAST HIGHWAY

The road runs a long way north of Madang and people will tell you that it will eventually reach all the way to Wewak. The tar stops at Malolo, but beyond there the road is in reasonable nick, although bumpy.

This would be a great road to cycle along. It's flat, mostly in reasonable condition and you're never too far from the beach. There are plenty of villages along the way where you could buy coconuts to drink. Staying in villages for a few nights might allow the budget to stretch for a night of luxury at the Malolo Plantation Resort.

North Coast Diving

There's more good diving along the coast north of Madang. Near Jais Aben Resort, there's the wreck of US tug/freighter *Henry Leith* in 20m of water. In 30 to 40m of water, the sunken wreck of the minesweeper *Boston* is also a favourite dive.

At the 'water hole', a lagoon is connected to the open sea by a large underwater tunnel. It's beyond the Malolo Plantation Resort and the enclosed lagoon has sand and is safe for children; it also offers dramatic snorkelling. At Bogia Bay, there's a Japanese Zero fighter upside-down in the water several hundred yards directly out from the jetty.

Hansa Bay also has some spectacular wreck dives. A medium-sized Japanese freighter (name unknown) has one davit projecting from the water (known as the davit wreck); it was sunk in 1943 by US bombers and the swim-throughs make an exciting dive in only 12m of water. Nearby in 10m of water is the mast wreck, with its mast protruding from the water; there is a gun on the bow, a large amount of ammunition on the deck and a field artillery piece in the hold.

The Madang dive shops organise dives to Hansa Bay and other north-coast sites.

Nobanob & Nagada Harbour

A little beyond the Siar village turn-off on the North Coast Highway, about 17km from Madang, there are two turn-offs. The right-hand turn leads to the Lutheran Mission complex on Nagada Harbour. The left-hand turn leads up to Nobanob Mission out-station which was used as a Japanese lookout during WWII. It's about a 20-minute drive. There is a pretty park here with a fine view over the north coast, Madang and the harbour; immediately below the park is one of the few remaining areas of virgin rainforest close to Madang.

There are two local guides who can show you around here, Damo Ikum and Dumit Benig. It is worth going on a guided walk with them for a few hours – they can take you to the nearby village of Guntabag or to another spectacular lookout (Tamolalakud Lookout). Damo is a great story-teller and a teacher of *tok pisin* (Pidgin), so he can lead you through the intricacies (or the simplicities) of the language. They can be contacted through the Madang Visitors & Cultural Bureau (☎ 852 3302).

Jais Aben Resort

About 20km from Madang and a couple of kilometres off the main road is the *Jais Aben Resort* (☎ 852 3311; fax 852 3560; PO Box 105, Madang). This is a pretty and secluded spot on its own little peninsula with beaches, lawns and a swimming pool. The resort specialises in diving; it rents equipment and runs boat tours to good dive sites. A couple of kilometres further north, off to the left of the road at **Amron**, is the site of the Japanese WWII strategic command headquarters.

Jais Aben staff can organise tours or sporting trips. A harbour cruise will cost K20 per person (assuming five passengers), a bus tour to Alexishafen and the WWII aircraft wreck will cost K20 and a half-day of local fishing will cost K150 (maximum four passengers). It rents diving equipment and offers diving trips (snorkellers can go along for K10) and water-skiing. Dive packages cost K155 for four dives or K215 for six dives. You can also hire canoes.

Accommodation is in self-contained units (half with their own kitchens) and there is a good restaurant and dive centre, all on the seafront. It's an attractive spot. The resort shares the promontory with the Christensen Research Institute (CRI), which provides facilities for worthwhile marine research.

Most people buy a package that includes diving but the rooms themselves go for around K80/106 a single/double. All sorts of packages are available, incorporating meals and activities. Weekend barbecue buffets average around K12. If you buy a meal, you can use the facilities, so it is also a good place for a day trip.

Getting There & Away The Jais Aben Resort people can arrange transport to/from Madang (whether or not you're staying at the resort) for K10 and they'll pick up from the airport for free. You can take a PMV to the turn-off for K0.50; some PMVs run you all the way in to the resort, otherwise it's quite a walk. You may be able to take a motorised canoe from Siar Island for about K5.

Kau Rainforest Museum & Wildlife Area

On the west side of the main coast road, not far from the turn-off to the Jais Aben Resort, is a rough track leading to the Kau Rainforest Museum & Wildlife Area, owned and operated by the Didipa clan (see The Didipa Clan & Forest Conservation aside below). Here you can learn about the traditional uses of plants for food and medicine and get some insights into the ecological relationships between local species (including humans). Did you know that the sticky juice of the Breadfruit tree can be used as glue? Or that the juices of two local vines can be used as contraceptives?

Alexishafen

Alexishafen Catholic Mission is off the road to the right, 23km north of Madang. Like so much of the area, it was badly damaged during the war but the old graveyard still

---

The Didipa Clan & Forest Conservation

The temptations for poor villagers to sell their natural birthright – their land – to multinational logging companies are immense. Usually unskilled in the ways of commerce or negotiation, villagers often have little knowledge of the true value of their timber on the international market or of the long-term impact such logging might have on their land.

But in 1963, when the PNG logging industry was still in its infancy, one clan, the Didipa clan, resolved to set aside over 300 hectares of its forest as a Wildlife Conservation Area. For 35 years the clan, led by prescient *bigman* Kiatik Batet, has protected the area from gardening, burning, logging and hunting (with firearms). Today, it is one of the last significant undisturbed forest remnants near Madang.

In 1992, the clan reinforced its pro-environmental stance and refused to sign an agreement with a Japanese company to log the area, despite pressure from the PNG government. A handful of Madang paradise birdwing butterflies, insects previously considered extinct, was discovered during an environmental impact study.

The clan, with the help of the Christensen Research Institute, is constructing a natural history museum and hostel to help retain traditional knowledge and create a research-cum-tourist asset. In recent years, other groups from all over PNG have studied the clan's methods. Its Kau wildlife area – a model for environmentally sound and culturally aware village development – is a popular attraction for travellers with an interest in environmental issues. ■

stands as a firm reminder of the number of early missionaries who died for their cause.

A little beyond the mission you can see the site of the old mission airstrip, now virtually overgrown. The WWII Japanese airstrip is a little off the road to the left, between the mission airstrip and Alexishafen. The jungle has almost reclaimed it and only the bomb craters and the odd aircraft wreck hint at the saturation bombing which destroyed the base. The wreckage of a Japanese twin-engined bomber is only a wingspan away from the bomb crater which immobilised it. Closer to the North Coast Highway is the fuselage of an early Junkers mission aircraft.

Malolo to Hansa Bay

The road continues north to the old Malolo (pronounced 'malollo') plantation, 42km up the coast, where you'll find the Malolo Plantation Resort. The black-sand beaches along the coast are the result of volcanic activity on Karkar and Manam islands. There's good swimming but watch out for the strong current which sweeps the coast. A traveller wrote that he had seen perfect surf at a beach near Bogia, but wouldn't say exactly where. There are magnificent views of Karkar Island from Malolo Plantation Resort and further up the coast.

About 20km on from Malolo, there's a large Catholic mission at **Magiya**. Just beyond here there's a road leading inland about 5km to **Aronis** village. About a kilometre from the main village is an aid post, near which is Manubyai Cave, home to a colony of horseshoe bats.

Salemben is a small village about an hour's drive inland, over some rough roads, from Malolo. Villagers offer guided bush treks, fishing expeditions and bird-watching from its Keki Tourist Lodge. **Balbe** (pronounced 'bal-bay') is another village in the Adelbert Ranges exploring ecotourism opportunities. There are excellent guides and the area is rich in culture and wildlife. Enquiries about Salemben and Balbe should be directed to the Madang Visitors & Cultural Bureau.

Bogia, 200km north-west of Madang, is the departure point for Manam Island. The road peters out a short distance before the mighty Ramu River. About 10km beyond Bogia, towards Hansa Bay, is **Kabak** where there is a nice beach at the old plantation. The reef has plenty of colourful fish.

Hansa Bay is a popular diving spot past Bogia, where the wreckage of 35 Japanese freighters and US aircraft reputedly lie in a shallow harbour – only some are locatable in reasonably shallow water and can be dived on; they've all been there since a US raid in November 1942. You can rent a dugout from a local village – either go to the black-sand beach at Awa Point or to the village of Sesemungam.

Get your guide to take you to the *Shishi Maru* – the upper deck is only 6m below the surface. Two anti-aircraft guns on the bow point towards the surface. Brass shell castings litter the deck and forward holds. Two fire engines are sitting in the hold, just before the bridge, where they were waiting to be unloaded. The *Shishi Maru* is about 60m long and must have been about 6000 tons.

There is a marine biology research station on **Laing Island** in Hansa Bay – it is a beautiful island with white sandy beaches and good snorkelling. Contact the Christensen Research Institute, near the Jais Aben Resort, or Madang Aquaventures at Smugglers' Inn in Madang for more information. Many of the small villages around Hansa Bay will also take visitors.

Places to Stay & Eat The *Malolo Plantation Resort* is a magnificently comfortable and beautiful place. The North Coast Highway, which once ran between the hotel and the beach, has been diverted, leaving an expanse of lawn leading down to a black-sand beach. Two thousand orchids have been planted, there's a very good restaurant (full breakfast K9, lunch K12 and dinner K25) and the staff are friendly and competent. There's a new and comfortable accommodation wing, a swimming pool and a tiny private island for picnics. The tame kokomo featured in a recent movie, *Robinson Crusoe*, filmed at nearby Baiteta village.

Accommodation is a very reasonable K90 for a single/double. Airport transfers from Madang are K10 (a PMV would be K3) and day tours are available – the resort has a good relationship with the villages in the area and it's quite safe to stroll along the beach at night. One of the managers, Rob, is a fully qualified dive instructor and can conduct PADI divemaster courses; dive gear can be hired for K25 a day (K35 with computer). Snorkelling gear and sea kayaks are also available. Simon Lusam is an accomplished local guide who can expound on birds, bush medicine, local culture and a host of other matters. Ask for him at the resort. If you go on one of the resort's early-morning tours, you stand a good chance of seeing birds of paradise.

Getting There & Away PMVs from Madang to Malolo cost K3. Bogia Company trucks go to Madang on Monday and Thursday and you might catch a ride with them either way. In Madang ask at Boroko Motors on Modilon Rd, where they refuel before heading back. It's more than three hours drive to Bogio. You can also get to Bogia by PMV for K6.

A traveller wrote that it's possible to get from Bogia to the Sepik. From Bogia take a PMV further along the coast to Boroi. Here, take a canoe to Watam, where there's a guesthouse. From Watam, near the mouth of the Sepik, there are infrequent passenger canoes up to Angoram.

INLAND

There are also some isolated and interesting places in central Morobe Province. Stations in the area include the remote Bundi, wedged between Mt Wilhelm and Mt Herbert in some of the roughest country in PNG. Some of the people living in these areas are almost small enough to be termed pygmies. Dumpu was the base from where the attack on Shaggy Ridge was launched during WWII. The Ramu is one of PNG's great rivers but it has never captured the imagination of tourists like the Sepik has, although the people

who live here also produce good woodcarvings.

Usino

There is an interesting place to stay near Usino – low-key, village-style accommodation for about four people, not too far from the Ramu River. It's necessary to contact the owners, Martin and Kupile Borkent and their daughter Marianne, in advance (PO Box 230, Madang). They don't have a phone, but if you have a contact number in PNG, Martin will ring you. The other option is to ask at the Lutheran Guesthouse in Madang; they'll probably have up-to-date information.

Martin has been trading in the area for many years and knows it like the back of his hand. Visitors can explore the rainforests and swamps, which are full of wildlife, and the Ramu River is about a 1½-hour walk away.

To get to Martin and Kupile's camp, catch a PMV from Madang or Lae to Usino Junction for K7, then ask for '*camp bilong Martin*'. There are two alternative routes, a main track which takes about 1¾ hours and a *draiwara shortcut* (drywater shortcut, or track only passable in dry weather). You'll need a guide for the shortcut.

Ramu Sugar Refinery

This is a major industrial development designed to make PNG self-sufficient in sugar. Apparently there is accommodation at the refinery and you can use the sporting facilities (golf, tennis, swimming) developed for the employees. Contact the administration office (☎ 474 3299).

Bundi & Brahmin
Bundi • postcode 522

Bundi is about a six-hour walk from Brahmin Mission and Brahmin is about 25km from the Lae-Madang Road. A PMV from Madang to Brahmin costs K6 and takes about 1½ hours. Island Airways flies from Madang to Bundi for K62.

There is a group of very simple bungalows at Bundi known as the *Mt Sinai Hotel*. The cost should be only a few kina per person.

MADANG PROVINCE

Teptep

Over 2000m up in the rugged Finisterre Ranges, Teptep is a small, isolated village on the border with Morobe Province which is becoming popular as a base for walks in the area. Guides are necessary (local people are not keen on unaccompanied strangers blundering through their land) and cost K5 a day. May to October are the best months for walking.

There's a *guesthouse* at Teptep, which charges about K15 per person and has meals available. Teptep is at an altitude where vegetables are grown, so the meals are good – if you choose the cheaper option. If you pay a little more for the deluxe menu, you get rice and tinned meat! Other villages in the area have more basic guesthouses. To book accommodation at Teptep, contact MAF in Madang (☎ 852 2229) or Lae (☎ 472 1555) or write to PO Box 1071, Madang.

MAF flies to Teptep a few times each week from both Madang and Lae. Island Airways also flies from Madang. You could walk in from Wantoat village; it takes about two days. Wantoat can be reached by PMV from Kaiapit on the Madang-Lae Road in Morobe Province.

ISLANDS

Long Island

The largest of the volcanic islands, Long is 414 sq km in area and 48km off the coast. It has two active craters, one of which contains a lake surrounded by crater walls up to 250m high. The population is only a few hundred but the island is renowned for its prolific bird-life and the many fish which swarm around its reefs. Turtles come ashore to lay their eggs at certain times of the year. Getting here isn't easy as there is no regular boat service. Island Airways flies from Madang (K97). A village guesthouse has apparently been built for visiting scientists and travellers might be able to stay there.

Karkar Island

William Dampier, the English pirate/explorer whose visit to the west coast of Australia preceded Captain James Cook's

visit by nearly a century, made an early landing on this 362 sq km island. Later Lutheran missionaries had a hard time both from malaria and the inhabitants.

The island has a population of 30,000, a high school and 20 community schools. It's one of the most fertile places in the country.

A volcanic eruption at Mt Kanangio temporarily evicted the missionaries but they came back, and today Karkar has both Catholic and Lutheran missions as well as some of the most productive copra plantations in the world. The volcanic cone is just 2m higher than Manam's at 1831m. The volcano erupted violently in 1974, leaving a cinder cone in the centre of the huge, original crater. It erupted again in 1979, killing two vulcanologists.

You can climb to the crater; it takes a full day. After the 1979 eruption, climbing had to be authorised and you were accompanied by a vulcanologist. That has changed but you still need to get permission from whichever village you begin the climb from. This is partly for your own safety (no-one can search for you if they don't know you're there) and partly because the crater is of religious importance for the villagers. Apparently the climb is easier from Mom village but there are better views if you start from Kavasob village. Be prepared for the intense heat of the sun bouncing off bare basalt, and if it rains watch out for flash flooding.

A road encircles the island and it takes four hours to drive right round. You can also walk around the island, but treat the river crossings with great caution. When it rains on the mountain, water comes down the rivers like a wall. A few years ago some unwary Australians were killed crossing a river. Karkar also has good beaches and places for snorkelling.

The high school and the airstrip are at the government station at Kiaim, which is the closest thing to a town on the island. Kulili, where boats from Madang dock, is about 15km away.

Places to Stay There is no formal accommodation on the island – in fact Madang shipping offices have signs warning you of this. Niugini Diving Adventures at the Madang Resort Hotel can arrange accommodation for about K30 and you don't have to go on one of their dives to do this. People have stayed in villages, at the high school and at Gaubin Hospital (ask at the Lutheran Guesthouse in Madang).

Getting There & Away A boat runs to Karkar daily from Madang's Rab-Trad (Rabaul Trading) wharf, stopping at Biabi (K7) and at Kulili (K8). Kulili is about 15km from the government station at Kiaim. Speedboats are always available to take you there faster, if you can afford them. Island Airways flies to Karkar from Madang for K50.

Bagabag Island

Bagabag, east of Karkar, encircles a sunken crater 36 sq km in area and is inhabited. During the war the Japanese used the 'fjord' to hide ships.

Manam Island

The island of Manam is only 15km off the coast from Bogia. The island is 83 sq km in area and is an almost perfect volcanic cone,

rising to 1829m. The soil is extremely fertile and has, at times, supported a population of 4000; occasionally the entire population has had to be evacuated as the volcano is still active. Most recently, the volcano erupted in December 1996 and February 1997, killing 30 people and wiping out Boda village. At night the crater glows and occasionally spurts orange trailers into the sky. There is a seismological observatory on the side of the cone.

There is a German mission (Tabele Mission) on the island. If you manage to make it to Manam, you will enjoy an incredible welcome by the local people, particularly the children. Bring your own food and ask your boat crew for somewhere to stay.

Getting There & Away Manam is 193km from Madang and not easy to get to. Bogia is the normal departure point; take a PMV from Madang for K6. Apparently, government and private boats leave Bogia for Manam virtually daily for about K5, although there is no schedule so you might end up waiting a few days; check at the district office. Be careful with your possessions on the boats.

The Highlands

Land Area 62,500 sq km
Population 1,560,000

The Highlands is the most densely populated and agriculturally productive region of Papua New Guinea. It is divided into five provinces – Eastern Highlands (around Goroka), Simbu (around Kundiawa), Western Highlands (around Mt Hagen), Enga (around Wabag) and Southern Highlands (around Mendi).

Strangely, it was the last part of the country to be explored by Europeans: they did not first encounter Highlands tribes until the 1930s. Until then, Europeans had thought that the centre of PNG was a rugged tangle of virtually unpopulated mountains. It was definitely a shock when a series of populated valleys, stretching right through the country, was discovered. Little development occurred before WWII, which almost entirely bypassed the region; it was not until the 1950s and 60s that the Highlands were really opened up.

Today, the region is a dynamic and fascinating part of PNG. Its people's lives are changing quickly, but many aspects of their traditional cultures remain, particularly in terms of social organisation. Clan and tribal loyalties are still very strong. It is possible to see dramatic *sing-sings* (celebratory festivals) and warriors wearing ostentatious traditional dress, but in most parts of the Highlands, and especially in main towns like Mt Hagen and Goroka, the people have taken on the trappings of the west – more particularly, through *sekonhan klos* (secondhand clothes).

Although some individuals and even some tribes are exceptions to the rule, traditional dress and decorations are now usually reserved for rare ceremonial or festive occasions which a visitor will be very lucky to see. Some of the big hotels organise theatrical sing-sings but these are usually rather sad and listless affairs.

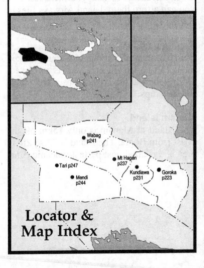

HIGHLIGHTS

- Climbing Mt Wilhelm to see PNG's northern and southern coastlines
- Experiencing a Highlands sing-sing
- Visiting the spectacular Goroka and Mt Hagen shows
- Exploring Goroka, the prettiest city in the Highlands
- Experiencing the cultures of the Huli wigmen and Asaro mud men
- Visiting the magnificent Lake Kutubu and the Wasi Falls, the highest waterfall in PNG

Wabag p241
Mt Hagen p237
Tari p247
Kundiawa p231
Goroka p223
Mendi p244

Locator & Map Index

The region is not a lifeless, open-air museum specially designed for photographers, as it might seem, but home to a number of vital, rapidly changing cultures, which are maintaining some things, adapting others and adopting still more with wholehearted fervour.

It has the most extensive road system in the country, half-a-dozen major towns and a growing cash economy based on coffee and tea. Gold and oil are now bringing enormous wealth to a few areas and rapidly changing both the economy and the lifestyles of the people.

The countryside is dramatic and beautiful, with wide, fertile valleys, countless streams and rivers and seemingly endless, saw-toothed mountains.

History

Most of the Highlands valleys were settled about 10,000 years ago; the presence of shells among archaeological deposits shows that, by this time, people were also trading with the coast. Some excavated sites date back to much earlier.

Kuk Swamp in the Wahgi Valley (Western Highlands Province) has evidence of human habitation going back 20,000 years. Even more significantly, there is evidence of gardening beginning 9000 years ago. This makes Papua New Guineans among the first farmers in the world. The main foods cultivated were likely to have been coconuts, sago, breadfruit, local bananas and yams, sugar cane, nuts and edible green leaves.

It's still uncertain when the pig and more productive starch crops (such as Asian yams, taro and bananas) were introduced but it is known that this occurred more than 5000 years ago, maybe as far back as 10,000 years. Domesticated pigs – which continue to be incredibly important, ritually and economically, in contemporary society – and these crops were probably brought to PNG by a later group of colonists from Asia.

The sweet potato was introduced to the Indonesian Spice Islands by the Spaniards in the 16th century and it is believed Malay traders then brought it to Irian Jaya, from where it was traded into the Highlands. The introduction of the sweet potato must have brought radical change to Highlands life – it is still the staple crop. Its high yield and tolerance for poor, cold soils allowed for the colonisation of higher altitudes, the domestication of many more pigs and a major increase in population.

As with the rest of PNG, the Highlands had tremendous cultural and linguistic diversity. The largest social units were tribes numbering in the thousands. The area controlled by a single group was usually small and there were apparently no empires or dynasties. Despite the political fragmentation, there were extensive trade links with the coast.

Evidence relating to the history of the Highlands before the arrival of Europeans is extremely scarce. It would be wrong to assume the situation found in the 1930s had remained unchanged through the centuries. Highlands societies were certainly not static. It is known some steel knives and axes were traded from the coast before European patrols arrived.

When the first Australian patrols arrived, minor warfare between the tribes was common, but the number of fatalities was probably relatively low because, in part, of the weaponry – bows, arrows and spears. Two of the most striking characteristics of Highlands culture were the intensive and skilful gardening (almost entirely the work of the women) and the fantastic personal adornment of the men, which was the most striking form of artistic expression.

The first direct European contact with the Highlands came as a result of the goldrush near Wau and Bulolo, which created speculation there would be more gold further afield. In 1930 Mick Leahy and Mick Dwyer set off south to search for gold in the region they believed formed the headwaters for the Ramu River. To their amazement the streams they followed did not turn north-west to join the Ramu but led southwards through the previously undiscovered Eastern Highlands.

When they finally reached the Papuan coast, they discovered that they were at the mouth of the Purari River. Rather than starting on the southernmost flanks of the Highlands, the streams that formed the Purari started just the other side of the towering Bismarck Ranges from the Ramu (on the map, less than 25km from the Ramu and around 80km from the north coast) and ran through populated valleys to the south coast.

In 1933 Leahy returned with his brother Dan and they stumbled upon the huge, fertile and heavily populated Wahgi Valley. After an

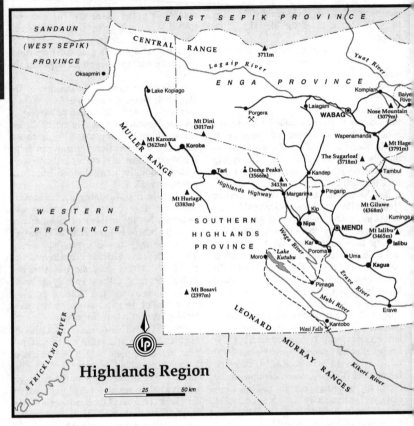

Highlands Region

0   25   50 km

aerial reconnaissance, they walked in with a large well-supplied patrol.

The first patrol built an airstrip at Mt Hagen and explored the area, but the hoped-for gold was never discovered in any great quantities. Jim Taylor, the government officer who accompanied this patrol, was one of the last direct links to those extraordinary times. A PNG citizen, he died peacefully at his farm outside Goroka in 1987.

The documentary *First Contact* includes original footage by Mick Leahy and is a priceless record of the first interaction between Highlanders and Europeans (see the

Films section in the Facts for the Visitor chapter).

Missionaries soon followed the miners, and the government and missions were established near present-day Mt Hagen and in the Simbu Valley, near present-day Kundiawa. Two missionaries were killed and in response a government patrol post was set up at Kundiawa and the Highlands declared a restricted territory with controlled European access.

During WWII, the mountains, once again, largely protected the Highlanders from outside forces. It was the 1950s before major

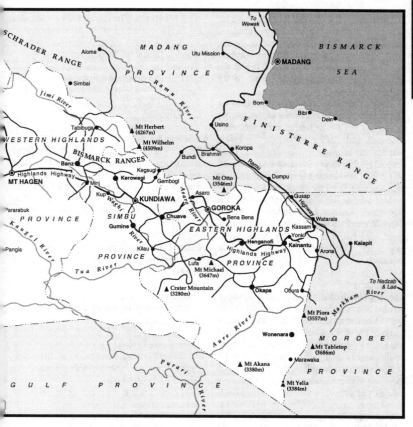

changes were really felt and many areas remained virtually unaffected until the 1960s and 70s.

The construction of the Highlands Highway had a major impact on the area, as did the introduction of cash crops, particularly coffee. The Highlanders have adapted to the cash economy with remarkable speed, perhaps due, in part, to western capitalism meshing with their existing culture; they have always understood the importance of land ownership and are skilful gardeners and clever traders. Material wealth, while handled very differently than in the west,

was still of crucial importance in establishing the status of a *bigman* (important man) and his clan.

The Highlands' dense population and the cultural differences between it and other parts of the country have caused more than a few problems. Ritual warfare was an integral part of Highlands life and to this day, payback feuds (to seek reprisal for both real and imagined injuries) and land disputes can erupt into major conflicts.

Highlanders and the coastal people have traditionally distrusted each other – this mutual suspicion still exists. The energetic

Highlanders think that the coastal people are lazy and unfairly dominate government bureaucracies. The coastal people see the Highlanders as aggressive and their numbers as threatening and feel that the Highlands have had a disproportionate share of the development pie.

Population pressures have pushed many Highlanders out to other parts of the country in search of work, where they are often resented and held responsible for rascal activity. As is usual with immigrants, these 'expat' Highlanders often take on the dirtiest and most demanding jobs – and tend to prosper, adding to the resentment.

A road linking Port Moresby with the Highlands (and thus Lae, Madang and potentially Wewak) would seem to be a pretty good idea but is highly unlikely given the extremely rough terrain and limited finances available.

Geography

The Highlands are made up of a series of fertile valleys and rugged intervening mountains. The mountains form the watershed for some of the world's largest rivers in terms of water flow (the Ramu, the Sepik, the Strickland, the Fly and the Purari) and form a central spine the length of the island. While there are higher mountains on the Irian Jaya side of the island, a number of Highlands mountains exceed 4000m in height; Mt Wilhelm, PNG's highest, is 4509m high. It's estimated that more than a million people live at an altitude higher than Mt Kosciuszko (2228m), the highest mountain in neighbouring Australia.

Arts

Highlanders do not carve bowls, masks or other similar items; their artistic talents are almost always expressed in personal attire and decoration or in the decoration of weapons. Pottery and bark paintings are now made in the Eastern Highlands and are available around Kainantu.

The best known weapons, although they were never intended for use as weapons or tools, are probably the fine ceremonial axes

from Mt Hagen. The slate blades come from the Jimi River area north of Mt Hagen on the Sepik-Wahgi divide and are bound to a wooden shaft with decorative cane strips.

'Killing sticks' from Lake Kopiago had an obvious and practical use: the pointed fighting stick is tipped with a sharpened cassowary bone to create a lethal weapon in close fighting.

Society & Conduct

The Highlanders are usually stockier and shorter than the coastal people but there is a large number of different tribes, language groups and physical types. Dress, personal decoration, weapons, house construction methods, and traditions vary widely within the region.

Bride Price Marriage is an occasion that is used to prove just how much you can afford to pay: the bride's clan has to be paid a bride price

Bride prices vary throughout the country and are usually higher in the cities; in Port Moresby, the average is more like K25,000, with wealthy people paying many times more. Kenneth Read's book *The High Valley* has an interesting description of the tense negotiations to establish a bride price and the related issue of prestige.

The old shell money has been seriously devalued since European contact, both because it has become more readily available and modern currency has been widely accepted. Pigs still retain their value – a pig is not just food, it's the most visible and important measure of a person's solvency. Cassowaries are also extremely important in the Highlands (although they're much less edible).

Payback Compensation, or payback, claims may also make demands on a clan's wealth. An eye for an eye is the basic payback concept (it is virtually a greater sin to fail to payback than to have committed the initial wrong), but sufficiently large payments of pigs and cash will usually avert direct bloodletting. Pigs have traditionally been used to negotiate an end to conflicts of many kinds and naturally the government and the courts prefer this kind of solution.

In Highlands society, where the clan is of much greater significance than the individual, a whole clan is held responsible for an individual's actions. In the case of a killing, revenge will be taken by the aggrieved clan, preferably by killing the murderer, but, if that proves too difficult, anyone in the murderer's clan will do.

To this day, violence will often only be averted by very substantial financial compensation, whether or not western-style justice has also been done. Car accidents are becoming an increasingly rich source of payback feuds.

Food Highlands women are highly skilled subsistence farmers, largely dependent on the sweet potato which is grown in neat round mounds about 1.5m in diameter (in the Wahgi Valley, they're square). The mounds are fertilised with ashes and can have very high yields.

Bananas, sugar cane, greens and yams are also traditional crops which are now supplemented by western vegetables. Hunting is relatively unimportant, but the pig is vital, both for protein and as a symbol of wealth.

Sing-Sings A sing-sing can be held for any number of reasons – celebrating paying off a bride price, a moga ceremony or even a mundane activity like raising money for a local school or church. Whatever the reason, the result will be much the same – a lot of people, brilliantly costumed, singing and dancing. Take plenty of film for photos.

Although sing-sings are not an everyday occurrence, you should definitely try to see one while you're in the Highlands. Around Mt Hagen they are held quite frequently, but finding where they are and getting to them

---

Mogas

If you need to be convinced that 'keeping up with the Joneses' and accumulating and displaying wealth are not peculiarly modern preoccupations, a visit to the Highlands should soon do the job. Wealth is enormously important in establishing status, and men of consequence in a village – the bigmen – are almost invariably men of affluence. Just being rich is not enough – other people have to know you are rich. As a result, much of the ceremonial life of the Highlands is centred around ostentatious displays of wealth.

The most vivid demonstrations are the *moga* ceremonies – in Enga Province the *tee* ceremonies are very similar. In many Melanesian cultures, and especially in the Highlands, the approved method of establishing just how rich you are is to give certain important goods away. The moga is part of a wider circle of exchange and inter-clan relationships.

In fact, wealth is never really given away, at least not in the western sense. Your gifts both cement a relationship with the receiver (from a related and allied clan perhaps) and pacify potential enemies. The receiver is effectively obliged to return the gifts and the receiver will attempt to outdo the giver's generosity. One way or another, the giver expects to have at least an equivalent number of pigs and kina shells (or good old cash) returned.

These ceremonies flow from village to village with one group displaying its wealth and handing it on to the next. Even enemies are invited, in the hope they'll be impressed by how much is given away.

During these festivals literally hundreds of pigs are slaughtered and cooked and all present indulge in an orgy of eating. Each clan attempts to surpass its neighbours by producing as many pigs as possible. Some indication of the economic significance of these feasts can be gauged by the fact that a decent-sized pig is worth around K500 and a sow can be worth even more.

You'll see the ceremonial grounds where these feasts are held as you travel the Highlands Highway, especially past Mendi in the Southern Highlands. They are distinguished by a fenced quadrangle, covering up to about half a hectare or so, surrounded by long houses (where guests sleep) with long pits dug in straight lines and filled with cooking stones (for cooking the pigs). Attempts to convince the Highlanders, many of whom live on the borderline of protein deficiency, that pigs could be rationed more sensibly, rather than used in this feast or famine manner, have been largely unsuccessful. ■

can be a problem. Many parts of the Highlands are still inaccessible to vehicles and the sing-sings are often in remote areas.

Other Highland ceremonies you may come across are the courting rituals known as *karim leg* or *turnim het*. Ceremonially dressed young couples meet in the long houses for courting sessions where they sit side by side and cross legs (karim leg) or rub their faces together (turnim het). While you may not get to see them 'for real', they are sometimes staged for tourists.

Highlands Shows During the 1950s, when the Highlanders first had serious contact with Europeans, the Highlands shows were instituted as a way of gathering the tribes and clans together and showing them that the people from across the hill weren't so bad after all. The shows were an amazing success, growing from the original concept of a local get-together into a major tourist attraction. As many as 40,000 warriors would gather in the show arena in a stomping, chanting dance that literally shook the earth. Drums thundered, feathers swayed and dancing bodies glistened with paint, oils and pig grease. It was like nothing else on earth.

Unfortunately, the shows have suffered a serious decline in quality. For the participants, the curiosity value of the gatherings has decreased, along with their pride in their traditional finery. With improved transport and better roads, it is also no longer such an effort to get from place to place, so people don't need to save up for an annual gathering.

Still, the shows go on and if you can see one, you're unlikely to be disappointed. It will certainly be one of the best available opportunities to get an overview of PNG's extraordinary cultural diversity. Mt Hagen and Goroka both now have annual shows, which have become major tourist attractions (see the Goroka and Mt Hagen sections). The Goroka show is the better of the two, partly because it is more than just a chance for sing-sing groups to perform; it has agricultural displays, stringband competitions and

other exhibits. But attending either show is an amazing experience.

Contact the Tourism Promotion Authority or the respective provincial governments for more information. Make sure you book accommodation as far ahead as possible and be prepared to pay twice the normal rate.

Things to Buy
Beautifully decorated bows and arrows are sold throughout the Highlands. Other traditional items you may see, sometimes for sale, are the fine kina pearl shells made from the gold lip pearl shell. These can be expensive, around K25. *Aumak* (wealth tally) necklaces, which are made of bamboo rods and were used to record how many pigs the owner had given away, are also sold but are much cheaper than a kina shell. In the Western Highlands, kina shells are sometimes mounted on a board of red resin; at traditional wealth displays, such as the moga ceremonies, long lines of these are formed on the ground.

People also sell excellent wickerwork incorporating striking geometric designs (trays and baskets, for example) from stalls along the Highlands Highway but, once again, they are not cheap, reflecting the amount of work that goes into creating them.

Coarsely woven woollen blankets, rugs, bedspreads and bags are available in several Highlands centres; they are hardly traditional but extremely attractive, nevertheless. Highlands hats are a necessary fashion accessory. The pottery at the Eastern Highlands Cultural Centre in Kainantu and the bark paintings at Okapa are more recent additions to the Highlanders' range of arts and crafts.

Getting There & Around
Air Air Niugini and MBA have regular connections with Goroka, Mt Hagen, Wewak, Madang, Lae and Port Moresby. There is also a comprehensive third-level network around the other Highlands centres.

MAF has an extensive network to many out-of-the-way places; its headquarters is in Mt Hagen (☎ 545 1477; PO Box 273). If you're planning a walk, find out if and when MAF flies in your direction, just in case you need to take an easy way out; MAF flies twice-weekly to strips south and west of Mt Hagen and three times a week to strips in the Baiyer River and Jimi Valley areas. There's also a useful flight on Tuesday and Thursday which originates in Port Moresby and goes to Tari, returning via Aiyura and Mt Hagen. At Tari you can connect with flights originating in Telefomin and Kawito.

Remember that MAF flies small planes, so don't expect to get away with too much over the 16kg baggage limit. Bad weather can play havoc with schedules.

PMV PMVs are frequent between all the major centres. They come in an assortment of sizes but most are comfortable and fairly new – they're no hardship at all. There isn't a lot of space for luggage, though, and if you have a large bag, it may be on your lap most of the way.

On less-important routes and over very bad roads, trucks are used as PMVs and are somewhat more spartan.

PMVs generally make their first trip early in the morning around 8 am, sometimes earlier. The best place to look for them is at the markets. Although there will often be some later in the day, their deadline for reaching a destination is sunset, which is around 6 pm; bear in mind that breakdowns can add unforeseen hours so give yourself some leeway if you have a deadline.

Many PMVs make return journeys within daylight hours, for instance they'll leave Lae for Goroka early and return around midday. PMVs meet a demand, so work out what the local people require. There will, for instance, be very early PMVs to get people to Saturday markets and returning PMVs after the markets; there'll be PMVs between Kundiawa and Mt Hagen later in the day after people have had a chance to shop, and so on.

Your safest bet is to be early. It's also not a good move to wander around most of the Highlands towns at night looking for accommodation; try to arrive in daylight, but if you don't, get the PMV to deliver you to the place where you plan to stay.

Expats frequently criticise PMVs and rarely use them, but those who do use them find them comfortable, cheap and safe. PMVs are a great opportunity to meet locals. Bad drivers are rare (they probably don't last) and most are surprisingly cautious. The following table shows approximate fares and journey times:

Route	Fare	Duration
Kainantu-Lae	K8	3 hours
Kainantu-Goroka	K4	1½ hours
Goroka-Lae	K12	4½ hours
Kundiawa-Goroka	K5	2 hours
Mt Hagen-Kundiawa	K4	2 hours
Mt Hagen-Goroka	K8	4 hours
Mt Hagen-Wabag	K6	3½ hours
Mt Hagen-Mendi	K8	3 hours
Mendi-Tari	K10	4 hours

Car You can drive yourself, at a suitably high price – see the Getting Around chapter. Rental firms often have restrictions on remote area use, which particularly applies to the Highlands.

Because of the risk of being held up by a roadblock manned by rascals, very few people drive at night. Roadblocks can even happen during the day, although this is not common. If you are forced to stop (don't unless you have to and be very sceptical if you are waved down), don't panic. They'll just want your money. This warning is not intended to induce fear and loathing. Talk to people and they'll fill you in on the current situation: you will be very unlikely to have any problems if you heed local advice. News travels very quickly and if there is trouble, it is usually part of a wider, well-known disturbance.

The Highlands Highway The most important road in PNG starts in Lae and runs up into the central Highlands. Where the highway ends depends on your definition. As a decent road, it now continues to Tari, in rougher condition to Koroba and in still rougher condition on to Lake Kopiago. The highway is now sealed as far as Mt Hagen and, in parts, between Mt Hagen and Mendi. New branches off the main road are being developed, although their condition varies widely.

From Lae, the highway runs out through the coastal jungle then emerges into the wide, flat Markham Valley.

It's a rather hot, dull stretch to the base of the Kassam Pass where the road starts to twist, turn and climb. At the top of the pass, there are some spectacular lookout points across the Markham Valley to the Sarawaget Range. The road continues through rolling grass hills to Kainantu, the only reasonable sized town before Goroka.

The road up from Madang joins the Highlands Highway just east of Watarais, but a new, shorter route which has recently been constructed between Dumpu and Henganofi is now open (but PMVs still prefer the older, better-known route).

From Goroka the road continues through the valley to Asaro, then climbs steeply to the high (2450m) Daulo Pass, about 25km from Goroka. It continues twisting, turning and generally descending all the way to Simbu Province and Kundiawa, about the mid-point between Goroka and Mt Hagen.

From Kundiawa the road descends to the Wahgi Valley and it's a fast run to Mt Hagen past the turn-offs to Minj and Banz. The road from Mt Hagen to Mendi is spectacular; you skirt Mt Giluwe, PNG's second-highest mountain at 4368m, and go through some beautiful valleys. On good days you can also see Mt Ialibu to the south of the road. Along the way, you'll see some enterprising people selling woven walls of bamboo or pitpit leaves – sort of prefabricated housing. There are also likely to be some roadside stalls selling attractive, though expensive, wicker-work.

The road becomes even more interesting after Mendi, as you pass ceremonial grounds, a suspension bridge over the Lai River and travel through the stunning Poroma Valley. It's a narrow gravel road in good condition, but you can't go too fast and

Islands in the Clouds

Isabella Tree, in her book *Islands in the Clouds*, gives a good account of travelling in the Highlands, and the passing parade of men, women and *pickaninis* (children):

Beyond Hagen, the territory was as new to Akunai as it was to me. Familiar patterns began to change. Village huts were longer and their roofs were so low that the thatch almost reached the ground. There were almost no iron roofs now, or square houses. We were gaining altitude and out here the nights were cold. Houses were designed with double walls of pitpit and small, low doorways to keep in the heat.

'Look at that,' said Akunai, giving the Engans some of the Simbu treatment. 'They have to crawl into their houses like pigs.' But the tone of his censoriousness had changed – from an ancient but familiar prejudice to an uneasy distrust of the unknown.

Busybee was amazed by the sight of his first *bus kanaka* in 'ass grass', and even more so by his youthful appearance. The man, walking casually along the road in a small woven lap-lap, tanget leaves and a neat black waistcoat, and shielded from the sun by a black umbrella, could not have been older than Busybee, who fell about laughing. Akunai was more diplomatic.

Everyone from Eastern Highlands thinks people in the western provinces must be wild men,' he said. 'But they probably think we're really weak or something and can't stand up for ourselves. They probably think we've forgotten how to fight.'

Increasingly, the men we passed were dressed this way, with a twentieth-century T-shirt worn above a traditional skirt. Most of them carried hunting *banaras* and *spias* in one hand. They stopped and stared when they saw a white woman pass in a truck – probably the first they had seen, other than a *missinari* or *voluntia*.

A group of children stood on a hillock and shot imaginary arrows, just as other children had done on the Highlands Highway four years before. But now the children around Akunai's village fired make-believe shot guns and automatic weapons; out here, they were Indians still, with no knowledge of *kaubois* and *raifels*. ■

you have time to soak in the views as you go through Nipa and Margarima. After Poroma you climb the 2900m pass overlooking the wide and fertile Tari Basin. It's then a quick run through the Huli's intensively cultivated gardens to Tari.

The road deteriorates after Tari and again after Koroba. If you're aiming for Lake Kopiago, you'll be lucky if you don't have to do some walking. There's very little transport, especially after Koroba: it's only an hour's drive or so to Koroba, but a two-day walk from Koroba to Kopiago. Beyond Kopiago it's definitely walking only. Koroba and Kopiago are small villages in interesting areas.

Other Roads Between Goroka and Mt Hagen, the old highway parallels the new one for part of the distance. An old road also runs to Mendi from Mt Hagen, on the other side of Mt Giluwe to the new Mendi Road. The new road runs through Kuminga, while the old road goes through Tambul.

A reasonable road runs north from Mt Hagen through the spectacular Baiyer Gorge to Baiyer River and a good road branches off the Mendi Road and continues on to Wabag and Porgera. From Wabag, there's a loop through Laiagam to Kandep and down to Mendi. It may not be passable because of washed-out bridges and slides. From Kandep, another branch goes down through Margarima, halfway between Mendi and Tari. This road is not often used and its condition varies, though it's never great.

A new road from Mendi to Pimaga is now open.

There's a breathtakingly precarious road north from Kundiawa to Kegsugl if you're intending to climb Mt Wilhelm.

Walking The best way to see the Highlands is to walk – there are networks of tracks everywhere. It is also possible to walk from the Highlands to the coast although with the exception of the route between Kegsugl and Madang, these routes are not for the fainthearted.

Most tour companies (see the Facts for the Visitor chapter) run walks in the Highlands, but if you're reasonably well equipped, don't mind roughing it and don't tackle anything too radical, there is no reason why you shouldn't do it yourself. This is a volatile, rugged area however, so it is important to talk to locals and local government officers, especially the *kiaps* (patrol officers) before you set out. In most cases, guides are necessary.

Eastern Highlands Province

Land Area 11,200 sq km
Population 320,000
Capital Goroka

Eastern Highlands Province has had longer and more extensive contact with the west than other parts of the Highlands. Its people have abandoned their traditional dress for day-to-day use, but you'll still occasionally see traditional dress at the Goroka market. Although the province is heavily populated, the Eastern Highlanders are a less cohesive group than people in other parts of the Highlands.

Their villages are recognisable for their neat clusters of low-walled round huts. The traditional design includes two peaks to the roof. On each of the peaks is a tuft of grass, one from the owner's area and the other from a neighbouring area. These tufts talk to each other in the night, so you can hear your neighbour's secrets.

Goroka is the main town and one of the most attractive places in PNG – a green, shady, well-organised city with decent shopping, transport and facilities. Kainantu, near the border with Morobe Province, is the second-largest town.

The steep and rugged mountains of this province form the headwaters for two of PNG's most important river systems: the Ramu River which runs parallel to the coast to the north-west, and the Wahgi and Aure rivers which run south and enter the Gulf of Papua as the Purari River. The province's highest point is Mt Michael at 3647m. Most of the population lives at altitudes between 1500 and 2300m. There are large areas of rolling hills covered with *kunai* (grass).

GOROKA

• *pop 20,000* • *postcode 441*

Goroka has grown from a small outpost in the mid-1950s to its current position as a major commercial centre. It's still a typical PNG town, clustered around the airstrip, but it's also spacious, attractive and conveys a sense of civic pride and community. There are several small parks and many tall pine trees.

The town is small enough to walk around and the atmosphere is much more relaxed than at Mt Hagen. It has something of the feel of an Indian hill-station. Along McNicholl St, across from the Lutheran Guesthouse, are several grand colonial houses in the 'Queensland' style, with spacious verandahs and large gardens; members of the judiciary live in them. It's a sign of Goroka's relative safety that there is no apparent security – although maybe that's just because the police barracks are across the road.

At an altitude of 1600m, Goroka's climate is a perpetual spring – warm days and cool nights. Temperatures can drop to about 10°C at night, especially in the dry season (May to November).

The town has an adequate range of facilities, including reasonable shopping, banks, a post office and the Raun Raun Theatre, an interesting performing arts complex. The PNG Institute of Medical Research, in the hospital grounds on Leigh Vial St, conducts major research programmes into PNG health problems.

Information

The Bird of Paradise Hotel (☎ 732 1144) on Elizabeth St is the best place to get information; its staff are particularly obliging.

Norman Carver of PNG Highland Tours & Treks (☎ 732 1602; fax 732 3302; PO Box 583) is a mine of information on the town,

the local area and even as far distant as Mt Wilhelm. See the Around Goroka section.

Wantok Tours (☎ & fax 732 3402; PO Box 568) also offers tours of the town and environs.

JK McCarthy Museum

JK McCarthy was one of PNG's legendary patrol officers and wrote one of the classic books on New Guinea patrolling – *Patrol into Yesterday*. The museum bearing his name is not far from the National Sports Institute, but a long way from the centre of town. It is small, but well worth visiting.

Among the exhibits, there is a variety of pottery styles, weapons, clothes and musical instruments, even some grisly jewellery, including several necklaces of human fingers! Perhaps the most interesting feature is the fascinating collection of photos, many of which were taken by Mick Leahy when he first reached the area in 1933. There are also some WWII relics, including a P-39 Aircobra left behind by the USAF after the war, now located behind the museum.

There is a shop with a selection of artefacts and handcrafts, including some striking modern paintings. It's open from 8 am to noon and from 1 to 4 pm on weekdays, from 2 to 4 pm on Saturday and from 10 am to noon on Sunday. Admission is by donation.

Raun Raun Theatre

If you have a chance, it is well worth seeing a performance by the Raun Raun Theatre (☎ 732 1116; PO Box 118). This highly successful Goroka-based theatre company undertakes national tours and has also performed internationally to high acclaim. The theatre building is in the park opposite the market, a short walk from town, and is an interesting and successful example of modern PNG architecture.

Mt Kis Lookout

Wisdom St, beside the post office, leads to a track that climbs to an excellent lookout, Mt Kis, so-called (apparently) because it is the lovers' leap of Goroka. It's a long, steep walk if you haven't got wheels, but there are two

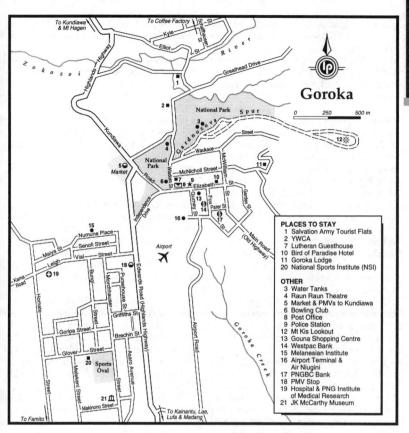

Goroka

0   250   500 m

PLACES TO STAY
1 Salvation Army Tourist Flats
2 YWCA
7 Lutheran Guesthouse
10 Bird of Paradise Hotel
11 Goroka Lodge
20 National Sports Institute (NSI)

OTHER
3 Water Tanks
4 Raun Raun Theatre
5 Market & PMVs to Kundiawa
6 Bowling Club
8 Post Office
9 Police Station
12 Mt Kis Lookout
13 Gouna Shopping Centre
14 Westpac Bank
15 Melanesian Institute
16 Airport Terminal &
     Air Niugini
17 PNGBC Bank
18 PMV Stop
19 Hospital & PNG Institute
     of Medical Research
21 JK McCarthy Museum

large water tanks halfway there, and a ladder you can climb (if you don't suffer from vertigo) to the top to catch spectacular views of the distant valleys through the pine trees and the Highlands mist. It's well worth the effort.

Market

Saturday is, as usual, the best market day. At the market, on the Highlands Highway, you'll see fruit and vegetables, rats, possums, ferns, fungi, pigs and feathers. Despite all this, it's not as colourful as the Mt Hagen market.

Goroka Show

Goroka Show, the best of the Highlands shows, is held over the Independence Day weekend (mid-September). It used to be held in even-numbered years but has now become an annual event. It attracts (well, hires) more sing-sing groups than Mt Hagen's and there are also bands and other cultural activities, as well as some elements of an agricultural show. Entry fee is K3 for general fairground entry, K15 for a day pass allowing you into the dancing grounds, or K25 for a full show pass – but this could go up. Watch out for pickpockets in the crowds.

Accommodation in Goroka can be very scarce around showtime, and prices tend to soar – a room at the National Sports Institute will probably increase from K20 to around K50 per night, and will be *very* noisy; many places are booked out months in advance – so make your arrangements early.

Places to Stay – bottom end

The modern *National Sports Institute* (NSI) (☎ 732 2391; fax 732 1941; PO Box 337), about a 20-minute walk from the centre of town, is a great place to stay. It's on Glover St, a block away from the JK McCarthy Museum. You get a small, clean 'student' room to yourself with sheets and blankets; you can take advantage of hot showers, satellite TV, tennis courts and other sports facilities. It is extremely popular during the Goroka Show which is held on the oval right next door – so if you are planning to visit at this time, book well ahead, and plan for a very full house.

There are 106 rooms at K20 per person, less with a student discount. Another K18 gets you three good meals in the dining room. Check in at the office or, after hours, see Sau Wai in room No 1.

The *Lutheran Guesthouse* (☎ 732 1171; PO Box 44) is right in the centre of town, behind the post office. It's a clean, comfortable two-storey house, centrally located and run by friendly people. Bear in mind that this is a church-run establishment and you will probably have to make some concessions. A bed, cooked breakfast and a good dinner costs K35; dinner is not available on Sunday.

The *YWCA* (☎ 732 1516; PO Box 636) is a residential hostel and usually full, but they keep one room free for visiting women (only). It's a pleasant, cheerful place where you're likely to make a lot of friends. It's about 750m north of the post office.

The *Salvation Army Tourist Flats* (☎ 732 1218; PO Box 365) in McGrath St is a fair way from the town centre and prefers to let by the week (K204), but will let by the day (K51). As with some other places, the rate increases during the Goroka Show. The flats are becoming a little rundown, but they're quite OK, and each has a stove, a fridge and attached bathroom. Two or four-bed flats are available.

The *Swiss Volunteer House* on Goripa St, not far from the NSI, might give you a bed, but prefers volunteers.

If all else fails, try the *Teachers College* (☎ 732 1039; 732 1257) which sometimes has cheap rooms available but is a long way from town and not really worth the trouble – unless you happen to be there in late June when the college has its festival, with students dressing up in traditional gear and practising their dancing.

Places to Stay – middle & top end

The *Bird of Paradise Hotel* (☎ 732 1144; fax 732 1007; PO Box 12), on Elizabeth St in the centre of town, is the top hotel in Goroka. This is the all-time pick for the best accommodation in PNG – not only for the excellent service and the top-quality amenities, but for the role it plays in the social life of the prettiest town in the Highlands. It is, however, a little beyond the means of most backpackers. All rooms have private facilities and all mod-cons and cost from K175 a single or double, plus K15 per extra person. There are some excellent weekend specials on rates – around 50% off. You can pay with Visa, MasterCard, Amex or Diners Club.

The Bird has a pool, a couple of restaurants and a few bars. If you are meeting someone in Goroka, it is the obvious rendezvous. There are squash courts and a gym for residents, and non-residents can attend the evening aerobic classes for just K3. On Sundays, there are often informal volleyball games by the pool.

The *Goroka Lodge* (☎ 732 2411; fax 732 2307; PO Box 343) runs a very poor second behind the Bird, although it is considerably cheaper. In the lodge section very small, spartan rooms with shared bathroom cost K41/56 a single/double, and better equipped rooms with attached bathroom in the motel section are K77/92. Meals are available in a licensed restaurant and on Sunday there's a barbecue; some nights there's a disco. The Lodge is a bit of a walk from the town centre,

Top: Mt Wilhelm, on the Madang-Simbu provincial border, is PNG's highest mountain.
Bottom Left: Traditional houses near Mendi, Southern Highlands
Bottom Right: Villagers with their pig, Daulo Pass, Eastern Highlands. Traditionally pigs
were used in rituals and for trade, and they are still valued highly today.

HOLGER LEUE

HOLGER LEUE

HOLGER LEUE

HOLGER LEUE

HOLGER LEUE

Top Left: A woman wears her *bilum* to carry goods, Goroka, Eastern Highlands
Top Right: Asaro mud man, Eastern Highlands
Middle Right: Coffee farmer near Goroka, Eastern Highlands
Bottom: Rest stop 'kitchen' at Daulo Pass, Eastern Highlands

down and up a couple of steep hills, but its staff will pick you up from the airport.

The *Goroka Holiday Lodge* (☎ & fax 732 1210; PO Box 985), south of the airport in Goroka, may be good value, but is a little far from the action of the town. They charge K40 per person or K60 for a double, accompanied children free. They will pick you up from the airport and offer various tours of the town and environs.

Places to Eat
By far the best place to eat is the Bird of Paradise Hotel – it seems to be the centre of activity in Goroka. This is where you meet people or just go for a quiet beer or a snack. The open-air *Deck Bar* is a good place to hang out and is open for breakfast, lunch and dinner. At lunch there's a buffet where you can help yourself to a wide range of salads for just K4.50 and there are various other inexpensive dishes. There's a reef 'n' beef buffet on Wednesday night and an oriental buffet on Saturday night. Pizzas are also available. The Bird also has the good, but expensive *Lahani Room* restaurant. Men will need to wear long trousers.

Spices, in the shops at street level under the Bird, is open during the day and sells excellent snacks. Other than these there are the usual kai-bars, and meals at the *Goroka Lodge*. The food at the Lutheran Guesthouse is excellent but only for guests. There's even a Big Rooster fried chicken franchise in the town.

Things to Buy
Some artefacts are sold from the footpath near the Bird of Paradise Hotel. If you've just arrived in the Highlands, this is an opportunity to buy that essential item of clothing, a Highlands hat. In recent years, there has been an influx of baskets in all shapes and sizes; they were once a handcraft only of the Mendi area. Something as big as a laundry basket might cost K80, but prices are negotiable. Tell the seller that if the basket you want is still unsold at the end of the day, you'll make an offer. There are a lot of other things, such as *bilums* (string bags), spears, bows and arrows and necklaces, none cheap but all negotiable. They will sometimes sell spears and arrows that can be separated into segments, which are more easily transported if you are travelling with a pack.

The art department at the Goroka Teachers College produces and sells prints, paintings and other artwork made using western tools and traditional concepts; artefacts are also for sale.

Getting There & Away
Air Air Niugini (☎ 732 1211), MBA, and MAF (☎ 732 1080) have offices at the airport. Airlink and Islands Nationair bookings can be made with the Air Niugini office.

Air Niugini has daily flights between Goroka and Port Moresby (K141) and flies to Madang (K66) five days a week. While there are direct flights from Mt Hagen to Goroka a couple of times a week, they do not fly the reverse route. To fly direct to Mt Hagen you must use MBA or Airlink.

Both Islands Nationair and Airlink have direct flights to Wewak (K121), Lae (K77), Madang (K66) and Mt Hagen (K70). In Mt Hagen you can connect with flights to Tari (K150 from Goroka). MBA also flies to Mt Hagen and Lae for the same fares.

There is no direct scheduled flight to Kundiawa.

Goroka Air Services (☎ 732 1681; fax 732 1722; PO Box 882) can provide charter services.

Road The main PMV station is at the market, but if you're going to Lae or planning to stay at the NSI, you may find the PMV stops on Edwards St, which runs parallel to the airport, more convenient. There are PMVs to Lae (K12; four or five hours); Kundiawa (K5); Mt Hagen (K8; around four hours); and Madang (about K20).

Budget (☎ 732 2858) is in West Goroka; Hertz (☎ 732 1710) is at the Bird of Paradise Hotel; and Avis (☎ 732 1084) is at the Air Niugini terminal. Apparently Avis will give you a discount if you book ahead through Air Niugini.

Getting Around

It's easy enough to walk around Goroka, but there are urban PMVs which circle the city and take you anywhere on the circuit for K0.50. Norman Carver or the Bird may also be able to organise transport for you.

AROUND GOROKA

You can arrange visits to coffee plantations or coffee-processing plants around Goroka. Try to line up a trip with a coffee buyer; many speak English, and it is an interesting way to visit Highlands villages and marketplaces. Get advice at the Goroka market.

Norman Carver of PNG Highland Tours & Treks (☎ 732 1602; fax 732 3302; PO Box 583) runs various day tours in the area and can cater the tour to your interests – whether they be bushwalking, cultural tours, trout farms or coffee plantations. He and his staff are very knowledgeable about the area and convey an enthusiasm that is contagious. He can also be contacted at the Bird.

Famito

About 10km south of Goroka is the Famito Valley – a lush, green and beautiful place. A rough road full of potholes leads through pretty villages and coffee plantations to the valley. You get the feeling of quiet, organised tranquillity, with well-maintained parklands leading to small hills and far distant mountains. There is a nine-hole golf course here with a well-stocked and comfortable clubhouse with panoramic views. Wander a bit further up the valley and you come across a rare sight in PNG – horses grazing peacefully in paddocks. If you ask the right people, you can organise horseriding expeditions through the valley. There is a pony club, polocrosse is often played at weekends, and nearby – to gently remind you of the machine age – is a go-cart track and a speedway association. Apparently one enterprising local has even started a model aeroplane club which buzzes around the area some weekends.

All these activities are open to visitors as well as locals – but you may need to be sponsored by a member of the various clubs.

You need transport to get to the valley, anyway, so probably the best place to ask about it is at the Bird.

Lufa

Lufa, south of Goroka, is a good base for climbing Mt Michael, named after those two original Highlands 'Michaels': Mick Dwyer and Mick Leahy. There is a cave near Lufa with some interesting prehistoric cave paintings.

Mt Gahavisuka Provincial Park

This is an area of around 80 hectares set in beautiful mountain scenery. Eleven kilometres from Goroka and 1km higher, the park is reached by a 4WD road (dry weather only) that turns off Highlands Highway on the Mt Hagen side, opposite the Okiufa Community School (look out for the sign).

The park includes a botanical sanctuary, where exotic plants from all over PNG have been added to the local orchids and rhododendrons. There are clearly marked walking tracks and a lookout at 2450m with a spectacular view. Facilities include picnic shelters, two orchid houses and an information centre. There is no admission fee.

There is talk of a fancy upmarket lodge being built on the cliff edge at the park – architects in Lae have supposedly prepared designs. But, as with many projects in PNG, so far there is much talk but little activity on the ground. Three different clans own land between Goroka and the park and they will all want their 'piece of the action' if a major tourist development takes place – and that may be the kiss of death for such a project.

Crater Mountain

In the tri-border area, where the Eastern Highlands, Simbu and Gulf provinces' borders meet, is the newly created Crater Mountain Wildlife Management Area. This is one of the best places in PNG to experience the spectacular countryside, the wildlife and the village culture; the villagers are welcoming.

The area encompasses 2700 sq km ranging from the lowland rainforests on the

Purari River to the forests on the slopes of Crater Mountain. Once inside the area, it is possible to hike between the various villages (with a guide), but the journey should only be undertaken by experienced trekkers. The easier option is to fly from village to village. Accommodation (K7 per night) is basic with village food available (about K4 per meal).

MAF can organise a return charter for a group of people for K280 or, if money is no object, you can charter a helicopter from Pacific Helicopters (☎ 732 1226) for K400 to K500 per person. The more intrepid can travel by PMV to Ubaigubi near Crater Mountain for K10 (but the trip takes 10 hours).

The area is managed by the Research & Conservation Foundation of PNG (☎ 323 0699; fax 323 0397). The site coordinator can be contacted care of MAF, PO Box 1080, Goroka.

Daulo Pass

The road out to Mt Hagen is fairly flat through Asaro, but it then hairpins its way up to the 2450m-high Daulo Pass. The pass is cold and damp but the views are spectacular, particularly if you're heading down from the pass towards Goroka.

KAINANTU
• *pop 3900* • *postcode 443*

The major town between Lae and Goroka, Kainantu is an important cattle and coffee production region. There was also some gold found in this area and very minor production still continues. The town, 210km from Lae and 80km from Goroka, is basically strung along the highway. Evenings can be quite cool because the town lies at 1600m.

The telephone service to Kainantu became totally unreliable and was replaced, for those businesses which can afford it, by satellite phones. So the telephone numbers listed in the telephone book for this area may not answer – you will have a devil of a job finding their satellite telephone numbers and if you do, the calls will be exorbitantly expensive.

The Eastern Highlands Cultural Centre

Asaro Mud Men

Many years ago, so the story goes, the village of Asaro (north-west of Goroka) came off second-best in a tribal fight. Someone at Asaro had a bizarre inspiration and the revengeful warriors covered themselves with grey mud and huge mud masks before heading off on their inevitable payback raid. When these ghostly apparitions emerged from the trees, their opponents scattered.

The mud men recreate this little caper for tourists, but unfortunately it has become rather commercialised and dull. The number of mud men appears to be in direct proportion to the number of kina-paying tourists. Mud men tours can be arranged by tour operators in the region.

One traveller wrote that Komiufa, about 5km from Asaro on the Highlands Highway, was a good place to see, very briefly, the mud men. Payment of K10 persuaded four men to don their masks and dance around for a couple of minutes. ■

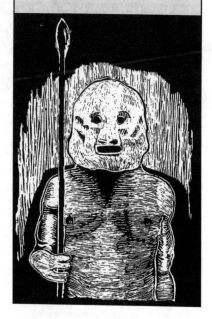

(PO Box 91), on the Lae side of town on the highway, is well worth visiting. It sells reasonably priced traditional crafts from the

Kuru & Pigbel

Kuru was a disease unique to the Fore area south-west of Kainantu. Attacking the central nervous system, the disease persisted in the body for about a year before causing death – it was dubbed 'the laughing disease' because the victims often died with a peculiar smile on their faces. It was remarkable in that it seemed to affect one particular language group and was limited to the women and children. The disease was known to have existed since the early part of this century, but it reached epidemic proportions in the 1950s when over 200 cases were reported. It took many years of epidemiological research, particularly by the PNG Institute of Medical Research (PNGIMR) in Goroka, to solve the puzzle of the disease's cause.

Its distribution was found to be linked to the diet and feasting behaviour of the clan. Specifically, it was caused by the ritualised cannibalism of the brain tissue of dead clan members by the women and children.

In recent times, due to changed dietary and ritual behaviour, there has only been a handful of new cases a year and the PNGIMR believes that the last reported case (and, it is hoped, the last case ever) died in early 1997.

Pigbel, or necrotising enteritis, is a disease of the intestines and was, until relatively recently, the commonest cause of death of Highlands children over the age of one. The children who died had a staple diet of sweet potato and rarely ate meat. The occasional feasting on pork sometimes involves the ritual killing of many pigs, and the meat may be kept and eaten for many days afterwards. One particular toxin, prevalent in the meat, has a more profound effect on children who have low-protein diets. The PNGIMR helped develop a vaccine against Pigbel and immunisation programmes since the 1980s have significantly reduced the number of cases. ∎

Eastern Highlands, such as pottery, hand-woven rugs, silkscreen prints and flutes; there's a small museum. This is an excellent opportunity to get to see the local arts and crafts at a grassroots level – the centre is owned and operated by the local community. It also trains people in handcrafts like print-making, dressmaking and weaving; it's open from 8 am to 4.30 pm on weekdays and from 9 am to 4 pm on weekends.

Places to Stay & Eat

The *Kainantu Lodge* (try the satellite number ☎ 640 4103; fax 640 4104; PO Box 31) is on a hill overlooking Kainantu on the other side of the disused airfield parallel to the highway. It's signposted and about a 20-minute walk from the PMV stop. It's a remarkably nice hotel for such an out-of-the-way place, with a swimming pool, bar and a restaurant. There's a Sunday barbecue lunch by the pool and a crackling log fire at night. Single or double rooms in the new wing cost from K112 and are very comfortable with superb views over the valley. The old wing has rooms for K87 and there are some budget rooms with a bath for K56. There are some-

times special offers, such as 10% weekend discounts, so check. If you want some peace and quiet in a pleasant spot, this would be ideal. They also have a free shuttle service to/from Goroka airport (a two-hour drive).

Getting There & Away

PMVs from Lae to Kainantu cost K8 and take three hours; from Kainantu to Goroka they cost K5 and take about two hours.

AROUND KAINANTU
Ukarumpa

• postcode 444

Adjoining a village of the same name, Ukarumpa is the PNG headquarters of the American-founded Summer Institute of Linguistics (SIL). It is in the Aiyura Valley about half an hour by PMV from Kainantu and is well worth a visit to see 'little America' in the midst of PNG. There's an excellent supermarket and the valley is a pleasant place for day walks, although it is best to ask if it is safe before heading off on your own. There's also a *guesthouse* (try their satellite ☎ 640 4400; PO Box 413) which charges around K25 per night. The SIL is planning a perimeter fence because of a number of rapes. However, there are SIL guesthouses all over PNG and all of them seem to be extremely well run and good value.

Yonki & the Upper Ramu Project

Situated 23km from Kainantu, Yonki is the support town for the Upper Ramu hydroelectric project. Commissioned in 1979, the project was financed by a K23 million World Bank loan and supplies power to Lae, Madang and much of the Highlands. You can arrange a free tour of the project which is 4km from the town.

Okapa

Highland Handcrafts (PO Box 225, Goroka) is at Okapa and sells, among other things, bark paintings.

About 12km from Okapa is the **Yagusa Valley**, where traditional culture is relatively intact. Here, the **Eastern Highlands Mission** (PO Box 225, Goroka) operates Christian schools, churches and a medical clinic in the mountain valley, with its lush

---

Summer Institute of Linguistics (SIL)

The SIL is a missionary organisation which aims to translate the Bible into every PNG language. You either love or hate the missionary presence in PNG – there seems to be no middle ground. But the good side of SIL is that it does record many languages, some of which are dying out and might otherwise be lost. While the generally accepted number of languages in PNG is between 700 and 800, the SIL claims to have evidence of 1300, which is certainly not beyond the bounds of possibility.

SIL's translator-missionaries, who are usually husband-and-wife teams, typically spend 15 to 20 years in a remote village, learning the language, developing a written alphabet and translating the Bible. The institute is working on 185 languages and has completed translations for 94.

An example of how local languages can rapidly disappear can be found in UNESCO's *Red Book on Endangered Languages*, which lists the language Aribwatsa and then notes, succinctly and poignantly, 'one very old woman left'. ■

---

trees, streams, waterfalls and wildlife. There are also some great walks. The mission has a *guesthouse* and a picturesque guest *treehouse* for visitors seeking a more remote and traditional look at the Highlands. It even has electricity provided by its own hydroelectric power plant. The nightly cost is K20, including meals. Contact the Bird of Paradise Hotel in Goroka for more information.

A daily PMV from Goroka to Okapa costs about K7 and takes three or four hours, more after rain because of the very bad road. The wet season is from December to April.

Simbu Province

Land Area 6200 sq km
Population 195,000
Capital Kundiawa

Travelling west from Goroka, the mountains become much more rugged and the valleys become smaller and less accessible. Some of the highest mountains in PNG are in this region, including Mt Wilhelm, at 4509m the highest of them all.

The province's name is said to date to the first patrol into the area. The story has it that steel axes and knives were given to the tribespeople, who replied that they were *simbu* – very pleased. The area was accordingly named Simbu, which was temporarily corrupted to Chimbu, and finally changed back to Simbu.

Despite its rugged terrain, Simbu Province is the most heavily populated region in PNG. The Simbu people have turned their steep country into a patchwork quilt of gardens which spreads up the side of every available hill. Population pressures are pushing them to even higher ground – to the detriment of remaining forests and, consequently, the bird of paradise. As in Enga Province, most people speak a similar language; Simbu-speakers make up the second-largest language group in PNG.

Kundiawa, the provincial capital and site

of the first government station in the Highlands, has been left behind by Goroka and Mt Hagen. It has a spectacular airstrip but its steep location, while picturesque, seems to have inhibited its development.

The Simbus have a reputation for being avid capitalists (who keep a good eye on their coffee profits) and also for being great believers in the payback raid. Minor warfare is still common in the Simbu region and aggrieved parties are all too ready to claim an eye for an eye. In Kundiawa, check out the painted signboard at the police station, which depicts a tribal battle with the police not doing terribly much to stop it.

The old customs are breaking down but, at one time, all the men in a village would live in a large men's house while their wives lived in individual round houses – with the pigs.

KUNDIAWA

• *pop 6000* • *postcode 461*

Although it's the provincial capital, you can cover most of Kundiawa in half an hour – and you won't be much better off for your efforts. There's a PNGBC bank, post office, some rather limited shopping and that's about it. Most people go straight through to Mt Wilhelm, Goroka or Mt Hagen. One of the main problems is the absence of reasonably priced accommodation. If you're heading for Mt Wilhelm, try to get to Kundiawa early in the day to ensure that you don't get stuck there overnight.

Many people have enthused about rafting on the Wahgi River near Kundiawa, but unfortunately no operators are currently offering it, partly because they have had groups harassed by rascals. Ask the local and foreign tour operators if anything has started up again. The scenery is excellent: the river goes through deep chasms, under small rope bridges and there are several good stretches of rapids and waterfalls.

There are a number of caves around Kundiawa used as burial places. Other large caves, suitable for caving enthusiasts, are only a few kilometres from Kundiawa while the Keu Caves are very close to the main road

near Chuave. The Nambaiyufa Amphitheatre is also near Chuave and is noted for its rock paintings.

In an unmarked, but roofed, grave on the other side of the road from the Air Niugini office lie the remains of Iambakey Okuk, a well-known bigman and politician during the 1970s and 80s.

Places to Stay & Eat

The *Kundiawa Hotel* (☎ 735 1033; PO Box 12) does not have much competition. Its prices are exorbitant: around the K90 mark for a double. It is noted for being rundown – peeling paint, unreliable hot water and noisy.

The only other alternative is the *Simbu Women's Resource Centre*, where the people are friendly but the prices high – K35 per person in a seven-bed room! It, too, is getting in need of a little renovation. No meals are available but there are cooking facilities. Follow the road past the hotel and the government offices, and turn left onto a muddy track as you go down the hill. It's a pink building.

The *Haus Kai Bilong ol Meri* or Women's Coffee Shop is the best place to eat, especially for lunch – it has good healthy food and a shady place to sit. Coffee is K0.60, kaukau pattie K0.50 and a reasonable lunch is K2, including fresh fruit juice or coffee.

Getting There & Away

Air The airport is quite spectacular as it's on a sloping ridge surrounded by mountains. Air Niugini (☎ 735 1273) has flights to/from Port Moresby (K140) on Monday, Wednesday, Friday and Saturday but no direct flights from other destinations.

PMV The fare to Goroka is K5, to Mt Hagen K4 and Kegsugl (for Mt Wilhelm) K5; each of these sectors takes around two hours. The Kegsugl Road may be closed for one or two days each week in the wet season (October to March) for road-clearing and local villages are in the habit of charging a 'royalty' for this service. PMVs for Kegsugl leave from the Shell station; others stop on the highway near the police station.

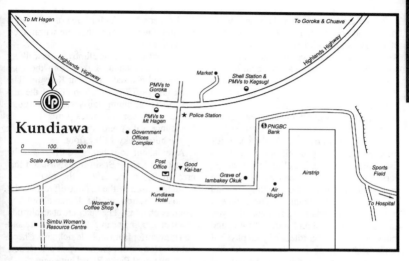

MT WILHELM

For many people, climbing to the 4509m summit of Mt Wilhelm is the highlight of their visit to the Highlands. On a clear day, you can see both the northern and southern coasts of PNG. Even if you don't intend to tackle the summit, it is worth staying near the base, from where you can explore the area and walk some of the way up the mountain.

While you're in the Mt Wilhelm area, a visit to **Niglguma** village or **Gembogl** is worthwhile. You can walk to Gembogl from Kegsugl in a couple of hours and, on the way, you pass through half-a-dozen villages, including Niglguma. Gembogl has suffered the inroads of corrugated-iron construction, so Niglguma is more interesting.

Climbing the Mountain

Although this is a popular climb, it's quite hard work, especially if your exercise has lately been limited to climbing into PMVs and sitting in boats. Care should be taken to prepare adequately for the climb and its dangers should not be underestimated. An Israeli trekker died in August 1995 after he sprained his ankle and stayed behind while his companions climbed to the summit. He

wandered off the trail, got lost, fell down a ravine – and his body was found about a week later.

If the weather is fine, the climb can be done in three days, but don't count on it. Frequently the weather is too bad to undertake the climb – so pack a good book to read in the huts. The best time of year is April to October (the dry season) because the start of the track can be very muddy in the wet. There are a number of ways of tackling the climb, depending on your wealth, health and available time: you can go with a tour company (talk to Norman Carver in Goroka or Trans Niugini Tours in Mt Hagen) which will provide a guide, porters, food and equipment; you can hire guides and porters; or you can do it all yourself.

The last option is feasible if you're reasonably fit and have some warm gear – but it is really not advisable to do it without a guide, no matter how fit you think you are. If you plan to climb the mountain in the dark, to reach the summit at dawn and see the views before the clouds roll in, a guide is almost a necessity. The track is marked with painted rocks which are visible during the day, but not at night.

People are keen to offer their services as guides and porters. James Mondo, a relative of Henry Agum who runs a guesthouse at Kegsugl, has been recommended. A porter costs about K10 a day, a guide about K20. If they stay overnight with you at the Pindaunde Lakes, you must supply them with food and blankets. John and Rose Banda, at the new guesthouse in Kegsugl, are good guides.

If you've just arrived from the coast, it's important to allow yourself time to acclimatise to the altitude before climbing. It can get very cold on top and can easily become fogbound, and even snow. Climbers (and guides) can suffer from altitude sickness, sunburn and hypothermia. It is vital that you have sufficient food and warm clothing and that you assess the weather and your physical state realistically. You would be most unwise to tackle it alone. In addition, make sure you have a hat and sunscreen (you can burn deceptively quickly at high altitudes), water containers (there's no water on the last stretch past the lakes), a torch with a spare globe and strong batteries, gloves and candles. Cooking gear might be useful – check in Kegsugl whether there are still utensils at the lake huts.

You might be confronted by a traditional landowner who asks for a fee of a few kina to climb the mountain; they are within their rights to do this.

The first stage of the climb entails walking up to the Pindaunde Lakes from the high school and disused airstrip at Kegsugl. The track takes off from the top end of the airstrip. After climbing fairly steeply through dense rainforest, the track turns into the Pindaunde Valley and continues less steeply up the hummocky valley floor.

After about four hours you'll reach the Pindaunde Lakes. Bushfires devastated this area in September 1997, the result of a drought caused by the El Niño effect (see the Climate section in the Facts about the Country chapter). The lakes are at an altitude of about 3500m; it can get very cold here and you may suffer from altitude sickness. Check out the views from the *haus pek pek* (toilet) at the National Parks Board huts here.

You are likely to be offered strawberries for sale along the first stretch of the walk. Buy the very sweet strawberries which apparently, like cabbage, cauliflower and broccoli, grow all year round because of the constant 'spring' weather.

From the huts, it's a long, fairly hard walk to the summit – about five hours. Some walkers reckon it is better to spend a day acclimatising at the lake huts and exploring the area before attempting the summit – this is wise advice. After the lakes, water is difficult to find, so carry your own. It can become very cold, wet, windy and foggy at the top. The clouds roll in soon after dawn so it is wise to start from the huts as early as possible, maybe 1 am, hence the torch on your shopping list. The ascent and descent will probably take you all day (coming down to the huts takes about three hours), but some people do go all the way back to Kegsugl (about 2½ hours from the huts).

Places to Stay

Kegsugl An excellent place to stay is *Henry's Place*, a guesthouse run by Henry Agum. It is the first house on the left above the old airstrip at Kegsugl. He has several six-bed dormitories, it's very clean and a bed

The little brown owl can often be heard in the Highlands at night-time

costs about K20 a night, but the showers are *cold*. There is an open fire in the kitchen and also cooking facilities – he will provide home-grown vegies and even a chicken if you ask him. Write to him care of the Kundiawa post office.

Lake Pindi Yaundo Lodge (radio ☎ 0561145 112037; fax 0561145 212037; PO Box 224, Kundiawa), better known as *Betty's Place*, is run by Betty Higgins and is about a kilometre from Kegsugl, near the start of the trail. It, too, is an excellent place and is situated on a ridge with superb views out over the valley. Betty used to be a stewardess with Air Niugini and is very helpful. Cooking is on a primus stove and lighting is by kerosene lantern (although apparently now there is electricity in the evenings and hot water showers). She charges K45 per person for dinner, bed and breakfast, or K25 for accommodation only, and can provide vegetables from her garden to use in the kitchen. Her place has its own trout farm; a luscious self-cooked trout can be had for around K4. She even provides a baby-sitting service if parents want to do some trekking. Her brother, Moses, is an excellent guide (K40 to the top).

Pindaunde Lakes There are a couple of huts owned by the National Parks Board, costing about K6 per person and containing beds, a wood stove and a kerosene lamp. The lamp isn't guaranteed, hence the candles on your shopping list. There may be no-one here, so see the ranger at Kegsugl for the keys before you leave, if you can find him (although keys will probably not be necessary). These huts are reportedly getting a little rundown and dirty now, and the place is getting trashed.

Henry Agum also has an A-frame here, where you can stay for around K10 a night; it is reputed to be more comfortable than the huts. Get the key from Henry before you leave Kegsugl and reserve a room for the return leg, as sometimes groups fill up the hostels.

Getting There & Away
Kegsugl, at the foot of the mountain, is about 57km from Kundiawa along a road that has to be seen to be believed. You can get there by irregular PMVs that cost K5 and take a couple of hours. They leave from the Shell service station in Kundiawa. The Bundi Road branches off to the right over a bridge, just before Kegsugl. The airstrip at Kegsugl, once the highest in PNG at 2469m, is now permanently closed. If you are heading for Betty's Place, ask the driver to let you off there. If you leave Goroka or Mt Hagen early in the morning, you can easily reach Pindaunde Lakes in one day (which leaves little time to acclimatise) and avoid having to overnight in Kundiawa. Alternatively, stay in Kegsugl.

WALKING TO MADANG

The turn-off for the Bundi Road and the trek to Brahmin (and Madang) is between Gembogl and Kegsugl. You turn right over a bridge, instead of left to Kegsugl. You can walk right down to Madang – but most people catch a PMV at Brahmin.

It's a hot but relatively easy route, following a 4WD track. Some vehicles have apparently gone the whole distance. A reasonable pace would get you to Madang in three fairly long days. Bring your own food, although you can get meals at Bundi.

The first stretch is largely uphill and there are very few villages. The first village you come to is **Pandambai**, where there's a store, and a missionary lives here. Next along is **Bundikara**, where there's an attractive waterfall and you can apparently stay in the village. There are great views from lookout points along the way. Some people take about five hours to get to Pandambai; others get to Bundikara in the same time.

From Bundikara it's 3½ hours to **Bundi**, where there is a group of lodges known as the *Mt Sinai Hotel*. From Bundi, it's 2½ hours to War, which is just after a suspension bridge, and from there it is a 3½-hour climb to Brahmin Mission. A PMV from Brahmin to Madang costs K6 or K7 and takes about 1½ hours. Brahmin is about 20km from the Lae-Madang Road.

Western Highlands Province

Land Area 8500 sq km
Population 385,000
Capital Mt Hagen

Continuing west from Simbu Province you descend into the large Wahgi Valley. Mt Hagen is the provincial capital and although it is not particularly attractive it does have the feel of a frontier town. The surrounding countryside is worth exploring.

The province's terrain varies between swamps in the lower Jimi Valley (about 370m above sea level) and a number of high peaks, including Mt Hagen at 4026m. Forest only remains on the mountain slopes, while the valleys and lower hills are grass-covered. This is the result of slash-and-burn cultivation and hunting fires. Gardens and stands of casuarinas are scattered through the hills and large tea and coffee plantations now dominate the most fertile valley floors.

The men usually have beards and their traditional clothing is a wide belt of beaten bark with a drape of strings in front and a bunch of tanket (or tanget) leaves behind. The leaves are known, descriptively, as *arsetanket*. The women can be just as decoratively dressed, with string skirts and cuscus fur hanging around their necks.

Today, that attire is usually reserved for sing-sings and political rallys, and bright lengths of printed cloth and T-shirts are more likely to be the everyday wear. Naturally, traditional dress is more likely to be seen in the smaller towns and villages than in main towns. At sing-sings both sexes will have beautiful headdresses with bird-of-paradise plumes and other feathers.

The Wahgi people keep carefully tended vegetable gardens and neat villages, often with paths bordered by decoratively planted flowers, ceremonial parks with lawns and groves of trees and colourful memorials to deceased bigmen.

Sing-sings are still an integral part of life and you should make every effort to see one.

MT HAGEN
• pop 18,000 • postcode 281

Mt Hagen is the provincial capital of the Western Highlands and although it is now commercially more important than Goroka, it is not nearly as attractive. It lies 445km from Lae and 115km from Goroka.

Mt Hagen was just a patrol station before WWII, but in the last 20 years, with the opening of Enga and the Southern Highlands, it has grown into an unruly city with a major squatter settlement and many itinerant workers. It's quite a shock to find a PNG city where the streets are packed with people.

Mt Hagen's ambience can vary from the more usual 'relaxed and quiet' to periods of heavy tension, particularly during elections or inter-clan disputes; there's a 'wild west' feel to the place. Payrolls for many businesses in the region now go by helicopter because trucks are ambushed so often. Aside from the rascal problem, the more traditional tribal warfare continues, exacerbated by the value of coffee and the over-population of the best land. Most people will know which areas to avoid at any given time.

The town acquired its name by a rather roundabout route. It is named after a nearby mountain, Mt Hagen, which in turn was named after a German administrator, Kurt von Hagen. In 1895 two Germans started off on a badly planned and ill-fated attempt to cross the island from north to south. They were murdered by two of their carriers, although one wonders if they would have survived the trip in any case. The carriers later escaped from custody. In the subsequent hunt for them, von Hagen was shot and killed near Madang in 1897; he was buried at Bogadjim.

Information

The Department of Lands & Surveys at the end of Kuri St has a good selection of maps, although they are less likely than the National Mapping Bureau in Port Moresby to have complete stocks.

Forster's Newsagent on Hagen Drive has a good collection of books and stationery. Keith and Maggie Wilson at Haus Poroman Lodge are good sources of information.

All the main banks have branches, as do the airlines. Mt Hagen hosts the headquarters for MAF.

Market

The Saturday market is one of the biggest and most interesting markets in PNG and, if you're lucky, you will still see some people in traditional dress. You're unlikely to see plumed headdresses but you may notice young men with leaves, feathers or flowers in their hair as a more subtle continuation of the tradition. Snapping a picture of anyone is likely to be followed by a demand for money – it's always best to ask permission first.

It is even rarer for women to dress traditionally than it is for men, but they make up for this with the sheer brightness of their dresses and bilums. Add a brilliant kerchief, several flowing scarves in various colours, traditional facial tattoos and you have a striking sight.

Don't forget to look at what is for sale; aside from a superb range of fruit and vegetables, there are pigs and even sometimes cassowaries, trussed up in lengths of bamboo.

Organised Tours

Trans Niugini Tours (☎ 542 1438; fax 542 2470; PO Box 371, Mt Hagen) organises package tours all over PNG – for example the Sepik, diving, the islands and the Highlands. It is well organised and a little expensive, but worth it. It is based in Mt Hagen – its head office is on Kongin St behind the hospital (and quite a walk from town) – so it also offers tours in and around the town.

Haus Poroman Lodge (see the Places to Stay section) also arranges excellent tours, ranging from treks up Mt Wilhelm to Sepik canoe trips and excursions to see the Huli people near Tari.

Mt Hagen Show

Although the Mt Hagen Show is not as big as the Goroka Show, it's definitely a must-see. It is now an annual event, held on the third weekend in August.

Make sure you arrive early in the day, say

! !

Warning

While the Highlands seem more relaxed than the urban jungles of Port Moresby and Lae, the razor wire and security guards at all Mt Hagen hotels are there for a reason. Being locked up at night in a guarded hotel compound may feel a little like being imprisoned, but it does lead to a better, and safer, night's sleep. Don't wander around after dark – there is not much to do in Mt Hagen at that time anyway, and there are no taxis.

Rascals are just as active in the Highlands as elsewhere in PNG and particularly on Friday pay nights, but the violence has a more subtle overtone here because it often relates to payback. The rascal's animosity may consequently be initially directed towards other locals or members of local clans, but add a few beers to the equation and the object of their aggression can very easily become the stranger in their midst. Stay away from situations where alcohol is being consumed. If you arrive in Mt Hagen by air, you may find your bags being searched for alcohol (or guns). The Western Highlands, Simbu and Enga provinces have officially been declared 'dry' to reduce alcohol's role in crime. But alcohol is still available at many tourist hotels and can find its way, often in the form of a home-brew, into the hands of rascals, with sometimes worrying results.

Rascal activity outside major urban areas seems to have died down dramatically (even on the Highlands Highway) in the past few years, but has not totally disappeared. Long-distance PMVs are still occasionally held up, but travellers say the benefits of PMV travel still greatly outweigh the disadvantages. Robbers are usually after money to buy beer, so keep K20 or so in your pockets, and hide the rest in a money belt – just in case.

Also see the Personal Safety section in the Facts for the Visitor chapter. ■

! !

before 8 am, to see the groups dressing and putting on impromptu performances for the people who can't afford a ticket into the grandstand. These performances are powerful and vigorous – even ribald – compared with the more formal stuff dished up for the dignitaries in the arena.

Bird-lovers might be relieved to know that there isn't a general slaughter just before showtime; most of the feather headdresses and costumes are extremely valuable heirlooms, many hired for the occasion.

As a visitor, you will be expected to buy a pass badge for the full three days. The price is high (K30) but without this contribution the show couldn't be held. All those groups have to be transported to Mt Hagen and accommodated; they are competing for some fairly large prizes. Also, paying the entry fee gives you the opportunity to stroll around the arena in a sea of colour and noise unlike anything on earth. It's absolutely mind-blowing.

The showground is quite a way from town, beyond the airport. You can get there by PMVs and on foot, but hitching a lift on showday isn't difficult.

Places to Stay – bottom end & middle

The *Haus Poroman Lodge* (☎ 542 2722 or 542 2250; fax 542 2207; PO Box 1182) is one of the nicest places to stay in PNG, no matter what budget you're travelling on. The place has atmosphere, class and comfort. The name means 'house of friends', which is appropriate – the staff are a very happy lot. It is located 9km out of Mt Hagen along a rough road which, in the mornings, can be misty and quite dramatically beautiful. The place itself is perched on a ridge, with superb views across the valley to the mountains beyond.

It comprises several separate lodges built in traditional style with thatched roofs and woven walls, but this is no simple village-style guesthouse: the rooms have their own bathrooms with hot showers, there is electricity and the place is very comfortable, well maintained and clean. Access to the lodges is via grassy paths which lead through pretty gardens and across a little stream. The original big building, also built in traditional bush materials, is now the dining and lounge area, with an open fire, a well-stocked library and a range of videos. It's a good place to sit and talk over a whisky or beer.

There are plenty of things to do in the surrounding area: there's a marked trail through the rainforest; you can visit the nearby village and watch traditional crafts being made; or make a three-hour trek through the Nebilyer Valley.

Keith and Maggie Wilson are the owners and Barbara is the manager: they will go out of their way to look after you. There is a choice of three types of accommodation, ranging from a backpacker dormitory to rooms with private facilities; a single/double in one of the round houses costs K70/90, a room in the lodge wing costs K40/55 and a bed in the dormitory hut costs K18 per person (you'll need a sleeping bag). Meals are extra, but are good value at K6 for a light breakfast and K25 for a three-course dinner.

Transport to and from Haus Poroman is included in the tariff, as long as you fit in with the other demands on the vehicles. If you let them know in advance, they'll also pick you up and drop you off at the airport. Keith and Maggie also have an office in Manda St which is the main pick-up and drop-off point for guests with things to do in town.

If you decide to stay closer to town there are a number of low-cost options.

The *Mt Hagen Missionary Home* (☎ 542 1041; PO Box 394) is across from the hospital, which is a short walk from the market. The home is friendly, very clean and charges K50 for dinner, bed and breakfast or K40 for bed and breakfast. The food is excellent. Missionary volunteers get a K10 discount.

The *New Town Lodge* (☎ 542 2872; PO Box 1006) is on the highway about a kilometre past the Highlander Hotel; it has been described as a 'friendly' place. It's very spartan and can get noisy, but is clean. Some PMVs run past, but walking out here at night could be unsafe. Small rooms are K40/50 a single/double (probably more during the Mt

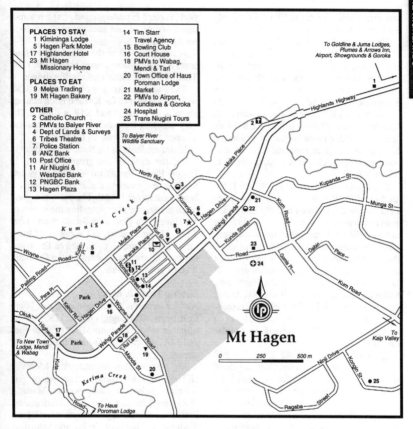

PLACES TO STAY
1 Kimininga Lodge
5 Hagen Park Motel
17 Highlander Hotel
23 Mt Hagen
   Missionary Home

PLACES TO EAT
9 Melpa Trading
19 Mt Hagen Bakery

OTHER
2 Catholic Church
3 PMVs to Baiyer River
4 Dept of Lands & Surveys
6 Tribes Theatre
7 Police Station
8 ANZ Bank
10 Post Office
11 Air Niugini &
   Westpac Bank
12 PNGBC Bank
13 Hagen Plaza

14 Tim Starr
   Travel Agency
15 Bowling Club
16 Court House
18 PMVs to Wabag,
   Mendi & Tari
20 Town Office of Haus
   Poroman Lodge
21 Market
22 PMVs to Airport,
   Kundiawa & Goroka
24 Hospital
25 Trans Niugini Tours

To Goldline & Juma Lodges,
Plumes & Arrows Inn,
Airport, Showgrounds & Goroka

To Baiyer River
Wildlife Sanctuary

Mt Hagen

0   250   500 m

To New Town
Lodge, Mendi
& Wabag

To Haus
Poroman Lodge

To
Kaip Valley

Hagen Show). They will pick you up at the airport if you book.

The *Goldline Lodge* (☎ 542 3333; fax 542 2000; PO Box 1070) and the *Juma Lodge* (☎ 545 1310; fax 545 1368; PO Box 740) are both small new guesthouses situated between the airport and town. Goldline charges K60/75 for a single/double and Juma K45/65 (with a K10 key deposit).

There are also backpacker beds at the Plumes & Arrows Inn (see below).

Places to Stay – top end
The *Highlander Hotel* (☎ 542 1355; fax 542 1216; PO Box 34) is part of the Coral Sea chain. It is located at the west end of the main street, not far from the town centre. It has three wings and all rooms have private facilities, TV, and tea and coffee-making equipment. Rooms range in price from K170 for a standard room to K190 for a premium room and K234 for the premier suite. The hotel is surrounded by pleasant gardens within an ugly (but safe) metal fence. There is a heated swimming pool; it's quiet and peaceful, but a little colourless. Corporate rates apply (15% discount) and you can ask for weekend rates for the standard rooms; if

you arrive after 5 pm (and haven't already booked), ask about stand-by rates.

The *Hagen Park Motel* (☎ 542 1388; fax 542 2282; PO Box 81) is rather more noisy and starting to look a little rundown. It now also has a casino and poker machines, so it tends to attract a rougher crowd. A budget room costs K55 (single or double), a standard room costs K75 and a deluxe room costs K95, but there isn't much difference between them. The dining room is near the pokies, so don't expect a quiet romantic tête-à-tête if you dine in. Breakfast is K12, and à-la-carte dinner is K19.

The *Plumes & Arrows Inn* (☎ 545 1555; fax 545 1546; PO Box 86) is a bit inconvenient for town, but is only a five-minute walk from the airport. It has a high stockade fence and feels like a fortress but has some very attractive gardens and a swimming pool. This is the headquarters for Tribal World, a company that organises upmarket tours in the Sepik region and around the Highlands. A-class rooms are K110, B-class K90 and backpacker beds K20. They have an Executive Advantage Club which offers an across-the-board 25% discount to regular travellers.

Kimininga Lodge (☎ 542 2399; fax 542 1834; PO Box 408) is on the Goroka side of town on the Okuk Highway, about 10 minutes walk from the centre, past the market. If you are coming from Goroka by PMV, get off before you get into town. It has three classes of rooms, but all seem overpriced: K110/125 a single/double with bathroom (class A); K95/105 with common bathroom (class B); and K75/85 for pretty basic rooms in the old wing with common bathroom (class C). A backpackers dormitory may still be available.

Places to Eat

The eating places in Mt Hagen are pretty well limited to the dining rooms of the accommodation houses.

The food at *Haus Poroman Lodge* is excellent. A light breakfast costs K6 and a big full breakfast is K9. Lunch is K10 and dinner is K25. Traditional mumus (usually pork, cooked in underground pits) are sometimes organised and backpackers can cook for themselves.

A full breakfast at the *Highlander Hotel* costs K12 and main courses are around K20. There's a Wednesday night buffet dinner.

The *Plumes & Arrows Inn* has good food, with decent snacks for K4, and main courses about K10 at lunch and K18 at dinner. The very pleasant lounge-dining room area has an open fire and Sepik art for sale.

If you are looking for somewhere to eat in town, the options are greatly limited. In Hagen Plaza, the *Plaza Coffee Shop* has sandwiches, omelettes and milk shakes – lunch costs from K3.50. The patio is a good place to regroup after pounding the streets of Mt Hagen. It's closed on Sundays and after 4 pm. *Melpa Trading*, in the centre of town on Hagen Drive, is a cut above the usual kai-bar and there are tables on the footpath. It stays open until late.

Getting There & Away

Air The airport is at Kagamuga, about 10km from town. Air Niugini (☎ 542 1183) has an office in town and both MBA (a new one) and MAF (☎ 545 1506) have offices at the airport.

Air Niugini flies to/from Port Moresby (K163) at least daily. Elsewhere, Air Niugini's schedule takes you to Madang (K83) on Monday, Tuesday, Wednesday, Friday and Saturday; Wewak (K102) on Wednesday, Thursday, Friday and Saturday; Goroka (K70) on Monday, Thursday and Saturday (to, but not from Goroka); and Lae (K107) on Wednesday, Friday and Sunday.

MBA flies to Port Moresby, Lae and Goroka for the same fares as Air Niugini, and also to Tabubil (K122) and Tari (K97). Islands Nationair also services Port Moresby, Goroka, Lae and Wewak for the same fares, as well as Kerema (K169) and Vanimo (K169).

MAF flies twice weekly to literally dozens of third-level airstrips. If you're planning a walk and want to know where along your route you could bail out or how you could make some shortcuts, talk to them.

Road PMVs heading east, to Kundiawa and Goroka, leave from the market. Those heading west, to Wabag, Mendi and Tari, leave from the highway near the Dunlop building. Wabag-bound PMVs (K6) can usually be found here as well; some continue on to Porgera (K15). There are regular connections to Mendi (K8; three to four hours), Kundiawa (K4; about two hours) and Goroka (K8; four hours). PMVs to Baiyer River (K3; around 1½ hours) leave from the corner of Moka Place and Kumniga Rd.

Hertz (☎ 545 1522), Budget (☎ 542 1355), Avis (☎ 545 1350) and Thrifty (☎ 542 2399) have representatives in Mt Hagen.

Getting Around
The Airport The airport is about 10km from town. Most accommodation places will collect you. A PMV from the airport to town costs K1. Walk out of the terminal, turn left and walk down to the small group of shops (if you went straight ahead you'd get to the Plumes & Arrows Inn), where PMVs stop. In central Mt Hagen, most PMVs stop at the market, with a few going through town along the highway.

Taxi There is no taxi service in Mt Hagen.

BAIYER RIVER
The 120-hectare Baiyer River wildlife sanctuary is 55km north of Mt Hagen and used to be one of the best places in the Highlands to visit and to stay. Sadly, it is now quite rundown and has become unsafe – so best to stay away. The lodge has closed, and the situation is unlikely to change in the near future.

If you do risk a visit, and everything has been maintained in the intervening period, you'll find the largest collection of birds of paradise in the world, nature trails through the forest and display trees used by wild birds of paradise.

Getting There & Away
Haus Poroman Lodge no longer makes day trips to Baiyer River for safety reasons – there has been a spate of robberies in the past few months. But if you want to risk it you may still be able to get a PMV from the corner of Moka Place and Kumniga Rd in Mt Hagen for K3. On the way you pass through the spectacular Baiyer River Gorge.

Enga Province

Land Area 12,800 sq km
Population 285,000
Capital Wabag

Beyond Mt Hagen to the north-west the roads deteriorate and the country is less developed although, as elsewhere in the Highlands, coffee is an important local industry. This situation is changing rapidly, especially with the development of the giant gold and silver mine at Porgera in the west.

Even in the 1960s, much of this region was still virtually independent from government control. It was part of Western Province until 1973. Control may have arrived, but tribal warfare can still occur. You may occasionally see circular, fenced areas filled with green-and-purple tanget bushes. These are the burial places of victims of tribal fighting.

Wabag is the provincial capital but it is still more an outlying town to Mt Hagen than a major centre in its own right. The province is made up of rugged mountains and high valleys, with the Lai and the Lagaip the main rivers. The people are fragmented into small clans, but the Enga language group – the largest in PNG – covers most of the province. Some tribes have close similarities with the people of the Southern Highlands.

Enga had a very bad reputation for rascals and while that seems to have died down, tribal fighting and other friction caused by 'outsiders' working at the mine can cause problems. Like the Western Highlands and Simbu provinces, Enga has been declared 'dry' to help control the situation. Unlike the other two provinces, however, there is a total ban in Enga, even at accommodation places. You may find your bags are occasionally searched by police for alcohol. The ban has helped to control the problem a little, but does not attack its root cause.

It can get very cold in Enga, so come prepared.

WABAG
• *pop 2100* • *postcode 291*

People tend to sit around a lot in Wabag – outside houses, by the roadside, wherever. Life in general is slow in PNG but it is even slower in Wabag. The stores have all the main necessities, but the cost of transport makes things a little expensive. There are two main stores: Bromley & Anton's (which does not have a sign) and Movenpick, which is slightly smaller, cheaper and has a kai-bar. The Moku Hardware store also has a small cafe upstairs. The shopfronts often have bars on the windows, which makes Wabag look like a town of bank teller's cubicles.

There's a large cultural centre in the valley. It's usually open from 8 am to 4 pm on weekdays but these hours can sometimes be erratic. It has an art gallery, a museum, and a workshop where you can see young artists making 'sand paintings', the principal artwork on display. Different-coloured sands are mixed with glue and applied to a hard surface, usually plasterboard, with striking visual effect. The adjacent museum has a large number of war shields, wigs and masks from many parts of PNG as well as Enga Province.

The annual Enga Festival is held in July at the local football oval – this is a relatively new event (the first was held in 1994). It is a mini-version of the equivalent in Mt Hagen and Goroka.

Both Wabag's water and the electricity supplies are erratic, so it is wise to keep a bottle of water and a torch handy.

Places to Stay & Eat
The *Malya Hostel* (☎ 547 1108; PO Box 237) is a short way out of town on the road to Mt Hagen and is run by the provincial government. Rooms cost K50, including breakfast, but this is negotiable; meals are available, but are totally uninspiring, and

there is a common sitting room with satellite TV. It isn't in great condition. Rooms have showers and toilets, but no basins, and there are rats in the ceiling.

The *Highlands Lutheran International School* (☎ 547 1059; PO Box 363; email jeggert@maf.org) is said to have better accommodation available for travellers.

The *Orchid Lodge* near Sari village has reportedly closed.

Getting There & Away
Air The Wabag airport closed some years ago, so you actually fly to Wapenamanda (call sign: WBM) which is an hour's drive away over a very rough road. Air Niugini flies from Port Moresby on Tuesday and Saturday for K174; the flights depart Wapenamanda for Mendi (K55) before returning to Port Moresby. It does not, however, have direct flights between Wapenamanda and Goroka or Mt Hagen. Be prepared to have your bags searched on arrival for alcohol or weapons – keep goodies like personal stereos out of sight, and politely demur if it's suggested that you might want to give a present.

Road From Mt Hagen the Wabag Road starts out in the same direction as the Mendi Road, then branches off to the north-west. It climbs over the Kaugel Pass, nearly 3000m high, before Wapenamanda and then Wabag, which is at about 2100m. The scenery on the three to four-hour trip is magnificent and the road is now sealed most of the way.

The PMV stop is at the top of the hill above the cultural centre. A PMV from Mt Hagen to Wabag costs K6 (but curiously it is only K4 in the reverse direction). The road to Porgera has been upgraded for mine traffic and is now good.

If you have a sturdy 4WD you can continue beyond Wabag to Laiagam and down to Mendi. PMVs cost about K4 from Wabag on to Laiagam. It's hard going and the road is often closed between Kandep and Mendi due to poor road conditions and washed-away bridges. If it is closed, you have an interesting 54km walk along the highest road

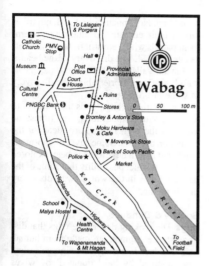

Wabag

in PNG ahead of you. It may be possible to stay at the mission about halfway along the road at Pingarip.

AROUND WABAG
• *pop 1250* • *postcode 299*

Porgera is a mining company town about 3½ hours west of Wabag. It has a large population of mining industry expats.

Porgera mine is the biggest producer of gold in PNG and also produces silver; mining is by both underground and open-cut operations. Seventy-five per cent of the mine is owned by foreign companies, the PNG government owns 20.1%, with the remainder owned by local landowners and the provincial government.

A 1996 report, compiled by the Mineral Policy Institute, Australian Conservation Foundation, Community Aid Abroad and the World Wide Fund for Nature, alleged the Porgera mine was discharging toxic tailings into the Strickland and Fly river systems. Assessing the environmental and social impact of the mine, the report claimed the river system was contaminated with arsenic at least 65km from the mine. The mine

owners deny the allegations and say there is no evidence of toxicity in the river downstream from the mine.

The report also called for an end to the discharging of tailings and waste rock sediments into river systems, saying the practice had been banned in the USA for at least 15 years.

The *Mountain Lodge* (☎ 547 9357; fax 547 9368; PO Box 63, Porgera) is about the only place to stay, other than in company-owned accommodation.

Getting There & Away The airstrip is frequently closed because of a landowners dispute, so check before planning your trip in too great a detail. If it is open, MBA can fly you Port Moresby-Moro-Tari-Porgera-Mt Hagen return on Tuesday and Thursday. Fares are: Tari K37, Moro K90, Mt Hagen around K100. If you can pull a few strings with mine management, you might be able to fly in from Mt Hagen on one of the company helicopters.

PMVs cost K15 from Mt Hagen or K9 from Wabag.

Laiagam
• *pop 700*

Laiagam has a botanic garden with a huge collection of orchids and a research centre.

Lake Rau

Lake Rau is a crater lake at nearly 3000m in the centre of Enga Province. It's a day's walk from Pumas, above Laiagam, and you will need a guide.

Southern Highlands Province

Land Area 23,800 sq km
Population 375,000
Capital Mendi

The Southern Highlands is made up of lush, high valleys between impressive limestone peaks. This region is particularly beautiful and traditional cultures thrive, especially in the Tari Basin, with many people retaining their traditional ways and dress. The head-waters of some mighty rivers, including the Kikori, Erave and Strickland, cross the province, and Mt Giluwe, 4368m high, is the second-highest mountain in PNG.

The most remote province of the Highlands, the Southern Highlands is still relatively undeveloped, although big oil and gas finds near Lake Kutubu and a huge alluvial gold mine at Mt Kare are rapidly changing that. Even in the past, it was at the end of the trade route from the Gulf of Papua to the Highlands.

Beyond the Wahgi-Mt Hagen area, both to the south-west past Mendi and north-west around Wabag, is the country of the wigmen – these are the Huli, the Duna and a number of other tribes whose men are famous for the intricately decorated wigs they wear. The proud Huli men of the Tari Basin, in particular, still wear their impressive traditional decorations. The Huli are the largest ethnic group in the Southern Highlands, with a population of around 45,000 and territory exceeding 2500 sq km.

The Huli do not live in villages, but in scattered homesteads, dispersed through immaculately and intensively cultivated valleys. The gardens are delineated by trenches and mud walls up to 3m high, broken by brightly painted gateways made of stakes. These trenches are used not only to mark boundaries and control the movement of pigs but also to secretly deploy large troops of warriors in times of war. As usual, the women do nearly all the work, while the men concentrate on displaying their finery. War was, and to some extent still is, a primary interest of the men.

The Mendi area is now the most developed part of the Southern Highlands (although the Tari area has more attractions and services for travellers), but it was not explored by Europeans until 1935 – the early explorers called it the Papuan Wonderland. It was 1950 when the first airstrip was constructed and 1952 before tribal warfare was

prohibited. Not unnaturally the Mendi tribes turned their energies to attacking government patrols who were still fighting them off as late as 1954. The discovery of the beautiful Lavani Valley in 1954 set newspapers off with high-flown stories about the discovery of some lost Shangri-la.

The Southern Highlands is starting to attract caving expeditions; the limestone hills and the high rainfall are ideal for the formation of caves. Some caves of enormous depth and length have already been explored and it is a distinct possibility that some of the deepest caves in the world await discovery in this region.

Society & Conduct

Wigs The striking decorative wigs that distinguish the wigmen are made from human hair. The hair is usually the wigman's own, supplemented by hair 'donated' by wives and children, who are consequently often short haired. The whole design is held together by woven string. It is possible to tell which tribe a man comes from by the way he wears his hair or decorates it.

The Huli wigmen cultivate yellow ever-lasting daisies especially to decorate their wigs and they also use feathers and cuscus fur. They often wear a band of snakeskin on their foreheads, a cassowary quill through their nasal septa and their faces may be decorated with yellow and red ochre.

Flutes similar to panpipes are a popular form of entertainment.

Brides in Black Mendi brides wear black for their wedding – they are coated in black *tigaso* tree oil and soot and they continue to wear this body colouring for a month after the wedding. The tigaso tree oil comes from Lake Kutubu and is traded all over the area.

During this time neither bride nor groom work, nor is the marriage consummated. This gives the bride time to become acquainted with her husband's family and for the groom to learn 'anti-woman' spells to protect himself from his wife.

Throughout the Highlands, women are traditionally distrusted by men, who go to extraordinary lengths to protect themselves and maintain their status. Sexual relations are not undertaken lightly. Contact with women is believed to cause sickness, so the two sexes often live in separate houses and the men often prefer to cook their own food. Boys are usually removed from their mothers' houses at a very young age.

Women travellers should bear these customs in mind because in many places they are still strictly upheld. Violence against PNG women is widespread.

Widows in Blue A dead man's wife, daughters, mother, sisters and sisters-in-law coat themselves with bluish-grey clay while in mourning. The wife carries vast numbers of strings of the seeds known as 'job's tears'. One string a day is removed until eventually, with the removal of the last string, the widow can wash herself of her clay coating and remarry. This is usually about nine months after the death.

Women's Houses The walls of women's houses are about 4m high, with kunai thatched roofs and walls of pitpit cane on the outside. The women sleep in semi-circular rooms at each end of the house and the pigs sleep in stalls along one wall. The sitting and cooking area is in the centre.

Long Houses Long houses, known as *haus lains*, are built along the sides of Mendi ceremonial grounds and used as guesthouses at sing-sings and pig kills. They can be up to 150m long, although 70m is the usual length, and they are built beside stone-filled pits where the pigs are cooked.

Warfare Land ownership is highly complex and very important – disputes over land are often at the root of conflicts. In general, people inherit land rights, not just from their parents, but from any known ancestor. All the descendants of a woman who planted a tree might have rights to its fruit; people will probably have rights to a number of widely scattered pieces of land.

Fighting arrows are carved from black-palm and are traditionally tipped with human bone. The tips were made from the forearm of a male ancestor so that his spirit could 'guide' the arrow to an enemy. Although casualties are fairly rare in traditional warfare, the men are fine bowmen and can shoot over long distances. They also carry bone daggers carved from the leg bone of a cassowary. Fights are still quite common.

Face Decoration Imbong'gu girls from the Ialibu area paint their faces red and their lips white for sing-sings. Their heads are crowned with a great range of bird feathers, including several raggiana bird of paradise feathers. The wigmen wear their wigs and blacken their faces with soot, whiten their beards and eyes and colour their lips and noses red.

MENDI
• *pop 6400* • *postcode 251*

Despite being the capital of the Southern Highlands, Mendi is a relatively small town, built around an airport. It shelters in a long green valley, surrounded by beautiful limestone peaks. Although it can supply all essentials, there is not much to keep you hanging around. It's really just the starting point for a trip to the Tari Basin or Lake Kutubu.

Friday and Saturday, when tribespeople crowd into town, are the best times to visit Mendi, although it can be rough on pay weeks.

The big oil project near Lake Kutubu is changing the face of the Mendi area. Oil began flowing through the pipeline down to the Gulf of Papua in 1992. The Chevron company is fulfilling its agreements with the local landowners, the Foi and Fasu people, which include building a road from Mendi to Pimaga and on to Moro, the company headquarters near the north-west end of Lake Kutubu. The Moro airstrip is now frequently serviced by flights from Mt Hagen and Port Moresby.

Information
Mendi has Westpac and PNGBC banks, a

handful of shops, supermarkets and kai-bars, a post office, a hotel and, being a provincial capital, a lot of government offices where it's difficult to find anyone at their desks.

There's an artefacts shop near Mendi Motors that sells hand-loomed products, baskets and weapons. It's not cheap, but the wares are of reasonable quality. A much better shop is in a village on the Mt Hagen Road, about an hour from Mendi. Mendi dolls make a good buy, although they are now rarely in the traditional designs, which had religious significance.

From the town centre there's a shortcut down to the market and the main road on a steep dirt path but it's slippery and almost impossible to walk with a pack after rain.

Places to Stay & Eat

The *Pentecostal Guesthouse* (☎ 549 1174; PO Box 15) is in town, not far from the airport. There are only a few rooms and church workers have priority, so it's sometimes full. The rooms are small but clean enough and there are cooking facilities and hot showers. It also has plenty of cockroaches in the bedrooms! It costs K10 for a bunk bed or K20 for a room to yourself (if available).

The United Church Women's Fellowship has the *UCWF Guesthouse* (☎ 549 1062; PO Box 35). It is a 20-minute walk from town and costs K15 in a shared room or K25 per person in a twin room with attached bathroom, which is a little steep for what you get. To get there, walk out onto Old Mt Hagen Road past Mendi Motors, take the left fork after the bridge, pass the turn-off to the large Menduli Trade Store and it's further up the hill on your right, near the hospital.

Muruk Lodge (☎ 549 1188; PO Box 108) is the revamped version of the old Mendi Hotel. It's comfortable and has a licensed restaurant. A single or double room costs around K95.

A few kilometres south of town, on the Highlands Highway just beyond the turn-off into Mendi, *Kiburu Lodge* (☎ 549 1077; fax 549 1350; PO Box 466, Mendi) costs about the same but is much nicer. Newly reno-

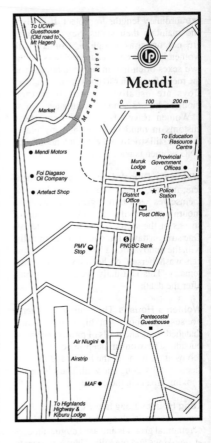

Mendi

vated, it has 12 rooms in quasi-traditional style (they have thatched roofs) and pleasant grounds and views. It is owned by the Kiburu people but is managed by the Global Group. Tours of the area are available, ranging from treks to helicopter flights.

Getting There & Away

Air Note that the Mendi airstrip is often unserviceable, particularly in the mornings, because of fog.

Air Niugini (☎ 549 1233) has daily flights to/from Port Moresby (K168), sometimes direct and sometimes via Wapenamanda (for

Wabag) or Tari. The Mendi-Tari leg costs K61.

MBA (☎ 549 1060) flies to/from Tari (K60) and Tabubil (K110) on Monday, Friday and Saturday; and Moro (K57) and Mt Hagen (around K70) on Wednesday and Saturday.

MAF (☎ 549 1091) and Southwest Airlines (☎ 549 1031) also fly regularly from Mendi.

Moro, a 20-minute flight away, is an hour's walk from the west end of Lake Kutubu. From there you can catch a boat to Tage Point (at the other end of the lake).

Road PMVs run back and forth between Mt Hagen and Mendi with reasonable regularity, taking three hours or so and costing about K8. The road to Tari goes via Nipa and is a spectacular four-hour drive costing K10. The new road to Pimaga and on to Moro should be completed by now and there will presumably be PMVs running this route. The Foi Diagaso Oil Company will have the latest information.

Mendi Motors might have cars to hire.

IALIBU
• *pop 1400* • *postcode 265*
About halfway between Mendi and Mt Hagen, Ialibu is the home of the Imbong'gu people, who also wear wigs. It is a major area for the production of sawn timber, and basket-making is a common village industry. Nearby is Mt Ialibu (3465m). The local people have built a cultural centre and museum made of river stones and local timber in the old style, with exposed posts and beams and woven walls. The museum reportedly has a 12-room guesthouse attached (☎ 540 1628). There are apparently some good walking trails near here.

LAKE KUTUBU
South of Mendi, Lake Kutubu has some of the Highlands' most beautiful scenery. According to legend the lake was formed when a fig tree was cut down by a woman looking for water. The story goes that what-

ever the tree touched turned to water – hence the lake.

The lake is beautiful, and the surrounding country is home to friendly people who still live a largely traditional life – currently changing fast because of the Chevron oil development. Butterflies and birds of paradise are common. You can swim in the lake and visit local villages or just soak up the beauty and peace. If you do visit Lake Kutubu, remember you are a guest of the people and tread carefully – try not to damage this beautiful spot.

The big Lake Kutubu oil project has changed the character of this area somewhat, and local people are used to dealing with (or hearing exaggerated stories about people dealing with) oil workers with fat wallets and expense accounts. Some prices asked to cross bridges or just walk across land can be outrageous, but getting angry won't help.

Walking to Lake Kutubu
If you have the time and inclination, the ideal way to get here would be to walk in from Nipa and fly out from Pimaga. Both methods end up costing much the same. See Lonely Planet's *Bushwalking in Papua New Guinea* for detailed descriptions of these walks, and a couple of alternatives, including walking to the lake from Tari.

From Pimaga From Pimaga you could walk about 22km on a dirt road to the southeastern tip of Lake Kutubu and an attractive village called Gesege (but check in Mendi that the new road hasn't altered this routing). This takes about four hours and a guide isn't necessary. From Gesege, you catch a canoe to the lodge at Tage Point. From Pimaga it might be possible to arrange a walk all the way down to Kikori in Gulf Province.

From Nipa The alternative is a fairly hard three-day walk from Nipa on the Tari-Mendi Road. It's an interesting walk that crosses several large rivers. The start of the trail is at Halhal, about 5km west of Nipa and accessible by PMV along the Highlands Highway.

The sections between Ungubi and Yalanda

involve some steep ascents and descents on rocky paths and it's hard going. A traveller describes the trail as 'wet, steep, slippery, leechy, snakey and isolated – absolutely fantastic but hugely tough'. You'll need a guide for these sections and possibly another from Yalanda to Tage Point.

KANTOBO

Kantobo village is on the banks of the Mubi River, near the eastern end of Lake Kutubu. It is home to the Muti clan of the Foimeana people. This is virgin rainforest, rich in bird and animal life. A 700 hectare Wildlife Management Area has been created with the help of the World Wildlife Fund around the nearby Wasi Falls. This is the local name for a series of waterfalls which includes the Bisi Falls, the largest in PNG, which plummet over 100m into a limestone basin. Also in the management area are the Maskimu Falls and Geagosusu Falls. There are many caves in this area, including some which were used for ancient burials, and some with a unique blind cave fish.

Places to Stay & Eat

Wasi Falls Lodge (PO Box 16, Moro) is a village-based tourist venture offering six traditional houses for accommodation. Situated in the wildlife management area, a little to the east of Kantobo, the houses come with electricity, gas stoves and fridges; meals can be provided. The lodge has a powered dinghy and canoes; the staff can organise tours to the falls and bird-watching or animal-watching expeditions. Ask for Richard Budu; the cost is K25 per person, including bedding, mosquito nets, and boat transfers to the lodge. There is also a one-off K10 entrance fee for the management area. Bookings can be made by writing direct or through the Tourism Promotion Authority (TPA; ☎ 320 0198; PO Box 1291, Port Moresby).

Getting There & Away

MBA flies to Moro from Tari (K61) or Port Moresby (K168). The Kantobo villagers can pick you up and drive you direct from Moro to Kantobo by 4WD for K92 (this is for a single person, sliding to K27 each for five or more people) – if you let them know you are coming. This is a spectacular two-hour trip over limestone roads around the southern side of the lake. From Kantobo it is another 25 minutes to the Wasi Falls Lodge.

MAF and Southwest Air can organise charters direct to Kantobo from Mendi; MAF can fly from Mt Hagen to Kantobo.

TARI

• *pop 900* • *postcode 255*

Tari is the main town for the Huli wigmen and the centre for the beautiful Tari Basin. The main attractions are the people and the surrounding countryside. The town really is just the airfield plus a handful of buildings. There is a post office, a few large but basic stores and a hospital; there used to be a PNGBC bank but it closed down because it got robbed by rascals too often.

The Tari area went through a boom with the Mt Kare alluvial goldrush in the late 1980s, but the main winners were SP Brewing, helicopter companies, Toyota dealerships and the top hotels in Port Moresby. About the only grassroots to benefit were prostitutes. Things have since quietened down but a big mine is being established by Australia's CRA and there are still plenty of individual miners hoping to strike it rich.

There's a tiny museum in a stockaded compound and most of the items in the small display are for sale. The place is a sort of old men's home and a couple of nice old guys will show you around and accept your donation. The covered structure in the compound is the grave of a former provincial premier, and you'll see similar (but usually smaller) structures all around the Tari area – people live under thatch but, when they die, they get corrugated iron to keep the rain off.

Saturday is the main market day but there are smaller markets between Wednesday and Saturday.

Places to Stay & Eat

Despite the small size of the town, the Tari area boasts some good places to stay.

The *Tari Women's Guesthouse* (try ☎ 540 8030, but it may not be operational) comes highly recommended. It looks rather like a store from the street but the guesthouse is in a building at the back. A bed in one of the small bunkrooms costs K20. There's a kitchen. As is usual at women's guesthouses, you might meet some articulate and politically aware women. Men can stay too.

The kai-bar at J & S Traders is better than the one at the supermarket and sells good chips. The Huli Bakery, next to the market, sells buns, tea and coffee.

In Hedemari, midway between Tari and Koroba, is the bush-material *Lakwanda Lodge* (PO Box 103, Tari), where you can stay for around K25 a night. A PMV from Tari costs K2 for the 40-minute ride. You may want to provide your own bedsheets here, and you'd be wise to bring some of your own food. There are good walks in the area and the guesthouse can provide a guide for about K10 a day and accommodation in other villages for K5. Nearby Ulirima village has been recommended. There's also the possibility of rafting on nearby Tagari River. The Thursday markets at Mari, near Hedemari, are worth experiencing. This is an interesting area, well worth visiting for the scenery and the culture.

Ambua Lodge is an upmarket place reminiscent of some of the famous game park lodges in Africa. It is about 45 minutes out of Tari by road and operated by Trans Niugini Tours. At 2100m, the lodge has a superb view of the land of the Huli, as well as a refreshing mountain climate. It attracts many bird-watchers and orchid enthusiasts. There are some pleasant walks that have been put in through the forest to a couple of nearby waterfalls, and the lodge can provide guides; Joseph Tano has been recommended. The lounge-bar is the kind of place where you could relax for hours, just watching the clouds roll by. There's even an outdoor spa.

Guests are accommodated in individual, luxury, bush-material huts. The huts have a great 180° view and are surrounded by flower gardens with a backdrop of mossy forest. It is a little incongruous to find such opulence in such rugged circumstances, but it's certainly impressive.

Needless to say, it isn't cheap. Most guests come on a package deal, but casual accommodation can be had for around K190 a night. Day tours to the surrounding countryside are available. They used to have a backpackers hostel as well, but unfortunately this building is now used to house security personnel. Bookings can be made through Trans Niugini Tours (☎ 542 1438; fax 542 2470; PO Box 371, Mt Hagen).

The lodge is off the main Tari-Mendi Road, and occasional PMVs run past. The lodge will meet your aircraft if you let them know.

Getting There & Away

Air Air Niugini flies from Port Moresby to Tari on Monday, Wednesday, Friday and Sunday via Mendi for K189. The Mendi-Tari leg costs K61 but note that you cannot fly the reverse route with Air Niugini.

MBA flies to/from Mendi (K60) and Tabubil (K103) on Monday, Friday and Saturday. On Tuesday and Thursday, it flies to Porgera (K37), Mt Hagen (K97) and return, then on to Moro (K61). On Wednesday, it

Tari

flies to Moro, Tari, Porgera and return. (The Porgera airstrip is not always open because of land disputes.)

MAF (☎ 540 8014) and Southwest Airlines also fly regularly out of Mendi. At the MAF terminal, there is a board showing 'true' flights – so check it out for changes to timetables and fares.

PMV PMVs can take a while to collect enough passengers to leave Tari but it's best to get to the market early in the morning if you're heading in the Mendi direction. PMVs to Mendi cost K10 and take four hours. PMVs also run from Tari to Koroba for around K4. Beyond this, most transportation is by plane or foot, although the roads have been pushed through to Lake Kopiago. There are actually two roads from Koroba to

Kopiago, both likely to close after rain and traffic is light. People from Kopiago sometimes come to the Tari market, so see if you can get a lift back.

KOPIAGO TO OKSAPMIN

From Lake Kopiago, you can walk to Oksapmin in West Sepik Province in four or five days. There's a mission guesthouse about 3km from Kopiago and a more basic council guesthouse in town.

Kopiago to Oksapmin is a hard and potentially dangerous walk, so don't undertake it unless you are pretty fit. See Lonely Planet's *Bushwalking in Papua New Guinea* for more details. If you are really keen, you can continue walking to Tekin, Bak, Bimin and down to Olsobip in Western Province, or to Telefomin.

The Sepik

Land Area 79,100 sq km
Population 425,000

The Sepik is one of the great rivers of the world and to travel on its broad waters is to experience the heart and soul of this amazing country. It has the same relevance to Papua New Guinea as the Congo to Africa and the Amazon to South America. This chapter first looks at the two provinces through which the river flows and later, the river, its tributaries and riverside towns and villages.

History

Very little archaeological evidence has been found to shed light on the early history of the Sepik. Because most people lived along shifting rivers or the coastal plains (which have flooded since the last Ice age), it is unlikely that much evidence will come to light. The population, as in other parts of PNG, was fragmented into different language groups and clans; violence between these groups is believed to have been commonplace. Today, most of these languages are spoken by fewer than 2000 people. The main Sepik language group is Ndu, including its sub-groups Abelam, spoken mostly around Maprik, and Passam, which is found mainly around Wewak.

The Sepik's first contact with the outside world was likely to have been with Malay bird-of-paradise hunters; the feathers from these beautiful birds were popular long before European ladies of society had their fling with them during the last century. The first European contact came in 1885, with the arrival of the Germans and the German New Guinea Company. Dr Otto Finsch named the river the Kaiserin Augusta, after the wife of the German emperor. Dr Finsch, after whom the Germans' first station – Finschhafen – was named, rowed about 50km upstream from the mouth.

During 1886 and 1887, further expeditions by steam boat travelled 600km upriver.

HIGHLIGHTS

- Cruising down the Sepik River, watching the bird-life and crocodiles
- Experiencing the lifestyle and culture of village communities
- Examining the architecture of *haus tambarans* and stilt villages
- Uncovering relics of the battles fought near Wewak towards the end of WWII
- Appreciating the distinctive trellises, rituals and festivals of the yam cult
- Swimming in the rock pools and long, secluded beaches between Vanimo and the Indonesian border

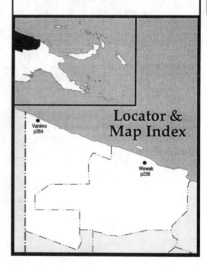

Locator & Map Index

Vanimo
p264

Wewak
p256

These early expeditions were soon followed by more mercenary explorers, traders, labour recruiters and missionaries.

The Germans established a station at Aitape on the coast in 1906 and between 1912 and 1913 sent a huge scientific expedition to explore the river and its vast, low-lying basin. They collected insects, studied the local tribes and produced maps of such

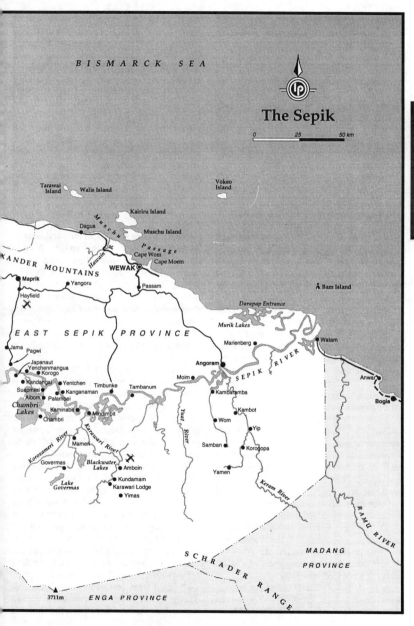

THE SEPIK

accuracy that they are still referred to today. Angoram, the major station in the lower Sepik, was also established at this time but WWI put a stop to activity for some time.

In 1924 Ambunti was the base for a German exploratory expedition to discover the economic potential of the area; it was further developed in the 1920s by the Australian administration. The early 1930s brought a small flurry of goldrushes in the hills behind Wewak and around Maprik, but development and exploration ceased with the explosive arrival of WWII.

The Japanese held the Sepik region for most of the war but the struggle for control was bitter and prolonged. As Australian forces pushed along the coast from Lae and Madang, the Japanese steadily withdrew to the west. In early 1944 the Americans seized Aitape and an Australian division began to move west from there. When a huge American force captured Hollandia (now Jayapura in Irian Jaya) in April 1944, the Japanese 8th Army was completely isolated.

The enormous number of rivers and extensive coastal swamps made for a drawn-out struggle along the coast. It was over a year later, in May 1945, before Wewak fell and the remaining Japanese troops withdrew into the hills behind the coast. Finally, with the war in its last days, General Adachi surrendered near Yangoru; he was so weak he had to be carried on a chair. The formal surrender took place a few days later on 13 September 1945 at Wom Point near Wewak. Of 100,000 Japanese troops, only 13,000 survived.

Since the war, government control has been re-established and extended further upriver, although the uppermost limits of the Sepik are still among the most unchanged and isolated parts of the country. It has been a volatile area since the Indonesian takeover of Dutch New Guinea (now Irian Jaya), although the location of the border was jointly mapped and marked in 1968. On several occasions large numbers of Papuan refugees have fled into PNG.

In 1984, more than 100 Indonesian soldiers deserted to the OPM (*Organisasi Papua Merdeka*, or Free West Papua Movement), sparking a major Indonesian operation which in turn drove over 10,000 Papuans into PNG. Refugees remain a political football. Only a small number have shown any interest in returning to Irian Jaya, so the PNG government has belatedly decided to settle them permanently. Unfortunately for the refugees, PNG doesn't have the necessary funds and Australia has refused to help. In the meantime, the refugees continue to live in extremely basic conditions in camps close to the border: Blackwater, near Vanimo, and Green River, near the Sepik River, are two of the largest camps.

Geography

The Sepik River is 1126km long and is navigable for almost its entire distance. It starts up in the central mountains, close to the source of PNG's other major river, the Fly, which flows south. The Sepik flows in a loop, first west across the Irian Jayan border, then north, before returning east across the border. It then runs through two PNG provinces: Sandaun (West Sepik), with its capital at Vanimo, and East Sepik, with its capital at Wewak.

At its exit from Irian Jaya, the Sepik is only 85m above sea level and from there it winds gradually down to the sea – a huge, brown, slowly coiling serpent. It has often changed its course, leaving dead-ends, lagoons, ox-bow lakes or huge swampy expanses that turn into lakes or dry up to become grasslands in the dry season.

As an indication of its age and changing course, the river has no stones or rocks within about 50km of its banks. Villages often have 'sacred stones' that have been carried in from far away and placed in front of the village *haus tambaran* (spirit house).

The inexorable force of the river often tears great chunks of mud and vegetation out of the river banks and, at times, these drift off downstream as floating islands – often with small trees and even animals aboard. There is no delta and the river stains the sea brown for 50km or more from the shore. It is said that islanders off the coast can draw fresh water straight from the sea.

For much of its length, the Sepik is bordered by huge expanses of swamp or wild sugar cane known as *pitpit*. There are hills further inland and eventually the Sepik climbs into wild mountain country near its source. Between the river and the coastal plain the Bewani and Torricelli mountains rise to over 1000m. There are no natural harbours on the Sepik region's coastline.

Climate

June to October is the driest time in most of the Sepik, but microclimates vary significantly, depending on topography and prevailing winds. Average annual rainfalls lie between 2000mm and 2600mm; you can expect drenching rain at any time on the river.

Arts

Traditional art was closely linked to spiritual beliefs. Sepik carvings were usually an attempt to make a spirit visible and concrete, although decorations were also applied to practical, everyday items, like pots and paddles.

Carving is rarely purely traditional – it is now more likely to be a mixture of traditional motifs, the individual's imagination and commercial good sense. Originally each village had its own distinctive style but a 'Sepik' style is now emerging, particularly in the more tourist-oriented villages.

Carving has become a vital part of the river's economy, and without it some villages would probably cease to exist. In some, it is the only significant source of cash. Coffee is grown in the Maprik region, but on the river there are no cash crops, no paid employment and rarely any agricultural surplus.

If a group arrives in a village with things to sell, a marketplace will materialise instantly. Considering the amount of labour and skill that goes into a carving, prices are very low. Depending on the size and quality of the piece, prices vary – you can buy hooks and carvings for as little as K5, and a mask can cost from K7 to more than K40.

THE SEPIK

Salvinia & Water Hyacinth

The water weed *Salvinia molesta* once threatened ecological disaster for the Sepik River system. Salvinia originated in Brazil, has small, fleshy fan-like leaves and can double in size in two days. You will see small chunks of it floating down the river and anybody who has spent time on the river will be able to point it out to you.

When it was introduced to the Sepik it went wild. In the early 1980s it covered 60% of the Lower and Middle Sepik's lakes, lagoons and barets, often forming a mat too thick for canoes to penetrate, isolating villages and preventing fishing. Herbicides were clearly inappropriate, and it grew much faster than it could be cut. It could well have forced the depopulation of the region, but it is now, fortunately, under control.

The solution was to introduce a weevil, *Cyrtobagus singularis*. The adult feeds on Salvinia buds and the larvae burrow through the plant which dies, becomes water-logged and sinks. Wide distribution of the weevil began in 1983. The results were dramatic and within months Cyrtobagus was winning the war – and it still holds the upper hand today.

The other major environmental problem on the Sepik is the ever-expanding water hyacinth, or *Eichorniae crassipes*. This attractive water plant is, in reality, one of the world's worst aquatic weeds; on the Sepik, it blocks water transport, turns clean water stagnant and provides breeding places for mosquitos.

A major project is trying to control the water hyacinth using sustainable and environmentally sound methods. Since 1993 three insects which will kill the water hyacinth, but not other plants, have been released. Over 180,000 water hyacinth weevils, *Neochetina eichorniae*, were released at various locations in PNG; two other insects, a moth called *Acigona infusella* and bug called *Eccritotarsus catarinensis* are also being tested.

It is hoped that such biological controls will limit the spread of these introduced species and the environmental integrity of the Sepik system will be maintained. ■

Bargaining in the Asian sense is unknown; it is considered rude and could be dangerous. The people are proud and it is not wise to denigrate someone's carvings. You can, however, always just walk away wistfully and show interest using body language (such as a longing backwards glance) to try to get a cheap price. Tact and diplomacy are ever necessary and a smile and a kind word often work wonders.

As you will soon discover, if you are a keen collector, you can very quickly end up with a lot of very heavy *diwai* (wood). Bear in mind that the airlines have baggage limits and, particularly in the case of light aeroplanes, there simply may not be room for a 3m statue. Air Niugini, however, has special freight rates for flying artefacts from Wewak to Port Moresby. See the Customs section in the Facts for the Visitor chapter.

Sea mail is the cheapest way to get a lot of wood home but will take at least three months and possibly much longer. Also, you can't mail (sea or air) anything longer than 1m. Air mail is very expensive. The other alternative is to have the item shipped home through a cargo agent. This isn't all that cheap as the smallest space you can buy is a cubic metre and you will have to make packing crates. There is also a great deal of paperwork, as carvings which are shipped (as opposed to mailed) need export clearance from the National Museum & Art Gallery in Port Moresby.

Getting There & Away
The standard way to get to the Sepik is to fly to Wewak from Mt Hagen, Madang or Jayapura (Indonesia) via Vanimo. There is now an Indonesian Consulate in Vanimo and a PNG Consulate in Jayapura, both of which issue visas. Second and third-level carriers have created an extensive network of air routes around the Sepik provinces.

Wewak is the most westerly port for the north-coast shipping routes and provides an important jumping-off point for those wanting to 'coast hop'. The *Melanesian Discoverer*, a luxury cruise ship operated by Melanesian Tourist Services (☎ 852 2766; fax 852 3543; PO Box 707, Madang), sails regularly from Madang up the Sepik, and Trans Niugini Tours (☎ 542 1438; fax 542 2470; PO Box 371, Mt Hagen) has a similar but smaller boat, the *Sepik Spirit*, which runs from its Karawari Lodge in Amboin. As you would expect, these cruises are not cheap, but if you have limited time and like a reasonable degree of comfort, they could be a worthwhile option.

There are, of course, no road links with the other provinces and the roads within the Sepik provinces are limited. But where there is a road there will be PMVs. The cross-border road between Vanimo and Jayapura was recently completed.

See the relevant sections in this chapter for more detailed information.

East Sepik Province

Land Area 42,800 sq km
Population 265,000
Capital Wewak

East Sepik Province is much more developed than Sandaun Province and includes the most-visited and heavily populated sections of the Sepik, as well as several large tributaries. Wewak, the provincial capital, is a thriving, important commercial centre, separated from the Sepik Basin by the Prince Alexander Range.

WEWAK
• *pop 25,000* • *postcode 531*
Wewak is an attractive town where you can happily spend a day or two in transit to the Sepik or Irian Jaya. Apart from good shopping and some reasonable accommodation options, there's an attraction that is rare for PNG coastal cities – golden sand, backed by swaying palm trees, right next door to town. Beautiful beaches stretch all along the coast.

Wewak is built at the foot of a high headland that overlooks the coast and nearby islands of Kairiru and Muschu. The hills behind the town climb steeply, so you don't have to travel far to enjoy a good view.

All the major banks and airlines are represented in Wewak. This is the spot to stock up with cash and food for a Sepik expedition. If you're going on to Irian Jaya and want some Indonesian currency, it's better to wait until you get to Jayapura.

Orientation

The headland overlooking Wewak is a largely residential area, and has some nice colonial-style homes which are getting a little rundown now; the New Wewak Hotel and the Seaview Motel are up here. The main commercial area is at the bottom of the hill behind the beach. The rest of town stretches eastward towards the airport, about 8km away. Like a number of other PNG towns, Wewak is irritatingly spread out; fortunately, there's an excellent bus system around town and a PMV system for longer distances.

The intersection of Boram Rd with the road leading down to the main wharves and the provincial government offices is referred to as 'Caltex', despite the service station on the corner now being of the Shell persuasion.

Wewak doesn't have a particularly well-sheltered harbour. There's a small wharf for local fishing boats and canoes right by the town centre, and a longer one for larger ships to the east of the Windjammer Hotel, along the bay formed by Wewak Point and Cape Boram; the main coastal road does a loop around it.

Information

The East Sepik Tourist Board (☎ 856 2005; fax 856 2677; PO Box 1074) in the Department of East Sepik may be able to provide limited advice. But it may be better to speak to people more directly involved in the tourism industry.

Ralf Stüttgen (see the Places to Stay section) has lived in PNG for 30 years and is an excellent source of information about the Sepik. But unless you stay at his place (and anyone planning a trip on the Sepik should), at least offer to pay for his time; people treat him as a sort of amateur consultant on everything from buying masks to establishing fish farms and that doesn't pay the bills.

Alois Mateus (fax 856 2525; PO Box 248), manager of the Ambunti Lodge, lives in Wewak not far from the SIL Guesthouse and is very knowledgeable about the Sepik, as is Joe Kenni (☎ & fax 858 3039; PO Box 35, Angoram), the owner of the Angoram Hotel. Both can help you organise your trip. Stephen Buku is an excellent guide and is now working for the Windjammer Hotel (but is still keen to work as a guide). He is amiable and knowledgeable and will answer any questions you may have if you encounter him at the hotel.

Telephones There are only three places for public telephones: at the post office, the hospital and the airport. All are coin-operated; there are no phonecard facilities. There is usually a queue at the post office telephones but local shopkeepers might assist – particularly Air Niugini. There is only one public phone at the airport and it is often broken or full of coins. The Air Niugini staff here are also very helpful and will let you use their phone.

Things to See & Do

Near the main wharf, the rusting remains of the MV *Busama* are rotting away in the sand. Further down at Kreer, on the road to the airport, there's a market and the wooden hulk of a Taiwanese fishing junk seized a few years ago for infringing PNG's coastal fishing limits. On the beach between Kreer Market and the hospital are some rusting Japanese landing barges which are rapidly disappearing. The **Japanese War Memorial** marks the mass grave of many troops; the soldier's bodies were later exhumed and returned to Japan.

Near the Windjammer Hotel, there's another Japan-PNG **peace park** with a memorial and fish pond. The nearest Pidgin gets to the concept of peace is *gutpela taim*, or good times. Peace sounds like the Pidgin *pis*, which means fish. So the locals usually refer to the park as the *pis park*, which is perhaps appropriate given the contents of the

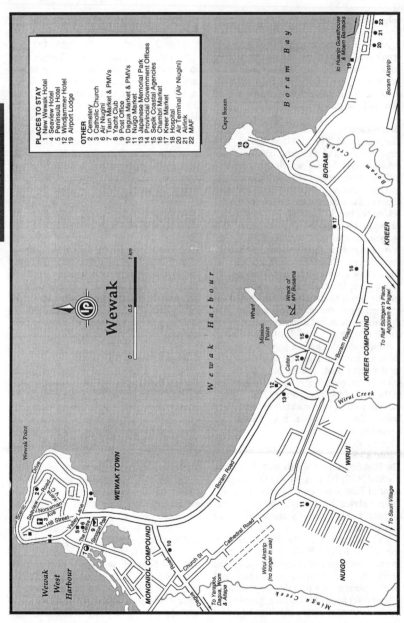

Wewak

0 0.5 1 km

PLACES TO STAY
1 New Wewak Hotel
4 Seaview Hotel
5 Peninsula Hotel
12 Windjammer Hotel
19 Airport Lodge

OTHER
2 Cemetery
3 Catholic Church
6 Air Niugini
7 Taun Market & PMVs
8 Yacht Club
9 Post Office
10 Dagua Market & PMVs
11 Nuigo Market
13 Japanese Memorial Park
14 Provincial Government Offices
15 Sepik Coastal Agencies
16 Chambri Market
17 Kreer Market
18 Hospital
20 Air Terminal (Air Niugini)
21 Airlink
22 MAF

Boram Bay

to Huarjo Guesthouse & Moem Barracks

Boram Airstrip

Cape Boram

BORAM Creek

KREER

Wewak Harbour

Wreck of MV Busama

Wharf

Mission Point

Caltex

Wirui Creek

Boram Road

KREER COMPOUND

To Raf Stüttgen's Place, Angoram & Pagwi

To Sauri Village

Wewak Point

Scenic Drive

Seaview Road

Norseman Ave

Hill Street

Valley Lane

The Cliffs

Boram Road

WEWAK TOWN

Wewak West Harbour

MONGNIOL COMPOUND

Church St

Cathedral Road

Wirui Airstrip (no longer in use)

To Yangoru, Dagua, Wom & Atape

WIRUI

NUIGO

Minga Creek

THE SEPIK

Top left: Goroka Market, Eastern Highlands
Middle: Renbo Stoa, Goroka, Eastern Highlands
Top Right: A woman displaying her flower headdress at Daulo Pass, Eastern Highlands
Bottom: Woman at Mando, Eastern Highlands

ADRIAN LIPSCOMB

LIZ THOMPSON

YVON PERUSSE

Top Left: Pandanus species can be found from the coast to sub-alpine areas. Its many uses range from a building and weaving material to a food.
Top Right: An East Sepik child with a coconut
Bottom: Strickland Gorge, Sandaun Province

pond. Curiously, the park is now enclosed by a wire fence.

Wewak's most vivid legacy of the bitter fighting in WWII is the **bomb craters** that pockmark the area. They are still visible around the Boram airport runway and the now disused Wirui airstrip (closer to town).

As in other places in PNG, there are many bits and pieces from the war scattered around Wewak. These include unexploded bombs; every now and then, someone burning the bush to make a garden sets one off. The replacement of Wewak's water mains took longer than expected, as the excavators kept encountering bombs. Infantry equipment, mainly Japanese, is a fairly common find.

There are five **markets**, in descending order of importance: Taun (at the end of the main street), Dagua (good for PMVs, not far from town), Kreer (on the airport road, just before it turns inland), Nuigo (not very interesting) and Chambri (really just an artefact stall on Boram Rd).

The view from the hills behind the town is superb. Those staying at Ralf Stüttgen's guesthouse don't have to go any further than their bedroom window to see it, but if you are staying in town, it's worth the trip. The deep, jungled valleys up here are reserved for hunting by the nearby villages, so while they are good for walks you should always ask permission first. Ralf can organise someone from the local village to go with you for a couple of kina.

Here and elsewhere around PNG you'll notice large nets spread across clearings on ridge-tops. Flying foxes (bats) fly through these gaps (because the clearings seem to be the lowest point to cross the ridge), into the net, become entangled and end up in the cooking pot. They are considered quite a delicacy, reportedly tasting like chicken.

There's decent **snorkelling** along the outer edge of the reef in the harbour. Much of the Sepik coastline is unprotected, so in season, from September to January, there can be small, occasionally surfable, waves to the east towards Turubu. Dabiar Beach at Forok village has been recommended.

There is an 18-hole **golf course** to the east

of town (beyond the airport) with a pleasant club house.

Places to Stay – bottom end

Ralf Stüttgen's Place (☎ 856 2395; PO Box 154) is situated in the hills behind Wewak. It is very basic and rather chaotic but is where most people planning a Sepik trip stay. His house is overflowing with dogs (which growl a lot but rarely bite), storage boxes, carvings, books and other odds and ends. Japanese helmets, rusty rifles, bayonets and other WWII memorabilia are scattered about, and outside are a couple of old car bodies and the remains of two Japanese machine guns pointing dramatically towards the oncoming traffic on the road below. In the middle of all this, he provides shoestring accommodation in two rooms, which, at a pinch, can accommodate 10 people, but there are rarely more than four guests at any given time.

Ralf's place is more like a mountaineering hut than a youth hostel – there is a 'deep-drop' toilet outside, no hot running water and the beds are basic bunks with thin mattresses. Even the telephone is a grudging concession to modernity – it receives incoming calls, but you can't ring out. But it is a homely, friendly place and only costs K15 per night. He will share his food with guests for a small charge and there's also an endless supply of coffee. Ralf's place has become an institution in PNG – it's a great place to meet all sorts of weird and wonderful people and get up-to-date information on the river. Ralf knows the Sepik well; if you can pin him down for a conversation, he has a wealth of anecdotes and facts. There are also some excellent travellers' notebooks which give useful insights into the experience of travelling on the Sepik and elsewhere in PNG.

Ralf's place is on a ridge overlooking the coast, just below a radio mast, hence the name of the area – Tower. Travel 15km inland from Wewak on the main road to Angoram and the Sepik and it's on the right-hand side of the road. Or take a No 14, 16 or 19 bus to Kreer Heights for K0.40, then hitch or take a rural PMV to Tower for K0.70.

THE SEPIK

Ralf Stüttgen

Ralf Stüttgen's experiences as a missionary, and colonial and post-colonial resident of PNG are, in many ways, typical of his era. His attitudes have been formed by an awareness and perception rare among expatriates.

Born in Berlin in 1939, he suffered the rigours of the war years and later experienced the divided city as a schoolboy. While at a Jesuit high school, he decided to become a missionary. Nevertheless, he shied away from joining the Jesuits because he felt he didn't have the required 'energy levels' – the result of a childhood battle with tuberculosis. He joined the Divine Word Missionaries and was based for seven years near Bonn as a seminarian. He was ordained in 1967.

In the same year he caught a migrant ship, the *Angelino Lauro*, to Sydney, where he trained for a further six months before continuing on to PNG in 1968. At this time he started to have doubts about the highly conservative values emanating from the Vatican and realised that he might have problems abiding with some of its dictates. However, he undertook missionary work on the Sepik until 1972, when he decided that his deep and irreconcilable philosophical differences were too great a burden.

ADRIAN LIPSCOMB

Ralf Stüttgen

He left the priesthood, and in 1973 married Theresa, from Kanduanum village on the Upper Sepik. Ralf then worked for the Department of Agriculture, and was based in various places around PNG. In due course, however, he moved back to the Sepik area and bought his present house near Wewak in 1980. In the same year, he was naturalised as a PNG citizen. Theresa and Ralf had a son, Ludwig (who now lives in Brisbane, Australia), and another child came a few years later, but Theresa passed away during the birth.

In January 1981 while accommodating some friends in his house, Ralf realised that there were many backpackers and shoestring travellers seeking accommodation and travel information in PNG – a niche he could fill. He established a guesthouse as the Wewak base for travellers intending to visit the Sepik. His small business thrived and is now widely known as *the* place for shoestring travellers to stay in Wewak. ∎

Although it is a long way out, it also means there are great views and at a 400m elevation it is markedly cooler than in town (you may need a sleeping bag) – low clouds often blanket the area at night. It's too far from town to walk but there's plenty of traffic and Ralf will pick you up or deliver you to the airport in his battered utility if you give him fair warning. It is a good spot to start your Sepik trip because all the PMVs go right past. This means you don't have to hang around the markets, and you can sit under the shady tree at the bottom of Ralf's driveway and enjoy the view while you wait.

A little more comfortable than Ralf's place, but just as difficult to get to, is the *Huanjo Guesthouse* (☎ & fax 856 2455; PO Box 503). It is still on the coastal plateau but out to the east of the airport and prison. Tony

Bias runs the place – he is an aspiring politician and an interesting guy to talk to. The guesthouse has seven rooms and 20 beds; rooms have fans and the shared bathrooms seem quite clean. Bed and breakfast costs K35. European-style dinner is available for K10. There is a pick up and delivery service to the airport. A bungalow and some self-contained units, which will be a little more expensive, are being built.

Places to Stay – middle

The *SIL Guesthouse* (☎ 856 2176/2416; PO Box 291), in Kreer Heights, is clean, secure and comfortable, as these places are in many PNG towns. It is, however, occasionally full, and SIL missionaries and workers have priority; if you make a booking two weeks ahead, they will reserve accommodation for you. They have seven comfortable, fully furnished two or three-bedroom flats with kitchens, bathrooms and satellite TV. They charge K50 for the first person, K20 per additional adult and K10 for children – so if there is a group of you, this is an ideal accommodation solution. To get there, take bus No 13, 16, or 19 to Kreer Heights and then ask. The bus driver may be accommodating and divert to take you almost to the door.

Places to Stay – top end

The *Windjammer Hotel* (☎ 856 2388; fax 856 2701; PO Box 152) was formerly known as the Sepik International Beach Resort (a name that never caught on). It is halfway between the town and the airport. It's great if you're interested in being right on the beach – it's only a couple of steps into the sea from some of the cheaper rooms – but this can be a distinct disadvantage if there's a surf running and you're trying to sleep. It also means that the rooms are susceptible to burglars who can walk along the beach and into the hotel grounds.

It's worth visiting just to see the carvings incorporated in the interior, including a magnificent crocodile bar. Its fence is actually also a stylised wooden crocodile but you may have difficulty recognising it as such. They have masks for sale and local people gather to sell their trinkets every afternoon.

There are three classes of rooms, becoming more expensive the further you are from the beach. All can sleep three people, maybe more. C class is pretty ordinary and you share bathroom facilities – a single/double costs K51/63; B class has air-con and private facilities and costs K61/73; A class is their top of the range but is still little better than your average country motel with TV and air-con, and is overpriced at K128/139. As with many hotels in PNG, the telephones in the rooms don't always work. A corporate discount of 20% (but you may have to fight to get it if you are not a regular) and a 10% discount for cash payment are available. There is a direct phone to the hotel at the air terminal.

The *New Wewak Hotel* (☎ 856 2155; PO Box 20), right at the top of the hill overlooking the sea, has 16 singles and 17 twin rooms, some with air-con, some with fans. Singles/doubles/triples are K63/84/104. It's in a great location with a *haus win* (gazebo-like structure) and views out over the water, but it seems to be getting more and more rundown every year; the recent introduction of poker machines has not improved its ambience.

The *Seaview Hotel* (☎ 856 1131; fax 856 2694; PO Box 103) has had several reincarnations. It was a hotel a decade or so ago, then it was turned into a police barracks, but it has recently been nicely renovated into a good hotel again. It is located halfway up Wewak Hill, near the New Wewak Hotel. It has excellent views, a swimming pool, a restaurant and a haus win. It is probably the nicest of the top-end places at K91/100/111 for a single/double/triple.

The *Peninsula Hotel* (☎ 856 2955; fax 856 2694; PO Box 103) is owned by the same people who own the Seaview and, despite a vast difference in quality, its room rates are almost the same. It is located in the middle of the CBD in Valley Lane, on a small rise at the foot of Wewak Hill. The rooms are older and less well maintained and it is noisier and has none of the views or beachfront amenities of the other top-end places. A single/double/triple costs K86/96/103.

The *Airport Lodge* (☎ 856 2373; fax 856 2418; PO Box 852) is a nice new place handily located only 100m from the airport and right on the beachfront. It is well maintained and clean. A single room costs K85 for bed and breakfast and dinner is available for K20. If you are catching an early flight this is the ideal place to stay.

Places to Eat

The eating options in Wewak are mainly hotel restaurants. The *Windjammer* is popular for lunch and dinner (although it sells meals all day) and is a good place for a beer. It also has a reasonably priced snack menu, with scones and coffee for K3 and toasted sandwiches and fries for K3; a main course for dinner costs around K15. The dining room leads directly onto the beach and on a windy day the surf can beat spectacularly against the outside patio. The *Airport Lodge* similarly has a dining room-cum-haus win right on the beachfront and is a pleasant place to have a snack, particularly while waiting for a flight from the airport.

The *Seaview* dining room has a similar menu – its toasted sandwiches are good, cold meat and salad costs K11 and a pepper steak for dinner is K14 – but it doesn't have the sea view that its name suggests. You need to step outside to the poolside to appreciate that. At the *New Wewak Hotel*, breakfast costs K7, lunch K8 and dinner around K15.

You can get some snacks at the *Yacht Club* and on Friday they have good meals from 4 to 7 pm. The *Garamut Supermarket* in the centre of town has an excellent hot bread kitchen, where you can fill up on delicious fresh cakes and soft drink for less than a kina. Other than that there are the usual kai-bars.

Things to Buy

A group of traders sets up a market at the Windjammer after about 4 pm. They sell jewellery and smaller pieces that are fairly commercial, but there is occasionally something interesting. It's worth a look.

At both the Taun Market and the Chambri bus stop you can buy baskets and *bilums* (string bags). Ralf Stüttgen has a good collection of carvings in his house, most of which are for sale at reasonable prices.

Getting There & Away

Air Wewak is a major hub for air transport around the Sepik and has frequent connections to Madang, Vanimo and the Highlands. The Air Niugini office (☎ 856 2433; fax 856 2203; PO Box 61) is in town and Islands Nationair, Airlink (☎ 856 3404) and MAF (☎ 856 2500; fax 856 2198; PO Box 977) are represented at the airport.

Air Niugini has daily flights to Port Moresby via Lae and Madang, and to Port Moresby via Mt Hagen on Monday, Tuesday, Thursday, Friday and Saturday. On Sunday, the international return flight to Jayapura starts at Port Moresby and calls in at Wewak. There is an Air Niugini flight to Manus,

which goes on to Kavieng and Rabaul, every Sunday.

Islands Nationair also flies to Rabaul return on Monday, Wednesday and Friday. Airlink plans to introduce a new service between Wewak, Timbunke and Karawari return, using BN2 eight-seater aircraft each Wednesday.

On Monday and Friday, MBA flies to Tabubil return. The third-level airlines like MAF offer some flights into the Sepik and service most airstrips at least weekly – MAF has bases at Anguganak and Telefomin. Remember these are usually unscheduled and many are charters on which you have to hope for a spare seat. They also fly regularly to Mt Hagen.

One-way fares from Wewak are: Aitape K94, Lae K155, Madang K111, Manus K148, Port Moresby K222, Tabubil K193 and Vanimo K107.

Road There are roads running west along the coast as far as Aitape, through the Torricelli Mountains and into the Sepik Basin, but they are frequently very rough. The roads to Pagwi and Timbunke are real teeth-rattlers and in the wet they must be a nightmare, sometimes impassable. When they are dry, conventional vehicles will survive, but a 4WD is essential after rain. The Aitape Road may also be impassable in very wet weather.

PMVs are quite infrequent, except on major routes such as from Wewak to Angoram and Maprik. Starting very early and being relaxed about arrival times is more important than ever. The PMVs are usually trucks and are often very crowded. Hitching is possible – most private cars act as de facto PMVs anyway – so if you're waiting on the side of the road, wave down anything that comes by (thumbing is unknown). You may well be expected to contribute the equivalent of a PMV fare, but you'll also meet some exceptionally generous people.

As in most PNG towns, the markets are the best places to catch PMVs; in Wewak go to Dagua or Taun markets. If you're going to the Sepik, the road going past Ralf Stüttgen's place is also a good spot to start. Most vehicles leave early, but you can often get PMVs to Angoram and Maprik in the early afternoon.

PMVs have numbers painted on the front and back. The number on the left-hand side refers to the route they are running, in theory, anyway. Always ask. No 1 takes the west coast road to Aitape, No 2 the Angoram Road, No 3 the Maprik-Pagwi Road. The number on the right-hand side gives an indication of how far along that road they run, eg, a No 2-4 will get you all the way to Angoram, a No 2-1 won't. A No 3-8 or higher should run to Pagwi.

Times and fares from Wewak are: Angoram (K8; three hours), Timbunke (about K10; three hours), Maprik (K10; three hours), Pagwi (K14; at least five hours), Aitape (K14; seven hours). These times can stretch a lot after rain.

Avis (☎ 856 2041) is located at the Windjammer and Hertz (☎ 856 2023) is at the Peninsula Hotel. Budget (☎ 856 3442) is at the airport and gives special rates to people with Airlink tickets. Remote-area surcharges may apply if you are going bush, which will make hiring substantially more expensive.

Boat Wewak is the westernmost port of call for Lutheran Shipping's *Mamose Express* and *Rita*, but its somewhat basic cargo freighters continue on to Vanimo from Wewak for K31/39 in deck/cabin class and for half that to Aitape. Boats usually leave weekly. From Wewak to Madang, the fare is K32/48 in deck/cabin class. Sepik Coastal Agencies (☎ 856 2343; fax 856 2796; PO Box 118) handles Lutheran's bookings and will have up-to-date arrival and departure times. Currently, the passenger boats arrive and depart on Saturday. You must buy tickets a few days in advance to ensure passage but they only become available seven days before departure. Their office is not far from the main wharf (coming from the wharf take the first turn on your left) and it's open from 7.30 am to noon and 1.30 to 5 pm on weekdays.

The MV *Thompson* is owned by the Wuvulu-Aua community and does a trading circuit between Wuvulu, Aua, Manus, Wewak and Madang, but there is really no fixed schedule. The fare from Wewak to Wuvulu is K14. For information and bookings see Sam Kewa (PO Box 612), whose office is located behind the kai-bar opposite the Air Niugini office in town.

The *Tawi*, operated by the Manus provincial government, was under repair, but normally plies between Wewak and Lorengau, the outer islands of Manus, Wuvulu Island and Madang. See the Manus chapter for further details.

Boats for Kairiru and Muschu islands leave from the wharf in town opposite the post office; the fare is K5.

Getting Around
Buses run frequently around town and are cheap, which is just as well, because everything is so spread out. They charge K0.40 for anywhere in town. There are major bus stops at all the markets. A few run all the way along Boram Rd but they are more frequent along Cathedral Rd. They run right past the airport – you can see the road and a shelter from the terminal. If you're going to Ralf's, get off at Chambri Market and start walking up the Sepik Road. Try hailing any passing vehicle.

The buses stop at dusk, which can mean you can be stuck at the airport, especially if you come in on the Air Niugini evening flight. The best solution is to let someone know you're coming – all the accommodation places can arrange for someone to pick you up from the airport. There are no taxis in Wewak.

AROUND WEWAK
Cape Moem
There are some good beaches for swimming and diving at Cape Moem, past the airport, but the cape is an army base, so you have to get permission to enter from the commanding officer (☎ 856 2060). Get a bus to Moem Barracks, then walk a kilometre or so along a dirt road to the right. Unless you're a keen diver, it's not really worth the effort.

At Brandi High School, to the east of Cape Moem, there's a collection of Japanese war relics.

THE SEPIK

Cape Wom

Cape Wom, about 14km to the west of Wewak, is the site of a wartime airstrip and where the Japanese surrender took place. There's a war memorial flanked by flag poles on the spot where Japanese Lieutenant General Adachi signed the surrender documents and handed his sword to Australian Major General Robertson on 13 September 1945. On the west side of the cape there's a good reef for snorkelling and a nice stretch of sand for swimming. It is a pleasant place for a picnic and has good views across to the islands.

Cape Wom can have rascal problems, so time your visit for when there are lots of people around, such as on sunny weekends. There's no transport all the way there, so you'll have to hitch; again, this is easiest when lots of people are going there. You could catch a PMV bound for Dagua (a small village further to the west) at Dagua Market and get off at the turn-off to the cape (at a small village known as Suara). From the turn-off it is a hot 3km walk.

The gates are open from 7 am to 6.30 pm; there's a ranger at the gates and you pay a small fee to enter.

The Coastal Islands

Just off the coast of Wewak are the two islands of **Muschu** and **Kairiru**. Kairiru is heavily forested and rises to nearly 800m. Its western end is volcanic and the sea has broken into an active crater at Victoria Bay, where there's good snorkelling, hot springs and waterfalls. At the north-eastern end of the island, there are two big Japanese guns. Kairuru is an untouched place (it is reserved as a hunting ground and there are no inland villages) and a good escape from Wewak.

Places to Stay There are apparently places on the islands where you can stay with local people for a few kina, but take your own food. On Kairiru Island, Joe and Edwick Sareo have been recommended, and St Xavier or St John's schools might have accommodation. On Muschu Island there's

the *Niarpop Guesthouse* run by a man named George, costing about K10 a night, and the *Auong Guesthouse*. There is also the *Keramarau Guesthouse* on Koil Island in the Schouten Group, about 50km from Wewak. For information on these places, contact the tourist board (☎ 856 2005).

Getting There & Away The mission boat *Tau-K* goes between Wewak, Muschu and Kairiru on Tuesday and Thursday or Friday. It arrives in Wewak about 9 am and leaves around 2 pm – don't rely too heavily on these times. The journey takes about two hours and costs K3 to Muschu and K7 to Kairiru. The boat docks at the wharf across the road from the post office. On the beach nearby there are often small boats and canoes. If you can get a lift as a passenger the fare is low, but chartering costs at least K50.

MAPRIK AREA
• *pop 1200* • *postcode 533*

Maprik town itself isn't a great place, but the area, in the Prince Alexander Mountains overlooking the vast Sepik Basin, is very interesting. It is noted for the Abelam people's distinctive haus tambarans, yam cult and carvings and decorations.

The population around Maprik is quite dense and there are many small villages, each with a striking, forward-leaning haus tambaran, a unique architectural style echoed in such modern buildings as Parliament House in Port Moresby. The front facade of the Maprik haus tambarans is brightly painted in browns, ochres, whites and blacks and in some cases they are 30m high. Inside, the carved spirit figures are similarly treated.

Yams are a staple food in this region and also have cultural significance – you will see them growing on their distinctive, cross-like trellis. Harvesting entails considerable ritual and you may see yam festivals or *sing-sings* during the July-August harvest time. The woven fibre masks, the region's most famous artefacts, are used in a ceremony where the yams are decorated to look like human beings, establishing a ritual link between the clans and their crops.

There are some interesting back roads linking villages between Maprik and Lumi, some with spectacular haus tambarans and good carvings; you can walk between villages. Ask permission before entering villages and then see the *bigman* (important man). Ask before taking photos and don't assume you can wander into the haus tambaran at will, especially if you're a woman. Traditionally haus tambarans were exclusively an initiated man's preserve, although these days the rules are sometimes bent for western travellers.

Places to Stay

Maprik The *Maprik Waken Hotel* is still operating but only on request; you must ask for the accommodation section to be opened. The *Waymbange Guesthouse*, with separate huts and shared bathrooms, may still be operating at K20 per person. Reportedly, there is also a *haus meri* (women's house) which charges about K10 and takes men also; ask for Lucy Goro. The Maprik High School may be able to accommodate you if they like you.

Kimbangoa Several travellers have enjoyed staying with Noah Washun in Kimbangoa village, near Maprik, for K6. They say he's friendly, knowledgeable and can show you around the area. He also pans for gold and can show you how.

Getting There & Away

From Wewak, the road climbs up and over the Prince Alexander Mountains, then continues 132km to Maprik. Maprik is actually 8km off the Wewak-Pagwi Road; the junction is called Hayfields, where there is a petrol station, a couple of trade stores and an airfield. A PMV from Wewak to Maprik (or a nearby village) costs K10, Maprik to Pagwi K5, or you can get one direct to Pagwi. The last stretch to Pagwi goes across the Sepik floodplain and is hard going in the wet.

Roads will eventually link Lumi with Aitape. A road already continues from Maprik to Lumi, although missing bridges and deep rivers can make it hazardous. A road link to Ambunti is also planned.

Sandaun Province

Land Area 36,300 sq km
Population 160,000
Capital Vanimo

Sandaun (formerly West Sepik) Province is so named because it's in the north-west of PNG – where the sun goes down. The province is little developed but agricultural activity in the Telefomin district and timber development around Vanimo, the provincial capital, have nonetheless brought rapid change. Gold is also mined in a couple of inland areas.

VANIMO
• *pop 8000* • *postcode 551*
Vanimo is located on a harbour formed around a scenic hill – almost an island – joined to the coastline by a tongue of flat land which has proved ideal for an airstrip. Its topography, with its peninsula and hill, is reminiscent of Wewak. The similarity continues as there are beautiful beaches on both sides. Vanimo, however, is much smaller and quieter, with invariably generous and hospitable people. In Vanimo, everything is within walking distance but when people see you walking they almost always stop and offer a lift. In PNG, smaller is better.

Malaysian logging companies Vanimo Forest Products and WTK are logging the province, to the mild dismay of some locals. Local business leaders aspire to a rapidly growing economy with talk of a relocated and longer international airport (no-one can say when) and the creation of a free trade zone around the town (the likelihood of which is dubious). The town has all the essentials: Westpac and PNGBC banks, a post office, a couple of reasonable supermarkets and several places to stay, one with backpacker accommodation. Since 1992, there has been an Indonesian Consulate in Vanimo.

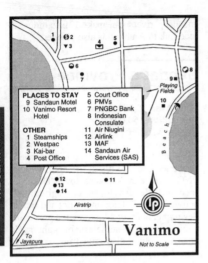

PLACES TO STAY
9 Sandaun Motel
10 Vanimo Resort Hotel

OTHER
1 Steamships
2 Westpac
3 Kai-bar
4 Post Office
5 Court Office
6 PMVs
7 PNGBC Bank
8 Indonesian Consulate
11 Air Niugini
12 Airlink
13 MAF
14 Sandaun Air Services (SAS)

Airstrip

To Jayapura

Vanimo

Not to Scale

Things to See & Do

You can do a pleasant two-hour walk around the headland, but make sure you're protected from the sun and carry some water. You're bound to find some good spots to snorkel. There's another good walk west along the beach from the airport. After about 40 minutes you come to a limestone headland draped with vines; wade around it to the beautiful beach on the other side. There's a rusting Japanese landing barge just offshore.

Narimo Island can be seen offshore from the Vanimo Resort Hotel (originally called the Narimo Hotel). This is an excellent place for picnics and swimming – take some water and a cut lunch. The hotel may be able to provide a boat to take you there (K5 per person return) or else ask about boat hire at West Deco village near the main wharf on the other side of the peninsula. Banana boat hire for a full day should cost between K40 and K50.

Places to Stay & Eat

The *Vanimo Resort Hotel* (☎ 857 1102; fax 857 1131; PO Box 42) is a short walk from the airport and across the road from a spectacular white-sand beach. Despite its location, it more closely resembles a trucking depot than a resort. It is rundown and overpriced and has recently devoted one of its back rooms to poker machines and gambling. The more expensive rooms have telephones, but don't expect them to work. There is a backpacker dorm for K15, budget rooms with shared bathrooms for K50 or rooms with bathrooms and air-con for K70/80. All include breakfast. You may get a cheaper rate if you negotiate – eg if you have an Airlink ticket. There is a restaurant which is meant to serve breakfast, lunch and dinner but never seemed to be open, except at breakfast time.

The *Sandaun Motel* (☎ 857 1000; fax 857 1119; PO Box 35) is significantly better but still little more than a country motel. But the staff are friendly. It's centrally located opposite the Indonesian Consulate and has a nice bar and a restaurant. Rates are from K120/135 for a single/double. The restaurant serves good Indonesian, Chinese and European food at reasonable prices and the beer is cold. A full breakfast costs K8.50 and fish and chips for lunch costs K7.50.

Visser Enterprises (☎ 857 1009; PO Box 201) has a guesthouse on top of the hill for about K75 a single. What this lacks in accessibility (it is a long steep walk), it gains in amenity – there is a great ocean view.

If you are a surfer or if you just want to experience village life in this part of PNG, Lido village (PO Box 31, Vanimo), about 8km out of town heading west, has a great surf beach, and a charming and comfortable *guesthouse* nearby. It is mainly for surfers and the pricing structure reflects a certain discrimination – K30 for surfers, K50 for non-surfers. The staff's definition of 'surfer' is pretty loose. They also hire surfboards and bicycles. This is a very pretty spot and well worth a visit. You may also be able to stay at the *Lote Pastoral Centre*, a nearby Catholic mission station.

In Vanimo, the only places to eat, apart from the two motels, are the kai-bars.

Getting There & Away

Air Air Niugini (☎ 857 1014; fax 857 1473;

PO Box 239), Airlink (☎ 857 1584), MAF (☎ 857 1091; fax 857 1127; PO Box 300) and Sandaun Air Services (☎ 857 1279) all operate from Vanimo.

Air Niugini flies to Wewak and Port Moresby on Tuesday, Friday and Sunday. The Sunday flight commences at Port Moresby and routes through Wewak and Vanimo to Jayapura before returning. If you're leaving PNG, remember to buy a K15 departure tax stamp at the post office. MAF has daily flights to Amanab, Green River, Aitape and Lumi; there are Wednesday and Friday flights to Telefomin, Tabubil and Oksapmin. Airlink flies to Wewak and Madang every day except Wednesday and Sunday, and to Mt Hagen on Monday, Wednesday and Friday.

One-way fares from Vanimo are: Aitape K90, Green River K75, Port Moresby K289, Madang K177, Telefomin K165, Tabubil K175 and Wewak K107.

Boat Lutheran Shipping's somewhat basic cargo freighters continue on to Vanimo from Wewak; one or the other makes the voyage most weeks. In Vanimo, get tickets at the wharf before departure.

To/From Irian Jaya At the time of research, the road from Vanimo to Jayapura was finished, but not yet open, and travel to Indonesia by land was strictly prohibited. The road should have opened by late 1997, however, and there will, no doubt, be a regular cross-border bus service.

Air Niugini has a regular flight to Jayapura every Sunday for K67 (one way). This means that if you want to cross the border for a quick 'look-see' by air, you must stay in Jayapura for a full week unless you return by other means.

The MV *Libby II* does a weekly run between Vanimo and Jayapura for K40 one way. It departs on Fridays at 4 am, arriving in Jayapura at 7.30 am. It caters mainly to Vanimo residents wanting a weekend of shopping in Jayapura. The return trip is on Sunday morning. Book through the Vanimo Resort Hotel.

Immigration & Customs The Indonesian Consulate in Vanimo (☎ 857 1371; fax 857 1373; PO Box 39) can issue a range of different types of visas. They are quite efficient and speedy. A four-week tourist visa costs K20 and can be issued in a day. They require two photographs. If necessary, this visa can be extended in Indonesia for a further two weeks. One reader suggests that 'if you are in a bind and don't want to spend an extra day in Vanimo, call the consulate ahead of time and ask them if it is possible to get the visa while the flight to Jayapura is in Vanimo. A staff member from the consulate is often at the airport, and they are very helpful'. He also advises travellers coming from Indonesia and planning to return to Indonesia to pick up a new visa on first arrival in Vanimo as this will save time and trouble later.

All travellers departing PNG (whether by air, sea or road) are required to pay the K15 departure tax – a tax stamp can be purchased at Vanimo's post office. See the Visas & Documents section in the Facts for the Visitor chapter for more detailed immigration information.

Getting Around
Everything in Vanimo is within walking distance. PMVs to the surrounding district congregate at the market or near the PNGBC bank in town. Apparently it's easy to get out to the border, especially on Fridays. You can probably hitch.

AROUND VANIMO
The coast between Vanimo and the Indonesian border is crammed with superb beaches, waterholes and lagoons, pretty creeks and picturesque villages. There are panoramic views up and down the coast and locals will direct you to several fine waterfalls.

Lido village has a good surf beach and a village guesthouse. **Waramo** village has developed an interesting cultural phenomenon in the form of firewood houses. Outside every house, there are several smaller and well-built houses stacked meticulously with cut firewood. This is regarded as a form of wealth and supplies of firewood are often bestowed on newly married couples. Sometimes there's several years' supply. The houses in these coastal villages are quite intricate and sometimes incorporate split levels with suspended verandahs. You can rent a bicycle at the Lido Guesthouse and cycle to nearby Yako village to see some excellent architecture.

In a small coastal cave near the northern-most border marker (just past Watung), you will find a curious sight: two piles of human bones – one of about twenty skulls and other human bones. Nobody seems to know their origins, although some locals suggest they may have been Japanese soldiers. The skulls are covered with graffiti (which suggests that they may not be culturally significant to the locals and supports the Japanese soldier theory). The nearby border marker – one of the 14 which the joint Australian-Indonesian border mapping party erected in 1968 – is also covered with graffiti.

The road to Bewani is reportedly rough, but passable, and there are good views and several waterfalls.

AITAPE
• *pop 3900* • *postcode 553*

Aitape is a tiny town which retains little evidence of its long colonial history. The Germans established a station here in 1905 and the jail they built in 1906 still stands above the town. It was used by the Japanese during WWII.

An Australian division relieved American units at Aitape in November 1944 and moved inland, against considerable Japanese opposition, to establish a base in the Torricelli Ranges. From there, they pushed the Japanese back slowly to the east until Wewak fell on 22 May 1945.

In 1974, 48 WWII aircraft dumped around Aitape were identified and, in a six-week operation, many were shipped back to California for eventual restoration and display at an aircraft museum. A lone B24 bomber is still displayed outside Aitape High School between Tadji airstrip and the town. There's a Japanese war memorial between the town and the Santa Anna Mission.

Tumleo and Seleo islands, about 5km from the coast, are rarely visited by travellers but worth seeing if you can find a boat heading in that direction.

Places to Stay
The *Aitape Lodge* (☎ 857 2055; fax 857 2020; PO Box 72) is a nice, quiet motel-style place with pretty gardens and views across the bay. It is owned by a Malaysian logging company which puts up its visiting staff there. With rooms starting at K90, it is grossly overpriced – it's not surprising that few travellers visit.

You could try the Catholic Mission or one of the outlying villages for cheaper accommodation.

Getting There & Away
The road between Wewak and Aitape is rough but certainly passable, except during the occasional bad wet season. PMVs can be caught at the local market to Wewak for K12.

There are two airstrips: Tadji (call sign TAJ) and Aitape (call sign ATP). Tadji airstrip is about 10km out of town and is where most flights land. It was the scene of much activity during WWII when 71 Wing of the Royal Australian Air Force flew Bristol Beaufort bombers from it – the original tarmac can still be seen in places through the vegetation. It is a bumpy landing on often-overgrown grass but the strip is longer than the Aitape airstrip which, although very close to the town centre, can only handle smaller aircraft. Islands Nationair has a small office next to the Aitape strip, but the local representative meets every plane at Tadji, and you can usually buy a ticket from them. There used to be a terminal building at Tadji but local landowners pulled it down when aviation authorities refused to pay rent. There is now just a clearing in the bush next to the windsock where trucks pull up to wait for flights – which are often late. Ask around for a lift into town.

One-way fares from Aitape are: Tadji-

Wewak K94, Tadji-Vanimo K90. MAF may have cheaper fares for these routes.

Local boats go to Vanimo most days for about K20.

TELEFOMIN & OKSAPMIN
Telefomin • postcode 555

The remote stations of Telefomin and Oksapmin were only established in 1948 and 1962 respectively. They are among the most isolated stations in the country, but missionaries are very active and traditional dress is now rare. There are some dramatic caves in the Oksapmin Valley – guides are necessary. Oksapmin is the main centre for the area where Southern Highlands Province meets Western and Sandaun provinces. This is a beautiful region with the Om and Strickland rivers and their spectacular valleys. The climb from the valley floor to the ridges is 3000m in some places. It's driest in November and December but can be very wet any time. The area's name derives from its two main clans, the Ok and the Min.

Places to Stay

There's an expensive *mission guesthouse* near Telefomin station. In Drolengam village, about a 20-minute walk south of the airstrip, there used to be a village guesthouse which may still be operating; it was run by Robinok and Solumnot.

There is other village accommodation around both Telefomin and Oksapmin, but talk to the district officer-in-charge. Some of the missions in the region accept visitors but advance notice is a very good idea.

The agricultural centre at Oksapmin has Peace Corps advisers and may welcome visitors.

Getting There & Away

There are frequent flights from Port Moresby and other destinations into Tari, and from there MAF has an extensive network into this area – you can make many connections to remote airstrips. But the schedules and fares change significantly from time to time for small destinations such as these – so check.

The area is of some significance to the Ok Tedi mine at Tabubil (a source of fresh food and labour), so there is a frequent air service. At the time of writing, MAF had flights from Vanimo to Telefomin, Tabubil and Oksapmin on Wednesday and Friday.

One-way fares are: Tari-Oksapmin K80, Oksapmin-Kopiago K40, Vanimo-Telefomin K165, Vanimo-Oksapmin K175 and Wewak-Telefomin K170.

It is possible to walk from Oksapmin to Telefomin in five days but it's very tough and should not be undertaken lightly. There's a road link to Tekap, a three-day track to Feramin (where there's an aid post) and another two or three days to Telefomin. Don't attempt this without a guide and make sure you contact the police or the district officer-in-charge before you set out.

It is, apparently, also possible to walk southwards from Oksapmin to Tekin, Bak, Bimin and down to Olsobib in Western Province. It's another tough five-day walk eastwards from Oksapmin to Lake Kopiago.

AROUND OKSAPMIN

There are now trade stores in the area with the usual tinned fish, rice, sugar and so on. The district is becoming important for the vegetables it grows and supplies to the Ok Tedi mining project near Tabubil. Other cash crops like coffee have also been introduced. This was a protein-deficient area and even spiders, grubs and beetles were eaten before the ubiquitous tinned fish was introduced. In the evenings you can sometimes see torchlight around the valleys as women search for frogs, mice and snakes.

An interesting circular walk can be made through the villages around Oksapmin to the west and back along the Arigo River. North of Oksapmin, there are very few people, but around town and to the south in the five high valleys of Bimin, Bak, Tekin, Teranap and Gaua there are over 10,000 people. For the most part their homes and gardens are at about 2000m. There's a sub-district office in the Teranap Valley.

Bimin is the most isolated of the valleys though it does have an airstrip. Gaua, too, is

THE SEPIK

isolated, but it is only a few hours walk over the mountains south of Teranap office. The other three valleys are linked by a 32km road from Teranap to Tekin, up the valley to Tekap through the gap to Bak Valley and down to Daburap. Known as the Opiago Road, it will eventually rundown to the Strickland River, go up the valley of the Tumbudu River and to Lake Kopiago.

It is hoped that the Highlands Highway will eventually extend to Oksapmin. With any luck, by then the Strickland Valley and gorge will have been designated as a national park.

Both the Om and Upper Leonard Schultz valleys have two airstrips and three aid posts, but they are still very isolated. There are Baptist missions in Telefomin and Tekin; Seventh-Day Adventists have moved into the Om River area.

Socially, the entire district is different to the Highlands. There are no ceremonial exchanges or bride price transactions. Big-men don't exist in the same way and there are few leaders of any lasting duration. The society is based on sharing, with power more or less equally distributed. Traditionally, wars were rare and small in scale and sorcer-ers held the most power. Male and female initiation, along with platform burial and certain forms of dress, have virtually died out and traditional dress is now only worn on special occasions.

The people in the Oksapmin area are known as having a shame rather than a guilt culture. When people, for any number of reasons, are shamed they often blame them-selves. Apparently, a high percentage of deaths are suicides: difficulties in marriage and problems with witches are major reasons, but in the past a factor was bereave-ment. Family members used to kill themselves at the loss of loved ones, but this no longer occurs.

Modern development and the problems caused by men leaving to work in other districts and then returning home have resulted in difficulties and disillusionment for people in the region, but it remains quiet and peaceful.

The Sepik & its Tributaries

The mighty Sepik reverted to its local name when the Australians took over from the Germans, who had named it the Kaiserin Augusta. Some people say Sepik means great river, but nobody is certain. There are few exploitable natural resources, so the Sepik has attracted little development, despite the relative density of the population. On the surface, most villages still appear relatively untouched by western influences and Sepik art is still vigorous and unique, although rarely traditional.

The art itself makes a visit worthwhile. The scale of the river, the impressive archi-tecture of haus tambarans, the beautiful stilt villages, the long canoes with crocodile-head prows, the bird-life, flower-clogged lakes, misty dawns and spectacular sunsets make a visit unforgettable.

Nowadays, however, there are many western influences. The Sepik peoples have a dynamic, living culture, not a museum culture, so change, both good and bad, is not surprising. Western clothing is the rule and the impact of the missions has been pro-found. Although in some villages there has been a revival of traditional ceremonies, including male initiation, this is alongside, or somehow mixed with, Christianity and western-style education. Many of the young men leave the villages, and if they survive the shanty towns in the cities and return, they bring with them both visible and invisible baggage. Travellers and artefact buyers have also left changes in their wake.

Although the Middle Sepik in particular is one of the most frequently visited parts of the country, it is not by any standards crowded with tourists and you are unlikely to be in a village at the same time as any other traveller. You may see the odd group sweeping past in a canoe or river boat, and perhaps a trader or missionary, but that will be about it. Only a small but steady number of travellers stay in the villages, especially independently.

Bear in mind that although in photos Sepik villages look idyllic, the photos do not show the heat and humidity (which can be extreme), the mosquitos (which can be unbelievably numerous and vicious), the village food (which is, to the western palate, monotonous and tasteless) or the (basic) housing conditions. Nor do they indicate the rewards of travelling at your own pace, meeting the people and experiencing such a rich and fascinating culture.

As a general rule, you're best not to try to do too much. Resist the urge to cast yourself as a heroic explorer. Although there are differences between the villages' carving styles, their organisation and appearance does not change significantly.

Rather than exhaust yourself paddling for days in the middle of a huge, monotonous river, you would be better off to give yourself time in a village, preferably a bit off the beaten track, so you can establish relationships and get a feel for the people's lives. This is difficult if you're looking at the world through a fog of sunburn, mosquito bites and exhaustion. Two or three villages on the Middle Sepik will be quite enough for most people and many find they enjoy themselves more when they get off the main river.

In a Sepik village, you can see a range of activities, including house-building, canoe-making, sago-cutting, processing and cooking, women's and men's fishing, gardening and crocodile-hunting. But don't expect entertainment to be provided. Villagers are never really quite sure why tourists visit anyway, so talk to people and get to know them and what they are doing. When you get to know each other, activities will start happening.

There is road access to the Sepik at only three points: Angoram on the Lower Sepik (except after heavy rain) and Timbunke and Pagwi on the Middle Sepik. The alternative is to fly in to airstrips like Amboin on the Karawari River or Ambunti on the Upper Sepik – but this is an expensive option. The most artistic villages are concentrated on the Middle Sepik and the most spectacular scenery is on the lakes or tributaries. If you want to see a reasonable amount of the river at not too considerable a cost, Angoram or Pagwi are the best bases to use although Timbunke and Ambunti are also worth considering.

The Upper Sepik extends from the river's source to just below Ambunti, the Middle Sepik covers from Ambunti to Tambanum and the Lower Sepik is the final section from Tambanum to the coast.

When to Go

June to October is the dry season, with the main wet season being December to April; most rain falls in January and February and the river level starts to drop after April. The region gets over 72cm of rain a year, so it can rain any time. Temperatures and humidity can be high, but it's usually pleasant on the river, where you're more likely to get a breeze.

The dry season is the best time to visit, since the mosquitos are less numerous. By August, the river level can drop significantly, and this may complicate the navigation of some tributaries and barets (artificial channels built as shortcuts across loops in the river). In the dry season, the Chambri Lakes can get very smelly: they shrink, fish die and weed rots. The people start gardening in June (when there is little likelihood of floods) and harvest their vegetables from September to November (which must be a relief from sago).

What to Bring

Whether you're going in a dugout canoe or on a cruise boat, you must carefully plan what to take. If you're travelling independently the issue becomes vital.

You need light cotton clothes – light enough not to be too hot, long enough to protect you from the sun and heavy enough to prevent mosquito bites (they'll bite through fine cheesecloth). You'll appreciate being able to tuck a long pair of pants into socks to protect your ankles from probing proboscises, especially in the evenings.

THE SEPIK

THE SEPIK

Natnat

Natnat is Pidgin for mosquito. The Sepik variety isn't particularly big or vicious but makes up for this with its numbers. It's not unusual to walk in the Middle Sepik and see the person in front of you with a back black with hitchhikers.

Needless to say, they aren't a problem while you're in the middle of the river, but once you're on the banks they descend in hordes. They are particularly bad in the evenings. The dry season (June to October) is much better than the wet, which is impossible to imagine. The mosquitos are not such a problem once you get up the tributaries, either. Higher altitudes, cooler weather and faster-flowing water might explain it, although the Blackwater Lakes seem particularly free of these nuisances.

The Sepik people have developed a number of strategies to cope. The simplest is to wave a plaited fan/whisk, a response that soon becomes a reflex action. Perhaps the greatest contribution the west has made is the cotton mosquito net. Before these were available, finely woven wicker baskets, which must have been unbelievably hot, were used. The other technique is to drive them away with smoke. Special aromatic, smoky woods are used (if possible) for fires lit under the long houses, so the smoke can drift up through the floor. This makes the long houses smoky, as well as hot, but anything is better than the mosquitos. Wherever people sit around, fires are lit. The Sepik may be the only place where smoke from a fire doesn't follow you – and the only place where you want it to. ∎

A broad-brimmed hat, sunscreen, sunglasses and insect repellent are essential.

A swimsuit is worth packing, although it won't be much use if you're staying in a village, as villagers are very prudish. For men a pair of shorts will be appropriate, women may find a *laplap* (sarong) best. Tennis shoes that you don't mind getting wet and muddy are ideal footwear; thongs or sandals are nearly as good.

Make sure you have a bag or case that is waterproof to store your camera and/or binoculars (if you are a bird-watcher). You might even consider an umbrella. Also see the What to Bring section in the Facts for the Visitor chapter.

Wewak and Vanimo are the only places in the area where you can change money. Make sure you have plenty of small denomination notes – especially K2 and K5 – as village people rarely have change.

Staying in Villages Those staying in villages will need a torch (flashlight), or preferably two, for night excursions. It's ideal if the torch casts a wide beam because you may need it for cooking at night. Take a spare globe and batteries.

It is essential to sleep well if you're going to survive the heat, food and mosquitos in good humour. That means you must have a mosquito net (nets will probably be supplied for tour groups) and a sleeping mat. There is an art to organising a mosquito net, but first you must ensure that it is large enough to allow you to sleep without touching the sides (a two-person net gives you much more room and if you're large, it's essential) and the mesh size must be very fine (less than 1mm). A well-ventilated inner section from a hiking tent is ideal, as it also gives you a bit of privacy. Good mosquito nets are available in Wewak for K10 to K20. There are also some useless nets on sale, so check them out carefully. Don't buy the circular type which hangs from one central point.

You will need a supply of cheap string or twine so that you can suspend the net from handy beams and walls. Sepik houses have no internal divisions, so your net becomes your bedroom. If you've hung a net and you're not using it, drape the sides across its roof. Make your entry as swiftly as possible, tuck the bottom edges of your net underneath your mat, and then make sure you've killed any *natnats* (mosquitos) that have come in with you. The mat is not just an optional extra. The floors of Sepik long houses are made of the outer casing of a palm, which is smooth, springy, airy and definitely not mosquito proof. The mat will also be very useful as a cushion in your canoe.

You must take at least some food. Although there are infrequent trade stores, they usually only sell tinned meat and fish, rice and tobacco. The local people will often (but not always) offer you a meal, but most of the year this will only consist of *saksak* (sago) and *makau* (smoked fish). The sago is, in most forms, vaguely suggestive of tasteless Plasticine, and smoked fish, while good, quickly loses its appeal. Coconut and banana (the starchy, cooking type) can enliven the picture a little, and there are taros and introduced vegetables late in the dry season. An English traveller with a taste for rice pudding recommends pouring condensed milk over your rice.

It is an unbelievably monotonous diet and you will be hard pushed to look that smoked fish in the eye for the 10th consecutive meal. If you do eat the locals' food and have nothing else to give in return, you should pay a kina or so per meal. Instead of paying, however, the best idea is to have packet soups, biscuits, jam and other western-style food you can share and trade.

Many villages have rats, and while they won't bother you in your mosquito net, they will eat through bags to get at your food. A tin, such as an old powdered-milk tin, is very handy for storing those noodles and beef crackers.

Villages often have rainwater you can drink, and it's handy to have a water bottle. The Sepik water may look a bit muddy, but it's quite OK, as long as it hasn't been taken directly downstream of a village. The volume of water is so huge and the number of people living alongside is so small that there aren't any problems with pollution. But water in the lakes and backwaters is suspect, especially when the level is low. If you want to be absolutely confident take along some purification tablets.

Make sure you have good maps. The available topographical maps of the area were produced in the mid-1970s and are very out of date. *Wewak, the Gateway to the Sepik* is a good map and is available in Wewak at the Christian Bookshop or from Ralf Stüttgen for K2.

If you're going on one of the tributaries, consider getting some detailed topographic maps at the National Mapping Bureau in Port Moresby. Although their detail on the river will not be much help, mountains don't change quite so quickly, so you should still be able to orient yourself.

There are aid posts along the river but you should have a medical kit to cope with emergencies. It's easy for a mosquito bite to become infected, for instance, and if you are planning a long trip, you should research how to identify and treat malaria.

Dos & Don'ts

The Sepik people can be fairly indifferent, even suspicious, when you first meet them. Younger men, particularly, often adopt a tough-guy image. It can take a while to get beyond this barrier.

Perhaps this is partly due to pushy travellers who rush in, grab a pile of carvings, struggle bitterly to save every toea and leave without making any contribution. And it's not just about money, but being friendly, taking time to talk, sharing food and maybe even a song.

The Sepik is not some sort of anthropological zoo and you cannot pass through as an anonymous observer. To the villagers, an outsider is a potential friend, but also a potential enemy. If you are to have a safe and enjoyable time, be ready to meet people and relate to them on their terms.

Try to behave in accordance with local customs. Dress and act conservatively, taking your cue from people around you. If you're in a village and would like to go for a swim, ask when and where the locals bathe; there will often be separate times for men and women and it is considered extremely rude to watch or take photos. Most Sepik villages are rigidly patriarchal.

Western men should be cautious about talking to women (you'll often embarrass them and may cause jealousy): talk to middle-aged men. And western women should be cautious about talking to men (this may be misinterpreted): talk to the women. It is always difficult to read peoples' characters, but watching their faces and learning their names will be a good start. Don't overuse their names in normal speech.

Don't argue or haggle over prices: it is considered rude. Bargaining is not a normal part of a business transaction in PNG the way it is in Asia and elsewhere. Above all, never belittle the item in an attempt to lower the price.

There may well be a 'second price' but if the vendor doesn't like you, you'll never be offered it. If the vendor is acting on behalf of someone else, they might not be able to change the price. If you think a price is too high or if you can't afford it, express polite regret and slowly walk away, maybe glancing back.

Try to arrive in a village well before dark, maybe mid-afternoon, so you have plenty of time to find somewhere to stay and get yourself organised. Apart from the fact that it's difficult to do things in the dark, the mosquitos come out at dusk and doing anything but sitting by a fire is torture.

Involving people in what you are doing is a good idea. For example, if you ask for advice on the best place to moor your canoe, the people who show you might feel some responsibility for the canoe's safety.

It is immensely preferable to stay with a family, rather than being isolated in a haus tambaran or *haus kiap* (house for *kiaps*, or patrol officers). It will be more enjoyable and secure. You'll often have to ask to stay with a family and if the village seems determined to have you sleep in an empty house, say that you're afraid to sleep alone. Ask adults (men if you're male, women if you're female) about accommodation, not kids.

Villagers go to bed early, perhaps as early as 8 pm, but if you sit up late they'll feel obliged to keep you company. They also get up early and complete many jobs before the day is too hot. If you ask what people plan to be doing the next day, you might be invited along on a fishing or hunting trip.

The amount you are expected to pay for accommodation varies. This is compounded by the fact that in many places, especially the more remote, you don't actually *pay* for accommodation, you give a gift to the people who have shown you hospitality. Of course, a gift is expected and some people will want

more than others, but discussing the price of accommodation in advance could well be considered bad manners.

Somewhere around K5 is usual, often less on the Upper Sepik, plus a couple of kina for food, if you don't have anything to trade. Tinned food, adhesive bandages and aspirin make welcome gifts, and one budding entrepreneur collected *kaurie* (cowry) shells from a beach near Madang and used them as gifts for Sepik carvers.

You will normally be expected to pay the man of the house, but this is not always the case. Because it's a gift you are giving, make it a whole note rather than a handful of coins, and give it nonchalantly. In purpose-built accommodation, such as a village guesthouse, there is likely to be a set fee, generally higher than you'd pay to stay in someone's house.

An exception to the idea of giving gifts is when you take a photo of a cultural item or event – there will be a fee, usually K2 or less but sometimes more if the people receive a lot of visitors or if they receive none. Ask before you take photographs.

Never take a picture of or in a haus tambaran (even if it is only under construction) before gaining permission from the men who are inevitably sitting around underneath. The nearest equivalent in western society is a church, so you should show respect. Ask before you enter, even the ground floor, and remove your hat. Women may not be allowed to enter, especially upstairs, although this rule is usually bent for westerners. Sometimes there will be a charge (usually K2 to K5).

On the Middle Sepik, you will usually be able to find someone who speaks a little English, often one of the children, but in most cases you will be very restricted in your communication without some knowledge of Pidgin. Beyond the Middle Sepik, Pidgin will be even more important.

Finally, remember that it isn't necessary to cover a lot of territory. You can have just as interesting a time staying in one village for a week as you would spending long, hot days paddling down the river.

Safety

Basically, it is safe to visit the Sepik but you should be a little cautious. Once you are out on the river, you are a long way from help. There have been reports of robberies and although these are rare, most locals don't like to travel alone.

You do have to watch your belongings, so you are best off leaving non-essentials like passports at somewhere like Ralf's place in Wewak. A pile of interesting things left in your canoe while you go for a wander will soon disappear.

Never display wealth – that includes personal stereos, jewellery, even fashionable clothes. Alcohol is the number one motivation for robbery in rural PNG, so if you carry it don't show it.

Although you might be safer travelling in a group (of westerners), you will inevitably be perceived as a group rather than as individuals, which will make it harder to make friends with villagers – which in turn increases the danger. Once you have made friends in a village, it is highly unlikely that you will have any problems there; you will be given help and information.

Mixed groups of men and women will always be safe to approach, but you should be sceptical about small groups of men.

Several homosexual attacks on lone male travellers, after they have paddled ashore in response to a friendly greeting, have been reported. There have also been stories of children threatening to tip canoes.

Be aware of the strict segregation of the sexes among Sepik people. Men should talk to men in a village, women to women. Women should *never* drink alcohol with men. Couples should not show physical affection.

A woman who travelled on the middle Sepik recommends making eye-contact with every woman you meet. As she was with a male guide, the village women found the situation initially confusing but she mixed almost exclusively with women in the villages and was usually accepted.

She recommends having a reason for being in a village, such as studying gardens or houses. Many village women resented the fact that she was allowed into a haus tambaran (which was taboo for them) and this created a barrier.

There are still crocodiles on the Sepik, although they are hunted heavily and are very leery of human beings. Their territories do not extend any great distance from the edge of the water – you are most at risk at dusk, if you are a long way from human

Beware of saltwater crocodiles: they are still found on the Sepik!

habitation, are within 20 to 30m of a river and have returned to the same spot several times.

A number of people have been bitten by snakes, mostly at night when stumbling around in the dark – take a torch and in long grass flick the ground ahead with a handy stick. Check the location of the toilet, which will be a separate shack a short walk away, and the layout of the washing place in daylight.

Travel on the Sepik

There are several ways to travel on the river: village canoes – as a passenger in someone else's canoe; do-it-yourself canoes – you buy a canoe and paddle it yourself; motorised canoes – you charter a canoe and a guide/driver; and tours on one of the boats cruising the river. There are no longer any passenger-carrying freighters on the Sepik.

Village Canoes The cheapest, most time-consuming method of travel is inter-village canoes with outboard motors and staying in the villages.

There is a reasonably constant movement of boats along the river, with people trading, going to markets and visiting friends and relatives. Predictably, the movement of these boats is entirely unpredictable. You may have to wait many days for someone heading in your direction, and without a reasonable grasp of Pidgin you will find it very difficult to make your intentions clear. There will often be a complete (deliberate?) lack of understanding and people will pressure you to charter a canoe (very expensive) and then load it up with assorted cronies anyway.

If you can get a ride, it will be very cheap: around K2 to K3 per hour. The best time is Wednesday or Thursday, when people are going to market. For Sunday travel, remember that some Sepik villages (Suapmeri, Mindimbit, Angriman) are Seventh-Day Adventist, with a strictly upheld Sabbath on Saturday. Catholics don't travel on Sunday.

The bottom line is that you need a lot of

time and patience to travel this way – and even then you just may not have any luck.

Do-It-Yourself Canoes You can buy a small dugout canoe and paddle yourself. This can be *very* physically demanding and is not recommended. It's not always easy to find a canoe in reasonable condition at a reasonable price and you'll need to have enough time to be open-ended with your plans.

Beyond the obvious advantages of being independent, there are also disadvantages aside from the physical demands. You will only be able to paddle downstream (the current is too strong to fight) and your view of the wide brown river, with high grass crowding to its banks, will soon become monotonous. Much of the really beautiful scenery is up the tributaries away from the Sepik floodplain. Without a translator you may well miss out on worthwhile explanations and, because the river changes course so quickly, some of the most important villages will be quite a distance inland – without a guide you could easily miss them. Look for coconut palms – they almost always indicate human settlement.

Ambunti is a reasonable place to buy canoes; it's difficult to buy canoes around Pagwi, but the nearby villages are more helpful.

Prices vary greatly depending on your negotiating skills and the canoe's condition. Make sure you know whether paddles are being included in the deal and think in terms of paying K20 to K60 for a canoe. Don't pay too little, or the canoe will probably sink, although that fate has also befallen travellers who paid a lot.

It takes a month of hard work to make a decent-sized canoe. They are an essential tool for the villagers, so usually they'll only want to palm one off if they no longer need it or can make a profit (that is, the canoe will be old, leaky and expensive). You must check the condition of the canoe carefully. Small cracks can be sealed with mud, but large ones may be a problem.

Depending on your competence with a canoe, you may consider having an outrigger attached (someone in the village should be able to do this at a moderate cost) or even joining two canoes together (although this will slow you down).

Although there are no rapids, manipulating an unwieldy dugout in a five-knot current can be quite challenging.

You must keep your eyes open for floating debris (which can be chunks of riverbank the size of small islands) and the occasional whirlpool – these aren't big enough to do any damage unless you are caught off balance.

The river is wide enough in places to have quite big waves, maybe up to a metre. The locals paddle standing up but it's not recommended you try this with your gear on board.

We've heard of several travellers having disasters with their canoes, often on the first day or two of paddling. Once you've bought a canoe find someone to show you how to manage it. Any leaks in the canoe might become apparent while you're learning and you'll have an expert on hand to show you

how to patch them. One traveller suggested taking along a guide for the first day's paddling.

Take along something to bail out the canoe. As well as leaks, downpours can swamp you. A trick worth remembering is to lay some sticks across the bottom of the canoe to make a raised base. Use this to keep your luggage out of the water that inevitably pools in the bottom. A traveller has suggested using banana leaves to cover your luggage when (not if) it rains.

Travellers have suggested the Green, May and April rivers as good places to start but all these are fairly strenuous expeditions, not to be undertaken lightly. It takes at least 10 days of solid paddling from Green River to Ambunti and around a week from April River. From Ambunti it takes a solid week to get to Angoram.

Motorised Canoes You can hire motorised canoes, especially in Ambunti, Pagwi and

Carving out a dugout canoe – one of the many ways of travelling on the mighty Sepik.

THE SEPIK

Angoram, where there is an increasing number of local entrepreneurs hoping to make their living this way.

This is much more expensive than paddling, but you can work out your own itinerary and travel upstream and the driver doubles as guide. Depending on the driver, this could be good or bad. There are a few rogues who do their very best to rip you off and some virtually force you to do what they think you want to do, entirely disregarding what you say. So, when planning your itinerary, the important thing is, first, to hire a guide you can trust – and here the advice of people like Ralf Stüttgen in Wewak is invaluable – and, second, discuss your itinerary with your guide and heed their advice.

Hiring a canoe will be more feasible if you have a decent-sized group – you may be able to organise this at Ralf's in Wewak. Most of the motorised dugouts, which can be over 20m long, comfortably hold six or seven people and their luggage. This kind of trip also entails staying in villages, although an honest and friendly guide will make life a bit easier and more interesting than if you do it by yourself.

If you charter a canoe you also have to pay for the driver to return to his base, whether you go or not. It is, however, much cheaper to travel downstream with a full load, as the petrol (also known as *benzin*) consumption will be considerably reduced. Petrol will be the largest single component of your expense; it's K5 or more per gallon and you can't negotiate your way around that. To get from Ambunti to Angoram, for example, is a five to seven-day trip and could vary between K300 and K600.

If you are paying for petrol on top of daily hire, ensure your driver fills up before you start (petrol is much more expensive away from the road heads): 15hp engines are recommended as they are faster and economical. Don't pay in advance for anything except petrol and check the price and quantity delivered. It's possible to hire flat-bottomed boats known as river trucks in Angoram and they're worth considering if you want to move quickly. They're much faster than a canoe, especially if the river is chopped up by wind – they plane over the top.

As a rule of thumb, bearing in mind that all sorts of factors can have an influence, travelling downstream in a large canoe takes about 1½ hours running time from Ambunti to Pagwi, about six hours from Pagwi to Timbunke, and five hours from Timbunke to Angoram. You can probably add at least 30% for going upstream. A boat is twice as fast.

You're not going to be superbly comfortable in a canoe but the biggest drawback is uncertainty – you can arrive at the river and find there are no canoes available and have to hang around for days.

Guides There are plenty of people with motorised canoes who will be only too happy to take you on a Sepik tour. You will probably need a couple of days at the beginning of the trip to negotiate a reasonable rate and to find a reliable guide/driver. Talk to as many locals as possible (store owners, district officers, police) and try to build up a picture of who is trustworthy, the going hire rates, how long a journey will take and how many gallons of petrol will be used.

A lot of so-called guides are just village people who happen to be on the spot when a traveller with a wad of cash comes along looking for a motorised canoe. There's no reason why you shouldn't have a great time with one of these instant guides, but there's always the risk that you'll be stuck with someone who doesn't know what they are doing or is not trustworthy. If you plan to start at Ambunti, the best way is to go there and seek guides out. Telephones are notoriously unreliable and there are all sorts of personal assessments that cannot be done over the telephone. Listen to the advice of those who know the river – people like Ralf Stüttgen, Alois Mateus in Ambunti and Wewak and Joe Kenni in Angoram. There are, however, a few guides with excellent reputations.

Joseph Kone can be contacted in Ambunti through Pacific Island Ministries (PIM). Kowspi Marek is also contactable through

PIM, but he usually runs tours from Pagwi. Another guide recommended by travellers is Bonny Simbawa. Cletus Maiban in Angoram has been guiding artefact buyers on the river for nearly 30 years. Steven Buku is another big name who is now working at the Windjammer Hotel in Wewak – but he is still guiding, and is a mine of information. Other names to note are Linus Apen and Valentine Mari. Henry Gawi comes from Tambanum and operates between Ambunti and Angoram; he can be contacted in Wewak on ☎ 856 2251 (or mail him care of the courthouse) or through Niugini Tours (☎ (02) 9290 2055) in Sydney, which often uses him. There are plenty of other honest and competent guides, but the above are names which crop up over and over again in travellers' letters.

It is important to be aware that while guides have many obligations to you as their client, you too have obligations towards them. Sometimes guides may be willing to tell you information that is strictly secret in the expectation that you will be discreet and will not try to double-check details of such things as rituals, or locations of sacred sites, with villagers. Saying 'but our guide said ...' could get them into all sorts of hot water and be the kiss of death for their career as a guide. It is not outside the bounds of possibility that their house could be burnt down (if the offence is considered sufficiently seriously). The guide must be trusted by both clients and villagers. Remember that sometimes villagers do not tell the truth and will ask you for money for goods and services. Your guide can tell you what to pay and to whom.

Organised Tours Depending on where you want to go and your ability to strike a bargain, it may not be much more expensive to join a tour, particularly if you have limited time and want to visit some of the more remote tributaries.

A number of companies organise groups to travel in large motorised dugouts and stay in the villages. Prices vary considerably. It would be worth writing in advance to get an idea of up-to-date costs and options.

Melanesian Tourist Services
    PO Box 707, Madang
    (☎ 852 2766; fax 852 3543)
    Operator of the luxury cruise boat *Melanesian Discoverer*, which travels the length of the river.
Trans Niugini Tours
    PO Box 371, Mt Hagen
    (☎ 542 1438; fax 542 2470)
    Operator of the luxury Karawari Lodge and the *Sepik Spirit* river boat. Some tours involve staying in villages.
Haus Poroman Lodge
    PO Box 1182, Mt Hagen
    (☎ 542 2722 or 542 2250; fax 542 2207)
Tribal World
    PO Box 86, Mt Hagen (☎ 544 1555)
    Some tours and also possibly a regular boat trip along the river.
Niugini Tours
    100 Clarence St, Sydney 2000, Australia
    (☎ (02) 9290 2055)
Terra Firma Associates
    PO Box 357N, North Cairns, Queensland, Australia (☎ & fax (07) 4055 0014)
Victoria Travel
    11 West Victoria Street, Santa Barbara, CA 93101, USA (☎ (805) 965 5183; fax (805) 966 1489; email exotic@west.net)

In between the tour companies and local operators there are two mid-range alternatives: Alois Mateus of Sepik Adventure Tours and Ambunti Lodge (☎ 858 1291; fax 856 2525; PO Box 248, Wewak; PO Box 83, Ambunti) can prearrange fairly inexpensive tours based in Ambunti; and Joe Kenni of Sepik Village Tours and the Angoram Hotel (☎ & fax 858 3039; PO Box 35, Angoram) can do the same from Angoram.

UPPER SEPIK

Above Ambunti, the villages are smaller and more spread out. The people have had less contact with western tourists and are often friendly and hospitable, although clumsy or downright rude foreign visitors have created bad feeling in some places.

Relations are not helped by the fact that many villagers have no real understanding of the value of money, so prices can be erratic. It's not a bad idea to take presents, such as salt, cigarette papers, tobacco, photos of your country and simple toys for kids.

Locals are often bemused by foreigners

who have no apparent reason for being there – you aren't a missionary and you aren't looking for oil, so what are you up to?

There is not nearly the same concentration of artistic skills that you find on the Middle Sepik, but it is still an interesting area – traditionally, different villages had their own cult or focal point for the spiritual world.

Nature lovers will find this the most exciting part of the river. From Ambunti the river narrows and the land it flows through becomes more hilly with denser vegetation. In many areas, trees grow right down to the water's edge.

There are few villages after Yessan and there is a long uninhabited stretch between Tipas and Mowi (perhaps two days paddling), although there are hunting lodges at relatively frequent intervals where you can stay.

The Upper Sepik is more isolated than the Middle Sepik, because there are no roads, so a visit requires detailed planning. You should definitely bring your own food. If you want to buy your own paddle canoe, a village up here would be a good place to look.

Villages around here tend to move and there are lots of deserted settlements. Their names also change.

Green River

This is a subdistrict station, close to the Sepik River in Sandaun (West Sepik) Province, due south of Vanimo and very close to the Irian Jaya border. It's about a three-hour walk to the river but there is a road and you may get a lift. There are also links to Telefomin and Oksapmin. This has been suggested as a starting point for a canoe trip, but you will be undertaking a major project: something like 10 days solid paddling to get to Ambunti.

Swagup

Well off the main stream, east of the April River, Swagup is the home of the insect cult people, who are still fairly isolated and have their own language. Their unique art usually incorporates the figure of a dragonfly, sago beetle, praying mantis or other insect. The

ferocious reputation these people earned in former times lives on.

There are crocs in the many swamps around here and the people are great hunters.

Maio & Yessan

The people here have a yam cult but they have been heavily influenced by missionaries. This area is quite swampy and marshy.

Maliwai

This village is on a small lake off the river. Going up the river, you encounter many villages known for their specialised religious cults. Here, the cassowary figures prominently and is carved into most things, regardless of function. It used to be customary in this village to cut off a finger joint when there was a death in the family.

Yambon

Not far from Ambunti, Yambon has good art and an interesting haus tambaran.

Ambunti

• *pop 1280* • *postcode 534*

Ambunti is an administrative centre of no great interest but there is an airstrip and a couple of reliable people who hire motorised canoes, so this is one of the best places to start a trip.

In general, canoes are cheaper to buy here than around Pagwi. If you're having problems, it might be worth hiring a motorised boat for a day – you *may* be able to find something in a nearby village.

Don't forget to approach the Sepik with lots of large and small denomination notes in your pocket (or better still, your money belt) – you may have trouble cashing travellers cheques in Ambunti.

Places to Stay & Eat The *Ambunti Lodge* (☎ & fax 856 2525; PO Box 83) has simple but clean singles/doubles at K25/50. There is a backpacker lodge for K15. Mattresses, sheets and nets are provided. Breakfast, lunch and dinner are available for K5, K8 and K16. In the lounge area, there are numerous Sepik artefacts on the wall.

The lodge runs half and full-day canoe trips and can put you in touch with a guide for longer journeys. If you contact the owner, Alois Mateus, directly rather than going through a tour operator, you may get a 20% discount.

There's the PIM guesthouse, also known as the *Akademi* (☎ 858 1302; PO Box 41), as well as the *SSEC guesthouse*, in a house once used by missionaries, which charges around K14 a night.

Across the river is the *Apan Guesthouse*, a bush-material building where basic accommodation costs K7 a night. Take your own food. If there are people from Apan in town, they'll paddle you across for a few toea, or someone will come and pick you up for K1. It's about half an hour by canoe.

Several people around town will let you stay in their houses, such as Alphonse Mava, who also has a motorised canoe.

Getting There & Away It is a four to five-hour trip over a long, arduous road to get to Pagwi from Wewak (security has not been a problem lately), then a two-hour canoe trip upstream to Ambunti. It is far better and more comfortable to fly to Ambunti by MAF from Wewak or Mt Hagen.

Malu

This village, near Ambunti, is interesting for its variety of fruit trees and flowers.

Avatip

Although this is the largest village on the Upper Sepik, it's not very interesting. The Germans burnt it down twice and the old carving skills have been totally lost.

The village has three initiations – the second is involved with the yam cult while the third is only for old men. Debating is of great importance here. Debates are held to discover the meanings of names, information which the owners of the names are very reluctant to part with.

MIDDLE SEPIK

The Middle Sepik region starts just below Ambunti and finishes at Tambanum. This area is regarded as the 'cultural treasure house' of PNG and almost every village has a distinct artistic style, although these styles are now tending to merge. The villages themselves are very similar so there is no pressing need to see them all. Although the whole middle Sepik region is of great interest, the largest concentration of villages is just below Pagwi. It is possible to visit a number of them on day trips.

Pagwi

Down the road from Hayfields, Pagwi is the most important access point to the Middle Sepik, although there is also a road to Timbunke.

There is little of interest in Pagwi, despite this vital role, and it's a rather ugly little place. There are a couple of rundown government buildings and galvanised iron trade stores and that's it. You can buy food (although it is mostly of the tinned variety) and the mark-up isn't too bad.

You can hire motorised canoes here, but use discretion. Steven Buku, whose home village is Yenchenmangua, 30 minutes away from Pagwi by motorised canoe, is one of the best guides on the Sepik. Contact him at the Windjammer Hotel in Wewak. Aldonus Mana from Japandai, a bit upstream, is another local operator who has been recommended.

Kowspi Marek offers four and five-day tours from Pagwi to more out-of-the-way places along the river and its tributaries, usually with a minimum of four people. You can set your own itinerary. Kowspi can be contacted through PIM in Ambunti.

An interesting and fairly comprehensive three-day tour could be made to the Chambri Lakes, downriver as far as Kaminabit, then back to Pagwi.

Day trips can be made to Korogo. Aibom, Palambei, Yentchen and Kanganaman are all interesting and within reach. It takes about six hours running time to Timbunke and another five hours to Angoram. Depending on your stops and side trips, you could do a five to seven-day trip down to Angoram for around K500.

People have, on occasion, paid outrageous

prices for canoes here, so you may have to make enquiries at nearby villages if you want to get something cheaper.

Places to Stay You can sleep with a family for K5 (this is a present, not a fee). Benjamin Jericho, Tobi, James Yambai and Jimmy Janguan have been mentioned as possibilities. The family who runs the petrol station may also help. Ask around: there are plenty of families willing to put you up.

Getting There & Away See the Maprik Area Getting There & Away section. It is a rough journey from Maprik to Pagwi (53km) and murderous in the wet. There are passenger canoes running between Pagwi and Ambunti most days.

Japanaut

This small village specialises in trinkets – little black masks or other carvings on shell or seed necklaces. Although every village has its own distinctive style there is also almost always some strange little item which is completely out of character.

Yenchenmangua

Yenchenmangua has an interesting haus tambaran and good artefacts.

Korogo

This is a commercially oriented village right beside the river, with a very impressive haus tambaran (described as a magical place). There is a pleasant two-hour walk to an interesting inland village.

The *Korogo Village Guesthouse* is unsupervised and people staying there have been robbed and even assaulted. If you can persuade a local to stay there with you, it will be safer (try Cletus Yambun), otherwise find another village.

Travel times from Pagwi are: half an hour by motor, half a day paddling.

Suapmeri

Variously misspelt as Swatmeri and Sotmeri, Suapmeri is famous for its mosquitos, less so for its carvings. There is little for sale,

although the village was famed for its orator's stools. Villagers say the mosquitos take the pleasure out of carving. Despite all this, it's an attractive village and is at the entrance to the Chambri Lakes.

You may be able to stay with a friendly family; ask for James Yesinduma. James knows everyone who lives on the river and speaks reasonable English.

It is very difficult to find your way through to the Chambri Lakes along the weed-filled barets, but James can arrange a guide. Rather than backtrack to Suapmeri, you can follow a channel that brings you out just above Kaminabit, but only if the water level isn't too low.

Travel times from Korogo are half an hour

Haus Tambarans

Tambarans are spirits, so the haus tambaran is the house where they live – or at least where the carvings that represent them are kept. You may also hear haus tambarans referred to as 'spirit houses' or 'men's houses' because only initiated men (and tourists) are allowed to enter. Once upon a time, a woman who ventured inside met instant death. Although western women are usually allowed inside, times have probably not changed for the village women.

Every clan has to have a spirit house and although they may have lost some of their cultural importance, they are still very much the centre of local life. On the Sepik, men while away the day lounging around in the cool shade underneath the building, carving, talking or just snoozing. On the Blackwater Lakes during the nine-month lead-up to their initiation, the initiates live in the upstairs section of the haus tambaran and are only allowed out at night when the rest of the village is asleep.

Haus tambaran styles vary: the high, forward-leaning style of the Maprik region is probably best known, but some on the Sepik are equally spectacular. They can be huge buildings on mighty, carved piles, 40 or 50m long with a spire at each end stretching 25m into the air. When the missionaries first arrived, some zealous individuals burnt down haus tambarans to destroy the village 'idols'. One brave district officer actually took the commendable action of charging a missionary with arson, and these days a more enlightened attitude is usual. ■

by motor, half a day paddling. To Aibom in the Chambri Lakes it's 1½ hours by motor, 1½ days paddling. If you can get a communal canoe from Pagwi it will cost around K5.

Indabu

This is a good place to buy carvings and bilums, as few people come to this small, friendly village. It is consequently also a good place to stay. People have stayed at Steven Buku's house for K5. Ask for him at the Windjammer Hotel in Wewak. Steven's uncle, Lawrence, might also help. Paias Sone is another guide from this village, but he doesn't speak English.

Yentchen

An hour by motorised canoe from Suapmeri, Yentchen is also a good place to stay. There is a big, clean haus tambaran for around K5.

The two-storey haus tambaran was copied from photographs taken at the turn of the century by German explorers of the building standing at that time. The top floor is only for initiates; the rest of the men stay downstairs. You climb upstairs between the legs of a graphic female fertility symbol and are blessed in the process.

Yentchen is noted for its wickerwork dance costumes – figures of crocodiles, pigs, cassowaries and two-headed men.

Palambei

You can't see the village proper from the river and it can be easy to miss: there are two or three huts and there may be some canoes on the bank. It's a hot 20-minute walk along a baret (dry in the dry season), but it is worth the effort because the village is beautiful. Built around several small lagoons full of flowering water lilies, the village has two impressive haus tambarans at either end of a ceremonial green. The surrounding ruined buildings, including a haus tambaran close to the green, were bombed by the Allies during WWII.

Stones, which must have been carried many kilometres, have been set up in the glade. There are also two virtuoso *garamut* drummers who will bring their hollow-log drums to life in an intricate duet. The village women make the best bilums on the river.

To travel here from Suapmeri takes 1½ hours by motorised canoe.

Kanganaman

A brief walk from the river, this village is famous for the oldest haus tambaran on the river. It has been declared a building of national cultural importance and has been renovated with help from the National Museum. It is a huge building with enormous carved posts.

Kaminabit

Kaminabit is not a particularly attractive village, not least because of the large lodge. There are, however, some good carvings. The lodge is used by a number of tour groups, including Trans Niugini, and is usually opened only for them. There is also a guesthouse in another western-style building which costs about K7. Ask for James Minja or Anton Bob. Dominic and Francesca have been recommended by several travellers.

From Aibom it takes one hour by motor canoe, and from Palambei it's 1½ hours by motor canoe. If you find a communal canoe from Suapmeri, it will cost about K5.

Mindimbit

The village is near the junction of the Karawari and Korosameri rivers. The Korosameri leads up to the beautiful Blackwater Lakes region. Mindimbit is entirely dependent on carving and there is some nice work, though there is no proper haus tambaran.

You can stay with a friendly family for K5 or so; ask for Peter Bai. They live in the downstream section of the village, which is spread out along the bank and a half-hour walk from end to end.

Timbunke

This is a large village with a big Catholic mission, a hospital and a number of other western-style buildings. There are also some impressive houses.

THE SEPIK

Trans Niugini's *Sepik Spirit* calls in here, so while there is a lively appreciation of the depth of the tourist wallet, there is also a good range of artefacts and carvings for sale.

People have had problems trying to find somewhere to stay and the mission is not helpful. The primary school is a reasonable place to stay, but isn't always available.

Tambanum

This is the largest village on the Middle Sepik and fine, large houses are strung along the bank for quite a distance. The people are renowned carvers. American anthropologist Margaret Mead lived here for an extended time. Cletus Maiban from Angoram has relatives here, who will probably be able to put you up. Henry Gawi has built a new guesthouse here with flyscreens, flush toilets, separate bedrooms, mosquito nets, running water and cooking facilities. Apparently, this is the largest guesthouse in the mid-Sepik, and is reportedly very comfortable.

Travel time from Timbunke is half an hour by motor.

LOWER SEPIK

The Lower Sepik starts at Tambanum and runs down to the coast. Angoram is the most important town on the Sepik. The Marienberg Mission station, which has been operated by the Catholics for many years, is about two hours downstream.

Near the mouth of the river, the Murik Lakes are vast semi-flooded swamplands, narrowly separated from the coast. Villages along this part of the Sepik are smaller, poorer and generally have had less western contact than many in the middle region.

The vast volume of water and silt coming down means that the landscape around the mouth of the Sepik changes rapidly. Many villages here are only a few generations old, built on new land.

Angoram
• *pop 1500* • *postcode 535*

If you want to see some of the Sepik and experience life in a village but don't want to undertake a long river journey, Angoram is the best place to visit. It's easily accessible from Wewak and there are plenty of beautiful and interesting places a few hours away (or a few days if you want) by motorised canoe.

Angoram is the oldest and largest Sepik station, established by the Germans before WWII. It is the administrative centre for the Lower and Middle Sepik and a pleasant, sleepy place. The town centres on a marketplace (as usual) and a large, overgrown, grassy area which was a golf course for the expats in colonial times. In the dark, watch out for the deep ditches running down to the river.

You cannot change money in Angoram, although there is a PNGBC bank and a small Westpac agency. There are a couple of reasonable trade stores.

Places to Stay The *Angoram Hotel* (☎ 858 3011; fax 858 3039; PO Box 35) is owned by Joe Kenni, a local bigman, businessman

---

Saksak

Saksak is Pidgin for sago, the staple food for the Sepik people and for all those who live in the swampy areas of PNG.

The preparation of sago is a long process and the end result is neither very appetising nor nutritional. Sago is basically pure starch, but in a land where it is often too swampy to grow anything else, it is vitally important. Certainly there is no shortage of it, since sago palms grow prolifically. On the Sepik, dry sago is usually mixed with water and fried into a rubbery pancake, although it can be boiled into a gluey porridge. Mixed with grated coconut it becomes quite palatable, but by itself it is almost tasteless. Supplemented with bananas, vegetables or fish, it will keep you going.

The sago palm is an ancient food source and it is difficult to imagine how and when it was discovered. First, a sago palm (which looks just like any other palm tree) is cut down, the bark is cut away and the pith is chipped and pounded out, producing what looks like fibrous sawdust. That's the men's contribution. Next the women knead the pith in a bark funnel with a rough filter, draining water through the pith to dissolve the starch. The starch-laden water is collected (often in an old canoe) and the starch settles in an orange, glutinous mass at the bottom. ■

and aspiring politician. Joe is a nice guy and is worth getting to know. The hotel is a rambling, old fibro building in bad need of renovation. It has air-con, but only when the town electricity is switched on, which it isn't during most of the daylight hours. Rooms cost K80, but Joe might do a major deal with you if you organise a river tour with him. The hotel also has a backpacker unit for K10 per person. Western-style food can be provided. Joe also runs Sepik Village Tours; he can organise short or long tours up the river and recommend guides.

Elijah Saun and Cletus Maiban, who are in competition, offer accommodation and motorised-canoe trips. They live in the area known as the Service Camp, a little upstream from Angoram proper, and are very different men. Elijah, a carver, is large and patriarchal, with an artisan's methodical competency. Cletus is quieter, but his family is lively, and he has an extensive knowledge of the Sepik.

Elijah's house adjoins his carving workshop on the riverbank. Mattresses, pillows, linen and mosquito nets are occasionally provided. It's a basic but nice place. Elijah has worked at the Windjammer Hotel in Wewak, so he knows how to look after guests. He charges K10 a night and his family will cook the food you provide.

Cletus's house is a little upstream from Elijah's. If you take his boat or one of his canoes on a Sepik trip, accommodation at his house is free; otherwise he charges about K10.

There are plenty of other people to stay with in Angoram, such as Raphael Maimba, and Peter Dimi, who lives across the river from town.

Getting There & Away Scheduled flights no longer call at Angoram and the airstrip is overgrown and unserviceable.

The road from Wewak to Angoram is the shortest access route to the Sepik. It branches off the Maprik road only 19km out of Wewak. The 113km, all-weather road is good by Sepik standards but you still shake, rattle and roll. The traffic is reasonably frequent, but if you're returning to Wewak you have to start very early – around 4.30 am. PMVs cost K8 and their stop is near the market.

Angoram is a reasonable starting point for Sepik trips, although it is really only relevant to those hiring motorised canoes (sooner or later you're going to have to go upstream).

Elijah Saun and Cletus Maiban also compete as river guides. Cletus is much more experienced, having guided artefact buyers for 30 years. On some trips he did the buying. He is an excellent guide, with good contacts all along the Sepik. If he is not available his sons, especially Jeffery, can take you on the river. Cletus has several motors of different horsepower, a couple of canoes and an aluminium boat.

Elijah is also very reliable. His canoe has a canopy, an innovation he designed.

Other people in Angoram offer motorised-canoe trips, notably Peter Dimi. Jimmy Bagu has been recommended, and you can also arrange trips through Joe Kenni. See the Places to Stay section for how to find them.

Travel times by motor upstream from Angoram are: Moim (two hours); Tambanum (four to five hours); Timbunke (five to six hours); Pagwi (nine hours).

Around Angoram

A good day trip is to go south on the Keram River to **Kambot**, stopping at either Magendo or Chimondo on the way. The cost for this is about K100. These villages are familiar with outsiders and there are no great art bargains, but the river is narrow and winding, and the banks are crowded with luxuriant growth. You can stay at the *Kambot Guesthouse*, run by Mr Mokmok, for K13 per night. Further south on the Keram is **Yip** station; south from here, there is beautiful rainforest with plenty of birds, especially around **Korogopa** and **Yamen**, on a Keram tributary.

A day trip from Angoram to **Moim** and **Kambaramba** and the beautiful lagoons nearby costs about K90. Further south on a tributary is **Wom**, a village built among grass lanes.

You can also make day trips to the **Murik Lakes** – they're about four hours away – or stay overnight at **Mendam**. As with most villages, you can usually arrange to sleep with a family at **Watam** village, on the coast near the mouth of the Sepik. The village is normally accessible from the main river, and apparently the seafood is wonderful.

TRIBUTARIES & LAKES

The Sepik River can become monotonous as it winds through its vast, flat plain, with pitpit crowding up to its banks. The most spectacular scenery is on the tributaries and the villages are generally smaller, friendlier and less visited. There are three main accessible tributaries in the Lower Sepik: the **Keram**, the **Yuat** and the smaller **Nagam**. The upstream tributaries require extensive travelling, meaning you either have to fly in or use a motor canoe. Most of these areas are more traditional; you should plan your journey with some care and bring your own food.

May (Iwa) River

May River is a small town more than halfway from Ambunti to the Irian Jayan border. There's an airstrip and a mission settlement; it's possible to begin a river trip at this point.

Canoes can be bought for around K40. The locals and missionaries will discourage you from going alone. The local guides don't like to go alone either – they travel in pairs and ask at least K12 each a day. The villages in this area are not often visited and relationships between them are not always amicable, but it could be a great trip.

Talk to the people at MAF or Ralf Stüttgen in Wewak; they might be able to give you the names of people to contact in the area. It's not a good idea to arrive unannounced and expect to be accommodated.

April (Wara) River & Wogamush River Area

Life on these tributaries continues in a more traditional manner than on the main river, with initiation rites and various social taboos and systems still intact. Both areas are good

for bird-watching, although the Wogamush perhaps is better.

There aren't many spare canoes, but you might be lucky enough to find one. Expect to pay around K50. There are villages at regular intervals and it takes about 21 hours (three or four days) of paddling to get to the Sepik. The river splits 2½ hours after Bitaram and the left fork is the quicker route to the main river. From the junction it will take you another three or four days to get to Ambunti.

One traveller recommends not paddling on the April River without a guide, or when it's in flood. His canoe overturned and he lost everything – walking barefoot for two days through the jungle and eating soggy beef crackers wasn't much fun.

It is rarely possible to fly to April River from Tari, although you might be able to hitch a lift on a charter. Talk to the people at MAF.

Wasui Lagoon

Also known as Wagu Lagoon, after the main village, this is a beautiful place, with many birds. The Hunstein Range is behind Wagu and there is beautiful rainforest. You can stay at the Wagu aid post for K5 or seek out Lucas Kiaui who might be able to help you.

Chambri Lakes

The Chambri Lakes are a vast and beautiful expanse of shallow water (they are partially drained dry in the dry season, making things pretty smelly and the water unfit for drinking unless treated). It's difficult to find your way in, as floating islands can block the entrances. James Yesinduma at Suapmeri can organise a guide for a few kina. Rather than backtracking via Suapmeri, you can continue east and come back out on the river just above Kaminabit, if the water is deep enough.

Indagu is one of the three villages that make up Chambri region. There is a haus tambaran here with a huge collection of carvings – mainly in the polished Chambri style – and also many ornamental spears. **Aibom**, another village on the lakes, is noted for its pottery. The distinctive Aibom pots sell from only a kina or two and the pottery fireplaces used all over the Sepik are made here.

If you're looking for somewhere to stay, Cletus and Esther Yambon (☎ 856 2005; PO Box 944, Wewak) can put you up at nearby Korogo village. They charge K8/12 for a single/double and can also organise tours of the lakes. Otherwise, ask for Anscar Kui at Aibom, who may be able to help you to stay at the mission. Jimmy Maik of Kandangai village (PO Box 106, Maprik) has accommodation.

From Pagwi, the shortest way into Chambri is via Kandangai, but if the water level is low you won't be able to get through.

From Suapmeri to Aibom, it takes 1½ hours by motor canoe, one day by paddle canoe; from Aibom to Kaminabit, it takes one hour by motor canoe and six hours by paddle canoe. It is possible to catch a village boat to Kandangai from Pagwi most days of the week (between 3 and 5 pm) for between K5 and K7.

Karawari River

The Karawari runs into the Korosameri (which drains the Blackwater Lakes) and then into the Sepik just near Mindimbit. For the first hour or so, the banks are crowded with pitpit. But the jungle soon takes over and the river becomes more interesting, with wide sand bars (in the dry), a range of bird-life, occasional crocodiles and attractive villages.

Amboin

For those with the money, the *Karawari Lodge* (Trans Niugini Tours, ☎ 542 1438; PO Box 371, Mt Hagen) at Amboin is recommended. It's a luxury base for exploring the Sepik. Built with bush materials and having some of the atmosphere of a haus tambaran, the lodge has dramatic views across the Karawari River and a vast sea of jungle. There are 20 twin rooms, all with panoramic views. Trans Niugini Tours offers various packages based on one or two nights stay at Karawari, sometimes with stays at nearby villages (far less luxurious). If your time is limited, this is an option worth exploring.

Amboin is usually reached by air (included in the packages) and from there you travel a short distance up the river to the lodge. The lodge river trucks will take you to nearby villages like Maraba, Marvwak and Simbut – where traditional Sepik-style tree houses are still used. There are also tours that utilise the lodge at Kaminabit and some that stay in the villages. Sing-sings and re-enactments of the Mangamai skin-cutting ceremonies are all part of the deal. Special tours for bird-watchers to the Yimas Lakes can be organised.

Mameri

About 40 minutes by motor canoe from Mindimbit and just before the turn-off to the Blackwater Lakes, Mameri has some particularly accomplished, dramatic and expensive carving. Check out Ben's work. He will also be able to organise somewhere for you to stay.

Blackwater Lakes

To enter the Blackwater Lakes is to enter a vast water world where villages are often built on stilts and the people pole their canoes through shallow, reed-clogged lakes. The bird-life is fantastic.

As you get higher, away from the Sepik, the temperatures become cooler and the scenery becomes more spectacular. **Lake Govermas** is covered in water lilies and surrounded by low hills, mountains, dense forest and three beautiful villages. It is impossible to find your way around the myriad channels without a guide.

Tour boats now come to the lakes and you might find that prices are a little too high in some places.

Sangriman This is an attractive, friendly village built on the edge of a reed-filled lake, but there are few artefacts.

Travel time from Mindimbit is about 1½ hours by motor canoe.

Kraimbit There is a new haus tambaran here and the locals are welcoming.

Govermas A place of 'dream-like beauty', Govermas also has one of the most impressive haus tambarans in the region and some excellent carving. It's about 1½ hours by motor canoe from Sangriman.

If you get as far as this, it's worth going on further to see Lake Govermas and the village of **Anganmai**, on top of a hill. On a tributary at the very south of Lake Govermas is **Mariama** village, where there's a good haus tambaran. Dennis Worry may be able to take you around in his motorised canoe and put you up in his house.

Gulf & Western Provinces

Land Area 133,800 sq km
Population 200,000

The two west Papuan provinces, Gulf and Western, are the least populated and developed in the country. The coastline is broken by a series of river deltas, while huge expanses of swamp run inland before rising to the foothills and then mountains of the Highlands. In the far west, the border with Irian Jaya runs north through the open expanses of seasonally flooded grassland. Two of the greatest rivers in the country, the Fly and the Strickland, run almost their entire length through Western Province.

History
The coastal people of the provinces have had a long history of contact with outside influences. The Gulf people traded their plentiful sago with the Motuan people's (from the Port Moresby area) pottery. The annual Motuan trading voyages along the south coast, known as the *hiri*, were regular, even after Europeans established Port Moresby. There were also trade links to the Highlands. Because of their easy access from the sea, the coastal villages were also the 'hunting grounds' for representatives of the London Missionary Society, who first arrived in the area in the early 1880s.

In 1842 Frenchman Dumont d'Urville, who had surveyed part of the north-east coast of New Guinea in 1827, charted the western side of the Gulf of Papua in HMS *Fly*. He discovered the Fly River and surmised that a small steam-powered boat could travel up this river into the interior of the country. It was some years before this idea was put into action, but when the ruthless Italian explorer Luigi d'Albertis successfully navigated the Fly in 1876, he quickly made up for lost time. In his tiny steamer, the *Neva*, he travelled over 900km upriver, further into the unknown than any previous explorer. He

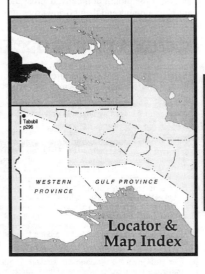

Tabubil
p296

WESTERN
PROVINCE

GULF PROVINCE

**Locator &
Map Index**

GULF & WESTERN

returned from this epic voyage with a huge collection of botanical specimens, insects, artefacts and even painted skulls from village spirit houses.

In 1901, the Reverend James Chalmers visited Goaribari Island on the Papuan Gulf and his boat was besieged by hostile tribesmen. Chalmers and 12 companions went ashore and, in short time, all had their skulls crushed with stone clubs. The rest of his crew managed to escape. Retribution from Port Moresby soon followed: the government ship *Merrie England* arrived at Goaribari and its crew killed 24 villagers and burnt down 12 *dobus* (men's long houses). A second punitive expedition a couple of years later was even worse, with between eight and 50 villagers massacred.

Although the Gulf and Western coasts were well charted and the Fly, Strickland and other major rivers were soon comprehensively surveyed, it was not until the late 1920s that the mountains north of the coast were explored. In 1927 Charles Karius and Ivan Champion set out to travel upriver from Daru, near the mouth of the Fly, to cross the central mountains and then go downriver on the Sepik to the north coast. Their first attempt failed when they ran out of supplies while trying to find a way through the jagged limestone mountains. A year later, they managed to complete their journey, considered to be one of the last great expeditions in Papua New Guinea.

Geography

The border region with Irian Jaya has vast, open, seasonally flooded grasslands to the south, rising to the mountainous spine. Ross Bluff (3727m), in the Star Mountains, is the

The OPM and Border Conflicts

The guerilla resistance movement OPM (*Organisasi Papua Merdeka*, or Free West Papua Movement) was established after the Indonesian takeover of Irian Jaya in 1963. The group was formed by indigenous Papuans who resented imposed rule by a different ethnic group. It has fought with varying degrees of success against tremendous odds, operating mainly around the border of Papua New Guinea and Irian Jaya.

Each time violence has flared, PNG has found itself squeezed between a practical need for good relations with Indonesia and an obvious sympathy for the rebels who are kindred Papuans. In balance, practicality has prevailed and PNG has done nothing to assist the rebels – even, on several occasions, handing alleged rebels back to the Indonesian authorities.

Because Indonesia has maintained tight control over news coming from Irian Jaya and the OPM has been dogged by factionalism since the late 1970s, it is difficult to separate fact from fiction in the fragmented accounts of the struggle which reach the press.

On a number of occasions, the OPM has been declared a spent force, only to reappear, seemingly undaunted. The OPM has attracted scant overseas support, but armed with traditional weapons and small numbers of outdated guns and captured rifles the rebels continue to operate.

Over the years the OPM has announced that it has killed hundreds of Indonesian soldiers and that many thousands of Papuans have been killed in indiscriminate retaliatory attacks. The Indonesian figures are much lower. There were major clashes in 1978, 1981 and 1983 – some provoked by Indonesia's ambitious transmigration scheme.

In 1984 over 100 Melanesian soldiers in the Indonesian armed forces deserted to the OPM, sparking a major Indonesian retaliation, which in turn drove over 10,000 Papuans into PNG. Years later these refugees, and those that have come both before and since, remain a political football. Few have shown any interest in returning to Irian Jaya, so the PNG government has belatedly decided to resettle them permanently. They have been settled primarily in UN camps at East Awin in Western Province and Blackwater in Sandaun Province. The 1990 census counted 6872 Irian Jayans in and around East Awin.

In 1996 the OPM took hostage a group of 11 British, Dutch and Indonesian nationals, who were investigating the establishment of a national park deep in Irian Jaya. The Dutch were a part of a World Wide Fund for Nature and UNESCO team. The hostages were forced to march through this mountainous region and most were in a bad state of health after several months of hardship and poor food. The International Red Cross tried to intervene, but to no avail, and finally the Indonesian Army moved into the area. Most of the hostages escaped and made their way to the Indonesian troops, but two Indonesian hostages – and eight OPM rebels – died in the ensuing action.

It seems unlikely that the real grievances of the Papuan people in Irian Jaya will be resolved in the foreseeable future – the conflict will almost certainly continue in one way or another. ■

The Sepik Provinces
Top: Carvings from the Blackwater Lakes region, East Sepik
Bottom Left: A Sepik woman in mourning
Bottom Right: Painted bark ceiling

Top: Mendam Village, Murik Lakes, East Sepik Province
Middle Left: Bridge at Timbunke, along the Middle Sepik
Middle Right: Dugout canoes are a popular form of transport along the Sepik River.
Bottom: Overlooking the Tauri Valley, Gulf Province

highest point of Western Province. To the south, the border with Australia in the Torres Strait comes within 7km of the PNG coast.

The Fly River starts high in the mountains and turns south-east towards the sea where it ends in a huge, island-filled delta. The Strickland River, nearly equal in size, joins the Fly about 240km from the coast.

Despite its size the Fly does not have the same interest for visitors as the Sepik: it is much more difficult to visit and there is not so much to see. Villages are usually some distance from the river because it tends to flood so far over its banks. In its 800km run to the sea, the Fly River falls only 20m. It flows (slowly) through 250,000 sq km of wetland where mosquitos appear to be the most successful inhabitants.

From the mouth of the Fly eastwards to the Purari River, the Gulf of Papua is a constant succession of river deltas, backed by swamps which run between 50 and 60km inland. The Turama, the Kikori, the Purari and the Vailala are among the great rivers that flow here. East of the Purari the land rises more rapidly from the coast; it's less subject to flooding and more heavily populated.

Arts

There are few artefacts created in Western Province now – the hourglass-shaped *kundu* drums of Lake Murray are very rare and the Kiwai people do not often carve.

However, art is still strong in the Gulf region. Unfortunately, when the missionaries first arrived in the Gulf area their attitude towards local culture was considerably less enlightened than it later became. Along with abandoning their spiritual beliefs and giving up head-hunting, the gulf villagers were also pressured to halt their artistic pursuits; in some cases, the missionaries actually persuaded them to burn and destroy their best work. Today, old artefacts are zealously protected.

In the Gulf region, from the mouth of the Fly around to Kerema, seven distinct artistic styles have been categorised. Once, the men's long houses in the delta villages were

veritable museums and although there are no 'fully furnished' spirit houses left, there is still a busy trade turning out figures, bull-roarers, *kovave* masks, headrests, skull racks (every home should have one) and gope boards.

Gope boards are elliptical in shape, rather like a shield, and incised with brightly coloured abstract patterns or stylised figures. Warriors were entitled to have a gope board for each act of bravery or to celebrate each successful conflict. Boards were often cut from the curved sides of old canoes and a board from your vanquished enemy's own canoe had particular significance, transferring some of its previous owner's strength to the victor.

Hohao boards are similar in their original role to gope boards but can be recognised by their squared-off edges, coming to a point at the top and bottom. These were particularly prevalent around Ihu and Orokolo at the eastern end of the Gulf but greater affluence in this region has caused the skill to virtually die out. It was also in this area that the *hehevi* ceremonies once took place. These were a cycle of rituals and dramatic rites that took a full 20 years to complete. The ceremonies stopped more than 50 years ago and the huge masks which were used in dances have also disappeared.

Society & Conduct

The people of the delta land build their houses on piles high above the muddy river banks. As the rivers change their courses, the people frequently have to move their villages. Traditionally, each village was centred around the dobu, also known as a *ravi*, in which weapons, important artefacts, ceremonial objects and the skulls of enemies were stored. While men slept in the long house, women slept in smaller, individual huts outside.

Today the long houses are no longer so culturally important; the Gulf people have been bombarded with Christianity for nearly a century and many traditions have been lost – including cannibalism.

Cannibalism had ritual and religious

GULF & WESTERN

GULF & WESTERN

importance, but it is also possible that it was provoked by endemic protein deficiency in the area. As on the Sepik and the Ramu, the main food is sago – the tasteless, starchy food produced from the pith of the sago palm. There is no shortage of sago, so nobody starves. But where sago is the staple food, severe protein deficiencies are common. Although the villagers supplement their diet with whatever fish they can catch and the small quantity of vegetables their inhospitable land will allow them to grow, this deficiency remains a serious problem.

In the hills behind the coastal swampland live the formidable Anga people, whose territory stretches right across to the south-eastern highlands in Morobe Province. The last major Anga raid took place at Ipisi near Kerema just before WWII. Today there is a government station at Kaintiba in the heart of their land and it is fairly peaceful.

The Kiwai people, who live on the islands in the mouth of the Fly, are noted for their sea-going abilities and interesting dances. They have close cultural links with the Torres Strait Islanders of Australia.

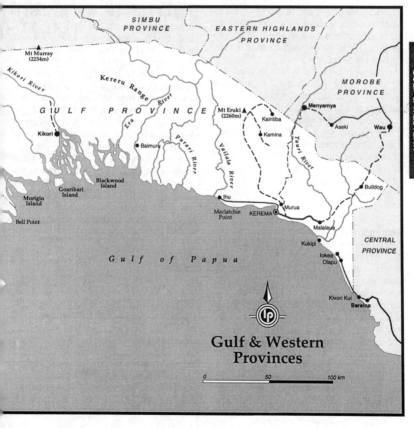

GULF & WESTERN

Gulf & Western Provinces

Gulf Province

Land Area 34,500 sq km
Population 75,000
Capital Kerema

KEREMA
• *pop 4000* • *postcode 311*

Kerema was primarily chosen as the provincial capital because of its climate – it is comparatively drier than elsewhere in the province. Facilities are limited but there is a PNGBC bank and two main stores: the Kerema Trader and Nings Trading. There is a sketchy road network, including a link to Malalaua, and nearby is a prawn fishery. More information may be available (if you are lucky) from the provincial tourism office (☎ 648 1084; fax 648 1150).

It is possible to travel by boat upriver from Kerema. For the shoestringer, Kerema is not really worthy the designation of a destination but is more a place to go through (and only if absolutely necessary).

The *Elavo Inn* might still have accommodation. Don't expect too much. The Catholic mission near the market may still offer rooms. As is so often the case in PNG, almost all villages will accept visitors and it is the women who provide the housing and the food.

Getting There & Around

Air Niugini does not fly to Kerema, but MBA flies there every day except Sunday, including its multi-stop Lae-Port Moresby run via Kaintiba and Menyamya on Monday. Annoyingly, neither airline flies between Daru and Kerema. MBA also services some of the smaller towns in Gulf Province. Non-discounted one-way airfares from Kerema in mid-1997 were: Port Moresby K139, Baimuru K80, Ihu K40, Kikori K112, Kuri K172 and Malalaua K40.

There are no passenger vessels sailing between Port Moresby and the gulf, and none of the major freight lines officially takes passengers. Your nautical options are limited to finding a smaller cargo boat out of Port Moresby. Alternatively, the MV *Purari* or MV *Mafaroe* may still be operating out of Malalaua. Village-hopping in smaller boats or canoes may also be possible if you have time.

The Hiritano Highway from Port Moresby now goes as far as Iokea (pronounced 'yoh-kea'); you can get there by PMV. There's a mission here where you can stay. From Lavare, a couple of kilometres west of Iokea, you can catch canoes to Malalaua (five hours). The trip through the swamps to Navara is very interesting. Apparently, it is also possible to go direct by canoe to Kerema from Iokea. There is a road link between Malalaua (about 2km from the river) to Kerema and there are PMVs. It is also possible to walk along the coast from Iokea at low tide. Government-funded ferries take people across the rivers; if they're on the opposite side, light a fire to attract their attention. Canoes may not operate during the wet season. People are very friendly – one traveller reported that it took him days to get to Kerema, not because of any shortage of canoes, but because people insisted that he stay the night with them.

People have walked into Menyamya (north in the Highlands) from Kerema but this would definitely not be a picnic stroll. You could also fly to Kaintiba and walk from there, picking up road transport into Lae. See the Menyamya & Aseki section in the Morobe Province chapter.

AROUND GULF PROVINCE
Malalaua

Malalaua can be reached from Port Moresby by air or a combination of PMV and canoe. The Toaripi Trade Store is the biggest in this small town. Malalaua is the southern end of the WWII Bulldog Track which goes through to Edie Creek near Wau. Walking from this end would be extremely difficult; first you'd have to get upriver to Bulldog and then you'd have a very difficult uphill walk to Edie Creek. Most of the few people who undertake this difficult trek come from the other direction (from Wau).

Pelicans are found in coastal areas of PNG

Ihu
Ihu is the main station between the delta country and Kerema and is planned to be the centre for the proposed Purari River power project. A road runs most of the way to the Purari and is surrounded by beautiful bush. Canoes apparently travel between Ihu and Baimuru and from Baimuru to Kikori, although they may not operate between January and September. There's a tractor road along the beach from Ihu to Murua. There are a couple of basic places to stay in Ihu but it is difficult to get information on them. The *Orokolo Guesthouse* may be worth trying. If you can get through (which is difficult), contact the Division of Commerce, Culture & Tourism (☎ 648 1056) in Kerema for information. Kela Trading has the main store in town.

Kamina
This is a beautiful place, between Kerema and Kaintiba. It's a difficult but interesting two-day walk to Kaintiba, through villages which have retained traditional culture. Guides are available for about K10 a day.

Kaintiba
Kaintiba, in the mountains behind the coast, is in Anga country. There is good walking in the area with frequent villages; many are within a day's walk of each other and many have some sort of mission where you can put up. From Kaintiba, it is a tough though interesting walk to Aseki and Menyamya, which are linked by road to Lae. See the Morobe Province chapter.

Kikori & Baimuru
These two small delta towns are set well back from the coastline. Kikori (pop 450) is one of the oldest stations in Papua, but Baimuru is now the larger of the two with a population of about 1400. Kikori is the coastal base for the Kutubu oil pipeline and there is a barramundi fishery at Baimuru. Both have small airstrips and it is possible to get from one to the other by boat through the maze of waterways. There are some interesting villages along the way.

The *Delta Lodge* in Kikori is worth trying for accommodation.

Western Province

Land Area 99,300 sq km
Population 125,000
Capital Daru

DARU
• *pop 8600* • *postcode 331*
Daru was the colonial headquarters for Western Division, the former name of the province, from 1893 but little has happened there since. It is on a small island of the same name close to the coast. Daru used to be a pearl and bêche-de-mer trading port and is still busy, with a growing fishing industry. Skins of crocodiles caught in the province are exported from Daru. There's a PNGBC bank, but not much of interest for travellers.

Place to Stay & Eat
The *Daru-Wyben Hotel* (☎ 645 9055; fax 645 9065; PO Box 121) is the only place to

WESTERN PROVINCE

stay and its restaurant has excellent seafood. For rooms with fans, TV and private bathrooms it costs an exorbitant K145/180 a night. If they know you're coming they'll collect you from the airport.

Getting There & Around

Air Niugini has an office in Daru (☎ 645 9058; PO Box 161). Both Air Niugini and MBA fly between Port Moresby and Daru. MBA also flies to Balimo and Kiunga. Non-discounted airfares from Daru as at mid 1997 were: Port Moresby K144, Balimo K80 and Kiunga K157.

The only regular boats going up the Fly are the ore barges from the Ok Tedi mine. Getting a lift on one is almost impossible, as you would first have to get to the mother ship anchored in the gulf, wait until a barge arrived and then negotiate a trip. It would be an interesting trip and the barges are apparently comfortable but the Fly, despite the huge volume of water coming down, does occasionally strand the barges. One crew was finally picked up a couple of months after its barge had run out of river and crewmembers had established a fine vegetable garden around their vessel.

A major drought in 1997, brought about by El Niño (the climatic event which has had a dramatic effect on weather patterns and has led to hot, dry conditions in southern PNG), caused the river to dry up to the point where the mine closed down temporarily because the barges couldn't navigate.

AROUND WESTERN PROVINCE
Balimo

• *pop 2300* • *postcode 336*

This relatively large missionary town is inland from Daru, on the Aramia River. The hospital here is supposed to be good. One of the nearby villages specialises in carvings, which can be bought in town. For accommodation try the mission or ask at the district office about staying in the cultural centre.

Bensbach

The Bensbach area is a vast floodplain, lightly populated because of heavy head-hunting in earlier years. But the area is alive with animals and birds, many of them amazingly fearless because they have had little contact with people. The Dutch introduced rusa deer into western New Guinea in the 1920s and, untroubled by natural predators, they have spread far into PNG – there are over 20,000 deer west of the Bensbach in PNG territory. Wallabies, crocodiles and wild pigs are also prolific and the bird-life is quite incredible. It's a photographer's paradise. Keen fishers will also enjoy themselves because the Bensbach River is renowned for the size and number of its barramundi, which feature frequently on the menu at the Bensbach Wildlife Lodge.

Place to Stay Only a few kilometres from the Indonesian border, the *Bensbach Wildlife Lodge* has been a major tourist attraction in Western Province – but only for well-off tourists. Near Weam, the lodge is 96km north of the river mouth, on the eastern bank of the Bensbach River. If you are a keen fisher or bird-watcher with a little money to spend, it's a must-see. The low-lying lodge was built with local materials and has 11 twin rooms flanking a central bar, lounge and dining room. It has had a difficult time in recent years and has been closed for some time; the owners hoped to have it operational in late 1997. The basic cost per person per night is K200, including meals and transport. You can't phone the lodge; contact John Renshaw in Port Moresby (☎ 323 4467; PO Box 6940, Boroko) for details.

Lake Murray

Lake Murray, in the centre of the vast Western Province, is the biggest lake in PNG; during the wet season it can spread to five times its 400-sq-km dry season area. There is a crocodile research station at the lake. Nomad, to the north, is one of the most remote and inaccessible patrol stations in the country.

Ok Tedi Mine

• *postcode 333*

Ok Tedi Mining Ltd has its headquarters at

Tabubil (☎ 325 9333; fax 325 9183; PO Box 1), and has been operating at Folomian on nearby Mt Fubilan since 1984. Until the Porgera mine opened in Enga Province, Ok Tedi was the largest gold mine outside South Africa. The operation involves an open-cut mine, less than 1km in diameter. A gold 'cap' has been mined first, most of which has been exhausted, followed by the main ore body of copper. The Australian company BHP and the PNG government are the main shareholders, but BHP manages the project.

The area's remoteness, in the Star Mountains near the Indonesian border, has created problems, as well as some odd juxtapositions. Local men wearing only penis gourds can be seen working on the site beside gigantic modern cranes and bulldozers.

In a mammoth undertaking to service the mine, a pipeline was built between Tabubil and Kiunga on the Fly River. A copper/gold slurry (50% water and 50% concentrate) is sent 140km through the pipeline to Kiunga where it is loaded onto barges and then taken a further 800km to the coast for loading onto ocean-going ships.

Tabubil
• *pop 10,000* • *postcode 332*

Tabubil was built to service the Ok Tedi mining community. It is more like a small Australian country town than a typical PNG village, which is understandable because it caters to a mining population including many Australians. The town is in a long, wide valley filled with rainforest and, in the early mornings, dense fog. A short walk to the west, behind the hotel, takes you to an escarpment which looks down on the Ok Tedi River.

Tabubil has a post office, well-equipped hospital, pharmacy, good supermarkets and an international school and is very much a 'company' town. Ninety per cent of Ok Tedi Mining Ltd's 2000 employees are locals, something reflected in the housing mix in the town. To prevent staff accommodating *wantoks* (relatives) in company houses built for a nuclear family, there is a regulation, applied to expats and nationals, that no outside visitors can stay in the houses without permission from the company. Partly as a result of this, and because of the higher wages in the town and its

The Ok Tedi Mine & the Environment

The Ok Tedi mine has not been without controversy, both in terms of its impact on people and on the environment. Work began on the site in the early 1980s, but a tailings dam, designed to trap waste by-products, collapsed in 1984, making a hell of a mess and raising significant environmental concerns as well as costing a fortune to fix. The accident also raised doubts about the capabilities of the project's engineers and management. The greatest impact was felt along a 20km stretch of the Ok Tedi River, where the terrain flattens out at the foot of the Star Mountains. About 80,000 tons of pollution a day flowed into the Ok Tedi and Fly rivers at the time, endangering not only the livelihoods of the people living along its banks but also the important breeding grounds for ocean fish near the river mouth. Sediment smothered vegetation over more than 100 sq km and caused the riverbed to rise.

With a view to eventually taking legal action for environmental damage against BHP, which manages the mine, a Melbourne law firm, Slater & Gordon, was instructed by over 30,000 PNG villagers to act on their behalf. In a controversial move, however, BHP lobbied the PNG government to make it illegal for anyone to bring damages against BHP or its affiliates such as Ok Tedi Mining Ltd in such cases. The PNG government complied.

Slater & Gordon successfully sought to have the case dealt with in Melbourne, Australia (primarily because that is where BHP's headquarters are, and that was where the critical decisions were made concerning Ok Tedi). However, the need for further legal action was averted when the landowners accepted an out-of-court settlement resulting in substantial compensation. BHP agreed to pay about K110 million to a provincial government trust. The provincial government was also given 10% equity in the mine, K40 million was allocated to the relocation of villages along the Ok Tedi and Fly rivers, various social and environmental development projects were initiated, and some K7.5 million was reimbursed to the villagers for legal costs. Precautions were also taken to ensure that future tailings do not flow into the river. ■

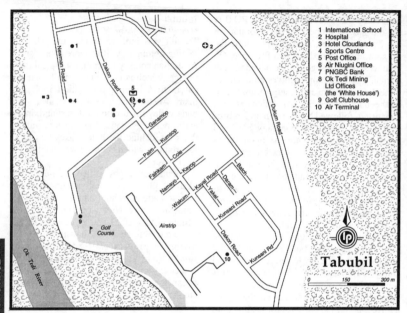

1	International School
2	Hospital
3	Hotel Cloudlands
4	Sports Centre
5	Post Office
6	Air Niugini Office
7	PNGBC Bank
8	Ok Tedi Mining Ltd Offices (the 'White House')
9	Golf Clubhouse
10	Air Terminal

WESTERN PROVINCE

work prospects, a shanty town has arisen around the edges, filling the niche of 'the wrong end of town'. It also means that it is more difficult for visiting backpackers to stay in private houses.

Electricity for the town is provided by the nearby Ok Menga hydroelectricity station (*ok* is *tok ples*, or local dialect, for river).

It is forecast that the mine's ore will run out in around 2010 – but this could be a significant underestimation. Planning is under way to find replacement industries to support the town when this eventually happens. Industries being investigated include rubber, ecotourism, clothing manufacture, pineapple processing, poultry, cashews and venison.

Things to See & Do The bird-life in the surrounding valleys is quite amazing – there are 16 species of birds of paradise within a 25km radius of the town.

There are good walks at **Lake Wangbin** –

but they can be a little rough. It is best to helicopter in and walk back downhill to Tabubil. You also need to seek permission from the local villagers who may ask you *not* to swim in the lake, which is a sacred site. The local villagers keep pet tree kangaroos which eventually end up in the pot.

The **Lukwi Caves**, 18km along the Okma Road, are worth exploring. There is a small waterfall covering the entrance to a 150m long tunnel which finally opens out into a narrow gorge.

The locals are friendly and visitors are welcome to join them in outings. There is also an excellent nine-hole golf course (with clubhouse) skirting the airport, a Hash House Harriers club, and a sports centre.

Places to Stay & Eat The *Hotel Cloudlands* (☎ 548 9277; fax 548 9301; PO Box 226) is similar to its Australian country-town equivalents, understandable because it is managed by an amiable Australian. It is comfortable and clean with an excellent swimming pool, bar and dining room. There are three standards of room – costing K80, K100 and K125. The top end is a nice air-con motel room; the bottom end is still very comfortable but merely a row of demountables (also with air-con, which is not really necessary in these cool mountains), with caravan-style bathrooms, dating to the early years of the town. There is to be a new wing added in 1998, which will mean that the top-end price will rise a little and apparently the demountables may come down in price to around K50.

The company mess is reportedly also a good place to eat, with good, cheap and filling food, and visitors are welcome.

Getting There & Around It is a busy airport and, if you ask around, you may be able to hitch a ride. Otherwise, MBA and (occasionally on a charter) Air Niugini fly to and from Tabubil. Non-discounted airfares are: Port Moresby K233, Tari K103, Mendi K110, Mt Hagen K122, Kiunga K59 and Wewak K193.

MAF also has irregular services in this area. There is an MAF agent (☎ 548 9025) at the Tabubil airstrip.

There is a rough road following the route of the pipeline between Tabubil and Kiunga – it's the only real road to either town. Massive convoys of trucks constantly ply the route carrying supplies back up to Tabubil. If you drive from Tabubil to Kiunga, be aware that these convoys have priority and will *not* stop for you. When you see them coming, you are obliged to get off the road and let them pass.

Four-wheel drives can be hired at Tabubil airport – but they are curiosities. They have flashing disco lights and long whip aerials with lights on top – because it is not unknown for the monstrous trucks which operate in the

---

> ### The Ok Counting System
> Gerry Schuurkamp notes in his book *The Min of the Papua New Guinea Star Mountains* that 27 is the numeric counting base for the Mountain Ok people:
> 'Fingers, hands, arms and the head play an important role in [this system], they all represent numbers. Counting starts with the little finger of the left hand as one *(maagup)* across to the thumb which is five *(egal)*, the wrist (six), forearm (seven or *ban*, which is also the word for an initiation ceremony because originally there were seven of these), elbow, biceps, shoulder, side of neck, ear, eye, with the bridge of the nose representing the midpoint of 14 *mit*, and then down the right side to the little finger of the right side (27 or *kakat)*.' ■

---

open-cut mine to crush minuscule 4WDs under their gigantic 4m-diameter wheels (they have limited visibility to the immediate front). Avis rents 4WDs for K136 per day plus K0.87 per kilometre.

Kiunga
• *pop 4000* • *postcode 335*

Kiunga's only reason for existence is as the river port for the Ok Tedi mine and Tabubil. From Kiunga, barges take the treated ore downstream to the delta where it is transshipped to waiting cargo vessels. On the return trips they bring supplies for the mine and the towns. There is a post office and both Westpac and PNGBC banks are represented. Many of the villages near Kiunga grow vegetables for the Tabubil market.

Place to Stay The *Kiunga Guesthouse* (☎ 548 1188; fax 548 1195; PO Box 20) has rooms for an exorbitant K195, including three meals and laundry, but there might still be cheaper old rooms available if you ask.

New Britain

Land Area 40,500 sq km
Population 316,000

New Britain Island, Papua New Guinea's largest, is divided into two provinces that are quite different in character and level of development.

East New Britain (ENB) Province ends in the densely populated Gazelle Peninsula where there has been lengthy contact with Europeans, education levels are high and the people are among the most economically advantaged in the country. The southern part of the province, around Pomio, is much less developed.

By contrast, the other end of the island, West New Britain (WNB) Province, is sparsely populated, little developed and did not come into serious contact with Europeans until the 1960s.

For most visitors, New Britain will mean Rabaul – the once-beautiful harbour city on the Gazelle Peninsula with its dramatic and recently malevolent cluster of volcanos. In September 1994 Tuvurvur and Vulcan erupted, spewing huge amounts of ash over Rabaul and the Simpson Harbour and Karavia Bay area, bringing about the death of one of PNG's biggest and perhaps most beautiful cities. Vulcan shot its load in a few days, but Tuvurvur was still blowing huge plumes of smoke into the sky at the time of this book's research, two and a half years later. The impact on the densely populated Gazelle Peninsula has been enormous.

History

The island of New Britain was settled around 12,000 years ago; volcanic glass traded from Talasea (WNB) has been found on Watom Island (ENB) and dated around 2500 years old.

Several hundred years ago, the Tolai (pronounced 'tol-eye') people, who make up two-thirds of ENB's population, came from

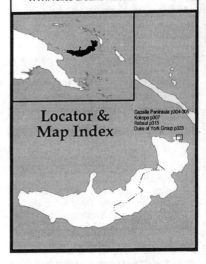

HIGHLIGHTS

- Walking around the ruins of the once-beautiful Rabaul
- Watching the volcano Tuvurvur blow plumes of smoke into the sky
- Catching a dinghy out to the Duke of York islands
- Snorkelling at Submarine Base
- Exploring the Japanese tunnels and other WWII relics around Rabaul

**Locator &
Map Index**

Gazelle Peninsula p304-305
Kokopo p307
Rabaul p315
Duke of York Group p323

southern New Ireland and invaded the Gazelle Peninsula in northernmost New Britain, driving the Baining, Sulka and Taulil people south into the mountains. The Tolais speak their own *tok ples* (local language) but have many cultural similarities to the southern New Irelanders.

English navigator William Dampier was the first European to visit, arriving early in 1700. Although he proved New Britain was an island, separated from the New Guinea mainland by Dampier Strait, it was not until 1767 that fellow Englishman Phillip Carteret discovered that Dampier's St Georges Bay was actually a channel and that New Ireland and New Britain were separate islands. St Georges Bay became St Georges Channel. A hundred years passed with only occasional contact, although whalers and sailors passed through the channel, sometimes pausing for water and provisions.

In 1874 German traders established settlements at Mioko Island, in the Duke of York islands, and in 1876 at Matupit Island in Blanche Bay. In 1875 the Reverend George Brown started a Methodist mission at Port Hunter in the Duke of York islands with a group of six Fijians. Apart from converting heathens he also worked as a keen amateur vulcanologist, linguist, scientist, an anthropologist and local explorer. Only one of his Fijian assistants survived the first turbulent years, but Brown left as a respected, even loved, man.

In 1878, Emma Forsayth, soon to be known as Queen Emma, arrived from Samoa and started a trading business at Mioko in the Duke of York islands, taking the first steps towards her remarkable fame and fortune (see the Queen Emma aside). Sacred Heart Catholics began a mission on the peninsula's north coast in 1882, and the following year saw the region's first coconut plantation near Kokopo and the founding of the Vunapope Catholic mission. In 1882 Captain Simpson sailed in on HMS *Blanche* and named the harbour where Rabaul would be situated after himself and the bay after his ship. On 3 November 1884, the German flag was unfurled on Matupit Island and a German protectorate was declared. The German New Guinea Company assumed authority – although it ultimately ran New Guinea more like a business than a government administration. Within a few years, it had relocated its headquarters around Blanche Bay to Kokopo, which it named Herbertshohe. The local name Kokopo ('the landslide') is now used.

In 1910, the Germans again relocated their headquarters to the new town of Rabaul, the only pre-planned town in PNG, because Kokopo had no deep-water harbour and

Simpson Harbour was suitable for off-loading plantation produce for export. Rabaul means mangrove in Kuanua (the Tolai tok ples) – so named because the town site was on the reclaimed land of a mangrove swamp. By WWI, the Germans had acquired more than one-third of Tolai lands for plantations.

On 11 September 1914, Australian troops landed at Kabakaul, east of Kokopo, and captured the German radio station at Bita Paka. It was in this operation that able seaman WGV Williams became the first Australian casualty of WWI; five of his compatriots also died, along with one German and 30 PNG soldiers, before the Australians had secured the radio station. A larger contingent of Australians died when their submarine mysteriously disappeared off the coast during the attack.

At the end of the war, the German planters had their plantations expropriated and were shipped back to Germany. They were compensated, as part of the war reparations agreement, in German marks, which soon became totally worthless in the hyperinflation suffered by Germany in the early 1920s. One unfortunate individual made his way back to New Britain, started again from scratch and once more built up a thriving plantation. He neglected to take out Australian citizenship and in WWII his property was expropriated once again.

Between the wars, Rabaul continued on its busy and profitable way as the capital of Australian New Guinea. However, in 1937 the Vulcan and Tuvurvur volcanos erupted, killing 507 people and causing enormous damage. Before this eruption Vulcan had been a low flat island hundreds of metres offshore (it had appeared from nowhere during the 1878 eruption), but when the eruptions ceased 27 hours later it was a massive mountain attached to the coast. Vulcan settled down after 12 days, but Tuvurvur blew smoke and ash for six years.

After this the Australian administration decided to move its headquarters to the safer site of Lae. The move had barely commenced when WWII arrived in Rabaul; its

NEW BRITAIN

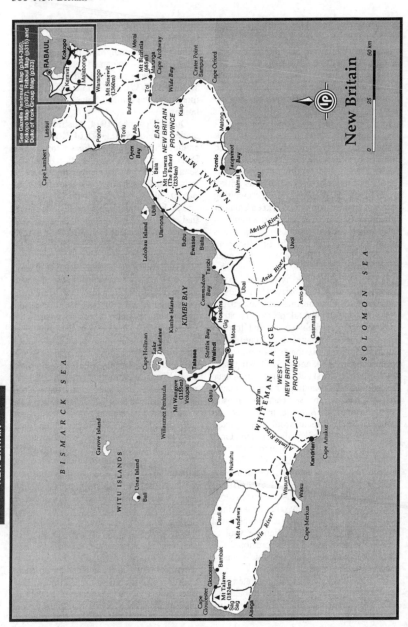

See Gazelle Peninsula Map (p304-305), Kokopo Map (p307) Rabaul Map (p315) and Duke of York Group Map (p323)

NEW BRITAIN

New Britain

BISMARCK SEA

SOLOMON SEA

Cape Lambert
Lassul
RABAUL
Kokopo
Keravat
Malabonga
Merai
Watom
Cape Archway
Mt Sinewit (1360m)
Mt Bitafrinia (685m)
Madonga
Cape Archway
Wide Bay
Crater Point
Sampun
Cape Orford
Warango
Tol
Kalip
Matong
Bulayang
Allo
Toriu
Pondo
Open Bay
Baia
Mt Ulawun (The Father) (2334m)
Jacquinot Bay
Pomio
Lau
Malmal
Ubili
Ulamona
Lolobau Island
NAKANAI MTNS
Bubu
Ewasse
Biala
Tarobi
Ubai
Melkoi River
Uvol
Ania River
EAST NEW BRITAIN PROVINCE
Cape Hollman
Lake Dakataua
Willaumez Peninsula
Mt Wangore (1155m)
Voupoi
Talasea
Kimbe Island
KIMBE BAY
Commodore Bay
Hoskins
Gig
Mosa
Walindi
Stettin Bay
KIMBE
WHITEMAN RANGE
WEST NEW BRITAIN PROVINCE
Gasmata
Arno
Garu
2027m
Nukuhu
Alimbit River
Cape Amukur
Kandrian
Wasum
Waku
Cape Merkus
Dauli
Mt Andewa
Pulie River
Bambak
Mt Talave (1824m)
Sag Sag
Alsega
Cape Gloucester
BISMARCK SEA
WITU ISLANDS
Ganove Island
Unea Island
Bali

0 25 50 km

impact was even more dramatic than that of the volcanos.

After the Japanese attack on Pearl Harbour, it was obvious that Rabaul would soon be in danger. All women and children were evacuated by the end of December 1941, but there were still about 400 Australian civilians in the town on 22 January, when a huge bombing raid heralded the coming invasion. The following day, a small contingent of Australian troops was completely crushed by a Japanese assault. Those who managed to escape found themselves cut off in the jungle and isolated on New Britain Island (the Japanese had already captured Lae and Salamaua on the mainland). In an amazing feat of endurance, patrol officers based in New Britain (including JK McCarthy, who retells the operation in his book *Patrol Into Yesterday*) shepherded the surviving troops along the inhospitable and roadless coast to New Britain's southern tip, where a flotilla of private boats rescued 400 of the 700 men who had survived.

Those left behind in Rabaul were not so fortunate – not a single one of them was ever heard from again. Over two years later the Japanese government revealed that on 22 June 1942, internees from a Blanche Bay compound were taken aboard the prison ship *Montevideo Maru*, which was bound for Japan. However, USS *Sturgeon* sunk the ship on 1 July near the west coast of Luzon in the Philippines and 210 civilians died. This was Australia's worst WWII tragedy in the Pacific.

The Japanese intended to use Rabaul as a major supply base for their steady march south. But, with defeats at Guadalcanal in the Solomon Islands and at Milne Bay and Buna on the New Guinea mainland, their naval power shattered in the Battle of the Coral Sea, they were soon on the defensive and Rabaul was made into a fortress. They dug 580km of tunnels into the hills – a honeycomb of interconnecting passages used for storage, hospitals, anti-aircraft guns, bunkers, gun emplacements and barracks. At the peak of the war 97,000 Japanese troops and thousands of POWs were stationed on the Gazelle Peninsula. They imported 800 Japanese and Korean prostitutes, the harbour was laced with mines and the roads were camouflaged with trees.

But the Allies never came. MacArthur had learnt the lessons of Guadalcanal and Buna, where the bitter fighting had led to enormous casualties on both sides – never again did the Japanese and Allied forces meet head-on. The Japanese airforce was unable to compete effectively with Allied air power and over 20,000 tons of bombs rained down upon the peninsula, keeping the remaining Japanese forces underground and impotent. When the war ended they were still there.

Above ground Rabaul was flattened. Photographs taken just after the Japanese surrender in 1945 show Mango Ave, Rabaul's main street, marked only by occasional heaps of bricks. Over 40 ships lay at the bottom of the harbour; it took two years just to transfer all the troops back to Japan.

Rabaul soon bounced back. After the war, as concepts of self-government developed, land became a major issue and there was considerable discontent. The Tolais wanted the return of all land 'bought' from them in the German days, when they were less sophisticated in their dealings with the west. A political organisation, known as the Mataungan Association, sprang up with the aim of subverting the Australian-managed local councils and self-government programmes. The Tolais were talking about self-government, but on their own terms – they successfully boycotted the first pre-independence election and demanded that their Mataungan leaders be given power. The problem has not gone away, but is not a central issue today.

Rabaul's volcanos have not been as easily put aside. In 1983 Rabaul seemed to be heating up, and by early 1984 the town was ready for evacuation. The threatened eruption failed to eventuate but the situation highlighted, once again, the town's precarious position.

On 19 September 1994 Tuvurvur and Vulcan exploded with relatively little warning. Metres of ash and rock now cover

NEW BRITAIN

Simpson Harbour and Karavia Bay and their adjoining lands, as well as the peninsula's northern coast. The false alarm of 1983 had helped develop a good evacuation strategy and only five people died, but 50,000 people lost their homes and one of PNG's most developed and interesting cities was again flattened. Rabaul is still a ruin and the lands around Simpson Harbour, Karavia Bay and as far back as Keravat are still suffering wet-season floods and enormous mudslides that can change the shape of the land daily. Everybody's lives have changed and the hardships suffered by ordinary people have been enormous. Where people once had jobs and homes, there is now just a weird expanse of broken buildings.

Rabaul was not just the provincial capital, it was also the centre for all the island provinces. Suddenly the little town of Kokopo, 20km further around the bay, has had greatness thrust upon it. History shows that Rabaul can rebuild itself but, for now, it's a desolate wasteland.

Geography

New Britain is a long, narrow, mountainous island. It is nearly 600km from end to end but at its widest point it is only 80km across. The interior is harsh and rugged, split by gorges and fast-flowing rivers and blanketed in thick rainforest. The highest mountain is Mt Uluwan (The Father), an active volcano rising to 2334m, which is north of the Nakanai Mountains. The north-eastern end

of the island terminates in the heavily populated, highly fertile and dramatically volcanic Gazelle Peninsula. Rabaul and Simpson Harbour are in the collapsed caldera of a giant volcano that has flooded with sea water; the volcanos that run around this old crater's edge are Kombiu (The Mother), Tovanumbatir (North Daughter), Turangunan (South Daughter), Rabalanakaia, Tuvurvur and Vulcan. Tuvurvur and Vulcan erupted to devastating effect in 1937 and September 1994.

Climate

New Britain lies across the direction of the monsoon winds so the rainy season comes at opposite times of the year on the north and south coasts. More than elsewhere in PNG the weather will affect your visit to ENB. The wet season brings massive mudslides and floods, which often cut off the Kokopo-Rabaul Road; walking and climbing opportunities are restricted during the season.

The Pomio and Jacquinot Bay area receives more than 6500mm of rainfall each year, while annual rainfall in the Blanche Bay and Simpson Harbour area is about 2000mm. The dry season is between mid-April and November.

Society & Conduct

ENB has 13 local languages, but two-thirds of the people speak Kuanua (the Tolai tok ples). Most people speak Pidgin and many

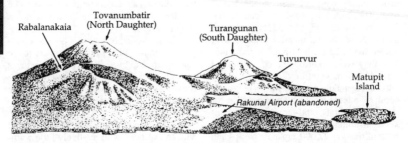

Volcanos of the Rabaul area.

also speak English. Most of the 184,000 people in ENB are Tolais. The Tolais invaded the Gazelle Peninsula from southern New Ireland several centuries before European contact. They still share many cultural similarities with southern New Irelanders, including the dances of the *tumbuan* (body masks) and *dukduks* (spirits).

The few Baining people left live in bark-walled houses, mainly in the Baining Mountains south of Rabaul in a relatively undeveloped part of the province. They traditionally perform fire dances which are a spectacular event – huge bark-cloth masks with emphasised eyes and features are worn by dancers who walk on hot coals. If you want to see a dance, ask at the ENB tourist office in Kokopo or call the Ulatawa Plantation (☎ 982 1294).

When Europeans came to the Gazelle Peninsula, the Tolais were a pretty wild bunch commonly involved in inter-clan warfare. Like most PNG islander communities, property and clan rights pass through the mother's side of the family. Chiefs and elders' council members are men, but women have enormous influence in village politics. Tolais don't live in communal villages as such. Rather, family groups live in hamlets and when children marry, they usually leave to start their own settlement nearby.

Traditionally, clan authority was wielded by *bigmen* (important men) who won their prestige through wealth or military prowess. A secret male society played an important role in village life, organising ceremonies and maintaining customary laws. Tolai ceremonies feature leaf-draped, anonymous figures topped by masks – tumbuans and dukduks, whose construction can take months. The building of tumbuans and dukduks is a highly secret rite, usually done in a secluded area that is fenced off and guarded by the 'owner' (shell money must be paid before the area can be entered). After Easter men build tumbuans and dukduks and this can take months. Spirits are both benign and malevolent and play a big part in clan law. A dukduk on your doorstep is a very foreboding sign. Tolais believe that the Duke of York islands are home to tumbuans and dukduks, which are roused by the rituals.

The most feared are the *masalais* (pronounced 'mussel-eyes'), which are spirits of the bush and water that live in certain rock pools and thickets. Masalais are powerful and vengeful. You should treat these ideas with respect when you speak with people, otherwise you will cause offence, and don't swim in a masalai's rock pool (a *dewel ples* in *tok pisin*, or Pidgin).

Shell money, or *tambu*, retains its cultural significance for the Tolai and is still displayed and distributed at traditional ceremonies, such as the *kututambu*. Little shells are strung on lengths of cane and bound together in great rolls called *loloi*. You can still see people using tambu to make small purchases at markets and roadside stalls. It takes a dozen shells to equal K0.10.

Traditional foods include taro, sweet potato and banana, but meals based around rice and tinned fish or bully beef have, like everywhere else in PNG, largely supplanted these staples (another legacy of WWII).

At one time Rabaul had a large Chinese community, and while many left after independence, others stayed on operating businesses. Since the 1994 eruptions, much of this community has relocated to Kokopo. The region has many Papua New Guineans from the less-affluent Highlands and Sepik regions, who have come to carry out unskilled work on the copra plantations.

East New Britain Province

Land Area 15,500 sq km
Population 220,000
Capital Kokopo

The volcanic eruptions of September 1994 completely altered East New Britain. Rabaul is utterly destroyed and the province now centres around Kokopo, 20km south-east of

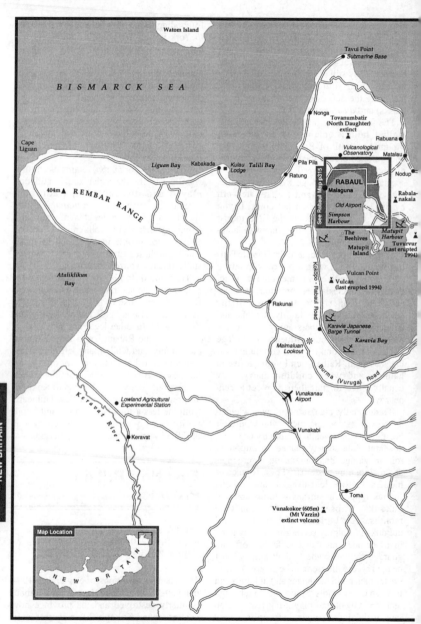

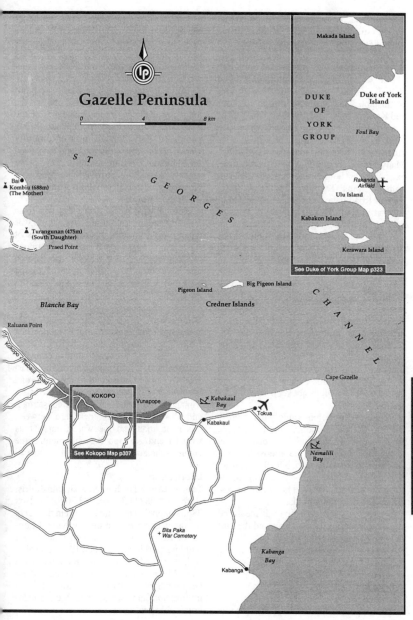

Gazelle Peninsula

0   4   8 km

S T

G E O R G E S

Bai
Kombiu (688m)
(The Mother)

Turangunan (475m)
(South Daughter)
Praed Point

Blanche Bay

Raluana Point

Kokopo / Rabaul Road

KOKOPO

See Kokopo Map p307

Vunapope

Pigeon Island

Big Pigeon Island

Credner Islands

C H A N N E L

Kabakaul
Bay

Tokua

Kabakaul

Namalili
Bay

Cape Gazelle

Bita Paka
War Cemetery

Kabanga
Bay

Kabanga

DUKE
OF
YORK
GROUP

Makada Island

Duke of York
Island

Foul Bay

Rakanda
Airfield

Ulu Island

Kabakon Island

Kerawara Island

See Duke of York Group Map p323

NEW BRITAIN

Rabaul. The region is serviced by Tokua airport (still called 'Rabaul' on some airline schedules), a further 20km past Kokopo.

Miraculously, Matupit Island, 1km offshore from Tuvurvur, was spared the wrath of the volcano, but the eruption levelled Rabaul and the northern coast. There's a lot of unstable land around Simpson Harbour and Karavia Bay. Vulcan covered the area of Karavia Bay in metres of ash and rock, which turns to mud in the rains; the wet seasons since have brought massive landslides. Many people are clinging on to a precarious existence, as houses and villages are lost with the rains. Travellers on the Kokopo-Rabaul Road have to negotiate up to 5m of earth at Vulcan's base, which shifts dramatically in the rains; huge rivers can appear in cracks in the semi-dry mud in minutes. The road can be open one day and cut by a broad ravine, 3m deep, the next. Slowly grasses are taking root in some parts of the rich volcanic ash – the start of the process which will eventually bring a more rigid shape to the topography.

At the time of research, Tuvurvur was still blowing huge plumes of ash into the sky, booming (which could be heard from New Ireland), rumbling and hissing literally every five minutes. If Tuvurvur follows the pattern of the 1937 eruption, when it huffed and puffed until 1943, it might keep smoking for several years yet.

Things are happening rapidly in the province, as Kokopo booms and the people rebuild. You can still stay in Rabaul, at one of the three hotels that are almost the only buildings to have survived, but all around are city blocks of utter ruin – including courthouses, a cinema, banks, a huge central post office and swimming pools.

The region's seismic activity is measured more conscientiously than ever and the vulcanology observatory posts daily bulletins. Tuvurvur's spectacular emissions of smoke and noise are not considered dangerous.

KOKOPO
• postcode 613

Kokopo wasn't ready to take on its new role as capital of the province; now the once-sleepy little town is full of people and its main road is choked with traffic. Rabaul's government services and almost all of its businesses have relocated to Kokopo, causing some tensions.

Tax concessions were granted to Rabaul-based businesses to move to Kokopo and the long-time Kokopo traders have found the new competition hard to manage. Many people in Rabaul's business community were Chinese, often relations, and have used their business clout to help each other quickly re-establish profitable businesses in Kokopo. Old racial problems simmer just under the surface.

Kokopo used to be a nice day trip from Rabaul, and neighbouring Vunapope was where you'd visit the historic buildings of the Catholic mission and hospital. But now, thanks to Kokopo's rapid expansion, the two towns are virtually contiguous, with Kokopo engulfing villages to the west and inland to the south.

Orientation
A coastal road runs around Blanche Bay, from Tokua airport through Kokopo to Rabaul. The old Burma Road also connects Kokopo and Rabaul, but leaves the coast near Vulcan and is used when the coast road is impassable. Kokopo and adjoining Vunapope are strung along this coast road, and Kokopo's central blocks are between this main road and the waterfront. At its western end Kokopo has the picturesque lawns of the golf course.

Information
Tourist Office The East New Britain Tourist Bureau (☎ 982 9038; fax 983 7070; PO Box 385, Kokopo) is in a small room in the street off the main road with the big white Chopsticks Restaurant and Taklam Guesthouse building marking the corner. It's not terribly well set up and moving from Rabaul has had its problems, but it's worth dropping in there because Samson Kakai has lots of local information and can arrange accommodation in the area.

Book A small yellow book called *A Guide to the History of the Kokopo-Rabaul Area*, written by local historian David Lindley and published by the East New Britain Historical & Cultural Society, has good local history information. The book is widely available in the province.

East New Britain Historical & Cultural Centre

This museum (☎ 982 8453; fax 982 8439; PO Box 50), near the Ralum Country Club (the golf course clubhouse), has a good collection of historical objects, photographs and many Japanese WWII relics. The objects are well displayed and accompanied by interpretive information.

Among the displays is part of the painted nose-cone of an American B17 bomber – 'Naughty but Nice' is the caption for the 1940s-style soft-porn painting; it's in remarkably good condition for a painting that lay in the jungle for many years until it was retrieved by a surviving crew member.

The museum is open from 8 am to 4 pm on weekdays (closing for lunch between 1 and 2 pm), and from 1 to 5 pm on weekends. Admission is K1.

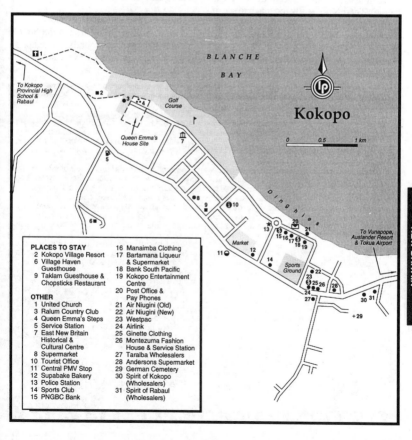

PLACES TO STAY
2 Kokopo Village Resort
6 Village Haven Guesthouse
9 Taklam Guesthouse & Chopsticks Restaurant

OTHER
1 United Church
3 Ralum Country Club
4 Queen Emma's Steps
5 Service Station
7 East New Britain Historical & Cultural Centre
8 Supermarket
10 Tourist Office
11 Central PMV Stop
12 Supabake Bakery
13 Police Station
14 Sports Club
15 PNGBC Bank
16 Manaimba Clothing
17 Bartamana Liqueur & Supermarket
18 Bank South Pacific
19 Kokopo Entertainment Centre
20 Post Office & Pay Phones
21 Air Niugini (Old)
22 Air Niugini (New)
23 Westpac
24 Airlink
25 Ginette Clothing
26 Montezuma Fashion House & Service Station
27 Taralba Wholesalers
28 Andersons Supermarket
29 German Cemetery
30 Spirit of Kokopo (Wholesalers)
31 Spirit of Rabaul (Wholesalers)

Kokopo

BLANCHE BAY

To Kokopo Provincial High School & Rabaul

Golf Course

Queen Emma's House Site

Market

Sports Ground

To Vunapope, Auslander Resort & Tokua Airport

NEW BRITAIN

German Cemetery

There's a small German cemetery set a little off the main road, opposite the Andersons supermarket. Many significant German planters are buried there, as well as other early settlers. This cemetery is looking a bit puny and vulnerable these days with all the development going on around it.

Queen Emma's Steps & House Site

Right where the road terminates at the Ralum Country Club is the site of Queen Emma's house, the larger-than-life Samoan-born planter who ran an empire here at the turn of the century (see the Queen Emma aside below). There's not really too much to see of Gunantambu, her grand home that was destroyed in WWII, but the breadth and height of the staircase indicates the mansion's grandeur; it has a commanding view from its hill-top site over Blanche Bay and the Duke of York islands.

Waterfront

Dozens of dinghies (banana boats) pull up on the beach. These boats come and go from all over the province, from the Duke of Yorks and even New Ireland, and the operators usually sleep through the midday heat under the big trees or gather in small groups playing cards and stringband music on their salty ghetto blasters. Regrettably, there's a lot of litter on this part of the beach, with packaging – the great gift of the developed world – making up almost all of it.

Vunapope Catholic Mission

It's worth having a look around the big old mission and hospital grounds in Vunapope. The grounds offer great views and there are

---

Queen Emma

Emma Forsayth was destined to become a legend in her own lifetime. Born in Samoa of an American father and Samoan mother, her first husband disappeared at sea. In 1878 she teamed up with Thomas Farrell, an Australian trader, and started a trading business at Mioko in the Duke of York islands. She was an astute businesswoman and soon realised that a plantation on the rich volcanic soil of the Gazelle Peninsula would be an excellent investment.

Emma acquired land at Ralum, near Kokopo, and became the manager and owner of the first real plantation in New Guinea. Emma's mansion house, Gunantambu, was on a hilltop at Ralum overlooking the Duke of York islands. When Thomas Farrell died he was succeeded by a steady stream of lovers.

She entertained like royalty. She had her own wharf where she met guests dressed in the finest European clothes, and took them up to the mansion to dine on imported food and champagne. By the time the Germans arrived in New Britain, Emma had extended her empire to include several plantations, a number of ships and a string of trade stores. She made clever use of her American citizenship to avoid possible German takeovers.

For many years, Emma was faithful to her lover Agostino Stalio, who is buried just outside Kokopo, but after his death she married Paul Kolbe. He died in Monte Carlo in 1913 and Emma herself died a few days later. Her empire soon fell apart and her fine home was destroyed during WWII. Kolbe and Emma's ashes were interred at the Forsayth family cemetery.

But there's mystery about their deaths: the dates in the death notice in the *Sydney Morning Herald* don't correspond with those on their tombstone. It's thought that Coe Forsayth (Emma's son) gave misleading information to the Australian newspaper. It's significant that Kolbe predeceased Emma, because she was known to be anxious about claims on her estate by Kolbe and his German relatives. She wanted her son and certain of her relatives to inherit her fortune.

Then in 1922 their ashes were removed from the cemetery, probably by Coe Forsayth. There are contradictory versions of this story, but legend has it that a white cutter appeared in Blanche Bay one day, and as the sun was setting the ashes were ceremoniously scattered over the sea from the deck of the cutter between the Duke of York islands and Ralum.

The cemetery was only rediscovered in 1955 and Emma's headstone was gone. Many years later, it was located in an old cemetery on South Head in Sydney, Australia, between the graves of JMC Forsayth (died 14 March 1941, 69 years) and Ida Forsayth (died 15 April 1947). Could JMC Forsayth be Coe? It seems likely. ■

many colonial-era buildings, including the grand church made of tin.

Market
Kokopo's market is colourful, although it's not a patch on the old Rabaul market, which was one of the best in the country. *Buai* (betel nut) and its condiments, *daka* (mustard sticks) and *cumbung* (lime), account for half of the stalls, with produce – fruit, vegetables, smoked fish and crabs – most of the remainder. At the rear tobacco growers sell dried leaves, and home-made cigars wrapped with sticky tape at the mouth-end sell for K0.10 each. Old Rabaul market sold many artefacts but there are few at Kokopo. The main PMV stop is just across the main road from the market. This area is busy with villagers bringing in produce from their gardens for sale and others taking it home again.

Activities
Swimming The town is fronted by beach. Kids swim at the beach near the hospital entrance at Vunapope and along the golf course beach, but try anywhere along Kokopo's straight coast or beyond in either direction. PMVs run along the road until 6 pm. The beaches here are nice – black sand and narrow, but shaded with overhanging trees – and in the midday heat you can lay about in the shallows and take in the shade.

Diving In Simpson Harbour, 10 of the 54 Japanese WWII shipwrecks are accessible, although some of them are quite deep. Many of them went down during one raid on 2 November 1943. Also in the harbour are a couple of plane wrecks and reef walls. Contact Michael Lee at Taklam Guesthouse (☎ 982 8370) to find out about diving trips. See the Rabaul section for more information on diving in the area.

Fishing There's great fishing in the Blanche Bay area and into the Duke of Yorks. Again, see Michael Lee at Taklam Guesthouse if you want to hire a boat or organise a trip. Of course it might be cheaper to hire a dinghy

for a few hours and buy a line from the trade store.

Golf Ralum Country Club (☎ 982 8240) is where to go if you feel like hitting a ball around the nine-hole golf course. The clubhouse has a bar, and offers darts and snooker. There's also a wonderful antiquated single-lane bowling alley with a German control panel. It has old knobs and dials and looks like it came from a 1930s rocket-science project.

Walking There's a few nice walks in Kokopo and the area abounds with interesting hiking possibilities. The East New Britain Tourist Bureau can tell you about routes, and can arrange a guide if necessary. You can walk from the beachfront cluster of shops along the strip of golf course beach and then onto one of the paths that cut back to the main road.

Organised Tours
Talk to Air Niugini about weekend packages to Kokopo staying at the Hamamas Hotel, Kaivuna Lodge or Kulau Lodge.

Paivu Tours (☎ & fax 982 8556; PO Box 44, Rabaul) offers a broad range of day activities and tours. There are many things to see on the peninsula and taking a day tour might be a good way to see it all.

Islands Nationair (☎ 982 8690; fax 982 9195; PO Box 717) offers helicopter flights over Tuvurvur and Vulcan from Tokua airport or Rabaul for K50 per person (four-person minimum).

Special Events
The pioneering missionary Reverend George Brown is celebrated on George Brown Day on 14 August with choral festivals in all districts.

The East New Britain PNG Independence show is scheduled for mid-September in Kokopo, as is the Tolai Warwagira Festival.

Places to Stay
In Kokopo there are quite a few options and more guesthouses opening all the time. Be

NEW BRITAIN

aware: as with elsewhere in PNG, the term 'resort' is used rather loosely.

The *Auslander Resort* (☎ & fax 982 8385) is in Vunapope, close to Kokopo. It's basic. There's a beach here and singles/doubles cost K33/43 in a bush-style building. You'll be given breakfast and dinner for K10.

The *Village Haven Guesthouse* is a bush-materials hut a bit behind town on a hill with great views. It's rustic and right in a village community, costing K40 with breakfast and another K5 for a kai-style dinner.

Kokopo Village Resort (☎ 982 8359; fax 982 8689) is new and at the western end of town. It's in a comfortable villa-style building overlooking Blanche Bay and the Duke of York islands, just near the beach. The smallish rooms cost K65/75 a single/double with breakfast and have air-con, TV, phone and fridge, but share bathroom facilities. There are some K100 double rooms that are a little bigger with private bathrooms. The upstairs rooms open onto a verandah with terrific views.

The rooms at *Taklam Guesthouse* feed off two central common rooms with attached kitchens and bathrooms. You can stay in a dorm-style room with air-con for K35 including a light breakfast. Single/double rooms with air-con cost K80/90. The common rooms have TV and guests can use the kitchens to prepare their own food. The big white building is centrally located on the main road, and Chopsticks Restaurant is underneath.

Places to Eat

There are only a few places to eat in Kokopo. You can fend for yourself at Andersons supermarket and get great fruit and vegetables and some 'exotics' at the Kokopo market. There are some kai-bars lining the streets, most of which are OK.

The *Muleshoe Restaurant*, in the Kokopo Entertainment Centre, has food served from a bain-marie. The menu board tells tales of steak and chips, fish and chips, and stew and the like. It's open for dinner too.

The restaurant at the *Kokopo Village Resort* (☎ 982 8359) serves sandwiches

(K3.50) and grilled fish or steaks (K9.50) for lunch. There's a broader menu in the evenings when generous mains include a crab salad for K14.50, chicken chow mein for K10.50 and grilled fish or steaks for K9.50.

Chopsticks Restaurant, under the Taklam Guesthouse, is open for breakfast, lunch and dinner. Bacon and eggs for breakfast costs K8, and Asian-style lunch dishes and sandwiches cost between K4 and K8. Dinner at Chopsticks is busy with locals and expats, and Mrs Lee senior serves up ample dishes of beef, chicken, fish and seafood, as well as soups and noodles. Mains cost around K10 to K12. Mrs Joyce Lee might join you for a chat as you eat, or her husband, John, might also pull up a chair. These two have seen it all in Rabaul (and beyond) and are good company.

Lunch and dinner are served at the *Ralum Country Club* from a bain-marie and cost around K5. Steaks and stews and chips make up much of the fare.

Getting There & Away

Air Tuvurvur buried Rabaul's old Rakunai airport. It's now a weird, flat, treeless place, and the kids from Matupit play golf across the open expanses.

The Kokopo-Rabaul area is now serviced by Tokua airport. It's about 20km east of Kokopo and 40km from Rabaul. Tokua can be closed if the wind blows Tuvurvur's dust over the runway, and flights around these closures are heavily booked. Construction is under way on a new terminal at Tokua, to replace the current tin shed, and the runway has also had some major upgrading.

Air Niugini has offices at the airport (☎ 983 9325, fax 9839052) and in Kokopo (☎ 982 9033; PO Box 120). Air Niugini is building new offices near the sportsground, but for now the office is in the post office building on the waterfront, opposite the Bank South Pacific.

Air Niugini flies to Tokua at least once a day from Port Moresby, and has direct connections to Hoskins, Kavieng and Buka. Air routes for other PNG destinations transit through Port Moresby. Fares from Tokua are:

Hoskins K98, Kavieng K97, Manus K188, Buka K124 and Port Moresby K231.

Islands Nationair is represented in Kokopo (☎ 982 8690; fax 982 9195) and at the airport (☎ 983 9336), and has flights to many of the smaller airstrips in the islands and on the mainland at least once a week. Islands Nationair flies to Lae direct for K198 and fares to New Ireland include Namatanai K57, Manga K57, Silur K58, Boang (Tanga Islands) K94, Londolovit (Lihir) K94 and Malekolon (Feni Islands) K95. Around New Britain fares are Hoskins K98, Jacquinot Bay (Pomio) K111, Bialla K118 and Uvol K147.

Airlink (☎ 982 8600), next to the Westpac bank in Kokopo, also offers these connections and charges the same fares, but has further connections to Goroka K235, Madang K221 and Mt Hagen K265 several times a week.

Boat Dinghies are the best way to get around the islands, and they tie up on the beach near the post office. Despite their size they travel far and wide, all over New Britain, through the Duke of Yorks and as far as Kavieng. These are work boats usually carrying supplies to remote trade stores and have no schedule, but you can pay a fare and jump aboard with a bunch of locals, or hire the boat and operator relatively cheaply.

See the Rabaul Getting There & Away section for shipping information.

Getting Around
The Airport This can be a bit of a problem, but PMVs do run to Tokua. The better hotels and guesthouses can provide transfers, but they'll charge you K20 to do the 40km run to Rabaul. A taxi fare from Kokopo should be around K8.

PMV The Gazelle Peninsula has most of ENB's 1200km of road and an excellent network of PMV routes. The PMVs have a number painted on them and often also a placard on the dashboard that indicates their route.

PMV Nos 1 and 8 run out along the coast road past the Karavia barge tunnel (K0.60), to Rabaul (K1), Bita Paka War Cemetery and to Tokua. PMV No 2 runs the 60-odd km to Warangoi (K3), and No 3 goes to Vunadidir (K1) and Toma (K2), offering the chance to see the inland of the Gazelle Peninsula and perhaps a glimpse of the Baining Mountains.

See the Getting Around section in Rabaul for information about PMV routes around Rabaul.

Car Car rental in PNG is very expensive and this is compounded in the Kokopo-Rabaul area by the fact that hirers only offer 4WDs. There are no renta-bomb outlets so if you're going to hire a vehicle it will cost you a fortune. All the rental companies charge a stiff per-kilometre fee on top of their rates. But if you can justify the cost, this is one of the best areas in PNG to have wheels, because there's lots to see and it's all fairly spread out.

Budget (☎ 983 9328), Avis (☎ & fax 982 8772) and Stan's Rent-a-Car (☎ 982 8367) have offices at Tokua airport; Hertz (☎ 982 1986) is opposite Kokopo market. Figure on around K120 per day and K0.80 per km. Budget will give you a 30% discount if you present your Air Niugini boarding pass.

There are only a few taxis and getting one can be a hassle but, during the day, some can usually be found at the airport.

AROUND KOKOPO
Bita Paka War Cemetery
Bita Paka War Cemetery is several kilometres inland, and the turn-off from the coast road is a few kilometres east of Vunapope. It contains the graves of over 1000 Allied war dead, including many Indians who came to Rabaul as POWs captured in Singapore. There are also memorials to the six Australian soldiers killed in the capture of the German WWI radio station at Bita Paka, to the crew of the Australian submarine that disappeared off the New Britain coast in the same operation, and to the civilians who went down with the *Montevideo Maru*. The cemetery and grounds are very well kept and the gardens are lovely.

NEW BRITAIN

Kokopo-Rabaul Road

The coast road goes past Raluana Point, around Karavia Bay before squeezing between Vulcan and the hills, and then around Simpson Harbour to Rabaul. Along this stretch are countless Japanese tunnels, Queen Emma's cemetery and mighty Vulcan. The road, where it passes Vulcan, is sometimes impassable after rains, and then the Burma Road carries the traffic between Kokopo and Rabaul.

Queen Emma's Grave Queen Emma's *matmat* is a few kilometres east of Kokopo in the Forsayth family cemetery. It's signposted and overlooks the road. The cemetery is very overgrown, and you really have to fight through the chest-high grass. All that remains of Queen Emma's grave is a cement slab with a hole in the centre – her ashes were stolen many years after they were buried here. The gravestones of her brother and her lover, Agostino Stalio, are in much better shape, the latter with a romantic inscription: 'Oh for the touch of a vanished hand and the sound of a voice which is still'.

About 1.5km north is the cemetery which holds the grave (in poor repair) of her brother-in-law, Richard Parkinson. Richard Parkinson is not as well known as Emma, but he wrote some of the earliest works on New Guinea Island anthropology and natural history, including a book titled *Thirty Years in the South Seas*, and was a botanist who planted many trees in the area.

Japanese Barge Tunnels The tunnels around Karavia Bay were once part of a network of rail track spread all over the local flat lands. The tracks connected barges and ships with munitions stores, headquarters and barracks. A road sign marks the way.

The main tunnel contains five barges, lined up nose to tail. It's hard seeing beyond your second or third barge without a torch so bring one along. They are all pretty rusty and there are bats in the tunnels.

Further around the bay is the wreckage of a huge crane, which the Japanese towed here from Singapore. It was bombed as soon as it arrived and was never used. Near the barge tunnel, Touman Resort is a village-run picnic area where you can swim.

Vulcan Vulcan's huge form rises on the roadside and its barren craggy slopes look awesome. During the 1994 eruptions, Vulcan threw up much more solid material than Tuvurvur, but stopped after 12 days. Ashmud cakes its slopes and huge cracks open as it dries.

When Vulcan erupted in 1937 a boat was moored in the bay. The boat became landlocked 70m from shore. Thanks to the 1994 eruption, it is now buried for some future archaeologist to find and puzzle over.

Burma Road & Malmaluan Lookout

The Burma Road leaves the Kokopo-Rabaul Road before Raluana point and climbs high up into the hills behind. It levels out on the tops of the hills and the Malmaluan Lookout is just off the road nearby. The views from here are some of the best in the area – you look out over Vulcan, the harbour, Matupit, Tuvurvur and the great rim of the ancient caldera. The road winds down again to meet the coast road north of Vulcan.

Peter ToRot's Cemetery & Memorial Church As the Burma Road begins to dip towards the coast, Peter ToRot's cemetery and memorial church loom up on the right. This place is Rakunai. Catholic catechist Peter ToRot ('Petro ToRot' is marked on his gravestone) was killed by the Japanese during their WWII military occupation. In the papal visit of 1995, ToRot was beatified (the Blessed ToRot), the first step towards being declared a saint (see The Pope & Peter ToRot aside on the next page).

Keravat

• *postcode 614*

Keravat is inland, due west from Kokopo and south-west from Rabaul. It has a national high school (a senior high school for matriculation), as well as the Lowland Agricultural Experimental Station, where research is carried out on coconuts, oil palms, cocoa,

The Pope & Peter ToRot

Much to the pride of the Catholic Church in PNG, one of its own is likely to become the first saint in the Pacific.

Peter ToRot was born in 1912 in Rakunai village, New Britain. In 1930 he enrolled in St Paul's College, and took on the tasks of a lay catechist, or a full-time assistant to missionaries. He was later appointed to the mission station in his village. In 1936 he married Paula Ia Varpit and three sons soon came along.

All was going well for the family until the Japanese invaded. In May 1943 the Japanese commander summoned ToRot and ordered him to reduce his pastoral work; 12 months later he was again summoned and this time forbidden to perform any religious duties. ToRot refused to comply and continued his pastoral work. He was arrested in April 1945, and thrown into jail. In July of that year, while still imprisoned, he was killed by a lethal injection from a Japanese military doctor.

The papal tour of 1995 was planned around a visit to Rabaul for Peter ToRot's beatification but the volcanic eruptions just months earlier forced a change of plan. Instead, the ailing John Paul II went to Port Moresby, ToRot's remains – his bones, rosaries and belt buckle – were exhumed and the beatification ceremony was held at Sir John Guise Stadium. Tolai pall bearers danced around a small casket containing his remains.

But other Tolais were outraged and many felt that exhuming ToRot's remains was insensitive to Tolai traditions. None of the correct ceremonies and rites were observed in the exhumation, and the lay community felt the church hierarchy, dominated by expatriates, was pushing its own interests in the affair.

Despite the controversy, the cemetery is a nice place. Its quiet order seems out of place against the devastation all around. Peter ToRot's remains now lie in a casket in the memorial church with a commemorative plaque that tells of his good deeds. ■

coffee and fruit trees. Nearby is Vudal Agricultural College.

RABAUL
• postcode 611

Rabaul is a weird wasteland, buried in deep black volcanic ash. The broken frames of its buildings poke out of the mud like the wings of a dead bird. Almost the entire old town is buried and barren and looks like a movie set for an apocalypse film or the *X-Files*. Streets and streets of rubble and ruined buildings recede in every direction. The scale of what

happened to Rabaul cannot be appreciated until you see it. If you were fortunate enough to walk its busy, noisy and colourful streets before September 1994, be prepared for a shock.

The main part of Rabaul is deserted, except for the three hotels, the Hamamas, Kaivuna and Travelodge, which were dug out of the mud. Down at its Malaguna end, near the Tunnel Hill Rd turn-off, the town suffered less damage and is where most of the few remaining people live. There's a new market there and several new trade stores and supermarkets have been built. East of here Rabaul is abandoned. Malaguna Rd still runs east-west and Mango Ave, the old north-south main drag, is now the only other road rendered suitable for vehicles. PMVs and other vehicles fight their way over its holes and unforgiving bumps at walking pace heading to Matupit, where the thousand-strong village community still lives right underneath the belching volcano. Tuvurvur's 1994 eruptions, miraculously, left Matupit almost unscathed.

Rabaul was the country's most spectacularly sited city and perhaps its most beautiful, built between Simpson Harbour and a dramatic backdrop of volcanos along the rim of an old flooded caldera. Rabaul's ruined city blocks are silent and empty now but they are full of ghosts.

Information

Tourist Office Rabaul has no tourist office. Try contacting the East New Britain Tourist Bureau in Kokopo (☎ 982 9038; fax 983 7070; PO Box 385).

Books An excellent book to read is *Pumice and Ash*, by expat Australian Sue Lauer (CPD Resources, 1995), a resident of Rabaul. It contains gripping descriptions of the days of the eruptions, of fleeing for Kulau Lodge and working on a relief team from Kokopo. There are excellent photos and reproductions of newspaper articles. The book is self-published and can be obtained by contacting the author (☎ (066) 24 5655; fax (066) 24 5656; CPD Resources, PO Box 4037, Lismore, NSW 2480, Australia).

Volcano Town, by RW Johnson & NA Threlfall (Robert Brown & Associates, 1985), looks at the 1937-43 eruptions and is also a good book. This is much easier to find and well represented on PNG bookshelves.

Simpson Harbour

The harbour is still magnificent and the tethered ships lie quiet in the still water. The Beehives, the tiny craggy islands in its middle, look striking from any angle. This is one of the few places of activity in the ruined town, and people fish off the wharves.

Namanula Road

Namanula Rd was the road that directly connected the northern coast to Rabaul, rising over the great caldera's rim. It runs east out of Rabaul off Mango Ave and used to meet the north coast road near Matalau.

The road is now badly busted up but there are plans to rebuild it (it will take a lot of rebuilding). You can drive a car *very* carefully – it's skinny and the edges have fallen sheer away leaving drops of 3m – to the Japanese War Memorial. There's space to turn around, but beyond there you must go on foot and at times you can feel a rope and tackle might be useful.

The **Japanese war memorial**, the main Japanese memorial in the Pacific, is looking a little dishevelled but has survived. Nearby is a huge kapok tree.

The remains of the small neighbourhood where Rabaul's rich and famous lived are further up the road. The panoramic views from this hilltop precinct are very sobering. When the Germans moved their headquarters across from Herbertshohe (Kokopo) in 1910 they built a plush neighbourhood up here too, as you can see from the stone gateposts and the crumbling staircase of a very grand **German residency**. There's also two little cement footpaths from the old car park to the lookout, built for *Misis Kwin*'s (Queen Elizabeth II) last visit to PNG.

From here, you can make your way down the buckled and torn-apart road to the steep north coast, where landslides are pushing houses into the Bismarck Sea. The road comes out near Matalau and joins the Nonga-Submarine Base coast road.

Tunnels & Relics

There are countless tunnels and caverns in the hillsides around Rabaul. Many of them are now closed, but a knowledgeable local guide can still take you around some amazing complexes. There are 580km of Japanese-built tunnels around the Gazelle Peninsula.

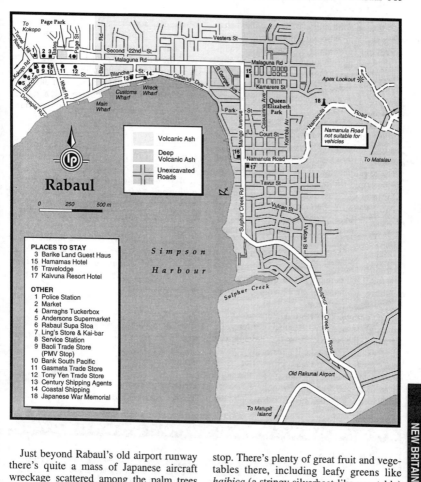

Rabaul

0   250   500 m

Volcanic Ash

Deep
Volcanic Ash

Unexcavated
Roads

*Simpson
Harbour*

PLACES TO STAY
3 Barike Land Guest Haus
15 Hamamas Hotel
16 Travelodge
17 Kaivuna Resort Hotel

OTHER
1 Police Station
2 Market
4 Darraghs Tuckerbox
5 Andersons Supermarket
6 Rabaul Supa Stoa
7 Ling's Store & Kai-bar
8 Service Station
9 Baoli Trade Store
   (PMV Stop)
10 Bank South Pacific
11 Gasmata Trade Store
12 Tony Yen Trade Store
13 Century Shipping Agents
14 Coastal Shipping
18 Japanese War Memorial

NEW BRITAIN

Just beyond Rabaul's old airport runway there's quite a mass of Japanese aircraft wreckage scattered among the palm trees and now semi-buried in earth. Take the track to the right. Local kids used to make a little money showing visitors to the remains, and you might still be asked to pay. There are two main chunks of wreckage, and various bits of engines, nacelles and undercarriage lie scattered around.

Market
The new market is at the Malaguna end of town, across the road from the central PMV stop. There's plenty of great fruit and vegetables there, including leafy greens like *haibica* (a stringy silverbeet-like vegetable) and every variation on the potato and root theme. There's also loads of buai if you get the urge.

Activities
Swimming There are pools at the Hamamas, Kaivuna and Travelodge hotels. The best beach for swimming is at pretty Pila Pila on the No 5 PMV route.

Diving The diving in the area is exceptional,

and the harbour is littered with sunken shipping and war relics. Right in Rabaul, at the end of old Turanian St, just beyond the swimming pool, there's a modern wreck – a small fishing craft that foundered about 20m from shore. It's home for many colourful, small fish and you can snorkel right through the main holds.

The Rabaul-based diving industry has suffered a bit of a downturn on account of being six feet under the mud. But Allan Jameson at Rabaul Battery Service (☎ 982 2574), opposite the police station on Malaguna Rd, can take people diving. You can contact Brian Martin at the Kaivuna Resort Hotel (☎ 982 1766). Kulau Lodge (☎ 982 7222; fax 982 7226; PO Box 65) staff can organise diving; it is probably the best set-up for casual divers.

Walking There are excellent walking routes around Rabaul, and you can spend hours just walking around the town overawed by its complete annihilation.

You can walk down to Matupit and back, although someone will probably offer you a lift, and the views from the vulcanology observatory also make it a rewarding walk.

If you're fit you can climb the badly broken Namanula Rd that meets the north coast road near Matalau. From here you can head north along the coast road, which rises over a pass and meets the Nonga-Submarine Base road – there are regular PMVs to Nonga hospital and some beyond – or you could walk the whole loop over Tunnel Hill Rd and take in the vulcanology observatory along the way. This would take about a day. Start early to avoid climbing in the heat and carry some water, a sandwich and a swimming costume.

Climbing You can climb all the volcanos, except for Tuvurvur. Vulcan is trickier than it looks from the roadside – its slopes are scored with deep cracks from mud-ash drying and contracting, which can be 4 to 5m deep and represent impossible chasms to the climber, who must descend again and find another route.

The best approach is on the northern face down near the water's edge (where the Japanese invaded). Rains can cause raging rivers in these huge cracks and the climb is unsafe in the wet season.

A warning: occasional tufts of grass are just starting to take root, but in a few years this quiet giant will again be covered in uncut grasses and vegetation, and the deep cracks will be much harder to see. You could easily disappear.

Organised Tours
See the Kokopo Organised Tours section.

What Was It like?
Rabaul had a hustle and bustle, but it was a laid-back kind of place that was very friendly. Streetlights shone at night and it was safe to walk about by yourself to the cinema (which is still standing, but barely), or to a restaurant or coffee shop. Rabaul had the biggest market in the South Pacific, an orchid park, playgrounds and swimming pools.

There was a great music scene in Rabaul and PNG's thriving local music industry was started there. Pacific Gold Studios was the first recording studio in the South Pacific. Even international bands and country and western performers came to Rabaul to record and perform at Queen Elizabeth Park.

The streets were stained buai-red and the shops faced their music speakers toward the street with the Moab Stringband on 11 (even though the amp only goes to 10) or Barike's latest blaring – there was a confusing din in the middle of the street. People would go into town on PMVs and hang-out around the cassette shops and trade stores, talk and chew, maybe go to the market for buai and bananas and that would be about it for the day.

Of course there were museums and a library, but Rabaul was more a cool place than a repository of high culture. There was always something happening – a dance or a gig – in town or at Matupit, or the Sea Wall Club on the Kokopo-Rabaul Road. It's very sad that it's all gone. ■

NEW BRITAIN

Special Events

Rabaul's Frangipani Queen Show is held in mid-July and scheduled to go ahead despite the interruptions.

Places to Stay

Rabaul In Rabaul there are the three upper-end hotels along Mango Ave. The scene inside these plush hotels is incongruous set against the receding devastation beyond. There's also one new cheaper option.

The *Barike Land Guest Haus* (☎ & fax 9821170; PO Box 944) is next to the market at the Malaguna end of town. Clean singles/doubles cost K40/60 with bathroom facilities. There are common areas with TV.

Meals are not available, but you can cook in the kitchen – the market is next door and Andersons supermarket is across the road and round the bend.

The *Hamamas Hotel* (☎ 982 1999; fax 982 1970; PO Box 214) has a range of rooms. The good value Budget Wing has singles for K55 and some doubles as well. The Pool Wing offers twin rooms for K90 and there's a new K90 double in the East Wing. The West Wing has generous rooms with queen-sized beds for K130. All of these rooms have air-con, tea and coffee gear, TV, phone, fridge and private bathrooms, and come with a terrific buffet-style breakfast. Hamamas has a pool, restaurant and public bar. The

Dead Town

What really happened? Rabaul is flattened – it collapsed under the weight of 1 to 2m of Tuvurvur's load and is now picked over for roofing iron and beams. It's abandoned like an empty film set. Silent. But three buildings remain, in the very middle of the vast destruction all around. It's not that they were rebuilt, they weren't badly damaged.

For several days after 19 September 1994 there were severe earthquakes as Tuvurvur and Vulcan went at it, and Rabaul was evacuated. Initially people ventured back to their homes to collect clothes and valuables, but soon the police and later the army prevented anyone from entering – except the looters. Looting had been a problem even during Tuvurvur's most furious days. The police and the army did some looting of their own (looting is a national sport). Buildings were slowly collapsing under the weight of ash-mud, one by one, for weeks and weeks. Gerry McGrade, Hamamas' proprietor, reckons the dead of night would be broken by the sound of a building groaning as it eventually succumbed to the weight on its roof.

Gerry defied the ban and went back to Mango Ave, while Tuvurvur was still throwing up a thick blanket of dust over the town each day. Gerry cleaned off the roofs of his buildings and set about cleaning up and repairing damage. He was one of two or three. Flash floods were bad in Rabaul and cars were swept away, but all the civic buildings were still standing and might have been saved.

The pressure of the situation on the government services was enormous – days of earthquakes and volcanic emissions and tens of thousands of people were on the move. There was no mains power, no phones, and Kokopo and Keravat were teaming with evacuees. Food had to be distributed and many local business people supported the relief effort.

But almost all of the destruction wrought on Rabaul is from human hands and from being abandoned to collapse into the earth. The proof of that is in the fact that the Hamamas and Kaivuna, while under stress, almost never stopped trading. If the authorities' response to the situation had been more appropriate, maybe Rabaul might have been dusted off not too much the worse for wear. Had the people been more restrained with their frenzied opportunism there might still be a town. But the terrible truth is all around in every direction. It's wasteful and sad.

You raise your gaze a few degrees and you see the rim of the old caldera with its five volcanos, one still smoking, and you remember where you are. Beneath the earth under your feet there are made roads, a sewerage system, parks and ovals, but above that everything has been laid to waste. It's black at night and the unnerving quiet is only broken by the wind and the scavengers moving through its bones.

Slowly, very slowly, people are coming back to Rabaul. The pretty town has suffered a lot in its short life and been reborn before. A lot of people said it was always going to happen and it'll happen again. Thrice in a 100 years the volcanos have boomed. People talk about better building standards and pitched roofs that would shed earth and they know it doesn't have to be a disaster whenever Tuvurvur coughs. This time it was. ■

management and staff at Hamamas are friendly and helpful.

Brian and Bev Martin who manage the *Kaivuna Resort Hotel* (☎ 982 1766; fax 982 1767; PO Box 395) are also very helpful. Kaivuna's height and location provide amazing views of smoking Tuvurvur, the harbour and the dead town. The views from the upstairs bar and attached verandah are the best. There are 32 assorted rooms and all have air-con with private facilities. Singles/doubles cost K120/130 plus 3% tax and include a good breakfast. They also offer cheaper 'stand-by' rates at K80/90. There is a restaurant and swimming pool. The bar is very pleasant for an evening drink and the food is good.

The *Travelodge* is about 12 months behind the others in its clean up, but it will soon look pretty shipshape. Singles/doubles/triples cost K85/95/105, but breakfast is not included. There's a pool and restaurant. The upstairs waterfront rooms have nice harbour views.

Nearby The new *Sub Base Resort* (☎ & fax 982 7200; PO Box 924) is where the Nonga road terminates at Tavui Point. It's a great site looking out over Watom Island. Accommodation is in free-standing bungalows artfully designed with a bush-materials look. The cheapest of these costs K110 and has either two singles or one queen-sized bed. Slightly bigger bungalows can sleep four and cost K125 per night. Sub Base Resort has an impressive restaurant and bar area. PMV No 6 runs along the Nonga-Submarine Base road and takes 10 minutes over Tunnel Hill to Rabaul.

Kulau Lodge (☎ 982 7222; fax 982 7226; PO Box 65) is on the beachfront of Talili Bay, past Pila Pila beach, and has been a local institution for a long time. This was the first port of call for many Rabaul evacuees during the eruptions. The No 5 PMV runs past, but takes 20 minutes to reach Rabaul. Kulau's cottages cost K135 and include double/twin bedding in fan-cooled rooms, with private bathrooms, phone, fridge and TV. They're nice, but beginning to look a little tired. The deluxe two-bedroom apart-

ments cost K195, and feature laundries and kitchens; they could sleep four or more.

Past Kulau Lodge along the coast road is the *Kabaira Beach Hideaway*, about 40 minutes from Rabaul. The accommodation is on the beachfront in a village environment. The rate is K30 per person, and breakfast costs K4 and dinner K8.

Places to Eat
Rabaul Apart from a few kai-bars at the Malaguna end of town, Rabaul's eating options are confined to the hotel restaurants and *Darraghs Tucker Box* on Malaguna Rd. Sub Base Resort serves food, as does Kulau Lodge.

Breakfast, lunch and dinner are served at the *Hamamas Hotel*. The lunch and dinner menus are semi-Asian with mains costing around K12 to K16. The food is good and the servings are generous. Chicken, beef, fish and seafood dishes are served, as well as tofu soups and a few eggplant variations for vegetarians.

The *Kaivuna* serves meals in its restaurant and pub-style lunches in its upstairs bar, and the food is very nice. Steaks, fish and seafood make up much of the dinner fare, and mains cost around K13 to K20. Chicken-in-a-basket and racks of lamb are available, and there's an impressive (and expensive) wine list.

The *Travelodge* also serves three meals a day. Sandwiches, omelettes and hamburgers are on offer for lunch, and cost between K3.30 and K7. In the evening steaks cost K17, lobster costs K23 and garlic prawns are K20. The Travelodge restaurant has a selection of entrees that includes sashimi, deep-fried camembert and oysters.

Nearby The *Sub Base Resort* has terrific open sandwiches and burgers, and beef or fish grills are available at lunch and are served with generous leafy salads. In the evening the menu includes mixed grills, pepper steak, chicken dijon and fried reef fish for between K14.50 and K16.50.

Kulau Lodge serves breakfast, lunch and dinner. For around K4 to K7 you can have lunchtime sandwiches, salads and omelettes, and for about K10 you could opt for grilled chicken, steak, lamb cutlets or reef fish. In the evenings mains cost around K14 to K17 and include lobster and mud crabs, seafood pastas, grilled pork chops and steaks, and chicken dishes.

Things to Buy

The reception areas of the hotels and guesthouses sometimes sell bilums and small carvings. The Tolais make great bilums that used to be available from Rabaul market.

Look through the few trade stores in Rabaul and in Kokopo for the classic T-shirts that the Tolais have always had a penchant for. Local screen printers have been knocking out great T-shirt designs for years, but since the 1994 eruptions the garments have had a bit of a theme running: 'Volcanic ash over Rabaul ... but we will survive', 'River of ash' and even 'My grandfather survived 1878, my father survived 1937 and I survived 1994'.

Getting There & Away

Air Rabaul is serviced by Tokua airport. See the Kokopo Getting There & Away section earlier in this chapter.

Boat See the Kokopo Getting There & Away section earlier in this chapter for information about dinghy travel around New Britain and through the nearby islands.

The Rabaul wharves were quickly back in operation after the 1994 eruptions, but the downturn in the copra and cocoa industries has meant that fewer freighters are sailing, and most of those don't officially take passengers. But you might get lucky. Shipping routes connect Rabaul with Kimbe, Kavieng, Buka, Manus and Lae.

Coastal Shipping (☎ 982 8518; fax 982 8519; PO Box 423) is on Cleland Drive in Rabaul, just near the wharves. Coastal has a few cargo boats that have facilities for passengers and are also the agents for Lutheran Shipping. Century Shipping Agents (☎ 982 1477; fax 982 1207; PO Box 606) is on the corner of Blanche St and Coastwatchers Rd

in Rabaul, and Pacific New Guinea Line (☎ 982 1955; PO Box 1764) is on George Brown St. Consort Express Lines (☎ 982 8720; PO Box 2224) is on Kamarere St.

Coastal has freighters, unscheduled but running approximately fortnightly, to Kavieng on New Ireland. The trip costs about K45/60 in deck/cabin class. These boats sometimes continue on to Lihir Island and the other island groups off New Ireland's east coast. Other freighters run to Nissan Island and on to Buka approximately weekly, and once a month there's a boat to Manus, via Kavieng.

To/From Lae Coastal Shipping has the *Lae Express*, which takes passengers, running between Lae and Rabaul via Kimbe. It departs Rabaul on Monday and takes about

---

Fish Bombs

PNG island villagers are always stumbling upon arms caches from WWII. The Bougainvilleans fight a war with their finds, but the Tolais bomb fish. It's an extraordinary community event.

Hundreds of villagers, young and old, line up along the shore with coat-hanger wire in their hands, others have baskets, and some wear swimming goggles. A man sits, almost ceremoniously, in a canoe 100m offshore as the tension builds. Somehow they know when the 'device' slips into the water and the villagers hush for a few seconds before a dull thud sounds offshore.

Initially nothing really seems to happen, but people chat excitedly as they slowly make their way into the water. After a minute or two you see the fish surface, belly up, and the people, moving quickly now, begin collecting them. Soon the water is boiling with a frenzy of dead fish and live people. Kids and adults get into this and there is abandon and gaiety in the air.

Swimmers emerge with coat-hanger-wire loops of 50 fish strung up eye to eye, and baskets brimming. The people are happy – they'll smoke much of this 'catch', which they will sell at the market.

Of course bombing fish is ecologically unsustainable. The reef gets mashed, corals are destroyed and the local fish populations plummet. But you try telling them that. ∎

48 hours to get to Lae. Coastal's *Kimbe Express* also sails to Lae via Kimbe, departing on Tuesday afternoon and arriving on Friday. It's a mixed passenger/cargo boat, with deck-class accommodation only. To Lae it's K46. Coastal's *Astro I* departs for Lae on Sunday, running via the south coast and stopping at Kandrian, among other places. This is not a passenger boat but there are a few cabins.

Lutheran Shipping has a weekly passenger boat, the MV *Maneba*, sailing from Rabaul direct to Lae once a month. Deck class costs K46 and cabin K54.

Getting Around
The Airport Tokua airport is about 40km away. PMVs run out to Tokua and the better hotels and guesthouses can provide transfers for K20.

PMV PMV Nos 1 and 8 run out along the coast road past the Karavia barge tunnel (K0.60), to Kokopo (K1), to Bita Paka War Cemetery and to Tokua. PMV No 2 runs the 60-odd km to Warangoi (K3), and No 3 goes to Vunadidir (K1) and Toma (K2). PMV No 4 runs to Keravat (K2), and No 5 runs across Tunnel Hill and along the north coast road, passing Pila Pila (K0.60) and Kulau Lodge (K0.80). PMVs No 6 and No 7 are based in Rabaul – No 6 goes to Nonga and Submarine Base (K0.70), while the No 7 fights its way down Rabaul's Mango Ave to Matupit (K0.50).

AROUND RABAUL
Tunnel Hill Rd climbs up over the old caldera rim and runs out westerly to meet the coast road of Talili Bay (during the German days it did go through a tunnel, but it was later opened out to a cutting). There's an intersection here. The road to the left goes past Pila Pila beach and Kulau Lodge, and the road to the right passes Nonga hospital and goes up to Submarine Base. There's a right-hand turn off the Nonga-Submarine Base road that goes over the mountain and along the north coast through Rabuana,

Matalau, Nodup and way down to Bai on the eastern slopes of Kombiu.

Sulphur Creek Rd is the extension of Mango Ave and goes down to Matupit.

Matupit Island
The September 1994 eruptions should have destroyed little Matupit (only barely an island and connected by bridge) but the prevailing winds brought Tuvurvur's load over Rabaul and left Matupit almost unscathed. Matupit is right beneath the volcano and from the beach you can see Tuvurvur's whole conical form and see it belch huge plumes of smoke into the sky from just a kilometre away.

There are some nice church buildings on Matupit and the 1000-odd Matupit Islanders take their religion seriously. Lovely painted statues adorn some of the churches' grounds.

You used to be able to climb up and into Tuvurvur. For a few kina a Matupit villager would paddle you across the water in an outrigger canoe and you'd climb up the volcano's western slope (then treed), over the rim and down onto the caldera's mud floor. It had vents expelling pungent gas. You wouldn't find a villager prepared to paddle you across now, but the volcano might settle down and be safe – locals will know.

You can, however, hire a canoeist to paddle you around to see Tuvurvur's southern slopes from the water, which have giant lava flows.

Praed Point
Before the eruptions there were communities at Rapindik and Talwat on the way out to Praed Point. A road rounded the point and connected them to the north-coast villages of Bai and Nodup. The people are gone and the road is badly damaged but you might be able to make your way out in that direction on foot or by 4WD.

The road went past the old airport buildings and around Tuvurvur's base. If the volcano is hissing and letting off clouds of smoke every 10 minutes, it might not be sensible and a bit too scary. There are (were) a couple of coastal guns at Praed Point –

ROWAN MCKINNON

ROWAN MCKINNON

ROWAN MCKINNON

Rabaul, East New Britain
Top & Middle: Tuvurvur continues to rumble, puff and hiss after its 1994 eruption
destroyed much of Rabaul and its surrounds.
Bottom: Children playing at the abandoned Rakunai airport.

ROWAN MCKINNON

LIZ THOMPSON

Top: Water taxis, Buka Passage, North Solomons Province
Bottom: A fisherman prepares his nets, New Ireland Province

when the Japanese invaded they were virtually the only defence Rabaul had, but they weren't used.

There are some hot springs at Rapindik, not far from the old airport right on the beach but they're too hot for bathing – it's really boiling water. The red colour of the beach is due to the iron from the boiling water.

Volcanos

Climbing one of the volcano cones is hot but rewarding work. You can also arrange a helicopter flight with Islands Nationair (☎ 982 8690; fax 982 9195; PO Box 717, Kokopo).

The Beehives (Dawapia Rocks)

The cluster of rocky peaks rising out of the centre of Simpson Harbour are said to be the hard core of the original old volcano. You can visit them by boat and there is some good diving and swimming. When Captain Blanche first visited Rabaul in 1882 these islands were much larger; the bigger one had a village of 200 people. The islands now have no inhabitants. Old photos of the village huddling under the tall rock look like illustrations from a book of ancient and apocryphal traveller's tales.

Submarine Base

Submarine Base is a great place for snorkelling and diving – the coral bed is flat and almost horizontal until it drops away straight down a 75m vertical reef wall. As you swim over this drop your heart races and it feels like you're leaping off a skyscraper. The Japanese used to provision submarines here during the war.

After returning from the area, one traveller said that they enjoyed their trip but 'never found the actual base'. Well, there isn't one. There are remnants of tunnels and rail track, guns and relics in the hills above, but it was a 'base' in so far as the Japanese pulled their submarines up to the vertical wall and then surfaced allowing soldiers to walk off over the reef.

Catch PMV No 5 from the central PMV stop opposite Rabaul's new market on Malaguna Rd.

Nodub and Bai

The north coast road turns off the Nonga-Submarine Base road and rises over a hill before meeting the coast. Along here are the villages of Rabuana, Matalau (where the remains of old Namanula Rd head back towards Rabaul between Kombiu and Tovanumbatir volcanos), Nodup and Bai.

At **Matalau** there's a monument commemorating the landing of the first Christian missionaries on New Britain on 12 October 1875. The road disintegrates badly after here, its once-flat and smooth form now twisted and buckled.

There are lava flows along here like natural staircases leading up Kombiu's slopes, and they are great to climb. These great slags were thrown from Tuvurvur and fell to earth over Kombiu's northern slopes (that's a long way). Villagers along here are watching their houses fall into the sea. Mudslides are common and houses pitched on Kombiu's steep slopes are in real trouble – these people fear the wet season, and hold on and hope.

The road threatens to become impassable for several kilometres but finally terminates at Bai. It's swallowed by a great ravine of mud and trees and broken houses, its bitumen appearing like pie crust.

It's a bit tricky getting out here. Only a couple of PMVs come along the route each day but there is traffic and you'd be offered a lift if you set out on foot.

Pila Pila

Pila Pila and nearby Ratung village are nice swimming beaches in Talili Bay. PMV No 5 runs past Pila Pila and Ratung.

Watom Island

Watom Island is an extinct volcano cone and site of one of the earliest settlements in New Britain. Volcanic glass traded from Talasea (WNB) has been found on Watom Island and dated at about 2500 years old. The island is also a good place for walking or snorkelling; it can be reached from Kulau Lodge or Nonga beach, near Nonga hospital. It's also possible to stay in villages.

NEW BRITAIN

The Pigeons

Between Rabaul and the Duke of York Group are the two Credner islands, commonly known as 'the Pigeons'. Small Pigeon is uninhabited. Either island would make a nice excursion for a picnic or to go snorkelling. To get here you could hire a dinghy from the Kokopo waterfront for a few hours.

JACQUINOT BAY

This region on the south coast of New Britain is beautiful, but little developed with no facilities for travellers. There are plans for a tourist development around **Pomio**. According to legends, the land here will one day be turned into an earthly paradise. There are enormous caves and underwater lakes in the area.

DUKE OF YORK GROUP

There are about 20,000 people living in the Duke of Yorks, about 30km east of Rabaul. These islands are beautiful and accessible, but they are little developed. The islands lie midway between New Britain and New Ireland, and Duke of York Island is the largest in the group. This was the site for the first mission station in the area, the place where Queen Emma started her remarkable career, and it is also blessed with some beautiful white-sand beaches, lagoons, reefs and scenery. Getting there is half the fun.

Local people are part of the cultural lineage that connects southern New Irelanders and Gazelle Peninsula Tolais; they have secret men's business and their islands are the haunt of dukduks and tumbuans.

Mioko Island

Mioko Island is where Emma and Thomas Farrell established their first trading station, and this is where one of the Duke of Yorks' two 'formal' places to stay is. The community at Mioko has one tiny trade store and a school, but it's got at least two churches. There are no vehicles on any of the islands except Duke of York Island, so there's no roads, just walking paths.

Queen Emma's first grand house was on the south-western tip of the harbour, but there's not too much to see – just some steps really. You can see photographs of this house in the Kokopo museum. There are two Japanese war graves nearby, but they are hard to find and you'll need help (you won't have trouble finding help).

There are two open-pit caves on the island's eastern flank and a coastwatcher's lookout cut into the clifftop nearby on the easternmost point. For many years hundreds of people hid in these caves to avoid being press ganged for heavy labour by the Japanese occupiers. The open pits were covered in bamboo frames and camouflaged with earth, leaves and debris. Conditions were very cramped, there were sanitation problems and diseases struck dreadfully.

Nearby, a tiny tunnel runs between the two cliff faces of the island's eastern tip. You can crawl between (it's rough going) for two views of the open sea and sky, and the cruel cliff below you. There's another passage leading into the darkness.

There's a *dukduk ples* (a place where dukduks are built) on a beach that you might be invited to see.

Place to Stay The 'resort' at Mioko is fantastic. It's two bush huts on a little spit of white-sand beach at the northern end of the harbour. Edward, the manager (on behalf of the school), will paddle across from the village on his outrigger and charge K5 per person per night (but he's thinking maybe K6 or even K7 is reasonable). You can lock the huts and you also get a key for the water tank.

You'll be brought a kerosene stove and lamp, bedding and a mosquito net, but you'll need your own food, a sleeping sheet and torch. The nights are hot with no overhead fan, but they are delicious in the shallows of the beach with the cool breeze across the harbour and the sky full of stars. You can see the lights of Vunapope's Catholic mission across the water.

Getting There & Away Airlink (☎ 982 8600) sometimes flies to Rakanda airstrip on Mioko Island for K26 but most people go by small boat.

It costs K5, or K20 if you charter, to catch a dinghy from Kokopo and the trip to Mioko or Ulu takes about an hour, although this will depend on the weather and the load in the trade boat.

Be warned, high seas can whip up on St Georges Channel and the trip can be very rough. If the seas do blow up (which won't happen without warning), the swells can be many metres high and you are likely to be terrified, but it won't bring a flinch to the face of the operator. There are no life jackets, so don't ask.

There have been deaths in these waters when high seas have rolled dinghies. In 1996, 12 of 15 people aboard one boat died, but locals say the operator was inexperienced.

The boats are 18ft to 23ft open fibreglass boats with a 40-odd horsepower outboard engine. They are fast, safe and exhilarating. As soon as there's a ripple in the water you are going to get wet – *very* wet – so keep your luggage off the boat's floor and under the tarpaulin. Try to sit at the rear of the boat and hang on! You sometimes see whales, dolphins and dugongs in St Georges Channel and flying fish will launch themselves next to your boat and 'outrun' you for 100m or more.

Ulu Island
Ulu Island is west of Mioko and much bigger. There are several settlements and a small guesthouse that has intermittent electricity. The charge is K10. Conditions are pretty rough on Ulu too, but there's a few extra stores that sell tinned fish and rice.

Duke of York Island
Port Hunter, at the northern tip of Duke of York Island, was the landing point for the Reverend Brown in 1875 and the site of his first mission. You can still see the crumbling chimney of his house, overlooking the entrance to Port Hunter's circular bay. Near the beach is the cemetery where most of his assistants ended up.

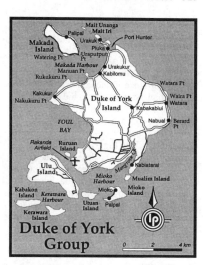

Duke of York Group

Kabakon Island
Kabakon Island, closest of the group to Rabaul, has a curious history. A German health fanatic named Engelhardt established a nudist colony here in 1903. He was soon dubbed *Mr Kulau* (Mr Coconut) by the locals because he supplemented his nude way to health with a diet of nothing but coconuts. At one time he had 30 or more followers on the island, but coconuts and nudism must get boring – he died alone just before WWI.

West New Britain Province

Land Area 25,000 sq km
Population 158,000
Capital Kimbe

While East New Britain has a high level of development, the island's other province is relatively untouched and little developed. WNB is PNG's highest timber and palm-oil exporter, and it has the country's greatest

NEW BRITAIN

proliferation of volcanos – five active and 16 dormant or extinct. Many people have come to WNB as labourers on oil-palm plantations; a quarter of the population was born outside the province – the highest proportion for any province in the country. WNB also has the highest birth rate in the country and there are considerable land pressures. There's tension between the province's villagers and settlers, who include many Highlanders. The rugged south is very wet with poorer soils and is less populated.

Most development is around Stettin Bay and the Willaumez Peninsula where the roads are concentrated. Much of the rest of the New Britain Island (apart from the Gazelle Peninsula) is thickly rainforested with oil-palm plantations and timber fellers making inroads. There are a few settlements and airstrips that service mostly plantation communities.

Travel in this province is difficult beyond the Kimbe area. Nearby Hoskins airport is well serviced by the first and second level airlines, but beyond here you must either spend a lot of money flying to airstrips or catch dinghies and trade boats along the coast and stay in villages. There are no tourist facilities beyond Stettin Bay and the Willaumez Peninsula (and few there too), so you would have to prepare well for a free-style trip into the unknown. There are rugged and virtually unexplored mountains for the insanely adventurous where you could loose yourself for weeks, or disappear altogether!

There's a few places to stay in Kimbe and there's the Walindi Plantation Resort, which is not cheap but does offer high-quality accommodation and outstanding diving.

KIMBE
• *pop 9000* • *postcode 621*

About 30km from Talasea and a bit less from Hoskins, Kimbe is the provincial headquarters and a major centre for palm-oil production. The projects in WNB have been resoundingly successful and have led to further developments in other provinces of PNG, notably in Milne Bay and northern provinces.

In Kimbe there's a hospital, post office, shopping centre, PNGBC bank and a daily market. Try contacting the Division of Commerce (☎ 983 5221; fax 983 5298; PO Box 427) for further information on the province.

Places to Stay
The *Palm Lodge Hotel* (☎ 983 5001; PO Box 32) is 100m from the wharf adjacent to the beach, a short walk from town. It's reasonably well equipped but pricey – K116.50/156.50 plus tax for air-con singles/doubles with TV, phone and fridge. Breakfast is included.

It may be possible to stay at the United Church or camp at the police station.

Getting There & Away
Air Hoskins airport is about 40km east of Kimbe and poorly serviced by transport. Air Niugini (☎ 983 5077; fax 983 5669; PO Box 181) flies to Hoskins once a day from Port Moresby (K173) and to Tokua (K98).

Airlink (☎ 983 5635) and Islands Nationair have flights once a week to the strips around WNB including Bialla (K54), Aumo (K133), Kandrian (K85), Gasmata (K66) and Jacquinot Bay (ENB; K83).

Boat Dinghies and trade boats are the cheapest and best way to get around the coast of the island, and they tie up in the harbour. You can use small-boat connections to get to Rabaul, the Duke of Yorks and New Ireland.

A number of ships, including Lutheran Shipping's passenger vessels, call in at Kimbe on the voyage between Lae and Rabaul – see those sections. Kimbe Bay Shipping Agents (☎ 983 5154; PO Box 27) in town should have information on these and other boats. There's also a government boat that makes an irregular 10-day voyage from Kimbe to Pomio, stopping in many small ports along the way. From Pomio you could pick up a boat to Rabaul.

The coastal road runs from Talasea through Kimbe to Hoskins. From Talasea to Kimbe or Kimbe to Hoskins by PMV costs about K5.

HOSKINS
• *postcode 622*

This small town is a major logging and palm-oil production centre. The oil-palm project is between Hoskins and Kimbe at Mosa, and the company estate is surrounded by smaller plots worked by people from all over the country. Palm oil is used in the manufacture of soap and margarine. There are a number of extinct volcanos in the area surrounding Hoskins, including some textbook-perfect cones, and a short distance inland, at Koimumu, there's an active geyser field.

Place to Stay

The *Palm Lodge Hoskins* (☎ 983 5113; PO Box 10) is also known as the Hoskins Hotel. It's close to the airport and has singles/doubles with fan for K87.55/118.45 and with air-con for K97.55/128.75. A full continental breakfast is provided. Dive Hoskins is associated with the Palm Lodge Hoskins. The *Po-Koe* is the 24-foot shark cat operated by Dive Hoskins, and it offers hire gear and diving trips. Contact Dive Hoskins at the Palm Lodge Hoskins.

TALASEA & THE WILLAUMEZ PENINSULA

The pretty little town of Talasea looks across the bay with its many islands from Willaumez Peninsula. The peninsula is an active volcanic region; there are even bubbling mud holes in Talasea. Lake Dakataua, at the end of the projection, was formed in a colossal eruption in 1884.

On Pangula Island, across from Talasea, there is a whole collection of thermal performers (geysers and fumaroles) in the Wabua Valley (*wabua* means hot water). It's only a short walk from the shops. In the hills behind Talasea are the wrecks of two US bombers, one of them a B-24 Liberator. Both are in reasonable condition.

Talasea is a centre for the manufacture of shell money. Obsidian (volcanic glass) from here is believed to have been traded from about 3000 BC until recent times. It went from New Britain to New Ireland, Manus and the Admiralty islands or even further afield, and was used in knives, spears and arrows.

Tribes inland from Talasea used to bind their babies' heads to make them narrow and elongated. Other tribes near Kandrian used Malay-style blowguns to hunt birds and fruit bats. The wooden darts are shot through a long bamboo tube.

Place to Stay

The *Walindi Plantation Resort* (☎ 983 5441; fax 983 5638; PO Box 4, Kimbe) is between Kimbe and Talasea on the east side of the peninsula. The plantation itself is a large, privately owned oil-palm plantation, right on the shores of Kimbe Bay, and there is a group of attractive and comfortable thatched bungalows. Kimbe Bay is fringed by volcanic mountains, some of which are still active.

Apart from the superb natural surroundings, which are very beautiful, the main attraction is the diving, which has many people raving about clear water, volcanic caves draped in staghorn coral and reef drop-offs. Fishing trips and day tours are also organised. All meals and accommodation are included for K205/290 single/double in very plush bungalows. A return transfer to Hoskins costs K45 per person. Diving costs K90 for a day and K45 for a half day including equipment, and there is night diving and snorkelling too.

AROUND WEST NEW BRITAIN PROVINCE

Mt Langila, on Cape Gloucester at the south-western end of the island, is still active and hiccups and rumbles every few months.

There are places to stay in and near **Kandrian**. The *Kandrian Guesthouse* (PO Box 14) is in town and charges K25/45 a single/double. Breakfast is K3, lunch K8 and dinner K10.

Another place is the *Akanglo Guesthouse*, which is in a beautiful location five minutes by boat from Kandrian. There's also the *Awa Guesthouse*, which is 45 minutes by boat from Kandrian. The Department of West

New Britain (☎ 981 7305) has district offices in Kandrian that can arrange boats and will have more information.

The Kimbe Islanders, off the Willaumez Peninsula, are expert sailors and canoe builders who live on the islands but tend gardens on the mainland.

The **Witu Islands**, west of the Willaumez Peninsula, are about 80km off the coast and are of volcanic origin. Unea has a 738m peak while Garove, the biggest island, has a beautiful bay formed when the sea broke into its extinct crater. Pirates once used the bay as a hideout.

During the first 10 years of this century a smallpox epidemic virtually wiped out the people on these fertile and quite heavily populated islands.

New Ireland Province

Land Area 9600 sq km
Population 101,000
Capital Kavieng

HIGHLIGHTS

- Exploring the villages and beaches of the Boluminski Highway
- Cycling around pretty Kavieng
- Swimming at the countless white-sand beaches
- Catching a dinghy to Nusa Island and beyond

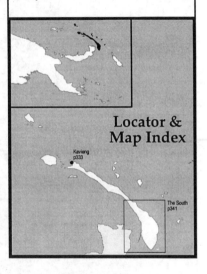

Locator &
Map Index

New Ireland is the long, narrow island north of New Britain. It's a beautiful and friendly place and, although little known and rarely visited, it has one of Papua New Guinea's longest records of contact with European civilisation. From the early 1600s, Europeans were sailing in St Georges Channel, which separates New Ireland from New Britain, and taking on fresh water at the island's southern tip at Cape St George. Later, the Germans developed lucrative copra plantations and the first real road in PNG – the mighty Boluminski Highway.

New Ireland has broad white-sand beaches, rivers of clear water tumbling down from the thickly forested central Schleinitz Range, friendly people and an easy-going pace. Kavieng is still much smaller than Rabaul was, before the New Britain town was demolished by volcanic eruptions in 1994, but has taken on the role of the 'happening' place in the islands. There are many people, expats and locals, who fled Rabaul and have settled in Kavieng – it's a nice place to flee to.

New Ireland Province has the world's potentially largest undeveloped gold mine at Lihir Island, the plantation estate home of former prime minister Sir Julius Chan in the rugged south and the intriguing traditions of Malangan (spelt variously) in the north, Kabai in the central areas and Tumbuan down south.

The province also includes a number of islands. The biggest is Lavongai (New Hanover) Island off the north-west end. Well offshore from the east coast are the Tabar, Lihir, Tanga, Green and Feni island groups. Further to the north-west is the large island of Mussau in the St Matthias Group and the smaller islands of Emirau and Tench.

Kavieng and Namatanai are the only towns on New Ireland, although Namatanai barely qualifies. Outside Kavieng and Namatanai, there are coastal communities on each side of the island but no real settlements bigger than a trade store or two. Kavieng has the island's only port.

History

The remains of rock shelters found near Namatanai suggest that New Ireland was inhabited 30,000 years ago. There's evidence of trade 12,000 years ago and Lapita ceramic items (3700 years old) have been

NEW IRELAND

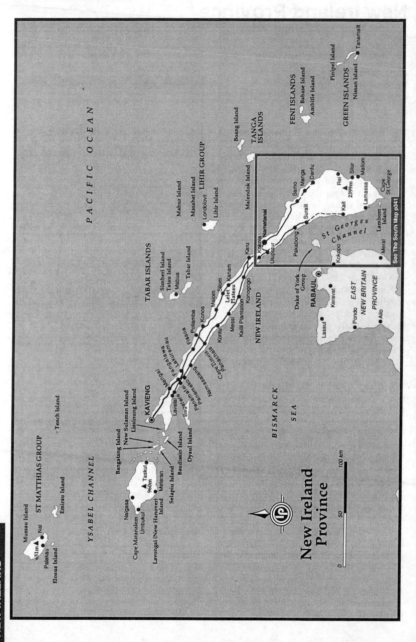

New Ireland Province

found at Eloaua Island in the St Matthias Group.

At the same time as they chanced upon the Admiralty Islands (Manus Province) in 1516-17, the Dutch explorers Schouten and Le Maire sighted New Ireland.

Methodists began arriving in 1875. The legendary Reverend George Brown arrived at Kalili during that year and started a mission at Port Hunter in the Duke of York islands between New Ireland and New Britain. Brown – a part-time vulcanologist, linguist, scientist, anthropologist and explorer – had some trouble getting established but is now a revered and celebrated man.

'Blackbirding' in the 1870s saw many New Irelanders forcibly removed to work on the plantations and canefields of Queensland (Australia) and Fiji, until church leaders and traders came under pressure to stop the practice.

During the German reign, New Ireland became one of the most profitable parts of the colony. Under German administrator Baron Boluminski, a string of copra plantations was developed along the east coast and the highway was built to connect them to the port at Kavieng.

Soon after WWII spread to the Pacific, New Ireland fell (on 23 January 1942) and Kavieng was developed into a major Japanese base. Most of the Australians in Kavieng managed to escape but those who chose to stay behind as coastwatchers were gradually captured as the Japanese extended their control over the island.

Like Rabaul, the Japanese held the island right until the final surrender and although the Allies made no attempt to retake New Ireland they inflicted enormous damage – Allied bombing killed many New Irelanders. Kavieng, the main Japanese base, was comprehensively flattened. The Japanese surrendered in Namatanai on 19 September 1945. Extensive redevelopment since the war has restored the productive copra plantations along the highway, and coffee, rubber and timber industries have also been developed. Kavieng is also an important fishing port.

Geography

The province has 149 islands spread over 230,000 sq km of sea. There are eight island groups and the six to the north and east mark the eastern end of the Bismarck Archipelago. The equator marks the northern province's boundary.

On New Ireland, the north-east coast is generally called the east coast, and the south-west the west. Anything south of Namatanai is known as the south.

The island is long, narrow and very mountainous. For much of its length, it's only about 10km wide but it's 350km long, with a high spine falling straight to the sea on much of the west coast and bordered by a narrow coastal strip on the east coast.

Midway down the island, the Lelet Plateau rises to 1481m and further south near Taron the Hans Meyer Range reaches 2399m. An earthquake-fault trench provides passage for the Weitin and Kamdaru rivers which separate the Hans Meyer Range from the Verron Range at the southern tip. These southern ranges are volcanic in origin, but there are no active volcanos on the island. Many of the islands in the province are extinct volcanos – Ambitle (Feni group) has geysers and Lihir has bubbling mud craters.

Climate

The south is pretty wet and has no real dry season, nor do Lihir and Mussau islands which receive more than 4m of annual rainfall. The area between Namatanai and Kavieng receives about 3m of annual rainfall and has a dry season between May and November. December to March is the cyclone season in northern Australia and the Coral Sea – it can bring strong winds and high seas.

Society & Conduct

The people of New Ireland are Melanesian and speak 19 local languages – all but one are related Austronesian languages.

There are three distinct cultural groups (with blurring at the edges) along the long island which are embodied in the traditions of Malangan, Kabai and Tumbuan cultures.

NEW IRELAND

Malangan Death Rites

Since the 1930s, people have been looking for malangan master carvers and they've been told to go to Tabar. The traditions originate there and the island's few carvers are still regarded as malangan masters. But Malangan culture is much more than carving.

Figures are carved (and occasionally built with bush materials) for the Malangan mortuary rites. There's just a few dedicated regular carvers on Tabar Island and Libba village near Konos, but otherwise carvings are only done for mortuary ceremonies in the villages.

Different clans have different funerary traditions, including interment, cremation and burial at sea (either sinking the corpse in the sea or setting it adrift). The *tatanu* or *tanuato* (soul) remains close to the body after death and it cannot go to the ancestors' world until the mortuary rites are performed. The spirit of a dead person enters the ancestors' world through the places that *masalais* (spirits of the bush and water) inhabit.

Secret men's societies carve malangans for months after someone's death until the mortuary rituals begin. The status of the deceased will determine the size of the ensuing festivities and feasting; countless pigs will be slaughtered for a bigman. The festivities go on for days and clans gather bearing fabulous gifts.

Carvings are also associated with the rites of passage of young men into adulthood. There's an excellent documentary film called *Malangan Labadama*, by Chris Owen, which shows a mortuary festival in all its extraordinary detail. ■

The word *malangan* has also been used to label the northern New Irelanders' carvings, and indeed a carving is called a malangan, but the word really refers to a complex system of spiritual ideas, rites and beliefs. The carvings are made by secret men's groups and revealed to the village in rituals associated with a death (see the Malangan Death Rites aside). The tradition of shark-calling is also practised on New Ireland and is particularly strong along the west coast (see the Shark-Calling aside).

In the island's south are the Tumbuan traditions. The people from the south invaded the Gazelle Peninsula and settled the Duke of York Islands several hundred years ago. Southern New Irelanders speak a *tok ples* (local language) that is similar to Tolai's Kuanua, with *dukduks* (spirits) and *tambuans* (body masks) common to all these cultures.

Around Namatanai and central New Ireland are the Kabai traditions, which have similarities with other cultures such as secret men's business and the building of spirit icons, but are less well understood.

As in most PNG islands, traditional clan power was wielded by chiefs and *bigmen*, but clan rites and land claims passed in a matrilineal system. Women in these cultures have considerable influence; some elderly women are powerful matriarchs in control of vast amounts of family land.

Lumber and copra workers have come to the province and given it the second-highest population of males in the country. New

APPRENTICE
MASTERCARVER

Shark-Calling

Along the coast of New Ireland, especially the west coast between Konogogo and Kontu, the ancient art of shark-calling is practised. Because of the documentary film *The Shark Callers of Kontu*, by Dennis O'Rourke, Kontu attracts what little attention the west coast gets. Some clans claim the skill for their own, but it was widely practised before the art was said to be nearly lost.

It's just astonishing that men have the ability to 'call up' a shark with only a loop-shaped rattle made of coconut shells splashing in the water and then beguile the shark into a tiny hand-held noose. The shark makes several passes of the canoe while the caller continues his incantations and weaves his spell with the rattle. When the shark comes close enough the caller snares it with the noose. The noose has a piece of wood fitted to it to cause drag in the water as the shark fights and tries to break away. The less artful bit comes next when the caller bludgeons the shark into some submission. Then the writhing 3m beast, with its teeth gnashing, is hauled into the tiny canoe where it continues to struggle and be bludgeoned until it dies.

It's believed that the shark won't come if the caller is impure or does not respect the shark; shark and caller are connected. Shark-callers 'own' certain sharks and only theirs will come to them.

Shark-callers are not unique to New Ireland but the island is famous for them. ■

Irelanders are well educated, highly literate and rarely visited by travellers.

KAVIENG
• *pop 7000* • *postcode 631*

Kavieng is a sleepy little town. This end of the island is quite flat and surrounded on three sides by sea so there are often cool breezes. The harbour looks across a broad channel to Nusa Island. There's nothing much to do here, but it's a very nice place to do nothing much.

Orientation

The town is spread out. Coronation Rd connects the airport road (Stanfield St) and the Boluminski Highway with the waterfront. Along Coronation Rd are the tourist office, Kavieng Club, Kavieng Hotel, Andersons

supermarket and Westpac bank. Shops extend for a few blocks to the east of Coronation Rd, but the prettiest parts of town are the long waterfront and the central golf course.

From the harbour you look west to Nusa, with a narrow passage separating it from Nusa Lik on the left. Further left (south) of Nusa and Nusa Lik is Nango Island.

Information

The New Ireland Tourist Bureau (☎ 984 1449; fax 984 2346; PO Box 103) is on Coronation Rd near the post office. Noah Lurang and his staff are friendly and knowledgeable.

Nusa Parade

Coronation Rd curls its way down to meet Nusa Parade that runs along the waterfront. At the intersection is a war memorial. The town and the bitumen end just past the Malagan Beach Resort to your right (north), and to your left (south) is the market, provincial government buildings, harbour proper with wharfs and customs buildings, a fishery and about 400m further down the road is the hospital.

North Just beyond the Malagan Beach Resort to the north, the road becomes *koronos* (crushed coral) and there are contiguous villages along the beachfront. You can walk up the road or along the thin strip of beach but be aware that these are private homes. The road is not a thoroughfare and only carries local foot traffic and very quickly you are in the intimate surrounds of the village. Even here in almost downtown Kavieng, young children look at you either quizzically or anxiously, but never without interest.

Visitors are rare and the locals will be very friendly if you say '*monin*' or '*apinun*' (even 'hello' is fine), but mind your manners. This is a great chance to see how many urban, educated, wage-earning Papua New Guineans live.

At the village of Patailu, the road bends inland to the right (east) and ultimately meets

NEW IRELAND

the road heading north to Kulangit and North Cape (the island's northernmost point).

South Nusa Parade runs past the market and further along on the left are the **provincial government buildings**, built on the site of Baron Boluminski's residence. His grand home was destroyed in WWII and all that's left is the jumble of paving stones that were once part of his stairway. Further along this waterfront ridge is a large Japanese gun still pointing futilely out to sea.

Down at the shoreline, a small workshop houses the castings which were to hold the stone grinding wheel for a mill which was part of the Marquis de Ray's incredible sham (see The Marquis de Ray & Cape Breton aside below). The wheel itself is in Rabaul but the castings are in remarkably good shape with their date of manufacture, 1852, clearly visible.

As you move south down Nusa Parade you pass the international wharf and customs buildings on the right and then 500m further on the left is the **Bagail Cemetery**, where Boluminski was buried. The tough guy's grave is right before you as you enter the cemetery (see the Boluminski aside).

Beyond the cemetery, 600m south, is the hospital and beyond that there's a road junction where a left turn (east) will put you on the road that becomes Court Rd and meets Coronation Rd.

Golf Course
The golf course is managed by the Kavieng Club, but golf in post-colonial Kavieng has taken on new meaning. There are no fences around the golf course and these days it serves as a central thoroughfare for local pedestrians. People sleep through the midday heat under its shady trees and picnic on its fairways. Some golfers play barefooted or bare-chested and might take in a snack under a tree between holes. Pet dogs walk alongside the players and chase golf balls down the fairway. Ironically, this once-great bastion of colonialism is now a potent symbol of egalitarianism.

The Harbour & Islands
Kavieng has a large and beautiful harbour. You can get a good view of it from the sandy beach in front of the Malagan Beach Resort, or you can go down to the waterfront and catch a dinghy (banana boat) out to an island. Dinghies have routes and fixed charges within the nearby islands or you can arrange a charter. You can negotiate a 'drop me off, pick me up later' trip.

Little **Edmago** is a tiny dot with palm trees, a white-sand beach all the way round

The Marquis de Ray & Cape Breton
The Marquis de Ray never set foot on New Ireland and yet he used the details of a ship's log to sell hundreds of hectares of land to gullible, would-be settlers. In 1879 he had raised A$60,000 on the basis of a flimsy prospectus, but many of his colonists paid with their lives as well as their savings.

The marquis had advertised Cape Breton, near Lambom Island off Cape St George, as a thriving settlement with fertile soil, perpetual sunshine and friendly natives. In fact, it was a tangled jungle where the rainfall was so heavy that, even today, there is virtually no development.

The marquis sent four shiploads of European land buyers to southern New Ireland. With only a few weeks' supplies and such useful equipment as a mill for an area where grain would never grow, the settlers soon started to die like flies.

The pitiful survivors were eventually rescued by Thomas and Emma Farrell (Emma Farrell would later become Queen Emma; see the Queen Emma aside in the New Britain chapter). Although most of the rescued settlers were sent on to Australia, one 16-year-old went on to become a successful New Britain planter. The grinding stone for the Cape Breton grain mill is buried in ash-mud in a park off Mango Avenue in Rabaul and some parts of the mill are in Kavieng. The marquis ended his days in a French asylum. ∎

and beautiful clear water over the coral. Further out is the island of **New Sulaman**, another local picnic spot where you can see copra being prepared. **Lissenung** (or Paradise Island) is another beautiful dot and there's accommodation here. See the Places to Stay section.

The sea between New Ireland and Lavongai is full of islands, most of them tiny, and it is possible to get from Kavieng to Lavongai by short hops.

Activities

Cycling New Ireland is suited to cycling.

The long straight Boluminski Highway is flat and sealed until Lakurumau village, and thereafter has a smooth crushed-coral surface. Tabo Meli's Rainbow Tours (☎ 984 2234; PO Box 305, Kavieng) does cycling tours of both coasts of New Ireland staying in village accommodation. The lodgings are grassroots style and cost about K20 a day and bike hire is K22 a day (K15 for students). You can take a guide for K20 a day.

The Kavieng Hotel and Malagan Beach Resort hire bicycles. For K3 an hour you can take in the harbour and villages to the north and ride along flat Nusa Parade which carries

PLACES TO STAY
13 Kavieng Guesthouse
18 Malagan Beach Resort
20 Kavieng Club
22 Kavieng Hotel

OTHER
1 Supermarket
2 Supermarket
3 Bakery
4 Haus Toksave Bookshop
5 M&M's Kitchen & Newsagents
6 Capricornia Variety Stoa
7 The Purple Shop
8 Service Station
9 Pakono Bus Service
10 Admiral Carteret Library
11 Tourist Office
12 Courthouse
14 Westpac Bank
15 Post Office
16 Andersons Supermarket
17 PNGBC Bank
19 War Memorial
21 Health Store
23 Agley Wharf (Small boats)
24 Market
25 Old Golf Clubhouse
26 Police Station
27 Tennis Courts
28 Provincial Government
   Buildings
29 International Wharf &
   Customs Buildings
30 Power Station
31 Bagail Cemetery
   (Boluminski's Grave)

NEW IRELAND

barely any traffic. Paths through the central golf course make good connections to the eastern part of town.

Fishing You can hire rods and tackle from the Kavieng Hotel or arrange a charter. Listen out in the lodge, hotel or club and you may get a chance to invite yourself along to a fishing trip.

Diving & Snorkelling There's great diving and snorkelling in the area, with lots of war wreckage (including a midget submarine) and fish and coral varieties. Divers sometimes hand-feed sharks.

Archipelago Diving (☎ 984 2531; fax 984 2531; PO Box 479) is the main diving operator in Kavieng. Archipelago rents all the gear and has diving courses as well, including an open-water course for K350.

Edith and Dietmar who run the Lissenung Island Resort (Paradise Island; ☎ & fax 984 2526; PO Box 536, Kavieng; email 101711. 3413@compuserve.com) are keen divers and the reefs around Lissenung Island are spectacular. They have a full gear hire facility and do night dives too.

Surfing Surfing in PNG is in its infancy but Kavieng is the most explored surfing loca-

tion in the country. There's an abundance of good breaks within a few minutes by dinghy or PMV from town. Contact the New Ireland Tourist Bureau, where you can pick up an information sheet on local breaks, or the Surfer Publishing Group (☎ 714-498 5922; fax 714-498 7849; PO Box 1028, Dana Point, CA 92629, USA), which can fax you information on Kavieng's surfing spots.

Also try the people at the Nusa Islands Retreat (see the Places to Stay section) for local surfing information.

Canoeing & Kayaking The waters off Kavieng are full of islands and you can approach the villagers on the beachfront north of town about hiring a canoe and paddler to visit Nusa or beyond. It's probably unwise to go alone because there are strong currents and the art of paddling a little outrigger takes some learning (see the Outrigger Canoes aside). Raging Thunder, based in Cairns, Australia (☎ 617 7051 8177), has sea kayaking tours from Kavieng.

Organised Tours
Contact Air Niugini for weekend packages, or the New Ireland Tourist Bureau for information on interesting tours of New Ireland that last from three nights to a week.

Outrigger Canoes

The silent, sleek craft that islanders still use are lightweight, beautifully built and glide through the water. The canoes can carry many times their own weight, are very stable with their outrigging and can handle swells, but piloting them is quite an art. You need to relax your body when you're sitting in a canoe because if you tense up, you tend to make the canoe wobble (which tends to make you tense up). But if you let your body relax, the craft becomes stable and you begin to see the attraction.

These ancient boats make no noise and once in motion, their sleek build and inertia make them almost effortless to propel. The whole experience is very meditative – the rhythms of the paddler, undulations in the water and the scenery around you can seduce you into a blissful state.

Canoes are made by hand and vary in design and decoration. A tree is felled near the water's edge, from where it can be floated to the builder's home, but most of the work is done at the tree site. The log must be cut to size and then the top is flattened with an axe. When the basic shape is formed, the builder will float the log home to hollow it out – an arduous process.

When the canoe's full shape has been fashioned, the builder will float it and test its ride. The canoe is trimmed and charred over a fire inside and out to harden the timber and bring out the resins to seal the pores. The charred material is scraped away and then the canoe is decorated, fitted with outrigging and given to some seven-year-old kid to go to school in. ■

Special Events

The Kavieng provincial celebrations are held in late February.

The week-long Luka Barok festival is held in late June or early July. Since 1992, it's been resurrecting old rituals (with elders' help) and includes *davan*, a ritual where girls are initiated into womanhood, shark-calling and feasting. The festival also pays homage to three American pilots shot down near Komalu and the village's parish priest who died a martyr's death in 1944.

George Brown Day is in mid-August and for four days in mid-September the New Ireland Independence Day and Malangan Show is held.

Ask at the New Ireland Tourism Bureau for more information.

Places to Stay

Kavieng The *Kavieng Guesthouse* (☎ 984 2312), on the corner of Emirau St and the airport road, charges K30 for a dorm-style bed and K35/45 for singles/doubles plus 3% tax. The guesthouse is clean and straight and has shared bathroom and kitchen facilities.

At the time of research, friendly Simon Baranko, who fled from Bougainville and re-established the Pakono Bus Service (☎ & fax 984 2611), was in the throes of converting his family home into an inexpensive *guesthouse*.

The *Kavieng Club* (☎ 984 2224; fax 984 2457; PO Box 62) is right next door to the Kavieng Hotel and offers good accommodation in a block set a little off the street. Delta Nates manages the club and there's seven rooms. Singles/doubles cost K42/50 in fan-cooled rooms and K50/60 for air-con rooms. All rooms have TV, fridge and private bathroom. The Kavieng Club has two bars and a restaurant, a garden area, snooker tables and TV lounge area.

The *Kavieng Hotel* (☎ 984 2199; fax 984 2283; PO Box 4), on Coronation Rd, is a lively and colourful place run by Shane Jenkinson. Shane's a friendly man with an irrepressible personality; he used to manage Rabaul's New Guinea Club but 30-odd years ago he was a British salty sailor/traveller type who was moving through Rabaul and couldn't bring himself to leave. A dorm-style bed in a fan-cooled room is good value at K30 per person. Self-contained single/double rooms cost K97/110 and have private bathroom, TV, phone, fridge, air-con and views over the golf course. All guests enjoy a free buffet breakfast. The Kavieng Hotel has a restaurant and attached bar, pool and large public bar. Shane hires out bicycles, golf clubs, fishing gear and windsurfing equipment and has a couple of old malibu surfboards and a 23ft dinghy he uses for fishing trips and sightseeing tours. Transfers to the nearby airport are free.

Malagan Beach Resort (☎ 984 2344; fax 984 1452; PO Box 238) is a pretty swish place on the beachfront. The grounds include a shady strip of beach overlooking Nusa Island. There's a restaurant and bar. The rooms cost K160/170/180 plus 3% tax for singles/doubles/triples. All rooms have air-con, private bathroom, phone, fridge and TV. The resort offers tours and hires bicycles, and you can practise the paddler's art on one of the two traditional canoes for hire. Airport transfers are free.

Around Kavieng Austrians Edith and Dietmar run the *Lissenung Island Resort* (☎ & fax 984 2526; PO Box 536, Kavieng; email 101711.3413@compuserve.com) on the tiny island (also known as Paradise Island). It's about 15 minutes by boat from Kavieng and they provide return transfers for K30. Lissenung is a private island with no electricity (a generator provides power during the day and early evening) and you can circumnavigate it on foot in 10 minutes. The two simple bungalows, each with two rooms, cost K45 per person. Breakfast costs K7, lunch K10 and dinner K13, and there's no self-catering. There's good snorkelling and diving here and they have a full gear-hire service.

The new *Nusa Islands Retreat* (☎ & fax 984 2247; PO Box 302, Kavieng) is based on Nusa Lik Island, across Kavieng Harbour from Kavieng. Its fan-cooled, traditional-style bungalows cater for between two and four people and cost about K30/50 a single/double. Meals are available for between K5 and K15; there are plans to build a restaurant. During the surfing season (November to April), bunkhouse accommodation with basic facilities, predominantly catering for surfers, will be available on the northern end of the neighbouring Nusa Laoeu Island. Rates will be about K20/40 a single/double; ask about the weekly rates. Visitors will be picked up from and dropped off at the airport and a ferry makes regular trips between the islands and mainland each day. The retreat offers a host of activities, including surfing, diving and traditional canoeing, and can arrange others.

Places to Eat

The market has a good range of fresh fruit and vegetables, and there's a bakery on Rose St. There are supermarkets around town including Andersons on Coronation Road. Most of the trade stores have attached kai-bars. Lobsters can cost as little as K3 if you buy at the market.

M&M's Kitchen is on Lavonga St and serves kai-style fare from a bain-marie. It's clean and busy.

The *Kavieng Club* has a restaurant that's open at lunch for sandwiches and light meals and offers a broader, predominantly Asian-style menu in the evening. Mains cost from K8 to K10. The restaurant serves up a K15 all-you-can-eat Chinese smorgasbord on Wednesday.

The *Kavieng Hotel* dishes up good food at breakfast, lunch and dinner. Sandwiches (K3.50) and cooked meals are available for lunch – grilled fish and steaks cost K8 to K10. The restaurant is busy in the evenings and the menu includes soups, chicken dishes and seafood. Mains cost around K10 to K14. The K15 Friday-night seafood buffet is legendary.

Malagan Beach Resort has a restaurant on the beachfront open for breakfast, lunch and dinner. A cool breeze blows through the lattice walls and the airy room is nicely decorated, but the muzak is inane and annoying. Seafood, chicken, fish and steak dishes are served for K12 to K20 and the adjoining bar has an impressive wine list.

Entertainment

Any organised evening entertainment will happen at the *Kavieng Hotel*, *Kavieng Club* or *Malagan Beach Resort*. Occasionally there's a band in town and dances are organised (or happen spontaneously) around the 1970s-stacked Wurlitzer in the Kavieng Hotel. If Shane gets the urge to dance, you'd better make some room.

Things to Buy

A small artefacts shop is intermittently open at the airport and has some small malangan pieces. There are collections at the Kavieng Hotel and Malagan Beach Resort and most are for sale. However, they're expensive and unwieldy items and difficult to travel with. Malangan art is very fashionable but acquiring your own piece and getting it home is not without its problems.

There are some good printed T-shirts in the town's trade stores and there are *laplaps* (sarongs), genuine stringband guitars (K50) and ukuleles, and loads of bully beef and tinned fish, too. There are also wonderful knick-knacks from Asia and elsewhere in these shops – cheap tin toys, weird fuel lighters and pocket knives. 'Romance' hair pomade comes in a great tin with a picture of a suave moustached and tuxedo-clad man.

Getting There & Away

Air Air Niugini (☎ 984 2135; fax 984 2337; PO Box 63), Islands Nationair (☎ 984 2332) and Airlink (☎ 984 2600) are represented at the airport terminal a couple of kilometres out of town.

Air Niugini flies daily to Kavieng from Port Moresby (K288) and Tokua (Rabaul; K97) and back again, except on Thursday and Sunday when it flies on to Manus (K131).

Islands Nationair flies to Kavieng from Tokua (K97), Namatanai (K132) and Londolovit on Lihir Island (K128) on Tuesday and Thursday (but flies between Namatanai and Tokua daily for K57).

Airlink also has direct connections to Hoskins (K155), Buka (K181) and Goroka (K252) at least once a week, as well as servicing many of the smaller airstrips around the islands.

Road There are a couple of bus companies that run PMVs down the Boluminski Highway; PMVs are a reliable and inexpensive way to head south from Kavieng. Contact Pakono Bus Service (☎ & fax 984 2611) in Kavieng.

Buses leave Kavieng at 9.30 am, run through Namatanai and arrive in Samo in the early evening. The following day, the return run leaves Samo at 6 am, passing Namatanai about 9.30 am and reaching Kavieng about 6 pm. The Pakono bus goes south from Kavieng, with many stops along the way, on Sunday, returning Monday, and Wednesday, returning Thursday. On Tuesday, Friday and Saturday they do 'specials' according to demand in a smaller 15-seater minibus. The fare between Kavieng and Namatanai is K14.

Avis (☎ 984 2454) and Hertz (☎ 984 2374) have offices next to the Malagan Beach Resort, with the Regent Garage (☎ 984 2090) next door to them. Budget (☎ 984 2045) is represented at the airport terminal and the Kavieng Hotel will hire vehicles also. Car rental in PNG is expensive and fuel in New Ireland is pricey (fuel outside Kavieng and Namatanai is scarce). If you're going to cross the steep, unsealed mountain roads from one coast to the other, you'll want a 4WD (especially in the wet). Figure on around K120 per day and K0.80 per km for a 4WD, but your airline boarding pass might entitle you to a discount. If you have a group or can justify the cost, New Ireland would be one of PNG's best places to have wheels.

There are some bicycles available for hire in Kavieng, but if you were planning spending some time on New Ireland and like the idea of touring between simple village guesthouses, consider bringing your own bike and pannier bags. Contact Tabo Meli at Rainbow Tours (☎ 984 2234; PO Box 305), who organises cycling tours of New Ireland, for good advice.

Boat The best way to get around the New Ireland coast and islands is by dinghy. These tie up at the small Agley Wharf, near the market, and regular dinghy routes connect with as far away as the New Britain coast. The open waters of St Georges Channel can get wild with high seas and strong winds; in these conditions, it's not for the fainthearted.

Dinghies and work boats run to the nearby islands, including a weekly boat making the overnight trip to Tatau in the Tabar group (K10), and two boats each week to Lavongai Island (K8). It takes about six hours by small boat to Mussau Island.

Consort Express Lines has freighters running weekly between Kavieng and Lae via Kimbe and takes passengers. It's one night to Kimbe (K41) and two to Lae (K54), deck class only. They usually depart on Sunday. Consort also has boats making the overnight trip to Rabaul (K48) but there is no fixed schedule. Its agent in Kavieng is Century Shipping (☎ 984 2239; fax 984 2041; PO Box 293), opposite the Malagan Beach Resort. There's no sign.

Coastal's freighters also call in at Kavieng but don't have a fixed schedule. There is a boat to Rabaul about fortnightly and one to Manus Island about monthly. Approximate fares in deck/cabin class are K40/60 to Rabaul and K45/90 to Manus. The Coastal agent is at the Kavieng butchery ('Haus Mit') on Coronation Road.

Getting Around

Getting around Kavieng is easy on foot, although rather spread out. PMVs around town cost K0.50 and some run to the airport. See the earlier information on cycling.

EAST COAST

The east coast is more developed than the west, with the Boluminski Highway running most of its length, although it carries only light traffic.

When WWI ended German rule, the

Boluminski Highway already ran 100km out of Kavieng along the east coast. Under the Australians, it was gradually extended and now reaches about 80km beyond Namatanai to Rei, before petering out into a 4WD track. The road is now sealed from Kavieng to Lakurumau village, 74km away.

The highway was (and is, where it's unsealed) paved with crushed coral and almost all the way along are copra plantations. There are many villages built beside the road, often right on the palm-fringed beach. Visitors to New Ireland are few and outsiders quickly become an interesting diversion. People are friendly, waving and shouting as you drive by, gathering around if you stop.

Nearly every village is built near one of the many streams that run down from the central mountains. These streams are cool, clean and delightfully clear and refreshing.

Cross-Island Roads

There are roads crossing from the east coast to the less-visited west coast. Although some of these trans-island roads can be very rough during the wet, none are very long because it's a very narrow island. From north to south, the crossings are:

Fangalawa to Panamafei The Fangalawa crossing runs from near Panamafei village on the west coast to the east coast a few kilometres on the Kavieng side of Lakurumau. It's in good condition but crosses the Schleinitz Ranges and is so steep that some of it is sealed for safety.

Poliamba to Panachais This track might be impassable even in a 4WD vehicle but it would make an excellent and easy walk. The track runs through a spectacular jungle-covered limestone gorge. At Panachais, there's a community school where you might find accommodation and there might be accommodation at Poliamba.

Karu to Konogogo This crossing is also steep and the road isn't in great condition. Take it slowly.

Namatanai to Uluputur/Labur Bay Beginning at Bo, this is the least hilly of the crossings. From the west coast it should be possible to find a boat to the Duke of York islands, although you might have to wait a day or so if you don't want to charter.

Boluminski Highway

There's no mains electricity outside Kavieng and Namatanai. On a clear night, the sky is ablaze with stars, revealing a million more flecks than you can see near our big, bright cities. A night on a cool New Ireland beach with a warm SP (no refrigeration) talking philosophy, religion and politics with a villager is a very nice way to spend the evening.

The guesthouses are simple bush material huts that cost about K20 a night and some-

---

Boluminski

Franz Boluminski was born in 1863 in Graudenz, west Prussia. He served in the German army in East Africa and in 1894 went to work for the German New Guinea Company in Astrolabe Bay near modern-day Madang. German rule was formalised in 1899 and, in March, Boluminski transferred into the German colonial service. He was posted to New Ireland at the new Kavieng station and promoted to district officer in 1910.

He built the Boluminski Highway by forcing each village along the coast to construct and maintain a section. He would do regular inspections and summon the villagers to push his carriage over any deteriorated sections. Punishments would be severe if repairs weren't soon under way. New Irelanders built a road not rivalled on the mainland until well into the 1950s.

When WWI ended German rule, Boluminski had a string of copra plantations connected to the highway running up to the deep-water port at Kavieng. He had made New Ireland one of the most profitable parts of German New Guinea.

However, Boluminski never saw the war or the ignominious handover of German New Guinea to Australia. He was overcome by heatstroke and died in 1913.

He was buried at Bagail Cemetery, in Kavieng, where there's an imposing but plain cross that bears the simple inscription 'Boluminski, 28 April 1913'. ■

times this will include kai-food or you may be asked to pay extra. They are all beautiful in a grassroots way and represent a great way to get into the local culture, but you have to be prepared to rough it a bit. Meals can be arranged, but take some supplies, a sleeping sheet and torch (if you ask for a mosquito net someone will usually find you one). There are small trade stores around but they sell mostly tinfis and rice.

In **Matanasoi** (or Liga) village, about 5km along the highway from Kavieng airport, a little pathway leads off the road to a limestone cave filled with crystal-clear water. During WWII, the Japanese used this grotto as a source of drinking water.

At **Sali** village, 55km from Kavieng, there's village *guesthouse* accommodation. There's a fantastic natural swimming pool upstream from the bridge at **Fissoa**, in the grounds of the Fissoa Vocational Centre. The water is exquisite – it's amazingly clear and quite cool. This spot is popular with swimmers and picnickers.

The big Commonwealth Development Corporation oil-palm project at **Poliamba** has created a new village and there's a *guesthouse* here. It's supposedly only for people connected with the project but you might get a room for about K40. See the administration office.

Libba village, just before Konos, is a good place to look for Malangan art. The village has a strong Malangan tradition and is home to master carvers. There's a village *guesthouse* here.

Konos is 140km from Kavieng and the approximate halfway point to Namatanai. This is the only major village along the road, and the loading point for timber ships. Konos has a village *guesthouse* that charges K20 per night and there's a lovely beach at **Pinis Passage** just on the Namatanai side of Konos. The waters between here and the Tabar group brim with large fish and sea creatures and, between September and January, you can see pods of whales migrating offshore.

The turn-off to Lelet Plateau, just after **Malom** village, is 165km from Kavieng and

25km south of Konos. There's another village *guesthouse* further down at **Dalom**.

Beyond here the road climbs a couple of times and occasionally deteriorates a little but generally continues to hug the coast.

Karu is about 40km before Namatanai and a few kilometres after a crossing to the west coast. There's a place to stay called the *Isi Isi Beach Village Guesthouse*. Thomas Molis runs this simple place adjacent to his trade store and charges K20 a night. The paintings and carvings in the church are creations of Kou, who has gone on to local fame as a singer.

A few hundred metres across Karu Bay from the village is the small **Mumu Island** (also known as Mumugas Island), which the traditional owners have proclaimed as a conservation area. Turtles come ashore to lay their eggs around the end of July. It's good for picnics and swimming. You can get across in a canoe for about K1.

Namatanai
• *pop 900* • *postcode 633*
Namatanai is a quiet little place, 264km south-east of Kavieng, but only 15 minutes by air from Tokua airport (Rabaul). Namatanai is the second-largest town on New Ireland but you won't find much more here than a hotel, a supermarket and a few stores. It was until recently a much prettier place, but all the big old rain trees were cut down after one of them fell on a policeman.

Namatanai was an important station in German days and the Namatanai Hotel is on the site of the old German station house. You can find the graves of Dr Emil Stephan, the German administrator, and Mrs Scheringer, wife of another German official from pre-WWI days, in the old graveyard down the road from the National Works compound on the other side of the airstrip.

Places to Stay The *Namatanai Hotel* (☎ 984 3057; PO Box 48) is currently closed but likely to re-open. It's right down by the waterfront, near the new wharf. Figure on around K90/150 for singles/doubles.

The guesthouse at *St Martin's Catholic*

NEW IRELAND

Mission, uphill from the town centre, has recently been rebuilt. Accommodation costs K20.

Getting There & Away Both Islands Nation-air and Airlink make the 15-minute flight from Rabaul at least daily, Monday to Saturday, for K30. You can also fly to Kavieng and the Eastern Islands from Namatanai – see also the Kavieng Getting There & Away section. To walk into town from the airport, turn right out of the terminal then take the next two left turns. It's not far.

Dinghies travel between New Britain and New Ireland's west coast, a short distance by road from Namatanai. From there they travel along the west coast to Kavieng and there'll be boats to Kokopo, Rabaul and the Duke of York islands, along this beach. You might have to be prepared to wait for a day or two, but once you're moving you can largely determine your own pace when island-hopping. Get some local help at Uluputur village to find a boat. The tricky bit is the little land leg across New Ireland from Namatanai to the west coast.

See the Kavieng section for more information on dinghy travel and road transport.

WEST COAST

A road runs along most of the coast and it carries even less traffic than the Boluminski Highway. For most of the way – from the Fangalawa-Panamafei crossing down to Konogogo village – it's in good condition, but some of the rivers have to be forded. In the wet season even a 4WD will have trouble with the some of the river crossings.

The water in the rivers is so clear that it doesn't even look like water – more like a floppy film of clingwrap. The rivers are cool to swim in and very refreshing, many full of fresh-water fish and prawns. There are some plantations and a couple of logging depots but most of the villages rely on fishing and gardening. Between Konogogo and Kontu shark-calling is practised.

There's just a couple of 'formal' places to stay on the west coast, but visitors are such a rarity you should have no trouble finding a place to sleep. While you probably won't have to pay for this, you should always leave a gift of about K10, plus some money or food if you have been given meals.

The population density is lower here than on the east coast, but there are still plenty of villages. Very basic food can be bought in these villages, but don't count on it.

From the crossing near Karu village and heading north up the coast, you come to **Konogogo**, known locally as Kono. There's a basic store and a Catholic school where you can usually stay.

From here, the undulating road runs to the big **Kalili Plantation**, where the country becomes flatter. This area gets nearly 5m of rain a year, falling year-round. Just north of the plantation's harbour there's a mission. The road crosses several rivers in this area.

Further north-west is **Messi** village, under the lee of a jungle-covered limestone escarpment. It's an unusually large village for New Ireland, with a basic medical aid station. In this area, the ground is covered with water-rounded black stones and pebbles – it looks like a formal Japanese garden. The Messi villagers tend gardens at the top of an escarpment, and the climb up it is tough but rewarding work.

Between Messi and **Kontu** there are many rivers, some of which must be forded. Kontu is smaller than Messi but it's still a reasonable size. Men might be invited to stay in the men's house but women might have to stay in the village (arrangements will be made). Shark-calling implements are kept in the men's house.

From Kontu, the road wanders inland and rises through some spectacular rainforest. At **Cape Timeis** the road runs near clifftops from where there are stunning views to the sea below and along the coast.

Further on, past Namasalang, you come to Panamafei village and the Fangalawa crossing to the east coast. North of here the coastal road deteriorates.

LELET PLATEAU

This high plateau is more than 1200m at its midpoint and is very different from the steamy coast. The climate is cool enough to grow vegetables and it can get quite chilly. It's rolling country and there are no rivers – perhaps that is why rain magic is practised. There's an enormously deep cave, as yet unfathomed, as well as some bat caves near **Mongop**.

The villages up here – there are only four – are larger than those on the coast. There is no commercial accommodation but you should be able to find somewhere to stay – take some rice and perhaps a live chicken as a gift for your hosts.

There's a road leading up to Lelet Plateau from the Boluminski Highway just after Malom village, about 25km south of Konos. Because there are a fair number of trucks bringing vegetables down, you should be able to arrange a lift. Try asking around at the Kavieng market. Walking up is another possibility.

THE SOUTH

The southern 'bulge' of the island is still relatively isolated because the roads are not too good. It is the birthplace of Tambuan culture. The people from southern New Ireland invaded New Britain's Gazelle Peninsula several hundred years ago. It's ironic that the south is so little known and poorly developed, while the sophisticated Tolais of East New Britain are Tambuan culture's greatest (or most visible) advocates. Even the Duke of York islands, another repository of Tambuan culture, are probably more accessible than most of New Ireland's south.

There's a move to list the impressive Weitin Valley, a rare rift valley, on the World Heritage register. This trench, where the Pacific and Indian ocean plates meet, provides passage for two mighty rivers, the Weitin and the Kamdaru. These rivers separate the Hans Meyer Range from the southern Verron Range. The southern ranges are volcanic in origin, but there are no active volcanos on the island. There are some high-altitude lakes.

Getting Around

Air Islands Nationair flies from Namatanai to airstrips at Manga (K63) and Silur (K80) once a week.

Road Along the east coast you can continue in a conventional vehicle from Namatanai through Samo to Danfu and from there to Rei by 4WD. It's possible, with great effort, to walk, canoe and boat right around the southern tip of the island. Logging companies are building roads in the south, especially on the west coast. A road already goes south to Pakabong and will extend to Wapi.

On the way southwards from Namatanai, Samo is where the road starts getting rough. After Warangansau village, there is a big hill to Manga and the road is almost deserted after this point. There is a mission and an airstrip at Manga and plantations at Muliana and Manmo, just after Muliana village. After Manga you come to Maritboan Plantation.

From the end of the road in Rei it takes about two days to Srar village – ask the way from the villagers. From Srar to Maliom is

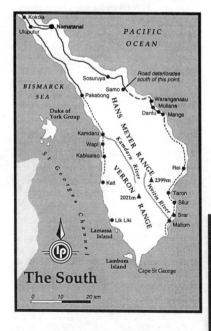

The South

fairly easy over a good, well-cut path. After Maliom the paths get difficult and some sections of the coast can only be negotiated by canoe. Canoes are reasonable to hire and easily obtained. There is a path across the southern part of the peninsula or, if you are lucky enough to pick up a boat, you can go around to Lambom Island by the cape.

Cape St George is worth seeing. Canoes around Lambom to Lamassa are easy to find and there is a path all the way along the coast to Pakabong – although it is better to get a canoe from Kabisalao to Wapi.

LAVONGAI & EAST ISLANDS

These are called the East islands despite the fact that they are *west* of New Ireland. La vongai Island doesn't really count among the East islands because it's the second-largest island in the province. It's a mountainous, isolated island with productive copra plantations on the volcanic soils of its coastline. Lavongai and the eight East islands make up this island group.

On little **Tsoi Island**, there's the *Mansava Adventure Lodge*. It charges K50 for accommodation, K8 for breakfast, K9 for lunch and K10 for dinner. There's swimming, snorkelling and fishing and WWII relics to see. Boat transfers from Kavieng cost K80 one way, but you could probably make your way out there much cheaper with the dinghy drivers down at Agley Wharf, near the Kavieng market.

EASTERN ISLAND GROUPS

There are five island groups strung off the east coast of New Ireland – Tabar, Lihir, Tanga, Green and Feni. They are only 30 to 50km offshore and clearly visible from the east coast.

Tabar Islands

The Tabar islands are the original home of Malangan culture and ceremonies and traditions are strong here. Edward Sale, Leppan and Maris Memenga came from Tabar and these carvers' works are regarded as masterpieces.

There are a few organised places to stay in the Tabar islands, including the *Ku Do Ku Don Village Lodge* and the *Tomlabat Adventure Lodge* on Tatau Island and the *Numb-Koko Village House* on Tabar Island. Contact the New Ireland Tourist Bureau (☎ 94 1449; fax 94 2346; PO Box 103, Kavieng) for more information.

There are boats that run from Konos to Tatau Island in the Tabar group and some from Kavieng to Tatau.

Lihir Group

Lihir Island has perhaps the world's largest undeveloped gold prospect. There are several thousand people working on the mine site at the moment, but this number will fall away when the mine is fully operational.

You could fly to Lihir very easily if you wanted to. See the Kavieng Getting There & Away section. From Namatanai, there's boats running to the mission on Lihir for about K10.

Tanga, Feni & Green Groups

The Feni islands are covered in dense, steamy jungle and are almost untouched. There are springs and geysers. The Tanga and Green island groups are similarly untouched. Who knows if anyone's been

---

The Johnson Cult

When the first elections for the House of Assembly were held in PNG in the 1960s, the islanders took to the spirit of democracy with gusto and decided they would vote for American president Lyndon Baines Johnson.

Lavongai went 'all the way with LBJ', but when the American president didn't show up, the islanders decided they needed take more direct action. They refused to pay their taxes and instead put their money in a fund to buy Lyndon Johnson. They raised a lot of money, but they never did manage to entice the American president to come and represent the people of Lavongai.

Eventually the Johnson Cult died out and the business was all but forgotten. And then someone started selling Johnson outboard motors. Well, you can imagine... ∎

there – maybe some sailors came by one time. Dinghy connections from the Kavieng waterfront would get you under way, and the region's airstrips are regularly serviced by the second-level airlines. See the Kavieng Getting There & Away section.

ST MATTHIAS GROUP

The islands of Mussau, Emirau, Eloaua and Tench are some distance north-west of New Ireland and put up determined resistance to European invasion. Tench was the last 'uncontrolled' part of the New Ireland region.

During WWII, there was an American base at Emirau with a larger force than the present-day population of the group. The people build large canoes without outriggers, which can carry 30 or more people. Tench is also famous for woven mats.

Islands Nationair and Airlink fly to Emirau and Mussau. See the Kavieng Getting There & Away section.

Manus Province

Land Area 2100 sq km
Population 38,000
Capital Lorengau

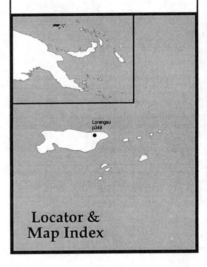

Lorengau
p349

Locator & Map Index

Manus Province consists of the Admiralty islands, of which Manus is by far the biggest, plus a scattering of tiny island groups that barely break the water's surface. The province is the most isolated and least visited in Papua New Guinea. Only New Ireland Province's barely touched St Matthias Group is more northern than the Admiralty islands and the Manus provincial boundary is marked in the north by 800km of the equator.

The province exports timber, copra and cocoa but is better known as an exporter of well-educated people. There's long been a culture that stresses the importance of education in Manus Province and it has paid benefits. Much of the local economy is supported by well-placed Manus Islanders in PNG's big centres who send money home. Manus Islanders are proportionally over-represented in high government and civil-service positions. The Manus premier once said 'our isolation is our strength', and maybe it's true.

History

No significant archaeological research has been undertaken on Manus, but there's evidence to establish that Melanesian people have been here for at least 10,000 years. The tiny Western islands (not even marked on many maps) and Wuvulu Island are peopled by the descendants of Micronesian settlers from the north. Obsidian (volcanic glass) from Lou Island was traded in the south-west Pacific for use in tools and weapons.

The islanders were sophisticated mariners and fishers with an extensive trade system. Their large sea-going outrigger canoes were up to 10m long, with two or three sails, and their fishing methods included fish traps and kite fishing.

The first European to come across the island was Spaniard Alvaro de Saavedra in 1527. Various Dutch and English explorers came past in the 17th and 18th centuries, but it was not until the late 19th century that serious contacts were made.

Phillip Carteret, an Englishman, dubbed the islands the Admiralty group in 1767. They were annexed as part of Germany's claim to New Guinea in 1884 but German law and order did not arrive on Manus until 1911. Some Spanish touches remain – the provincial airport is on Los Negros Island.

Lutherans founded a mission in 1915 and

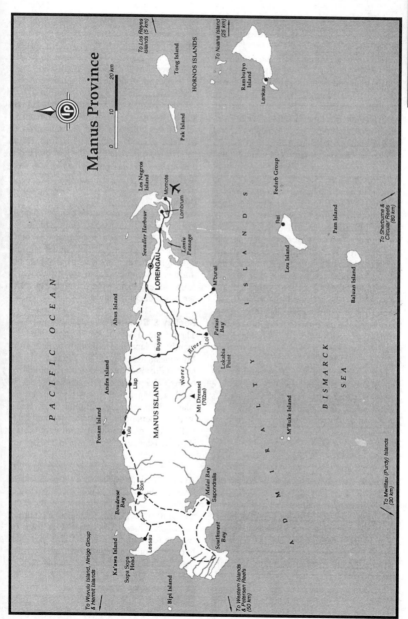

Manus Province

the Catholics came in 1920, but it wasn't until the mid-1930s that the Seventh-Day Adventists began arriving.

Manus was still pretty wild and 'untamed' until WWII began in the Pacific, and then things changed dramatically. Manus was taken without struggle by the Japanese in April 1942. In February 1944, American and Australian forces launched a six-week campaign to recapture the island, causing a great deal of damage to villages.

The Americans constructed a huge naval base at Lombrum, dock facilities were built around Seeadler Harbour and an airstrip capable of handling heavy bombers was built at Momote. From here the Americans staged their invasion of the Philippines.

Untold millions of dollars were lavished on the base and, at times, as many as 600 Allied ships were anchored in Seeadler Harbour. All in all, a million Americans and Australians passed through. A year after the war ended, the Allies had gone, but not before they had scrapped everything. This display of western technology and profligacy had quite an impact on the local people (American anthropologist Margaret Mead described it in her book *New Lives for Old*, published in 1956).

The experience of WWII was quite a revelation for the isolated islanders and led to a series of cargo cults (see the Cargo Cults aside), while also sparking an interest in education and new ideas.

Geography

Manus is the smallest province in the country – its 208 islands cover just 2100 sq km of land area – but it has more than 220,000 sq km of sea. The Admiralty islands comprise PNG's biggest island group (in number) with 57 separate islands. Manus Island is by far the biggest, measuring 104km long and 28km wide, and the highest (Mt Dremsel reaches 702m). And then there is a bunch of tiny coral atolls, most of which are uninhabited.

The low-lying eastern end of Manus is uplifted coral in formation, as is nearby Los Negros Island. Seeadler Harbour is a deep water anchorage that extends from Los Negros Island right around to the provincial capital Lorengau, which served the American navy's huge Lombrum base in WWII. Southwest Bay is a flooded caldera and there are large limestone caves in the central area of the island.

Other islands – Rambutyo, Lou, Baluan and M'Buke – are spent volcanos; an active underwater volcano called Tuluman erupted between 1953 and 1957. The Hermit, Heina and Ninigo groups to the west are coral atolls and reefs, while Wuvulu Island is way over in the west.

Climate

Despite its proximity to the equator, Manus Province's daily temperatures are a moderate 24°C to 30°C, although humidity is high. Lorengau gets nearly 4m of annual rainfall, although it has drier months from September through December. There are strong winds from November to March which can make sea travel uncomfortable.

Society & Conduct

The people of Manus Province are predominantly Melanesian, although settlers from Micronesia dominate in the Western islands. Manus Province has the smallest population of any PNG province; the islanders speak 30 local languages. Trade has long linked the islands despite their geographic dispersion – atoll-dwellers have no arable land and trade fish and lime for fruit and vegetables. Wuvulu islanders grow taro in ponds dug into the coral.

Trade links, called the *kawas* system, allowed people to become specialised in their produce. The Manus people (sometimes referred to as Titans) occupy the south and south-west islands and share a common language, Titan. They depend entirely on fishing for their livelihood. The Matangol live to the south, east and north and although they fish, they also depend on some agriculture. The Usiai are inland people and exclusively gardeners. There is further specialisation between those who make canoes, nets, pottery, coconut oil, obsidian blades and wood carvings. Ritual, magic and friendship play an important part in the kawas system and although it's no longer strong, its traditions remain the basis of the local culture.

Unlike in most PNG island cultures, a patrilineal system of inheriting land and clan rights dominates Manus Province. Margaret Mead first studied the Manus people in her book *Growing up in New Guinea* (1942) and came back after WWII. Mead was once highly lauded in academic circles, but her work is no longer fashionable. However, her writings still give fascinating and readable insights into traditional society.

Extensive tattoos are common among Manus people, with some designs displayed in the public domain and others reserved for

Cargo Cults

The recurrent outbreaks of 'cargo cultism' in New Guinea are a magnetic attraction for assorted academics.

To many New Guineans, the strange ways and mysterious powers of the Europeans could only have derived from supernatural sources. In religious systems where it is necessary to invoke the help of spirits to ensure, say, a good yam harvest, it is logical that the same principles be applied if you want manufactured goods.

Cult leaders theorised that the Europeans had acquired their machines and wealth from some spirit world and there was no reason why they too could not acquire similar 'cargo'. Some went further and insisted that the Europeans had intercepted cargo that was really intended for the New Guineans, sent to them by their ancestors in the spirit world. One cultist even suggested that the whites had torn the first page out of their bibles – the page that revealed that God was actually a Papuan.

If the right rituals were followed, the cult leaders said, the goods would be redirected to their rightful owners. Accordingly, docks were prepared or crude 'airstrips' laid out for when the cargo arrived. Other leaders felt that if they mimicked European ways, they would soon have European goods – 'offices' were established in which people passed bits of paper back and forth. But when locals started to kill their own pigs and destroy their gardens (as a prerequisite for the better days to come) or to demand political rights, the colonial government took a firm stand. Some leaders were imprisoned. However, arresting cult leaders simply confirmed the belief that an attempt was being made to keep goods rightfully belonging to the New Guineans, so some cultists were taken down to Australia to see with their own eyes that the goods did not arrive from the spirit world.

The first recorded cargo cult outbreak was noted in British New Guinea in 1893. A similar occurrence in Dutch New Guinea dates back to 1867. Cargo cult outbreaks have occurred sporadically ever since. One of the largest outbreaks took place in the Gulf area just after WWI; it was known as the Vailala Madness and was considerably spurred on by the arrival of the first aeroplane in the region – as predicted by one of the cult leaders.

The cults took another upswing after WWII, especially in Manus Province, when people witnessed even more stunning examples of western wealth. Seeing black American troops with access to desirable goods had a particularly strong impact.

Some of the cult leaders can be regarded as early nationalists and in several cases the cults developed into important political movements. In Manus Province in 1946, a movement started by Paliau Moloat (called the New Way, or Paliau, Church) was initially put down as just another cargo cult. But Paliau was a clever, if enigmatic, man and went on to live a long life in public office. His movement eventually became seen as one of PNG's first independence movements and a force for modernisation.

Paliau was imprisoned in the early days, but in 1964 and 1968 he was elected to the PNG House of Assembly. From 1978 he was the leader of Makasol, which was both a political lobby group and a religious movement. Paliau Moloat was seen by his followers as the last prophet of the world.

He died on 1 November 1991, in his Lipan village on Baluan Island, in Manus Province. He had one of the longest and most influential political lives in PNG history and is now fondly remembered as one of the country's greatest sons. ■

certain people. A common place for a tattoo is in the middle of the forehead and Manus people often have slit ear lobes, also.

Despite its relative poverty, Manus has a good education system. Four years of secondary schooling is compulsory and students unable to attend the secondary schools in the province use the radio 'School of the Air'. More than a third of the population have received at least six years of schooling. English is widely spoken, even in remote villages.

Carving has virtually died out in the province, although the people of Bipi Island still do some – you can see examples in the Lorengau council office. Wooden bowls, stone spears and arrowheads were produced on Lou Island, while shields and spears decorated with shark's teeth were produced by Micronesian people on the western islands. Dancing is the most popular form of cultural activity.

MANUS & LOS NEGROS ISLANDS

One of the first things you'll notice about Manus and Los Negros islands is the distinctive call of the chauca bird. The birds are common here and unique to the region, as is a variety of sea snail with a vivid green shell. Another local you'll hear is a *rokrok* (frog) with a bizarre croak that sounds like a faraway person nailing down a tin roof!

Only two degrees south of the equator, Manus is a steamy, sleepy island, with inland jungle on the central limestone hills which rise to about 700m. There are many sharp ridges and streams. Los Negros is more fertile than the main island.

Orientation

The airport is at Momote on Los Negros Island, and a road serviced by PMVs (public motor vehicles) connects it to Lorengau, 35km away on Manus. A bridge crosses the narrow Loniu Passage between Los Negros and Manus.

Lorengau (population 4700, postcode 641), the provincial capital, is the only town of any size on Manus but is still a small place.

The town straggles along a nice bay, with the provincial government buildings at one end and the market and main wharf at the other. Most of the town is centred around the market and wharf end, and a pleasant 1km walk east along the waterfront will take you to the provincial government buildings, with the Kohai Lodge and Lorengau Guesthouse a little further on.

Information

The Manus Tourism Bureau (☎ 470 9361; fax 470 9218) is in Lorengau's provincial government buildings. It's not well set up, with little printed information, but the staff are friendly and helpful.

There are both PNGBC and Westpac branches in Lorengau and the town has the only hospital in the province (although there are many aid posts). You'll find the post office and payphones opposite the foreshore park.

Things to See & Do

There are the remains of the US base at Lombrum (now home to a much smaller PNG navy coastal patrol) and rusting relics scattered around; you can see some relics from the bridge across Loniu Passage.

Near Loniu Passage is **Loniu Cave**, which, with the passage, makes for an interesting afternoon's diversion.

Good places to swim include **Salamei Beach** on Rarah Island, a couple of kilometres from Lorengau, and **Tulu** village, on the Manus coast west of Lorengau and accessible by boat from Lorengau and Andra Island. There's a **waterfall** and delightful **swimming hole** in the Lorengau River about 5km upstream from town.

Manus is a great place for shell enthusiasts. The vivid shells of the unique Manus green snail are featured on the provincial flag.

Buyang, a village in the centre of the island, is a place where you might see traditional dancing. **Worei**, in the south near the coast, is on the Worei River where you can make canoe trips and there's a guesthouse near Lokabia Point.

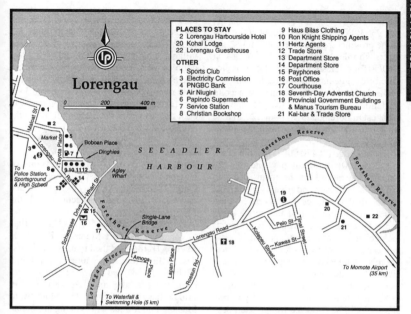

PLACES TO STAY
2 Lorengau Harbourside Hotel
20 Kohai Lodge
22 Lorengau Guesthouse

OTHER
1 Sports Club
3 Electricity Commission
4 PNGBC Bank
5 Air Niugini
6 Papindo Supermarket
7 Service Station
8 Christian Bookshop

9 Haus Bilas Clothing
10 Ron Knight Shipping Agents
11 Hertz Agents
12 Trade Store
13 Department Store
14 Department Store
15 Payphones
16 Post Office
17 Courthouse
18 Seventh-Day Adventist Church
19 Provincial Government Buildings
   & Manus Tourism Bureau
21 Kai-bar & Trade Store

With the north coast bordered by a reef, the diving around Manus is superb. Visibility is excellent and there is a fantastic variety of sea-life, with many large fish, as well as some wartime wrecks. Whales are sometimes seen between January and March.

Ron Knight (☎ 470 9159/9323; PO Box 108, Lorengau) is an experienced and professional diver, although he isn't a registered instructor. He will take groups diving and hire out equipment (bring your own regulator) but you must be qualified. You'll find his store on a road leading to the waterfront near the market.

Organised Tours

Talk to Air Niugini about some interesting weekend packages that include two nights accommodation at the Lorengau Harbourside Hotel.

Trans Niugini Tours (☎ 542 1438; fax 542 2470; PO Box 371, Mt Hagen) offers tours around Manus Province.

Special Events

The Manus Provincial Show is celebrated over three days in late August.

Places to Stay & Eat

Tourism in Manus is being actively encouraged and there are plans to open village guesthouses on Manus and some of the outlying islands. At present, accommodation can be found at village social clubs or private houses. The rates are negotiable but you shouldn't have to pay more than K15 for a room at a village club. Take some food, partly so you can repay the local hospitality.

Los Negros On Los Negros Island, not far from the airport, is the *Momote Tavern* (☎ 470 9061; PO Box 196). It's a long way from Lorengau but is accessible by PMV. It's at a nice location right by a beach on the island's southern coast. The rooms cost K40 and are attached to a popular villagers' bar, so it could get rowdy in the evenings.

Manus The *Lorengau Guesthouse* (☎ & fax 470 9363; PO Box 525) is about 400m east of the provincial government buildings, and offers simple lodgings in five rooms at K40/50 for singles/doubles. A kitchen is provided for guests and portable fans are available for the rooms. It's no-fuss accommodation, but clean and straight, and the cheapest in Lorengau. It's about a 20-minute walk into the town centre from the guesthouse.

Kohai Lodge (☎ 470 9004; fax 470 9263; PO Box 100) is almost opposite the Lorengau Guesthouse on the main road into town. It's a pleasant and friendly place, on a small hill that catches the breeze. Singles/doubles with air-con *and* fan cost K88/92 and they come with a fridge. Breakfast is included in the room rates. The long block at the rear has better rooms for the same price. There's a lounge and dining area (with bar), nicely decorated with some good books to read, and a restaurant serving lunches for K7 to K9 and dinner from K10.50. If you ring ahead, you'll be collected from the airport.

The *Lorengau Harbourside Hotel* (☎ 470 9093; fax 470 9392; PO Box 89) has a resort-style main building but the accommodation is in a few free-standing buildings. There's a pool, bar and restaurant and a small artefacts shop. It's a very comfortable place to stay and the rates include a free buffet-style breakfast. The Harbourside is centrally located, near the market, harbour and shopping centre, with four room types and all with bathroom, air-con, fridge, phone and TV. Singles/doubles cost K105/120 in the central wing, K115/130 in the courtyard, K120/135 for one harbour-view wing and K125/140 in the other. While it's comfortable and well located, the Harbourside is overpriced. The restaurant serves good food but, again, it is expensive: crumbed fish costs K13, chicken in mushroom sauce K15, steak dianne K15.50 and chilli crabs K19. Airport transfers are K20.

Around Lorengau The *Lohowai Village Guesthouse* (☎ & fax 470 9363; PO Box 525, Lorengau) offers simple budget accommodation and is owned by Levi Polomon, owner of the Lorengau Guesthouse. It's about 10km outside Lorengau, near Sabon village, and charges K35/60 for singles/doubles with shared bathroom facilities. There's a kitchen which guests can use or you can eat kai-style meals for K10 per person. Levi is a Lorengau town trader and commutes in each day, so you could catch a lift or use the regular PMV to get to town (K1).

Getting There & Away

Air Momote airport (☎ 470 9092) is on Los Negros Island, 35km east of Lorengau. Air Niugini flies there everyday except Wednesday and it has good connections with the PNG mainland and Manus.

On Monday and Tuesday, Air Niugini flies to Manus from Port Moresby (K254) via Madang (K134) and then returns. On Thursday, it flies from Port Moresby via Tokua (Rabaul; K188) and Kavieng (K131) and back via Madang and Lae (K178). On Friday, the route is from Port Moresby to Madang and Manus and back again. Saturday, it goes from Port Moresby to Lae to Manus and back again. Sunday, the route is Port Moresby to Madang to Wewak (K148) to Manus (K148) and then back to Port Moresby via Kavieng and Tokua.

Boat The Lutheran Shipping freighter MV *Maneba* goes from Lorengau to Madang, taking 24 hours and costing K26.70/33.90 (students K13.35/16.95) in deck/cabin class; to continue on to Lae takes another 24 hours and costs K59.10/69.20 (students K29.55/34.60). Coastal Shipping runs about once a month between Rabaul (K60/105) and Manus, via Kavieng (K40/95). Contact Ron Knight (☎ 470 9159/9323; PO Box 108) in Lorengau.

The *Tawi*, operated by the Manus Provincial Government, is currently under repair but normally plies between Lorengau, the outer islands of Manus, Wuvulu Island, Wewak and Madang. You can get information from the marine office, a red building near the Neruse wharf where the *Tawi* docks.

The MV *Thompson* is owned by the

Wuvulu-Aua community committee and does a trading circuit, but really has no fixed schedule. Ask around – its comings and goings might suit your schedule.

Getting Around

PMV There's a good road system and it's possible to drive from Lorengau to the south coast and several inland villages. PMVs cover the road network and regularly run to the naval base at Lombrum and airport at Momote. They're not too frequent, however, and you shouldn't feel too shy about flagging down any vehicle outside of Lorengau.

Car Car rental in PNG is expensive. The Avis agent is Cyril Fitzgerald (☎ 470 9207; PO Box 253, Lorengau), who often meets incoming Air Niugini flights. His office in Lorengau is near the Lorengau Harbourside Hotel. Avis charges the usual high rates, plus a K15 a day remote-area surcharge. Budget (☎ 470 9250) is also represented in Lorengau.

Boat Lorengau's waterfront is the place to catch dinghies (banana boats). These are open, 20ft-long fibreglass boats with a 40hp outboard motor. There are good dinghy routes around Manus Province (trade routes have linked these islands for a long time) and many islands to visit.

Sadly it seems the giant outboard-powered canoes are gone from the Lorengau waterfront, and these days dinghies are the only boats tying up. There are also larger work boats which take passengers. In Lorengau, dinghies are usually found in the harbour near the creek mouth at the end of the little street from the market (Boboan Place). The work boats usually dock at Neruse wharf, but try the main wharf as well.

You can charter boats with a driver for about K60 a day. Fuel is expensive and the cost will depend a bit on where you want to go. The seas can get rough and travelling by boat at these times can be scary. From November to March, prevailing winds blow and the seas will be, at best, uncomfortable

for travel. The fishing is great, particularly along the north coast.

OTHER ISLANDS

On **Andra Island**, north-west of Lorengau and K10 from there by dinghy, there's a village guesthouse. The accommodation will cost about K10 and you have to take your own food. The friendly Andra people might cook for you but you should be prepared to pay or leave a donation. There's likely to be some fresh fish or lobster involved.

Bring goggles and a snorkel because there's fine reefs, corals and fish to see; you can also practise paddling a canoe. For more information, go to the Manus Tourism Bureau or find Paula Nakam in the health department in the same provincial government buildings. Andra is her home island.

There's a more up-market guesthouse on **Ahus Island**, near Andra but a little closer to Lorengau. It costs about K40 per person. Contact Ron Knight in Lorengau (☎ 470 9159/9323; PO Box 108) for more information.

Lou Island (pronounced 'low') is an old volcano and particularly fertile and beautiful, also hosting hot springs. Located south-east of Manus Island, Lou was once an important source of obsidian which was traded throughout the south-west Pacific. In Rei, the main village, there's a guesthouse charging about K20 a night. Several dinghies run from Lorengau each day (fewer or none on Sunday) and the trip takes about 1½ hours. The fare should be about K20.

You can get a boat south from Lou to tiny **Pam Island** where there's a village guesthouse. East of Lou is the Fedarb group, which includes beautiful **Sivisa Island**. About 15km north of Sivisa is **Tilianu Island** atoll, inhabited by seafarers who still use large canoes with sails. Dive parties camp here and about the only food available is lobster!

Wuvulu Island

Wuvulu Island has to be the most remote part of the country. It's much closer to Wewak, the capital of East Sepik Province, than to

Lorengau but there's more than 200km of open sea between Wewak and Wuvulu. There are no rivers or creeks discharging into the sea so the water is incredibly clear – visibility can be around 50m. The people are Micronesian and mostly Seventh-Day Adventists. They still make distinctive canoes, some large enough to hold 40 people.

There are two villages on the island, Aunna (literally 'sunrise') and Onne (literally 'sunset'), and the diving and snorkelling are superb.

Organised Tours There is talk of developing dive packages including the Walindi Dive Resort (West New Britain), Kavieng (New Ireland) and Wuvulu, so ask around. Sea New Guinea (☎ 612 267 5563; fax (02) 267 6118; 100 Clarence St, Sydney 2000) in Australia might have information.

Places to Stay & Eat *Wuvulu Lodge* (PO Box 1071, Wewak, East Sepik Province) has accommodation for 12 people at about K40 for full board. There's diving equipment for hire. Onne has a guesthouse, which charges about K10 for basic accommodation.

Getting There & Away Wuvulu is very difficult to get to. There are no scheduled air services and the only boat that used to pull in with any frequency was the Manus government's *Tawi*, but that was never very often and it's currently being repaired anyway. A traveller who reported heading off from Wewak on the *Tawi* returned a couple of days later because the captain couldn't find Wuvulu! It's marked 'position approximate' on many maps.

The MV *Thompson* is owned by the Wuvulu-Aua community committee and does a trading circuit between Wuvulu, Aua, Wewak and Madang. It doesn't really have a fixed schedule, so ask around.

North Solomons Province

Land Area 9300 sq km
Population 170,000
Capital Buka

The islands that comprise the North Solomons (Buka, Bougainville and a scattering of smaller atolls) are more closely related to the neighbouring, independent Solomon Islands than they are to Papua New Guinea – just as the name suggests. The province is the farthest flung from the mainland and the international border between the Solomon Islands and PNG passes just a few kilometres south of Bougainville Island.

Bougainville is the major island, green, rugged and little-developed. Until the secessionist rebellion, the province had the most productive economy, best education levels and most efficient government in the country. Between 1972 and its closure in 1989, the Panguna mine produced 45% of PNG's export earnings and paid the government about K55 million each year in taxes and dividends.

You should seek the advice of your country's diplomatic representatives in PNG or your department of foreign affairs before making any travel plans. Air Niugini flies to the province regularly but suspends its Buka service when things get a bit hot. The whole region is besieged by the crisis.

The province is under military control because of the fighting between the Papua New Guinea Defence Force (PNGDF) and the Bougainville Revolutionary Army (BRA). All air and sea traffic comes through Buka, the provincial government headquarters. Ironically, the army presence makes Buka especially safe because there's no alcohol allowed and no rascals around. The fighting is confined to the south of Bougainville Island (often called 'the mainland'); any access to Bougainville requires a military permit and all movement in the PNGDF-controlled area is plotted through a series of checkpoints. It is a messy guerilla

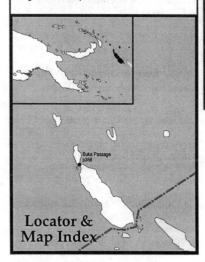

HIGHLIGHTS

- Catching a dinghy across fast-flowing Buka Passage
- Visiting the nearby islands around Buka
- Tiny Sohano Island with its lawns, gardens and panoramic views

Buka Passage
p358

Locator &
Map Index

war on a large, mountainous and thickly jungled island, and people are getting killed. Stay off Bougainville unless you're travelling with a local person who knows exactly what they're doing – and even then, think about it.

History

There's evidence that human settled on Bougainville at least 28,000 years ago.

Spanish mariner Luis Vaez de Torres passed through in 1606 but Bougainville acquired its name from the French explorer Louis-Antoine de Bougainville who sailed up the east coast in 1768. In Buka Passage, the locals greeted him with cries of '*buka,*

buka', which Bougainville promptly named their island. Buka means 'who' or 'what'.

European settlements were established as the German New Guinea Company began trading in the late 1800s. Bougainville and Buka were considered part of the Solomons group, a British possession, until 1898, when they were traded to Germany. Marist Catholics started a mission at Kieta in 1901, the Methodists campaigned out of Siwai from 1920 and the Seventh-Day Adventists came to Lavelai in 1924.

Australia seized the North Solomons, along with the rest of New Guinea, at the start of WWI, but by the start of WWII the only development was still on the coast.

The Japanese arrived in early 1942, swiftly defeating the Australians and holding most of the island until the end of the war. Buka became an important air base, Shortland Island (part of the Solomon Islands) was a major naval base and Buin, at the southern tip of Bougainville, was a base for ground troops. Australian coastwatchers scored some notable successes on Bougainville, particularly during the battle for Guadalcanal.

In November 1943, American troops captured the west-coast port of Torokina and Australian forces started to fight their way south towards Buin. The war ended before they came into direct confrontation with the Japanese but the cost of the war in Bougainville was staggering – of 80,000 Japanese troops only 23,000 were taken prisoner; 20,000 are thought to have been killed in action and the remaining 37,000 died in the jungles of disease and starvation.

After the war, the district headquarters was transferred from Kieta to Sohano Island in Buka Passage but found its way back to Kieta in 1960. Then, in 1964, a major copper discovery at Panguna revitalised Bougainville. More than K400 million was invested in the development of the mine and its ancillary operations. A new town, roads, a power station and a port were constructed, and thousands of workers descended. The district headquarters and mine workers were based at Arawa. The mine was developed by Bou-

gainville Copper Ltd (BCL), a subsidiary of Australia's CRA, itself a subsidiary of the British Rio Tinto Zinc.

Secession & War In the 1960s and early 1970s, the North Solomons began a push to break away from Australian colonial control, climaxing in land disputes over the proposed Panguna mine and the landowner's right to share in the mine's profits.

In the years prior to independence, Bougainville pushed for an independent grouping of the Bismarck Archipelago, but that plan quickly faded. In 1974 secessionist movements sprang up, with Father John Momis becoming one of the leaders. North Solomons leaders won the right to establish a provincial government but the following year the PNG House of Assembly did not include this provision in the constitution. On 1 September 1975, two weeks before independence was proclaimed, rebels raised a 'Republic of North Solomons' flag at Kieta. Parliament quickly made a first amendment to the constitution: the provincial government system was established. The 'me too' reaction from the rest of the country burdened PNG with an unwieldy provincial government system which was remodelled in the early 1990s.

The Panguna mine produced huge profits, and huge royalties flowed to the landowners and the PNG government. A small group of traditional landowners was doing very well out of the mine but not much community development was taking place. And the environmental destruction caused by the mine was affecting many more people than those directly compensated for it. There was a growing feeling that the people had been cheated in the initial negotiations with CRA – that they had cheaply signed away their land without realising the consequences.

In 1987 the Panguna Landowners' Association was formed, led by Pepetua Sereo and Francis Ona. It demanded better environmental protection, huge back-payments of profits from the mine and US$10 *billion* in compensation. These demands were not met and in 1988 the BRA, an offshoot of the landowners' association, began to sabotage the mine. Relations between the locals and police sent to protect the mine deteriorated sharply. Several politicians, including the premier, were beaten up by police, and mine workers and police from other parts of PNG came under attack from the BRA. The BRA's numbers were bolstered by sympathisers from other parts of the country, local thugs and even a religious cult.

Increasing attacks on mine workers resulted in the mine's closing in 1989 – an enormous blow to the PNG economy. After the mine closed, a state of emergency was declared, the PNG army moved in and the conflict spread to the rest of the island. Whole villages were moved into 'care centres', areas outside of BRA control. To ensure that the people moved, the army burned their villages; stories about rape and murder flooded out of Bougainville. The Panguna issue had become a civil war – at the height of the conflict, there were 60,000 people displaced.

In 1990 the PNG government withdrew its forces and instituted a blockade, resulting in great hardship for the Bougainvilleans. The BRA declared independence, forming the Republic of Meekamui on 17 May, although no other nations recognised it. News from the island since then has been highly unreliable. The BRA brought over supplies from the nearby Solomon Islands and the PNG army, in retaliation, caused international tension by raiding suspected BRA bases in the Solomon Islands, killing a few innocent people. The PNGDF landed on Buka on 13 September 1990 and on Bougainville on 13 April 1991 and now controls most of Bougainville Island.

But in all the confusion, there has been some blurring of allegiances, with the BRA factionalising and splintering and some PNGDF soldiers, sometimes with no effective chain of command, going feral. The PNGDF has had trouble paying and feeding its Bougainville troops and morale has been poor. The south of Bougainville is now a very dangerous place with everybody suspicious of everybody else.

In April 1995, there was some real hope with the election of Theodore Miriung as premier. He had been a lawyer, national court judge, senior public servant and member of the BRA and was widely respected both in the government and with Bougainville sympathisers. But some members of the BRA saw him as a traitor and held and harassed him. On 12 October 1996, Miriung was assassinated while eating an evening meal with his wife and children. The country was shocked; it was assumed that the BRA had killed him. An inquiry revealed the killers were PNGDF soldiers, although where their orders came from is still unclear. Miriung was buried as a martyr and Bougainville plunged into darkness again.

In February and March 1997, the controversial Sandline Affair hit the headlines. In a highly covert operation Chan contracted a mercenary company, Sandline International, to solve the secessionist problem by military means. When the deal became known, there was international condemnation of Chan's actions. See The Sandline Affair aside in the Facts about the Country chapter.

Geography

Bougainville is a volcanic island, about 200km long and covered in jungle. The Crown Prince, Emperor and Deuro ranges make up the central spine and the volcanic Mt Bagana frequently erupts. Mt Balbi, the island's highest point at 2685m, is a dormant volcano; Benua Cave is perhaps the world's largest at 4,500,000 cubic metres. The island has many natural harbours, with large swamps on its western edge.

Buka Island is formed almost entirely of coral, pushed above the sea. It's separated from Bougainville Island by a tidal channel, Buka Passage, only 300m wide and a kilometre long. Buka is generally low-lying, apart from a southern hilly region.

The province has another 166 islands spread over 450,000 sq km of sea. The province is the most earthquake-prone area of the country – a quake caused major damage at Torokina in 1975.

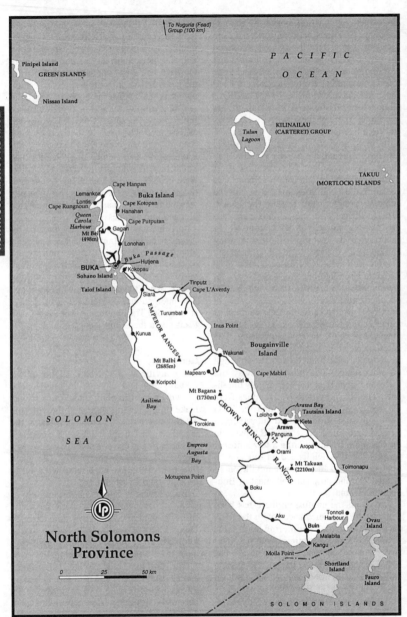

North Solomons
Province

0   25   50 km

Climate

North Solomons Province is hot (its northern boundary is the equator) and wet, with some areas getting more than 5m of annual rainfall. The drier period in Buka is between May and October but some places don't have a dry season.

Arts

Apart from intricately woven Buka baskets, there are few artefacts still made on Bougainville. Buka baskets are made from jungle vine; the variation in colour is made by scraping the skin off the vine. They're some of the most skilfully made baskets in the Pacific and are now woven all over the province (and in the Highlands too), but traditionally they were made by the Siwia and Telei people of south-west Buka Island.

Society & Conduct

The people of Bougainville and Buka are often collectively referred to as 'Bukas'. The Bougainville people are instantly recognisable anywhere in PNG because of their extremely dark skins, said to be the blackest in the world. There are 23 different languages in the North Solomons; those of Buka and northern Bougainville are Austronesian. Pidgin is the second main language but most people you meet speak good English. The people of Takuu (or Mortlock) and Nukumani islands are Polynesian.

North Solomon Islanders have a matrilineal system of clan membership and inheritance rights. Their education and affluence has led to a reluctance to work on copra plantations, and copra labourers are imported from other parts of the country. Many people still live in bush-material housing in villages and depend on shifting agriculture for their food.

BUKA ISLAND

A road runs up the east coast of Buka Island, connecting the copra plantations. An airstrip was built in the south-east of the island near Hutjena and has since been upgraded to handle Air Niugini's F-28s. Queen Carola Harbour, on the west coast, used to be Buka's main port, but because all air and sea traffic must pass through military checkpoints at Buka, Buka Passage has become the de facto port for the province.

Buka & Buka Passage

• postcode 355

Buka town became the provincial capital because of the strife down south. It used to be a tiny place but it now has many new buildings and residents. There are lots of people moving through Buka, including military personnel, mediators, aid workers and construction crews, although the expat population is almost none.

Buka has throngs of armed soldiers and resistance fighters (disaffected Bougainvilleans fighting alongside the army) who all look like extras in a Sly Stallone movie.

When you step off the plane at Buka airport your luggage, including your hand luggage, will be searched for weapons and contraband. You need to go to the movement office, at Forward Base HQ in town next to the main wharf. Here, you'll be issued a pass to move around freely on Buka Island if you know where you're staying and have a ticket out. This is normally quite a simple rubber-stamping procedure, although the officers might still be searching luggage at the airport if you're too quick. Getting authority to be in the province is important. Even if the movement office is closed, you must keep going back – you can be arrested if you have no pass.

You need to be keenly aware of the precarious situation in which most people here live. Be *very* careful when asking people their views on the war. While there's broad support for the Bougainvilleans, people cannot speak freely. If they express any of these sympathies, it's quite possible that they (or their family) could get into serious trouble from the PNGDF. The walls have ears in this part of PNG and so does the bush, the water and the air.

Having said that, Buka is safe, interesting and very beautiful. The water in the passage is exquisitely clear and the fishing, snorkelling and swimming are excellent. The people are very friendly and they'll engage you in interesting conversations in well-spoken English.

Orientation & Information Most of the shops and services are on, or just off, the main waterfront strip of town. Dinghies congregate near the market and the passage is abuzz with these small craft plying between the town, Kokopau village (opposite on Bougainville Island), where you can go without any further clearance, Sohano Island at the southern mouth of the passage and the islands beyond.

Air Niugini has an office on the road running west with the Buka Enterprises trade store on the corner, Islands Nationair has an agent further off the strip on the road running west from the post office on the corner, and Kathleen Morok at Jayes Enterprises is the Airlink agent.

Everything in Buka closes at 3 pm and there's a water curfew between 6 am and 6

pm, after which only military and government vessels are allowed to move in Buka Passage.

Things to See & Do Riding in a dinghy in Buka Passage is a thrill in itself. The deep passage runs at about 8 knots when the tide is running fast, causing undulations on the surface and little localised currents and whirlpools. You can jump on a dinghy, pay the local fare and head to many of the little islands near the southern mouth of the passage. There are good swimming spots out on these islands and the fishing over the reefs is excellent. The fare to Sohano Island is K0.50.

There's wonderful snorkelling in Buka Passage but you have to pick your tide times, and perhaps even get some local advice, or you'll wind up lost at sea. Beware: even when the tide is not running fast, you might find that you're swimming at full tilt just to break even with the current and you'll tire quickly. Those who aren't strong swimmers might prefer to watch.

There are good walking trails just outside town but don't think about wandering off on your own – take a local with you.

Place to Stay Kathleen Morok at Jayes Enterprises (☎ 983 9734; PO Box 325, Buka) runs a small B&B-style *guesthouse* in her home behind town at the end of the airstrip. She's friendly and charges K70 per person (three single rooms only), including all meals and laundry.

Getting There & Away Air Niugini flies to Buka on Tuesday, Thursday and Saturday from Port Moresby via Tokua (Rabaul). The fare from Port Moresby is K297 and from Rabaul is K124. Islands Nationair (☎ 983 9734; PO Box 325, Buka) flies the same route for the same fare on Monday, Wednesday and Friday. Airlink has connections with Buka from Nissan Island (K80), Hoskins (K182), Tokua (K124), Namatanai (K154), Kavieng (K181), Lae (K282), Madang (K327), Mt Hagen (K350) and Goroka (K320) at least once a week.

1	Islands Nationair
2	Premier's Office
3	City Pharmacy
4	Post Office & Payphones
5	Service Station
6	PNGBC Bank
7	Police Station
8	Movement Office Forward Base HQ
9	Chris Textiles
10	Newsagent
11	Air Niugini
12	Jayes Enterprises
13	Marenco Trade Store
14	MS Hakena Trade Store
15	Trade Stores
16	Buka Luman Soho Lodge

SOHANO ISLAND

Sohano Island is a few minutes by boat from Buka and was the provincial capital from WWII until 1960.

It's a beautiful place with lawns and gardens, a Japanese monument and lots of war relics, steep craggy cliffs and panoramic views over town, the passage and Bougainville Island. Sohano has a few pleasant swimming beaches and lots of big, timid crabs which will be hiding down their huge holes in the sand, unless they haven't seen you coming. It has plenty of colonial-period buildings in good condition and Buka's hospital is there also. There's a rather gentrified atmosphere on the island; the only reminders of the civil war are helicopters breaking the silence high above Bougainville en route to Buka airport.

Sitting on the cliff edge and watching the water race through the narrow Buka Passage lulls you into a blissful torpor. Then, on some impossible primeval cue, a thousand tiny flying fish will launch themselves in perfect choreography and glide just above the water for 100m before again, in perfect formation, disappearing below the surface.

The weird **Tchibo Rock** stands just off-shore from Sohano's northernmost point and figures in many local legends. It's said to have magical properties.

Place to Stay

The *Buka Luman Soho Lodge* (☎ 983 9937/9757; fax 983 9934; PO Box 251, Buka) is a nice place to stay, and while it's not cheap, it's actually one of the better value-for-money accommodation options in PNG.

The laconic Joe Moni runs the lodge, which has two buildings; a fan-cooled room in the older wing costs K80/100 single/double with shared bathroom facilities. Rooms in the new wing cost K90/110 for a single/double with air-con and fan, private bathroom, phone, TV, tea and coffee-making facilities. All prices include free laundry, breakfast and a three-course dinner. Ask about the bigger, but more expensive, rooms, including a family room.

BOUGAINVILLE ISLAND

The following information is included in case the situation in Bougainville dramatically improves and travel onto the island is once again allowed. But this information is likely to be out of date since Bougainville has been off-limits for eight years and there's been considerable damage to the towns in the south.

There's a road running down the east coast of Bougainville from Kokopau on the Buka Passage to Kieta. Not all of the rivers are bridged and the road fords several of them. From Wakunai there's a three-day trip to climb Mt Balbi (2685m). From its summit, you can see the active Mt Bagana (1730m).

Kieta & Arawa

Kieta • postcode 352
Arawa • postcode 351

Kieta and Arawa, virtually contiguous, have been severely damaged and remain off-limits. Coming north from the old airport you first go through Toniva, a suburb of Kieta, then central Kieta, which is now virtually a suburb of Arawa, and then 10km east (over the Kieta Peninsula) to Arawa, the main town.

The *Kieta Hotel* has been severely damaged but is said to be still functional and may be able to take guests when the blockade is lifted. Prices will be very, very high.

Four kilometres north-west of Arawa is **Loloho** on Arawa Bay, the port to which the copper concentrate was piped down from Panguna, the site of the power station and home to many of the mine workers. There's an attractive beach.

Panguna

• postcode 353

High in the centre of Bougainville is one of the world's largest artificial holes – Bougainville Copper Limited's gigantic open-cut mine at Panguna.

A geological expedition discovered copper reserves at Panguna in 1964, and by 1967 the size of the deposit was large enough to justify cutting an access road from Kobuna. Progress from that point was rapid:

War Weary

The people of Bougainville are tired of the war. There are some die-hards but mostly people want peace first, then negotiations. There's still very broad support for the BRA and moves towards independence but heavy hearts declare that won't happen and the best they can hope for is an end to the fighting and some return to normality.

There's no electricity in the south of Bougainville and the island's schools, roads and hospitals are mostly ruined, although a restoration programme has seen some rebuilt, mainly in PNGDF-controlled areas in the north of the island. North Solomons Province was one of PNG's most developed areas but, thanks to 'the crisis', Bougainville Island has free-fallen back to primitivism.

Many Bougainvilleans have left over the last nine years and resettled in other parts of PNG – their abandoned homes and cars are falling apart where they left them. The PNGDF herds people into 'care centres' which it claims offer protection from the BRA (the PNGDF burnt houses and villages to 'encourage' people to go to the care centres). The BRA claims the centres are concentration camps used to subdue local people and isolate the BRA from its community support base.

Francis Ona, one of the founders of the BRA, is still the leader of the independence movement but even some local people see him as a stubborn megalomaniac who is not altogether sane. He claims that sorcery and voodoo will help the BRA defeat the PNGDF. The BRA fights mostly with crude home-made weapons.

But the enigmatic Ona (who has a K200,000 price on his head) knows that he can't *lose* this war, even if he can't win it. The rebel guerillas are too easily hidden on the thickly jungled and rugged island and they can blend in with the local villagers who support them. The PNG government can keep sending troops to the conflict (and even mercenaries), but as long as the rich Panguna copper mine stays closed, Ona and the rebels know that they can keep PNG governments on their knees.

For now the fighting continues and more and more ordinary people are getting hurt and killed, degraded and brutalised. The PNGDF is undisciplined, poorly trained and Bougainville troops sometimes don't get paid or fed.

The only hope for an end to the war is internationally sponsored talks. The BRA has serious (and justifiable) questions about the government's credibility in its own mediations. The desire to end the violence is keenly felt on both sides, but the war will not end until outsiders bring some sense to the situation. ■

in 1969 construction of the mining project started, advance sales of copper were made, the temporary road was upgraded and port facilities were constructed. At the peak period of construction, before the mine started commercial operation in 1972, 10,000 people were employed. Before it was closed by the BRA, 4000 people (about one in five were foreigners) worked for Bougainville Copper.

Buin

• postcode 359

Buin, in the south of the island, has suffered less damage than Kieta and Arawa. It is very wet all year-round, with more than 4m of annual rainfall. During WWII, Buin hosted a large Japanese army base; the area is packed with rusting relics of the war.

The extensive Japanese fortifications came to nothing because the Australians landed north of Torokina and moved south, instead of making the frontal attack the Japanese had expected. You can see much wreckage at Lamuai and on the Kahili Plantation, which you can walk to from Buin.

There's a road south from Aropa to Buin that takes about three hours by vehicle. You could complete a circuit and come back through Panguna if you had your own transport, but the road fords several fast-flowing rivers, which would be pretty tough going after rain.

Around Buin

The Japanese had plans to resettle a huge number of civilian Japanese in the area – at a place called Little Tokyo. Tonnoli Harbour is beautiful.

The road to Buin from Aropa comes to an intersection; the road to the right (east) heads back to Arawa through Siwai and Panguna, the left (west) road goes to Malabita village and the road straight ahead goes to Kangu. About a 15-minute drive from here is a small overgrown bunker on the right and a track just past it. This goes through to an open area with a couple of pill boxes and a gun pointing forlornly out to sea.

Admiral Yamamoto's aircraft wreck is the most historically interesting wreck in the area. Admiral Isoroku Yamamoto, who planned the attack on Pearl Harbour, left Rabaul in a Betty Bomber on 18 April 1943, accompanied by a protective group of Zeros. He did not realise that US fighters would be waiting for him near Buin.

The wreckage of the Betty still lies in the jungle, only a few kilometres off the Panguna-Buin Road. It was well signposted, near the village of Aku, 24km before Buin, and a path had been cut through the jungle from the road. It's a one-hour walk.

In 1968, only 400m from the Buin-Kangu Hill Road, an American Corsair fighter was discovered where it had crashed in November 1943, its pilot still in the cockpit. Just down the beach from the hill is a Catholic mission which has a small plantation with three more bombers.

OUTER ISLANDS
There is a scattering of islands far away from Bougainville and Buka which, nevertheless, come under North Solomons jurisdiction. Some are as easily accessible from New Ireland as they are from the North Solomons.

The **Nuguria (Fead) Group**, about 200km east and north of New Ireland and Buka respectively, has 50-odd islands with a total area of only five sq km and a population of not much more than 200 Polynesians.

Nukumanu (Tasman) Islands are about 400km north-east of Bougainville and much closer to the extensive Ontong Java Atoll in the Solomon Islands. Nukumanu, with an area of less than 3 sq km, is the largest island in the group. The population is about 300 Polynesians.

About 195km north-east of Bougainville, the ring-shaped reef of the **Takuu (Mortlock) Islands** has about 20 islands, virtually midway on a line drawn from the Carteret Group to the Tasman Islands. The people, who are related to the Nukumanu Islanders, number around 600 and are predominantly Polynesian. They speak a language very similar to New Zealand Maori and no-one knows quite how or why.

Only 70km north-east of Buka, the **Kilinailau (Carteret) Group** comprises six islands on a 16km circular atoll. The population of about 900 are Buka people who are thought to have supplanted earlier Polynesian inhabitants.

The **Green Islands** are on an atoll, measuring about 16km by 8km, which lies approximately 70km north-west of Buka. Nissan is the large curved island and the smaller ones lie within its curve. Nissan and Pinipel Island, a little further north, are the only inhabited islands in the group; their combined population is about 3200. The textbook-perfect atoll was evacuated during WWII and a large American airbase operated here. After the war vast quantities of supplies were dumped there.

Glossary

arse tanket – a bunch of tanket leaves stuck into a belt to cover a man's backside, also called *arse gras* (Highlands)

bagarap – broken; literally 'buggered-up'
bagi – the red shell necklace used for trade in the *kula ring* islands
balus – aeroplane
banana boat – trade boat or dinghy
banaras – bow and arrows
baret – artificial channels or canals constructed across loops in a river (Sepik)
benetii – cassowary (New Britain); see also *muruk*
bigman – an important man, a leader
bikpela – big, great
bilas – jewellery, decorations, finery
bilum – a string bag
boi – boy
brada/barata – brother
buai – betel nut
buk tambu – the bible
bukumatula – bachelor house (Trobriand Islands)
bung – meeting, marketplace (Kuanua and Pidgin)
bus – bush
buskanaka – bush villager

cuscus – an arboreal, nocturnal marsupial like a large possum

dewel – devil
diwai – wood
doba – leaf money from Milne Bay Province
dukduk – spirit and ritual costume

echidna – spiny anteater and member of the monotrene family
em nau! – great! fantastic!; literally 'him now!'

garamut – drum made from a hollowed log
gavman – government
guria – earthquake, nervous
gutpela – good

haibica – a stringy silverbeet-like vegetable
haus lain – long house (Highlands)
haus sik – hospital
haus tambaran – spirit house
haus win – open-air structure like a gazebo; literally 'house of wind'

inap – enough
isi – softly, gently, easy

kai-bar – a cheap takeaway food bar
kaikai – food
karim leg – a courting ceremony involving crossing legs with a partner; literally 'carry leg' (Highlands)
kaukau – sweet potato
kiap – patrol officer (of colonial origin)
kina – unit of PNG currency, large shell traded from the coast as an early form of currency
kisim – get
kokomo – a hornbill bird
kula ring – a ring of trading islands in Milne Bay Province
kumul – bird of paradise
kunai – grass, grassland
kundu – an hourglass-shaped drum skinned with lizard or snake skin
kwik piksa leta – fax; literally 'quick picture letter'

laplap – a sarong or wrap-around
lapun – elder, a term of respect for an older person of either sex
liklik – small, a little
liklik haus – toilet; literally 'small house'
loloi – rolls of shell money strung on lengths of cane (East New Britain)
longlong – confused, crazy
lotu – religious service, worship
lusim/larim – to leave

makau – tilapia fish (Sepik)
malangan – the practice of making totemic figures (also called malangans) to honour the dead; also known as *malagan*

masalai – a spirit of the bush or water, a devil (East New Britain and New Ireland)

maski – doesn't matter, as if to say 'forget it' or 'don't worry about it'

masta – white adult male (colonial)

mausgras – beard, moustache, whiskers

meri – wife, woman

misis – European woman

missinari – missionary

moga – the ceremony surrounding the giving away of goods to display one's wealth (Highlands)

Mokolkols – a nomadic tribe from East New Britain

Motu – the indigenous people of the Port Moresby area, the language spoken by these people

mumu – traditional underground oven

muruk – cassowary; see also *benetii*

mwala – decorated armlets made from cone shells used for trade in the *kula ring* islands

nambawan – number one, the best

natnat – mosquito

nogut – no good, bad

OPM – Organisasi Papua Merdeka, or Free West Papua Movement

payback – compensation paid for a wrongdoing, but in reprisal more than revenge

pikinini – baby, child

pikus tri – fig tree

pinis – finish

pis – fish

pisin – bird

pitpit – wild sugar cane

PMV – public motor vehicle

Police Motu – an early colonial lingua franca, derived from the *Motu* language

pukpuk – crocodile

raskol – a bandit, criminal or thief

rausim! – go away! get out of here!

ria – a volcanic fjord, as found near Tufi

rokrok – frog

saksak – sago

salvinia – a weed (*Salvinia molesta*) found in many waterways

save – understand, think

sing-sing – a celebratory festival/dance

solwara – ocean, sea

spia – spear

story board – a narrative carving done on a wooden board

susa – sister

susu – milk, breast

tambaran – ancestral spirit, also called tambuan, tabaran or tabuan

tambu – forbidden or sacred, shell money (Tolai)

tapa – beaten bark cloth

taro – tuberous root vegetable similar to a sweet potato

tasol – that's all, only

tee – ceremony where men give away goods to display their wealth (Enga)

toea – a unit of PNG currency (100 toea = 1 *kina*), a shell necklace also used as currency

tok pisin – the Pidgin language

tok ples – local language, first language, pronounced 'talk-place'

Tolai – the main inhabitants of East New Britain's Gazelle Peninsula, pronounced 'tol-eye'

tumbuan – large, feather-draped body mask

tupela – two, both

turnim het – a courting ceremony involving rubbing faces together, literally 'turn head' (Highlands)

voluntia – volunteer

wantok – fellow clanspeople, kith and kin; literally 'one talk' or 'one who speaks the same language'

yam – tuberous root vegetable similar to a sweet potato

Index

TEXT

364

LONELY PLANET PHRASEBOOKS

Building bridges,
Breaking barriers,
Beyond babble-on

Listen for the gems

Speak your own words

Ask your own
questions

Master of
your
own
image

- handy pocket-sized books

- easy to understand Pronunciation chapter

- clear and comprehensive Grammar chapter

- romanisation alongside script to allow ease of pronunciation

- script throughout so users can point to phrases

- extensive vocabulary sections, words and phrases for every situations

- full of cultural information and tips for the traveller

'...vital for a real DIY spirit and attitude in language learning' – Backpacker

'the phrasebooks have good cultural backgrounders and offer solid advice for challenging situations in remote locations' – San Francisco Examiner

'...they are unbeatable for their coverage of the world's more obscure languages' – The Geographical Magazine

---

Arabic (Egyptian)
Arabic (Moroccan)
Australia
  Australian English, Aboriginal and Torres Strait languages
Baltic States
  Estonian, Latvian, Lithuanian
Bengali
Burmese
Brazilian
Cantonese
Central Asia
Central Europe
  Czech, French, German, Hungarian, Italian and Slovak
Eastern Europe
  Bulgarian, Czech, Hungarian, Polish, Romanian and Slovak
Egyptian Arabic
Ethiopian (Amharic)
Fijian
French
German
Greek

Hindi/Urdu
Indonesian
Italian
Japanese
Korean
Lao
Latin American Spanish
Malay
Mandarin
Mediterranean Europe
  Albanian, Croatian, Greek, Italian, Macedonian, Maltese, Serbian, Slovene
Mongolian
Moroccan Arabic
Nepali
Papua New Guinea
Pilipino (Tagalog)
Quechua
Russian
Scandinavian Europe
  Danish, Finnish, Icelandic, Norwegian and Swedish

South-East Asia
  Burmese, Indonesian, Khmer, Lao, Malay, Tagalog (Pilipino), Thai and Vietnamese
Spanish
Sri Lanka
Swahili
Thai
Thai Hill Tribes
Tibetan
Turkish
Ukrainian
USA
  US English, Vernacular Talk, Native American languages and Hawaiian
Vietnamese
Western Europe
  Basque, Catalan, Dutch, French, German, Irish, Italian, Portuguese, Scottish Gaelic, Spanish (Castilian) and Welsh

---

LONELY PLANET JOURNEYS

JOURNEYS is a unique collection of travel writing – published by the company that understands travel better than anyone else. It is a series for anyone who has ever experienced – or dreamed of – the magical moment when they encountered a strange culture or saw a place for the first time. They are tales to read while you're planning a trip, while you're on the road or while you're in an armchair, in front of a fire.

JOURNEYS books catch the spirit of a place, illuminate a culture, recount a crazy adventure, or introduce a fascinating way of life. They always entertain, and always enrich the experience of travel.

ISLANDS IN THE CLOUDS
Travels in the Highlands of New Guinea
Isabella Tree

Isabella Tree's remarkable journey takes us to the heart of the remote and beautiful Highlands of Papua New Guinea and Irian Jaya – one of the most extraordinary and dangerous regions on earth. Funny and tragic by turns, *Islands in the Clouds* is her moving story of the Highland people and the changes transforming their world.

Isabella Tree, who lives in England, has worked as a freelance journalist on a variety of newspapers and magazines, including a stint as senior travel correspondent for the *Evening Standard*. A fellow of the Royal Geographical Society, she has also written a biography of the Victorian ornithologist John Gould.

'One of the most accomplished travel writers to appear on the horizon for many years . . . the dialogue is brilliant' – **Eric Newby**

SEAN & DAVID'S LONG DRIVE
Sean Condon

Sean Condon is young, urban and a connoisseur of hair wax. He can't drive, and he doesn't really travel well. So when Sean and his friend David set out to explore Australia in a 1966 Ford Falcon, the result is a decidedly offbeat look at life on the road. Over 14,000 death-defying kilometres, our heroes check out the re-runs on tv, get fabulously drunk, listen to Neil Young cassettes and wonder why they ever left home.

Sean Condon lives in Melbourne. He played drums in several mediocre bands until he found his way into advertising and an above-average band called Boilersuit. *Sean & David's Long Drive* is his first book.

'Funny, pithy, kitsch and surreal . . . This book will do for Australia what Chernobyl did for Kiev, but hey you'll laugh as the stereotypes go boom'
– Time Out

LONELY PLANET TRAVEL ATLASES

Lonely Planet has long been famous for the number and quality of its guidebook maps. Now we've gone one step further and in conjunction with Steinhart Katzir Publishers produced a handy companion series: Lonely Planet travel atlases – maps of a country produced in book form.

Unlike other maps, which look good but lead travellers astray, our travel atlases have been researched on the road by Lonely Planet's experienced team of writers. All details are carefully checked to ensure the atlas corresponds with the equivalent Lonely Planet guidebook.

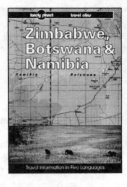

The handy atlas format means no holes, wrinkles, torn sections or constant folding and unfolding. These atlases can survive long periods on the road, unlike cumbersome fold-out maps. The comprehensive index ensures easy reference.

- full-colour throughout
- maps researched and checked by Lonely Planet authors
- place names correspond with Lonely Planet guidebooks
  – no confusing spelling differences
- legend and travelling information in English, French, German, Japanese and Spanish
- size: 230 x 160 mm

Available now:
Chile & Easter Island • Egypt • India & Bangladesh • Israel & the Palestinian Territories •Jordan, Syria & Lebanon • Kenya • Laos • Portugal • South Africa, Lesotho & Swaziland • Thailand • Turkey • Vietnam • Zimbabwe, Botswana & Namibia

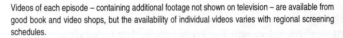

LONELY PLANET TV SERIES & VIDEOS

Lonely Planet travel guides have been brought to life on television screens around the world. Like our guides, the programmes are based on the joy of independent travel, and look honestly at some of the most exciting, picturesque and frustrating places in the world. Each show is presented by one of three travellers from Australia, England or the USA and combines an innovative mixture of video, Super-8 film, atmospheric soundscapes and original music.

Videos of each episode – containing additional footage not shown on television – are available from good book and video shops, but the availability of individual videos varies with regional screening schedules.

Video destinations include: Alaska • American Rockies • Australia – The South-East • Baja California & the Copper Canyon • Brazil • Central Asia • Chile & Easter Island • Corsica, Sicily & Sardinia – The Mediterranean Islands • East Africa (Tanzania & Zanzibar) • Ecuador & the Galapagos Islands • Greenland & Iceland • Indonesia • Israel & the Sinai Desert • Jamaica • Japan • La Ruta Maya • Morocco • New York • North India • Pacific Islands (Fiji, Solomon Islands & Vanuatu) • South India • South West China • Turkey • Vietnam • West Africa • Zimbabwe, Botswana & Namibia

The Lonely Planet TV series is produced by:
Pilot Productions
The Old Studio
18 Middle Row
London W10 5AT UK

For video availability and ordering information contact your nearest Lonely Planet office.

Music from the TV series is available on CD & cassette.

PLANET TALK

Lonely Planet's FREE quarterly newsletter

We love hearing from you and think you'd like to hear from us.

When...is the right time to see reindeer in Finland?
Where...can you hear the best palm-wine music in Ghana?
How...do you get from Asunción to Areguá by steam train?
What...is the best way to see India?

For the answer to these and many other questions read PLANET TALK.

Every issue is packed with up-to-date travel news and advice including:

- a letter from Lonely Planet co-founders Tony and Maureen Wheeler
- go behind the scenes on the road with a Lonely Planet author
- feature article on an important and topical travel issue
- a selection of recent letters from travellers
- details on forthcoming Lonely Planet promotions
- complete list of Lonely Planet products

To join our mailing list contact any Lonely Planet office.

Also available: Lonely Planet T-shirts. 100% heavyweight cotton.

LONELY PLANET ONLINE

Get the latest travel information before you leave or while you're on the road

Whether you've just begun planning your next trip, or you're chasing down specific info on currency regulations or visa requirements, check out Lonely Planet Online for up-to-the-minute travel information.

As well as travel profiles of your favourite destinations (including maps and photos), you'll find current reports from our researchers and other travellers, updates on health and visas, travel advisories, and discussion of the ecological and political issues you need to be aware of as you travel.

There's also an online travellers' forum where you can share your experience of life on the road, meet travel companions and ask other travellers for their recommendations and advice. We also have plenty of links to other online sites useful to independent travellers.

And of course we have a complete and up-to-date list of all Lonely Planet travel products including guides, phrasebooks, atlases, Journeys and videos and a simple online ordering facility if you can't find the book you want elsewhere.

www.lonelyplanet.com
or
AOL keyword: lp

LONELY PLANET PRODUCTS

Lonely Planet is known worldwide for publishing practical, reliable and no-nonsense travel information in our guides and on our web site. The Lonely Planet list covers just about every accessible part of the world. Currently there are eight series: *travel guides, shoestring guides, walking guides, city guides, phrasebooks, audio packs, travel atlases* and *Journeys* – a unique collection of travel writing.

EUROPE

Amsterdam • Austria • Baltic States phrasebook • Britain • Central Europe on a shoestring • Central Europe phrasebook • Czech & Slovak Republics • Denmark • Dublin • Eastern Europe on a shoestring • Eastern Europe phrasebook • Estonia, Latvia & Lithuania • Finland • France • French phrasebook • German phrasebook • Greece • Greek phrasebook • Hungary • Iceland, Greenland & the Faroe Islands • Ireland • Italian phrasebook • Italy • Mediterranean Europe on a shoestring • Mediterranean Europe phrasebook • Paris • Poland • Portugal • Portugal travel atlas • Prague • Russia, Ukraine & Belarus • Russian phrasebook • Scandinavian & Baltic Europe on a shoestring • Scandinavian Europe phrasebook • Slovenia • Spain • Spanish phrasebook • St Petersburg • Switzerland • Trekking in Greece • Trekking in Spain • Ukrainian phrasebook • Vienna • Walking in Britain • Walking in Switzerland • Western Europe on a shoestring • Western Europe phrasebook

Travel Literature: The Olive Grove: Travels in Greece

NORTH AMERICA

Alaska • Backpacking in Alaska • Baja California • California & Nevada • Canada • Florida • Hawaii • Honolulu • Los Angeles • Mexico • Miami • New England • New Orleans • New York City • New York, New Jersey & Pennsylvania • Pacific Northwest USA • Rocky Mountain States • San Francisco • Southwest USA • USA phrasebook • Washington, DC & the Capital Region

CENTRAL AMERICA & THE CARIBBEAN

Bermuda • Central America on a shoestring • Costa Rica • Cuba • Eastern Caribbean • Guatemala, Belize & Yucatán: La Ruta Maya • Jamaica

SOUTH AMERICA

Argentina, Uruguay & Paraguay • Bolivia • Brazil • Brazilian phrasebook • Buenos Aires • Chile & Easter Island • Chile & Easter Island travel atlas • Colombia • Ecuador & the Galápagos Islands • Latin American Spanish phrasebook • Peru • Quechua phrasebook • Rio de Janeiro • South America on a shoestring • Trekking in the Patagonian Andes • Venezuela

Travel Literature: Full Circle: A South American Journey

ANTARCTICA

Antarctica

ISLANDS OF THE INDIAN OCEAN

Madagascar & Comoros • Maldives • Mauritius, Réunion & Seychelles

AFRICA

Africa - the South • Africa on a shoestring • Arabic (Moroccan) phrasebook • Cape Town • Central Africa • East Africa • Egypt • Egypt travel atlas • Ethiopian (Amharic) phrasebook • Kenya • Kenya travel atlas • Malawi, Mozambique & Zambia • Morocco • North Africa • South Africa, Lesotho & Swaziland • South Africa, Lesotho & Swaziland travel atlas • Swahili phrasebook • Trekking in East Africa • West Africa • Zimbabwe, Botswana & Namibia • Zimbabwe, Botswana & Namibia travel atlas

Travel Literature: The Rainbird: A Central African Journey • Songs to an African Sunset: A Zimbabwean Story

MAIL ORDER

Lonely Planet products are distributed worldwide. They are also available by mail order from Lonely Planet, so if you have difficulty finding a title please write to us. North American and South American residents should write to Embarcadero West, 155 Filbert St, Suite 251, Oakland CA 94607, USA; European and African residents should write to 10a Spring Place, London NW5 3BH; and residents of other countries to PO Box 617, Hawthorn, Victoria 3122, Australia.

NORTH-EAST ASIA

Beijing • Cantonese phrasebook • China • Hong Kong • Hong Kong, Macau & Guangzhou • Japan • Japanese phrasebook • Japanese audio pack • Korea • Korean phrasebook • Mandarin phrasebook • Mongolia • Mongolian phrasebook • North-East Asia on a shoestring • Seoul • Taiwan • Tibet • Tibet phrasebook • Tokyo

Travel Literature: Lost Japan

MIDDLE EAST & CENTRAL ASIA

Arab Gulf States • Arabic (Egyptian) phrasebook • Central Asia • Central Asia phrasebook • Iran • Israel & the Palestinian Territories • Israel & the Palestinian Territories travel atlas • Istanbul • Jerusalem • Jordan & Syria • Jordan, Syria & Lebanon travel atlas • Lebanon • Middle East • Turkey • Turkish phrasebook • Turkey travel atlas • Yemen

Travel Literature: The Gates of Damascus • Kingdom of the Film Stars: Journey into Jordan

ALSO AVAILABLE:

Travel with Children • Traveller's Tales

INDIAN SUBCONTINENT

Bangladesh • Bengali phrasebook • Delhi • Hindi/Urdu phrasebook • India • India & Bangladesh travel atlas • Indian Himalaya • Karakoram Highway • Nepal • Nepali phrasebook • Pakistan • Rajasthan • Sri Lanka • Sri Lanka phrasebook • Trekking in the Indian Himalaya • Trekking in the Karakoram & Hindukush • Trekking in the Nepal Himalaya

Travel Literature: In Rajasthan • Shopping for Buddhas

SOUTH-EAST ASIA

Bali & Lombok • Bangkok • Burmese phrasebook • Cambodia • Ho Chi Minh City • Indonesia • Indonesian phrasebook • Indonesian audio pack • Jakarta • Java • Laos • Lao phrasebook • Laos travel atlas • Malay phrasebook • Malaysia, Singapore & Brunei • Myanmar (Burma) • Philippines • Pilipino phrasebook • Singapore • South-East Asia on a shoestring • South-East Asia phrasebook • Thailand • Thailand's Islands & Beaches • Thailand travel atlas • Thai phrasebook • Thai audio pack • Thai Hill Tribes phrasebook • Vietnam • Vietnamese phrasebook • Vietnam travel atlas

AUSTRALIA & THE PACIFIC

Australia • Australian phrasebook • Bushwalking in Australia • Bushwalking in Papua New Guinea • Fiji • Fijian phrasebook • Islands of Australia's Great Barrier Reef • Melbourne • Micronesia • New Caledonia • New South Wales & the ACT • New Zealand • Northern Territory • Outback Australia • Papua New Guinea • Papua New Guinea phrasebook • Queensland • Rarotonga & the Cook Islands • Samoa • Solomon Islands • South Australia • Sydney • Tahiti & French Polynesia • Tasmania • Tonga • Tramping in New Zealand • Vanuatu • Victoria • Western Australia

Travel Literature: Islands in the Clouds • Sean & David's Long Drive

THE LONELY PLANET STORY

Lonely Planet published its first book in 1973 in response to the numerous 'How did you do it?' questions Maureen and Tony Wheeler were asked after driving, bussing, hitching, sailing and railing their way from England to Australia.

Written at a kitchen table and hand collated, trimmed and stapled, *Across Asia on the Cheap* became an instant local bestseller, inspiring thoughts of another book.

Eighteen months in South-East Asia resulted in their second guide, *South-East Asia on a shoestring*, which they put together in a backstreet Chinese hotel in Singapore in 1975. The 'yellow bible', as it quickly became known to backpackers around the world, soon became *the* guide to the region. It has sold well over half a million copies and is now in its 9th edition, still retaining its familiar yellow cover.

Today there are over 240 titles, including travel guides, walking guides, language kits & phrasebooks, travel atlases and travel literature. The company is the largest independent travel publisher in the world. Although Lonely Planet initially specialised in guides to Asia, today there are few corners of the globe that have not been covered.

The emphasis continues to be on travel for independent travellers. Tony and Maureen still travel for several months of each year and play an active part in the writing, updating and quality control of Lonely Planet's guides.

They have been joined by over 70 authors and 170 staff at our offices in Melbourne (Australia), Oakland (USA), London (UK) and Paris (France). Travellers themselves also make a valuable contribution to the guides through the feedback we receive in thousands of letters each year and on our web site.

The people at Lonely Planet strongly believe that travellers can make a positive contribution to the countries they visit, both through their appreciation of the countries' culture, wildlife and natural features, and through the money they spend. In addition, the company makes a direct contribution to the countries and regions it covers. Since 1986 a percentage of the income from each book has been donated to ventures such as famine relief in Africa; aid projects in India; agricultural projects in Central America; Greenpeace's efforts to halt French nuclear testing in the Pacific; and Amnesty International.

'I hope we send people out with the right attitude about travel. You realise when you travel that there are so many different perspectives about the world, so we hope these books will make people more interested in what they see. Guidebooks can't really guide people. All you can do is point them in the right direction.'

– Tony Wheeler

LONELY PLANET PUBLICATIONS

Australia
PO Box 617, Hawthorn 3122, Victoria
tel: (03) 9819 1877 fax: (03) 9819 6459
e-mail: talk2us@lonelyplanet.com.au

USA
Embarcadero West, 155 Filbert St, Suite 251,
Oakland, CA 94607
tel: (510) 893 8555 TOLL FREE: 800 275-8555
fax: (510) 893 8563
e-mail: info@lonelyplanet.com

UK
10a Spring Place,
London NW5 3BH
tel: (0181) 742 3161 fax: (0181) 742 2772
e-mail: lonelyplanetuk@compuserve.com

France:
71 bis rue du Cardinal Lemoine, 75005 Paris
tel: 1 44 32 06 20 fax: 1 46 34 72 55
e-mail: 100560.415@compuserve.com

World Wide Web: http://www.lonelyplanet.com
or AOL keyword: lp